The war in the East. An illustrated history of the conflict between Russia and Turkey with a review of the Eastern question

A J. 1826-1881 Schem

T. C. Morrison

T. C. Morrison
1020 North Avenue 51
Los Angeles Calif.

To My good old friend

V E Theodoroff

A noble & worthy
Comrade &
proletarian democrat
progressive & liberal.

255-284, 339-359, 413-423,
439-467

ALEXANDER II.—CZAR OF RUSSIA.

ABDUL-HAMID II.

SULTAN OF TURKEY.

THE

WAR IN THE EAST.

AN

ILLUSTRATED HISTORY OF THE CONFLICT

BETWEEN

RUSSIA AND TURKEY,

WITH A

REVIEW OF THE EASTERN QUESTION.

By PROF. A. J. SCHEM,

Assistant Superintendent of Public Schools, New York City; Late Professor of Ancient and
Modern Languages in Dickinson College; Editor of a "General Cyclopedia," of the
"Statistics of the World," of the "American Ecclesiastical Year Book;"
Associate Editor of the "Cyclopedia of Education," Etc., Etc.

Illustrated with Engravings from Original Designs.

PUBLISHED BY
H. S. GOODSPEED & CO.,
NEW YORK, & CINCINNATI, O.

E. H. JONES, St. JOHN, N. B.; J. O. ROBINSON, LONDON, ONT.;
B. R. STURGES, BOSTON; J. W. GOODSPEED, CHICAGO.

PREFACE.

THE author of this work has made the Eastern Question for nearly twenty years a subject of constant and special study. As a member of the editorial staff of the New York *Tribune*, and contributor to other daily and weekly papers of New York, he has had many occasions to discuss it editorially in its various aspects, and as editor of and contributor to several cyclopædias and other publications, he has made himself familiar with the entire literature on this subject. A large amount of information had in this way been accumulated when the new Eastern war began. The general interest which the civilized world takes in this new effort to solve the Eastern Question, appeared to him a suitable occasion to combine the results of his former studies with a history of the Eastern war, into a comprehensive work on the Eastern Question and the Eastern war.

While every part of the subject embraced within the scope of this work may be supposed to enlist the attention of our readers, the interest of all undoubtedly culminates in the history of the Russo-Turkish war. This great conflict in the East ranks with the Civil war in our own country, and the Franco-German war, among the most memorable wars which the present generation has witnessed or is likely to witness. A compendium of such a war, it is therefore believed, will be a welcome volume in the library of many households. This work gives due prominence to the more interesting features of the conflict. It gives an account of every battle, using in the description of the more important battles, graphic accounts of eye-witnesses. Its biographical notices of distinguished Russian and Turkish generals are very full, and embrace almost every name that is mentioned in the progress of the war—as a glance at the pages of the book will show. A distinguished artist, who has resided in both Turkey and Russia, and who is familiar with the customs and manners of the different races who inhabit these countries, as well as with the places and fortifications in both, has designed many of the illustrations which embellish this book.

The narrative of the war is preceded by a historical outline of the Eastern Question; a brief sketch of the past and present condition of both Russia and Turkey, and a history of the Bosnian insurrection of 1875, and the Servian war of 1876. Conjointly, these chapters contain information most needed for understanding the development of the Eastern Question prior to 1876, and enable the reader to conceive a clear idea of the causes, importance, and aim of the war.

The peace which has been concluded between Russia and Turkey can not possibly end the Eastern Question, but is more likely to be the beginning of a series of new questions and conflicts of which it is impossible to predict, or even to guess, the duration or the end. Even now, while this book is going to press, and while the ink with which the Treaty of San Stefano was signed is hardly yet dry, the air is full of the noise of conflicting demands and of rumors of wars, in which all the principal nations of Europe are in danger of being involved. The so-called peace has brought only dissatisfaction. The demand for its modification in the interests of other powers than Russia went up even before its terms were fully known. Even the former tributary States of Turkey, which, having gained their independence, might have been supposed to have received the greatest benefits from the treaty, find that they have reason to feel wronged, or to believe that their rights and interests have not been properly regarded; the claims of one State, which deserved as high consideration as those of any of the others, and which enjoyed a wide and warm sympathy in Western and Southern Europe, have been ignored. Two powerful nations, which had great interests at stake in the adjustment of the affairs of Turkey, find themselves, under the new arrangements, dictated by Russia in the presence of a situation which they can not tolerate. Their claims are acknowledged to have more or less of justice by their neighboring powers, and even by Germany, which has been regarded as the adviser of Russia, and its supporter, in a moral sense. The same dispatches which report the diplomatic remonstrances of these powers and the replies, the propositions and counter-propositions which are circulating among the Courts of Europe, bring accounts of their measures to support their claims by force, if they should adjudge that necessary or expedient. In the meantime Russia keeps its armies in front of Constantinople, and England approaches it with its war-vessels, either party being determined not to retire till the questions at dispute have been settled.

The parties to the new controversy have great resources and powers of endurance, and are nearly evenly balanced. They have also great schemes at heart, and vital interests at stake, all of which are involved in the present dispute. The contest, if they should come to blows, will be long and desperate. It will, in its turn, cause new questions to be brought up, and may lead to new conflicts, involving as principals parties which hold only a secondary place in the present discussions; for a protracted war on the borders of Turkey can not fail to arouse the diversified nationalities of Austria to an effort to realize their aspirations.

It is therefore evident that the Russo-Turkish war of 1877–'78 was only a single incident in a long chain of events; that the questions which seemed most immediately involved in it, were only as the single threads of an entangled net of international complications and issues, of which the unraveling has hardly yet begun. It is impossible to understand adequately either the events of the war or the questions without having first acquired some comprehension of the events and complications and issues to which they are related, and of which they are essentially a part. The effort is made to give such a comprehension, not only in the introductory historical chapters which lead up to the war, but further in the chapters following the narrative of the war.

In these chapters are treated the important issues connected with the Eastern Question, which yet await their solution; the decline of the Ottoman power, and the deterioration of the Turkish race, which promise to produce for it further losses of territory and continued enfeeblement; the physical and moral condition of the Christian nationalities of Turkey, and their probable capacity to build up self-supporting States to take the place of the Turks; the prospective growth of Russia, and the aims and tendencies of Panslavism; the dangers which the co-existence of so many discordant races involves, not only for Turkey, but also for Austria; the conflicting interests of the two greatest Empires of the world, the British and the Russian, in Asia. Finally, a suggestion is attempted of a method in which a final solution of the Eastern and all other international complications may be reached in the general recognition of the principle of self-government by nationalities.

As the Eastern Question is by far the most important of all the international complications which keep the Old World in an unsettled condition; and as for many years to come it can hardly fail to constitute a conspicuous and interesting element in the history of Turkey, Russia, Austria, England, and many other States of Europe, Asia, and Africa, a full statement of all issues involved in it will conserve, it is hoped, for this work some value as a reliable guide through the continuing difficulties of the Eastern Question, even when the interest in the bloody war shall have begun to subside.

A. J. S.

CONTENTS.

CHAPTER III.

CONDITION OF RUSSIA.

CHAPTER IV.

HISTORICAL SKETCH OF TURKEY

CHAPTER V.

PRESENT CONDITION OF THE TURKISH EMPIRE AND THE OSMANLI TURKS.

CHAPTER VI.

THE TRIBUTARY STATES AND THE SUBJECT PEOPLES OF TURKEY.

CHAPTER VII.

THE INSURRECTION OF 1875, AND THE WARS OF 1876.

SECOND BOOK.
THE EASTERN WAR OF 1877–1878.

CHAPTER I.

THE RUSSIAN DECLARATION OF WAR.

CHAPTER II.

PASSAGE OF THE DANUBE AND THE BALKANS.

CHAPTER III.

THE RUSSIAN ADVANCE IN ARMENIA.

CHAPTER IV.

THE RUSSIAN REVERSE IN ARMENIA.

CHAPTER V.

THE BATTLES AROUND PLEVNA.

CHAPTER VI.

THE FALL OF PLEVNA.

CHAPTER VII.

THE SECOND CAMPAIGN IN ARMENIA.

CHAPTER VIII.

THE OPERATIONS BEFORE BATUM AND IN THE CAUCASUS.

CHAPTER IX.

ON TO CONSTANTINOPLE.

CHAPTER X.

MONTENEGRO AND THE GREEK PROVINCES

CHAPTER XI.

NAVAL OPERATIONS.

CHAPTER XII.

DIPLOMATIC HISTORY OF THE WAR.

CHAPTER XIII.

INNER HISTORY OF TURKEY DURING THE WAR.

CHAPTER XIV.

ARMISTICE AND PEACE.

THIRD BOOK.

THE EASTERN QUESTION AT THE CLOSE OF THE WAR—AN OUTLOOK INTO THE FUTURE.

CHAPTER I.

THE DOOM OF TURKEY

CHAPTER II.

THE NEW STATES OF THE BALKAN PENINSULA

I. BULGARIANS AND GREEKS.

CHAPTER III.

THE NEW STATES OF THE BALKAN PENINSULA.

II. RUMANIANS AND SERVIANS.

CHAPTER IV.

PANSLAVIC HOPES AND TENDENCIES.

CHAPTER V.

THE PERIL OF AUSTRIA.

CHAPTER VI.

ENGLAND AND RUSSIA.

CHAPTER VII

THE NATIONALITY PRINCIPLE AND THE FINAL ISSUE OF THE EASTERN QUESTION.

CHAPTER VIII.

COMPLICATIONS ARISING AT THE CLOSE OF THE WAR.

APPENDIX I.

APPENDIX II.

LIST OF ILLUSTRATIONS.

LIST OF MAPS AND PLANS.

A COFFEE-HOUSE IN CONSTANTINOPLE.

INTRODUCTION.

IMPORTANCE OF THE EASTERN QUESTION AND THE EASTERN WARS.

The War of 1877-'78 one of the most important Wars of the Nineteenth Century—Vastness of the territory involved—Great Issues at stake—Eastern Europe on the eve of a Radical Transformation

A WAR between two countries so extensive and so powerful as Russia and Turkey will never fail to enlist the profound interest of the civilized world, and to fill a conspicuous place in the history of the century. Russia and Turkey are among the largest empires of the earth. In point of extent, Russia is the second, and Turkey the sixth, in point of population, Russia the third and Turkey the fourth among all the States. Their aggregate population exceeds one hundred and twenty millions, or nearly one-tenth of the human race; their united area fully occupies one-fifth of the entire surface of the land. Thus in every Russo-Turkish conflict the world again witnesses the horrors of war on a larger scale, and these horrors must be expected to be all the more frightful, as the Turks and even large portions of the Russian troops have not yet experienced that influence of the Christian religion and of the civilization of the nineteenth century which fortunately distinguishes to some extent the wars in Western Europe and in North America from those of former times and of other countries.

The Eastern war of 1877-'78 has enlisted an even more general and more profound interest than its predecessors. For two years its outbreak had been anxiously looked forward to, because it was thought that it might lead to results of more than ordinary importance, and might take its place among the more memorable wars in the history of the human race. The power of the Turks has long been on the wane, and the opinion has been widely spread that they would not be able to retain much longer their hold of their Christian provinces The rising in 1875 and 1876 of all the tribes of the Servian nationality appeared to be fraught with the most serious danger to the Turks, and awakened the full measure of that sympathy which is accorded to the struggle of any oppressed people for independence. When Russia, in 1877, took up arms in support of its Slavic brethren, it was commonly expected that the time for a radical change in the territorial division of Eastern Europe was near at hand. A decided defeat of the Turks, it was thought, might involve their entire expulsion from Europe, and a reconstruction of their European dominions. In any permanent change of this kind, however, other great powers are directly concerned. Austria can not be indifferent to the final fate of the Slavic tribes of Turkey; England can not but be anxious about the final fate of Constantinople and the Suez Canal; both Austria and England have very good reason to watch with suspicion any further aggrandizement of Russia; and no one believes that any lasting change in the map of Europe can be effected without the consent of the powerful German Empire, and its great statesman, Prince Bismarck. The movements of English, Austrian, and German diplomacy have therefore been watched by public opinion with almost as great eagerness as the progress of the war, and the changing prospects of a still further extension of the seat of war have largely added to the general interest which has been taken in it.

A peculiar interest attaches to this war in its religious aspect. The civilized world has fortunately learned to discard religion from politics, and the legislation of the United States, which grants equal rights and equal protection to persons of all religions, is duly appreciated and more and more adopted by the States of Europe and America. The Turks might have received the full benefit of this progress of religious toleration, and the fact that the Mohammedan religion forms a broad line of distinction between them and the civilized world might have been ignored, if the Government had been just toward its Christian subjects. This, however, has not been the case. The shameful oppression of the Christian provinces, after having lasted for centuries, has not yet ceased. Mohammedan fanaticism has again reflected itself in the horrible Bulgarian atrocities, and the war against Russia had hardly begun when the Turkish Government manifested the design of proclaiming a holy war of all Mohammedans against the Christian enemy. Such acts could not but arouse a strong feeling of antipathy against the Mohammedan Turks throughout the Christian world. They recalled to the Christian nations the past wars between the Cross and the Crescent, and their final result, the complete victory of progressive Christianity, which is now the religion of almost every civilized country, over the decrepit Islam, which for centuries has been losing ground wherever it came into contact with Christians. The examples of Spain, of Hungary, of large Slavic territories, and of Greece, all of which have fully emancipated themselves from Mohammedan rule, and of Servia and Rumania, which have at least achieved an actual independence, were looked upon as proofs that a Mohammedan government can not and should not conduct the developing civilization of a Christian race, and that the Christian tribes which are still kept down by Turkish rule, are fairly and fully entitled to a liberation from the shackles which thus far have obstructed their progress. The warlike spirit which animated the Crusader against the infidel conquerors of the Holy Land may no longer exist in the present generation, but just in proportion as the Turks choose to remind the Christians of their triumphs in former religious wars, they will revive in millions of minds the sorrow for the Mohammedan conquest of the sacred places hallowed by the history of the Old and New Testaments, and will swell the already powerful current of an anti-Turkish public sentiment. Even those who dread a further advance of Russia, more than the continuance of Turkish rule, have demanded and will demand satisfactory guarantees for the freedom of the Christian provinces from any further oppression by a Mohammedan government.

The fact that the Turks not only belong to an alien religion, but that they are an alien race in Europe, has greatly added to the hereditary hatred with which the conquered tribes and the neighboring nations have looked upon them. But this difference of race has received a much greater significance in the light of modern science. The progress of comparative philology which has shown the degree of kinship existing between all the principal languages of the world, has revealed the remarkable fact that from the days of the Persian Empire one family of nations, speaking languages nearly akin to each other, have run far ahead of all other nations in power and civilization. The Persians, the Greeks, the Romans. in the past, and all the Teutonic, Romanic, and Slavic nations of the present, are members of this family, which has been variously designated by linguists as the Aryan, Indo-Germanic or Indo-European. In its irrepressible progress, this family of nations has now

2

obtained control of the government of nearly all Europe, America, Australia, and the larger portion of Asia, and it is still steadily advancing. The Turks do not belong to it, but to an entirely different race, which in the progress of civilization has thus far greatly lagged behind, and, on account of its obvious inferiority, has been steadily losing ground for centuries. The inference has been drawn from this historical argument that the Turks have not only been unsuccessful in the past, but that as an inferior race they will also be constitutionally unfit in future to raise the countries over which they rule to a level with the Aryan nations of Europe and America. The Eastern wars from 1875 to 1878, and the inner history of Turkey during this time, have therefore been scrutinized with close attention by thousands of eager observers, to whom they appear as a new test of a theory which, if true, is certainly of a very grave importance for the welfare of millions of men, and which undoubtedly may claim, in the face of the history of the last two thousand years, a very thorough investigation.

FIRST BOOK.

TURKEY, RUSSIA, AND THE EASTERN QUESTION PRIOR TO 1877.

FIRST BOOK.·

TURKEY, RUSSIA, AND THE EASTERN QUESTION PRIOR TO 1877.

CHAPTER I.

A HISTORICAL OUTLINE OF THE EASTERN QUESTION.

The Crusades—Conquest of Eastern Europe by the Turks—The Turks Threatening the Christian Nations of Europe—Emperor Maximilian's Plan of a General Coalition against the Turks—Decay of Turkey and Rise of the Russian Empire—Aspirations of the Christian Races of Turkey for the Recovery of their Independence—History of the Russian Policy in the East—The Interest of Austria and England in the Eastern Question—International Treaties and Joint Action of the Christian Powers—The Great Crisis

THE Eastern Question, or the question as to the destiny of South-eastern Europe, has for many centuries been a prolific source of great excitement and of bloody war. It has presented itself to the people of Europe and of the civilized world, under greatly varying aspects, but it has rarely lost its interesting character, and recently it has become once more the most exciting feature in the international complications of the world.

The fate of the East became a subject of anxious concern for all Christian nations of Europe, when the followers of Mohammed began to conquer in Asia the places hallowed by the life and death of Christ. The conquest of the Holy Land from the Infidels was truly for the Christian people of Europe an Eastern Question, though it was not called by that name, and no Eastern war has ever awakened a greater enthusiasm, or finds even at the present day a larger number of attentive readers than the crusades. These religious wars have turned out to be a great promoter of civilization, and have largely contributed to the ascendency which the Christian nations of

(27)

Europe and America now enjoy over all others; but in a military point of view they resulted in a complete failure. Not only were no lasting conquests made by the Christians, and not only were the Eastern States established by them very short-lived, but the final withdrawal of the Christians from Asia was followed by the invasion of Eastern Europe by the Mohammedans, by the decay of the East-Roman Empire, and finally, in 1453, by the fall of Constantinople.

Then the Eastern Question assumed for the nations of Europe a new shape. The conquest of Constantinople had only increased the greed of the Mohammedans for more land, and Austria, Hungary, Poland, and Russia had long to suffer from the impetuous invasions of the Turks. The Turkish wars of the fifteenth, sixteenth, and seventeenth centuries, though not so famous as the crusades of the middle ages, and the great Eastern wars of more recent times, still live in the recollections of the nations which suffered from them, and the people still sing many popular songs celebrating the great heroes who saved large portions of Europe from falling under Turkish rule. The Eastern Question for the monarchs of that age consisted in devising plans of defense from the horrors attending and following Turkish invasions. Sometimes bold plans were formed for not only repelling the Turks, but for expelling them altogether from Europe. Such a plan, among others, was devised by the Emperor Maximilian I., the last imperial representative of medieval chivalry. It provided for a joint war, not only of the Christian nations of Europe, but of Persians and Tartars, which was to last for three years. It was to begin in 1518 simultaneously in Africa and in Hungary. In Africa, the Emperor of Germany and the king of Portugal, aided by the French fleet, were to liberate the princes of the Northern States from Turkish rule and to enlist them in the common alliance. In Hungary, the king of Poland, at the head of his own troops, and of Hungarian, Bohemian, Moravian, Silesian, Austrian, Bavarian, and other auxiliaries, was to conquer the border provinces of European Turkey. In 1519, the kings of Poland and France were to unite their forces in Bosnia, conquer Adrianople and Philippopolis, and plunder Greece, in order to raise the money for paying the Wallachian and Tartar auxiliaries. In Africa, the kings of England and Denmark, and the Grand Master of the Teutonic Order, supported by a Muscovite army, were to fight a decisive battle near Algiers, and conquer the Nile. In the third year of the war, the victorious army of Africa was to join the kings of France and Poland, and to put an end to the Turkish Empire by the conquest of Constantinople. A new census was to be taken in all the countries of Christendom, in order to distribute among them, pro rata of the population, a new Turkish tax, which was to meet the expenses of the war. After the destruction of the Turkish Empire, the king of Persia was to be rewarded for his help by one-half of Asia Minor, Caramania, and Armenia, while the other half of Asia Minor, Egypt, and Syria were to be given to the Austrian nation. It is not known how the Emperor intended to divide the European dominions of the Sultan; probably the want of agreement about the Turkish inheritance was as great in the sixteenth as in the nineteenth century. At all events the plan was not carried out at all, and the Turks remained, for many more years, a terror for the Austrian and other neighboring nations.

At last the time came when the Turks ceased to be a terror to the nations of Europe. Their empire began to decline with the death of Solyman, in 1566. Several great defeats destroyed the spell of their military fame and furnished the welcome proof that they were not invincible. Moreover, it soon became apparent that the great progress of military science in Central and Western Europe was largely improving the efficiency of the Christian armies, while the reign of several weak Ottoman rulers reflected itself in the declining discipline of the Turkish troops. Though the Turks continued to meet with a few successes, their wars began to assume less of an aggressive and more of a defensive character. Their territorial losses began to exceed their gains, and no important addition of territory was made to the Empire after the beginning of the eighteenth century. But the most momentous among all the causes of Turkish decline was the rise of Russian power. The Russians were among those nations of Northern Europe which had had to struggle against the advancing Turks for their very existence. Thus the Russian and the Turkish Governments became hereditary enemies, and this enmity became all the more intense, after Peter the Great, about the end of the seventeenth century, had raised Russia to a level with the most powerful countries of Europe. The policy of Russia, with respect to Turkey, was from that time unmistakably more aggressive. The Czars were anxious, not only to avenge the Turkish aggressions of the past, but to extend their dominions at the expense of the Turks. Throughout the eighteenth and the nineteenth centuries, the two countries have been in an almost chronic state of enmity and war, and as during all this time Russia has been steadily advancing in extent and in power, and Turkey has been just as steadily progressing in its decay, it has more and more become the general belief that if the two powers should be left fighting out this hereditary war single-handed, the Turks would finally be at the mercy of the Russians. This result appeared all the more inevitable, as Russia had not only a steadily increasing preponderance of power in every new war, but was, moreover, aided by the outspoken sympathy of the Christian population of European Turkey In proportion as the Ottoman Government became weaker, the demands of the Christian population for liberation from Turkish oppression became more outspoken. Thus the Christians of European Turkey and the Russians became natural allies, because they had at least one common interest, the weakening of the Turkish Government. The Christians of Turkey hailed every Russian victory as a forerunner of their own independence, and looked upon the Russians as their natural and most powerful patrons. The Russians, on the other hand, could not be blind to the great access of strength which such a patronage would give them in every new war against the Turks. Accordingly, when in 1774 the Turkish Government was compelled to conclude the fatal treaty of Kainardji, one of the articles of peace, which was insisted upon by Russia and conceded by Turkey, was the establishment of a Russian protectorate over the Danubian principalities, and a right of Russian guardianship over the Greek churches of Turkey. A treaty so humiliating for the Turks, of course stimulated the aspirations of the Christians for freedom, and these aspirations were greatly strengthened by the greater acts of cruelty and oppression in which the Turkish Governors of Christian provinces thought they could indulge in view of the growing weakness of the Imperial Government at Constantinople. Finally the aspirations of the Christians found vent in the wars of independence, which began early in the present century, and resulted in the entire freedom of Greece, and the actual independence of Servia, the latter obtaining full self-government, and having only, like Rumania, to pay a tribute to the Turk. If other provinces were, less successful, repeated insurrections in Bosnia, Albania, Bulgaria, and Crete at least reminded the Turks that their rule in these provinces was not less detested, that in any new war against the Russians the sympathies of the Christians would be with the enemies of Turkey, and that any opportunity

KILID BAHR, ON THE EUROPEAN SHORE.

KEY OF THE DARDANELLES.

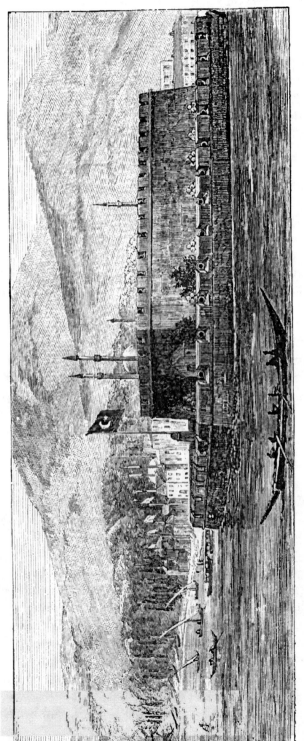

TCHANAK KALESI, ON THE ASIATIC SHORE.

KEY OF THE DARDANELLES.

for establishing the independence of the Christian provinces would be eagerly seized.

The Christian powers of Europe have often deemed it their duty to support the demands of the Turkish Christians. The peace of Carlovitz, in 1699, compelled the Sultan, for the first time, to treat with the European powers in accordance with the received rules of international law, and thus gave to the Turks, much against their own will, a place in the family of European States. In virtue of this position the Christian powers have frequently found an opportunity to force their diplomatic advice upon the Porte in behalf of the oppressed races; and, once at least, in the case of the Greeks, they have actually co-operated in the establishment of an independent State. More recently, the appointment of Christian Governors for the Christian provinces, and the conferring of some kind of provincial autonomy, was demanded of the Porte, and the whole of Europe, including all governments and all political parties, supported the Christian races in demanding it. But even if this concession had been made, it would not have sufficed to convert the Christians into contented, peaceful subjects. Their desire has long been overwhelmingly for the expulsion of the Turks from Europe, and in this demand they have been openly supported by the outspoken sympathy of many millions in the European countries. Every prospect of an entire expulsion of the Turks from Europe, and the erection of one or several independent Christian States in the place of European Turkey, would be hailed by many thousands with boundless enthusiasm. The popularity of this project might long ago have hastened its execution, if all the men of influence and of intelligence among its patrons were not aware of the great difficulty of determining beforehand what is to be substituted for the destroyed Turkish Empire in Europe. The Christian races of Turkey themselves have troubled themselves very little about this question. The friends of independence in each province have mostly been so absorbed with plans for achieving their own freedom, that hardly any of them appear to have given much thought to what should become of the whole of the European dominions of the Sultan. Garibaldi, who takes an ardent interest in the liberation of the Christian tribes, and has repeatedly offered his services for achieving it, has proposed the erection of a republican confederation of all the races after the model of Switzerland, allowing each nationality a provincial autonomy. This view has some friends, but there is not at present, and will not be for many years to come, the slightest prospect of its success, for the Christians of Turkey have no republican sentiments, and the monarchs of Europe can not be expected to favor it. It is, however, taken for granted that whenever the power of the Turks in Europe should actually come to an end, a conference of the great powers would assemble and arrange the future form of government. While Greeks, Albanians, and Bulgarians live almost exclusively under Turkish rule, and may therefore be enabled, by a dissolution of the Turkish Empire alone, to recover their independence as a nationality, it is different with the Servians and the Rumanians. Millions of people of the same descent, and still speaking the same language, belong to the Austrian Empire—partly to Austria proper and partly to Hungary. Both nationalities are sufficiently numerous to constitute States of considerable size—if ever it should become possible to unite in a political union all the people speaking the same language. Now this project has not only been broached, but it has found influential adherents, both in Turkey and in Austria. The example of the kingdom of Italy, which has not only absorbed the petty States ruled by native princes, but has even succeeded in wresting from the powerful Austrian Empire the large and flourishing provinces of Lombardy and Venetia, has greatly encouraged the enthusiasts to believe in the restoration of a united Servian and a united Rumanian nationality. It is evident that any attempt to carry out this visionary scheme is an act of open hostility against Austria. Every progress, which a tendency in this direction should make among Austrian subjects, would threaten the Austrian Empire with a territorial loss such as was inflicted upon it by the Italians. There have been Austrian statesmen who, in view of the impending decay of the Turkish Empire, have indulged the hope that Austria might risk patronizing the nationality movements among the Servians and the Rumanians, with a view of making the two reconstructed nations integral parts of the polyglot Austrian Empire. The execution of such a project would, however, revolutionize the entire policy of the house of Austria. It would equally offend the two ruling races, the Germans and the Hungarians, whose leading principle is to strengthen the preponderance which they already possess by the gradual absorption of the smaller Slavic tribes. In whatever light, therefore, this nationality movement, which some enthusiasts have started among the Rumanians and Servians, may be viewed, it has given to the Austrian Empire an entirely novel interest in the fate of the Servian and Rumanian nationalities, and it has thus still more complicated the difficult Eastern Question.

The same is the case with another movement of recent date—the so-called Panslavism. As the word indicates, this means some kind of union between all the sections of the Slavic race. Some Slavs have viewed it as a merely literary union among all speaking Slavic languages, but more commonly it is regarded as a political movement, and in this sense it has made, and is making, a great stir in Europe. Though the Panslavists disagree in many respects among themselves, they are all agreed that all people speaking Slavic languages should live under Slavic rule, and that the direct rule of Germans, Magyars, and Turks over Slavic tribes should come to an end. The first Panslavic agitators were revolutionists, who wished to overthrow, not only the rule of Germany, Austria, Hungary, and Turkey over their Slavic subjects, but even the rule of the Russian Emperors, and unite all the Slavs in one vast republican government. One of the most prominent leaders of this movement, Bakunin, is well known in the United States, which he visited after his escape from Siberia. At present this party, though not extinct, has comparatively little influence upon the march of events. Among the Panslavists who now take a conspicuous part in the politics of the East-European States we may distinguish three sections. The one contents itself in Austria, Hungary, and Germany, with the demand that the Slavic populations be placed under Slavic administrations, with a legal protection of the Slavic tongue as the mother tongue of the provinces and districts in which it prevails. The German Reichstag often hears these demands from the leaders of the Poles; the Austrian Reichsrath from the leaders of the Czechs, Poles, and other Slavs; the Hungarian Diet, from the leaders of the Servians. A second party of Panslavists is frank enough to aim directly at the overthrow of the non-Slavic Governments which rule over Slavic populations, and at a reconstruction of a number of independent Slavic Empires which are to be closely united for mutual protection among themselves, and with the giant representative of Slavism, Russia. The third party regards as the easiest road to the realization of the Panslavic schemes the union of all the scattered Slavs with Russia. Many German, Hungarian, and Turkish statesmen and writers agree in charging the Russian Government with employing paid emissaries to spread Panslavic views of this latter kind in

Austrian and Turkish provinces. At all events, Panslavic agitations have made a mark in the history of all the States of Eastern Europe. In European Turkey, not only the Servian nationality, embracing the Bosnians, Herzegovinians, and Montenegrins, but the Bulgarians, speak Slavic languages, and are therefore accounted as members of the Slavic world. Among both, Russian Panslavists have been hard at work, and the impressions made by them are visible in the history of late events. Midhat Pasha, when Governor-General of the vilayet of the Danube, had several Panslavic agitators executed, and openly accused them of being Russian agents. In Austria, and especially in Hungary, the progress of this Panslavic agitation has long been anxiously watched, and the feelings of sympathy which the horrors of Turkish rule do not fail to call forth, even in Austria, are to a large extent neutralized or entirely overcome by the fear of a growing Russian preponderance.

The Panslavic idea offers advantages to Russia so great and so obvious that Russian statesmen can not be expected to overlook them, whatever reserve the regard for international relations and duties may outwardly impose upon them. But whatever the relations of the Government of Russia to the Panslavic agitations may have been, the policy which she had steadfastly pursued, in her wars against Turkey, has been thoroughly Russian, not Slavic or Panslavic. Her chief aim in weakening Turkey has always been to build up a strong Russian Empire. Since Peter the Great all the Emperors appear to have followed a definite plan in their struggle for aggrandizement. In order to raise her people above the level of merely agricultural nations, and develop their commerce and industries, Russia, with unwavering steadiness, has endeavored to gain a firm footing on the Black Sea. This aim has gradually been reached by the conquests of the eighteenth century, and Russian vessels can now, from the Black Sea, proceed to the Mediterranean. But one great drawback remained. The connection with the Mediterranean can at any time be interrupted by the closing of the Bosphorus and the Dardanelles, which are controlled by the Turks. Therefore, the conquest and occupation of Constantinople would be an immense advantage for Russia, for it would fully carry out the intentions of Peter the Great, and complete the work which the founder of Russian greatness began. It can hardly be doubted that the Russian statesmen who have desired, for more than a century, the possession of Constantinople, have been guided chiefly by this consideration, though other reasons may have co-operated to make the desire as strong and as wide-spread as it is at present among the Russian people. When the Turks had destroyed the East-Roman Empire, the Czar of Russia became, in the place of the Emperors of the East-Roman Empire, the protector of the Greek Church; he appeared as their natural successor, and it is not surprising that at the outbreak of every new war against the Turks, the Russian peasantry should hope, with feverish anxiety, for the news that the Czar had made his entrance into the city of Constantinople, which they call Czargrad, or city of the Czar, and that mass should once more be celebrated in the great church of St. Sophia, now the chief of the Mohammedan mosques. It is also known that one of the great empresses of Russia, Catharine II., conceived the plan of reviving the Byzantine Empire, and that one of her grandsons had to learn for that purpose the modern Greek language. But the chief consideration for the Russian statesmen and emperors during the last two centuries has been the desire to get full control of a sea coast, as an indispensable necessity for developing fully all the resources of the vast empire.

As the intentions of Russia, with regard to Turkey, have long been, and will be in future, of prime importance for the final solution of the Eastern Question, it will be interesting to hear the views of a distinguished Russian writer. Professor Martens, of the University of St. Petersburg, has made the history of the relations between Russia and Turkey a special study, has published, for the first time, a number of official documents relating to it, and has reviewed the whole subject in a treatise which is, at all events, a valuable contribution to the history of the Eastern Question. The design of the article is to show that the views generally entertained of the aims and policy of Russia with reference to Turkey have been mistaken It sets forth that within the present century, at least, Russia, so far from seeking to destroy the Turkish Empire, has insisted upon its being maintained; and that while it has held it a supreme duty to protect the Christian subjects of the Porte, it has always endeavored to accomplish the object through the united action of the powers, always hesitating to act alone till the attempt to secure co-operation had failed. The article deserves attention, both on account of the new views it gives of Russian history and policy in the East, and because its positions are supported by citations from documents which are now for the first time made known to the public.

Prof. Martens' first endeavor is to show from the public declara-

tions of Russian statesmen that ever since the pacification of Europe,
after the wars of Napoleon made concert possible, it has sought to
exercise its right only in concert with the powers, and has steadily
endeavored to secure the permanent well-being of the Christians of
Turkey by placing them under the collective protection of Christian
Europe. In 1815, at the time of the meeting of the Congress of
Vienna, the Russian Government addressed a note to the allies,
urging them to extend the obligations of the law of nations over
Turkey, and particularly to exact of the Porte a correction of the
practice of reducing prisoners of war to slavery. The invitation
was not heeded, and the affairs of Turkey were not considered in
the Congress. At the beginning of the Greek insurrection, in 1821,
Russia sought to interest the powers in behalf of the revolted Greeks.
In one of the notes on the subject the Government, referring to the
possibility of its being impelled to act, said that the Russian armies
would march, not to extend the frontiers of the Empire, or to gain
a preponderance for which it had no ambition, but to restore peace,
confirm the equilibrium of Europe, and secure to the countries of
European Turkey the benefits of a happy and inoffensive political
existence. In 1825 the Government, in a circular note on the same
subject, declared that " in associating ourselves with our allies, we
adopt a measure of which the first effect is that no event can be
turned to our exclusive profit, or can disturb the equilibrium of
Europe; on the contrary, all the results will be common, and all the
intervening powers will participate in a just and even proportion."

At the negotiation of the treaty of Adrianople, Russia proposed
conditions intended to secure the peace of Europe for several years.
After the constituting of the kingdom of Greece, it continued to seek
to secure for the Christian populations the protection of the powers,
sometimes by friendly overtures to the Porte, sometimes by invoking the concert of the powers. While the preliminaries for the
treaty of Paris were under negotiation in Vienna in 1855 and 1856,
the powers insisted that Russia should give up its claim to the right
of protecting the Christian subjects. Russia interposed no objection
to the demand, as appears by the protocol of the 15th of March,
1855, save to exact the condition that the religious rights of the
Christian populations should be placed under the protection of all
the contracting powers. Again, on the 5th of January, 1856, the
Russian Cabinet declared that the Emperor desired to raise his voice,
in common with the other European powers, in favor of his co-

religionists, and to be associated with them in deliberations having for their object to assure to the Christian subjects of the Sultan their religious and political rights; and in March following, in signifying the adhesion of his Government to this policy, Prince Gortchakoff declared in the Conference that it was convinced that nothing was better fitted to facilitate the government of his Empire by the Sultan than for him to do what he could to add to the happiness and satisfaction of his Christian subjects.

While Turkey and some of the other contracting powers have held that the treaty of Paris prohibited interference with the internal affairs of the Turkish provinces, Russia holds that the prohibition is based upon the promise of reforms which was given by Turkey in the publication of the Hatti-Humayun, and that its obligation is dependent upon the due and efficient execution of these reforms; and it insists that the other parties to the treaty acted upon the same view, when, on the occasion of the Mussulman outbreaks in Syria in 1860, they permitted French troops to be despatched to the province to restore order, and the Porte accepted the intervention as " a manifestation of the sympathies of the allied powers." Again, on the occasion of the Cretan insurrection, in 1866, Russia endeavored to induce the Porte to adopt measures for the improvement of the condition of the people of the island, but was not supported by the powers, and its efforts were fruitless. In a despatch of the 12th of May, 1869, Prince Gortchakoff again laid down the doctrine, which the Russian Government had never ceased to insist upon, that the collective authority of the great powers, in order to be effective, should be exercised collectively, and that a combined action afforded the best means of introducing improvements in the condition of the Christians, to be carried out through the agency of the Porte. A number of facts which have only recently been brought to light, tend, according to Prof. Martens, to show that the Russian Government has become convinced that the continuance of the Turkish Empire on the Bosphorus affords the conditions least disadvantageous to the commercial and political interests of Russia, and that its later policy has been governed by this conviction. In the war of 1828, when the Russian armies had reached Adrianople, and the complete downfall of the Turkish Empire seemed imminent, the Czar Nicholas appointed a commission to consider what should be done in the expected contingency. Count Nesselrode laid before this commission, on the 4th of September, 1829, a memorandum, frankly setting forth the view of the Russian Government, in which he said : " We have always considered that the preservation of the Ottoman Empire would be more useful than injurious to the true interests of Russia, and that any condition that could be substituted for it would only balance for us the advantage of having a weak State for a neighbor ;" but, if the fall of the Turkish Empire was inevitable, or the rule of Turkey should be replaced by a new combination, then Russia should invite its allies " to deliberate in common with it on this great question. To desire to solve it without their participation, while their strongest interests were involved in it, would be to affront their honor, and charge ourselves with a too great responsibility." The commission had also to consider a memoir by Councillor Dashkoff, a distinguished specialist, the burden of which was to show that Russia needed no new acquisitions of territory. This paper sets forth that the present Russia should occupy itself with securing its frontiers and developing its resources, rather than in seeking after new lands. A policy involving the destruction of the Turkish Empire must be regarded as against the true interests of Russia. It was not denied, that in times past, Russia had entertained designs of conquest against Turkey, but those times were forever at an end, and the Russia of the eighteenth was not the Russia of the nineteenth century. A plan was also laid before the commission which had been proposed by the Count Capo d'Istria, for the reconstruction of the Balkan peninsula and its division into five States, according to the nationalities and the race affinities of the people, with governors chosen from five European princely houses of the second rank to rule over them, which should form a confederacy to be represented by a Congress meeting annually in Constantinople, which, with an enlarged territory, was to be constituted a free city. Without taking formal action on this plan, which it is known, however, was not acceptable to them, the commission concluded as the result of their deliberations: 1. That the advantages afforded by maintaining the Ottoman Empire outweighed the inconveniences occasioned by it ; 2. That the fall of Turkey would be against the true interests of Russia ; 3. That it would therefore be wise to prevent such an event, and for that purpose to make use of every opportunity to conclude an honorable peace.

When the existence of the Ottoman Empire was again put in peril between 1830 and 1840, by the operations of Mehemet Ali, pasha

MIDHAT PASHA.

PRINCE GORTCHAKOFF.

of Egypt, Russia concluded a defensive alliance with the Porte, sent a fleet and an army corps to Constantinople, and at a later period acted in co-operation with England, Austria, and Prussia, to defend the Empire against its dangerous enemy. The Russian policy at that time was defined in a note from Count Nesselrode to the Czar, June 7, 1833, in which he said: "Our system in regard to the East has had for its principal tendency to give a greater consistency to certain parts of the Turkish Empire."

When the condition of Turkish affairs had reached its worst, and there seemed no possibility of preserving the Empire, the Czar sought a consultation with the Austrian Government, as the power which had the most direct interest in the affairs of the Balkan peninsula. At an interview with the Austrian Ambassador, on the 8th of February, 1833, after describing the sad situation of the Porte, with its internal disorders complicating the dangers from without, and expressing his willingness to come to its help if that was desired, he added, "but that is all that I can do. I can not give life to a dead body, and the Turkish Empire is dead; but," he continued, "if it falls, I do not want any of its remains, I have no need of them." In the same year the treaty of Munchengratz was concluded between Russia and Austria, in which the two powers mutually engaged themselves to persevere in the policy of maintaining the existence of the Ottoman Empire under the actual dynasty, and to consecrate to that end, "in a perfect accord," every means of influence and action in their power. In contemplation, however, of the possible extinction of the Turkish Empire, a secret article was added to the treaty providing that the two powers should act in concert and in a perfect spirit of solidarity in reference to everything that concerned the establishment of the new order of things which it would be necessary to arrange. In 1839, Mehemet Ali again rose against his suzerain and put Constantinople in peril. England and France now appeared as the champions of Turkey, both being actuated by suspicions of the designs of Russia. Under these circumstances the Czar repeatedly instructed his representatives at London, Paris, and Vienna to use all their influence to confine the conflict between Turkey and Egypt to as narrow limits as possible, so that it should not compromise the general peace of Europe. At the same time he sought to induce the Cabinet of Vienna to make the convention of Munchengratz the basis of the policy on which the two powers should continue to act together. The Government instructed its

3

Ambassador at Vienna to represent that the Czar was then, as before, firmly resolved to employ every means in his power to maintain the existence of the Ottoman Empire under the actual dynasty; to oppose every combination which could attack the independence of the authority of the Sultan; to accept no order of affairs which might imperil the actual existence of the Ottoman Empire; and, finally, to agree with Austria upon the most efficacious measures to be adopted in common, between the two imperial courts, to prevent the dangers which a sudden change in the existence of the Ottoman Empire might bring to those parts of their estates which bordered on Turkey. The Czar, it is explained, thus decided to take the side of the Sultan, not because of any particular friendship to him, but because he was convinced that if the Turkish Empire was destroyed, Mehemet Ali would be able to build up a new living State, dangerous to Russia. The Czar at this time declined to join in a call for a conference of the great powers, because it was convinced that France and England were seeking objects opposed to Russian interests, or in other words, that they did not wish to secure the repose of the East, as much as to fetter the Russian power. The Russian Government proposed to Austria, in 1843, to communicate confidentially to the powers the terms of the convention of Münchengratz, which provided for the maintenance of the Turkish power in Europe, hoping thereby to dissipate the prejudices and suspicions prevalent in England against Russia. The Austrian Minister would not agree to make it known, and the convention remained a secret until it was very recently revealed. It is doubtful if publication, even at the time it was suggested, would have had any influence upon English feeling, which had already begun to become an element of party division. The prevailing opinion that Russia opposed the closing of the Dardanelles and the Bosphorus to ships of war is contradicted by Prof. Martens, who cites from the Imperial archives evidence that no power contended with as much energy for the closing of the straits as Russia. The Government repeatedly instructed its representatives, while the negotiations were going on, to insist upon this point, and the Czar Nicholas is said to have declared categorically that the security of the Turkish Empire, and of the Russian possessions on the Black Sea, could not be guaranteed unless it was carried. On this point, Russia was opposed to the Austrian Cabinet, who sought to separate this question from that of the integrity of Turkey.

The Russian Ambassador made explanations of the views of his Government to Lord Palmerston, which, while they did not remove the jealousy and apprehension of the Russian purposes entertained by the British Government and people, led the Premier to declare that both England and Russia had often had cause to regret that the duty of solving the Eastern Question had not been given to them alone. The Czar gave his full assent to a note intended to influence the domestic policy of the Turkish Government, which was drawn up by Prince Metternich, the Austrian Prime Minister, in 1841. In this paper it was announced that the intrinsic defects of the Turkish system, growing out of the want of homogenity of the people and the weakness of the Government, were aggravated and intensified by the efforts to introduce reforms in the European fashion, which the Sultans were endeavoring to carry out " without any other support than a profound ignorance and an immense mass of illusions." The document contained the strange doctrine that " States in decay are, as a rule, less able to govern themselves under happy circumstances than in misfortune, which has become for them a normal condition, a species of second nature," and gave the advice that the Turks should establish their Government upon respect for their own religious institutions, consult and act upon the emergencies of the moment, and " remain Turks. Accord to your Christian subjects the most complete protection ; exercise toward them a genuine tolerance ; do not suffer Pashas and subalterns to molest them ; do not meddle in their religious affairs, but be their sovereign protector in all their privileges ; keep all the promises that you made in the edict of Gulhane." Russia repeated substantially the same advice in a note addressed to the Porte about a month later. It was mistaken advice ; but the fact exists that the two powers held the views it embodies at the time it was given. Prof. Martens, at the conclusion of his review, sums up the principles of Russian policy in the East to be : 1. Russia has always considered the fate of the Christian subjects of the Porte a matter of common concern to all the European powers ; 2. In case the great powers reach no common understanding, that one of them, whose interests are drawn most directly into sympathy by disturbances in the East, has the moral and judicial right to intervene in the internal affairs of Turkey ; and, 3. The prime and real object of Russian policy in respect to the Ottoman Empire has been nothing else than the improvement of the condition of the Christian populations without distinction of race and faith.

The growth of Russia, at the expense of Turkey, and the plans of further aggrandizement, which are commonly attributed to it, have nowhere aroused so great jealousy and so bitter enmity as among some of the leading statesmen of England. Russia and England are at present the two great Empires of the world. If we say that the Emperor of Russia and the Queen each rule over a territory of more than 8,000,000 square miles, or more than double the extent of the United States, and that the Empire next to them in point of size has less than 4,000,000 square miles, it will be seen how far both, in this respect, have run ahead of the remainder of the world. A position like this is well adapted to engender feelings of rivalry and jealousy. Both Empires are still continuing to annex new territory, and in the race for the highest place among the States, neither would like to be greatly distanced by the other. In Asia the borders of the two Empires now almost meet, and many British statesmen have long been haunted by the fear that the disappearance of this small neutral zone, which still separates British India from the latest Russian conquest, may soon be followed by a collision of the two great Empires. In such a case Russia would have the great military advantage over England that all the parts of the Russian Empire are a compact whole, and that nets of railroads may enable the Government to bring within a short time vast bodies of troops to any point. India, on the other hand, is separated by an immense distance from England, and it will take a much longer time to obtain reinforcements from England. The route to India has of late been greatly shortened by the construction of the Suez Canal, and an alliance with the power in whose dominions lies the canal, is therefore of obvious advantage to England. Formerly the importance for England of Constantinople, in case of a war with Russia, was frequently discussed, as the shortest land route between England and India would lead through Germany, Austria, and Turkey. Since the construction of the Suez Canal, Constantinople is no longer so much talked of; but it is urged that as Turkey is the irreconcilable enemy of Russia, it is the manifest interest of England to maintain the Turkish power as much as possible, as in the present state of international relations, England can at any time compel the alliance of the Turks. All this reasoning, it will be seen, depends upon the supposition that there may be at some future time some tremendous war between Russia and England; that in this war, Turkey can not help siding with England, and that therefore England must keep

Turkey as powerful as possible, and that she must, as much as possible, prevent any further aggrandizement of Russia. It is, however, only the statesmen of one party, the Tories, who hold these anti-Russian views. The other great party in England, the Liberals, are decidedly unfavorable and hostile to Turkey. They insist that in any speculation on the future, the utter rottenness of the Turkish Empire can not be overlooked; that it would be unworthy of England to disregard the terrible wrongs of the Christian provinces and their just claims to independence; that the fears of an impending conflict between Russia and England are greatly exaggerated; that wise statesmanship may remove the danger of a very serious complication, and that with regard to Turkey, an alliance between England and Russia might furnish at once the best solution of the Eastern Question by putting an end to the rule of the Turks over Christian provinces and Christian races. The controversy of the great political parties of England on this question has been carried on with great bitterness, and the Eastern Question has thus been in England for years the subject of the most venomous parliamentary war. The attitude of the ruling party of England with regard to any new complication between Russia and Turkey is a matter of grave importance; the changing ascendency of the two parties makes the great solution of the Eastern Question all the more obscure. In 1853, the anti-Russian party engaged with Turkey, France, and Sardinia in the Crimean war, which resulted in the defeat and humiliation of Russia. When the Bosnian insurrection of 1875 inaugurated the new Eastern war, the anti-Russian party was again in power, and great apprehensions were therefore again felt that this war might assume very large dimensions.

It is evident that the powers most directly and immediately interested in the solution of the Eastern Question—the Christian races of Turkey, Austria, Russia, and England—widely and radically differ in their views. The Christian races agree in the demand of an entire expulsion of the Turks from Europe, and of the substitution for the Turkish dominion in Europe of a number of independent States, based upon the nationality principle. The real designs of the Russian policy are, to a large extent, shrouded in mystery; but it is fully admitted by Russia, that she wants a greater development of her naval strength and, therefore, free naval communication with the Mediterranean. The views of the Russian Government with regard to the Turkish rule in Europe have undergone many changes;

but the unchanging element in them is the desire of Russia to see
the Balkan peninsula, if not in her own possession, at least occupied
by weak and impotent States. The attention of England is mo-
nopolized by the question whether Russia plans any movements which
might endanger the British interests in the East. Austria is chiefly
concerned in preventing the establishment of powerful States on
her southern border, which might increase the dissatisfaction of
the Slavic and Rumanian population of Austria. None of the
other States of Europe has so direct and immediate an interest in
Turkish affairs as the powers just mentioned. France has taken
the Catholic subjects of Turkey under her special protection, and
was formerly very active in the affairs of the East, but has been
compelled by its own internal condition, since 1870, to refrain from
conspicuous participation relating to them. In general, the European
States can not be supposed to be favorably disposed toward an extension of Russian rule in South-eastern Europe; for, even the
present extent of the Russian Empire is believed by most of them
to involve great dangers for the future. But in case of general wars
arising out of complications in the East, some States may always
expect to derive greater advantages from an alliance with Russia,
than from joining an anti-Russian combination. Thus, the German
Government has been for many years on intimate terms with the
Government of Russia, and may be expected to aid Russia, at least
indirectly, in her Eastern policy, as long as she can rely on a similar
aid from Russia in case of new complications with France. Even
the Emperor of Austria attributed so great importance to friendly
relations with the Czar of Russia, that he formed, in 1872, an agreement with the Emperors of Russia and Germany, which has been
known as the Tri-Imperial Alliance, or the Alliance of the Three
Emperors, and by which it was stipulated that they should act in
common in international complications, and that neither should take
an important step without first consulting the others.

The progressing decay of Turkey on the one hand, and the diverg-
ing views of the great powers of Europe, in regard to the future of
the Balkan peninsula, on the other, naturally awakened an immediate
interest of all Europe in any Turkish war, and generally led to the,
at least diplomatic, interference of other governments. When the
intervention of England and her allies had ended the Turkish-
Egyptian conflict, the treaties of 1840 and 1841 formally admitted
Turkey into the political system of European States. The attempt

of Russia to extort from the Porte in the Crimean war (1853–1855) certain guarantees of the rights of the Greek Christians in Turkey, induced England, France, and Sardinia to take sides with Turkey, on the ground that the very existence of Turkey and the equilibrium of power in Europe were endangered by Russia. The Treaty of Paris (1856), while it expressly denied the right of the powers to interfere in the domestic concerns of the Empire, defined the privileges of the tributary States, and made the powers guarantees of their preservation, and referring to concessions which the Porte had promised to the people of the provinces still subject, by implication gave the powers the right to exert a moral influence in favor of their being carried into effect. On the other side, the treaty worked to prevent Russia or any other State acting singly from constituting itself the especial guardian of the rights and interests of the Christian subjects, and made the same a matter of general European concern. The first occasion on which the provisions of the treaty afterward came up for discussion, was on the occasion of the massacre of Christians in Syria, in 1860, when a French corps was sent, with the unwilling consent of the Porte, to restore order. It would have remained in Syria after the emergency which justified its presence had passed, had it not been for the force of the objections which were set up under the Paris treaty. The next occasion was during the Cretan insurrection in 1866, when an intervention which would have been a clear violation of Turkish sovereignty and of the Treaty of Paris, seemed imminent for a considerable time, and was barely prevented. In 1870, Russia, taking advantage of a time when one of the parties to the Treaty of Paris could not make effectual opposition, and the others were not prepared to resist its demand by force, insisted upon an essential modification of some of the provisions of the treaty, and obtained them at the London conference a few months afterward. A few comparatively unimportant points touching the Eastern Question were brought forward in the transactions of the three succeeding years. The agitation of the demands of the Bulgarians for ecclesiastical autonomy, which was settled in 1872, prompted some of the powers to make representations of their views to the Porte, but their offices were not accepted.

In 1873, the Russian Government, after a correspondence, the friendliness of which has been especially remarked upon, obtained from the Porte the grant to Russian subjects residing in Turkey, of considerable privileges and immunities in addition to those which they had before enjoyed. In 1873, the Porte complained of Rumania for encroaching upon the rights of the Sultan by concluding treaties with foreign powers without consulting with its suzerain. In the course of the correspondence which ensued, the Austrian, Russian, and other Governments informed the Porte that they could not suffer the important interests which they had upon the Danube to be interfered with by exaggerated pretensions of suzerainty on the Bosphorus, and that they intended to carry on their negotiations directly with the Rumanian Government. The Turkish Government replied that the Treaty of Paris must be maintained; but that if Rumania would submit its case, and the provisions of its treaties, to the Porte, arrangements could be made satisfactory to the parties. About this time, also, the Rumanian Government attracted attention by holding military maneuvers of a character which seemed more befitting an independent State than a principality which owed allegiance to a superior government. A correspondence took place between Turkey and Montenegro in 1874, respecting some murders committed by Turks upon Montenegrins at Podgoritza, in which Russia and Germany sought to promote intervention, but the Porte refused to tolerate it, and the affair was finally settled between the two parties immediately concerned.

Finally, the Herzegovinian insurrection, breaking out in 1875, threatened to bring up the whole Eastern Question in all of its complications, and actually produced that result in the end. The successive steps that were taken to ensure the speedy suppression of the insurrection, to prevent its spread, to keep the other provinces from participating in the movement, and to induce Turkey to satisfy the public sentiment of Europe, and their failure, are recorded in the pages that follow. The moral aid of Great Britain, as the power supposed to be most influential with the Turkish Government, was invoked in behalf of the reasonable requests of the Christians, and was given, in the British signature to the Andrassy note; but when the British Government was asked to go further and sanction a threat of force by signing the Berlin note, it declined; for it was determined not to consent to a new European war upon Turkey under any pretext. After the failure of the conference proposed by England, and of the protocol, Russia professed to consider that it had fulfilled all the conditions of the Tri-Imperial Alliance, and could be no longer held bound by the restrictions of the Treaty of Paris, and decided to go to war upon its own responsibility.

We have now reviewed all the different elements which constitute the Eastern Question—the hatred of the Turks by the Christian provinces and the anxious hope of the latter for deliverance from Turkish rule; the sympathy of Russia with the Christians of Turkey, and her desire for the crippling of Turkey, and for her own aggrandizement; the distrust with which Austrian and Hungarian statesmen look upon the movements going on among the Slavs; the jealousy of the ruling British statesmen against the designs of Russia. In the entire history of the Eastern Question during the nineteenth century it has been assumed as granted that the Turks alone would not be able to arrest the progressing decay of their Empire. The parties concerned have regarded Turkey as "the sick man" whose consumptive life has been with difficulty prolonged by artificial means. The implacable enemies of the Turks have represented all the reforms that have been attempted by them, as meaningless and insincere; her patrons have had to admit that they were insufficient to avert the impending danger. When the Eastern Question, in 1875, once more began to expand into another Eastern war, it was the common opinion that without aid from England or Austria it would be extremely difficult, and perhaps impossible, for Turkey to resist the combined onset of her own Christian subjects and of the Russians.

Before we enter into a narrative of this war, a brief historical sketch of the belligerent powers and their present condition will be needed to understand fully the great events on the scene of hostilities.

CHAPTER II.

HISTORICAL SKETCH OF RUSSIA.

Origin of the Russians—The Republic of Novgorod—Occupation of Russia by the Mongol Tartars—Rise of the Principality of Moscow—Ivan the Great, the First Prince who called Himself Czar—Ivan the Terrible—Michael Romanoff—Peter the Great—Anna—Elizabeth—Catherine the Great—Alexander I.—Nicholas I —Alexander II.

THE Russian Empire has attained its present vast extent and power by a career of aggression and conquest which it has carried on almost uninterruptedly since the fifteenth century. Russia first came into notice as a State in the ninth century. The country known as Sarmatia to the ancients, had been occupied by different tribes, the principal of which were Slavs and Finns, while the Scythians dwelt in the south-east, around the Caspian Sea. Novgorod, the oldest of the Russian towns, often called "the Mother of the Russian cities," was a flourishing republic in the ninth century, inhabited by Slavs, and surrounded by Finnic settlements. It became involved in dissensions, and the Slavs, with some of the Finnic tribes, invited Rurik, a chief of the Varangian tribe called Rus, to come and assist them and reign over them. Rurik came about the year 862, with two of his brothers, both of whom died shortly afterward, put down the dissensions, and made himself master of the country. The sovereign authority remained in the hands of his descendants for nearly two hundred years. The name of the tribe Rus. to which Rurik belonged, is perpetuated in the present name of the Empire. The story of Rurik, which is supposed to embody the history of the foundation of the Empire, is symbolized in a monument of original and peculiar design, which was erected in the principal square of Novgorod in 1862, in commemoration of the thousandth anniversary of that event.

Oleg, who succeeded Rurik as regent, annexed the principality of Kiev, designing to make the city of that name the capital of the State, and made war upon the Khazars, who lived between the Dnieper and the Caspian Sea. Sviatoslav, 957 to 972, continued the wars against the Khazars, attacked the Bulgarians and other tribes as far as the Black Sea, and extended the borders of the State

(52)

MONUMENT ERECTED AT NOVGOROD

COMMEMORATING THE 1000TH ANNIVERSARY OF THE FOUNDING OF THE RUSSIAN EMPIRE.

TYPES OF RUSSIAN SOLDIERS

to the Sea of Azov. Upon the death of this prince, the territory was divided among his sons, and continued to be divided, with the exception of short intervals of union, till the nation became in effect a kind of a confederacy, of which the different members were rivals to each other, and in dissension. Losses of territory were suffered from the aggressions of the Lithuanians, Poles, Teutonic Knights, and other rival States, till finally, in 1237, the country was overrun, and the greater part of it taken possession of and made tributary by the Mongol Tartars, followers of Genghis Khan. The city of Novgorod maintained its independence during the greater part of the two and a half centuries of the Tartar occupation, but with smaller extraneous territory and diminishing influence. One of its sovereigns, Alexander Nevskoi, 1247 to 1263, distinguished himself by victories over the Swedes, Livonians, and Lithuanians. This little State remained, during its whole existence, really a republic, its prince, or executive, possessing merely such authority as was freely granted to him by the people. "The supreme power," says Wallace, in his "Russia," "resided not in the prince, but in the assembly of the citizens called together in the market-place by the sound of the great bell." This assembly made laws "for the prince as well as for the people," entered into alliances, imposed taxes, and performed all the other functions of government, including the election of magistrates and the judgment and deposition of them when it thought fit. It was its attachment for their old institutions, and its unwillingness to accept despotism instead of them, that brought upon Novgorod the savage destruction inflicted upon it in the sixteenth century by Ivan the Terrible.

The principality of Moscow—from which Russia was for a long time known abroad as Muscovy—rose into prominence during the fourteenth century, and began to absorb the other Russian States. Ivan I., 1328 to 1340, united with it the principality of Tver. Demetrius was engaged in hard-conflicts with the Mongols. Vasili II., 1389 to 1425, incorporated Nijni Novgorod, and Suzdal, and Vasili III., 1425 to 1462, added Halicz, Mozhaisk, and Berovsk. The principality of Moscow, as thus formed, at the accession of Ivan III., the Great, in 1462, was the nucleus around which has grown the present Empire. It occupied a territory of nearly seven hundred miles in length from north to south, and two hundred miles in breadth from east to west, situated between the 51st and 61st degrees of north latitude, with the cities of Nijni Novgorod, and Tver nearly marking its extreme eastern and western limits. Ivan the Great, 1462 to 1505, delivered the land entirely from the Tartars, made the Khan of Kazan tributary, annexed Novgorod, Perm, Pskov, and several other Russian principalities, and carried the Russian arms into Siberia, in 1499, but was defeated in a war with Livonia by the Teutonic Knights in 1501. Ivan was a haughty prince, the first of the rulers of Russia to assume the title of Czar, and laid great stress, in his intercourse with the other sovereigns of Europe, on his equality with them. He built the Kremlin at Moscow, introduced improved arms, began to develop the mines of precious metals, and introduced Russia to foreign intercourse. His successor, Vasili IV., 1505 to 1533, by the final incorporation of Pskov, in 1510, completed the extinction of the semi-independent principalities into which the Empire had been divided, and made the Tartars of Kazan tributary. At the close of his reign, Russia extended from near the fiftieth degree of north latitude to the Arctic Ocean, and from the Ural Mountains to the eastern borders of Finland, Livonia, and Lithuania. Ivan IV., the Terrible, 1533 to 1584, who united with the most heinous crimes some splendid virtues, and was at once a scourge and a benefactor to Russia, reconquered Kazan, subdued Astrakhan, and united the country of the Don with the Empire. Siberia was conquered during his reign by a Cossack freebooter, Yarmak Timofeyeff. As an offset to his victories, he was forced to cede Livonia to the Swedes. So marked a mixture of good and evil as was this sovereign has seldom appeared in history. His temper was so violent, his cruelties were so excessive, that he might well have been called mad, and he was totally unscrupulous in many matters of morals. He ordered the city of Novgorod destroyed, and its inhabitants butchered, in a fit of rage, on account of the discontent it had manifested against his despotic rule, so that from the most flourishing city and commercial mart of the North, it became an obscure village, above which it has never since risen. On the other hand, he delivered Russia from the last traces of Tartar rule, made conquests over the Mohammedans, opened the country to foreign trade, introduced printing, instituted clerical reforms, assembled a Parliament, and drew up a code of laws, worthy to be well spoken of. Michael Romanoff, the founder of the present reigning dynasty, extended the Siberian conquests nearly to the Pacific, and his son Alexis restored or annexed to the Empire, Tchernigov, Smolensk, Kiev, and the Ukraine.

At the accession of Peter the Great in 1689, the Russian Empire had attained the dimensions of a great realm, and presented a shape approaching that which it exhibits at the present time. Its European possessions had been extended to the Caspian Sea and the Caucasus Mountains, and it had acquired territory in Asia extending from the fiftieth degree of north latitude to the Arctic Ocean, and covering one hundred degrees of longitude. Peter devoted his attention principally to the development of the material resources and the improvement of the civilization of his country. The story of his journeys in Europe, and his working disguised in ship-yards, and inspecting the armaments and workshops of different nations, in order to become personally acquainted with the arts which had made them strong, and introduce them to his own country, has been told very often, and is known to every reader. To him, more than to any of his predecessors or all of them together, is due the wonderful progress which Russia has made, and the position it has attained among the nations. He added to the territory of the Empire, Ingria, part of Karelia, Esthonia, and Livonia from Sweden, Daghestan and other territories on the Caspian Sea, from Persia, and the towns of Baku and Derbent. The Persian acquisitions were lost under Anna, 1730 to 1740, but in recompense she made the Kirghiz tributary, completed the incorporation of Siberia to Behring's Straits, and added the Aleutian Islands. Elizabeth, 1741 to 1762, gained some districts of Finland. At the close of her reign, the extreme western boundary of the Empire was the Baltic Sea, its extreme eastern point was near the coast of North America, and it stretched through more than one hundred and sixty degrees of longitude. Catherine the Great, whose reign from 1762 to 1796 was a long and splendid one of unprincipled conquest, added nearly two hundred and twenty-five thousand square miles of territory to the Empire, including the country of the Kirghiz, Courland, the Crimea, Azov, and Russian Poland. To this sovereign is ascribed the origin of the policy which has been imputed to Russia, of systematic aggression against Turkey, for the sake of acquiring Constantinople, and establishing a new Christian Empire of the East.

Alexander I., 1801 to 1825, was distinguished for his conspicuous participation in the wars against Napoleon, in the course of which the boundaries of the States of Europe were changed very often. Russia gained and lost, along with the rest of the States which were engaged in these wars, but permanently lost little. At the end of the reign of Alexander, it had gained all the provinces of Georgia, the district of Bialystock, Finland, the Aland Islands, a part of Bothnia, and the peninsula of Alaska, in North America. Alexander, with the Emperor of Austria and the King of Prussia, formed the Holy Alliance, under the operation of which the aspirations of the people for freedom, awakened by the career of Napoleon, were trampled down, and the States of continental Europe were placed and kept for a whole generation under the rule of petty sovereigns who were mostly foreign to them, and whom they hated, but were prevented by the powers of the Alliance from removing.

The reign of Nicholas, 1825 to 1855, was severe and prosperous at the beginning, but ended in misfortune. Until the occurrence of the war in the Crimea, Russia shared with Austria the predominance in the councils of the European States, and was the object of anxious regard and dread on the part of the other great powers. The rule of this Czar was aggressive and domineering toward other nations, and intensely despotic toward his own people. He instituted the cruel policy which has resulted in crushing out entirely the nationality of Poland, and abolishing its separate administration. In pursuance of this policy, he banished tens of thousands of Poles to Siberia, and gave the appearance of reality to the purpose he is said to have expressed of making a Siberia, that is a waste, of Poland, and a Poland, that is a well populated country, of Siberia. Not only were Poles sent to Siberia; men from all parts of the Empire, accused of every kind of offense, but chiefly of those of a political character, were consigned to that inhospitable region as to a prison, until the dread of being sent to this place of exile became a common misery to all distinguished Russians. Nicholas co-operated with Austria in repressing the popular uprisings of 1848, and in endeavoring to perpetuate the system of autocracy which had been imposed upon Europe by the Holy Alliance. He lent efficient aid in the cruel suppression of the Hungarian revolution, and to this is owing in part the present attitude of the Hungarians of unwavering and intense hostility to every Russian interest and every friend of Russia, and their disposition to favor the Turks. Under this sovereign, Russia suffered the most disastrous defeats it has encountered since its conquest by the Tartars, in the Crimean war, when France, England, and Sardinia assisted the Porte in repelling its attacks upon the Turkish sovereignty. Russia lost in this war a part of its territory in Bessarabia and around the mouths of the Danube, and was obliged to submit to restrictions upon its privileges in the Black Sea, to forego all its claims to the right to interfere in behalf of the Christian subjects of Turkey, and to see its predominance in the councils of Europe disappear, to be replaced first by that of France, later by that of Germany. It is worthy of remark that the efforts of Nicholas to repress the progress of popular development have all failed, and that the condition of Europe is, to-day, the reverse of what he would have had it. Hungary is free and self-governed. Austria has suffered the introduction of popular institutions, and every State in Europe enjoys a constitutional government, except Russia. The additions to Russian power made by Nicholas were the gain of Erivan and Nakhitchevan, and of the exclusive control of the Caspian Sea.

The reign of the present Emperor Alexander II. has been one of the most prosperous and liberal in Russian history. Previous great Czars have sought chiefly the development of the material resources and the moral and physical strength of the State as a political unit. Alexander's policy has been aimed at the culture and the amelioration of the condition of the people. The emancipation of the serfs is one of the noblest acts of humanity on record. Except for the wars with the Turkomans of Central Asia, which, like our wars with the Indians and the wars of the British in India, have been rather wars of necessity than of conquest, his reign has been one of peace, and under it the country has made great advances in the arts and sciences. It has been marred by continued cruelties in Poland, by the despotic efforts to repress the local languages of the provinces, and by religious persecutions, which seem to be still pursued as a part of the settled policy of the Imperial Administration to make the population of the Empire a unit in religion, language, and customs. The present reign has been distinguished also by the development of the Panslavic idea in the steady cultivation of the doctrine of the unity of the Slavic race, and by efforts to create a public opinion in all the Slavic States in and out of Russia in favor of the separation of the people of that race from political associations with other races, and their organization into distinct States to be ruled or protected by Russia. Alexander has added to the Russian Empire the territories of the Khanates of Central Asia, and the region of the Amoor River in extreme Eastern Asia; but has, on the other hand, ceded by sale to the United States the territory of Alaska in North America.

The following tables exhibit at a view the steady growth of Russia in territory and population :

			English Square Miles.
In 1462 the Czardom of Muscovy contained about.....			382,700
In 1505 Russia contained about..			510,300
In 1584	"	"	.. . .	1,530,800
In 1650	"	"	'	5,038,800
In 1689	"	"	....	5,953,000
In 1730	"	"	. ...	6,888,500
In 1775	"	"	.. . .	7,122,300
In 1868	"	"	... .	7,866,500
In 1877	"	"	. . . .	8,391,800

The population of the Empire in 1722, when the first census was taken, was fourteen millions; in 1742 it was sixteen millions; in 1762, nineteen millions; in 1782, twenty-eight millions; in 1796, thirty-six millions; in 1812, forty-one millions; in 1815, forty-five millions; in 1835, sixty millions; in 1851, sixty-eight millions; in 1858, seventy-seven millions; in 1875, 86,486,000.

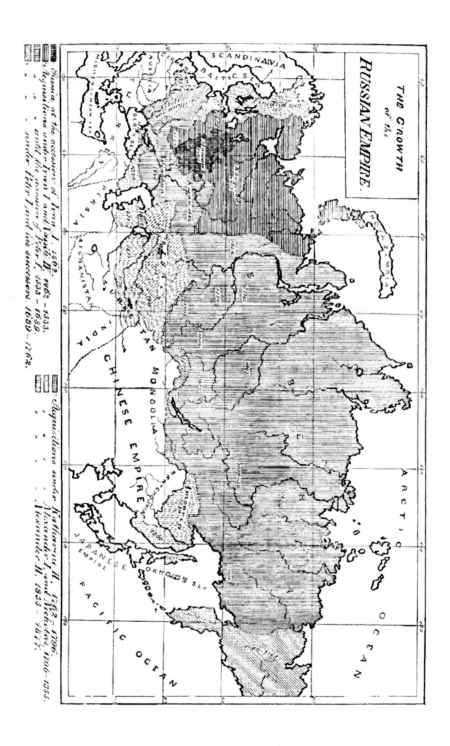

THE Growth
of the
RUSSIAN EMPIRE.

Russia at the accession of Ivan I, 1462.
Acquisitions under Ivan I and Vasili II, 1462 - 1533.
until the accession of Peter I, 1533 - 1689.
under Peter I and his successors, 1689 - 1762.

Acquisitions under Katharine II, 1762 - 1796.
Alexander I and Nicholas, 1796 - 1855.
Alexander II, 1855 - 1877.

RUSSIAN PEASANTS.

CHAPTER III.

CONDITION OF RUSSIA.

The Races of Russia—Backwardness of Civilization—Abolition of Serfdom—Public Instruction—Russia the only State in Europe without a Representative Form of Government—The Policy of Russianization—Religious Intolerance—Agricultural Resources—Scarcity of Large Towns—The Village Commune—The Provincial Assembly—The Russian Church and the Dissenters—The Army, Navy, and Finances of Russia.

THE dominant population in Russia is of the Slavic race. Four-fifths of the entire population of the Empire belong to this race, and it predominates in a large majority of the provincial governments. To it belong the Great, Little, and White Russians, inhabiting Russia proper, and numbering forty-nine millions, the Bulgarians, Servians, and other Slavic people living in different parts of the Empire, and the Slavs of Poland and Lithuania, who number some seven millions. The Slavs are, for the most part, attached to the orthodox Greek Church, but the Poles are Roman Catholic. Next to the Slavs in importance and influence are the Finns, numbering 3,038,000, and the Lithuanians, numbering 2,343,000. Jews are found in the commercial centers, most largely in Poland, to the number of 2,800,000, and Armenians and Greeks in the southern Asiatic and European parts of the Empire in lesser numbers. Russians form the predominant race in Siberia, but there are many Mongol tribes in that region, mostly Pagans or Buddhists in religion. The rest of Asiatic Russia, from the southern borders of Siberia down to the Persian frontier, is inhabited by the Mohammedan Tartars, Turkomans, and Caucasians, all more or less dissatisfied with Russian rule, but kept in subjection partly by interest, partly by force   The Slavs and Finns are loyal to the Empire, but the Poles and Mohammedans can not be relied upon.

Russia, as well as Turkey, is behind the most advanced nations in civilization. Russia has only emerged from barbarism within the past two hundred years, and although it has within that period established several centers of the highest civilization, is still obliged to see a large part of its rural population lingering in a state of primitive simplicity as to knowledge and the arts. The Russians

4

are of the same religion, the Christian, and the same great race, the Indo-Germanic, or Aryan, with the most advanced nations of the world, and may readily sympathize and co-operate with them in all general movements. Since the days of Peter the Great, they have striven to emulate other nations, and have thus been drawn into the atmosphere of civilization. Having risen by its vast strength to the rank of one of the Great Powers of the world, and to be associated on equal terms with the leaders of civilization, while it still remained far behind in culture, Russia has felt itself instinctively and peremptorily compelled to try to make itself equal in all respects to its neighbors. With this object it has made all possible efforts to promote the intellectual and social advancement of its people. Rulers, the higher classes, and the people, have all joined in the efforts according to their capacity and degree of understanding of its object, and great progress has been made. Serfdom has been abolished, a great social reorganization has been undertaken, education has been promoted, and a literature has been developed, respectable and voluminous enough to receive the attention and the praises of foreign critics.

The abolition of serfdom was an event in the progress of the Empire quite as important, and destined to have as influential a bearing on the civilization of the country as the abolition of slavery in the United States. It was effected by a decree of the Czar Alexander II., issued on the 3d of March, 1861, and was a measure carried out solely in the interest of civilization. It was applied to the whole Empire, and elevated to freedom twenty-two million serfs belonging to private owners, and a still larger number belonging to the crown, making free in all 44,225,075 men and women, or more than one-half the population of the Empire, who had before been attached to the soil as a part of the real estate. Provision was made at the same time for the assignment of a portion of land to the emancipated serfs; and in order that the great act might be accomplished without injustice, a plan was devised for the reimbursement of the former owners for their loss in estate. The serf was held to pay twenty per cent. of his capital value directly to the holder to whom he had been attached; while the Government advanced the remaining eighty per cent within five years, to be repaid by the freedman in forty-nine years. All of the arrangements for abolition were completed at the end of July, 1865, when serfdom may be said to have technically ceased to exist in Russia. It appears, however, by a report recently published in the *Golos*, of St. Petersburg, that there are still two million serfs in the country whose emancipation has not been effected, either in consequence of the high price of the land or of their own unwillingness to accept the new state of things.

The system of Public Instruction has been gradually developed, and although it is still imperfectly and insufficiently applied, has been greatly improved within a few years. The schools are not all under one head of administration, as is the case in most other countries; but each ministry has a number of special schools under its own control, while some are conducted by the clergy, thus preventing full unity in organization. Primary instruction is regulated by the law of 1874, which provided for the establishment and conduct of four classes of schools: primary schools under the direction of the clergy; similar schools, both public and private, under the direction of the Minister of Public Instruction; elementary schools, supported by the communes and under the control of other ministries; and Sunday-schools The usual elementary branches are taught in these schools, and the use of the Russian language is obligatory. District or circle schools are established in the center of every circle for the children of the merchants, trades-people, and other inhabitants of the cities, in which some degree of academic instruction is afforded, and teachers' institutes have been established in connection with them. The Empire—except Finland, which has its own administration; the Caucasus, which is administered by its Governor; and Central Asia —is divided for school purposes into nine districts, in which the provision of schools and the attendance are very unequal. The average of the whole is about one school for every 3,100, and one pupil for every eighty inhabitants. Secondary instruction is afforded in 455 gymnasia of various grades and under different administrations, which were attended in 1877 by 87,775 pupils; and instruction in special branches is furnished by upward of three hundred theological, military, naval, technical, and other schools. The eight universities had in 1875 five hundred and sixty-nine instructors and 6,408 students. A beginning has been made for introducing compulsory education at St. Petersburg.

The Press is held under a strict censorship, the direction of which is in the office of the Minister of the Interior, with special censor-commissions or single censors in the principal cities. Under the rules of this office the publication is forbidden of articles against the dogmas of the orthodox Church, against the form of government or the person of the Czar or any member of his family, and of slanders upon any private person. The publication of any information concerning the Imperial family is forbidden until permission has been granted. The censorship applies to books and music as well as to newspapers. Of late years the severity of the censorship has undergone a practical relaxation, so that journals have been allowed considerable freedom in the discussion of political and social topics, so long as they do not criticise the pet schemes of the Government. The Press laws have been enforced with constant rigor against the papers in the Baltic provinces and Poland, which have spoken too freely against the Russianizing measures of the Government; and several papers in different parts of the Empire were suspended in 1875 for their indiscreet utterances. In the year 1873, 409 periodicals were published in Russia, of which twenty-two received a support from the Government. Literary activity has only recently been largely developed in Russia. It has, however, already become quite vigorous; books are rapidly multiplying, and a high standard of merit has been reached, insuring to Russian works favorable attention in the most cultivated literary circles. The most prominent works are of fiction, which have a marked, distinctive character, of science, and of Oriental philology, in which Russian scholarship has made a very creditable mark.

In point of political administration and religious liberty, Russia is behind every other civilized nation. Alone among the important European States, it has not yet attained a representative government. The Czar exercises the authority as well as bears the title of an autocrat, and governs the Empire through boards of his own appointment, which carry out his will. It has been the policy of the Government to allow conquered or annexed provinces to preserve for a time their old institutions. The Grand Duchy of Finland keeps its ancient Constitution, reserved to it by a special grant. In other conquered provinces, administrative independence has been gradually taken away. Thus Poland had a separate Government till 1864, when it was placed under the rule of a Council of State, and is now, under a new regulation, governed directly from St. Petersburg. A beginning was made several years ago, for the organization of Provincial Legislatures, but they have never attained any real efficiency. The Empire is divided into General Governments, or viceroyalties, governments, and districts, besides a number of provinces which, on account of the thinness of their population, have not been organized into regular governments. The Governors-General, or Viceroys, are appointed by the Emperor, and represent him, and have supreme control of all affairs, and the direction of all under-officers. Even the judgments of the courts are subject to their revision. Each general governor has to assist him a civil governor and council, who, however, have no independent functions. Only in local parish and district affairs has any one but the Czar authority. Here, for a paradox, we have popular government in its simplest and purest form. The whole country is divided into communities which are called *Mir*, and these are formed into *Valosti*, or districts of about two thousand inhabitants each. The communes and districts elect their own officers and assemblies, which discuss and decide all questions relating to such affairs as the division of the field, the arrangement of tenancies, the distribution of taxes, accounts, recruiting, the admission of new members, complaints to the Czar, and the like. The communal assemblies meet three times a year. The people of the villages also choose tribunals which have jurisdiction of small offenses and disputes relating to property below a certain amount.

Some of the most remarkable manifestations of Russian ideas and policy have been seen in the measures of the Government for the Russianization of the non-Russian people, in political system, religion, and language. The gradual abolition of the institutions of Poland has been mentioned. A similar process has been adopted in other parts of the Empire. Great stress has been laid upon securing the universal use of the Russian language. Compulsion has been employed to make it the language of the schools and the Church, and to banish other languages from the books and the newspapers. The idea of making a single language current, and generally understood throughout the Empire, is in accordance with a general tendency of our times; but to resort to force, and infringe upon domestic rights, as has been done in Poland and the Baltic provinces, is certainly not consistent with even a moderate degree of civilization. It may be a benefit to confer upon the barbarous tribes of the East a language of civilization and literature, but the attempt to force it upon an unwilling people, already in possession of such cultured languages as the Polish and German, is reprehensible.

Both Russia and Turkey are countries of vast natural resources, which are as yet almost wholly undeveloped. Agriculture is the leading pursuit in either Empire. In Russia it must always be the main reliance of the mass of the population; and in comparison with the extent of agricultural development which the land is destined to receive, other industries will be of less importance. The capabilities of the land of Russia for agriculture are, however, by no means commensurate with the extent of the territory. A large part of the soil must be forever untillable. The northern slope, extending from the Ural-Baltic table-land to the Arctic Ocean, lies under a climate which imposes rigorous limits upon the amount and variety of production; a large part of it is occupied by swamps, or the *tundras*, and the extreme northern border is frozen during nearly the whole year. The middle zone, between the Ural-Baltic and the Ural-Carpathian tablelands, is occupied in the western part by extensive forests of fir and large tracts of fodder grass, but in the east contains great swamps. The soil of this district is very fertile, and capable of productive cultivation. Much of Asiatic Russia, as in the steppes of Turkistan and the Caspian, is desert, chilled by Arctic winds during most of the year, and scorched by a burning sun during the rest. In Southern Russia lie the great wheat-fields which have made this Empire the third principal grain-producing nation on the earth, only the United States and France exceeding it in production.*

Besides wheat, the leading agricultural products of Russia are rye, barley, oats, buckwheat, and millet, which are consumed in the country, and hemp and flax, which form considerable items in the export trade. The cultivation of the sugar-beet, and the manufacture of beet sugar, make a considerable figure in the table of productions. Tobacco, Indian-corn, and vines in the Crimea and Bessarabia, and along the river Don, and garden products form

---

* The amount of grain production of the three States we have named, was, according to the reports published by the English Board of Trade at the beginning of 1877 · For the United States, 1874, 308,000,000 bushels; for France, 1873, 230,000,000 bushels; and for Russia, 1872, 158,000,000 bushels The grain trade of Russia, however, does not seem to be increasing, but rather diminishing, under the pressure of competition from the United States, Canada, South America, and India. A few years ago, England drew from Russia a far larger supply of grain than from any other country. Suddenly, in 1874, according to a statement made in England, the exports of the United States made a great bound forward, and every year since, they have more and more exceeded the Russian, until in the agricultural year ending with the harvest of 1876, the United States and Canada sent to England nearly one-half its whole foreign imports, while Russia sent it only one-seventh. "In fact," it is stated, "while the Russian imports have fallen one-third, American have trebled since 1872" The cultivation of wheat is very imperfect in Russia, as the same returns from which we have quoted state that the average crop is only five and a half bushels, while in the United States it is twelve and one-half bushels, to the acre. The chief point of export for Russian wheat is at Odessa, on the Black Sea.

smaller, but by no means unimportant items. The wooded districts give large supplies of timber—firs in the North; oaks, limes, ashes, and maples in the South, which are floated down the rivers to the more scantily-timbered districts.

The grass-covered plains afford excellent facilities for raising live-stock. Horses are abundant and of excellent quality, good animals for general service being obtained from the Cossacks, Kalmucks, and Kirghiz, strong and hardy horses from Viatka, Kazan, and Finland, while a more highly-bred class are raised in the breeding-stables encouraged by the Government. A census report records the number of horses in the whole Empire at about eighteen million head. Of other live-stock, Russia contains about twenty-one million head of cattle, forty-five million sheep, and nine million pigs.

The Government has taken pains to encourage manufacturing in-dustry, and has gained a good measure of success. The more im-portant manufactures are those of textile fabrics of wool, linen, hemp, and cotton, and of leather. Many minerals and metals are found in the country, and a large industry is employed in the min-ing and manufacture of coal, coal-oil, iron, copper, bronze, zinc, and other metal and metallic products in smaller quantities. The Govern-ment endeavors to foster the industries and encourage the production of the country in every way, but the high rates of taxation which other exigencies demand are a great drawback to enterprise.

The great rivers are valuable aids to commerce. To them the Government has added a system of railroads, of which 12,945 miles had been constructed on the 1st of January, 1877, and about 1,324 miles more were under way. The length of telegraph lines on the 1st of January, 1876, was 58,675 miles, and the number of post-offices was 3,415. Foreign commerce and the coasting trade are carried on by a fleet of twenty-five hundred and twelve sea-going vessels, and the rivers of the Empire bear three hundred and eighty-five steamers. A peculiar feature in the distribution of population is the small number of large towns. In the whole of European Russia proper—this term excluding Finland, the Baltic provinces, Lithuania, Poland, and the Caucasus, which are countries annexed and not socially Russian—there are only one hundred and twenty-seven towns of more than ten thousand, twenty-five of more than 25,000, and eleven of more than 50,000 inhabitants; and only one-tenth part of the entire population are dwellers in towns, while in England more than one-half the inhabitants live in towns.

The peculiar feature of the Russian social organization is the Village Commune, or *Mir*. This institution has primarily to do with the allotment of the land among the inhabitants who are entitled to share in its use, but its functions have been extended to embrace nearly all the concerns of the local life. The lands of the Commune are held in common by all of its inhabitants, each family of whom has a fixed, inalienable right to a home and its proportionate share of the privilege of tillage and pasturage. If the amount of land is more than sufficient for the wants of the village, as is the case in many communes, these rights are practically unlimited. If there is no excess of land, the rights of each family are defined, and whoever wishes to enjoy more than his share, must pay for the privilege. Besides superintending the division of the land, the Commune is charged with the duty of assessing the taxes and transmitting the moneys received from this source to the Central Bureau. Each Commune is charged with an amount of taxes proportioned to the number of its male inhabitants as they appear in the official lists, and in its turn distributes the charge among the persons entitled to share in the communal privileges. The lists for the whole Empire are revised at irregular intervals, when the Commune makes a new division of the lands and a new assessment of the taxes. As important changes may often take place in the relations of the families between the periods of revision, which have averaged fifteen years, the Communal Assemblies are sometimes called upon at shorter periods to make adjustments of distribution in favor of equity, and each Commune does this in its own way. The affairs of the Commune are administered by the Village Assembly, of which all the heads of households are members. The authority of this body having never been legally defined, has become extended so as to cover nearly all the details of the village life and some personal matters. According to Mr. D. Mackenzie Wallace, in his "Russia," "It fixes the time for making the hay, and the day for commencing the plowing of the fallow-field; it decrees what measures shall be employed against those who do not punctually pay their taxes; it decides whether a new member shall be admitted into the Commune, and whether an old member shall be allowed to change his domicile; it gives or withholds permission to erect new buildings on the Communal land; it prepares and signs all contracts which the Commune makes with one of its own members or with a stranger; it interferes, whenever it thinks necessary, in the domestic

ODESSA.

A COSSACK.

affairs of its members." It elects the village officers, and allots the lands In illustration of its authority in matters more particularly personal, Mr. Wallace says : " If a peasant becomes a drunkard, or takes some equally efficient means to become insolvent, every family in the village has a right to complain, not merely in the interests of public morality, but from selfish motives, because all the families are collectively responsible for his taxes. For the same reason, no peasant can permanently leave the village without the consent of the Commune, and this consent will not be granted until the applicant gives satisfactory security for the fulfillment of all his actual and future liabilities. If a peasant wishes to go away for a short time, in order to work elsewhere, he must obtain a written permission, which serves him as a passport during his absence ; and he may be recalled at any moment by a Communal decree. In reality he is rarely recalled so long as he sends home regularly the full amount of his taxes."

The Commune is supplemented by the *Zemstvo,* or District Assembly, a body which was created about ten years ago by an Imperial Ukase, to have the charge of those public wants which it is beyond the reach of the Communal Assembly to provide for. It has the care of the repairs of the roads and bridges, of the provision of means of conveyance for public officers, of educational and sanitary affairs, looks after the condition of the crops, provides against the danger of scarcity, etc. It consists of an assembly of deputies, who are elected every three years by the landed proprietors, communes, and municipal corporations, and which meets every year, and of a permanent executive bureau elected by the assembly from among its members. Nobles and peasants are chosen to this body, and meet in it on a footing of equality, and without apparent antagonism ; the nobles, however, being the more conspicuous on account of their superior education and experience. The Provincial Assembly is a body whose members are chosen by the several district assemblies of the province, to take cognizance of those matters which concern more than one district.

These bodies are denied all political functions, so much so that, according to Wallace, the Government, very soon after it created them, " showed that it would not allow the assemblies to exert even a moral pressure by means of petitions and political agitation. As soon as the *Zemstvo* of St. Petersburg gave evidence of a desire to play a political part, the assembly was at once closed by Imperial command, and several of the leading members were banished for a time from the capital."

The Russian Church is a branch of the Oriental Greek Church, and is in communion with the four Patriarchates of Constantinople, Antioch, Jerusalem, and Alexandria. Its concerns were formerly regulated, like those of the other Eastern Churches, by a Patriarch, who resided at Moscow. The Patriarchate was allowed to die out in the reign of Peter the Great, and its place was supplied by an ecclesiastical council or synod, whose members were appointed by the Emperor. This body, the "Holy Synod," is the nominal governing body of the Church. It is a permanent college, or senate, of prominent dignitaries of the Church, who are nominated by the Czar, and are removable at his pleasure. Its acts are subject to the revision of the Czar, and take effect, when they are promulgated, as acts of the Government, rather than of the Church. The Czar appoints to every office in the Church, leaving to the bishops and prelates only the privilege of proposing candidates. He does not, however, assume to decide theological or dogmatic questions, but allows the synod to exercise its full discretion on such points. The duty of deciding and passing judgment in case of new heresies, likewise rests with the synod, but the judgment having been given, the Czar must command its execution before it can be carried into effect. If the questions at issue are critical, the opinions of the four patriarchs are sought, and in extreme cases a council may be called, the final result being, however, in every case dependent on the Czar to give it force. Each province, or government, forms a diocese administered by the bishop, assisted by a council, which, like the Holy Synod, has no independent authority, but simply represents the bishop. The ecclesiastical administration is in the hands of the "Black Clergy," or monks, while the parish priests, or "White Clergy," a poor, uneducated, little considered class, do most of the hard work, but do not share in the higher honors of the Church.

The Raskolnik, Dissenters, or Nonconformists, form a large body. They were separated from the Church in the latter part of the seventeenth century. Believing that the Church was departing from the primitive faith and introducing innovations in doctrine, the first Nonconformists refused to follow it, and assumed an attitude of protest against the innovations. They were excommunicated and subjected to persecutions, which continued till they were relaxed by Catherine the Great, since whose time they have been tolerated. They have been divided on the question of the recognition of the Old Church as a true Church, into " Old Ritualists" and Bezpopoftsi, or " Priestless people." The Old Ritualists accept their episcopal and priestly succession from the Old Church, but the " Priestless people," believing that that Church has destroyed itself by its departure from the faith, and has lost all authority, refuse to accept the sacraments and other rites, on the ground that there is no longer any priesthood. They have been split into a great variety of sects.

The Old Ritualists are not really very far removed from the orthodox Church, differing only in a few particulars of doctrine, which are regarded, now that the heat of controversy has passed, as of minor importance. The Government has adopted a policy of conciliatory measures to induce them to return, having among other things offered them special churches in which they could indulge their particular preferences of ritual, on condition of accepting the regularly consecrated priests, and submitting to ecclesiastical jurisdiction, but has not met with much success. The " Priestless people" were treated with severity until the accession of the present Czar. He has adopted toward them a milder policy, under the influence of which they have become less fanatical and exclusive, but show no signs of returning to the State Church.

There are also in Russia numerous sects called heretical. Two of them, the Molokáns and the Stundists, seem to be allied in faith to some of the evangelical bodies of Protestantism, the Molokáns being likened by Wallace to the Presbyterians, while the Stundists are generally spoken of as the Russian representatives of the Baptists. Besides these there are a variety of sects, professing all shades of doctrine, from those which accept the Scriptures as the basis of belief and the inspiration of their leading members as authentic means of interpreting them, to those which regard nervous excitement as a manifestation of religion, and practice rites which do not admit of description. Little is really known concerning many of these sects. The accounts of them which have reached the public have been generally furnished by strangers or persons prejudiced against them, who are not above exaggerating their more offensive peculiarities. They have been for many years under the observation of the police, and the Government has at times instituted severe measures to suppress them.

The Old Ritualists and Priestless people are estimated to number about seven millions of adherents; and the Molokáns, Stundists, and "fantastical sects" about three millions more. "If these numbers be correct," says Wallace, "the sectarians constitute about an eighth of the whole population of the Empire. They count in their ranks none of the nobles, none of the so-called enlightened class; but they include in their number the third and wealthiest part of the merchant class, the majority of the Don Cossacks, and all of the Cossacks of the Ural!" According to the official statistics of the Russian Government, the aggregate number of all sectarians is only about 1,200,000, an estimate which nearly all foreign writers on Russia agree in considering as too low. The Roman Catholic Church has in the Russian Empire a population of about seven and a half millions, who live almost exclusively in the provinces formerly belonging to Poland, and belong almost wholly to the Polish and Lithuanian nationalities. There were formerly in these provinces several millions of Uniats, or members of the Greek Church, who had united with Rome, but had been permitted to retain some rites and disciplinary laws of the Greek Church. These Uniats have been induced by the Russian Government to rescind their connection with Rome, and to re-unite with the Russian Church. The last remnant, the diocese of Chelm, in the kingdom of Poland, took this step in 1876 and 1877. Protestantism is the dominant religion in Finland, in the Baltic provinces, and the German settlements which are scattered through the south of Russia. The entire population connected with it is about 2,600,000, exclusive of the Grand Duchy of Finland, which is also almost wholly Protestant. The Jews are very numerous, especially in the provinces formerly belonging to Poland; they number about 2,800,000. The number of Mohammedans has been greatly increased by the enlargement of the Russian rule in Central Asia, where the bulk of the population belongs to the Islam; their total number in Russia now exceeds 7,000,000. The number of Pagans has been reduced to about 500,000, and continues to decrease. Excepting the case of the Uniats which has just been referred to, the Russian Church has made but little progress among Catholics, Protestants, Jews, and Mohammedans, but an increasing number of the members of these religions are entering the service of the National Government, an indication that the national unification of the Empire is making more rapid progress than the religious. Russia is frequently charged with being extremely intolerant in matters of religion. It is said that the State Government regards it as a crime to apostatize from the Greek Church to any other, and that any one who has once joined the Greek Church is not allowed to leave it again. The policy of the Russian Government with regard to the Baptists, which has often been mentioned in the religious journals of the United States, attracted the attention of the Evangelical Alliance, and caused a deputation from this body to be sent to St. Petersburg. The emigration of the Mennonites of Southern Russia to the United States was occasioned by a violation of their conscientious scruples by Russian laws, and the nonfulfillment of the pledges of the Government to respect them. With regard to these and other charges of intolerance, it must, however, be mentioned that some of them are declared by prominent Russians to be absolutely false, and that most of the Russian writers, including representative men of the Russian Church,* declare in favor of the principle of religious toleration.

The Russian armies are recruited in accordance with the military law of 1871, by an annual conscription, to which all able-bodied men of twenty-one years old and over are liable. Substitutes are not allowed, but special facilities are afforded to young men who have gained a certain degree of education, to become officers or pass over to the reserve. The period of service is fifteen years, six of which are spent in the active army and six in the reserve. All able-bodied men are liable to be called out in time of war to serve in the militia. In 1877, the Russian army was computed to number 28,645 officers, 662,073 combatants, and 97,380 non-combatants on a peace footing, and 44,894 officers, 1,626,780 combatants, and 169,080 non-combatants on a war footing. Besides its regular force, the Government commands a large supply of irregular troops, the most important of which are the Cossacks, who own their land in common, and are exempt from taxes, but are bound to perform military service, in lieu of the liability to taxation. They serve fifteen years in the active army and seven years in the reserve. The total number of irregular troops on a peace footing is 1,740 officers, 33,827 combatants, and 1,512 non-combatants. On a war footing there are 3,505 officers, 131,290 combatants, and 5,698 non-combatants

---

* A defense of the Russian Church against the charge of intolerance, by a Russian writer, is given in the New York *Churchman*, April 7, 1877. This writer, in particular, denies that real punishment has ever been inflicted upon persons who left the State Church, and that the right of propagating religious doctrines is exclusively possessed by the State Church.

The administration of the army is lodged with the War Minister, who is responsible only to the Czar. Its organization is complete, its equipment good, and its discipline efficient. Military institutes of different grades are provided for the instruction of the officers, as preparatory, middle, and higher schools, and special schools for the instruction of under-officers.

The military affairs of Finland are administered on a separate system from those of Russia. The province is expected to furnish a certain number of men on the demand of the Emperor as Grand Duke of Finland.

The Russian navy consisted in 1876 of the Baltic fleet, 77 vessels; the Black Sea fleet, nine vessels; the Caspian Sea fleet, eleven serviceable vessels; the Siberian fleet, eleven vessels; the White Sea squadron, three vessels; and the Sea of Aral flotilla, twenty-six serviceable vessels. These vessels are manned by about 1,490 officers and 11,600 seamen. The iron-clad fleet consisted of 29 vessels, having a total tonnage of 74,793 tons, carrying 184 guns. The most powerful of the iron-clads is the " Peter the Great," a mastless turret-ship carrying four 35-ton Krupp guns. A fleet of vessels of a new kind, called Popoffkas, or circular monitors, is in process of construction after designs by Admiral Popoff. They are intended for defense, as floating fortresses, and will not have a speed of more than eight or nine miles an hour. The sailors of the navy are enlisted for nine years, seven of which must be spent in active service and two in the reserve.

The finances of the Empire are in a wretched condition. The aggressive policy of Russia involving the necessity of maintaining a large standing army and navy, has proved to be an expensive one. Most of the railroads have been constructed by the Government through regions in which the commercial traffic would not begin to pay for the expense, and the system has required the borrowing of large sums of money. Two-thirds of the expenditure of the Empire, or about the whole amount of the revenue from direct and indirect taxation, is applied to the army and navy, and the payment of the interest on the public debt. According to the budget estimates, the amount of the revenues for 1876 was £81,448,320; and of expenditures £79,443,630, showing a small balance on the credit side of the account. Between 1822 and 1876, the Government borrowed upward of one hundred and thirty-five million pounds sterling to meet deficits in the annual accounts and provide capital for the construction of railroads; and the estimated amount of the public debt of the Empire on the first of January, 1876, was £250,962,000, or upward of twelve hundred million dollars. Besides this, the country had a legal-tender currency of £113,044,783, standing at from ten to fifteen per cent. discount. A sinking fund has been formed, and the financial condition has been improving for several years. But every war imposes new and difficult burdens upon the financial bureau; and it is evident that Russia could not endure a great long war without suffering a critical strain on its credit.

A few of the provinces and peoples of Russia have been brought into especial notice in connection with the war, and deserve a more particular account.

The Cossacks have received more attention from travelers than any other class of Russians, and are more often mentioned, since they make themselves more conspicuous in the campaign and in battle than any other Russian soldiers. The name Cossack is said to be Turkish in origin, and to signify robber. However true the application may have been in the beginning, the Cossacks are now rather brave, daring soldiers, and accomplished and effective scouts than robbers, although even now no legitimate booty ever comes amiss to them. The Cossacks were a number of free tribes who inhabited the country of the Ukraine and the valleys of the Dnieper, Don, Volga, and Ural Rivers, who were able to preserve a measure of independence during the period when Russia and Poland and Turkey were contending for dominion over the region, and who, when they submitted to the Russians, were permitted to preserve most of their customs and privileges, on condition of their serving in the Russian armies. They are allied to the Russians and Tartars in origin, and are most probably the descendants of refugees who fled from Russia during the twelfth and succeeding centuries, to escape the oppression of the landed lords, and of those who were afterward driven away by the cruelties of Ivan the Terrible (1533 to 1584). Communities were formed of the fugitives, of which one of the chief bonds of connection was that all the members, of whatever tribe they might be, should profess the orthodox religion and speak the Russian language. In the latter part of the sixteenth century, the Cossack bands on the Don formed a union for the defense of the Christians against the Turks and Tartars, and built a number of rallying stations or winter camps along the Don, which are now represented in the peculiar Cossack villages of that region.   Colonies of Cossacks have been established by the Russian Government for purposes of settlement and defense in the Ural, and parts of the Caucasus, and in Central Asia, where they prove useful pioneers of civilization, and good agents for the preservation of order as against the unruly native populations and predatory bands.   They have language and religion in common with the Russians, but are quite different from them in customs, manner of life, and character.   Though professing Christianity, they are not at all particular in religious matters.   The Cossacks of the Upper Don pursue agricultural occupations; their houses are surrounded by fruit gardens, and their women take delight in the cultivation of flowers.   The whitewashed houses of their villages, just visible through the trees, present a very attractive appearance. The interior of the houses corresponds with the outside, and is scrupulously clean, and contains comforts and conveniences in pro- portion to the wealth of the owner.   The Cossacks of the Lower Don live by fishing, raising horses, mining for salt, metals, and coal, and vine-culture.   They are gayer and more extravagant than their northern countrymen, and are fond of display.   As a whole, the Cossacks are free, roving in disposition, fond of wild adventure, are quick in movement, and fight with great vigor, but without much regularity or system.   As soldiers, they form to the Russian service some such an arm as the Bashi-Bazouks form to the Turkish service, but a comparison with the Bashi-Bazouks is unjust to them; they are better disciplined than the Bashi-Bazouks, have principle, and are not naturally cruel.   When not in fight they are genial and pleasant companions, and are well spoken of by travelers who have had intercourse with them.   Mr. Bryce, an English traveler who recently ascended Mount Ararat, and who was accompanied by Cossacks during his whole journey, describes them as "merry, simple, good-natured fellows."   His verdict is sustained by the majority of the travelers who have had intercourse with them away from the battle-field.   In home life they are jovial, and exceedingly fond of their families, and will play with their children for hours with an enjoyment equal to that of the children.   The uniform of the Cossack soldier is very picturesque.   The upper garment con- sists of the Circassian tunic, or *chekmen*, fastened down the breast with frogs, with cartridge-cases on the right and left.   Beneath this is the *bechmet*, a kind of long waistcoat, reaching down below the

COSSACKS.

RUSSIAN SOLDIERS.

tunic, and which is of silk when the Cossack is in full dress. The head-dress is the *papakka*, a cap made of sheepskin. The several regiments are distinguished from one another by the color of the *bechmet* and shoulder-straps, the top of the *papakka* and the colors of the cartridge-cases being also of the same hue. To protect him from the rain the Cossack carries a large mantle, called a *bourka*, made of a peculiar kind of cloth manufactured in the mountains, which is said to be light, warm, impervious to moisture, and everlasting in wear. By night this *bourka*, which possesses also the invaluable property of driving away all insects and vermin, serves as a bed, and when not in use is rolled up and strapped on behind the saddle. The *bocklik*, a cap made of the same kind of cloth, is the complement of the *bourka*, and is provided with two long tails, which when it rains the Cossack twists round his neck. In bivouac also the *bocklik* is worn as a night-cap. The arms carried by the Cossacks are the *schachka*, or long mountain sword, with no guard to the hilt; the *kindial*, or short dagger, two pistols stuck into a waist-belt, and a Berdan rifle without a bayonet. The horse furniture consists of a light saddle, somewhat resembling in appearance the Arabian pattern, but without the high wooden cant peculiar to this latter. The framework is covered with a skin of soft and exceedingly supple leather; the two girths are broad but thin leather bands, each about nine inches in width, and are attached to the saddle at a considerable interval apart. A thick-woolen rug is placed below the saddle, while, finally, a leather cushion, stuffed with horse-hair, secured on the top of the saddle by a third girth similar to the two already described, forms the seat for the rider. The bridle has only a single rein, the horse moving generally with his head down and his neck stretched straight out. The horses themselves are small, usually about fourteen hands in height, but they are well-proportioned, robust, and able to get through much hard work without knocking up.

The province called Bessarabia includes the country lying between the Pruth and Dniester Rivers. It is named after a tribe called the Bessers, who invaded it in the seventh century. It formerly belonged to Moldavia, but was given to Russia in 1812. So much of the territory as included the mouths of the Danube was given back to Turkey by the Treaty of Paris, in 1856, the powers insisting that Russia should surrender the control of every part of that important stream. Three-quarters of the population are Moldavians, or

Rumanians, and are naturally inclined to favor incorporation with Rumania whenever it is made an independent State. On the other hand, Russia has never been satisfied with its surrender of the south-western section, and claims the right to restore it to the territory of the Empire.

The name of the Caucasus is given to the whole region between the Black and Caspian Seas, which is occupied by the Caucasus Mountains and their outlying spurs. The Caucasus range of mountains begins on the north shore of the Black Sea, and stretches in a south-westerly direction for about seven hundred miles. It is divided, according to Mr. Douglas Freshfield, who has carefully examined its geography, near Tiflis into two branches, so as to give the whole range the shape of the letter Y, the two arms of which stretch from the point of division to the Caspian Sea. The southern branch is the longest and highest; but the northern branch has also some very high peaks, and marks the boundary line between the two divisions of the province, Ciscaucasia and Transcaucasia. It is a region of very ancient historical, and more ancient mythological, interest. The Prometheus of the old Greek fables was chained to a rock on one of its mountains; Medea, whose fate in connection with the expedition of Jason for the golden fleece has been commemorated in classical tragedy, had her home within its bounds. It figures also as a land of enchantment in the stories of the "Arabian Nights" and other legends of the Saracens. Its tribes, men of great vigor, having an indomitable spirit, maintained their independence against all attempts to conquer them till the present century, when Russia, having obtained a foothold in Georgia, in the year 1800, gradually extended its control until the whole region was subjugated on the surrender of Shamyl in 1859. The spirit of the inhabitants was not subdued, however, and after 1863 nearly half a million of them, refusing to submit to Russian rule, left the country and settled upon homesteads which were offered to them by their co-religionists in Turkey. Again in the war of 1877, the independent spirit of the Mohammedan tribes, supported by such helps and encouragement as the Turks found opportunity to afford them, kept the country in so restless a condition that, although no formidable insurrection was actually developed, considerable forces had to be detailed from the Russian armies to keep order, and the movements of the invading columns were embarrassed by the apprehension of danger in the rear. The Caucasian district is inhabited by several tribes, Mohammedan, Christian, and Pagan, of whom the Mohammedans have been so reduced by emigration and other causes, as to number now only about one-third of the whole. The majority of the population have ·learned to be contented under Russian rule, and are loyal to the Government. Even the Mohammedans, until excited by the events of the war and the appeals of the Turks, had not for many years shown any spirit of resistance. Ciscaucasia, or the country lying on the northern side of the Caucasus, is inhabited by the Tchetchentzes, Ossetes, and Tcherkess, or Circassians. The Tchetchentzes, a Mohammedan tribe, numbering about 150,000 persons, dwell in the Terek Valley, and between the Caspian and Vladikavkar, and are considered the tribe the least to be relied upon. They were the last of the Caucasians to submit to the Russians, having adhered to Shamyl during the war of final conquest till he was compelled to surrender. Their tribes are not connected by any bond of union, and they are given by travelers a bad character, being described as untrustworthy and mischievous, though daring, given to irregular and guerrilla warfare, and incapable of maintaining a steady campaign. The Ossetes, who dwell west of the Tchetchentzes, and inhabit the country around the Pass of Vladikavkar, are a tribe of 65,000 persons, of whom 50,000 are nominally Christians, of a quite opposite character from their neighbors. They are regarded by many ethnologists as belonging to the Indo-Germanic race, and have maintained peaceful relations with the Russians for more than a century. West of the Ossetes are the Tcherkess, or Circassians, who are divided into three branches, the Kabasdans, the Tcherkess proper, or Adighei, and the Adhaz, or Abkhasians. The Kabardans are Mohammedans, and were formerly the most influential of the Circassian tribes, and were the first to accept Russian rule. They, as well as their neighbors the Ossetes, took no part in the war led by Shamyl, but have-been constantly loyal to Russia. The Karatchai, who live near the sources of the Kuban, took the Russian side in the last revolt, and are regarded as peaceable. The Adighei, or Tcherkess, as the Russians call them, or Circassians proper, have been most hostile to the Russians, but the majority of the race have emigrated to Turkey, and are represented in its army with an unenviable notoriety by the Tcherkess bands, whose name has become associated with all that is disorderly and barbarous in military life. West of the Adighei, and on the southern slopes of the mountains, and around the Black Sea coasts, live the Svanetians, a small, disaffected tribe, and the Abkhasians, a much larger tribe, who gained considerable importance in the summer campaign of 1877. The Abkhasians possess a separate history, dating back several centuries, and speak a different language from the other tribes, are brave, and somewhat unruly. They formerly professed Christianity, which was introduced among them in the sixth century, and were attached to the Greek Church, but many of the leading families afterward embraced Mohammedanism. The multitude have practically lapsed into heathenism, so that little remains of the old Christianity except a few superstitious rites and some ruins of churches. In 1863 and 1864, after the great Circassian emigration, the Russians proposed to them that they should again embrace the Christian faith, as a condition of their remaining on their lands. Thousands of them took advantage of the offer and were baptized in crowds, " with a kind of switch dipped into a tub of water, by a priest on the balcony of a house, while the procession passed below." This conversion was without sincerity, and had little effect in attaching the people to Russia.

The contentment of the upper classes with Russian rule was severely tested several years ago, by the abolition of the privileges of the Caucasian nobility, which was particularly hard on the Abkhasians. Formerly a complete system of vassalage existed. The land was allotted among a very large number of princes and nobles, each of whom possessed twenty or thirty houses, with numbers of dependents, over whom he exercised absolute sway. This system was abolished about 1871, when the nobles were deprived of all rights over the people, and their lands were divided, without any compensation being given to them, among the peasants to cultivate. Notwithstanding, this measure was a real reform akin to the abolition of serfage in Russia, and a benefit to the country. Many of the deprived nobles were indignant at the loss they had suffered, and were made ready for revolt. Upon a superficial view, the district should have afforded an excellent field upon which to direct the efforts to excite an insurrection, which the Turks attempted. Transcaucasia, or that part of the Caucasus which lies south of the mountains, is described by Mr. Bryce, in his " Transcaucasia and Ararat," as being on the whole "a fairly contented and peaceable part of the Czar's dominions," in which "there does not exist nearly so much bitterness of feeling among the subjects as there is toward ourselves [the

British] in India." The important province of Daghestan lies in the fork of the mountain range. The Lesghians, as the inhabitants are called, are a steady, industrious people, engaged in the culture of the soil, and the manufacture of iron and weapons, are partly Mohammedan and partly Christian, and have some literary culture. They opposed the Russian encroachments steadily, and with regular warfare, but having been overcome, submitted manfully, and have given themselves to peaceful pursuits. Shamyl, the great Caucasian leader in the last war with Russia, whose history is as full of romance as that of any hero whose exploits have been recorded in story, was a native of this province The southern part of the district was formerly included in the kingdom of Georgia, which has been named Grusia since its annexation to Russia. The people are mostly Christians, are loyal to the Russian Government, and are of the higher class of Eastern populations. At Baku, on the Caspian Sea, in the midst of a region abounding in naphtha wells, are situated a seat of the fire-worshipers, and temples in which the holy fires are kept perpetually burning.

The Caucasians have a traditional celebrity for physical beauty, and their women have been sought out for centuries by wealthy Mussulmans to be made favorite wives and the chief attractions of their harems. The people of many of their tribes undoubtedly present a very fine bodily aspect. The Tcherkess, with all their moral deficiencies, are a very handsome people, with fine forms, small hands and feet, broad shoulders, aquiline noses, bright eyes, pure black beards, elastic gait, proud bearing, and picturesque dress. The weapons of the richer braves are highly ornamented with gold and silver and precious stones. The women wear a clear blue silken shirt, embroidered with gold and silver, and gathered at the waist with a costly belt, veil themselves in a white veil covering them from head to foot, and practice tight-lacing from childhood. The custom of "blood revenge" is characteristic of the people. The feud is transmitted from generation to generation, and is permanently terminated only by stealing a child of the hostile family, taking care of him until he has grown up, and then restoring him to his father, when the bitterest enmity is changed into the warmest friendship.. This custom is mitigated by the power of Circassian hospitality, which permits one to be entertained even by his fiercest enemy, and to be quite secure so long as he is his guest. The boys are taught.

war-like exercises and dexterity, and are instructed in theft, with the full knowledge that they will be punished if they are caught stealing.

Georgia and Russian Armenia, which form the extreme southern part of the Transcaucasian Province, contain about 280,000 Armenians. They are separated, only by an arbitrary territorial line, from the Armenians of Turkey, with whom they have common manners and characteristics, and the same religion.

THE CIRCASSIAN CHIEFTAIN SHAMYL.

REDIF PASHA.

CIRCASSIANS.

CHAPTER IV.

HISTORICAL SKETCH OF TURKEY.

Origin of the Turks—The Seljukian Empire—Rise of the Ottoman Turks—Conquest of
Constantinople—Growth of the Turkish Empire in Europe, Asia, and Africa—Turkish
Policy with regard to Conquered Nations—Climax of the Ottoman Power under
Solyman—Spell of Turkish Bravery Broken—Struggle of the Subjected Races for
Independence—The Sick Man.

THE Turks came from those regions of Central Asia that have furnished the majority of the stocks which have successively occupied different parts of Europe and Western Asia, from the Aryan invasion down to the present time. They emigrated to the neighborhood of the Aral and Caspian Seas early in the Christian era, and were first mentioned in connection with western history in the sixth century, as forming an alliance with the Roman Emperor Justin II. They came under Mohammedan influence during the tenth century. In the eleventh century they advanced into Persia, subjugated the best districts of that country, and from there spread over Syria and the greater part of Asia Minor. Their principal chief, who became paramount, was Seljuk, from whom they received the name of Seljukian Turks. The Seljukian Empire attained its greatest extent and prosperity under Melek, the grandson of Seljuk, when it included, besides the districts already named, Armenia, Georgia, and Lower Egypt. After Melek's death it was divided up into smaller States, which became rivals, were encroached upon by the Ottoman Turks, and were finally extinguished in the thirteenth century by the irruption of the Moguls, under Genghis Khan. About the beginning of the thirteenth century, a band of Oghuze Turks emigrated from the main body in Khorasan, Persia, to the mountains of Armenia, whence a part of it removed and settled near Angora, still acknowledging the suzerainty of one of the Seljukian Sultans. A Sultan of this part of the band, Othman, or Osman, having made considerable conquests from the Greek Empire, established his independence in 1299, and founded the State which has since been known as the Turkish, or Ottoman Empire. The present dominant race of Turks are called Ottomans after him. Under Orchan, the successor of Othman, all of Western Asia was occupied, and Gallipoli, the first of the acquisitions of the Turks in Europe, fell into their hands in 1357. From this point the Ottomans gradually advanced in Europe, slowly at first, more rapidly as they gained strength. They took Adrianople, the most important European position of the Greek Empire, in 1361, Philippopolis shortly afterward, defeated the Servians and Hungarians in 1365, then conquered several towns on the Thracian coast, and Nissa, a point which plays an important part in the wars of the present, made Servia and Bulgaria tributary to them in 1375, and Wallachia in 1391, exacted a tribute from the Roman Emperor himself, and captured the most important fortresses on the Danube in 1394. Their most formidable antagonists during this period were the Hungarians, with whom they fought many bloody battles. This brave people have, for several centuries, borne the credit of having at this time saved Western Europe from being overrun, like the East. Murad II., from 1421 to 1451, reduced Salonica and important positions in Greece. Finally, Mohammed II., the successor of Murad, captured Constantinople after a short siege, on the 29th of May, 1453, the Emperor Constantine being slain in the final assault, and the Ottomans gained the seat and throne of the Roman Empire.

Had Europe been united to resist the advance of the Turks, this great disaster might have been avoided, and the invaders have been driven back into Asia. But the princes and rulers of the petty States outside the line of immediate danger were too busy with their own little jealousies to give proper attention to a peril which menaced the whole; so the Ottomans were allowed to establish themselves almost without molestation. All Europe was thrown into a panic by the conquest of Constantinople. Terror ruled everywhere; but nearly every State seemed to be in a quarrel either between its own factions or with some of its neighbors, and the Turks were allowed to complete the conquests they had made, and to add the rest of Greece, Bosnia, Albania, Herzegovina, and the States in Asia which were not already in their own possession. The States further west, so far from helping their fellow-Christians against the invader or sympathizing with them, were willing to form alliances with the Turks if that would help them to gain an advantage over a rival. The Ottoman Empire reached its greatest extent under Solyman, the Magnificent, and Selim II., his successor, when it extended on the east to the Tigris and Euphrates, included Egypt and the Barbary States, Arabia, Rhodes, and Cyprus, and took in a large part of Hungary on the west. A series of wars for the conquest of Hungary was begun during the reign of Solyman, in 1521. The young King of Hungary was killed on the battle-field of Mohacs in 1526, and immediately three aspirants for the crown began their rivalries for the succession instead of resisting the invader, so that the Turks had every advantage on their side. In 1529, Buda, the principal Hungarian fortress, was occupied, and the Turks approached Vienna without resistance, and were prevented from capturing it only by disorders within their own ranks. A peace was concluded in 1533, by which Ferdinand of Austria, as King of Hungary, was obliged to pay tribute for that State. He refusing to continue the tribute, the war broke out again in 1541, and Ferdinand was compelled after six years of war to purchase peace by the surrender of the Hungarian territory as far as Stuhlweissenburg, Buda, and Gran, and the payment of an annual gift of fifty thousand ducats for the rest of the kingdom. Solyman renewed the war with Austria in 1551; the country was again invaded, and the Turks made incursions into Carinthia and Styria. Ferdinand again bought a truce in 1562, by which the Turks were left in possession of their conquests, and he gave up his claims over Transylvania, and submitted to the payment of a yearly tribute of thirty thousand ducats. Solyman made war again upon Maximilian, the successor of Ferdinand, and again carried all his points in the truce of 1567.

These wars occurred during the wars of the sixteenth century between France and Germany. The French king, desiring to see the Hapsburgs crippled, threw their influence on the side of the Turks, and even entered into alliances with them; and when the Emperor Charles V., as King of Spain, endeavored to subjugate Algiers and Tunis, the French lent a part of their fleet to assist the Turks. In return, the French were granted commercial privileges in Turkish waters which were denied to other nations, and gained a small degree of influence at the Ottoman court. War broke out between Turkey and Venice in 1570, the end of which was the surrender of the island of Cyprus to the Turks, and the payment of an indemnity by the Venetians. In this war, France was again friendly to the Turks.

Circumstances brought Turkey and Poland into close relations during a part of the sixteenth century. Poland leaned on Turkey for protection against the growing power of Russia. Turkey was glad to detach all the neighboring States it could from alliances with Austria. The result was that the Porte for a time exerted an influence in Polish affairs extending even to the nomination of the king. The alliance was gradually broken up by the operation of other natural causes, and in the following century it was the King of Poland who saved the West a second time from being overrun by the Moslems. Another war between Turkey and Austria, beginning in 1593, in which the Turks advanced to Komorn, the extreme limit of their previous advances, ended in 1606 with the Treaty of Sitnatorok, in which Austria bought a release from the tribute it had paid for Hungary, and the frontier districts were more clearly defined. In a war with Venice, which began in 1645, the Turks gained the city and castle of Candia after their fleet had been vanquished twice. A war with Austria which followed, ended in the peace of Vasvar, or St. Gotthard, renewing the peace of Sitnatorok. Poland was next engaged in war with the Turks, and the king, Michael Caribert, concluded a disgraceful peace after a single defeat. His successor, John Sobieski, refusing to be bound by the terms Michael had granted, renewed the war and gained better ones. This king did signal service to the West a few years afterward, when the Turks, again at war with Austria, having marched up to the walls of Vienna, and being about to capture that capital, he came to its relief, defeated the invaders conclusively, and saved the city and Austria, September 12, 1683. In the next year, Austria, Poland, and Venice concluded a "holy alliance" against the Porte, and attacked its possessions in Hungary, Dalmatia, and the Morea, and on the Dniester defeated the Turks in several great battles, took some of their most important border forts, and after a war of about sixteen years' duration, concluded in 1699 the peace of Carlovitz, the most creditable treaty which any Christian power had yet made with Turkey. It was the first treaty in which the payment of a tribute in some form to the Porte was not stipulated for, and was also the first in which neutral Christian powers acted as mediators, England and Holland having given their services in that capacity to promote the conclusion of an honorable peace.

Russia began to be prominent in the wars against Turkey early in the eighteenth century. Previous to this time some border wars had occurred between the two powers, which grew out of the depredations of the Tartars and Cossacks, but they were insignificant in comparison with the wars with Austria, Poland, and Venice. The war beginning in 1710, in which the Czar twice bought his security against yielding a disgraceful peace by bribing the Grand Vizier, is noteworthy as having led indirectly to the wars with Venice and Austria (1714 to 1718), in which the Austrian Prince Eugene gained the brilliant victory of Peterwardein (1716), and in consequence of which a new adjustment of boundaries was made at the Treaty of Passarovitz, to the disadvantage of Turkey. A war with Russia and Austria (1736 to 1739) resulted, after the peace of Belgrade, in gains of territory for Russia, and losses for Austria.

In 1768, the Turks interfered in behalf of the Catholic party of Poland, to check the growth of Russian influence in that kingdom. The war which ensued was a disastrous one for them, and ended in their losing the Crimea, and yielding to Russia Keitch, Jenikala, and Azov, the free navigation of the Black Sea and the Sea of Marmora, and other important commercial privileges, and paying an indemnity. The Crimea was finally occupied by the Russians in 1783. The Turks nearly lost Constantinople in this war, and it was saved to them only by the interference of England and Prussia.

This occasion marks the introduction of the policy of making the affairs of Turkey a subject of European concern, and also the origin of the British doctrine that the integrity of Turkey must be maintained. During a part of the period of the French Revolution, the attitude of parties was curiously reversed, and the Porte was engaged in a defensive alliance with Russia and England against the aggressions of the French in the East. The alliance ceased in 1802 upon the conclusion of the peace of Amiens between France, Turkey, and England.

Turkey and Russia were again engaged in war in 1806. At first the Turks were supported by the French, and Russia by England. Both these alliances were broken up before the end of the war. The Emperor Napoleon of France engaged in secret plots with the Czar Alexander, for the dismemberment and division of Turkey, and England concluded the peace of Dardanelles with the Porte. The peace of Bucharest, concluded in May, 1812, made the river Pruth the boundary between Russia and Turkey, established the freedom of the Lower Danube to the trade of both countries, and assured to Servia the position as a semi-independent tributary State, for which it had been striving since 1804.

The revolution in Greece began in 1821. The campaigns of the Turks were accompanied with barbarities, which, like those perpetrated nearly fifty years later in Bulgaria, excited general abhorrence, while the bravery of the Greeks aroused for them the sympathy of the Western peoples. The powers tried to put an end to the war by negotiation, without taking an active part in it. Their overtures were rejected by the Porte, and England, France, and Russia sent their fleets to the Mediterranean to prevent further hostilities. The Western fleets met those of Turkey and Egypt in the Port of Navarino in 1827, became engaged with them, and entirely destroyed them. Russia declared war against Turkey in 1828, but concluded with it the peace of Adrianople in the next year. The independence of Greece was established and confirmed, and its boundaries were defined by the London protocol of 1830.

The downfall of the Turkish Empire had been looked upon for several years as a certain event of the future. Napoleon and the Czar had discussed it as early as 1807. In 1833, Sir Archibald Alison wrote in the *Quarterly Review*, that "the Ottoman power has, within these twenty years, rapidly and irrecoverably declined" It had suffered by internal dissensions as well as by foreign wars. The Viceroy of Egypt had given it much trouble by his efforts to secure independence, and had gained a degree of strength which, together with his steady pursuit of the idea of a sovereignty of his own, made him a very insecure vassal; and the Turkish court, to save itself from destruction, had been obliged to plot and execute the murder of the Janizaries, which, while it removed a pressing danger, also deprived the Empire of a strong military arm. For the last fifty years, European diplomacy with reference to Turkey has consisted chiefly of endeavors on one side to find opportunities and occasions for destroying it, and efforts on the other to maintain it; and its continued existence during that period has been mainly due to the jealousy entertained by England, France, and Austria against Russia and against each other.

In 1831, Russia assisted the Porte in suppressing a rebellion of Mehemet Ali, the Pasha of Egypt. This vassal rebelled again in 1839, and was supported by France. England, Austria, Prussia, and Russia came to the help of the Porte and engaged in a quadruple alliance in 1840, to protect the integrity of the Turkish Empire. Among the results of these proceedings was the negotiation of a treaty permanently closing the Bosphorus and the Dardanelles against all foreign vessels of war, so long as the Porte should enjoy peace. The Crimean war, the last of the great wars of Turkey previous to that of 1877, originated in a dispute between the Greek and Latin Churches at Jerusalem, regarding the right to the control and use of the "Holy places" of that city. Louis Napoleon of France is accused of having instigated and promoted the controversy. He supported the Latin priests. The Czar Nicholas of Russia took up the cause of the Greeks, and pressed it with a demand to be recognized as the protector of all the Greek Christians under Ottoman rule, which was very offensive to Turkey. During the discussions of the subject among the powers in 1853, Turkey was spoken of as the "sick man" who must soon die and leave his estate to be administered upon. The Czar proposed to the British Envoy at St. Petersburg a division of the estate, in which the Danubian principalities (Moldavia and Wallachia), Servia, and Bulgaria, should become independent States under Russian protection, and England should receive Egypt and Candia. England refused to countenance this scheme. The Czar then made a formal demand upon Turkey to make an engagement "to secure forever to the Orthodox Church and its clergy all the rights and immunities which they had already enjoyed, and those of which they were possessed from ancient times." The Porte refused to make such an engagement, and diplomatic relations between the two powers were suspended in May, 1853. The Russians entered Moldavia in July, 1853, and declared war in the next November, the Sultan having declared war on the 5th of October.

England, France, Austria, and Prussia united to support the Porte against the Russian demands, and through their representatives adopted a protocol at Vienna in April, 1854, which affirmed the duty of maintaining the territorial integrity of the Ottoman Empire, and of also securing, by every means compatible with the independence and sovereignty of the Sultan, the civil and religious rights of his Christian subjects. France and England supported Turkey with their arms, and Sardinia joined these allies at the beginning of 1855. The war was signalized by the brilliant victories of the allies at the battles of the Alma, Balaklava, and Inkerman, and the capture and destruction of the fortress of Sevastopol, in the Crimea, offset by the single victory of the Russians in the capture of Kars, in Armenia. Negotiations for peace were begun, which resulted in the conclusion of the Treaty of Paris on the 27th of April, 1856. Seven powers were parties to this treaty, viz.: Austria, France, Great Britain, Prussia, Russia, Sardinia, and Turkey. The treaty recognized Turkey as one of the powers of the European system, standing before the public law and in diplomatic negotiations on an equal footing with all the other powers; engaged the contracting powers to respect the independence and integrity of the Ottoman Empire, and to make every assault upon the same a question of common interest; and stipulated that in case of a difference arising between the Porte and any of the powers threatening the continuance of their good relations, the other powers should be given an opportunity to mediate before resort to arms should be had. It recited the fact that the Sultan had issued a new firman (the Hatti-Humayun), designed to improve the condition of his subjects without distinction as to religion or race, and had of his own accord communicated the same to the contracting parties, and declared it to be clearly understood that this act could not in any case give the said powers the right to interfere, either collectively or separately, in the relations of His Majesty the Sultan with his subjects, nor in the internal administration of his Empire. The treaty declared the Black Sea neutral and open to the commerce of all nations; re-established the rule which excluded the vessels of foreign powers from the Dardanelles and the Bosphorus so long as Turkey remained at peace, and prohibited both Russia and Turkey from keeping vessels of war in the Black Sea, except such a number as they should both agree to be necessary as a police. It confirmed the position of Servia, Moldavia, and Wallachia in the condition of semi-independence which they had gained, with the full enjoyment of all the privileges and immunities which they had acquired, pledged the Porte to preserve them all, and the other contracting powers to guarantee their preservation.

In 1860 France intervened to protect the Christians from a violent persecution which had broken out against them in Syria, but was prevented by England from occupying that country. In 1866, an insurrection broke out in the island of Candia, or Crete, which the Turkish Government suppressed after a long effort, marked by many cruelties, but without interference from any of the powers. In 1870, Russia took advantage of the powerless condition of France, caused by its entanglement in the war with Germany, to declare that it would be no longer bound by the limitations imposed by the Treaty of Paris upon the size of its fleet in the Black Sea, and proceeded to increase the number of its vessels in those waters. In 1876, in the course of the diplomatic correspondence concerning the Bosnian insurrection and the Servian war, it declared that the Treaty of Paris had been broken, and was no longer binding upon it.

A WALLACHIAN.

A GROUP OF TURKS.

(1) TURKS.   (2) ALBANIANS.   (3) DRUSES.

CHAPTER V.

PRESENT CONDITION OF THE TURKISH EMPIRE AND THE OSMANLI TURKS.

The Ruling Nationality in Turkey—Distribution of Races—What Prevents the Assimilation of the Ottomans with the More Civilized Nations—Abortive Attempts at Reform—Religious Toleration—Work of Protestant and Catholic Missionaries—The Educational Condition of Turkey—Agricultural and Mineral Resources—Tenure of Land—The Army and Navy—Desperate Condition of the Finances.

THE Turkish Empire ranks in point of extent and population among the largest States of the world. It is only surpassed by the British, Russian, and Chinese Empires in both respects, and by the United States and Brazil in point of population. But it occupies a very different position if we compare its internal condition with that of other States. In this respect it is greatly inferior to any other country of Europe. The Turkish Government has shown itself utterly unfit to establish an efficient administration. Turkey has come to be known as the "sick man," and the continuance of its existence depends wholly on the disposition toward it of the great powers of Europe.

The ruling nationality in Turkey, the Ottoman, or Osmanli Turks, belong to the Turanian race. The only other nationality of Europe which belongs to the same race are the Hungarians, or Magyars. But while the latter have for nearly a thousand years been identified with the other nations of Europe in religion, have constantly received large admixtures of the Aryan race, to which the remainder of Europe belongs, and have succeeded in obtaining a high degree of culture and political capacity, the Turks have during the whole period of four hundred years during which they have lived in Eastern Europe, remained foreign and hostile to the Aryan nations of Europe, and present to-day the most remarkable example of that backwardness in progress and civilization which charactertizes almost the entire Turanian race. Still greater is the breach which the religion of the Turks constitutes between them and the remainder of Europe. They have been during all these four hundred years the only sovereign nation of Europe which professes the Mohammedan religion.

(101)

The Mohammedan States, without any exception, have long been in a state of decline and decay. The inferiority of their culture to that of the Christian nations is still more marked than the inferiority of the Turanian race to the Aryan. Thus both by race and religious affinity the Turks belong to a system of States which is constantly receding before the advance of a superior civilization, and it is only natural that public opinion in the more civilized States has accustomed itself to look upon them as a people who are not only strangers and foreigners in Europe, but who should give way to nations which in every respect are their superiors.

The Ottomans, or Osmanli Turks, predominate very largely in the Asiatic part of the Empire, but in the European part they form only one-eighth of the whole population. Affiliated with them are the Arabs, whom they conquered, and whose religion they have embraced. The Arabs number less than one million of the sixteen millions of the population of Asiatic Turkey, but they constitute the whole of the settled population (aside from the African races proper) of the African dependencies. Next in importance in Asiatic Turkey are the Armenian, Greek, Syrian, and Chaldean Christians, the Turkomans, near relatives of the Turks, Kurds, and Druses. The Slavic races constitute one-half the population of European Turkey. They number about four millions and are four times as numerous as the Turks. After them come a million Turks, 900,000 Greeks, 820,000 Albanians, 200,000 Armenians, 70,000 Jews, and 11,000 Tartars. The actual proportion of Mohammedans is, however, larger than appears from these figures; for a considerable number of the Slavic people, particularly in Bosnia, have professed the Mohammedan faith, and about two-thirds of the Albanians are of that religion; so that the Mohammedans number about one-third of the whole.

A curious fact in relation to the different races which people European Turkey is the irregular manner in which they are distributed and mingled. "No locality," says Baker, in his "Turkey," "can be found where the population is exclusively of the same nationality, but a rival race crops up here and there and jostles its neighbors. We find, for instance, a quarter where the majority of the population is Bulgarian, but among them in considerable numbers are Turks, Greeks, Circassians, and Gypsies. In another quarter the majority are Albanians, but they again have to bear the friction of Bulgarians, Wallachs, Greeks, and Turks; and so on all over the country. Each of these nations has its own language, religion, and customs; and it therefore follows that the difficulty of governing the mass lies in a direct ratio to the number of races represented in it; and when it is borne in mind that in Europe alone no less than eight distinct nationalities, each with a considerable population, and several others of smaller degree can claim the rights of Turkish subjects, some idea may be formed of the obstacles in the path of good government in Turkey." Mr. Baker illustrates the difficulty which the Government experiences in dealing with this variety of races by supposing the embarrassments which England would encounter if it had fifteen Irelands to manage instead of one.

The Turks, according to the latest review of the distribution of population as given in No. 7 of Peterman's *Mittheilungen*, for 1876, are to be found as a compact population only in the Vilayet of the Danube and the sanjaks of Rustchuk, Tultcha, and Varna. They are less numerous in the Rhodope Mountains. On the shores of the Ægean Sea and the Sea of Marmora and on the south-east shore of the Black Sea, they are greatly outnumbered by the Greeks, especially in the direction of Constantinople. The Bulgarians occupy the country south of the Danube, their southern boundary being a line passing through the towns of Nissa, Prisrend, Ochrida, Kastoria, Niagostos, Salonica, Adrianople, and Burgas, on the Black Sea. They are also scattered in various districts of Albania, Wallachia, and the Dobrudja. The Servians (including Bosnians, Herzegovinians, and Montenegrins) occupy the space between the Bulgarian Morava, the Save, and the Dalmatian frontier as far as Albania. On the right bank of the Morava, their villages are interspersed with Rumanian settlements. The Albanians inhabit the country south of Montenegro down to the frontier of the Greek kingdom. Other races in European Turkey are the Zinzars, nearly related to the Rumanians, most of whom live among the Albanians in Epirus and Thessaly; the Armenians in the Turkish towns; the Magyars, or Hungarians; the Nogai Tartars in the Dobrudja; the Gypsies in Rumania, Albania, and Bulgaria; the Jews, Russians, Arabs, Poles, and Germans. The last three races are, however, but scantily represented.

The greatest drawback to the assimilation of Turks with Europeans is polygamy, which imposes upon the people social ideas and customs opposite to those which prevail in the West. Under the practice of polygamy, and more by its influence than by any other

6

assignable cause,* the Turks, once the formidable conquerors of the fairest part of the world—particularly those of the wealthier classes, whose opportunities to enjoy a plurality of wives have been the best—have sunk into a kind of indolent stupor and listlessness. Lassitude characterizes their actions in private and public. The whole country bears evidence of the indifference and lack of energy which seem to have become one of the inherited qualities of the Ottomans, and to be growing more obvious with each generation. It is generally admitted that the stock of the Imperial family is worn out, so that there is not one in the whole list of eligible candidates for Sultan who is really competent for the position. The other families of high station are not much better off. With a few exceptions, the really competent higher officers of the nation are men who have risen from a low origin, or are foreigners, whose Ottomanized names are the only things about them that are Turkish.

Another influence which keeps Turkey apart from the western nations of Europe is found in the fanaticism and lack of intelligence of the Mussulmans of the remote provinces, who oppose every effort of the Government to carry out reforms, and defeat it unless it is supported by a stronger force than can be afforded. Assimilation is further hindered by the imbecility and corruptibility of the provincial administrators, who, remote from the seat of Government, and holding their positions by a tenure regulated rather by the caprice of the court than by any consideration of their fidelity, think more of filling their purses and having an easy time than of governing well.

The Porte has made several attempts to introduce constitutional reforms into the Empire; they have not been supported by efficient measures to execute them, and have been left inoperative, and the misrule they were to abolish has hardly been disturbed by them. Observing and remembering these successive failures to accomplish any salutary object, the people of Europe have acquired the habit of regarding any Turkish promise to do away with an evil or to improve administration anywhere as a nullity. Yet some improvement has been realized from these efforts.

The first promise of general reform was made by Sultan Mahmoud II., in November, 1839, in a document which was called the Hatti-Sherif of Gulhane. Sixteen years passed, in which noth-

---

* The direct influence of polygamy upon the deterioration of the Turkish people is treated of fully in another chapter.

ing was done to carry out the provisions of this charter, when it was renewed and extended by Sultan Abdul Medjid in the charter called the Hatti-Humayun, promulgated in February, 1856. The renewal of the charter was mentioned in the Treaty of Paris as the consideration on which the powers admitted Turkey to the company of European States, and guaranteed to it its rights as an independent and inviolable power. The charter thus renewed, professed to secure liberty of worship and equality of rights to the Christian inhabitants of Turkey, and promised that the laws should be codified, the administration of justice reformed, that the collection of the taxes should be regulated, and that banks, public institutions, and public improvements should be established or prosecuted. More than twenty years longer elapsed, during which the charter was not carried out, although an immediate execution of its provisions was repeatedly promised whenever and wherever manifestations of local dissatisfaction became formidable, when it was again renewed, with additional features, all in favor of liberty and liberality, in the Constitution of December, 1876. This constitution copies the best features of the fundamental law of the most enlightened governments, and would, if faithfully executed, make Turkey one of the freest States. It has, moreover, gone, in part, into actual operation, and the experiment of applying it has been begun with an earnestness which should have obtained for it a fairer trial than Turkey has been allowed to give it.

The first Turkish Parliament has been chosen, and has actually sat and deliberated under the new Constitution. It is a respectable body in point of ability and culture. Among its members are cultivated scholars and statesmen of enlightened views and farsightedness, who are capable of giving credit to any legislative body on the earth. Whatever may be its shortcomings, it is a real Parliament, representing its constituencies, and is a beginning. Russia has not yet had a Parliament, or taken steps to call one. The Grand Duchy of Finland has one, it is true, but it is an institution which the country possessed before it was incorporated with Russia, and which has been preserved to it, in distinction from the usage which has prevailed in other parts of the Empire, by especial concession.

Turkey has made great advances in the direction of religious liberty. From being one of the most intolerant of despotisms, it has become, so far as governmental declarations can make it, one of the most tolerant of States. The equal right of Mussulman and non-Mussulman subjects has been repeatedly declared, with every variation of language and particulars. Only in respect to the liability to conscription has a distinction been made, and the distinction has in this case been based on obvious considerations of policy. This distinction was practically abolished in 1876, when the Government gave notice that it would accept, and did accept, Christian volunteers; and under the new policy Christian corps have been actually organized among the Turkish defensive forces The enrollment of Christians for military service equally with Mohammedans has, furthermore, been definitely and permanently provided for in the new Constitution of 1876.

Non-Mohammedans are eligible and have been frequently appointed to offices of high trust and profit. They may be found in stations near to the household of the Sultan, and in close connection with the cabinet. The appointment of Christian Governors or responsible administrators in the provinces is far from being an extraordinary occurrence; and in the Parliament which met in 1877, all the religions of the Empire were fairly represented. Thus, among the deputies returned from Constantinople at the election of the second of March, were five Turks, four Christians, and one Jew; and of the Christians, one was a Greek, one was a Roman Catholic Armenian, and two were Gregorian Armenians.

Christians and Jews form their societies and congregations, build churches and synagogues, and worship with entire freedom, so far as the Government is concerned, throughout the Empire. Their ecclesiastical organizations and administrations are respected and upheld by the laws, the jurisdiction of their tribunals as to internal affairs, and their discipline are respected; and no obstacle is opposed to the exercise of his legitimate authority over his own people by any bishop, priest, rabbi, or pastor, be he Greek, Armenian, Roman Catholic, Jew, or Protestant. Christians are, however, not protected from popular outbreaks or oppression by local officers, and this is the text of most of their complaints of grievance. It shows that the Government is inefficient and badly administered. It is worthy of remark that the Jews make stronger complaints of worse treatment which they endure at the hands of the professed Christians of Rumania.

The work of the Missionary Societies is countenanced by the Government, and receives as much protection as the Porte affords to any of its subjects. The operations of American Societies in particular have been very successful. Armenia, Asia Minor, and the regions around Constantinople are dotted with the churches of the American Board, and Syria with those of the Presbyterian Board. The Methodist Episcopal Church has a smaller mission work in Bulgaria, the United Presbyterian Church one in Syria, and the United Presbyterian Mission in Egypt has been very prosperous, and has become quite important. Flourishing schools for boys and girls, young men and young women, are connected with these missions at important points, and are recognized as valuable auxiliaries to the education of the people. Robert College, of the American Board, at Constantinople, is a well-established institution in high repute, enjoying the confidence of the people and the Government. It has a faculty of American teachers of recognized scholarship, and competent Armenian, Bulgarian, French, Greek, and Turkish professors, and is well attended, the majority of the students being Bulgarians.

.The Syrian Protestant College at Beyrut, which grew out of the Presbyterian Mission in that city, is another institution which is assuming prominence. It has literary and medical departments, an astronomical observatory, and a faculty of excellent instructors, who are for the most part graduates of the Union Theological Seminary in New York City. It is surrounded by other schools of the Presbyterian Mission, with two English schools and the school of the Kaiserswerth Deaconesses. The colleges of the American Board at Harpoot and Aintab, and the schools of the United Presbyterians at Osiout, Egypt, are younger institutions which promise well. Besides the higher institutions, nearly every Mission station has its primary or academic school, well attended and appreciated. The Missionary Societies have built up, in connection with their Missions, extensive publishing enterprises. The American Board issues from its presses, books, tracts, and papers in the various languages which are spoken in the Empire. The works in Armenian, published by this Society, which are numerous and meritorious, deserve especial commendation. The Presbyterian presses at Beyrut sent forth in 1876 thirty-eight thousand, four hundred and fifty volumes, comprising 13,786,980 pages of Bibles, tracts, and other books, including a series of text-books and a number of juvenile works.

The missionaries of these Societies often bear witness, in their communications to the Home Boards, to the respectful treatment which they receive from the Government, and the general harmony of the relations which exist between them and the responsible officers with whom they have to deal. The Rev. Dr. E. E. Bliss, of Constantinople, in a paper which he has recently published* on the "Indirect Results of Missionary Labor in Northern Turkey," says, speaking of the battle which has been going on, for some twenty-five or thirty years past, on questions of religious liberty: "The world knows, too, or should know, that although the victory has not been so completely and finally on the side of liberty as has been desired, or as has, sometimes, in the joy of notable success in special issues, been claimed, yet religious liberty is to-day enjoyed in a remarkable degree compared with what was the case thirty or forty years ago." The presence, the teaching, and the steadfast maintenance of their principles by the missionaries, he adds, "have had a very great influence, not only in directing the attention both of Government officials and of the mass of the people to the question at issue, but in spreading enlightened and just views, and in securing right action in regard to it" The Rev. Mr. Fuller, of the American Board, writing from Aintab, March 22, 1877,† says: "The Government is now nervously anxious not only about the safety, but even the *opinion* of foreigners, and they are very prompt to render us any aid we ask. We have nothing to fear while the present Government stands, except it be from some vicious or fanatical person planning secret mischief, or from some suddenly excited and reckless mob. The Moslems always seem friendly to us, and great numbers call on us, and show marked tokens of respect, yet in these times some sudden passion may outweigh it all."

Another letter from a missionary of the same Society, of December 29, 1876, speaks of an annual celebration having just been held by the Protestants of Turkey, in commemoration of the issuing of the firman granting them religious toleration. Dr. Bliss published in the *Missionary Herald* for February, 1877, an article on the "Attitude of the Missionaries in Turkey," which shows how they have gained and hold the respect and confidence of the Moslem officials, simply by adherence to the principle of abstinence from all interference in political affairs A prejudice once existed against them founded on the suspicion that they were political agents, but this has long since disappeared, and men now "recognize the fact that the doctrines preached by the missionaries will, through their stimulat-

---

* † *Missionary Herald*, 1877.

ing and elevating power, at length exert an influence in the domain of politics; but they admit the distinction between the legitimate influence of religious doctrine and political propagandism" The missionaries had not, however, hesitated to denounce acts of oppression coming under their observation, by whomsoever committed; they had remonstrated with Turkish officials and ecclesiastical rulers in such cases; had brought wrong acts to the notice of the Government, and had even, in important cases, appealed to European and American public opinion and the friendly offices of foreign Governments, but had done such things openly and above-board, and avoided incurring prejudice. During the exciting events of 1875 and 1876, while holding aloof from political schemes, the missionaries in Bulgaria endeavored to discharge all the duties of Christian philanthropy; they advised the people against any attempt at insurrection, and as soon after the massacres took place, as it became safe, they visited the principal places in the ravaged district. They afterward did all in their power to make known to the Turkish Government and the Christian public, the greatness of the ravages committed, and at the time of writing were administering succor to the suffering survivors. These acts were done with the full knowledge of the Turkish authorities, but exposed the missionaries to no suspicion of sinister designs.

The Rev. N. G. Clark, Secretary of the American Board, at the close of June, 1877, published in the papers a statement concerning the condition of the missionaries at Erzerum, Armenia, who were almost in the center of the military operations in Asia, to the effect that the Turkish authorities were everywhere, so far as was known, considerate and obliging; that while the missionaries had been given the largest liberty to go or stay, they had so far decided to stay; and that they had been able to prosecute their work, in spite of the unsettled condition of affairs, with but little interruption, and with a larger measure of success than in any former year; and that they had "not expressed a tithe of the anxiety shown by their friends at home."

The missionaries of the Roman Catholic Church are also conducting a large number of schools, some of which are in a flourishing condition. The funds are supplied by foreign missionary bodies, by the Congregation of the Propaganda, and the French Government, which contributes 40,000 francs a year. The Austrian Government has been the great protector of the Armenian Catholics.

Their colleges and schools are ably conducted by the celebrated
Order of the Mekhitarists, who give instruction in Armenian,
French, and Turkish, and have furnished some of the best Turkish
scholars among the Christians in the Government service. In the
great towns are Propaganda colleges, on the French system, in
which French is the chief language for instruction

An edition of the Bible was printed in Arabic by the American
Bible Society in 1846, and is widely circulated in the East, and a
Roman Catholic translation, in high Arabic, is in process of publi-
cation from the Jesuit Press at Beyrut.

The tolerance which permits this development of missionary
enterprise is of recent origin, for it is only about thirty years since
beheading was the punishment prescribed by law for a Mussulman
who changed his religion.

The Turks have been brought, by their contact with the Western
people, to appreciate the advantages of European civilization, and
observe the superior strength it gives. They have striven to imitate
it, and to adopt outwardly some of its more obvious features. They
have, further, been forced, by the pressure of the Western powers
in behalf of their Christian subjects, to adopt, as we have seen,
certain reforms in law and methods of administration, tending to
make their system of government seem more liberal These changes
are as yet mostly superficial, and mark the adoption of the forms of
which they are imitations, rather than of the principles which inspire
European civilization, yet they are encouraging. They show that
the Turks may be taught to try to assimilate with the Western
people; and it will be hardly possible to maintain such liberal
amendments as the Porte has made in its laws and usages, without
in time imbibing some of the spirit with which similar legal and
political principles have been applied in other countries. If the
Turks are still behind in the application of constitutional freedom,
we must remember that it is not yet thirty years since the majority
of the States of Europe which now talk so earnestly of forcing this
boon upon the subjects of the Porte, exchanged the irresponsible
government of an absolute king for that of a Parliament and
ministry responsible to the people; and if Christians are badly
treated in Turkey, that it is a still shorter period since Protestants
were subject to intolerant legislation in several Catholic States, and
Catholics suffered from intolerant laws in several Protestant States.

The schools of Turkey are practically left in the charge of the

P showing the distribution of the principal *Races* and *Religions* of *Turkey*.

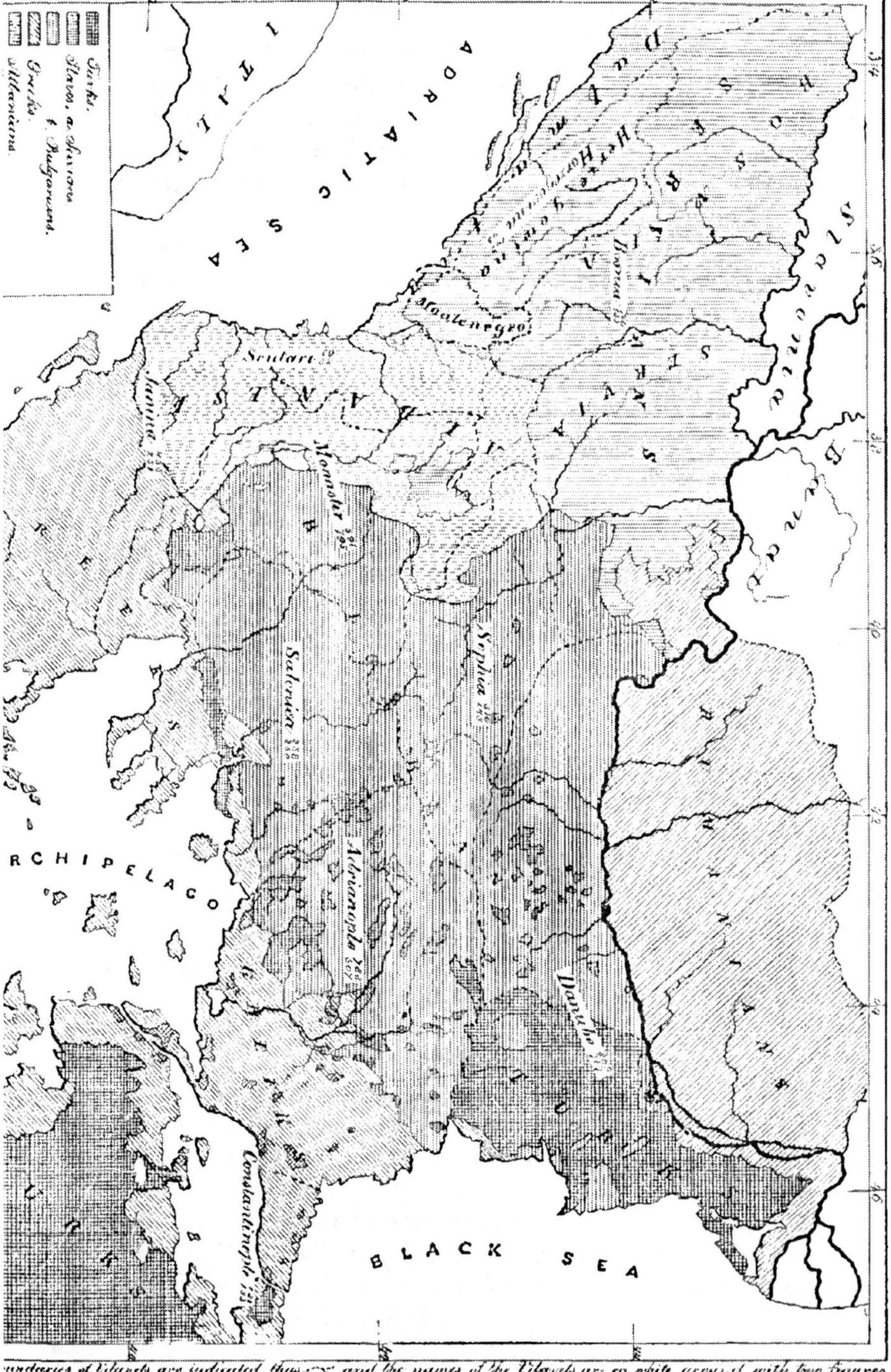

BLACK SEA

ADRIATIC SEA

ARCHIPELAGO

TYPES OF ASIA MINOR AND ARMENIA.

1. BANDIT OR BRAVO OF AIDIN.   2. TURK OF TREBIZOND.   3. TURKISH NOBLEMAN OF ERZERUM.

several religious denominations. Besides the schools of the Missionary Societies, to which we have already referred, schools are conducted by French and Italian Roman Catholic missionaries, the Greek and Armenian churches, and the Jews. The Medresses, or colleges attached to the Mohammedan Mosques, afford instruction in the Turkish language, Arabic and Persian, the Koran, and Commentaries upon it, and teach, though in a very defective manner, theology, law, philosophy, rhetoric, morals, history, and geography. Primary schools have long been established in most of the towns. An effort was made in the educational law of 1869 to provide a general system of instruction, but like most of the promising schemes of the Government, it has been of little effect for want of execution. It made education obligatory for boys of between six and eleven, and for girls of between six and ten years of age, and required every village and every ward of a town to have at least one primary school. For secondary schools, it provided that every town of more than one thousand houses should have a preparatory school, with a three years' course of instruction, and that the chief town of every province should have a lyceum, with a six years' course. It directed that separate schools be established for Mohammedans and for Christians wherever the population was sufficient to warrant it, with instruction to be given in the Koran or the Christian religion, according to the faith of the pupils, as a part of the regular course. It also made provision for normal schools. The school system was placed under the control of the Imperial Council of Education, and it was directed that the school authorities in the provinces and departments be composed in equal numbers of Mohammedans and persons of other religious belief. According to the latest accounts, there were in Constantinople 454 primary schools of all denominations, with 33,000 pupils, and in all Turkey 95 superior primary schools, with about 7,600 pupils. A university, with faculties of literature, law, and natural science and mathematics, was opened at Constantinople in 1870, and the capital and its vicinity are provided with several special and technical schools. Among these is the School of Administration, established in 1862, a lay institution, which educates Mussulmans for appointments as governors, or magistrates, of small districts.

The literature of Turkey dates from the beginning of the Osmanli dynasty, and had assumed form before Constantinople was captured. It is founded on Arabic and Persian models, and, although it is respectable in quantity, it holds a very inferior place in a comparative history of the literature of the world. Its most flourishing period was in the sixteenth century. Literature and science have received increased attention within the last generation, and Turkey has many men of letters who are well known and well esteemed abroad. Several scientific and literary societies have been established at Constantinople, and publish journals and magazines of merit. The publication of a " Universal Cyclopedia," in sixteen volumes, in Arabic, based in part upon " Appleton's New American Cyclopedia," has been begun at Beyrut by Mr. B. Bistanys, a convert of the Presbyterian Mission at that place.

All parts of Turkey enjoy a climate and a capacity for agricultural development not excelled by those of any country. Egypt, Syria, and Asia Minor were the most fruitful countries of ancient times, and surpassed any countries of Europe in wealth. They have grown poor through misgovernment and the neglect to which it leads. The European parts of the Empire are not so well situated, for their climate is less favorable; but the soil is good, and the land is capable of a culture at least approaching that of the best parts of Europe. Husbandry is in a state of primitive simplicity, the tillage is rude and imperfect, and the taxes, or rather the tax-gatherers, are oppressive, so that the farmers are hardly able to earn more than a bare subsistence. The forests produce timber of fir, pine, beech, oak, lime, and ash; the fields, millet, rice, cotton, rye, barley, and Indian corn; the orchards, the best fruits of the temperate zone. Asiatic Turkey produces all the grains of a southern climate, cedars, cypresses, and oaks on the mountains; sycamores and mulberries on the lower hills, and olives, figs, citrons, oranges, and pomegranates in the plains. The figs, olives, and vine products of Asiatic Turkey and the prunes and rose extracts of European Turkey, form important articles in the commerce of the world. Mines of various metals are numerous in both Turkeys, and were worked in ancient times with profit. At present they yield but little, and that is got in large part by working over the *débris* which the ancients have left. The country was once better watered than it is at present, and supported large herds of cattle. It is now, in consequence of the removal of the trees, as is generally supposed, subject to scorching droughts, but the pasturage is good in the valleys. Manufactures are not numerous or extensive, but the Turks make certain preparations and fine articles of value, in which they defy competition and command

.the markets of the world. There are no official statistics of the foreign commerce of the Empire, but it is quite important, and is said to be increasing. The exports are estimated at about ten million pounds sterling. They consist chiefly of grain products, wool, goats' hair, drugs, dye-stuffs, fruit products, perfumery, and fancy articles.

A railway system was begun in 1865, of which on the first of January, 1876, 1,137 miles were open—965 miles in European, 172 miles in Asiatic Turkey. The telegraph lines have a total length of 17,618 miles. The post-office is in its infancy, and is as yet mostly in the hands of foreigners. There are only four hundred and thirty post-offices in the whole Empire.

Russia is a primitive country, which is passing through the first stages of its development. Turkey is a country once highly civilized, rich, and progressive, which has fallen into decay. In this respect the promise of the future is with Russia.

The lands of Turkey are divided into Vakuf, or Church property, private lands and domain lands. The *Vakuf* property consists of that which actually belongs to the ecclesiastical establishments, and of that which lapses to the ecclesiastical boards in default of direct heirs to the owner. The law affords easy means of preventing the lapse of estates of the latter class, by permitting sales to persons who have direct heirs, and by affording facilities for the conversion of Vakuf into fee-simple titles. Private property, called *Mulkh*, is held by a tenure equivalent to our freehold tenure, by a title acquired directly from the Government, and registered in the owner's name. A law recently enacted permits the owner of a mulkh selling it to reserve a perpetual charge upon it, which is called a *Gedik*, and is, in effect, a sort of mortgage. The domain lands are *Miri*, or lands appropriated to the State Treasury, unoccupied or waste lands, escheated or forfeited lands, the domains and lands assigned to the Sultan, his family, and various offices and officers, and the military fiefs. The tenure of the last has been abolished, and nearly all the lands formerly held by it have passed to the Government. Under recent enactments, the transfer of landed property is simple and expeditious; the evidence of it can be made by the registry as secure as in any other country, and the purchaser can in most cases, where he finds the title complicated, receive a fresh one from the Government. Previous to 1867, foreigners purchasing land in Turkey had to hold it in the name of some Ottoman subject, but a law passed in that year gave them the right to hold in their own names. The proprietors of estates are usually non-resident, and cultivate their lands through tenants, to whom they are let usually on the *metayer* system, or on shares. The tenant often becomes indebted to his landlord for borrowed money. As he is never able to pay the debt, and the landlord can not afford to discharge him and lose the capital represented by the debt, he becomes practically a fixture on the estate, and goes with it to a new purchaser, who is expected to take over the debts. The tenant is thus in the position of being able to compel the landlord to support him, whether he be a profitable occupant of the land or not. As the landlord has in addition to supply grazing for ten animals for each tenant, the advantages would seem to be on the side of the latter ; yet very few of the rayahs, or tenants, are well-off.

The taxes in Turkey are of several kinds. First, is the tithe, or tax of one-tenth on all the agricultural produce of the country. The collection of the tithes is farmed out, or sold annually to the highest bidder. The first purchaser of the privilege will often sell his right to others at a profit, and they may sell again at a profit. The Government receives comparatively little revenue from this source, while the farmers of the tithes are enriched. The amount of the tithes is not oppressive, but the people deem it a grievance that worthless speculators should thrive so well at their expense with so little profit to the country. They are, moreover, subjected to inconveniences and delays and hinderances growing out of the method in which the tithes are collected, by means of which they are likely to suffer considerable losses. The *Verghi*, which is known by different names in different districts, is fixed at a certain amount for every province, and is imposed in various forms, sometimes as a property-tax, sometimes as an income-tax, sometimes as a house or a capitation-tax. The *Bédel* is a tax paid by non-Mussulman subjects of the Porte in consideration of their exemption from military service. The principle on which it is levied is not uniform, but generally has some reference to the population of the district The *Saymé* and another tax paid in butter and cheese are assessed upon goats, sheep, cattle, and swine.

The customs duties are levied in accordance with a tariff on certain articles of merchandise, and include, in all cases, an additional charge of eight per cent on imports and one of one per cent. on exports. A duty of eight per cent. was formerly levied on articles of native produce passing from one port of the country to another, but it has been abolished.

The Turkish army is recruited by conscription, for which until recently only Mohammedans were liable, Christians having been admitted to the army only since 1876. The whole, even of the Mohammedan population, is, however, not available for ordinary service. About a million, constituting the population of Constantinople and other cities, escape on one ground of privilege or another ; about three millions, constituting the nomad tribes, are not amenable to conscription ; the Mussulmans in Crete can not be spared from the island for fear of risings of the Greeks. It is estimated that by reason of the various exemptions, about one-third of the Mohammedans escape the conscription, leaving only about twelve millions as the total population from whom the draft must be made. The military forces are divided into three classes of troops, called the active army or Nizam, the reserve or Redif, and the sedentary army or Mustaphiz. Soldiers in the active army, after four years of service, may return to their homes and are free to marry, but are still liable to be called to their regiments for two years' longer service. After six years they pass to the reserve, where they serve three years in the first ban, and three years in the second ban. The soldiers of the reserve are called out to drill for one month in every year. After twelve years of service in the active army and the reserve, the soldier passes to the sedentary army, where he is enrolled for eight years longer, but is called out only in case of war. According to the estimates of 1876, the active army, or Nizam, consisted of 210,000 men, of whom 150,000 were in actual service and 60,000 were furloughed ; the reserve, or Redif, of 192,000 men, of whom half were in the first and half in the second ban ; and the sedentary army, of about 300,000 men, giving in all a force of 702,000 men. The actual available force of the Empire was, however, probably not more than about 460,000 men. For the purposes of the reserve force, the military population are divided into one hundred and twenty battalion districts, in each of which a battalion of each ban is organized, giving in all two hundred and forty battalions. Soldiers drafted into the active army may be relieved by payment of a commutation. The active army is organized, including the corps of Yemen, in Arabia, into seven corps, into which the additional forces from the reserve are embodied when they are drawn upon.

In addition to its regular forces, the Government has organized irregular troops, called Bashi-Bazouks, contingents from the Circassians settled in Turkey, and Tartars from the Crimea, Spahi-squadrons, Kurds, and Bedouins, all of which are under the loosest discipline. The Bashi-Bazouks are recruited principally in the Asiatic and African provinces In times of war they form a considerable part of the effective force, being attracted to the army by the prospect of booty. In the last war with Russia they numbered 8,000 foot and 16,000 horse. Having no settled home, they are genuine vagabonds. The conspicuous part which they have played in the present war, justifies the insertion of the following description of them by one of the correspondents from the seat of war : "The Bashi-Bazouk is commonly ill-mounted ; very few of them, except recruits from Syria, riding horses that show any trace of blood. Their horses are always kept bridled, even when eating their food. The saddles are of one pattern, but the bridles are as various as their owners' tastes. Some riders prefer halters. The men are from all parts of the Turkish Empire—Kurds, Albanians, and Arnauts predominating among them. Their clothing may be rich or may be rags. It may be also of shades of dinginess, or every variety of vivid colors. An enormous shawl or girdle around the waist is universal. They have the merited reputation of being the greatest pillagers in the world, and this girdle is the hiding-place and receptacle of their booty. Their bodies have sometimes been found with gold to the value of a thousand or eighteen hundred dollars hidden in its folds. They are not hard to discipline as to military maneuvers, but they baffle every attempt to put any restraint upon them after they break ranks. During the Crimean war no punishment would keep them from insulting, striking, and wantonly bayoneting English soldiers whom they met in public places. Their bitterest hatred is for Russians ; their sweetest hope the plunder of Moscow. Their officers can animate them to fury with that word, which is received by shouts (with their hands upon the pistols in their belts), of the Arab word for " Let us hope it—*Inshallah !* " Their arms are rude and various. They depend upon the Government they serve for a distribution of lances and carbines, but every man carries his own *yattaghan*, and has two, three, or four enormous pistols."

The Spahis, though likewise free and irregular, form a more respectable order, and consider themselves a kind of aristocracy among the troops of this class. They are mostly recruited from the older

Mohammedan families of Bosnia, Turkish Croatia, and Bulgaria. They have a picturesque appearance, but will not submit to discipline, nor are they fit to operate in a regular campaign against a disciplined army. They are employed chiefly in guerrilla service in the mountain districts, or anywhere that personal daring is of more value than subjection to rule and the command of an officer.

The Bedouins and Kurds are free at home, acknowledging only a nominal allegiance to the Empire, and a close allegiance only to their own chiefs. They are likewise free in the army; contented to stay so long as they are allowed to fight and plunder without restraint, but ready to fold their tents and march away whenever any attempt is made to exercise discipline over them.

The Turkish navy consisted, at the end of 1875, of twenty iron-clad ships and seventy other steamers, with four steam transports. Three of the iron-clads were considered vessels of extraordinary size and strength. The navy is manned by thirty thousand soldiers and four thousand marines, recruited by conscription or voluntary enlistment, who serve for eight years.

The Sultan has the right to call upon Egypt and Tunis for contingents of troops. The Egyptian army consists of about twenty thousand men of various branches of the service, and the navy of two frigates, two corvettes, three large yachts, and four gun-boats. The army of Tunis consists of 4,600 regular and 11,500 irregular troops, and its navy of three small armed vessels, one transport, and two monitors in course of construction.

The financial condition of Turkey is really desperate. For nearly thirty years the expenditures of the Government have exceeded the revenues by between thirty-five and forty millions of dollars. Loan after loan has been borrowed, defaults have been made in payment of interest, and the credit of the Government is at the lowest stage. The foreign debt is represented by fourteen loans, contracted between 1854 and 1874, amounting in the aggregate to 184,981,783 pounds sterling, and the internal and floating debt is variously estimated at from nine million to thirty million pounds sterling, or five times as many dollars. The Turkish Government in effect announced its bankruptcy in October, 1875, when it gave notice that the payments of interest upon the debt would be reduced for five years to one-half the stipulated amount. It confessed in the decree which conveyed this notice that it had been in the habit of making new loans to pay the coupons on the old ones, but could do this no longer. It had, therefore, to make a temporary reduction of inter-est, on the plan of paying one-half wholly in cash, and providing for the other half by the issue of fresh securities bearing five per cent. interest, payable simultaneously with the cash half of the original coupon falling due. If at the expiration of five years the bonds representing the second half of the coupons should not have been redeemed, the payment of them would be further delayed until the foreign loan following next in order for redemption should be ex-tinguished. Default was made in the payment of the cash interest promised under this arrangement, and a further announcement was made in July, 1876, that no payments would be made until the in-ternal affairs of the Empire had been settled. The Government was out of money, and, of course, could not borrow. It provided for its wants by an issue of paper money. The first issue was fixed at three million Turkish pounds, but in four months more than twice that amount had been put into circulation.

The character and bearing of the views of the Turkish leaders of opinion have undergone considerable modifications within the pres-ent century. The Turks of the old school, bigoted, fixedly attached to the old ways, and who would tolerate no change whatever, dis-appeared as a force in the State when the Janizaries were abolished in 1826. A few of this stamp remain, but not enough to form a party. The change in the conditions of the Empire and in its rela-tions to other States have brought a new class of men to the front, who seek to meet the emergencies of the times with new views and new ways of management. They are still, however, steadily at-tached to the past, and still seek to adhere to the old traditions and usages, only consenting to change or adapt them so much as may be necessary for the preservation of the State in its integrity and inde-pendence. The prominent Turks of the present day are classified into two parties, called respectively the Old Turks and the Young Turks. The Old Turkish party seeks to restore as much as is possi-ble of the old patriarchal condition of the East, and to maintain it with all the means at command. Among its objects it seeks to pre-serve the ancient usages and regulations with reference to women, and has so far succeeded in preventing any alterations in them. It insists especially on avoiding all entanglements with foreigners, even to the extent of setting limitations upon the trade with foreign coun-tries. With this object—and on this point it has shown considerable worldly wisdom—it advocates and supports those measures, which will

BASHI-BAZOUKS.

KURDS.

content the Christian populations; for it has been learned by experience that every oppression of the Christians leads directly to a
complication with some one or other of the European powers. One
of the most prominent members of the Old Turkish party was the
late Grand Vizier, Ali Pasha, who was dispatched to Crete at the
time of the insurrection there in 1867, and addressed a memorandum
to the Porte recommending reforms, which is pointed to as containing one of the best expositions of the principles of his party. In
this paper he showed that the principles of the Treaty of Paris,
which were supposed to have prevented all danger of foreign interference in the affairs of the Empire, had ceased to be effective and
could no longer protect it. A new doctrine of government had been
set up and acted upon, which recognized the rights of peoples to be
arranged under governments according to their race and national
affinities, which would be used to the disadvantage of Turkey and
for the advancement of the designs of Russia.

The Russian Government had not given up its designs upon the
East; it would not now carry them out by war, for it had found a
better way; it would excite discontent among the Christian population of the principalities, and while assuring the other powers that
it was seeking to promote the welfare of its fellow-Christians, would
seek to dismember Turkey by the operation of internal dissension.
If such a condition as the one which then prevailed in Crete were
produced, and continued, the powers would sympathize with the
professions of Russia, while Turkey would be entirely isolated, and
would be compelled "to hold those persons who are most necessary
and most useful for the reproduction and agriculture of the nation
under arms, and to appropriate its entire income to this object, so
that not a penny would be left us for the culture of the land, nor a
minute for working out good laws for the weal of the State and the
nation; and thus our enemy would hasten the attainment of his destructive purpose; for it is evident that the Mohammedan population, which alone furnishes troops, could not long endure this
condition; that the treasury could quite as little bear to have all its
income turned to unproductive ends, and that the host of ten millions of subjects, who heartily desired to rise and be free, would not
remain long in obedience and subjection."

A remedy for these difficulties and dangers could be found if the
Government would grant to its non-Mohammedan subjects an enlargement of their opportunities for culture, of their sphere of

7

action, and of their privileges, so that they could find at home what they now had to seek abroad, and that they should "not see anything to envy in the situation of the subjects of foreign States, and should learn to regard themselves no longer as subjugated by an Ismaelitish State, but as servants and subjects of a superior monarchy, which protected all alike." Three specific measures were proposed as likely to produce this result directly; that all the offices and public positions in the State be thrown open to all alike, so that Christians should find all the bars to promotion removed from before them; that schools be established and thoroughly organized, in which the children of Mohammedans and Christians should be instructed together, and Greeks should no longer have to send their children to Greece, and Bulgarians to Russia, to learn principles of hostility to the Ottoman Empire; and that mixed civil courts be established, with a code for the trial of all mixed suits. "In fine," said this remarkable memorandum, "the fusion of all our subjects, except as to purely religious affairs, is the only means by which we can overcome the jealousy between our different populations and avoid the dangers that threaten us."

The representatives of the Old Turkish party are, with few exceptions, men of high character and standing. The "Young Turkish" party is composed of young men who have been educated abroad or under European teachers, and have cast off the religious prejudices and authority of their fathers, and who have acquired enough of the superficialities of French culture to unsettle them in their old principles without their having imbibed any of the fundamental principles of European knowledge and life. The serious idea on which the party rests is that the prosperity of the Empire and the operation of the measures which are necessary to restore it to a sound condition are hindered by the too rigorous traditional constructions which are placed upon the religious law, and it has sought to obtain from the doctors authoritative determinations and modifications of the law better adapted to the present exigencies. Some of the Young Turks have regarded the reigning dynasty as an insurmountable barrier to the regeneration of the Empire. The party arose about twelve or fifteen years ago, in an opposition to the administration of Ali Pasha, at a period when the Government was contracting large loans and spending extravagantly, and after the hopes which had been awakened upon the accession of Abdul Medjid had been dispelled. The increasing number of appointments of Christians to offices in the service of the State especially excited its animadversion, and gave occasion to the publication, in the journals which were started in Young Turkish interests, of numerous articles breathing the most intense hostility to the Christians and sounding the praises of the Ottoman Empire, its power and its glories. Equally with the "Old Turks," the "Young Turks" shun entanglements with Europe, and seek to prevent the introduction of European notions; but they go about their work in a different manner and with a different spirit.

The party has never been very numerous, and its life has been rather social than political, its political objects only occasionally rising to the surface. Its representative men are described as being polished and prepossessing in their manners and appearance, but many of them crafty, untrustworthy, and without the sense of personal honor or principle. The leaders have once or twice come under the displeasure of the Government for excess in their manifestations, and have been subjected to voluntary or involuntary exile. All of them who were under punishment were pardoned by Abdul Hamid, and allowed to return to the capital, where, all the political questions about which they had contended having been settled, it was thought they would not be likely to do harm, but might be of service in exciting the fanaticism of the people against the foreign enemy. Both parties participated in the deposition of the Sultan Abdul Aziz. Of the leaders in that movement, Midhat Pasha and Zia Bey were ranked as Young Turks. Hussein Avni Pasha and Mehemet Rushdi Pasha as Old Turks. The principal advisers of the Sultan Murad were Young Turks, and to them is due the promulgation of the Constitution of Midhat Pasha. The Government which succeeded that of Midhat Pasha was under Old Turkish influences The most prominent upholders of the constitutional principle in Midhat Pasha's cabinet were sent away after its accession, one to be Governor-of-Syria, one to retirement, one to prison, and Midhat himself to exile.

The Turks in Europe are of a mixed race, and present a variety of physical traits according to the nationality whose blood they share, hardly any of which can be considered distinctive. Generally they are characterized by a strange expression of the eyes, lankness of the limbs, and in the cities by colorlessness of the skin. The Asiatic Turks have well-shapen heads, black or brown hair, fine forms, and a calm, placid expression of countenance. Both Asiatics and Europeans are eminently pious, and observe strictly all the requisitions of the Mohammedan ritual with regard to worship, prayer, fasts, alms, and other acts of ceremonial and worship. They set a high value upon the privilege of pilgrimage, and hold the Koran in such respect as to ascribe the working of wonders to the mere reading of it. Their other characteristics will be revealed in the course of our history.

The style of dress in Turkey has been greatly modified by the adoption of European fashions. The old Turkish turban was a woolen cloth wound around the fez, and was worn green by Mohammedans, black or blue by Christians and Jews. The cloth is now dispensed with, and the fez is generally worn alone. The trousers were distinguished by their excessive fullness. The upper part of the body was dressed in a vest or jacket called the *Anteri*, and the Dolman, or *Chekman*, with pendant, slitten sleeves, which was generally red and embroidered with braidings of golden yellow silk. Over all was worn the *Benish*, or cloth coat. In the harem the Turk wore a dressing-gown with a long robe (the *Kusk*) over it, with socks and morocco shoes, or half boots. In modern times, the Turks in the higher ranks around Constantinople will be found dressed in a correct European costume, except that they adhere to the picturesque and pleasant fez, instead of adopting the European tall hat. The women wear a red or yellow shirt, reaching to the knees, under which are worn full and gathered trousers, a long overdress which is gathered at the waist by a shawl, woolen hose and slippers. On their heads they wear a fez or little cap, and on the street a white cloth, the *Yashmak*, which covering the head leaves the eyes free; further, the whole face is concealed by an ugly mantle called the *Fereye*.

Turkish houses present a blank wall to the street, with no window or other opening except the entrance-way. This leads to a court-yard, which is really the front of the house. The rooms are built around it, in such a way as to leave the women's quarters in a secluded position and separated from the rest of the house. The court-yard is beautified, and the house furnished with comforts and luxuries according to the means of the owner; there may be none, or they may be—as they generally are with wealthy Turks—in excess. The street appearance of the house gives no clue to what is inside of it. The roughest and most forbidding mud wall in appearance may be the shell of a palace, exhibiting the highest degree of splendor inside, or the interior may be nearly as rude and meagre as the outside.

CHAPTER VI.

THE TRIBUTARY STATES AND THE SUBJECT PEOPLES OF TURKEY.

Rumania—Union of the Principalities of Moldavia and Wallachia into one State—Education, Literature, Army, and Finances—Characteristics of the People, their Dress and Manner of Living—Servia—Its History and Present Condition—The Omladina—The Servian Church—Dress, Customs, and Domestic Usages—Bosnia and Herzegovina—The Bulgarians—They Regain the Autonomy of their National Church—Progress of Education—Circassian Colonies in Bulgaria—Montenegro—Sketch of its History—The Albanians—The Miridites—The Greeks of Turkey—The Districts in which they Predominate—Their Control of Turkish Commerce—Greeks in Asia Minor—Crete—The Armenians—Maronites—Druses—Egypt—Its Advance toward Independence—The Suez Canal and other Works of Improvement—Tripoli and Tunis.

THE European tributary States of Turkey at the beginning of 1877 were Rumania and Servia. The principality of Rumania is composed of the former provinces or principalities of Moldavia and Wallachia. It has an area of 45,642 square miles, and a population of 3,864,848. The principality lies entirely north of the Danube, and presents an irregular figure, whose shape may be compared to that of a piece of a quarter of an apple with the core taken out. The sharp curve of the Carpathian Mountains and Transylvanian Highlands entering from the north and west to the center of the figure the State would present were its shape symmetrical, may represent the line formed by cutting out the core. Wallachia, the southern province of the principality, lies between the Danube and the Transylvanian Highlands, touching Servia on the west, and presents its greatest length from east to west. Moldavia, lying between the Carpathians and the river Pruth, presents its greatest length from north to south, touching on the north the country which was once Poland. A narrow strip of country, extending north and east from the Danube and Pruth, gives the principality a small frontage on the Black Sea. The mountains on the north and west separate Rumania from Austria-Hungary, and the Pruth separates it from Russia, but neither mountains nor river separate Rumanians from Rumanians; for a large proportion of the population in Austrian Transylvania and Bukowina, and Russian Bessarabia are of this stock.

The inhabitants of the predominant race are commonly called Wallachs, or more recently Rumanians. They are a mixed people, combining the blood of the ancient Dacians, a branch of the Thracian stock, with that of the Roman colonists, who were settled in the province of Dacia after its conquest by Trajan, mingled with that of the various races and tribes which have overrun the country from the days of the Roman dominion down to the present time. By the treaties of Adrianople and Paris, the two principalities of Moldavia and Wallachia, commonly called the Danubian principalities, acquired a condition of semi-independence, by which they gained control of their own internal administrations, while they paid a tribute to Turkey. In 1859, they effected a substantial union by choosing the same person as Hospodar, or Prince.

The union has been gradually made closer, and has been recognized by the Great Powers and by Turkey. The government of the principality is a constitutional monarchy, with representative chambers and a responsible ministry. The present prince is Charles of Hohenzollern-Sigmaringen, who has assumed the title of Charles I. The people speak a language more like the Latin than any other modern tongue, and have some physical and mental characteristics which they may have derived from the ancient Romans, along with the language and name of that people. They are generally attached to the Greek Church, and are farmers, practicing the rudest methods in agriculture. Education is in a low state. A compulsory school law exists, but the schools are few and thinly attended. In 1875 there were four thousand teachers and fifty-five thousand pupils in all the schools, and the higher education was represented by twenty-two high-schools of different grades, a larger number of theological, technical, and private schools, and the two Universities of Bucharest and Jassy. The Wallachs have a small literature, the oldest specimen of which is a historical fragment of the date of 1495. The following century produced some theological literature, but the Bible was not translated into their language till 1643. Recently a number of learned and poetical works have been produced, some of the latter of which have been considerably admired. Political discussions have been active during the present century, leading to the establishment of several newspapers, and the production of minor works of a political character. The principality has a number of contemporary poets and writers of romances, who, however, have not commanded any great fame abroad.

The Rumanian army consists of 22,463 infantry and 12,184 cavalry. The revenues of the principality in 1876 were 97,894,427 francs, its expenditures were 97,891,427 francs, and its debt on Jan. 1, 1877, was 515,841,278 francs, or about one hundred million dollars.

The typical Rumanian is a man of slender stature and symmetrical shape, and has a brown oval face, not unhandsome, and often with noble features His eyes are dark and expressive. His mouth is well cut, filled with showy white teeth, and shaded with a mustache. The full beard is seldom worn, being in this, as in the other principalities, peculiar to the priests. The man takes much pride in his long hair, hanging down over his shoulders. The hands and feet are small and neatly formed. The women are quite handsome

K. E Franzos says of them in his "Half Asia"*: "The Rumanian girl reaches her full bodily development in her thirteenth or fourteenth, at most in her fifteenth year; and she presents often a handsome, elegant figure. The Roman type, although partly obliterated by marriages with the Slavs, is manifested in the well-developed nose, in the fine and sharply-defined mouth, in the black, shining hair, in the peculiar, but not unpleasant, bronze tint of the countenance. If you observe her in her gala-dress, with her chemisette of linen, adorned with artistic embroidery, with the national frock cut out of a single piece, which, fastened by a girdle at her waist, swells over her hips in thick folds, and falls to her ankles, with the light, tunic-like, generally blue mantle; if you listen to her conversation, which will remind you in almost every word of the speech of ancient Rome —it will not require the exercise of much imagination to think that you are in the presence of a Roman peasant-girl of the time of Cicero."

The men wear over linen breeches, a white, wide-sleeved shirt, open at the breast, and falling nearly to the knees. It is confined at the waist by a broad leathern band, in which are worn the knife, pipe, flint and steel, tobacco-pouch and wallet. Over the shoulders is worn a jacket of sheepskin, with the wool outside ; a longer cloak, also of sheepskin, is worn in many places in the winter. Sandals, similar to those of the Romans, are worn on the feet in pleasant weather, but in wet weather their place is supplied by boots reaching up to the knee. A broad-brimmed straw hat is worn on the head in summer, a sheepskin cap in winter. On festive occasions,.

---

* "Halb Asien," Leipsic, 1876.

the well-to-do Wallach completes his costume by a doublet fanci-
fully embroidered, which lends to his dress a decidedly Romanesque
appearance.

The houses of the Wallachian peasants are wooden buildings,
thatched with straw, often only of a single story, but where there
are two stories, with the upper story surrounded with a veranda.
In poorly-wooded districts the dwellings are often dug out of the
ground, and covered with an earthen roof. In the regions exposed
to the overflow of the Danube, the houses often consist of rude
timber huts, placed upon four stakes, so as to be lifted above the
reach of the floods.

The aristocracy of Rumania are called Boyars. They are the
modern representatives of the ancient aristocracy of the land, and
date, according to one authority,* from the time when every one
who bore a weapon had a right to rank himself in that class. The
name originated among the descendants of the Roman colonists in
the eighth and ninth centuries, when the warrior who went into
battle with a scythe-chariot, drawn by oxen, was designated as a
bovis herus, or Boyar, the same as those who went with horses
were called *cavalli heri*, or cavaliers. Others derive the title from
Bulgar, Bulgarian.† Among the original privileges of a Boyar was
exemption from taxes. The title and its privileges were personal,
and did not descend At a later period the title was given to the
holders of certain offices, and once given was continued for life,
even though the term of official service were but one year. Under
Turkish rule it became a matter of sale. Under the present Government it is given, according to a regular system, as a symbol of
rank and office. The Boyars are now of two ranks, the great and
small Boyars. The total number of Boyar families of both ranks
in the two provinces forming the principality was 6,000 in 1865.
The Boyars live like other European aristocracy, so far as their
means permit them, and copy French fashions and French manners
to such an extent that they have made Jassy and Bucharest "the
city of pleasure," to be among the gayest capitals of Europe.

The principality of Servia is the relic of what was a considerable
State in the middle ages, but which became subject to the Turks
after the battle of Kosovo, in 1389. The Servians proved to be
discontented subjects, and gave the Turks much trouble. They

---

* Hellwald and Beck—"Die Heutige Turkei," I , 132.

† Franzos, *Allgemeine Zeitung*, Oct. 24, 25, and 26, 1877.

CHARLES I.—PRINCE OF RUMANIA.

MILAN—PRINCE OF SERVIA.

gained a condition of semi-independence in 1811, and have retained it, except for a short interval during the wars of Napoleon, to the present time. The maintenance of all the privileges which had been gained by both Servia and Rumania was guaranteed by the great powers in the Treaty of Paris in 1856, but Turkey retained the right to keep garrisons in certain of the Servian forts. The principality has been ruled by the families of the Karageorgevitch and Obrenovitch, between whom a bitter rivalry exists. The present ruler is Prince Milan Obrenovitch IV., who was enthroned in 1868. The Government is a constitutional monarchy, with a representative chamber, called the Skupstchina, and a responsible ministry.

Servia has an area of about 16,600 square miles, and a population of 1,320,000. It has made great advances in civilization within the last ten years, particularly in the building of roads and in education. Until 1876 it had no debt, but a balance in the treasury. In that year it borrowed a small loan to enable it to carry on the war against Turkey. Its standing army consists of four thousand men, and its entire military strength is rated at about seventy thousand men. Education is provided for in a public school system, under the control of the Minister of Education, which embraces primary schools, academical and collegiate schools, a normal school, a high-school at Belgrade, and special and professional schools. The Servians have a literature in which they take pride. Their old literature, which is in the old Slavic or Church language, dates back to the eleventh century, and is rich in songs and ballads. Their modern literature is also quite copious and creditable, and dates from the eighteenth century. The secret society called the Omladina was originally formed for the purpose of cultivating the national literature, but it has been converted into a political organization, and is the most steady and influential promoter of the agitations for securing the complete independence of the country.

The Greek Church is established, but religious freedom prevails under the restriction that no one is permitted to leave the Holy Orthodox Church to join another. The religious and spiritual life is wholly under the influence of the cloisters, from which the Metropolitan and the Bishops are appointed. The Archbishop of Belgrade is head of the Church, is independent of the Patriarch of Constantinople, and has under him the three bishops of Shabatz, Ushitza, and Negotin, who with him constitute the National Synod. The clergy consist of seven hundred worldly priests, and one hundred and twenty priests in the cloisters. The number of cloisters was forty-one in 1875; but by an order passed in that year they are to be reduced to five.

The Servians have sharply-defined faces and robust bodies, are rather large than small in stature, broad-shouldered, but seldom gross. They have well-proportioned heads, with rather high crowns, well-shaped foreheads, somewhat prominent cheek-bones, medium-sized noses, which are generally straight, but sometimes repressed, and are very often finely developed. Their hair is generally blonde or brown, and luxuriant in growth. The men commonly wear their hair cut short, long hair and the full-beard being left to the priest-hood. The people in the cities sometimes wear side-whiskers, but the peasant wears only a mustache. The ladies in the towns set a high value on black hair, and are not loath to use dyes to get it.

The women are of medium size, and have regular features without being handsome, although very fine, faultless faces are often met with in the cities. The women are, as a rule, better-looking than their sisters in Montenegro, but the men lack the lightness and elasticity of movement which characterize the warlike mountaineers. The dress of the Servians varies greatly in different districts, and often in different neighborhoods. In the country, garments of folded white linen, a colored belt and brown or light-colored woolen outside coats, are worn extensively by both sexes. The Servian peasant wears, in summer, large breeches reaching in full folds to the ankles, over which is a woolen shirt open at the breast, and held in at the waist by a red cloth belt. Over the belt he wears a brown leathern girdle, in which he carries a pistol or two, a brass gun-stick, a dagger and a handkerchief, and a cartridge-box. On his right side hang a short knife in a leather sheath, a flint and steel, and an oil-box. If the man is going away to any distance, he puts on a short, striped vest, and over it a thick, braided woolen jacket, and completes his armor by adding a long Albanian flint-lock, or a more modern improved gun, if he has one. On his head he wears a low, red fez, with or without a tassel, and on his feet dark, knit hose and sandals of untanned leather.

In Western Servia, the peasants commonly wear wide, slit breeches of brown cloth, which are narrowed like gaiters just below the knees. In the south, some Albanian fashions are adopted, such as the bandage of white cloth around the fez, the short brown or black jacket, with slitten sleeves, and the broad red cloak for rainy weather. The sheepskin cap of the Bulgarians is worn in the south-east, and Rumanian fashions prevail in the east.

The dress of the merchants and official people in the cities, when it has not been modified by European styles, is very rich. The breeches are cut in the Turkish fashion, of blue cloth, and embroidered with black braid. The red vest is richly braided with gold-thread, the winter coat is bordered with fur, and a variously-striped shawl, several yards in length, woven of yarn, cashmere, or silk, is worn as a girdle. The arms and other articles of dress and ornament are enriched in a corresponding degree.

The principal variations in the costumes of the women are in the head-dresses. Flowers, pieces of gold or silver, to which the women of the cities add a small fez, arranged in a great variety of ways, form the principal parts of the head-dresses of girls. The women wear diadems, helmets, or similar designs, which are trimmed with metallic pieces, feathers, or other ornaments, and are crowned, in the cities, with a fez surrounded with a switch of hair. The costume of the peasant women is in other respects very simple. The most important article is the shirt, of home-made stuff, reaching from the neck to the ankles, and embroidered with wool in front and on the arms and sleeves. Two striped aprons, worn in front and behind a belt, and often a short jacket open in front, with the shirt, make up the home dress. The overdress, which is seldom worn in the house, is a sleeveless coat of white cloth, varied with stripes, rosettes, and other designs. The feet are clothed with colored stockings and sandals. The picturesqueness of the costume is enhanced not only by the fanciful head-dress, but also by the many other ornaments which women know how to use with effect.

The women of the cities combine the Oriental and Western fashions in their dress. An embroidered shirt and neckerchief cover the bust, and are revealed, with the accompanying nosegay or golden pin, through the open front of the sack. A heavy brocade sash is thrown around the waist, and hangs with richly-ornamented ends in front of the colored silken dress, which is made in the European style. An embroidered pocket-handkerchief, a fan, a bouquet, wide bracelets, a necklace of pearls or gold, and the usual rings, complete a picture, whose beauty is, however, sadly marred by the senseless fashion of dyeing the hair and staining the eyebrows and lips.

The Servian country-houses are structures of timber-work, or consist of a lower story of stone and an upper story of wood, surmounted often with a very high roof of thatch or tiles. They are rather scantily furnished in the interior, where the weapons of the head of the family occupy the place of honor among the household ornaments. The windows are seldom furnished with glass, but paper in wooden frames is made to supply its place. On the larger estates the house of the head of the family, which serves also as the dwelling of the unmarried members of the household, is surrounded by the smaller houses of the married members. These consist generally only of a bed-room, the main hall affording living-room and dining-room for the whole family. The whole group of buildings, including also the granaries of basket-work set up on stakes, is surrounded by a fence of pickets. The Servian character is distinguished by strong family affection, patriotism, and love of freedom, and an inclination to mysticism. The family life is conducted after the patriarchal style. The head of the household presides over the whole circle of relatives and dependents, adjusts their differences, regulates their labors, superintends the division of the proceeds, and cares for all as for himself. When he dies his son takes his place, or if he declines the responsibility, some one else is chosen in his stead. All the members of the household are united by common interest, and when any one goes away from the estate he is entitled to receive a commutation proportioned to the amount he has contributed by his services to the general weal. While the condition of the women is subordinate, the depth of the affection which exists between brother and sister, and the esteem in which it is held, form one of the most peculiar and creditable traits of the Servian character. So firmly-seated and widely-extended and recognized is it, that out of it has grown the strongest sanction that a Servian can give to his pledge or his word— " As true as my brother (or my sister) lives." Akin to it is the bond of brotherhood or sisterhood which two young men or young women may take for each other, which is often sanctioned by open and formal ceremonies, and is held for life.

The Servians have the qualities of good soldiers, but are withal patient and peaceful, honorable, enduring, and firm. They are not easily cheated, and are not inclined to cheat. If they believe a thing to be right, they will adhere to it, and will suffer legal restraint rather than yield. They are proud, and avoid menial occupations and mechanical trades, but are fond of military and official life, and readily enter mercantile callings. Their merchants enjoy a wide field of trade. They have houses in Bucharest, Trieste, Pesth, and

Vienna, and visit all the larger fairs of Southern Hungary with their goods, which consist rather of raw materials than of manufactured articles.

Bosnia and Bulgaria are former independent kingdoms, which have been subjugated by Turkey, and are ruled as Turkish provinces or vilayets, by Governors appointed by the Porte. The majority of the people of Bosnia are attached to the Greek Church, but the Roman Catholic population is large, and the wealthier classes and landowners are generally Mohammedans. The kingdom of Bosnia survived that of Servia nearly a hundred years, although it had become tributary to Turkey, but was finally overthrown in 1463 The King and a number of the Waywodes were put to death, over two hundred thousand of the inhabitants of both sexes were sent into slavery in Asia Minor, and thirty thousand of the young men were enrolled in the corps of the Janizaries. The people, of whom the mass remained true to the Greek faith, were despoiled of their lands, which were divided among the Mohammedans. An opportunity was given, however, to the native landowners to save their estates by professing the Mohammedan religion, and many of them did so. These proprietors were the ancestors of the Mohammedan Bosnians, the *begs*, or landowners, or *agas*, if their estates are very large, of the present day, who are only in a few instances Turks, but are generally Slavs of the same race with the Christian Bosnians. Bosnia occupies an isolated position with reference to the rest of Turkey. The Christian States of Servia, jutting in from the north and Montenegro from the south-west, almost cut it off from the other provinces, leaving only the narrow sanjak of Novi-Bazar as a connecting link. The Servian language is spoken through most of the province, but the Turkish, as the official language, is somewhat affected by the more pretentious begs. The country is mountainous, with broad, fertile valleys. About four-tenths of the land is considered tillable, and this part is productive of remunerative crops, the best known of which are the "Turkish prunes;" yet the resources of the country, which are capable of an extensive development, are almost entirely unimproved. There are but few highways worthy of the name. The principal means of communication are by bridle-paths, with causeways over the swamps that are almost as dangerous as the morasses themselves, and dilapidated bridges over the streams that offer little choice above fording the waters. The country was, before its conquest, provided with good roads, the remains of which may be found in various quarters, and a few of the ancient Roman bridges are still in use. A single railroad has been built from Banialuka to Rasnice, and four telegraph lines have been completed.

Bosnia contains several cities of moderate size, the principal of which is the capital, Bosna Serai or Serayevo, a handsomely-situated and well-appearing town of 45,000 inhabitants, with about two hundred minarets and mosques and considerable trade.

The Mohammedan Bosnians live together only in the larger towns, where they are engaged in trade, and control most of the commerce of the province. The landowners live scattered about on their estates, in the broader valleys The Christians live in the smaller villages, and in the higher and less fruitful valleys, and on the table-lands. The Bosnians are of fine stature and physical appearance, with handsome, expressive features, are pious, brave, and hospitable. Bishop Strossmayer characterizes the Mussulman landowners as a fine and generous body of men, brave, high-spirited, and resentful against wrong; but truthful, honest, and never, like the Turk, cruel in their vengeance. The costume of the Bosnians is like that of the Morlaks, a Slavic tribe living in the maritime districts of Austro-Hungary, and is marked by variety in color, material, and fashion. Polygamy has never gained prevalence among the begs. The women go veiled in public, but enjoy at home a freedom and privilege greater than those of the Turkish women. The young women are allowed to receive attentions from the young men, and the young man who contemplates marriage is permitted to spend the evening with his betrothed, while she sits concealed from his view by a wall or shutter. It is related of the Bosnian women by a Turkish historian that when the first captives were taken to the Turkish court at Brussa, before the capture of Constantinople, they appeared to the chiefs like living genii from Paradise.

The education of the people is limited, and science and literature have made but little progress among them. In the few schools which have been established by the Greeks, Turks, and Bosnians themselves, instruction is hardly given beyond reading and writing. The Mohammedans have schools for boys, but not for girls. They have also higher Koran schools in connection with their more important mosques, and the Roman Catholics have schools at the Franciscan monasteries. It is estimated by good authorities that only one per cent. of the population can read, hardly any one can write, and there is not a printing-office in the province. Although the Bosnians have no literature of their own, they have a share in the popular songs, tales, and fables, in which the Servian folk-lore is peculiarly rich.

The Bosnians are discontented, unquiet subjects, and have given trouble by frequent insurrections. Even the Mohammedan begs have not cast aside the ties of country and race "They have never," says Mr Malcolm MacCall, in his work on "The Eastern Question," "forgotten their Christian ancestry; and in many a Mussulman household among the valleys of Bosnia and on the slopes of the Balkans are fondly cherished traditions and memorials of the faith which their forefathers bartered in exchange for the rights of freemen. . . . . The Slav Mussulmans are fanatical, no doubt, but it is the fanaticism of caste rather than of religion. Of Islam, in its theological and religious aspect, they know little and care less Let the Slav Mussulmans of Bosnia and Bulgaria," he adds, "be convinced that the abolition of the Turkish rule does not mean the abolition of their hereditary rights, and they will view the exit of the Ottomans not with equanimity merely, but with warm approval."

The unhappy disposition of the people is chiefly owing to the backward state of the country and the inconveniences under which it suffers. Prof. Gottfried Kinkel, of Basel, in his lecture on "The Christian Subjects of Turkey in Bosnia and Herzegovina," shows that they are chiefly due to the unjust distribution of the land, in which the actual tiller is not permitted to enjoy any interest of proprietorship. This author expresses the belief that quiet can never be restored to the country until the present system is swept away, and a new distribution is made among the actual inhabitants, who are also the heirs of the former rightful owners of the soil.

Herzegovina is geographically, ethnographically, and historically connected with Bosnia. It is more mountainous than Bosnia, and has a smaller relative area of tillable soil, the amount being three-tenths for Herzegovina to four-tenths for Bosnia. In the fifteenth century Herzegovina was known as the Bosnian Province of Kosatchina. The Prince Stefan Kosatcha, who ruled the province during the reign of the Bosnian King Tomer Ostojiksh Christitch, asked and obtained from the German Emperor, Frederick III., the title and rank of Duke. From that time the province has borne its present name, Herzegovina, derived from the Hungarian word *Herczeg* (German, Herzog), Duke. Under Turkish rule it has been at times, as now, a separate vilayet, and at other times a part of the vilayet of Bosnia. The capital and principal city of Herzegovina is Mostar, a town of 15,000 inhabitants, on the Narenta River, founded in 1440.

The dress of the Bosnian rayah is similar in cut to that of the Turk of the same rank, but the Bosnian is not permitted to wear bright red. He wears a fez, which is often wrapped with a dark red cloth; a brown doublet, full breeches of white or dark blue felted goods reaching to the knees, a blue or dark red sash, and sandals. He can not carry arms without paying a tax and getting a license therefor, so that his chibouk, or Turkish pipe, and his tobacco-pouch constitute the only ornaments he has corresponding to the glittering pistols and daggers of his Servian and Montenegrin neighbors.

The women wear a costume which is after the fashion of either the Servians, Morlaks, or Turks. In the latter case it consists of a fez, a colored jacket with sleeves open before, exposing an under bodice which partly covers the opened shirt; trousers of dark stuff reaching to the ankles, and stockingless feet, with slippers or low-cut shoes. The rayah lives in a house of wood and mud or of stone, according as either material is more abundant in the neighborhood; sleeps in his clothes, and does not forget to be obsequious to the Mussulman

The Bulgarians are not confined to the province marked Bulgaria on the maps, but form the bulk of the rural population of the country from Western Macedonia to the Black Sea, and from the Danube to the Sea of Marmora. They are of the Ugro-Finnish race, and came down in the days of the Roman Empire from the regions of the Volga, whence their name, and took possession of the region which they still occupy. This region being inhabited by a Slavic people, the Bulgarians mingled with the natives and assimilated with them, adopting their customs and the essential features of their language, while they still retained the physiognomy of their own race. Bulgaria formed a kingdom of considerable importance in the middle ages, but was subdued by the Hungarians in the middle of the fourteenth century, and finally by the Turks in 1392. The Bulgarian Church gradually fell under the influence of the Greeks, who are the dominant race of the districts lying south of the Bulgarian region. The Greek clergy finally gained the control of the ecclesiastical organization and ritual, and sought to banish the Bulgarian language from the churches and

BULGARIANS.

NICHOLAS I.—PRINCE OF MONTENEGRO.

schools, and to substitute their own ritual in worship. Their efforts aroused a spirit of discontent and opposition to which the Bulgarians had long been strangers, and led to the organization of a movement about thirty years ago for the restoration of the National Church and the establishment of a national system of popular education. In 1870, the Sultan issued a firman re-establishing the Bulgarian Church upon its ancient foundations, and conceding to it a complete organization of native ecclesiastical administration, courts, and ritual, which produced a happy effect on the disposition and condition of the people. The new rule gave them a set of officers of their own, who would have much to do with the management of local affairs, and also furnished them, in their priests and bishops, an agency of their own faith and nationality in whom they could confide, and who would sympathize with them, through whom to communicate with the heads of the province and of the Empire.

The reorganization of the schools, although it was a part of the same movement, in effect preceded that of the Church. Permission was obtained from the Government for the establishment of schools distinct from those of the Greeks in some of the district towns. Slavic books were printed and imported from abroad, and the revival of education became very rapid, so that there were in 1870, in the sanjak of Philippopolis, 337 schools of four grades, with 385 teachers and 16,500 pupils, and a special training-school for teachers at Philippopolis. The teachers receive salaries ranging from $350 to $700 per annum; education is free, the schools being supported by subscriptions and the proceeds of bequests made for that purpose, and appropriations from the ecclesiastical revenues. Efforts have been made to induce the Ottoman Government to establish a special board of instruction for Bulgaria, but so far without success.

The popular schools are supplemented by the excellent schools of the American missions at Philippopolis and Eski Sagra, and by Robert College at Constantinople, which is largely attended by Bulgarian youth seeking a higher education. The Bulgarian ladies have also made efforts for the advancement of education among their own sex, which have been rewarded with a measure of success.

Literary enterprise is not very active among the Bulgarians. One of the most important of their journals is the *Makedonia*, the organ of the National party. The people are represented as anxious to receive education, and the Bulgarian students at Robert College are said to take the lead in scholarship.

8

The most serious cause of complaint which the Bulgarians have recently had to make against the Turkish Government has arisen from the enforced settlement of the Circassians among them. The Porte, in providing for the Mussulman refugees from the Caucasus who sought its protection in 1864, after the Russians had subdued that country, settled one hundred and twenty thousand Circassians in Bulgaria, scattering them among the Bulgarian people in such a manner as to split up the most compact Bulgarian masses into weaker communities and thus injure their force and influence. Land was seized for the colonists, and the Bulgarians were compelled to assist them in building houses and settling themselves. In addition to this original sway, the Circassians have proved very troublesome neighbors, have destroyed the security of persons and property in their neighborhood, and have become, as a writer who has recently described the situation in the province* says, a thorn in the flesh of the Bulgarians, "against whom they have to put up iron bars and keep numerous fierce dogs, precautions which do not always avail."

The Bulgarians have generally been quiet subjects, and have submitted for several centuries to political and ecclesiastical oppressions with such patience as to have acquired a reputation for servility and lack of energy which they do not deserve; with a patience, too, which contrasts strangely with the outburst of frenzy to which they gave way in the summer of 1877, and makes that phenomenon all the more remarkable. They labor industriously when they work, yet do not get along as well as they should, for they faithfully keep all the feasts and fasts ordered by their religion, which, with the Sundays, take up about one hundred and eighty days, or half the year. Nevertheless, the Bulgarian settlements of the better class bear evidence of considerable thrift and comfort. The Bulgarians live in simple style, are fond of brilliant costumes—of which every village has its own colors—and are addicted to ceremony, especially at weddings and funerals. They are fond of dancing, and have a bagpipe and music like those of Scotland. An equality is acknowledged in their families between man and wife and the other members of the household, which is quite foreign to the Slavs of the neighboring provinces. Frequently, according to Kanitz, the woman shows herself, by her superior ability and energy, to be qualified to be the effective head of the house. The Bulgarians in the cities of the Danube are engaged in mercantile occupations or shop-keeping,

---

* Mr. Archibald Forbes, in the *Nineteenth Century*, November, 1877.

or follow handicrafts. Very few of them practice in the professions or fill official positions; many enter the service of the Church as priests or monks. Those who live in the highlands or towns of the Balkans raise cattle or prosecute industries; the people of the plains are farmers. The manufacture of the attar of roses is largely carried on south of the Balkans, and the milder climate of these regions make it favorable to the production of silk, tobacco, wine, fruits, and other profitable crops.

The Bulgarians have made considerable progress during the last ten years in enterprise, education, and all that tends to better their condition. It is, however, far less than the progress which Servia has made, and not as great as that which Rumania has made.

The Montenegrins are the most warlike people of the Slavic race. Turkey claims a sovereignty over their principality, but has never been able to exercise it, except for very brief periods, for four hundred years. The people are in a state of chronic warfare against the Turks, and have more often beaten them than been beaten by them; and although less than two hundred thousand in number, and possessing only 1,700 square miles of territory, they have maintained their independence with a heroism that has won for them the admiration of the world. The principality of Montenegro, Tchernagora, · or the Black Mountain, was founded in 1484, when Scutari, having been taken on the south, and the Herzegovinians on the north having submitted to the Ottomans, Ivan Tchernoyevitch, with his followers, rather than give up their independence, abandoned the plain country and retired to the rocks and mountains. A monastery was built at Cettigne, to be the center of the new commonwealth, and a printing-press was set up in it, only twenty-eight years after the first printed book had been made, and before Oxford or Cambridge or Edinburgh had a press Here the fundamental law of the State was adopted, which included, according to Gladstone, the conditions " that in time of war against the Turk-no son of Tchernagora could quit the field without the order of his chief; that a runaway should be forever disgraced and banished from his people; that he should be dressed in woman's clothes and presented with a distaff; and that the women, striking him with their distaffs, should hunt the coward away from the sanctuary of freedom."

Ivan died in 1490, and was succeeded by his son George, who, upon his retirement in 1516, assigned the sovereignty of the principality to the metropolitan or bishop. From his accession, " a long series of twenty prelates," says Gladstone, "like Moses, or Joshua, or Barak, or the son of Jesse, taught in the sanctuary, presided in the councils, and fought in the front of the battle." Several of these prince-bishops were admirable statesmen, a fact which is well shown by the success with which they maintained the independence of the country against foreign foes whose armed detachments outnumbered its entire population, as well as against domestic traitors, and by the attachment and confidence with which the population always rallied around them. The bishop was assisted by a civil governor, who attended to secular affairs until the present century, when the office was abolished. A code of laws was promulgated, and a complete system of judicial administration was established about the beginning of the present century. Prince Danilo, who succeeded to the sovereignty in 1851, wishing to marry, avoided consecration as a bishop, and effected a permanent separation between the ecclesiastical and the civil authority. His administration was very successful. He published a statute-book in 1855, maintained the neutrality of the country during the Crimean war, though at the cost of internal commotion, and conducted a successful campaign against the Turks in 1858, after having refused a proposition made to him by the Western Powers in 1857 to acknowledge the suzerainty of the Porte in return for some advantage promised to the State.

The independence of the country was acknowledged by the powers in 1858, and its representative was admitted to the commission which sat at Constantinople in 1859, for the adjustment of boundaries, but in the face of the protests of the Porte. Prince Danilo was assassinated in 1860, and was succeeded by the present Prince Nikita, or Nicholas. The Montenegrins are stalwart, active men, of unsurpassed bravery; their dress is picturesque, and bristles with arms, for they go prepared for conflict. They speak the Servian language, and are attached to the orthodox Greek Church, but are not as devout as warlike. They maintained, until very recently, several peculiar customs of a primitive society, the most remarkable of which was that of the bond of brotherhood, by which two champions pledged themselves to stand by each other, with the condition that if either were hopelessly disabled in battle, the other should cut off his head to save it from capture and outrage by the enemy. The principality contains 374 villages and hamlets, a church for each, several cloisters, some of which are not used, and seventy-two schools. Cettigne, the capital, is a town of five hundred inhabitants, picturesquely situated at the foot of a steep mountain. Montenegro has no standing army, but the twenty thousand men are all soldiers by habit, ready for duty at a moment's notice, and the women are little behind them in bravery and capability of defending themselves and their homes.

The Montenegrins have maintained their wars against the Turks for about four centuries, and have never suffered themselves to be overcome. Gladstone remarks in his paper on Montenegro in *The Nineteenth Century*, that the Turks never venture to attack the principality with an equal force, but aim to bring against it double the number of men that it can muster; and he gives several striking illustrations from past and present wars of the pertinacity with which the Montenegrins have maintained their position. In 1712, the Turks brought a force of not less than fifty thousand men, which Prince Danilo met with 12,000 men, and routed with a loss to the Turks of 20,000, to the Montenegrins of only 318 men. In 1768, the Turks again invaded Montenegro with an army variously rated at 67,000, 100,000, and 180,000 men. The Montenegrins met them with ten to twelve thousand men, killed twenty thousand Turks with three thousand horses, and captured "an incredible booty of colors, arms, ammunition, and baggage." The brilliant character of the Montenegrin victories of 1876 is admirably set forth by Gladstone in the following summary:

"On July 28, the men of Tchernagora encountered Mukhtar Pasha, and for once with superior force. Four thousand Turks were killed, but only seventy men of Montenegro. Osman Pasha was taken; Selim was among the slain. At Medun, on August 14, 20,000 Turks were defeated by 5,000 of these heroic warriors, and 4,700 slain. On September 6, five battalions of Montenegro defeated Dervish Pasha in his movement upon Piperi, and slew 3,000 of his men. On October 7, Mukhtar-Pasha, with 18,000 men, drove three Montenegrin battalions back upon Mirotinsko Dolove. Here they were raised, by a junction with Vukovitch, to a strength of 6,000 men. Thus reinforced, they swept down upon Mukhtar, and after an action of sixteen hours, drove him back to Kloluk, leaving 1,500 dead behind him. On October 10, Dervish Pasha effected an advance from the south, until he found himself attacked simultaneously at various points, and had to retreat, with a loss of 2,000 men. On October 20, Medun was taken, and the Ottoman General fled to Scutari, leaving garrisons in Spuz and Podgoritza. The armistice arrested this course of disasters, when the southern army (Dervish) had been reduced from 45,000 to 22,000, and the northern (Mukhtar) from 35,000 to 18,000."

An illustration of the practical respect which the great powers show for Montenegro was given during the wars of 1875 and 1876, when, until July of the latter year, Austria permitted the Turks to use its port of Klek for landing their troops, because the comity of nations allowed them thus to assist a friendly State in quelling an insurrection in one of its provinces; but when Montenegro declared war against Turkey in July, 1876, the port was closed against the Turks, because, as the Austrian Government presented the case, Montenegro was a sovereign State, engaged in regular warfare, and standing on an equal footing with Turkey, and Austria, as a neutral, could not assist either belligerent.

The Montenegrins, whether they be tall, portly figures, as is the prevailing type, short and thick-set, or slender, as some are, are robust and active, possessing all the qualities of the best physical manhood. They have, for the most part, brown or black hair, which is cut short in front and left long behind, and dark, fiery eyes. Occasionally a blonde is found, with blue eyes. The beard is generally worn only in the mustache, though recently whiskers have come into fashion, but the chin is shaved. The men have fine, expressive, weather-bronzed countenances, but the women's faces wear the marks of hard work, care, and fatigue. Handsome women are as rare as fine, hearty-looking men are numerous. The whole training of the men is directed to making them strong, active, and enduring as warriors.

The Montenegrin costume is very picturesque. The cap is in the shape of a low cylinder hat, without a brim, the sides of which are of black silk or gauze, the black color having been adopted as a symbol of mourning for the subjection of the Servian nation. The top of the cap is red, and ornamented with a golden star, to which is added a semicircle or rainbow, symbolizing the hope of the ultimate restoration of Servian nationality, and the initials of the name of the reigning prince. To a red waistcoat, embroidered with black or gold, is added the *gunj*, a long, folded, white cloak, and in case of a well-to-do Montenegrin, the *jelek*, a sleeveless doublet, which with numerous black, red, and golden ornaments, is often made to cost a very high price. The dagger, pistol, and other weapons are carried in a red belt, which is bordered with a silver-worked binding. The plaited full blue breeches reach to the knee, where they are attached by an ornamental band to a kind of gaiter, or to an embroidered white stocking. The feet are protected by sandals of untanned leather, which are wrapped around with a network of thongs so as to facilitate the task of climbing the rocks. Both men and women wear over the shoulders a long fringed shawl, called the *struka*, which is used as a protection against rain and cold, and as a covering at night. Frequent washing does not agree with the Montenegrin's idea of heroism; consequently he is said to be far from clean, and his linen heroically dirty. An English writer, who estimates the value of a complete Montenegrin suit at £20, or one hundred dollars, says that when he expressed his surprise that the men could afford such a sum, he was told that a dress would last a life-time.

The women of the poorer classes wear a long shirt fastened with a belt, a woolen apron, and the *struka*, or shawl. Those in better circumstances wear a vest, open in front, with sleeves, a sleeveless jacket of blue or violet silk embroidered with gold braid, a silver belt, a silk apron, and a black hood. The young women wear, instead of the sleeveless vest, a bodice and a cap, which is destitute of the stellar ornament and semicircle, and dispense with the belt.

The Montenegrin looks upon war—war against the Turks—as his proper calling. During intervals of peace he is a hunter—in the old time he would have been a highwayman—and leaves all labor and mechanical work to the women and to foreigners. Under the enlightened rule of the later princes it has begun to be considered respectable to engage in a few kinds of business. If he has not the means to live a gentleman's life during peaceful times, the Montenegrin will go abroad and earn his bread; but he will return home at the first sign of war and enlist under the banner of his nation. Nothing but extreme necessity will induce him to emigrate permanently from his beloved country.

The houses of the Montenegrins are built on the mountain sides, or cliffs, both for safety and so as to encroach as little as possible on the soil fit for cultivation. The houses of the poorer classes are of rough stones, laid without mortar, and seldom of more than one story. The houses of the middle classes are of two stories, with the stable and store-rooms below and the living rooms above. The houses of the well-to-do classes are of a better order; and, lastly, the kula, or tower, the place of refuge for the neighborhood, where all the families can retire in case of invasion, is a peculiar feature of Montenegrin life, which takes us back to the warlike days of the middle ages. A hereditary aristocracy exists in the country, embracing two ranks, the Waywodes and the Serdars, or Cavaliers. The family life is quite the opposite to that which prevails in Servia. Here the household is contracted to the narrowest circle of blood-relatives, and is destitute of that community of interest which beautifies Servian life. The land goes generally to the youngest son, because he stays longest in the family, while the eldest seeks a home elsewhere, receiving, as his share of the inheritance, only his father's arms. The condition of the women is lower than in Servia; they have the burden of labor and of the maintenance of the household, and are contented to bear it as part of the order of things, while their manly relatives fulfill their destiny in fighting the Turks.

The first school was established in Cettigne in 1834. There are now in the principality seventy-one institutions, a seminary for priests and teachers, and a girls' high-school. Education is free, and the State supplies books and other requisites.

The Albanians, Arnauts, or Shkipetars, who inhabit the Adriatic province south of Montenegro, are of the old Illyrian or Thracian stock, and have given Turkey some of its greatest men and best soldiers. They are divided into a number of tribes, most of which may be referred to two stocks—the Geg in the north, and the Toskari in the south and center of the country. The majority of the people are Mohammedans. That part of them who are of Greek or Slavic descent are, for the most part, attached to the Greek Church; and the Roman Catholics are numerously represented. The Roman Catholics of one district, who are called Miridites, were in insurrection in the spring of 1877, but soon yielded to the force that was sent to quiet them.

The Albanians are, as a rule, a handsome, noble-looking race of men, of medium height or tall, strong, well-formed, rather slender than stout, with a proud, theatrical bearing. Their heads are long, their foreheads broad, their noses lengthened and straight. Their method of dressing the hair is peculiar. A wide border is clean shaven all around the head, so that only a small tuft remains on the crown; this is twisted into a loose switch, is turned up under the fez, and so lies on the back of the neck as a sort of chignon. Often the whole front of the head is shaven from ear to ear, and the remain-

MONTENEGRINS.

GREEKS.

ing hair is allowed to fall down over the back. The beard is trimmed to a mustache. A little, but not important difference is observed in the dress of the Northern and Southern Albanians. The fez is worn everywhere. The fustanella of Epirus, a plaited skirt of white cloth reaching to the knees, is about equally in vogue with the sailor's breeches of blue cotton of the North. The brown sailor's cloak, or *capota*, of wool mixed with goats' hair, is likewise generally worn A cloak of white woolen, without collar or sleeves, and leaving the breast and body exposed, called the *flokate*, is worn in Toskeria, or Southern Albania, by young and old, at all seasons It is evidently designed to represent the sheepskin; its white texture is plentifully besprinkled with red threads corresponding to the stains of blood, and triangular pieces are attached to the upper part of the arm-holes, which, reaching to the middle of the arms, suggest the skins of the sheeps' fore-legs. This garment is worn close to the body down to the waist, whence it hangs in full folds. Some other tribes wear a white woolen coat without a collar, open in front and reaching to the middle of the thighs, fastened at the waist by a belt; in other districts, short breeches and gaiters prevail, the latter being highly ornamented, and calling to mind the *Cothurni* of the ancients. The Albanians are fond of all kinds of dress ornaments, and indulge in them lavishly. The dress of the women is very similar to that of the Montenegrin women.

In thought and feeling the Albanians are barbarians; they set a light value on human life, and are ready to kill for a slight offense; and every murder calls the custom of "blood vengeance" into exercise, when the assassin and all that are his have to flee, and the family of the murdered man pursue him till the law of vengeance is satisfied, after which friendship may be renewed with solemn ceremonies. Their favorite occupation is war; they were formerly enlisted in the armies of several of the principal States of Western Europe, but are now found mostly in the Turkish armies. The family life is characterized by community of goods and the subordination of the women, whose condition is little above servitude. They perform all the labors and are so accustomed to their situation as to consider any deference paid to themselves as unworthy of a man. They often accompany their husbands to the battle-field, where they take care of the wounded, and sometimes take up arms themselves. There are many Albanian legends of heroic women. Girls are considered marriageable when twelve years old. The marriage is a matter of sale, and the price of a wife averages about one hundred piasters A modification of the custom of marriage by capture, or of stealing the bride and carrying her off by force, still prevails among some of the mountain tribes of the North.

The Albanians in the mountain districts live in two-story stone houses, in which the living-rooms are in the upper story, the stable, etc., in the lower. A tower is often attached, which is reached from the house by a kind of draw-bridge. This feature, as well as the whole style of the buildings, suggests the time when the houses were fortifications. The habitations in the agricultural districts consist of a hedged enclosure, containing several small buildings, one of which is used for the dwelling, the others for cattle and store-houses. The Albanian language includes several dialects, which seem to be mixtures of various tongues, representing all the races which have ever inhabited or ruled the country. It is written by the Northern tribes in Roman, by the Southern tribes in Greek characters.

All of the Grecian States and Islands formerly belonged to Turkey. The kingdom of Greece, consisting of the Morea, most of ancient Hellas, the island of Negropont, or Euboea, with the Sporades lying near it, and the Cyclades, gained its independence in 1827. The Ionian Islands were added by cession from Great Britain, in 1864. The area of the kingdom is 19,353 square miles, and its population in 1870 was 1,457,894. The little State has made considerable advancement since it became free, both material and in the arts, but its small size and scanty population prevent the development of great statesmanship or enterprise. The Greek population of Turkey are scattered through the districts representing the ancient States of Thessaly, Epirus, and Macedonia, in Southern Rumelia, along the northern, western, and southern coasts of Asia Minor, and upon the islands of the Eastern Mediterranean, including the large islands of Cyprus and Candia, or Crete. The northern line of the regions in which the modern Greek language is spoken in Turkey, in Europe, starts at Philates on the Adriatic, opposite the island of Corfu, extends through Yanina, Konitza, Kastoria, and across the Lower Wardar, near Salonica; thence through the middle of Rumelia to Agathopolis, or Akhteboli, on the Black Sea. The Greeks are a trading people, and are most numerous in the towns and commercial centers and along the sea coasts, leaving the rural parts of the interior to be inhabited mainly by Bulgarians. They have a genius for political intrigue, and before the kingdom of Greece was separated from Turkey, exercised a powerful influence on the Porte. Although much less numerous than the Bulgarians in Rumelia, they have enjoyed so much prominence over them, and have so exercised the mastery of •the Bulgarian Church and schools, as to give rise to exaggerated ideas of their numbers. According to Baker, there is a marked difference in customs and social ways, between the Greek settlers in the towns of the Black Sea coast and those of the Macedonian frontier, the former being more Oriental than the latter, and not so advanced in civilization, while in neither district is the manner of living of the people high, or even comfortable according to Western ideas. The Greeks of the Black Sea coast make but little complaint of Turkish mismanagement, while in Macedonia it is a common topic of conversation, and the popular mind is still embittered by the remembrance of the atrocities committed during the Grecian war of independence. Yet Baker relates, in his "Turkey," that even during the excitement attendant upon the Herzegovinian insurrection, the Christians of Salonica gave an amateur concert for the benefit of the Turkish wounded, which was attended by the Turkish Governor-General and his staff, with other Turks, the proceeds of which were three hundred pounds sterling.

The Greeks also form an important part of the population of the sea coasts of Asia Minor. Being a trading and sea-faring people, they congregate at the commercial towns and the shipping points throughout the Levant. They share with the Armenians in the general trade of the country, but so far, at least, as the Turkish populations are concerned, they control that which depends on the sea. Before the Turkish conquest, Asia Minor was a Grecian country. As this region was occupied by the Moslems some centuries before Constantinople fell into their hands, the mass of the Greek population removed to Europe. For several centuries, Asia Minor has been, except as to its commercial towns, an almost purely Turkish country. Since, however, the Empire has entered into more general relations with Western Europe, and its trade has been developed, the Greeks have increased in numbers and been more conspicuous, and at present their influence is growing very fast.

The island of Crete (now commonly called Candia) has attracted more attention in recent years than any other of the Greek provinces of Turkey. It lies in the Mediterranean Sea, south-east of Greece, and is the central and largest of the series of islands which, stretching from the southern points of Greece to the south-western angle of

Asia Minor, seem to enclose the Archipelago, or Ægean Sea. It is about one hundred and fifty miles long, and from six to thirty-five miles wide, and presents a mass of mountains, the highest of which, Mount Ida, near the center of the island, is 7,674 feet in height. The island is extraordinarily rich in associations with the most ancient mythology and classical traditions of the Greek race. The inhabitants, who number about one hundred and sixty thousand, are reckoned to be three-quarters Christians and one-quarter Mohammedans. In many points of government the Cretans have less to complain of than the people of some of the other provinces; the taxes are not heavy; no military service or poll-tax is required of them, and local liberty is to a great extent secured. Nevertheless, a bitter jealousy prevails between the Christians and Mohammedans; and though all avowedly possess equal rights and privileges, the Mohammedans receive the practical favor of the Government, and are enabled, or are supposed to be enabled, to domineer over their fellow-subjects. Discontent has prevailed very widely throughout the island for many years, and culminated in the insurrection of 1866, which came very near precipitating a new crisis in the Eastern Question, and which the Government put down only after a long contest and with great difficulty. The Government has endeavored to pacify the people by making them a few concessions and giving them Christian Governors; but the affairs of the island have continued to be very disturbed. The danger of a new outbreak seemed very imminent throughout the wars from 1875 to 1877, so that much of the attention of the Government was directed toward devising means to preserve order, and a force had to be spared from the active army to be ready to repress any disturbance, should one break out.

The Greeks of Turkey preserve, in only a slightly modified degree, all the predominant traits of their ancestors. The modern Greek language is quite as nearly like the ancient Greek as are any of the languages of Latin Europe, the German, or the Russian language, to the tongues from which they are descended. The social customs, folk lore, superstitions, manners, art-tastes, utensils of domestic and agricultural use, and dress of the present Greeks bear a striking resemblance to those of the ancients. A systematic effort has been making in the Kingdom of Greece since the revolution to restore as much of the ancient classical life as is consistent with modern conditions, with a success that is remarkable, and is almost complete with respect to the language.

The red cap of the modern Greek preserves the sailor's cap which is painted in the same color on the ancient vases, and the Phrygian cap of old is worn by the shepherds of Arcadia. Greek brides wear a stomacher formed of silver pieces sewed together, which recalls the silver breast-plate of Minerva. The ear-rings, necklaces, and bracelets of the women are like those of the ancients, and they sprinkle their hair with gold-powder and stain the tips of their fingers with red, just as they did in the days of Homer. The ancient Phrygian dress, which the Greek colonists adopted in early days, is still worn in Asia Minor, by both Turks and Greeks. Even the turban, which till recently has been held as a distinctive mark of a Turk, is not Turkish, but is a gift of the Asiatic Greeks to their conquerors.

According to Kohl, in his "People of Europe," the Grecian Palikar, or countryman, wears a colored vest, open before and embroidered on the edges, and over that a short jacket of the same material, richly embroidered, while from his shoulders hangs a colored, embroidered over-garment, with open, free-flowing sleeves. A broad belt, colored and ornamented, is buckled around his waist, in which he carries his pistols and dagger. From his waist depends to below his knees a white linen skirt, folded into numerous narrow plaits, which is called the *fustanella*. The fustanella of the islanders is often blue. The legs from the knees down are covered with white hose, or with tight, colored gaiters adorned with embroidery or tassels, the feet with red, pointed shoes. A coarse, brown, hooded cloak embroidered with blue, covering the whole upper part of the body, completes the costume. The dress of the women is different in different places. It generally consists of a woolen frock, reaching from the neck to the feet, which is girdled at the waist with a broad, shawl-like cloth. A shorter over-garment completes the costume. The fez is worn by both sexes.

Colonies of Circassians have been settled around the Black Sea since 1864, when the Russians having conquered the Caucasus, forced the former inhabitants of that region to remove from their homes. A part of these people, who refused to accept the lands on the steppes which were offered them by Russia, were given homes and a refuge on the soil of Turkey. They are supposed to number at this time about two hundred thousand souls in European Turkey, where they are settled principally along the Black Sea coast. They are strict Mohammedans, live in the simplest style in obscure villages, cultivate the soil in a careless manner, are courteous and hospitable in an eminent degree, and, like the ancient Spartans, are proud of their skill as thieves. Their women are brought up to be sold to foreign harems, and look forward, says Baker,* " to entry into that life as a young lady in England does to 'coming out.' " Their families being represented in the household of the high officers and wealthy people at Constantinople, they have influence at court and know how to use it, both for their own advancement and for protection against the consequences of their depredations and disorderly conduct.

The Armenians are the descendants of the people who once owned and ruled the whole of Armenia, those parts which are included in Russian and Persian Armenia, as well as the Turkish provinces. They have an ancient and honorable history, of which traces are found in connection with the records of the most flourishing periods of the Assyrian and Egyptian Empires. In the thousand years around the beginning of the Christian era, they played an important part in the affairs of the Eastern nations. They now form an integral part of the population of the three Armenias, so much so as to give them the character of a Christian district, surrounded by Mohammedan tribes, but are probably more numerous at the present day in other parts of their three sovereign States than in the home of their fathers. Their present total number is variously estimated at from 3,000,000 to 6,000,000, and it is thought that there are about two and a quarter millions of them in the Turkish Empire alone.

The Armenians claim that they were the first to embrace Christianity *as a nation*, and the claim seems to be well established by the evidence cited by the historian, St. Martin. " About the year 276," says Dean Milman, " Christianity was the religion of the king, the nobles, and the people of Armenia." This was thirty years before the accession of Constantine made Christianity fashionable in the Roman Empire. Ever since that period the Armenians have been known as Christians, and have formed a distinct branch of the Christian Church, next among the Oriental Churches in importance after the Greek Church. The services of the Church are still performed in the ancient Armenian language, a tongue which the people fondly believe to have been the original speech of the human race. Nine orders of clergy are recognized, the chief of

---

* "Turkey," p 101.

which is the Catholicos, or Patriarch. The principal convent of the Church is at Etchmiadzin, in the Russian province of Erivan, and the patriarch who resides there is recognized as the head of the whole Church, everywhere except in a small district on Lake Van, which has a patriarch with rival claims to supremacy. Other patriarchs reside at Jerusalem and Constantinople. The Patriarch of Constantinople is the civil head of all the Armenians in Turkey, and is practically independent of the Catholicos at Etchmiadzin, but recognizes an inferiority in rank to him. The Patriarch of Etchmiadzin has immediate jurisdiction of all the Armenians in Russia and Turkey. He is elected by the synod, subject to the approval of the Czar.

The remains of the ancient prosperity and supremacy of Christianity in Armenia are found all over the country in the shape of the ruins of churches and other ecclesiastical buildings. The numerous changes and conquests to which the country has been subjected have, however, driven the majority of its proper inhabitants away, so that the Armenians are now widely scattered. Wherever they go, however, they carry with them the love of their country, and cherish their religion and literature. Wherever they are found, too, they generally form a respectable part of the population. They are the merchants of all the interior towns of Turkey and in Persia, and parts of Russia and South-eastern Europe share with the Greeks the trade of the great commercial towns, and have extensive business relations at home and abroad. They often also attain official positions, where they prove to be at least as efficient and faithful as native Turks and Russians; and it is worthy of note that General Melikoff, the active commander of the Russian forces in Armenia, and General Tergukasoff, who proved himself probably one of the most skillful general officers in the Russian army, are both Armenians.

The Armenians have a literature of considerable antiquity, which they prize. They have also made much literary progress recently, and had, at the close of the year 1871, thirteen newspapers, published at Constantinople. They have received much attention from American Missionary Societies, which have built up flourishing missions and schools among them at Van, Bitlis, and Erzerum, in Armenia, and at several points in Asia Minor.

A branch of the Armenian Church, called the United Armenians, acknowledge the supremacy of the Pope. They are noted for the flourishing schools which have been established by the celebrated Order of the Mekhitarists, and which have educated some of the best Turkish scholars among the Christians in the Government service.

The mountains of the south-eastern coast of the Black Sea are inhabited by a people of the Grusian or Georgian stock called the Lasis. They are described by Kasbek* as a people of prepossessing appearance, remarkably neat in their clothing, of considerable intellectual development, and as living in much comfort.

The houses of the common people throughout Armenia are generally earth huts, partly dug out of the sides of the hills, partly consisting of adjoining outside structures of timber, covered with a roof of sod. It is a feature of the regions in which this style of building prevails, that while to one looking over the country from certain positions, it will appear quite uninhabited, one coming into it from other directions will find the same spots full of houses and people. The more wealthy inhabitants live in houses of a better style.

The Maronites are a sect of Christians in Syria, who acknowledge the authority of the Pope. They number about one hundred and forty thousand persons, are generally farmers, poor, honest, and hospitable. They are governed by a patriarch, whose election is subject to the confirmation of the Pope and bishops. Their priests are allowed to marry, and number about twelve hundred. They have four hundred churches, and about one-half of the two hundred convents of the Lebanon district, in which are from 20,000 to 25,000 monks. They have also nunneries, which are built at a distance from the convents, and have no intercourse with them except on the occasion of administering the sacraments. The Maronites speak the Arabic language, and have selections from the Bible and other sacred books in their tongue. These people were united in the former part of the last century as to civil and political government into a community with the Druses. The two sects afterward became separated from each other and alienated, and finally hostile. A personal quarrel between Maronites and Druses, in 1859, became the occasion of a war of extermination by the Druses upon the Maronites, which led to the outbreaks of 1860 in Syria, and brought an interference and settlement by foreign powers. Since that time a special Governor has been provided for the Lebanon district.

The Druses are a people of a peculiar race and religion, numbering

---

* Colonel Kasbek, "Three Months in Turkish Grusia."

in all about seventy thousand persons, who live in the mountains of Syria. They have religious books and methods of worship, which they are not willing to expose to strangers, so that a complete account of their doctrine and usages is hard to obtain. Their government is partly feudal. They are warlike and courageous, a people of simple and primitive habits, who earn their subsistence by cultivating the soil and working at mechanical trades. The women occupy a comparatively high position, in which their rights are recognized and protected; their occupations are weaving and spinning. The man is the husband of one wife. The villages of the Druses are usually built in mountain passes, where they rise in terraces up the sides of the hills. These people form a considerable part of the population, and exercise much influence in the towns at the foot of Mount Hermon.

The Kurds are a race of Mohammedans who inhabit the large territory called Kurdistan, which, lying south of Armenia, is mostly included in Turkey, but partly in Persia. Their numbers are variously estimated at from eight hundred thousand to three million persons. About one hundred thousand of them are Christians of the Nestorian Church. They have a light complexion, an animated physiognomy, sharp, delicate features, and neat frames; are good horsemen, skilled in the use of arms, and fond of plunder, although hospitable. They are partly settled and partly nomadic. Their houses are of stone, often furnished with a kind of tower; besides their homes, they have retreats in the fastnesses of the mountains, to which they retire when danger is present in the country. They are divided into numerous tribes, which are often at war with each other, and some of which, especially those in Persia, are very wild. They acknowledge the general authority of the Sultan, but will not submit to a close government. Women have a higher position among them than among either the Turks or the Persians. They do not veil themselves, except among the higher classes, and are treated with comparative respect and deference. The Kurdish costume is like that of the Turks. The men wear a cloak of black goats' hair and a red cap wound with a silk shawl which falls over the shoulders. Travelers give varying accounts of the character of the Kurds, according to the degree of culture or the friendly or hostile moods of the tribes which they meet. The Kurdish irregular troops in Armenia have given a very disgraceful account of themselves in the present war.

9

The most important African tributary of Turkey is Egypt. Egypt proper contains an area of 212,607 square miles, and a population of about five and a quarter million persons. Nubia, which is politically a part of Egypt, though ethnographically distinct, contains a population of about two and one-half millions more. The Khedive has made large additions to the dominions of the country by conquests along the Upper Nile nearly to the equator, which swell the extent of the territory subject to Egypt to a total of 869,389 square miles, and the population to 16,922,000. Egypt is the most ancient country in the world of which the history survives, the records inscribed upon its monuments extending back to a period which is reckoned, according to the various methods of computing chronology, at from three thousand to five thousand years before Christ, and far antedating all other existing records, except the books of Moses, and, perhaps, one or two documents recently exhumed from Nineveh. It was conquered by the Persians 525 B.C., then by Alexander the Great, then by the Romans, 30 B.C. Under the Roman Empire it became an important Christian State, and Alexandria was a noted seat of theological learning and institutions. It was conquered by the Saracens, A D. 683, and by the Turks in 1517. It has advanced gradually toward independence since Mehemet Ali became Viceroy in 1806. The Khedive is absolute sovereign, subject to the chiefly nominal allegiance which he owes to the Porte, and governs with the assistance of a Council of State, of four military and four civil dignitaries. The revenue of the country was calculated in the official budget of 1874 at about $49,559,850. It maintains a separate army and navy from those of Turkey. Its commerce is large, but consists, to some extent, of goods carried in transit. The exports for 1873 amounted to $72,500,000, and the imports to $30,000,000. The total debt of the Viceroyalty as fixed by Messrs. Goschen and Joubert, representing the English and French creditors in 1875-'76, is £76,000,000, or $380,000,000: This large amount of indebtedness has been incurred through extravagance in constructing internal improvements and building up business enterprises which, although they promise to contribute to the future prosperity and resources of the country, impose at present a heavy load upon the Government and the people. The principal work of improvement is the Suez Canal, which has been cut across the Isthmus of Suez, and connects the Mediterranean and Red Seas. The total length of the canal is ninety-two miles; it has capacity for vessels drawing twenty-five feet nine inches of water, and was built at a total cost of $94,393,645. More than thirteen hundred miles of railway have been built in Egypt proper; the telegraph wires extend over 5,500 miles, and other lines of railway and telegraph are contemplated, which will be pushed into the heart of Africa. A system of irrigation canals has been constructed, which involved the removal of sixty-five per cent. more material than the Suez Canal. Great harbor works have been begun at Alexandria, which will cost when completed more than ten millions of dollars. In addition to these public works, the Khedive has built sugar refineries and cotton manufactories and numerous palaces and public buildings. Besides the University at Cairo, and the schools connected with the Mosques, which have a reputation co-extensive with the Mohammedan world, but which are not much above the level of other Mohammedan schools, Egypt has a number of schools formed partly after the European model, which are of a better grade and better attended than the similar schools in Turkey. Among them are several special and technical schools; two girls' schools, formed by the wives of the Khedive; elementary schools, and a school for the blind. Several excellent schools, an academy, and a theological school, the two latter at Sioot, in Upper Egypt, have been established in connection with the Missions of the United Presbyterian Church of North America. Several schools have been also established by the Roman Catholics, the Greek, Italian, German, and French residents. As a whole, Egypt offers better facilities for education than any other predominantly Mohammedan State.

The leading races inhabiting Egypt are the Arabs and the Copts. The Arabs are by far the most numerous race, numbering between four and four and one-half millions. The Arabs of the better class in the cities are a courteous people, strict Mohammedans, and fair representatives of the East, as pictured in the "Arabian Nights," many of the scenes of which are laid in Cairo. The rural Arabs, called Fellaheen, or Fellahs, form the chief part of the peasantry, or working people of the country, and are among the most miserably situated people on the earth. Their life is one of the meanest drudgery, by which they gain a bare subsistence. They are subject to all sorts of oppression and extortion from the local officers, who being instructed to return a certain amount of revenue to the Government, collect the amount and their own commissions by force. Flogging with the bastinado to compel the payment of taxes is a regular feature of Egyptian peasant life. It has come down from time immemorial, and is more a custom than a sign of real oppression. The Fellah, though he may be perfectly able, prides himself upon refusing to pay the taxes, until he has compelled the collector to administer a certain number of blows to him, and would be ashamed to yield too easily. With all their misery, the Fellahs are a fine, muscular race, well-proportioned, " with fine oval faces, bright, deep-set, black eyes, straight, thick noses, large, but well-formed mouths, full lips, beautiful teeth, broad shoulders, and well-shaped limbs," and are " the most patient, the most home-loving. and withal the merriest race in the world."* The women have much beauty when young, but wither rapidly after they have passed their teens. Girls are considered marriageable at from twelve to eighteen years of age. The condition of the peasantry appears to be the same now that it was five thousand years ago, and seems to have undergone no change during the whole history of the country, through all its various dynasties.

The Copts are descendants of the Ancient Egyptians, and until recently spoke a language whose derivation from that of the ancient inhabitants was shown both in its structure and in the form of its written characters. They are Christians, and form a distinct branch of the Christian Church, the Coptic Church. This Church is Monophysite in doctrine, that is, it ascribes but one nature to Christ, and is similar in its general doctrines and practices to the Abyssinian Church. It is governed by a Patriarch, chosen by itself, and bishops, and possesses an independent translation of the Bible in the Coptic language. The Copts associate readily with the Mohammedans, from whom they are distinguished chiefly by wearing a black turban, and have adopted many Mohammedan customs. As a consequence, they intermarry freely with Mohammedans, and conversions to Islamism are easily made, and frequent among them. Thus the purity of their stock has been impaired, and it is probable that a considerable part of the race is represented among the population who are classed as Arabs.

The Egyptian Government has employed European and American officers of tested ability in various branches of administrative and practical work, with great advantage to the interests of the country. Some of its native officers have received a good European education. The Minister of War, who is the third son of the Khedive, has

---

* McCoan, "Egypt as It Is," (London, 1877).

completed a university course, and received the degree of D.C.L. from the University of Oxford, in England.

Tripoli and Barca, with Fezzan, constitute a province lying west of Egypt, and between it and Tunis. The area of the province is about 344,400 square miles, or considerably more than that of the German Empire, but the population will hardly reach a million, of whom all but a few thousand Christians and Jews are Mohammedans. Although the country consists largely of desert, it could easily support a much greater population. A fraction of the province, called Cyoenaica, contained in ancient times as many inhabitants as the whole now has. Tripoli is wholly subject to Turkey.

Tunis, the farthest west of the African provinces of Turkey, lies northwest of Tripoli, between that province and Algeria. It has an area of about 45,000 square miles, and a population of between 1,200,000 and 2,000,000. The Bey holds his title as a fief of the Sultan, without whose authority he can not declare war, conclude peace, or cede territory, whose name must appear on all the coinage, and to whom he is obliged to pay a tribute, and to furnish a contingent of troops when demanded. Practically, except as to the acknowledgment of the Sultan's authority, the payment of the tribute and furnishing the contingent, he is independent. The climate of the country is good, the soil is fertile and productive, and trade in a considerable variety of products is active and profitable The exports in 1876 were valued at $3,292,000, and the imports at $2,274,000. A large part of the trade, as well as of that of Tripoli, is by caravans with the interior of Africa, whence are brought senna, gums, ostrich feathers, gold, and ivory. Forty miles of railway are in operation within the province, and French telegraph lines have been extended to various parts of the country, connecting it with Algeria and Europe.

CHAPTER VII.

THE INSURRECTION OF 1875, AND THE WARS OF 1876.

Complaints of the Christian Subjects of European Turkey—The Insurrection in Herzegovina and Bosnia—Efforts to Suppress it—The Great Powers seek to Prevent its Spreading—Futile Efforts of Diplomacy—Schemes of Reform—The Andrassy and Berlin Notes—The Massacre of Consuls at Salonica, and the Bulgarian Atrocities—Views and Reports of Mr Gladstone, Mr Baring, and Eugene Schuyler on the Massacres in Bulgaria—Servia and Montenegro make War upon Turkey—Details of the Campaign—Defeat of the Servians—An Armistice Granted—Conference of the Powers at Constantinople—Lord Salisbury, the British, and Count Chaudordy, the French, Representative at the Conference—The Turkish Constitution—Plan of the Conference for the Settlement of Difficulties—It is Rejected by Turkey—The Protocol—It is Rejected—Conclusion of Peace between Turkey and Servia—The Turkish Parliament.

CHRISTIAN tenants in the European provinces of Turkey have frequently complained of oppressions inflicted upon them by the Mussulman landowners, under whom they hold, and their grievances have often been the occasion of local disturbances. Such complaints were more than usually numerous in Herzegovina and Northern Albania in the spring of 1875. Many Christian families at this time fled to Montenegro for security against the hard treatment they were receiving. In the middle of July, the people of two small villages on the Narenta River, near Nevesigne, offered resistance to the collection of taxes. The Turkish troops undertook to quell the disturbance, but the insurgents defeated them after a fight of fifteen hours, and occupied their position. This success having been gained, others were encouraged to join in the resistance ; the revolt spread to the neighboring towns, and finally involved all of Southern Herzegovina, to the borders of Montenegro. Every advantage gained over the Turks helped to increase the number of the insurgents The families and cattle of the people were sent to Montenegro and Dalmatia, while the able-bodied men joined the military bands. The begs, or landowners, likewise formed their dependents into bands to oppose the insurgents, and an irregular war of outrage and plunder ensued. The Turkish Government tried to quiet the disturbance by sending a commission to inquire into the grievance of the people

SVETOZAR MILETITCH.

LUKA PET-KOVITCH.

SERVIAN SOLDIERS.

and offer redress, but without success. It then sent a force of troops, which were dispatched by sea and landed, with the permission of the Austrian Government, at the Austrian seaport of Klek, and marched the short remaining distance to the scene of the insurrection. On the 6th of August the insurgents surrounded the Turkish fort at Trebigne, and cut it off from its supplies. The first troops landed at Klek were sent to the relief of this place, which they effected, defeating and dispersing the insurgents on the 20th of August, and clearing the way to Mostar.

In the meantime, the insurrection had spread to Bosnia. It broke out at Banialuka, in the northern part of that Vilayet, on the 16th of August. Some mounted Turks had ridden through this town and killed a number of Christian workmen while quietly attending to their business The complaints of the friends of the murdered men before the magistrates not having been attended to, an excitement arose over the affair, which led to an open conflict between the Mohammedans and Christians in the streets of the town. The Christians were beaten, and fled to the nearest towns for safety. Bands of Bosnians were immediately formed for resistance at various points. Their proceedings were, however, for several months conducted without any energy, and with no fixed plan.

Immediately on the occurrence of the outbreak in Herzegovina, the Governments of Germany, Austria, and Russia, after consultation with each other, notified Turkey that she must suppress the insurrection at once ; when the movement extended to Bosnia, they offered their friendly offices to the Porte, stipulating, however, that concessions to the wants of the Christian population would be essential to an effective pacification. The Porte at first declined this offer ; but France and Italy afterward joined in it, and on the 22d of September the Ambassadors of the five powers proposed that the Consuls of their respective Governments should go into the insurgent districts and confer directly—with the chiefs of the insurrection respecting a cessation of hostilities. The Porte assented to this proposition, and named Server Pasha as its representative to attend the conference. The meeting was to be held at Mostar, on the 3d of September. The Consuls of the five Western Powers and the Turkish representative attended punctually, but not an insurgent. was present. The chiefs had previously held a consultation on the 27th of August, at the cloister of Kosierovo, and had resolved upon a better organization of the insurrection, and had decided, as to the proposals of the Consuls, that they would listen to them, but avoid giving any definite answer to them.

The chiefs who participated in this council were Liubibratish, who was at that time the recognized head of the movement ; Lazar Sotchitza, Luka Petkovitch, Bozevitch (an Albanian), and Peko Paulovitch (a Montenegrin), who subsequently displaced Liubibratish as leader. The Consuls having failed to bring the insurgents to a conference, next agreed to separate into groups and visit the chiefs at their places of resort. One group—consisting of the Consuls of Russia, France, and England—was to go to Nevesigne, while the other group—consisting of the Consuls of Germany, Austria-Hungary, and Italy—should go to Trebigne, the Turkish agent attaching himself to either group as circumstances should demand. Several conferences were held without result. The insurgents insisted upon a suspension of hostilities, and refused to take part in any conference in which a representative of Turkey participated. At the end of September the Consuls returned to Mostar, where they were instructed to remain and await the development of events. Server Pasha was instructed by the Porte to receive courteously all the communications which they might make to him, but to enter into no engagements which might commit his Government. Through September and the succeeding months of the fall, till the closing in of the winter, the insurgents harassed the Turkish troops continually, attacking them at difficult points along the paths of the mountains and forests, surprising their convoys and capturing or destroying their provisions and animals. A brilliant surprise inflicted upon the Turks by Peko and Liubibratish with two thousand insurgents at Prapatnitza in the latter part of September was followed by a considerable addition to the strength of the insurrection from Bosnia.

Another event of a different character added to its force. The Turks had promised immunity to those who had participated in the insurrection who should return to their homes. A number of refugees, relying upon the assurances thus given, returned early in October from Dalmatia and Montenegro to Papovopolie, where they were arrested as rebels and executed.

On the 1st of October the Turks had in the insurrectionary districts and on the borders of Servia nearly 100,000 men, of whom 16,000 regular troops were in Herzegovina, while the insurrectionary forces numbered not more than between 10,000 and 14,000 men.

Nevertheless, the movements of the insurgents were nearly always successful. The country was a difficult one and strange to the Turks, while the Herzegovinians were familiar with its ways and managed their movements with skill.

On the 11th of October Shevket Pasha marched from Trebigne with a brigade of Turks against the insurrectionist position on the Zubtchi. He met a force of 2,000 insurgents near Grab on the 13th, defeated them and occupied their position, but was not able to pursue them, and returned to Trebigne. At the close of October, Peko Paulovitch and Sotchitza with 5,000 men held the road between Goranitchka and Piva, while 3,000 insurgents at the Duga Pass controlled the communications of the fort at Nicsic. Rauf Pasha, who had been appointed to the command of the troops in Herzegovina, dispatched Shevket Pasha with about 5,000 men to the relief of Goranitchka. This expedition was repulsed in the engagements of the 10th and 11th of November, and Rauf Pasha w nt in person to the relief of the fortress. He surprised the insurgents at the cloister of Piva, and accomplished his purpose. The relief of Nicsic next engaged attention. It was effected at the cost of hard fighting by a combined operation, in which Rauf Pasha marched up through the south end of the Duga Pass while Selim Pasha pressed down from the north end. Winter set in about the middle of December, and all important military movements were suspended.

Political discussions in Servia centered around the questions which grew out of the relations of the country to Turkey. The party of Young Servia kept up a constant agitation for the union of the Serbs and their kindred stems for war against Turkey, and the erection of a great Servian Kingdom, and was very strong, both in the Skupstchina and among the people. Prince Milan recognized the weakness of his country as compared with a great power like Turkey, and believed that the policy advised by the Young Servians would be disastrous and destructive of the best interests of the State, if not of its existence. He therefore favored a policy of peace. His career was made very uncomfortable by the hostility to his views of the agitators for war among the people, in the Skupstchina, and even in his cabinet, and was troubled by movements to displace him and set up another prince, supposed to be more ready to yield to the views of the war party. At the breaking out of the Herzegovinian insurrection in July, 1875, the conservative ministry of Stephanovitch was in power, but could not command a majority in the Skupstchina. The prince dissolved the Assembly. The new elections resulted adversely to the ministry, and they offered their resignations on the 16th of August. Prince Milan requested them to remain in office until the Assembly should meet. The Skupstchina was opened at Kraguyevatz on the 28th of August, with a majority decidedly hostile to the ministry. A new ministry was appointed from the national party, with Ristitch at its head. Prince Milan delivered an address to the Assembly on the 10th of September, in which he described the situation of Servia in the existing trouble as a hard one, and complained of the moving of Turkish troops on the frontiers, but expressed the hope that good results would follow the conferences of the Porte with the Western Powers. A circular, issued by the ministry to the provincial officers, ordered them to prevent all acts which might disturb the friendly relations of Servia with the Porte. The Skupstchina voted a reply to the address of the Prince, promising him all the means necessary to protect the liberties of the people and the security of the country, and speaking of the possibility of war as something to be contemplated only in case it should be necessary for the national defense. On the 28th of September, the Skupstchina, in secret session, granted the ministry a credit for making precautionary military preparations. The next day the Skupstchina was adjourned by the Prince to Belgrade. The ministry were very abruptly dismissed a few days afterward. Prince Milan, meeting the members of his cabinet in the ministerial chamber, complained that they were inciting the country to war, and desired that they should be more prudent. Minister Ristitch replied, that if the policy of the cabinet was not satisfactory to the Prince, the members would be obliged to tender their resignations. On the next day, October 4th, the Prince came into the palace of the Skupstchina, accompanied only by an adjutant. After exchanging a few words with the ministers, he went alone into the hall of the Skupstchina. The ministers followed him. Milan was received by the chamber with a deep silence, in the midst of which he arose and announced that his ministers had given him their resignations, and he had accepted them. Upon this announcement, the ministers retired from the hall. Milan continued, that having no ministers through whom to communicate with the Skupstchina, he was obliged to address it in person. He then asked the deputies, "Have you con-

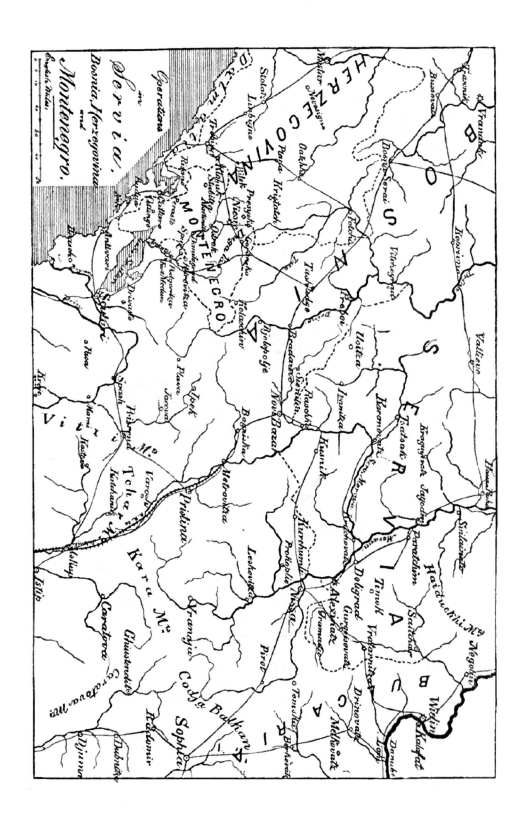

Servia,
Bosnia, Herzegovina
and
Montenegro.

English Miles

ADVANCE SENTINELS.

fidence in me?" The astonished members of the Assembly, after some hesitation, replied, "Yes." The Prince then asked, "Are you for war?" The deputies responded at once, with enthusiasm, "Yes, yes!" The Prince replied that he did not desire war, and declared that in view of the situation of the country and the respect due to the views of the great powers, he could not wish for it. His remarks were received coldly, and the session of the chamber was adjourned. Three days afterward, Prince Milan invited all the deputies to his palace, and calling their names from the list of members of the Skupstchina, put to each singly the question, "Who is for war, who not?" The members, thus appealed to on their individual responsibility, were not as ready for war as they had been in the chamber, and only twelve of them answered in the affirmative, while the rest expressed themselves as opposed to war. The Prince then asked, in the same manner, "Who is in favor of our giving support to the insurrectionists?" and the majority likewise voted against this line of action. A new ministry was appointed on the 9th of October, under the direction of Kalievitch, former President of the Skupstchina. It represented the same political views as the former Ristitch ministry, but its members were personally more agreeable to the Prince. Kalievitch introduced his cabinet to the Skupstchina on the 10th, with an address, which embodied a warning against indulging a self-confidence, which the difficulties of the situation and the slender resources of Servia would not justify, but admitted the duty of guarding the honor and interests of the country and preparing for the future; and uttered the hope that the ministry, supported by the Skuptschina, would be able to say to the Prince: "You have trusted us, and we have not deceived you. Servia and the Servian cause have received from us all that in these times we have been able to give them." This address, and the measures of reform which the minister outlined, particularly those looking to the improvement of the defenses of the country, were received with acclamations. The Skupstchina adjourned on the 30th of October.

The Turkish Government adopted energetic military measures to prevent the further spread of the Herzegovinian insurrection. Besides the forces which were kept in constant activity in Herzegovina, and added to as often as was necessary, it stationed large detachments throughout Bosnia, and put a formidable corps of observation along the Servian frontier. The presence of this latter body added to the warlike excitement in Servia, helped to protract it, increased the difficulties which Prince Milan had to encounter in preserving his policy of peace, and called for the presence of bodies of Servian troops on the other side of the line.   These troops on both sides were withdrawn in November.

The Porte tried also to satisfy the insurrectionists by measures of conciliation. It made many pleasant promises and offered several fair-seeming schemes of reform, but these offerings failed to produce any perceptible effect; they rather received the contempt of the insurgents, because they had become habituated to regard it as an established custom with the Porte to make promises which it would fail to see executed.

On the first of September the Sultan issued a firman to the Governors-General of the provinces, admonishing them to see that the laws were fully and promptly executed, and ordering the impartial trial of all offenders, so that all the subjects of the Porte without distinction might enjoy the greatest security and justice.   On the second of October an Iradé was issued providing for the relief of the poorer farmers from one-fourth of the tithes which had been recently imposed, and from the arrears of taxes up to the financial year 1873–'74. It also projected a scheme for the representation of the people in the government of the vilayets by a General Assembly of deputies from every district, which should meet once a year to discuss concerns of public interest, and should have consideration of matters relating to the imposition of taxes and the appropriation of the revenues. Deputations from these annual assemblies, consisting of persons selected by the Sultan for that purpose, should go from time to time to Constantinople to present directly to the Porte the wishes of the people.

On the fourteenth of December the Sultan issued an Iradé instituting reforms not only for Herzegovina and Bosnia, but for the whole Empire.   It contained provisions relating to the election of judges and administrative officers by all subjects of the Porte without distinction; for the transfer of lawsuits to the civil courts, and measures to prevent arbitrary collection of taxes; to reform the titles to real estate, and restrict the exaction of services for public works; it assured to the people of all religions, and the heads of all religious organizations, the right to the free exercise of their respective religions and ecclesiastical functions; guaranteed privileges for the foundation of schools, and declared all public offices open to non-Mohammedan subjects; graduated the amount of the fee for exemption from military duty, and secured the right of holding real estate to all non-Mohammedan subjects, together with respect for testamentary provisions.

The three Imperial powers—Russia, Austria, and Germany, who had long since formed a convention and agreed to act in concert in affairs relating to Turkey—had become very anxious to prevent a reopening of the Eastern Question, which was now threatened by the progress of the Herzegovinian insurrection and the growing excitement in the tributary States. They agreed, therefore, that a note, formally expressing their views as to what measures were necessary for the pacification of the Turkish Empire, and for the security of civilization, should be formally drawn up in their name and presented to the Porte. The framing of this note was entrusted to the Austrian Prime Minister, Count Andrassy. Hence it is commonly known as the Andrassy note.

The Andrassy note, which is a very long and elaborate document, began by relating the efforts which the European Governments had made for the restoration of peace in the disaffected districts, and the pains which they had taken at the same time to avoid the appearance of an interference in Turkish affairs It referred to the reforms promised in the Iradés of the 2d of October and the 14th of December, as embodying good principles, but as requiring effective administration to render them of practical value, and declared that they would be useless until the country should have been first pacified. It then detailed the complaints of the Christian inhabitants of Bosnia and Herzegovina, and named the measures which it was necessary to make of effect in those provinces before the hope of a valid peace could be realized, viz: (1). Complete freedom of religion ; (2). Abolition of the farming of the taxes ; (3). A law guaranteeing that the revenue from the direct taxes of Bosnia and Herzegovina should be applied for the good of the provinces under the control of boards constituted in the sense of the firman of December 14th; (4). The creation of a special commission, composed in equal numbers of Christians and Mohammedans, to superintend the execution of the reforms proposed by the powers as well as those which had been promised by the Porte; (5). The improvement of the agrarial condition of the rural population. The note reminded the Turkish Government that it had not succeeded in putting down the insurrection by arms, and expressed the general conviction entertained by Christians that the coming spring would reinforce it; that Bulgaria and Crete would increase the movement, and Servia and Montenegro would be drawn into it. The task of the powers who wished to preserve the general peace had become difficult under these complications. They could not secure peace by enjoining the governments of the principalities, or by pointing to the promises of the Porte, for these promises had been broken so often that nobody would longer regard them; but if they could point to indisputable, practical reforms, in actual operation, their task would be greatly simplified.

The Andrassy note was completed early in November, 1875, was communicated to all of the great Western Powers, and received their approval. It was not, however, formally delivered to the Turkish Government for several weeks, Reshid Pasha, the Minister of Foreign Affairs, asking indulgence under various pretexts. The threatening attitude of Servia and Montenegro was pleaded as offering an impediment to the action demanded in the note; this was removed by the withdrawal of the forces of both sides, from the Servian frontiers. Then the Iradé of the 14th of December provided for the introduction of some of the reforms indicated, and the note had to be revised and changed to meet the new situation thus created, and again approved by all the powers; so that it was not till the 31st of January, 1876, that Count Zichy, the Austrian Ambassador at Constantinople, was able finally to place it in the hands of Reshid Pasha. The Ambassadors of England, Germany, France, Italy, and Russia informed the Turkish Minister that their Governments supported the Austrian propositions in all of their points. A few days afterward the Ambassadors were informed that a new *firman* instituting reforms, was in preparation for Bosnia and Herzegovina. This document appeared on the 11th, and ordered the immediate institution in the insurgent districts of complete liberty of worship; reform in the system of taxation; the sale of waste lands to needy inhabitants on easy terms of payment; the institution of mixed commissions in the capitals of Bosnia and Herzegovina to insure the prompt execution of reforms; and an increase in the sums applied to works of public utility in proportions to be fixed by the mixed commissions. It also offered a general amnesty to all disaffected inhabitants who would return within four weeks to their obedience. The Government further promised to have the houses and churches of the returning refugees, which had been destroyed, rebuilt, and to

help those who should return to a new start in business. The answer
of the Porte to the Andrassy note was delivered to Count Zichy on
the 20th of February. It promised to give immediate attention to
the introduction of the measures suggested by the powers as to four
of the points, and as soon as possible as to the other. The position
of the Turkish Government on this subject was also fully explained
in a circular note which it addressed to its Ambassadors at the European Courts, calling their attention to the provisions of the Iradé of
the 11th, as embodying most of the principles declared in the Andrassy note. The application of the direct taxes to meet the requirements of the provinces, demanded by the powers, was mentioned as
involving the difficulty that it could not be brought into harmony with
the general system of administering the Turkish finances, but the
Government would endeavor to make a satisfactory adjustment of
that point also.

On the 1st of January, 1876, Mukhtar Pasha succeeded Rauf
Pasha, as commander of the Turkish forces in Herzegovina, and
established his headquarters at Trebigne. The winter's rest was disturbed only by a few unimportant engagements, when the insurgents
attacked the provision-trains of the Turks, or surprised their detachments as they struggled along the rough bridle-paths which serve as
substitutes for roads in that poorly improved region. Some accessions of Montenegrins came to the insurgents at Zubtchi and Banyani, about the middle of January. Liubibratish was displaced from
the leadership of the insurrection, and the position was formally
assumed by Peko Paulovitch. This officer undertook to give a military organization to the insurgent forces. He arranged his force
into detachments, over each of which he placed a chief, who should
be responsible for the strict execution of his orders. Attached to
his personal staff were the Archimandite Melentitch Perovitch and
the Catholic Curé Don Juan Musich._ His subaltern commanders
were Milcevitch, Tripko Kikatovitch, Sava Angelitch, Stolan Babitch,
Luka Petkovitch, and Maksim Bacevitch. The band of Lazar Sotchitza continued independent.

The most noteworthy of the engagements during the winter was a
sharp action which took place at Muratovizza on the 16th of March,
when five battalions of Turks, going to provision the fortress of
Goransko, were attacked by 1,150 insurgents under Peko Paulovitch,
defeated, and pursued with considerable loss.

During the winter another attempt was made by the European

Consuls, who had remained at Mostar ever since the failure of their summer conferences, to negotiate with the insurgents for a suspension of hostilities. By advice of their Governments, they invited the Herzegovinian leaders, February 9th, to confer for a restoration of peace on the basis of the propositions of the Andrassy note. But the insurgents had lost all faith in diplomatic negotiations as well as in Turkish promises of reforms, as means of bettering the condition of their country, and refused to consider these terms. The leaders met at the Suttorina, February 26th, and issued a manifesto declaring their views on the subject. No reforms, they said, would be of any effect, for the Mohammedans would baffle every attempt that could be made in that direction, and would revolt if an effective effort were made; they sought freedom and independence; for these they would fight, not negotiate, and would not lay down their arms till they were gained, and Herzegovina was granted independence.

Baron Rodich, Governor of Dalmatia, on behalf of the Austrian Government, visited both the Turks and the insurgents in the interests of peace. The Turks were ready to consider the subject of a suspension of hostilities, if the provisioning of the garrison at Nicsic was secured. The insurgents firmly maintained the position they had assumed Deputations of refugees declared that they would resist to the last, and that their families should starve in other countries rather than be again subjected to abuse at home; and the chiefs themselves communicated their ultimatum in the beginning of April. They demanded that all the Turkish troops in Herzegovina should be concentrated at six specified posts; that the Christians and insurgents should be allowed to keep their arms till the Mohammedans were disarmed; that provisions should be furnished the people to last them till the next harvest; that the collection of the taxes should be suspended for three years; that the Christians should have one-third of the lands held by the rayahs on lease, awarded to them; that the reforms proposed in the Andrassy note should be immediately and fully carried out in the peaceful parts of the country, so that it could be seen how the Mohammedans would act with reference to them; and that a commission of the European powers should be established to watch the introduction of the reforms. An informal suspension of hostilities ensued from the 28th of March to the 10th of April.

At the opening of the campaign in the spring of 1876, the insurgents were able to enter the field with a force recruited from the Slavic peoples abroad, improved in organization, and well armed.

MR. EUGENE SCHUYLER.

MR. WALTER BARING.

The Turks had, including the garrisons of the forts, about 22,000 men fit for action. The insurgents had cut off the communication of Nicsic with Montenegro whence it had been provisioned during the winter, and the supplies of its garrison had run out. Mukhtar Pasha tried twice to relieve it, and succeeded on the second attempt, only after four days of hard fighting and with heavy losses. The other garrisons were supplied with less trouble, for the insurgents had given all their attention to Nicsic, and that port was provisioned again in June without resistance.

The Servian Government during the earlier months of 1876 maintained an attitude of quiet observation, in the midst of popular agitations in favor of war. The ministry favored a peaceful policy; the Skupstchina was inclined toward war. As measures of precaution, a sum was voted for the equipment of the army, and a levy of men fit for service was ordered. The expressions of Prince Milan to the Austrian representative at Belgrade, were, however, of a peaceful term. The public excitement continued to grow. The capital was illuminated on the 14th of March in honor of the Herzegovinian victory at Muratovizza. Liubibratish, the former leader of the insurgents, had organized a force of various nationalities in aid of the insurrection, which was captured in March by Austrian officers on the territory of Dalmatia. With it was captured the Fräulein Markus, a Dutch lady, who, inspired with enthusiasm for the Slavic cause, had given it money and was now giving it her personal assistance. On her release she went to Belgrade and was received there with an ovation. A few days afterward (April 9th) a warlike demonstration was given by the Omladina in the shape of a charivari to the Austrian representative at Belgrade, for which the Austrian Government demanded and received an apology. Finally, the Prince was forced, in May, to appoint a new ministry more in sympathy with the public feeling. This ministry was called after two of its most prominent members, the Ristitch-Gruitch Ministry.

The massacre of the French and German Consuls by a Mohammedan mob at Salonica on the 7th of May greatly increased the excitement among the Christian population of Turkey, and led to renewed protests by the Great Powers. The riot at Salonica was occasioned by the appearance at the railway station of a young Bulgarian girl whom Emin Effendi, a prominent Turk of the town, had procured for his harem. The mother of the girl had followed

10

her on the same train without either knowing that they were so
near. Their surprise and demonstrations on meeting each other
attracted the attention of the crowd, which was mostly composed
of Christians, and the cry was raised that the girl had been forced
to become a Mohammedan and enter Emin Effendi's harem. In the
tumult which ensued, an empty carriage belonging to the American
Consul, which was standing by the station, was seized by the Christians, and the girl was put into it and carried off to a place of safety.
The Mohammedans were indignant, and the streets were filled all
the afternoon and the next morning with crowds calling for vengeance for the insult that had been offered to Islam. The French
Consul, apprehending riot, went, accompanied by the German Consul, who was his brother-in-law, to call upon Emin Effendi to induce
him to use his influence to restore order. The Effendi was at the
Mosque, and the Consuls sought him there. Their appearance in
the sacred place excited the mob to ferocity. The higher Turks
tried to protect them without avail. They were fallen upon and
savagely murdered The Western Governments took the matter
up immediately and demanded satisfaction for the outrage, and supported their demand by the dispatch of war vessels to the spot.
The most prominent participants in the murders were punished,
and an indemnity was paid to the families of the murdered Consuls.

Attention had by this time become painfully directed to the unhappy situation of the Bulgarian people. Manifestations of their
discontent appeared in February, in the shape of demands for relief
from the burdens imposed upon landholders, supported in a few
places by the organization of bands of insurgents. Military forces,
composed partly of regular troops, but mostly of Circassians and
Bashi-Bazouks, were dispatched to the province to repress these
manifestations. The irresponsible irregular soldiery, who are subject to only the loosest discipline, began a career of plunder, outrage, and destruction, which has few, if any, parallels in the annals
of civilized warfare. They made no distinction between orderly
and disorderly inhabitants, spared no age nor either sex, but exercised violence upon all according to their caprice. The stories that
were told of the rapine, murders, burning of houses and villages,
outrages upon women, and abductions of girls, were almost incredible, and were so considered and not believed at first, but they have
been confirmed in their worst details by unimpeachable testimony.

These atrocities excited universal astonishment and horror when their full extent and nature had been made known. Mr. W. E. Gladstone, late Premier of the British Cabinet, was prompted by them to write a pamphlet full of burning denunciation of the administration in power in Great Britain, for its attempt to palliate the enormity of the offenses and its toleration of the Turkish Government, which, knowing that they had been committed, had not taken efficient measures to bring the perpetrators of them to justice. In this pamphlet, he pronounced them "the basest and blackest outrages upon record within the present century, if not within the memory of man," and characterized them as "crimes and outrages so vast in scale as to exceed all modern example, and so unutterably vile as well as fierce in character, that it pains the power of heart to conceive, and of tongue and pen adequately to describe them."

Mr. Gladstone's denunciations are justified by the testimony of responsible persons who visited the scenes of the outrages, questioned the friends of the victims, and looked upon the wasted villages. Among these persons were missionaries of the American Board, the correspondent of the London *Daily News*, and Mr. Eugene Schuyler, United States Secretary of Legation at Constantinople. A strip of country south of the Balkan Mountains, about thirty miles wide and one hundred miles long, was wholly or partially desolated, and in this district seventy towns were given up to massacre, plunder, and fire. The number of persons who were murdered, in most cases with fiendish brutality, was estimated by Mr. Baring, an agent sent by the British Minister at Constantinople, to make inquiry on the subject, at twelve thousand, and by Mr. Eugene Schuyler at fifteen thousand at "the lowest."

Four days were spent in ravaging Panijurishta, or Otlukloi, which was regarded as the focus of the insurrection. The town was filled with inhabitants of the neighboring towns, whose houses had been already destroyed, and who had taken refuge here. Twenty-nine hundred people were slain, of whom two thousand were refugees from the other towns, and nine hundred were inhabitants of Panijurishta. About one-third of the place was destroyed. The churches were desecrated in every manner that sacrilegious ingenuity could suggest. An old blind man, who had earned the good-will of the whole town, was shut up in his house and burned; another man was deprived of his eyes; and a third was first mutilated upon the altar, then covered with petroleum, and burned. "The sinners," says a correspondent of the Cologne *Gazette*, relating the story of the outrage, "whom Dante places in hell along with his old teacher, Buenetto Latini, were true saints, as compared with the Turkish hordes of Panijurishta." ' Similar scenes were enacted, with such differences in details as might be occasioned by differences in the size and situation of the towns, through the whole of the ravaged district. The culminating outrages were committed at Batak, a town of about nine thousand inhabitants, situated in the Rhodope Mountains, about nine hours' journey south of Tatar-Bazardjik It was one of the most prosperous and enterprising towns of the region, and was engaged in extensive manufacturing industries. The Bashi-Bazouks came to this place on the 12th of May, and spent five days in their work of devastation. Mr. Djorbajik, a chief officer of the town, was impaled on a spit, and roasted alive; women were stripped, deprived of their jewels, outraged, and all were killed. Finally the town was burned and utterly destroyed, and its inhabitants given to wholesale massacre, which only twelve hundred succeeded in escaping.

This place was visited by the correspondent of the London *Daily News*, with Mr. Schuyler, on the 18th of August, three months after the massacre took place. The correspondent describes the scene as of the most horrible character. Approaching the town the party found skulls, of which the writer of the account counted one hundred from the saddle, all of women and children. "We entered the town," he continues, "on every side were skulls and skeletons charred among the ruins, or lying entire where they fell in their clothing. There were skeletons of girls and women with long brown hair hanging to the skulls. We approached the church. There these remains were more frequent, until the ground was literally covered with skeletons, skulls, and putrefying bodies in clothing. Between the church and the school there were heaps. . . . . . The whole church-yard, for three feet deep, was festering with dead bodies partly covered. . . . . I saw many hands, heads, and feet of children of three years of age, and girls with heads covered with beautiful hair. The church was still new. . . . . There were three thousand bodies in the church-yard and church. . . . . In the school, a fine building, two hundred women and children had been burned alive. All over the town there were the same scenes." The skulls were all separated from the bodies, showing that the women and girls had been beheaded.

Similar outrages, but less heinous, were committed north of the

Balkans, near Tirnova and Gabrova, where it was estimated that three thousand Bulgarians were murdered. An attempt was made to palliate the outrages on the ground that previous atrocities had been committed by Bulgarians. This is contradicted by Mr. Schuyler, who says in his report: "I have carefully investigated this point, and am unable to find that the Bulgarians committed any atrocities, or any act which deserves that name. I have vainly tried to obtain from the Turkish officials a list of such outrages. . . . . No Turkish women or children were killed in cold blood. No Mussulman women were violated. No purely Turkish village was attacked or burned. No Mussulman's home was pillaged. No mosque was desecrated or destroyed."

Mr. Walter Baring was sent to Adrianople in July, to investigate the truth of the reports of the insurrection and outrages, and ascertain their exact extent. His report, which was published on the 19th of September, is doubtless as favorable to the Turks as adherence to the truth would allow it to be, but it in no way mitigates the horror excited by the accounts from which we have just quoted. Mr. Baring confirmed the assertion that a real insurrection had been planned, and stated that the schoolmasters, many of whom had been educated in Russia and were Pan-Slavists, and the priests were the leading movers in it. A meeting of eighty agitators had been held at Otlukoi on the 31st of March, at which the general rising was appointed for the 13th of May. Their plan was to destroy as much of the railroad as possible; burn Adrianople, Philippopolis, Sofia, Tatar-Bazardjik, and several other places, and occupy others; attack the Turkish and mixed villages, and kill all Mussulmans who resisted and take their property, and to force all the Bulgarians into the insurrection. None of this was done, for the movement was suppressed, and the massacres were perpetrated before the time appointed for the plans to be carried-into effect. "No sooner," says Mr. Baring, "did the regular troops appear on the scene than the insurrection was at an end, and much bloodshed and useless destruction of property would have been spared had they only been despatched somewhat earlier." After describing the scene at Batak in nearly the same terms as were used by the correspondent of the London *Daily News*, Mr. Baring expressed the belief that the Turkish authorities were not aware, before he visited the place, of the horrors that had been committed there; for the town was remote and difficult of access, and no one had gone there "who was

likely to give the authorities a faithful account of what he saw."
Finally, in summing up the evidence, Mr. Baring was constrained
to say that "the manner in which the rising was suppressed was in-
human in the last degree, fifty innocent persons suffering for every
guilty one." The total number of Mussulmans killed during the
whole disturbance was about 163.

A commission was despatched by the Turkish Government to
visit the scene of the outrages and investigate their character. It
succeeded in making an estimate of the magnitude of the crimes so
moderate as to appear ridiculous by the side of the verified accounts
of the English and American observers. Tribunals were instituted
for the trial of the Bulgarian agitators, numbers of whom were
executed. Some of the Bashi-Bazouks and others who participated
in the outrage were executed; but Shevket Pasha, who had command of the district, was continued in high command through the
whole of 1877, and Achmet Agha, who commanded the troops at
Batak, received the order of the Medjidie. With all its efforts at
explanation and its pretenses to do justice, the Porte failed to remove the evil impression which the cruelties made upon the world,
and was not able to disconnect itself fully from the responsibility
for them.

The situation in the disaffected provinces had grown no better,
but rather worse. The three great powers who had taken the lead
in action with reference to Turkish affairs, decided that a new representation should be made to the Porte. The Prime Ministers of
Russia, Germany, and Austria met at Berlin on the 12th and 13th
of May, and agreed upon the memorandum which is known as the
Berlin note. This paper set forth that the Porte by accepting the
Andrassy note had pledged itself to Europe to carry out its suggestions, and that the powers had a right to demand the fulfillment of
its pledge. The Sultan had done nothing in this direction, and the
massacre at Salonica was attributable to his weakness. An armistice
of two months should at once be concluded with the insurgents, at
the end of which, if the object sought by the powers were not
gained, it would be necessary to consider what effective measures
should be taken in the interests of a general peace, and to prevent
the development of further difficulties. The note was promptly approved by France and Italy. Great Britain declined to give its
sanction, on account of objections to the clause respecting "effective
measures."

ABDUL-AZIZ—LATE SULTAN OF TURKEY.

ABDUL-AZIZ ON HIS WAY TO PRISON.

The massacre at Salonica was followed by a change in the ministry at Constantinople. The ostensible head of the new cabinet was Rushdi Pasha, appointed Grand Vizier, but it was largely under the influence of Midhat Pasha, one of the most eminent and able of the Mussulman statesmen, who took a place in the council without a portfolio. Before the end of May the ministry co-operating with the Softas, or students of Mohammedan theology, procured the deposition of Sultan Abdul Aziz. Alleging that the faculties of the Sultan had become disordered, so that he was not only not fit to engage in public business, but that his continued rule threatened ruin to the Empire and the Mussulman cause, the conspirators obtained from the Sheik-ul-Islam, the supreme authority in Mohammedan law, a decision that it was lawful to depose him. Armed with this decision, the ministers arrested the Sultan, and took him a prisoner to the Palace of Top Kapu, and afterward to the Palace of Tcheragan. Murad Effendi, the eldest son of the late Sultan Abdul Medjid, and nephew of the deposed Sultan, the legal heir to the throne, was installed Sultan under the title of Murad V., on the 30th of May. On the morning of the 4th of June, Abdul Aziz was found dead in his chamber in the Palace of Tcheragan. A council of nineteen physicians of different nationalities was called to hold an inquest over him. They decided, unanimously, that he had killed himself by cutting his veins with a pair of scissors.

The probability of war between Servia and Turkey became every day more strong. The Ristitch-Gruitch ministry were in favor of war, but they hesitated to take the decisive steps, because they saw that the country was not sufficiently prepared for it, and that it lacked the means of making speedy preparations. A decree for the issue of a loan of twelve million francs was issued on the 24th of May. The Russian General Tchernayeff was appointed a general in the Servian army, with the understanding that he would be the commander-in-chief. On the 26th of May an alliance was concluded with Montenegro. On the 9th of June the Porte asked what these and other warlike movements meant. The Servians replied that they desired to preserve peace, and had no design of disturbing the integrity of the Porte. They agreed to send a messenger to Constantinople to consult with the Porte concerning the demands of the situation. On the 29th of June, the Servian agent in Constantinople presented to the Porte a demand which Servia and Montenegro had agreed to make, that Turkey should entrust the pacification of Bosnia and the

Herzegovina to those States, in consideration for which Servia should receive Bosnia and Montenegro, and Herzegovina, they agreeing to render homage and pay tribute to the Porte for those districts, as Servia already did for her own territory. This demand was, of course, refused. Prince Milan went to join the army on the 29th of June. He issued a proclamation to the people, in which he said that he had intended to send an Ambassador to Constantinople to seek .an understanding with the Porte, but that that power had showed, in every way, that it did not wish for an understanding. It had sent troops upon troops to the frontier prepared to enter Servia at any time. Servia must avert this danger, and itself enter the insurgent provinces to restore peace and order. It would respect the religion and integrity of Turkey. On the 2d of July the country was declared in a state of siege.

The Prince of Montenegro also raised the banner of war, and placed himself at the head of his troops for an active campaign on the 2d of July. Montenegro had not taken an open active part against Turkey, during the whole insurrectionary movement, until the alliance with Servia was negotiated in May. The Herzegovinian insurrection had excited a lively sympathy in Montenegro, and the Turks had accused that State of giving it help and encouragement. Nevertheless, the Turks relied upon the Montenegrins to provision their garrison at Nicsic, during the winter of 1875-'76, and it was provisioned by them from day to day, until its communications were cut off by the insurgents. Early in 1876, the Turkish Vali of Herzegovina had made a vain attempt to induce the Prince of Montenegro to take arms against the insurgents. The Montenegrin declaration of war was based upon the allegations that the Turks had quite blockaded the southern.frontier of Montenegro, that they had shown hostility to the State, had interrupted its trade, and kept it continually uneasy; and that it was impossible for them to carry out the reforms which they had promised to introduce in Herzegovina.

When the war was declared, the Turks had available, for operations against Servia and Montenegro, a force of about one hundred thousand men. About twenty thousand men were in Herzegovina, north of Montenegro, under Mukhtar Pasha, and between four and five thousand men were posted south of Montenegro. On the Danube were about fifty thousand men, commanded by Eyub Pasha, and including the divisions of Osman Pasha and Fazyl Pasha. Between fourteen and fifteen thousand men were in North-western and South-western Bosnia. Besides all these forces, there were about thirty thousand men about Philippopolis, commanded by Abdul Kerim Pasha, who had been sent up against the Bulgarian insurgents. Large additions were made to these forces, for which even the remote Asiatic corps were drawn upon, as soon as war was declared

The Servian forces were posted in four bodies: The army of the Drina, twenty thousand men, under General Alimpitch; the army of the Ibar, about twenty thousand men, under General Zach; the southern army, which was their principal force, about forty-five thousand men, under General Tchernayeff; and the army of the Timok, twenty thousand men, under General Lieshanin.

The Servian divisions all moved immediately after war was declared. Gen. Lieshanin crossed the Timok with six thousand men on the 2d of July, intending to advance against Widin. He was repulsed near Karaul with serious losses, and obliged to return. On the next day Osman Pasha crossed into Servia, and forced the Servians to abandon their fortifications on the right bank of the Timok, but was not able to pursue his advantage.

On the morning of the 3d of July, Gen. Alimpitch crossed the Drina with fifteen battalions, and marched with three columns upon Bielina. He captured the fortifications, but was driven out of the town after having entered it, and compelled to retreat in disorder. He returned to his original position, strengthened his defenses, and pushed forward from day to day, until, finally, after the evacuation of Little Zvornick by the Turks, he gained possession of both banks of the Drina. Gen. Zach crossed the frontier near Javor, on a rough road, very difficult for artillery, to advance upon Sienitza. He met a Turkish force under Mehemet Ali Pasha, July 6th, was repulsed and obliged to retreat. He was wounded in the engagement, became discouraged in consequence of his defeat, fell sick, and was relieved by Col. Tcholak Antitch.

Gen. Tchernayeff, of the army of the South, having ordered Col. Milan Ivanovitch to make a demonstration against Nissa as a feint, marched himself, with the larger part of his army, against Ak Palanka, which point, with Pirot, he captured on the 6th of July. He had expected to excite a rising among the Bulgarians and receive reinforcements from them. He was disappointed in this, and on the 10th of July evacuated Ak Palanka and Pirot, and returned to Servia. The remainder of July was occupied with movements and skirmishes which were unimportant in their nature and had no important results

The Montenegrins entered upon their campaign with vigor. The larger part of their little army was massed on the northern frontier, ready to march into Herzegovina and co-operate with the insurgents there. A small force was kept near the southern boundary of the State to hold in check the Turkish garrisons in the neighboring towns of Albania. The first operations were directed against Gatchko and the columns of Selim Pasha. On the 11th of July a sharp engagement took place between a part of their force and a command of Selim Pasha's; on the same day Prince Nicholas occupied Stolatz, and another force drove a Turkish command near Klek. The Montenegrins were successful in engagements with Selim Pasha on the 16th and 17th of July, but on the 18th they were attacked by Mukhtar Pasha, with a stronger force, and defeated. Mukhtar Pasha, following them to cut off their retreat, was surprised by them shortly after leaving the cloister of Plana on the 28th. The Bashi-Bazouks were struck with panic and ran away, and some of the regular forces shared their disorder. The Montenegrins, perceiving this, fell upon the Turks with vigor, cut them up severely, and captured Osman Pasha, the commander of one of their columns. Mukhtar Pasha retreated to Trebigne, and called for reinforcements. On the 2d of September he again crossed the Montenegrin frontier and intrenched himself at Saslap, where a Montenegrin force stood opposed to him, but no important engagement took place.

In the south the Montenegrins had blockaded Medun. Mahmond Pasha attacked them on the 15th of August and was routed. He was court-martialled and superseded by Dervish Pasha, who, on the 6th of September, made an attempt against Rogatzi, on the north bank of the Moratcha. The Montenegrins fell upon his force from their superior positions on the rocks, and routed it with a terrible loss. Another attempt, September 11th, against the heights of Welie Brdo, on the right bank of the Zeta, likewise met with disaster.

Toward the end of July the Turks began a combined operation against the line of the Timok, in which were engaged the command of Achmet Eyub Pasha, supported by the divisions of Suleiman Pasha and Osman Pasha. The principal objective points on this line were Gurgussovatz and Saitchar, with their dependent posts.

On the 28th of July, Osman Pasha made a demonstration against the advanced posts of Gen. Lieshaniu, and forced him to retreat to Saitchar. As this place could not long hold out against an earnest attack, it was ordered to be evacuated. The inhabitants removed all of their effects, and left the neighborhood. Gen. Lieshanin retired with his forces to the west, and left Saitchar to be occupied by Osman Pasha on the 6th of August.

In co-operation with this movement, Hafiz Pasha attacked the Servians at Gramada, and compelled them to withdraw to Gurgussovatz, while Suleiman Pasha, crossing into Servia near Pandiralo, obliged Gen. Horvatovitch to abandon his posts on the border and concentrate his force at Tresibaba, south of Gurgussovatz. The two Turkish columns were now joined. Achmet Eyub Pasha took command in person, attacked Tresibaba, drove Horvatovitch into Gurgussovatz, and compelled him to evacuate that place also on the 6th of August.

These movements had been made with the view of advancing upon Alexinatz, the ultimate object of the Turkish campaign from Widin. But the Turks had hardly possessed themselves of the two chief points on the line of the Timok than their plans were changed, and it was decided that the advance against Alexinatz should be made from Nissa, on the southern, or Bulgarian Morava. Accordingly, Gurgussovatz and Saitchar were evacuated, and by the 20th of August, Horvatovitch was again in possession of all the posts he had occupied near the former place.

The Turks, having concentrated their forces at Nissa, with Abdul Kerim Pasha in command, began their attacks against Alexinatz on the 19th of August. Six days of hard fighting ensued, till the 24th, which have collectively received the name of the battle of Alexinatz. The Servians fought with vigor, and held all their essential positions. The Turks, having failed to carry their point, and having learned that Horvatovitch was coming up from Gurgussovatz to attack their right flank, fell back exhausted, on the morning of the 25th, upon Katun. The Servian loss in these battles was 1,613 killed and wounded; that of the Turks was considerably greater, but is not exactly known.

Abdul Kerim Pasha again changed his plans, and determined to gather his army on the left bank of the Morava, extending it further to the west, and going around Alexinatz and Deligrad, to descend the valley on that side. He proceeded to attempt this movement on the 28th of August. Tchernayeff was surprised on the 1st of September, and an engagement ensued by which the Servians were compelled to retreat in disorder. The Servians would have been placed in great peril, but the Turks, suffering from a shortness of supplies, were obliged to remain quiet while Tchernayeff reorganized his forces. Unimportant engagements occurred on the 7th, 10th, 11th, and 13th of September. On the 16th, hostilities were suspended for ten days by the operation of an armistice.

While the military movements were in progress, changes of much importance had taken place in the Turkish Government, and the condition and relations of the belligerent parties had been made the subject of new negotiations with the Great Powers. The reign of Murad V. as Sultan was brief and inglorious. The deposition and death of Sultan Abdul Aziz had been followed on the 15th of June by the murder of Hussein Avni, Minister of War, and Reshid Pasha, Minister of Foreign Affairs, while at a cabinet council, together with the Grand Admiral and a retainer of one of the ministers, by the assassin Hassan Bey, who was seeking to gratify a personal animosity. In less than three months, Murad proved to be physically and mentally incompetent. He fell into fits of melancholy and stupor, and was declared incurable. The Sheik-ul-Islam was again consulted, and decided that it was lawful to depose him. He was accordingly deposed on the last day of August. Abdul Hamid, a younger brother of Murad's, the next in the order of succession, was named as the new Sultan, and was girded with the sword of Othman on the 7th of September. He issued an Imperial *Hat*, or decree, on the 9th of September, confirming the former ministers and higher officers in their positions, and making the promises of reforms which are customary with the new Sultans of Turkey. Abdul Kerim Pasha having gone to the field to take the command of the army, Halil Redif Pasha was appointed Minister of War in his place, and Savfet Pasha was appointed Minister of Foreign Affairs in place of the assassinated Reshid Pasha.

The Servian Government about this time narrowly escaped being placed in an embarrassing position through the indiscreet action of Gen. Tchernayeff and his officers, who, at a festival given at Deligrad on the 16th of September, proclaimed Prince Milan King of Servia. That more than an after-dinner compliment was intended was assured by the formal publication of the proclamation on the next day to the army, and the reading of an address to King Milan I., Obrenovitch, as "in the name of the heroic Servian people." A deputation was

GENERAL TCHERNAYEFF.

GENERAL ALIMPITCH.

TURKISH SPIES BROUGHT INTO THE SERVIAN CAMP.

sent up from the army to communicate the proceedings to Milan, and to invite him to accept the honor which they had tendered to him. The act was disquieting to the neighboring powers, and might have been made a serious obstacle to the progress of the negotiations, but that Prince Milan disavowed all complicity with it, and caused the deputation from the army to be sent back before it had reached the capital.

Skirmishing had been going on through September between the Turks and Servians on the Morava and around Alexinatz. It had hardly been interrupted by the nominal suspension of hostilities between the 16th and 25th. The first important engagement was the battle of Weliki Shiliegovatz, on the 19th of October, one of the results of which was that the Turks got a better position as against the Servians. It was followed on the 23d by another movement, by which the Turks gained positions on the Djunis stream, enabling them to divide the Servian army. The Servians were again defeated on the 29th of October in the battle of Trubarevo. General Horvatovitch was driven back upon Krushevatz, and General Tchernayeff was compelled to retreat to Deligrad and abandon Alexinatz. On the next day the Turks fired upon Alexinatz, and were not answered. On the 31st they fired upon it again, and, receiving no reply, entered the place, to find it empty of men and provisions.

The Servian army was in a desperate condition. It had suffered many defeats and had been compelled to abandon the strongest fortified position of the country. It had also been disturbed by internal dissensions and quarrels between its Russian and Servian elements, and was so demoralized that it was nearly broken up. The Servian cause seemed certain to be lost, when Russia saved it on the evening of the last day of October, by presenting to the Porte an ultimatum demanding immediate assent to the armistice.

Quite different was the situation at this time in Montenegro. The suspension of hostilities had been well observed here. On the 9th of October, Mukhtar Pasha made an attack on the Montenegrins, but they turned upon him, drove him out of his intrenchments, and sent him into Turkish territory. The Turks were also defeated in lighter engagements at Liubigne and Bilek. On the southern border of the State, Dervish Pasha undertook to invade the country along the Zeta. He had advanced a short distance when he was attacked at Zagarash, October 16th, and decisively defeated. Fort Medun capitulated on the 21st of October, and not only was Montenegro free from the presence of the Turks, but the Montenegrins had gained positions on Turkish territory.

The progress of events in the Balkan peninsula was observed with interest by the people of all Europe. The Russians sympathized deeply in the struggles of their Slavic brethren, and gave them moral and material aid, so that especially in the latter part of the campaign the Servian army was considerably reinforced by Russian recruits, and largely under the command of Russians as officers. The Government took no pains to repress these manifestations, but rather encouraged them by public utterances in favor of the Slavic cause, and by making preparations which indicated that war in their behalf was not improbable. In its diplomatic communications it spoke more freely of righting the wrongs of the Slavic people, less of the necessity of preserving peace. The English people were powerfully moved by the reports of the outrages which had been committed in Bosnia and Bulgaria by the unrestrained Turkish soldiery, and made, through the press and public meetings, demonstrative protests against the conciliatory course of their Government. The British Government, committed to its traditional policy of preserving the integrity of the Turkish Empire, and opposing whatever might look like aggressive movements by Russia, was slow to support the other powers in their demands upon the Ottoman Government for guarantees of the reforms which it could not be denied were necessary, and was often credited with having suggested to the Porte the ingenious counter-propositions with which it answered every successive demand of the powers and evaded immediate decisive action. The other powers professed to regard the questions at issue solely from the point of their own interests, and to favor what would most readily restore and preserve peace, but declined to commit themselves in advance as to what their course would be should matters come to a breach.

While the summer campaigns were going on in Servia, the powers were trying, at both Belgrade and Constantinople, to arrange a settlement. The Servians averred that they were fighting for Slavic freedom, and would accept no other solution. The Porte pleaded that it was preparing, as fast as possible, a scheme for reforms and self-government that would embrace the whole Empire, and could not be hurried. Finally, on the 14th of September, Savfet Pasha communicated the terms on which the Ottoman Government would make peace. They were: That the Prince of Servia should pay homage to the Sultan ; that four fortresses which had been given up to him in 1867 should be again occupied by the Turks ; that the Servian militia should be abolished, and the number of troops allowed for the preservation of order in the interior of the principality, limited ; that Servia should return to their homes all the refugees from other provinces within its territory and destroy the fortresses which it had recently built ; that the amount of tribute paid by Servia should be increased so as to cover the interest on a war indemnity ; that the Turkish Government should be allowed to build and operate a railway from Belgrade to Nissa, and that the relations with Montenegro should be the same as before the war. The powers replied on the 23d, ignoring all the points of the Turkish position, asking self-government for Bosnia and Herzegovina, a seaport to be given to Montenegro, an improved organization for Bulgaria, with a Christian governor to be appointed by the Porte, and as to Servia, a restoration of the *status quo*, except that an indemnity might be charged for the damage occasioned by the war. An informal suspension of hostilities was obtained from the 16th to the 25th of September.

On the 7th of October the representatives of the powers called for an armistice of six weeks. The Porte responded with a proposition for an armistice of six months, and at the same time communicated the draft of a Constitution which had been prepared for the whole Empire, embodying the principles and more important provisions of the most liberal constitutions of European States, together with laws which had been framed for the better organization of the civil administrations and courts of justice, and for the more equitable collection of taxes in the provinces.

General Ignatieff, the Russian Ambassador at the Porte, had returned to Constantinople after an absence of several weeks, and renewed the demand of his Government for a concession of the autonomy of the provinces and the introduction of the promised reforms, and for an armistice, during which the reforms should be carried into execution. While he was waiting for the answer of the Sultan, the Turkish victories at Trubarevo had placed the Servian army in imminent peril. He was then instructed by his Government to present the Russian ultimatum. He had an interview with Savfet Pasha on the afternoon of the 31st of October, at which he stated that the rising in Servia and Montenegro had excited in the Russian nation a lively, enthusiastic interest. The Czar, who shared in the sympathies of his people for the Christian inhabitants of the Balkan peninsula, had endeavored with the other powers to restore peace and order. They were all agreed that the States involved in the complications should be restored to as good a condition as they enjoyed before the war, and that continued bloodshed was useless. The Czar could not suffer any longer protraction of the negotiations respecting an armistice; therefore he had decided to withdraw his entire embassy from Constantinople, if within forty-eight hours from this time an unconditional armistice of from six weeks to two months, embracing all the combatants, and involving an entire suspension of military operations, were not in operation. Having delivered the note, General Ignatieff made ostensible preparations to leave Constantinople. The next day (November 1st) he received the answer of Savfet Pasha conveying the unconditional agreement of the Porte to an armistice of two months, beginning with that day. On the 4th of November, Earl Derby, in behalf of the British Government, issued a circular note calling for a conference of all the great powers, at which the Porte should also be represented, to meet at Constantinople. The circular proposed as a basis for the deliberations of the conference:—the independence and territorial integrity of the Ottoman Empire; a declaration that the powers will not seek for any territorial advantages, exclusive influence, or special concessions; the basis of pacification to be the terms which had been proposed to the Porte on the 21st of September, including the restoration of the *status quo* in Servia and Montenegro, and the undertaking by the Porte in a protocol to be signed at Constantinople with the representatives of the mediating powers, to grant to Bosnia and Herzegovina a system of local or administrative autonomy, with guarantees of a similar kind to be provided against maladministration in Bulgaria; the reforms already agreed to by the Porte in February, 1876, to be included in the administrative arrangements for Bosnia and Herzegovina, and, so far as they might be applicable, for Bulgaria. The powers all gave their assent to the proposition for a conference, Turkey responding last, with hesitation, and only at the pressing request of England, on the 18th of November. Lord Derby had proposed that each power should send a special Ambassador to attend the conference, in addition to its regular representative at the Porte. Austria sent Baron Calice to act as the associate of its Ambassador, Count Zichy; France, Count Chaudordy, to support Count Bourgoing; England, the Marquis of Salisbury, to act with Sir Henry Elliot, and Turkey recalled Edhem Pasha from Berlin to assist its Foreign Minister, Savfet Pasha. Of these special envoys, the Marquis of Salisbury was a distinguished statesman and publicist of England, a writer of considerable fame. He had been Secretary of State for India in the third Cabinet of Lord Derby, 1866 to 1867, and had at the time of his appointment on this mission held the same position in the Cabinet of Mr. Disraeli (or Earl Beaconsfield) since 1874. He was known to take a warm interest in the welfare of the Christian subjects of Turkey, being associated with Earl Derby as one of the members of the cabinet who opposed the tendency of their chief to regard the question from the Turkish point of view; and in connection with this mission, he visited several of the continental courts to consult with their ministers regarding the measures which it would be possible to take in the interests of peace and humanity.

Count Chaudordy, the French envoy, had been in the French diplomatic service a large part of the time since 1850. In 1870, as representative of the Foreign Office at Tours, he published several circulars in answer to the notes of Count Bismarck, and repelled the charges made by the German Chancellor that the French had been guilty of violations of the Convention of Geneva. He was chosen a member of the Chamber of Deputies in 1871, and took his seat on the Right. At the time of his appointment to Constantinople, he was Ambassador to Madrid.

A preliminary conference was opened on the 12th of December, of the representatives of all the powers except Turkey, to arrange a programme of the conditions which it should be judged necessary to require for the protection of the Christians of the Balkan provinces. This conference adjourned on the 21st, having agreed to demand the restoration of the *status quo* as to Servia and Montenegro, with the addition of the cession of Little Zvornik by Turkey to Servia, and the rectification of the boundaries of Montenegro, by giving to it those angles of Herzegovina which project into its territory about Trebigne and Nicsic; a considerable extension of Bulgaria to the west and south, and the division of the territory thus enlarged into two Vilayets, with local self-government, under a Governor-General for the two provinces, to be appointed by the Porte with the approval of the powers, a provincial assembly, militia, police force, and *gendarmerie*, composed of Christians and Mussulmans; the union of Bosnia and Herzegovina into one

11

province, with similar privileges of administration; and the institution of an international commission, to be appointed by the guaranteeing powers, to watch over the introduction of the reforms, and be supported by a foreign *gendarmerie.*

The conference proper was opened on the 23d of December, Savfet Pasha, Turkish Minister of Foreign Affairs, presiding. The Turks had prepared a dramatic incident to add effect to their part of the proceedings. As soon as the preliminary formalities of the opening of the conference were over, salvos of artillery were heard. The President explained that this demonstration was in honor of the adoption of the new Constitution, the proclamation of which placed Turkey on that day in the rank of Constitutional States. This Constitution was the work of Midhat Pasha, who had, a short time before, succeeded Rushdi Pasha as Grand Vizier, and was promulgated as the fundamental law of the whole Empire. It embodied the leading principles of the most liberal constitutions of Western Europe. Proclaiming the Empire indivisible with the Sultan as Caliph and sovereign supreme and inviolable; it declared the inviolability of personal freedom, property, and the domicile, the freedom of religious worship, while Mohammedanism should be the religion of the State, the equality of all subjects before the law, and their right to speedy and impartial justice, the freedom of the press and instruction, while primary instruction should be made obligatory. It made the ministry responsible, and established a legislative Assembly, to consist of Senators appointed by the Sultan for life, and a Chamber of Deputies, whose members should be chosen by the people by secret ballot, in the proportion of one deputy for every fifty thousand inhabitants, and should serve for four years; the deputies to be free in their votes and unrestricted in the expression of their opinions; the Legislature to be in session every year from November till March. It established elective provincial assemblies, to legislate for the provinces, cantonal and municipal councils, made regulations for the courts, consisting of a High Court, for the trial of official offenders, a court of cassation or accounts, and ordinary courts, and secured the independence of the judges. The Constitution was declared unalterable, except by a vote of two-thirds of both chambers, with the approval of the Sultan.

On the 28th of December, the armistice was extended till the 1st of March. The terms agreed upon in the preliminary conference were rejected by the Porte as involving violations of the Con-

THE MARQUIS OF SALISBURY.

EDHEM PASHA.

stitution just adopted, and being incompatible with the sovereignty of the Empire.

A new proposition was presented to Turkey, in which the cession of Little Zvornik to Servia, and the points in reference to the additions to Montenegro were modified so as to meet the expressed views of the Porte. The plan for the reorganization of Bulgaria was wholly changed. The demand for a reserve of the power of approval of the appointment of the provincial governors was limited to five years of operation, and the scheme for a commission to watch over the introduction of the reforms was modified so as to make the commission a mixed one. The plenipotentiaries declared that if these propositions were rejected, they would leave Constantinople. On the 20th of January, 1878, Savfet Pasha read a note in the conference, announcing that Turkey declined to accede to the propositions, and giving the reasons for its action. The conference was then declared closed. The special Ambassadors shortly afterward withdrew from Constantinople.

On the 25th of January, Savfet Pasha issued a circular, explaining that the Porte had rejected the proposals made at the conference, first because they were part of a programme which had been settled beforehand at a conference from which Turkey was excluded; and, second, because in making them the plenipotentiaries had entirely lost sight of one of the fundamental conditions of the conference—non-intervention in the affairs of the Turkish Empire, and had demanded conditions such as no Government could accept which wished to preserve its independence, and that, too, when a Constitution had been granted, assuring to the whole Empire privileges which the powers demanded for certain provinces only.

On the 31st of January, Prince Gortchakoff, Chancellor of the Russian Empire, issued a circular note reciting the failure of all the attempts to pacify Turkey_and_of_the conference, and inquiring what the powers intended to do next.

On the 5th of February, Midhat Pasha, the Turkish Grand Vizier, was dismissed; Edhem Pasha was appointed in his place, and a new cabinet was formed. The act was a general surprise, and was variously accounted for. An official circular stated that it was because the Vizier had failed to oppose plans against the prerogatives of the Sultan and the public tranquillity which it was his duty to prevent.

In March, the Russian Government invited the powers to agree to a protocol to be signed by them and Turkey, pledging the execution of the reforms demanded and promised, failing the realization of which, within a reasonable time, the powers should come to an understanding as to what should be done. This was agreed to by the other powers, and the protocol was signed March 31st by the representatives of England, Russia, France, Germany, Austria, and Italy In this paper the Porte was invited to conclude the pacification of the principalities " by replacing its armies on a peace footing, excepting the number of troops indispensable for maintaining order, and by putting in hand, with the least possible delay, the reforms necessary for the tranquillity and well-being of the provinces, the condition of which was discussed at the conference;" the readiness of the Porte to realize an important part of the reforms was recognized ; a proposition was made to watch over the manner in which they should be carried into effect; and the intention was reserved, if the condition of the Christian provinces were not improved, to consider what further steps would be necessary. The protocol was presented to the Porte for its signature April 3d, and was immediately rejected with decision. In a note conveying its rejection formally, the Turkish Government said it could not see how it had deserved so ill of justice and civilization as to see itself placed in a humiliating position without example in the world. " The Treaty of Paris," reads the note, "gave an explicit sanction to the principle of non-intervention. This treaty, which binds together the powers who participate in it, as well as Turkey, can not be abolished by a protocol in which Turkey has no share. . . . . Turkey feels that she is now contending for her existence," but "strong in the justice of her cause, and trusting in God, she determines to ignore what has been decided without her and against her ; resolved to retain in the world the place which Providence has destined for her in this regard, she will not cease to encounter the attacks directed against her, with the general principles of public right and the authority of a great European act, which pledges the honor of the powers that signed the protocol of the 31st of March, a document which, in her eyes, has no legal claim to exact compliance." This note was presented to the Russian Government on the 12th of April. On the 24th of the same month Russia declared war against Turkey. Before proceeding to narrate the action of the Russian Government, it is necessary to mention a few other events, which had a bearing upon the situation and attitude of Turkey.

Negotiations for peace were begun in January between Turkey and Servia and Montenegro, independently of the action of the powers. Peace was concluded with Servia on the 27th of February, on the basis of the maintenance of the *status quo ante bellum*, the granting of an amnesty, and the evacuation of Servian territory by the Turkish troops within twelve days. Servia agreed to erect no more fortifications, to hoist the Ottoman flag by the side of that of Servia on the existing forts, and to prevent armed bands from crossing the frontier The terms were approved by the Great Skupstchina, at a session called especially to consider them, on the 28th of March. The Montenegrins demanded a rectification of their frontier, with additions to their territory, the cession of the seaport of Spizza, the free navigation of the Lake of Scutari and the river Bayana, the restoration of the Herzegovinian refugees to their homes, and a new *modus vivendi* with Turkey. The Porte declined to accede to these demands. They were modified, and the negotiations were resumed, to be broken off finally on the refusal of Turkey to cede Nicsic to Montenegro.

The insurrectionary movements in Bosnia were renewed early in the spring, when bands of insurgents appeared in several quarters, and a number of skirmishes took place. The most prominent of the new leaders was Col. Despotovitch, a Servian by birth, who had served in the Russian Imperial Guard and the Servian army.

The first Turkish Parliament under the new Constitution was opened March 19th, by the Sultan in person. The Sultan, in the "Speech from the Throne," said of the conference: "The disagreement between my Government and the powers rests rather in the form and method of application than in the substance of the question. All my efforts will be devoted toward bringing to perfection the progress which has already been realized in the situation of the Empire, and in all the branches of its administration. But I consider it to be one of my most important duties to remove any cause which may be detrimental to the dignity and independence of my Empire. I leave to time the task of proving the sincerity of my intentions of reconciliation." The reply to this address was discussed in the Chamber of Deputies in secret session, when, it is said, the speakers were unanimous in favor of rejecting absolutely all foreign intervention in the internal affairs of Turkey.

SECOND BOOK.

THE EASTERN WAR OF 1877–1878.

SECOND BOOK.

THE EASTERN WAR OF 1877–1878.

CHAPTER I.

THE RUSSIAN DECLARATION OF WAR.

The Russian War Manifesto—Prince Gortchakoff's Circular—The Turkish Reply—The Army of the Pruth, its Composition and Commanders—Total Strength of the Russian Armies—Crossing of the Pruth—Occupation of Galatz and Braila—Convention between Russia and Rumania—Turkish Protest—Declaration of Rumanian Independence—Strength of the Rumanian Army—The Seat of War—The Defenses of Turkey—The Danube and its Fortresses—The Turkish Quadrilateral—The Country beyond the Balkans—Strength and Condition of the Turkish Forces—Operations on the Danube

THE prompt and determined rejection by the Ottoman Porte of the London protocol as being a violation of the independence of Turkey, left little, if any, hope for the preservation of peace. Though it was not immediately followed by a declaration of war on the part of Russia, warlike movements began at once. The Russian army in Bessarabia rapidly advanced toward the Pruth, and the Turks were hastening the erection of works in front of Kalafat, with a view, it was thought, to cross to the Rumanian side. When, on April 20th, the Emperor of Russia left for Kishenev, it was generally understood that his arrival at the headquarters of the Russian army would be immediately followed by a declaration of war. Having reached Kishenev, the Czar, on April 23d, reviewed his troops on the banks of the Pruth, and on the following day he issued the anxiously awaited manifesto to his army, which informed the world that peace was at last broken, and that the two great countries of Eastern Europe were in a state of war. Few public documents of the

(211)

nineteenth century have been read with a more intense interest, and
however much views differed on the justice of the cause for which
the Emperor pleaded, it was felt on all sides that this manifesto
would rank among the most notable addresses issued since the days
of the French Revolution.   The manifesto is as follows:

"Our faithful and beloved subjects know the strong interest we
have constantly felt in the destinies of the oppressed Christian population of Turkey.   Our desire to ameliorate and assure their lot has
been shared by the whole Russian nation, which now shows itself
ready to bear fresh sacrifices to alleviate the position of the Christians in the Balkan peninsula.

"The blood and property of our faithful subjects have always
been dear to us, and our whole reign attests our constant solicitude to preserve to Russia the benefits of peace.   This solicitude
never failed to actuate us during the deplorable events which occurred in Herzegovina, Bosnia and Bulgaria.   Our object before all
was to effect amelioration in the position of the Christians in the
East by means of pacific negotiations; and in concert with the great
European Powers, our allies and friends, for two years we have made
incessant efforts to induce the Porte to effect such reforms as would -
protect the Christians in Bosnia, Herzegovina and Bulgaria from
the arbitrary measures of local authorities.   The accomplishment of
these reforms was absolutely stipulated by anterior engagements contracted by the Porte toward the whole of Europe.

"Our efforts, supported by diplomatic representations made in
common by the other Governments, have not, however, attained
their object.   The Porte has remained unshaken in its formal refusal
of any effective guarantee for the security of its Christian subjects,
and has rejected the conclusions of the Constantinople conference.
Wishing to essay every possible means of conciliation in order to
persuade the Porte, we proposed to the other Cabinets to draw up a
special protocol, comprising the most essential conditions of the Constantinople conference, and to invite the Turkish Government to adhere to this international act, which states the extreme limits of our
peaceful demands.   But our expectation was not fulfilled.   The
Porte did not defer to this unanimous wish of Christian Europe,
and did not adhere to the conclusions of the protocol.

"Having exhausted pacific efforts, we are compelled by the
haughty obstinacy of the Porte to proceed to more decisive acts, feel-

ing that our equity and our own dignity enjoin it. By her refusal, Turkey places us under the necessity of having recourse to arms.

"Profoundly convinced of the justice of our cause, and humbly committing ourselves to the grace and the help of the Most High, we make known to our faithful subjects that the moment foreseen when we pronounced words to which all Russia responded with complete unanimity has now arrived. We expressed the intention to act independently when we deemed it necessary, and when Russia's honor should demand it. In now invoking the blessing of God upon our valiant armies, we give them the order to cross the Turkish frontier.

" ALEXANDER."

On the same day, Prince Gortchakoff addressed a circular to the Russian Ambassadors at Foreign Courts, in which he undertook to justify the action of Russia as a legitimate and necessary consequence of the Porte's refusal to accept the London protocol. The Russian Chancellor has long been admired as a writer of diplomatic notes, many of which are regarded as masterpieces of this kind of literature, and it was therefore to be expected that the circular in which he was to explain the causes of what every one thought would turn out one of the most memorable wars in the world's history, would be worthy of his reputation. The consummate ability of this document was indeed admitted on all sides, even by those who did not believe in the soundness of its reasoning. Like the Emperor's manifesto, it is an indispensable part of any history of this war, and we therefore give it here entire. It is as follows:

"Since the beginning of the Eastern crisis the Imperial Cabinet has exhausted all the means in its power in order to bring about, by the co-operation of the Great Powers of Europe, a lasting peace with Turkey. All the proposals successively made to the Porte as a result of the understanding arrived at between the Cabinets of Europe, have been met by it with obstinate resistance. The protocol signed in London on the 19th (31st) of March in this year has been the last expression of the united wishes of Europe. The Imperial Cabinet had suggested it as a last effort of conciliation. It had made known by a declaration bearing the same date, and accompanying the protocol, the conditions which, if loyally and sincerely accepted, and executed by the Ottoman Government, might bring about the re-es-

tablishment and consolidation of peace. The Porte has just answered
this declaration by a new refusal. This contingency had not been
foreseen in the protocol of London. In formulating the wishes and
decisions of Europe, the protocol had confined itself to a stipulation
that in case the Great Powers should be deceived in their hope of
seeing the Porte energetically adopt the measures destined to improve the condition of the Christian populations—measures unanimously recognized as indispensable to the tranquillity of Europe—
they reserved to themselves the right of consulting together as to the
means most suitable for insuring the well-being of these populations
and the interests of general peace.

" Thus the Cabinets had taken thought of the contingency that
the Porte should not fulfill the promises which it had made, but not
that the Porte should reject the demands of Europe. At the same
time the declaration made by Lord Derby, after the signing of the
protocol, had established the fact that as the British Government had
only consented to sign the protocol with a view to the interests of
the general peace, it was to be understood at the outset that, in case
this object should not be attained—especially the reciprocal disarmament and peace between Turkey and Russia—the protocol should be
considered as null and void. The refusal of the Porte, and the motives
on which this refusal is founded, leave no ground for hoping that
she will now defer to the wishes and advice of Europe, and afford no
guarantee for the adoption of reforms, suggested for the improvement of the condition of the Christian subjects of the Porte Peace
with Montenegro is thus rendered impossible, and it is impossible,
also, to complete the conditions which would bring about disarmament and pacification. In these circumstances, all prospect of successful attempts at conciliation is at an end. There remains no other
alternative than either to prolong a state of things which the powers
have declared incompatible with their interests, and with those of
Europe in general, or to try and obtain by force what the unanimous
attempts of the Cabinets have failed to obtain from the Porte by
persuasion. Our august master has resolved himself to undertake
the work, which His Majesty had invited the Great Powers to undertake in common with him. His Majesty has therefore ordered
his armies to cross the frontier of Turkey. In taking upon himself
this task, our august master fulfills a duty which is imposed upon him
by the interests of Russia, whose peaceful development is seriously
impeded by the permanent disorder of the East. His Imperial

Majesty is persuaded that in taking this step he is consulting at the same time the views and the interests of Europe."

Prince Gortchakoff also wrote to Tevfik Bey, the Turkish Ambassador at St. Petersburg, notifying him of the assumption of hostilities by Russia:

"The earnest negotiations between the Imperial Government and the Porte for a desirable pacification of the East not having led to the desired accord, His Majesty, my august master, sees himself compelled, to his regret, to have recourse to force of arms. Be, therefore, so kind as to inform your Government that from to-day Russia considers herself in a state of war with the Porte."

The note also stated that Turkish subjects residing in Russia had the option of leaving the country or remaining, and that in the latter case they would enjoy the full protection of the laws. The Ambassador having been offered passports for himself and the members of his embassy, took leave of the Russian Government in a courteous note, and the rupture of diplomatic relations between the two countries was completed. The Turkish Government immediately published a reply to the Russian declaration of war. After reviewing the part played by Russia during the insurrection of 1875, and the war of 1876, the Porte appealed in this document to the mediation of the powers on the strength of the eighth article of the Treaty of Paris in the following terms:

"The Sublime Porte falls back on Article 8 of the Treaty of Paris, which is in these terms: 'Should there arise between the Sublime Porte and one or more of the other Signatary Powers any misunderstanding threatening the maintenance of their relations, the Sublime Porte and each of the powers, before having recourse to the employment of force, will give the other contracting parties an opportunity of preventing this extremity by their mediatory action.' Although it is not the Ottoman Government which threatens to take the initiative of aggression, and although, consequently, it was by rights the part of the Russian Government to appeal to these stipulations of the Treaty of Paris, this Imperial Government, in order to avoid all misunderstanding, applies to the Signatary Powers of that treaty for them to use their good offices in the grave circumstances in which it is placed, by applying the Article before mentioned, and thus putting an end to the dangerous tension affecting the relations of the two States by means of such mediatory action in conformity with right and treaty. Apart from all treaty stipulation, the action of the powers would even be justified on the ground on which, according to the declaration of her *Chargé d'Affaires* at Constantinople, Russia desires to found her present military action, in alleging the refusal of the Porte to agree to the proposals made to it by all the powers, and to the document signed by them, and by pointing out that her conduct thus conforms as well with the provisions of Article 8 of the Treaty of Paris as with the motives for the rupture assigned by Russia. The Sublime Porte expresses the conviction that the friendly powers, true to the feeling of benevolent interest which they have never ceased to manifest to the Ottoman Empire, will seize this opportunity to arrest the breaking out of a great war, thus sparing these countries the painful extremities with which they are threatened, and Europe herself the trouble and danger resulting from a conflict between two States—a conflict of which the Sublime Porte can justly repudiate the entire responsibility."

Although the outbreak of a new Eastern war had for years been regarded as probable, and during the last two weeks as unavoidable and immediate, a profound impression was produced by the official declaration. It was fully and generally understood that momentous results might follow its issue. Attention was called by many leading newspapers of Europe, to the remarkable silence of the Imperial manifesto as to the suspected intentions of Russia to annex, if victorious, considerable portions of Turkish territory. But few persons were found in the countries of Christendom who expressed a warm and unreserved sympathy with the Turks. The bitterest enemies of Russia did not deny that the Turkish Government had contracted great guilt by the failure to improve the wretched condition of its Christian subjects, and that the stubborn refusal of the Porte to listen to the advice of the Great Powers of Europe was foolhardy and reckless. The enthusiastic sympathy which the Mohammedan world expressed with the hazardous step of its foremost representative was, of course, of no practical avail, and was apt to hurt the Turks more than to benefit them, because it might be expected to produce a strong reaction in the Christian countries. Russia met with the wildest applause from all the Slavic nations except the Poles, and if any further proof had been needed that the much-talked-of Pan-Slavic agitations had not been altogether devoid of consequences, it was now furnished by the comment of the Slavic press on the Eastern war. In the Christian countries outside of the Slavic world, public opinion was greatly divided. Strong anti-Turkish sentiments were expressed by those who were deeply convinced of the prime importance of restoring the ascendency of the Christian religion in the East, as the first condition of its political and social regeneration; by those who believed in a special mission of the Eastern Church, for aiding in the reunion of the Christian Church; by those who had been waiting upon the fall of the Ottoman Empire as a fulfillment of Biblical prophecy; by many liberals, especially in England, who believed, with Mr. Gladstone, that the Turks were irremediably cruel and oppressive, and that England ought not to hold out to them any hope of material or moral aid; by radicals, like Garibaldi, who demanded the expulsion of the Turks to make room for the introduction of self-government. Strong anti-Russian sentiments, on the other hand, were uttered by those who, in the rapid aggrandizement of Russia, saw a danger for its more highly cultivated neighbors, and for all Europe. All parties, however, agreed in picturing in the most sombre colors the horrors which the world must be prepared to witness in the coming war.

The obstinate refusal by the Porte of all the demands of the Constantinople conference and the London protocol had been partly inspired by the firm belief of the Turkish statesmen, that if war was once declared between Russia and Turkey, England would be forced by her own interest to take part in it on the side of Turkey. This hope was not fulfilled. In the answer to the Russian note which was on July 1st addressed to Lord Loftus, the British Ambassador in St. Petersburg, Earl Derby, the British Secretary of State for Foreign Affairs, strongly disapproved the action of Russia, and especially entered a solemn protest against the assumption that it was acting with the concurrence of Europe, and in the interest of other powers, but he confined himself to this declaration and abstained from any intimation of an active participation in the war, at present or in future. In the violent debates which the declaration of war called forth in the English Parliament, the ministers qualified their policy as one of neutrality, and even deemed it expedient to defend themselves from the imputation of being indifferent to the ill-treatment of the Christians in Turkey. The other Governments of Europe, as well as that of the United States, promptly issued official declarations of neutrality.

In Russia, the events of 1875 and 1876 had produced great excitement. This was aided and increased by Pan-Slavic agents throughout the Empire. It was well-known that Pan-Slavic committees had collected moneys and provisions in Russia for the Servian cause, while large numbers of Russians had entered the service under General Tchernayeff. In the middle of November, 1876, the Czar had ordered the mobilization of the greater part of the European army, as well as of the entire army of the Caucasus, and, consequently, two large armies were concentrated by Russia on its Turkish borders.

The army of the South, or of the Pruth, was placed under the command of the Grand Duke Nicholas, a brother of the Emperor, with its headquarters at Kishenev, and was concentrated on both banks of the Lower Dniester, and between this river and the Pruth. General Nepokoitchitzky was appointed chief of the staff, which was very numerous, and was increased by the addition of a fully-equipped bureau for the administration of the Slavic provinces south of the Danube, which were to be captured. The powers, military and political, of the Commander-in-chief were very great, and in order to make him as much as possible independent of interference from St. Petersburg, he was authorized to decide for himself as to the strategical movements to be executed ; to appoint governors for the provinces which should be occupied ; to make promotions in the army up to the grade of lieutenant-general, and to grant certain decorations. This army was composed of four corps:—the eighth, under Lieutenant-General Radetzky ; the ninth, under Lieutenant-General Baron Krüdener ; the eleventh, under Lieutenant-General Prince Shachovsky ; and the twelfth, under Lieutenant-General Vannovsky, and included eight divisions of infantry, of two brigades, or four regiments each ; four divisions of cavalry, each consisting of four regiments and a brigade of mounted artillery ; and eight brigades of field artillery.

Besides this force, a second army was formed for the defense of the coasts of the Black Sea, and was placed under the special command of Lieutenant-General Semeka, with its headquarters at Odessa. It was composed of two corps:—the seventh, under Lieutenant-General Ganyetzky II., and the tenth corps under Lieutenant-

GRAND DUKE NICHOLAS.

EVENING PRAYER IN A CANTONMENT OF RUSSIAN SOLDIERS
AT KISHINEV.

General Prince Voronsoff. The strength of the two armies in men, horses, and guns, was:

	Men	Horses	Guns.
Army of operation (four corps), . . .	144,000	32,800	432
Second army (two corps), ...	72,000	16,400	216
	216,000	49,200	648

. The following additional troops were also available: the third and fourth brigades of chasseurs, under Major-General Dobrovalsky, and Major-General Zviazinsky, respectively; the Bulgarian militia, Major-General Stolyetoff, composed of Bulgarian refugees in Rumania; the combined Cossack division, Lieutenant-General Skobeleff; nine Cossack regiments of the second class; the Don-Cossack batteries, No. 8–11, and No. 15; two mountain batteries of 8 guns each; the third brigade of sappers; the third and fourth battalions of pontooners; a park of siege artillery, consisting of 400 guns; two companies of marines with 24 torpedo-boats in parts all ready to be put together; two squadrons of field *gendarmes;* fourteen transport divisions of 350 wagons each; a reserve depot of 12,000 horses; and the escort of the Grand Duke commanding, consisting of the first sotnie of Guard Cossacks of Terek; the first sotnie of Guard Cossacks of Kuban, and two companies of Plastuni (Kuban Cossacks on foot).

Forty-eight hours before the declaration of war, small Russian detachments had crossed the Pruth and occupied several important positions in Rumania, including the railroad station at Jassy, and the railroad bridge over the Sereth at Barboschi. It was all the more important to secure this bridge and protect it by batteries, as it was to be supposed that the enemy would make every effort to destroy it. Its importance lay in the fact that it was the sole means of communication by railroad, between the two sides of the river, over which the greater part of the army of operation had to be brought in order to assume the offensive along the whole line of the Danube. The Turks, however, made no attempt to destroy the railroads of Rumania, not even the Barboschi bridge. It was supposed that their policy on this point was governed by a desire to give to Rumania no pretext for forming an alliance with Russia.

Immediately upon the declaration of war the Russian troops began to cross the Pruth in two wings or columns. The left wing was composed of the eleventh and seventh corps. The 11th corps had been stationed shortly before the outbreak of the war at Kubai, in

12

the extreme south-western corner of Bessarabia. Beginning its march on April 24th it reached Galatz and Braila on May 4th. The advanced guard of these corps had been in these towns as early as April 25th. Reni was also occupied. The 7th corps marched from Tatar Bunar on Kilia and Ismail, the last troops reaching these places on May 5th. The right wing, which was composed of the 8th, 9th, and 12th corps, and to which the headquarters of the Grand Duke Nicholas had been attached, marched on the line Kishenev, Byrlat, Tekutch, Buseo, Bucharest. The headquarters were located on May 6th at Jassy, and on May 15th at Ployeshti.

· Rumania had remained neutral during the wars of 1875 and 1876, and had attracted but little attention from the outside world. But as the probability of a Russo-Turkish war increased, and Russia began to mass her forces on the Rumanian border, its position became a very doubtful one, lying as it did directly between the two belligerent powers. The progress of events forced it to take sides with one party or the other, and on April 16, 1877, Prince Charles concluded a convention with Russia, in which he assured to the Russians a free passage, and the treatment due a friendly army. The Czar, on the other hand, bound himself to respect the rights of Rumania. According to an additional convention, the Russians were allowed to use Rumanian roads, railways, rivers, and telegraphs. The resources of the country were placed at their disposal for the supply of the army. The Rumanian authorities were to assist in erecting camps and forwarding baggage. Russian military trains and telegrams were to have the precedence of ordinary traffic. The Russians were empowered to complete unfinished railroads, and the necessary ground for this purpose was to be ceded to them. The chief of the Russian Military Traffic Department was empowered, subject to the approval of the Rumanian Minister of Works, to dismiss Rumanian railway officials. The Russians were allowed to establish military stations and hospitals anywhere except in Bucharest. Rumania would, if required, provide material for the construction of boats, ships, and bridges. Articles intended for the Russian army would be admitted into Rumania, duty free. The Rumanian authorities would assist in capturing Russian deserters. All the expenses incurred through the passage of the Russians were to be paid in cash within two months. An explanatory report annexed to the convention said Russia was obliged to intervene in Turkey because Mussulman fanaticism and the weakness of the Turkish Government allowed no hope of reform, and as Russia desired to respect the inviolability of Rumania, the present convention was concluded.

When the existence of this convention became known, in the latter part of April, the Turkish Government informed the Rumanian agent at Constantinople, that in view of the above convention, and the entrance of Russian troops into Rumanian territory, the Porte no longer regarded the Prince and the Rumanian authorities as free agents, but considered that they were in the power of the enemy, and could therefore hold no more official communication with them. Rumanian subjects in Turkey were at the same time placed under the direct jurisdiction of the Turkish authorities. In consequence of this action the Rumanian agent retired from Constantinople. The Porte also addressed a note respecting the attitude of Rumania to the powers, in which it accused Prince Charles of having "betrayed the interests of his country, and the confidence of his suzerain, besides disappointing the hopes cherished by Europe when it established the united principalities."

Such faithlessness could not, according to the note, be too strongly condemned. On May 21st an order of the day was unanimously adopted in both the Rumanian Chambers, declaring the independence of the principality, and recognizing the existence of a state of war between Rumania and Turkey. Prime Minister Cogalniceano addressed a note to the powers on the 3d of June, notifying them of the new attitude of the country. The Turkish Government, in a note of June 5, protested against the Rumanian declaration of independence, and asserted that "it intended to preserve its rights without regard to the actions or the words of the rebellious Government of Moldavia-Wallachia, and it reserved for itself the right to use such measures against the principalities as seemed proper in its estimation." The strength of the Rumanian army was variously estimated. The most probable estimate was that which placed it at 38,000 infantry, 8,200 cavalry, and 120 field guns. On May 10th Prince Charles published a decree, assuming the chief command of his troops, and appointing as his chief of staff, General Slaniceano; as commander of the first corps, Gen. Lupu; and of the second corps, Gen. Radovici.

Early in May three more corps were added to the Russian army of operation, viz.: the fourth corps, from Minsk, under the command of Lieutenant-General Zotoff; the thirteenth corps, from Shitomir, under Lieutenant-General Hahn; and the fourteenth corps, from Kiev, under Lieutenant-General Zimmerman. Besides these troops, there were a large number of separate regiments of Cossacks, pioneers, engineers, and others; and the marine equipage included twenty-four small screw-steamers, which were taken along in parts and put together on the Danube. Taken all in all, the army of the Danube was composed as follows:

	Men	Cannon.
16 Infantry Divisions..............................	254,784	768
2 Brigades of Sharpshooters	7,632	..
9¼ Cavalry Divisions	38,711	114
7 Separate Regiments of Don Cossacks.....................	4,900	..
6 Separate Batteries of Don Cossacks	?	36
Total.	305,027	918

The engineers, the marine detachments, the siege artillery, and various other detachments were not included in these numbers. Counting them at 20,000 men, we would have a total of 325,000 men. Allowing 75,000 men for the sick and wounded, there would still remain 250,000 men, with 170,000 rifles, 23,000 sabres, and 918 cannon. This army was increased by the Rumanian and Bulgarian contingents to 200,000 rifles, 27,000 sabres, and 1,038 field-guns.

The valley of the Danube, which had again become the seat of war between Russia and Turkey, has been the scene of many battles. The Emperor Trajan for several years carried on war against the Dacians, who lived between the Theiss, the Pruth, and the Danube, occupying the territory of the present Rumania and Transylvania. In the year 103 he conquered the Dacians completely, and made their country a Roman province. He did not, however, take possession of what is now called the Dobrudja, recognizing its poverty and sterility as well as its uselessness in a strategical point of view. But in order to protect the rich and fertile country south of the Danube against invasions, he erected a triple wall of earth at the point where the solid ground between the Danube and the Black Sea was narrowest. Since that time the Danube has been the scene of many wars between the different nations living upon it. In the war of 1854 Trajan's wall played a very important part. The Turks, in the beginning of the war, abandoned the Dobrudja, but made a halt at the wall, where they inflicted two severe defeats on the Russians on April 10th at Kostelli, and on April 22d at Tchernavoda.

The river Danube forms the northern boundary of Turkey proper from the Iron Gate, in the Carpathian Mountains, to its mouths at the Black Sea, a distance of 584 miles measured along the navigable channel. The river, at the outbreak of the war, presented a formidable defense for Turkey. General McClellan, in the *North American Review*, speaking of it, says: " Below the Iron Gate the Danube, except when divided by islands into several arms, is nowhere less than nine hundred paces in width, often more than double that. In places it is from seventy to eighty feet deep, often shallower, but always a deep river, nowhere fordable. There is only one place, at Tultcha, where a sandbar reduces its depth so much as to render a pile bridge practicable; at all other points bridges must be supported upon boats. The current averages about two and one-half miles per hour. As a rule the right, or Turkish bank commands the left bank, which is often marshy to the water's edge. The points suitable for crossing large bodies of troops are few, and are generally covered by fortifications on the Turkish bank."

Turkey, besides completely commanding the Black Sea with her navy, had a fleet of seventeen gun-boats on the Danube. The smaller boats were lightly armored, so as to resist the shot from field cannon, but the larger vessels were strongly plated to resist the heavy fortification guns which the Russians transported by their long land route, the only one open to them. Besides this fleet, the Turks had three monitors with movable turrets. Along the Turkish shore there was a line of strong fortresses, which in 1828 and 1853 had resisted the attacks of the Russians, and between them was a chain of smaller forts, capable of holding back, for a short time, any force which the enemy could throw across the river.

The fortresses on this line were indicated as follows, commencing at the west: Ada-Kale, on a rocky island of about eight hundred acres, situated in the middle of the river, where the channel is bounded on each side by nearly perpendicular rocks two thousand feet high, and utterly inaccessible to an enemy with even the smallest cannon. This fortress is above the cataract of the Iron Gate, and is so placed as to be able to prevent the passage of any gun-boat down the river, or of any land force along the only road— the "Trajan Way"—which is an admirably built modern Macadam road, over the same ground upon which the Roman Emperor built a military road in A.D. 78. The next fortress is Widin, one hundred miles below Ada-Kale, on the right bank, opposite Kalafat, a Rumanian fortress.

Widin, which is one of the most important posts on the river, is built on hills, and has a population of about thirty thousand. It was very strongly fortified with works containing from two hundred to three hundred cannon. Kalafat, immediately opposite, was also strongly fortified, as were besides two high hills beyond the town. The Turks certainly missed a grand opportunity in not occupying Kalafat and the hills surrounding it, and using it as a bridge-head. This could have been done the more easily as the Rumanian troops had retired from it on the 26th of April, and from that date up to May 4th, when they again entered it, it remained entirely unprotected. The fortresses next in order are Lom, Rahova, Nicopolis, and Sistova, dividing about equally the distance between Widin and Rustchuk. Rustchuk is, like Widin, one of the strongest points on the river, and formed, with Silistria, Varna, and Shumla, what was known as the celebrated Turkish quadrilateral. It has been the scene of numerous sieges, and has been destroyed and rebuilt several times. The town of Giurgevo, opposite to it, was built in the early part of the present century, as a bridge-head for Rustchuk. A correspondent of the London *News*, who passed down the river on April 25th, wrote, that for a distance of three miles along the margin of the stream—from far above the town to the bluff far below it—the bank was thickly studded with earthwork batteries, some looking due across the river, some facing up-stream, others fronting down-stream, so that the cannon mounted behind the massive parapets could sweep with front and flanking fire the whole broad bosom of the Danube so thoroughly that a row-boat could not run the gauntlet of their iron hail-storm. But the brink of the river was not the only locality that was thus protected. Behind the low bluff along the bank an undulating plateau, about two miles broad, extended backward to a continuous rising ground having a series of knolls upon its surface. On each of these knolls was an intrenched work. So far as the correspondent could see with his glass from the river, the ridge above was "a great intrenched camp, with an elaborate earthwork redoubt on each flank, and another in the center." The fortifications thus consisted of three lines, all of which "are extremely formidable." The next fort is Turtukai, half way between Rustchuk and Silistria.

Silistria, the second fortress of the quadrilateral, is one of the strongest fortified towns in the East. It is a very ancient city, and in the vicinity are the remains of fortifications which were erected during the Byzantine Empire. In 971 the Emperor routed the Russians under Sviatoslav. In 1773 it was again besieged by the Russians, and still again in 1779, when they suffered severe losses. In 1810 it capitulated—the first and only time but one in history. In 1828 another siege was laid and continued several months, the Russians at last retiring. In 1829, however, it was reduced, and held as a pledge for the payment of an indemnity by the Porte. When new troubles with Russia were apparent in 1849–'50, the fortifications were greatly strengthened by the addition of twelve detached forts, of which, the one on the hill commanding the town, is said to be one of the best military works of the time. In April, 1854, it was invested by an army of 50,000 Russians, which was afterward increased to 70,000, and a siege begun which continued until near the 1st of July. A bombardment was kept up for three weeks, midnight attacks were made, 30,000 men attempted to gain the town, but all without success. The Russians retired and retreated across the river. It is recorded that 50,000 shot and shell were thrown upon the town, while the Russians lost 12,000 men and had 20,000 laid up in hospitals. Below Silistria are Tchernavoda, Hirsova, Matchin, Isaktcha, and Tultcha. On the Rumanian side are Braila, Galatz, Reni, and Ismail Of these forts, Braila, Matchin, and Tultcha are especially important, as they command the Dobrudja. Another place of importance to the Dobrudja is the small port of Kustendji on the Black Sea.

The second line of the Turkish defense was the Balkan range of mountains, which rises to a height varying from 5,000 feet in the west to 2,000 feet in the eastern extremity. The distance from the Danube to the top of the Balkans is about fifty or sixty miles, across a rough and broken country. The declivities of the mountains themselves are covered with forests. The climate is very cold and bleak. The best pass through the mountains is from Tirnova to Slivno. Besides the few passes known to and defended-by the Turks, there are quite a number of secret passes known to the Bulgarians only. The most important fortresses at the northern base of the Balkans are Shumla and Varna, the former considered one of the strongest points in Turkey, at which a number of roads converge. Varna is a port on the Black Sea, also strongly fortified, and connected by railroad with Rustchuk. Beyond the Balkan range the country slopes gradually down to the Sea of Marmora. A railroad connects Adrianople with Constantinople, a distance of seventy miles. The land approaches to Constantinople are protected by a range of steep hills, extending from

Kara Bournu on the Black Sea, to Silivri on the Sea of Marmora. Here it was that Attila was stopped and hurled back in his victorious career.

Very little was known of the strength and the disposition of the Turkish forces at the beginning of the war, as nothing like an *ordre de bataille* exists in the Turkish army. According to all reports, however, the army of the Danube, inclusive of the garrisons, and exclusive of the troops stationed at Nissa, did not exceed 200,000 men. From this number the troops assigned to garrisons should be deducted: for Widin 15,000 men, for Rustchuk and Silistria each 12,000 men, for Varna 15,000 men, for Shumla 20,000 men, and for the other smaller fortresses 30,000 men, making together 104,000, which would leave for the army of operation hardly more than 90,000 or 100,000 men. Included in this number were 20,000 irregular troops. In May, the Sultan ordered a draft of 200,000 men, in which, for the first time, the Christians and the inhabitants of Constantinople were to be included. Large concentrations of troops had taken place only around Widin, Rustchuk, and Shumla, while a corps of 20,000 men was said to have been stationed in the Dobrudja. At the outbreak of the war considerable movements of troops took place from Widin and the Dobrudja, toward the center, in the direction of Rustchuk and Silistria, while at the same time the reserves, which had been stationed at Adrianople and Sophia, as well as a part of those at Constantinople, were moved across the Balkans. After these movements of troops had been completed the strength of the forces stationed at Shumla and forward of it, on the line of Rustchuk, Silistria, and Sistova, was estimated at about 128 battalions, 600 men each, 20 squadrons and 116 field-guns, inclusive of the garrisons of the fortresses of the Danube. The Dobrudja corps, inclusive of the garrison of Varna, was estimated at the highest at 39 battalions, 8 squadrons, and 42 guns, while the troops concentrated around Widin were estimated at 60 battalions, 16 squadrons, and 150 guns, making in all 227 battalions, 44 squadrons, and 338 field-guns. The *Preussische Militär Wochenblatt* (Military Weekly), in its issue of May 23d, gave the same numbers, estimating the strength of battalions as varying between 300 and 1,000 men, and that of squadrons at 150. It summed up the entire force, inclusive of garrisons, at 159,000 infantry, 6,600 cavalry, and 338 guns. To this must be added about 20,000 Circassians and an unknown number of irregulars. The regular infantry were all armed with breech-loaders, and the artillery consisted of

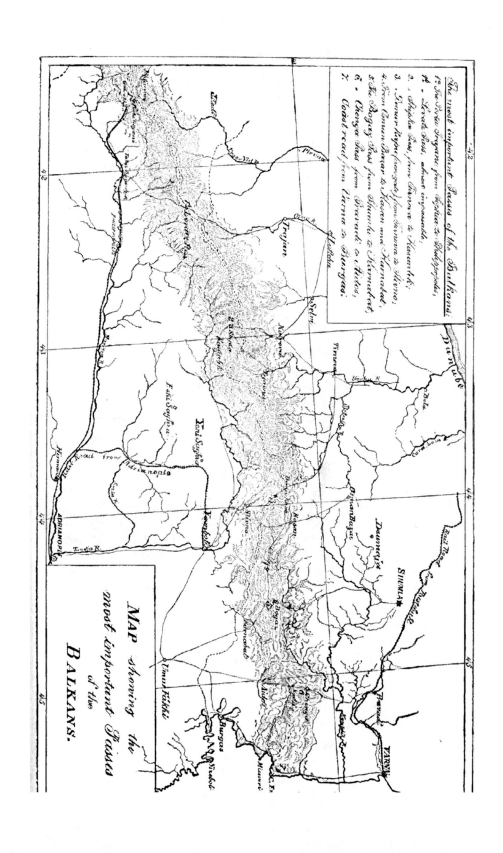

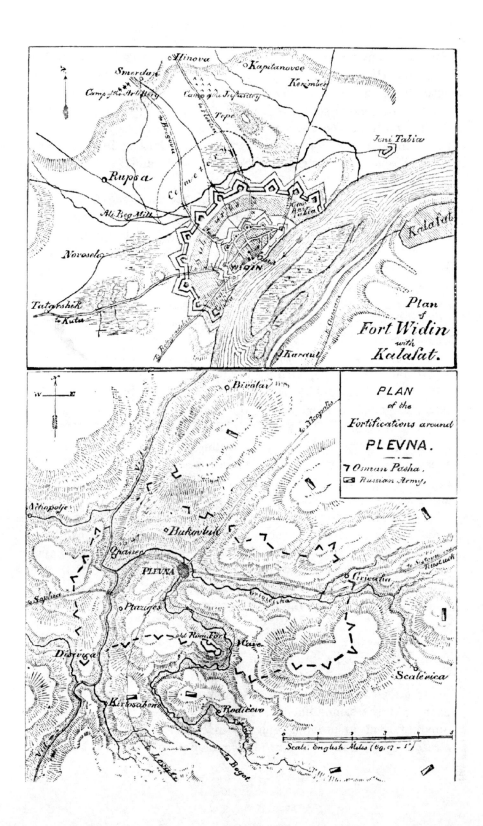

Plan
of
Fort Widin
with
Kalafat.

PLAN
of the
Fortifications around
PLEVNA.

Osman Pasha.
Russian Army.

Scale. English Miles (0g. 07 = 1")

Krupp cannon, the most of which were said to have been paid for by Abdul Hamid from his private purse. The commander of the entire Turkish forces in Europe was Abdul Kerim Pasha, and the chief of his general staff, the Ferik Aziz Pasha. The commander of the army of the Danube was the Mushir Achmet Eyub Pasha; in the Dobrudja, Ali Pasha; in Varna, Blum Pasha; in Rustchuk, Tahir Pasha; in Silistria, the Ferik Selami; and in Widin, the Mushir Osman Pasha.

Besides the above, the Russian *Invalide* and the *Preussiche Militar Wochenblatt* estimated that the following troops were in European Turkey in the middle of May: 6 battalions, 4 squadrons, 12 guns around Nissa, as a corps of observation against the mobilized Servian army; Mushir Zamik Pasha with 36 battalions, 20 squadrons, and 42 guns, as a general reserve in Constantinople, of which, however, a considerable number were sent to the coast of Caucasia; Mushir Suleiman Pasha with 37 battalions and 54 field and mountain cannon in Herzegovina, with his headquarters in Trebigne; Veli Pasha with 26 battalions, 1 squadron, and 36 guns, together, 18,000 men, in Bosnia, with his headquarters at Serayevo; Ali Saib with 25 battalions and 42 field and mountain guns, 18,000 men, in Albania against Montenegro and the Miridites, with his headquarters at Scutari; Achmet Pasha with 25 battalions, 4 squadrons, 30 guns, on the boundary of Greece; Mehemet Ali with 14 battalions, 2 squadrons, and 18 guns, in Rascia, between the southern boundary of Servia and the eastern boundary of Montenegro; 16 battalions and 18 guns on the islands of the Ægean Sea, principally in Crete, where the Mushir Rauf was in command. The army in Europe then numbered in all about 412 very unequal battalions and 75 squadrons, making together 290,000 men and 12,000 horses, and 590 field and mountain guns, with a few field and mountain batteries. Of the irregular troops, only 12,000 Arnauts in Rascia and Albania, and 20,000 Circassians with the army of the Danube, could be counted on as reliable.

As soon as the Russians had secured the shores of the Danube from Kilia to Braila, they began to erect shore batteries and earthworks along the whole line, those at Barboschi, Braila, and Galatz being armed with heavy guns brought for this purpose from Kishenev. At the same time torpedoes were placed by the Russians opposite Reni, in order completely to blockade the passage of the stream at this bend. On May 3d, two monitors, stationed at Matchin, began to bombard the Russian positions at Braila. The firing continued on the 5th and 6th, and was answered by the Russians at first with their field artillery, and as their heavy siege guns began to arrive, with them also. The Turks afterward also bombarded Galatz, but with little effect. On May 11th a Russian battery above Braila had the good fortune to blow up the "Lufti Djelil," a Turkish monitor, which had two turrets, and was one of the largest on the river. It was destroyed by a shell from a Russian mortar going down the funnel into the engine-room, exploding and communicating the destruction to the powder magazine. The loss of the Turks was 150 men, the entire crew, and 5 guns.

Artillery duels took place also at various other points, particularly between Reni and Isaktcha, without, however, doing any serious damage to either side.

The Turks began to bombard several Rumanian towns from their positions opposite. Thus, on May 8th, Kalafat was bombarded from Widin, Oltenitza from Turtukai, and on the same day a Rumanian coast guard at Giurgevo was attacked by a Turkish monitor. A party of Bashi-Bazouks landed at Piketi, near the mouth of the Shyl, and burned several Rumanian merchantmen, but were driven back by Rumanian cavalry.

The Rumanian troops, in consequence of the undecided position of the Government, were, on the first day of the war, withdrawn from Kalafat and Giurgevo, but early in May they again took possession of these places, so that on the 8th they were able to answer the Turkish fire from Widin and other points.

A greater activity became perceptible in the movements of the Russian troops on the Rumanian railroads after the 10th of May. On the 14th, the headquarters of the commander-in-chief were removed from Jassy to Ployeshti, where the Grand Duke was received by Prince Charles of Rumania. A report which had been in circulation of the formation of a Bulgarian legion, three thousand strong, in Bessarabia, and its march to join the Imperial forces, received apparent confirmation from the appearance of a Bulgarian company of honor drawn up at the railroad station during the ceremonies of reception. On the 15th, the Grand Duke visited the Prince, and held a conference with him at Bucharest.

A daring feat against the Turkish iron-clads was performed on the 25th of May. The situation of the largest of the Turkish monitors having been ascertained, a party of Russians under the command of

Lieut. Dubashoff, and accompanied by a Rumanian officer, set out in the night toward the spot. A correspondent of the Leipsic *Gartenlaube*, who accompanied the Russians as far as the river bank, and witnessed the action while awaiting their return, thus describes what followed:

"Suddenly a shot was heard and then a second. The light of the second showed to me for an instant a Turkish guard on board the monitor. Now a shot was heard from the Rumanian shore. Five minutes afterward I again heard the paddling of wheels in the water, and soon one of the little steamers landed. One of the officers held one end of the wire, which I had before seen fastened to the torpedo.

"'Everything worked capitally,' an officer said. 'We took the monitor in the rear, while the others came in front. We reached the keel unnoticed,' and pointing to a dripping artillery-man, 'our diver there adjusted the thing in the right place. Those fellows must sleep very hard. They really had only one man on guard. He it was who challenged the other boat in Turkish. Our Rumanian friend, who really speaks Turkish very well, took the part of an officer belonging to the fleet, who was returning from Matchin rather tipsy, and told the guard not to make any fuss about it. When the steamer moved off, the Turk began to fire, but then, of course, it was too late. Here are the others.' . . . . After a while the officer holding the wire, asked: 'Is it time?' The engineer answered with a nod. . . . . . 'Back, back all!' some one cried out, and we all rushed up the bank, where the battery was standing. Then there was an explosion so terrible that even now it seems to resound in my ears. After a short interval, another and then still another and louder explosion, and that was all. . . . . The monitor had been literally blown into shreds by the terrible effect of the torpedoes filled with dynamite."

The Emperor Alexander arrived in Ployeshti on the 6th of June, accompanied by his sons, the Grand Dukes Alexander, Vladimir, and Sergius, as well as by his military staff and his diplomatic and political chancery.

From this time until the crossing of the Danube no action of any importance took place, although artillery duels were kept up almost constantly between the batteries on the opposite shores. The Russians continued their advance rather slowly during May and June, considering their first spurt to the Danube. Their tardiness was chiefly owing to the impassable condition of the Rumanian roads, which, in consequence of incessant rains, had become almost bottomless, while the Danube, at as late a date as the beginning of June, was sixteen feet above its normal height. But all preparations for crossing were made. Four Russian pontoon-parks were sent by rail from Galatz to Bucharest and thence to the Danube. Wooden vessels were constructed at Slatina and Galatz, and after they had been brought by rail to Slatina on the Aluta, were all moved down the Aluta to Turnu-Magurelli, on the left bank of the Danube opposite Nicopolis. Torpedo boats were brought from Galatz to Slatina and to Fratesti near Giurgevo, in order to blockade the river, as soon as the crossing was possible, while gun-boats were brought up in parts to be put together and employed in scouting duty.

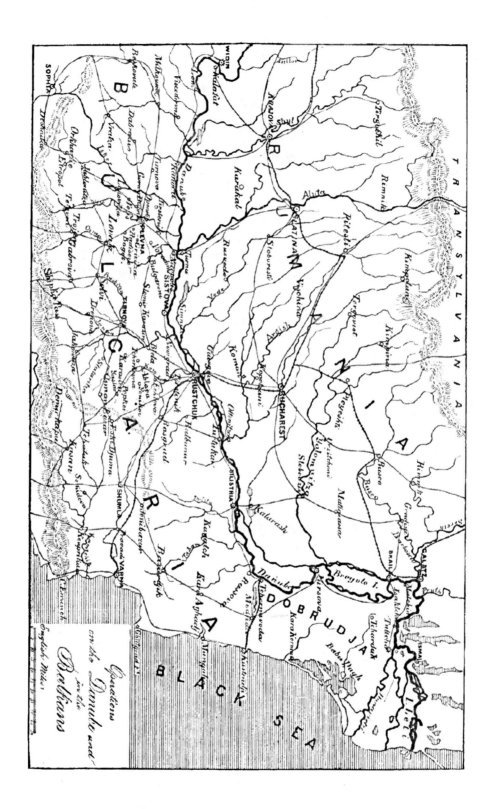

Operations on the Danube and in the Balkans

English Miles

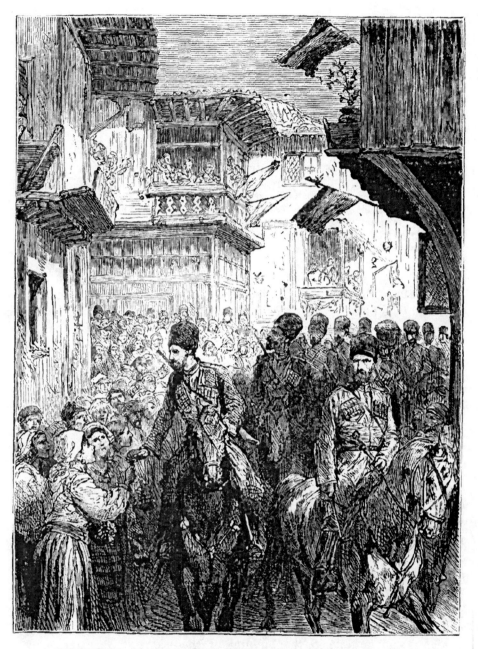

CIRCASSIAN CAVALRY PASSING THROUGH A TURKISH TOWN.

CHAPTER II.

Passage of the Danube at Galatz—Bombardment of Rustchuck—The Russians Cross at Sistova—Inactivity of the Turks—Proclamation of the Czar to the Bulgarians—Capture of Braila and of Tirnova—The Balkan Passes—Gourko Crosses the Balkans—Capture of the Shipka Pass—Advance of Gourko into Rumelia—The Russians Capture Lovatz—Storming of Nicopolis.

As the passage of the Danube was delayed from day to day, the Czar became impatient, and ordered the passage from Galatz and Braila to take place within three days, directing that everything be in readiness by that time, as he intended to be present to witness the passage. General Zimmermann, commanding at those points, pleaded for delay, and the Emperor reluctantly yielded. The passage was finally effected on June 23d. It was described as follows by the correspondent of the New York *Herald:*

"The programme was adroitly planned and carried out. It had been ascertained by Russian spies that the Turkish forces at Matchin were in no condition to oppose a crossing, if made in force, and that only straggling bands of Bashi-Bazouks were to be met among the low lands along the river. Accordingly before dawn a few barge loads of Cossacks were sent across from Galatz to Ghiacet. The crossing was assisted by small steamers, which performed the journeys with the barges as rapidly as possible. In this manner a sufficient number of these brave horsemen were soon across and mounted. They remained close to the river, having their sentries out to give notice of an approach of the enemy. The guns in the forts at Galatz fully covered the cavalry, and the gunners stood ready to serve their pieces at a signal from the Cossacks. So far as can be learned, the building of the bridge at Galatz partakes of the nature of a feint, because the great body of troops crossed into the Dobrudja at Braila.

"Meanwhile the same movement had been made at Braila. The barges at this place were not so large as at Galatz, and many valuable Cossack ponies either fell or leaped from them into the river, but they were mostly saved by being lassoed and thus towed to the shore. In some instances the horses swam ashore at the call of their masters, who remained on the barges. After considerable delay several hundred men were landed and formed on a grassy slope about a quarter of a mile from the river, the intervening land being so marshy that the horses were led over it with great difficulty. All being ready at both points, the telegraph was put in requisition from Braila, and a simultaneous movement took place, the Cossacks advancing with great rapidity into the Dobrudja. The force landed at Braila had by far the more difficult task, for they were compelled to extend their line to the utmost, while the detachment from Galatz advanced along the main road and larger paths, outside of which it would be impossible for an enemy to approach or to flank them, because of the marshy condition of the country. In less than two hours the two lines of horsemen had formed a junction, the distance between Galatz and Braila, measured on the inside of the bend in the river, being only eighteen miles. Thus was formed a cordon of Cossacks between the river's bank and the enemy. The prominent part which the Cossack was thus made to play in the first real aggressive movement into the enemy's territory in Europe is worth noticing. It fully justifies all that has been written about the important service which he, as a horseman, is likely to render to Russia in the war. This brings the Cossack squarely to the front, and makes of him what the Uhlan was to the troops of Prussia, ' *l'éclaireur par excellence.*'. Under cover of this Cossack cordon, the pontoons were towed into position, and the bridges at the two points were soon laid, every plank being ready and every man having a particular service to perform. The Galatz bridge was much more easily built than the one at Braila, because at the latter place, on the Dobrudja side, the long stretch of swamp land before referred to had to be planked for the passage of the artillery. The foot soldiers did not wait for this event, however. No sooner had the last plank been laid in the main structure than the men already drawn up in battalions were ordered to prepare for the crossing. Eight thousand men and two batteries of artillery then passed over as rapidly as possible, each battalion forming directly it had reached the dry ground. By the time the guns were ready to be brought over, preparations for landing them across the marsh were finished. The enemy in the shape of scattered, irregular cavalry, had shown themselves at various points, and when the main body of troops had formed and the batteries had been placed, the Cossacks were ordered forward to drive back the videttes. An advance was then made toward Matchin, the object being to attack at once, before the place could be reinforced. The Turks were found posted on a range of hills to the north-westward of the town. The batteries on these hills opened on the invading Russian troops, and a strong detachment of irregulars sallied out to meet their inveterate foes, the Cossacks. They did not risk a close encounter, however, and a few shells from the Russian battery posted on the assailed flank dispersed the Bashi-Bazouks and caused their inglorious retreat under cover of the batteries on the hills. Without delay the Russians were ordered to advance and charge the batteries. After a severe hand-to-hand fight the outlying fortifications were captured and the guns turned upon the fleeing Turks.

" The second assault followed as soon as the men could be re-formed, and, with the aid of the newly-acquired field-pieces, the heights were carried by storm. These most desperate struggles, in which the fighting was in many instances hand to hand, continued until late in the afternoon Driven from their intrenched position the Turks fell back on Matchin. Nightfall of Friday settled down over the hills and valleys, and the victorious invaders deemed it wiser to rest on the successes of the day than to attempt to follow up the retreat of the Turks. But the Russians bivouacked for the night in the deserted camp. The camp fires burned brightly and could be seen, doubtless, from the village of Matchin, distant only two and a half to three miles. During the night the utmost activity prevailed in the camp, and it was soon generally known that Matchin was to be attacked on the morrow. It was impossible to ascertain the losses, but from their exposed position it is probable the Russians lost more men than the Turks. Prisoners captured place the number of the Turkish garrison at 6,000 men, but it is believed that this estimate is too large. The Turkish force probably numbered 5,000, including the irregular cavalry. On yesterday (Saturday, June 24th) morning the battle was renewed During the night the Turks had made great efforts to strengthen some earthworks which were in front of the eastern or most feasible approach to the village, but after a few shells had been thrown into the intrenchments and the town the Turks evacuated the former. The Russians advanced and occupied the town only to find that it had been abandoned by the main body of the Turkish troops during the darkness.

Therefore by six o'clock on Saturday morning the Russians held the key to the Dobrudja."

The Russian left wing at the time of the crossing comprised divisions of the 4th, 13th, and 14th corps. These corps had been originally concentrated in Bessarabia, and were sent to the front to relieve the 7th and 11th corps as soon as the reserve corps of 50,000 men had been mobilized for the defense of Odessa, the Crimea, and the northern coast of the Black Sea. The troops that first crossed the Danube belonged to the 14th corps. In the following week, considerable activity was manifested throughout the Russian lines. Large bodies of troops were moved down from Slatina to the Danube, where they took up positions between Turnu-Magurelli and Simnitza. At the same time the artillery fire was resumed by the whole Russian line. The fiercest fire was at Rustchuck, where it was commenced on June 24th, and as the *Herald* correspondent described it: "It soon seemed as if every Russian gun was fired simultaneously, for the earth fairly trembled with the roar of the artillery and the shells flew over the doomed city with an awful and indescribable sound." The Turkish batteries promptly replied to the fire. The Russian fire, which seemed to have for its particular object the center of the city, caused great devastation. Mosques were destroyed and even hospitals and the foreign consulates were demolished. The house of the British Consul fared decidedly the worst, so that at last, in order to save his house from total destruction, the Consul raised the American flag, but even that expedient was without avail. On Monday the entire population left the city and fled to the interior. The town was completely destroyed by the terrible fire, although the fortifications remained practically intact. The Turks in reply partly destroyed Giurgevo, into which, it was stated, they threw 1,500 shells within two days. At Nicopolis also the firing was very severe. On Monday, June 25th, the Russians occupied Hirsova. Having observed that everything was very quiet there, a party of Cossacks first crossed the Danube near Kalaiash unopposed, advanced cautiously toward Hirsova and found it had been evacuated. On Tuesday, June 26th, the Russians succeeded in crossing from Simnitza to Sistova. This crossing, of great importance, as it opened the way for the hosts assembled along the Aluta, is described as follows by the correspondent of the London *Daily News :*

"With the darkness General Dragomiroff began his dispositions.

A COSSACK RECONNOISSANCE IN THE DOBRUDJA.

The first work was to plant in made emplacements a row of field-guns all along the edge of the flats to sweep with fire the opposite banks. This was while his infantry was being marched over the flats down into the cover of the willow wood. The darkness and the obstructions were both so great that all was not ready till the first glimmer of gray dawn. There was no bridge, but a number of river boats, capable of holding from fifteen to forty men each. These were dragged on carriages through the mud and launched in the darkness from under the spreading boughs of the willow trees. The troops embarked and pushed across as the craft arrived. Drag-omiroff stood on the slimy margin to bid his gallant fellows God-speed. He would fain have shown the way, for, although a scientific soldier, it was his duty to remain till later The grateful task devolved on Major-General Yolchine, whose brigade consisted of the regiments of Valinsk and Minsk, the Fifty-third and Fifty-fourth of the line. The boats put off singly, rowing across for the little cove, and later the little steam-tug was brought into requisition.

" For once the Turks had not spent the night watches in heavy sleep. Their few cannon at once opened fire on the boats, on the hidden masses among the willows and on the columns marching across the flat. Nor was this all. From the slopes above the cove there came at the boats a smart infantry fire. The Turkish riflemen were holding the landing place. Yolchine has not gained experience and credit in Caucasian warfare for nothing. His boat was leading. The Turkish riflemen were in position about fifty yards from the shore. He landed his handful and bade them lie down in the mud. One or two were down previously with Turkish bullets. He opened a skirmishing fire to cover the landing boats that followed. One by one these landed their freights, who followed the example of the first boat load.

"At length enough had accumulated. Young Skobeleff was there, a host in himself. Yolchine bade his men fix bayonets, stand up and follow their officers. There was a rush and a cheer that rang louder in the gray dawn than the Turkish volley that answered it. That volley was not fired in vain, but the Turks did not wait for cold steel. Yolchine's skirmishers followed them doggedly some distance up the slope, but for the time could not press on far from the base. Busily, yet slowly, the craft moved to and fro from shore to shore. The Russian guns had at once opened, when the Turkish fire showed that there was no surprise; but, however heavy a fire may be, it will not all at once crush another fire. The Turkish shells kept falling in the water, whistling through the willows, and bursting among the columns on the flat. One shell from a mountain gun fell into a boat containing two guns, their gunners, and the commandant of the battery. The boat was swamped at once, and all on board perished. This was the only serious casualty, but numerous Russian soldiers were falling on both sides of the river. Nevertheless the work was going steadily on, and when, soon after seven o'clock, I went to meet Prince Mirsky on the high ground before Simnitza, the report was that already the whole brigade of Yolchine had reached the other side, that a Russian battery was there, and that Dragomiroff himself had crossed. We stood for some time surveying the scene.

"Cast your eye down there to your left front athwart the flats, and note the masses of troops waiting there or marching on toward the cover of the willows. See the long row of guns in action there by the water's edge, covered by the battalions of infantry, in this case a mischievous conventionality, owing to the exposure, for the Turkish cannon will not just yet be wholly silenced. Note how deftly the Russian shells pitch into that earthwork on the verge of Sistova. But the gallant gunners stubbornly fight their guns under the rain of fire, and when one gun is quiet another gives tongue. And what a mark! Half an army corps out there on the flat, with no speck of cover save that patch of willows down there. Hark to the crackle of musketry fire on the wooded slopes rising out from the cove. No wonder Yolchine's skirmishers are moving, for that Turkish battery on the sky line is dropping shells with fell swiftness among the willow trees. Sistova seems stark empty. It might be a city of the dead. But the Turkish gunners cling to their posts and their guns with wonderful stanchness, amid clouds of dust thrown up by the shells which burst around them. Nor are the single pieces among the trees wholly quiet. Shells are dropping among the troops on the flat and the ambulance men are hurrying about with brancards or plodding toward the military surgery with heavy, blood-sodden burdens. You may watch the shells drop into the water, starring its surface as they fall as if it had been glass. What a wonder that one and all should miss those clumsy, heavy-laden craft which stud the water so thickly. A shell in one of these boats would produce fearful results among the closely-packed freight. Not less fell havoc would it work among the soldiers further on, massed there under the shelter of the clay bank.

" One realizes how great would have been the Russian loss if the Turks had been in any great force in the Sistova position, and how, after all, the Commander-in-chief might have been forced to take a denial, accepting the inevitable. But as the affair stands, the whole thing might have been a spectacle specially got up for the gratification of Simnitza enjoying the effect from the platform high-ground overhanging the flats. The laughter and bustle there are in strange contrast with the apparent absence of human life in Sistova, opposite. But then, Sistova was a victim lashed to the stake. Those on Simnitza Bluff knew their skins were safe.

" Prince Mirski has received his reports and final instructions: He gives word to his division to move down on to the flats, to be in readiness to cross. Previously, their march finished, they had been resting on the grassy uplands behind Simnitza. As we leave the plateau the cry rises that a Turkish monitor is coming down the Danube. Sure enough, near the head of the island is visible what seems to be a large vessel with two funnels moving slowly down the stream. Now the ferryboats may look out. Now is the opportunity for some dashing torpedo practice. But the Russian officers evince no alarm—rather, indeed, satisfaction The fact is, as we presently discern with the glass, that seeming monitor is really two large lighters lashed together, which the Russians are drifting down to assist in transporting the troops. No person is visible on board, yet some one must be steering, and the course held is a bold one. Slowly the lighters forge ahead past the very mouths of the Turkish cannon in the Sistova battery, and are barely noticed by a couple of shells. They bring to at the Rumanian shore higher up than the crossing place, and wait there for their freight. Prince Mirski takes his stand at the pontoon bridge to watch his division file past and greet the regiments as they pass him.

" But in front of the Ninth division comes a regiment of the brigade of riflemen formed specially for this war, and attached to no army corps. This brigade is armed with Berdan rifles, and comprises the finest marksmen of the whole army. Prince Mirski's division is made up of four historic regiments which suffered most heavily in Sebastopol during the great siege. They are the regiments of Yeletsk, of Sefsk, of Orloff, and of Brianski, the Thirty-third, Thirty-fourth, Thirty-fifth, and Thirty-sixth of the Russian line. Very gallantly they marched down the steep slope and across the bridge on to the swampy flats. Soon there greets them the scarcely

enlivening spectacle, the surgery of the second line, where the more
serious cases were being dealt with before forwarding them to the
house hospitals in Simnitza. As we passed, about twenty shattered
creatures were lying there on blood-stained stretchers waiting
their turn at the hands of the doctors. More than one I noticed required no further treatment than to be consigned to a soldier's
grave. Beyond the first swamp we met a fine young officer of the
Guards carried on a stretcher with a shattered leg. But the plucky
youngster raised himself jauntily on his elbow to salute the general,
and wrote a telegram in my note-book to acquaint his friends that
he was not much hurt. A little further on, as we were passing the
rear of the guns, the Grand Duke Nicholas the younger, son of the
Commander-in-chief, rode off from the battery to greet our general.
The members of the Imperial family of Russia do not spare themselves when other subjects of the Czar are exposing themselves on
the battle-field. In Russia it is not the fashion that lofty station
gives exemption from the more dangerous tasks of patriotism. , The
young Grand Duke had been across the Danube and was in high
spirits at the success of the enterprise.

"Going still forward toward the willows we all but stuck, horses
and all, in the deep, holding mud. It was admirable to see the
energy with which the heavily-laden soldiers of the infantry column
battled on doggedly through obstruction. I should have said earlier
that the troops were in complete marching order, and that for this
day they had discarded their cool, white clothing, and were crossing
in heavy blue clothing. Two reasons were assigned for this. One,
the greater warmth to the wounded in case of lying exposed to the
night chills. The other, that white clothing was too conspicuous.
The latter reason is rubbish. Blue on the light ground of the Danube
sand is more conspicuous than white. Everywhere, British scarlet
is more conspicuous than any other. The true fighting color is the
dingy kharki of our Indian irregulars.

"And what of the Turkish monitor? She had been hemmed in
by a cordon of torpedoes within the side channel to the south of the
island of East Vardim. Although she was puffing and blowing
furiously in her circumscribed area, a Russian battery moving down
the river bank on the Rumanian side, shelled her into a melancholy
victim of the acknowledged supremacy of the newest war machine.
So the resistance terminated, and what followed is mere routine work.
Iron pontoons began casually to make their appearance both from up-

stream and down-stream, and accumulated about the crossing places, being used for the time as ferryboats. A complete pontoon is in reserve at Simnitza, and will be on the water's edge to-night and be laid to-morrow. Probably there will be two bridges, for this is the crossing place of the main column, and will be the great Russian thorough-fare to and from Turkey. Simultaneously with the pontoon boats appeared on the scene the Emperor's brother, the Grand Duke Nicholas, with Gen. Nepokoitchitzky, and spoiled my prospects of dinner by requisitioning the whole hotel. The Emperor did not turn up.

" It is useless to waste more words. The crossing has been effected by a *coup de main* with marvelous skill and finesse. Until the last moment no hint was given. The foreign *attachés* were all abroad. The Emperor and suite were ostentatiously at Turnu-Magurelli, and yet further to promote the delusion, the Nicopolis position was assiduously bombarded the day before. The successful effort has probably cost only 1,000 men killed and wounded."

With this crossing effected, the Russians had made a great step forward. Throughout Europe, and particularly in England, the achievement created considerable excitement. Speaking of its importance, the London *Times* said :

" Since the days when an Emperor capitulated at Sedan, and a great army went into captivity from Metz, no event has created so intense an excitement as the passage of the Danube in force by the Russian army. In all the wars that have raged in the revolutionary period, which extends from 1848 to the present time, there has been no movement more colossal, more dramatic, and at the same time more closely affecting the interests of Europe and the future course of history."

The Russians, being now fully in the enemy's country, found the Turks chiefly massed on their left wing, in the garrisons occupying the fortresses of the quadrilateral. Away beyond their right wing was Osman Pasha with his garrison at Widin, who might at any time, however, move up into a more threatening proximity to them. They had to consider, before advancing in force, the necessity of protecting their wings, especially the left, where the Turks were very strong, and of guarding their communications over the river. Apparently, a division of their force so as to carry out both purposes would be a hazardous operation, and leave both columns too weak to perform their work efficiently. Yet the temptations to go forward were very strong. Directly before them lay the road to Adrianople and Constantinople, the thought of which is associated with so many dreams of glory to the Russian mind. From Sistova they might march to the Yantra, and along its borders to Biela, whence three roads diverge to Rustchuk, Tirnova, and Plevna; thence up the valley of the Yantra to the larger city of Tirnova, the ancient capital of the Bulgarian Czars, the meeting-place of the roads of Western Bulgaria, which is connected with Shumla by a road, and is the starting-point of two passes over the Balkans; further up the Yantra valley-road lay the towns of Drenova and Gabrova, from the latter of which places a good road leads, by way of Selvi and Lovatz, to West Bulgaria. From Gabrova also rises the mountain pass which leads over Shipka to Kasanlik in the Tundja valley, whence Adrianople may be reached either by marching down the Tundja, or by the shorter, more direct road through Eski Sagra and Kharskoi. The latter road has the advantage for a hostile force, that the railways from Yamboli to Kharskoi and from Adrianople to Philippopolis can be most quickly reached by it. The Russians received unexpected help in carrying out the bold policy which they concluded to adopt, from the unaccountable supineness of the Turkish generals.

Immediately after the crossing of the river, the Czar issued a proclamation to the Bulgarians, in which he promised to the Christians complete protection against all violence. Russia, he said, was fulfilling its sacred mission to protect the rights of the different nationalities, and to pacify all races and worshipers. The Mussulmans also were promised protection and justice; only the well-known authors of the atrocities which had been committed would be severely punished.

At the same time that the crossing from Simnitza took place, the Russians made a serious demonstration at Turnu-Magurelli, a little higher up the stream, which might have been turned into a real attack, had a fair chance offered. The Russian forces were so distributed in the neighboring villages that they could fall with ease upon Simnitza or Turnu-Magurelli, and the last moment it was uncertain which place would be chosen. On June 28th, the Emperor and the Grand Duke Nicholas took up their headquarters at Simnitza, and a few days afterward at Tsarevitza, near Sistova.

The Turks remained completely inactive during the month of July, Abdul Kerim insisting that he had a plan which would eventually result in the total defeat of the Russians. This inactivity at one time seemed to threaten the Turkish army with the loss of the campaign, without a single battle being fought. It permitted the Russians to establish themselves in sufficient strength, to secure a fortified crossing-place, Sistova, to isolate the fortresses of Rustchuk and Silistria, and to secure the passes of the Central Balkans. In these operations they were universally successful, meeting with but little opposition, as will be seen from a detailed account. The advanced guard of the army coming from Simnitza having secured the massive bridge over the Yantra, at Biela, on July 1st, a cavalry detachment under General Gourko, after a short engagement with about 3,000 Turks, captured Tirnova on July 7th, which place was strongly garrisoned by a large detachment of infantry. During the following days the main army secured a strong position along the line of the Yantra, with its front toward Osman Bazar and Rasgrad, while to secure its rear, detachments of Cossacks scoured the country to the west as far as Lovatz and Plevna. At the same time preparations were made for the operations against the passes of the Central Balkans by General Gourko, after he had previously occupied Gabrova, where most of the roads north of the Balkans crossed each other

The Balkan Mountains, which the Russians had now reached, formed the second line of defense for the Turks. They are for the most part impassable, being crossed by only a few known passes, which were all held and strongly fortified by the Turks. Besides these passes, however, there are a number of bridle-paths and secret passes, known only to the Bulgarians. The passes may be properly divided into two groups, radiating respectively from Shumla in the east, and Tirnova in the west. The Tirnova group comprises the Shipka Pass and the Tvarditza Pass. The Shipka Pass is reached from Tirnova by a road running through Gabrova, and is at its summit 4,500 feet above the sea. From this pass there is a beautiful view on the valley below, where the town of Kasanlik lies, almost hidden by the numerous rose gardens, from which is drawn the material for the attar of roses, which is manufactured here. The Tvarditza Pass is reached from Tirnova by a road through the valley of the Saltar to Elena, whence a path goes over the mountains to the village of Tvarditza into the valley of the Tundja, and along the left bank of this river to the town of Kasanlik. It is about 4,000 feet high. A little beyond Tvarditza the Balkans branch off into three separate ranges, the Kutchuk or Little Mountains, the Stara Planina or Old

Mountains, and the Emineh Dagh, running to Cape Emineh; and through these run the various passes belonging to the Shumla group. In the hollow between the Kutchuk and the Stara Planina branches of the Balkans, surrounded on every side by the steep hills, lies the town of Kasan, called by the Bulgarians Kotel (kettle), from the peculiar shape of the gorge enclosing it. Through this gorge passes the road from Osman Bazar, crossing on its way the Binar and Kutchuk ranges. West of Kasan lies the famous pass of Demir Kapu or Iron Gate, a narrow and gloomy defile of unusual strength. The chain may also be crossed from Kasan by another route, running south-eastward through the narrow defile of Kotlenski Buaz, and entering the town of Karnabad from the west. The latter place is, moreover, accessible by another pass, the Dobrot Pass. This, although the most direct approach from Shumla, can be reached only by taking or masking that fortress, which completely commands the road leading to it. This pass is 2,000 feet high. The road leading to Aidos over the Nadir-Derbent Pass, starts from Pravadi on the Varna Railroad. The first part of the line of march is the most difficult of the eastern routes. By this pass Gen. Rudiger, in 1829, crossed the Balkans, while his colleague, Gen Roth, avoided the mountains by taking the shore road from Varna to Missivri. Besides these is the Topolnitza Pass in the Western Balkans, near Etropol, which has more than once played an important part in the history of mediæval Europe

On July 12th, General Gourko set out from Tirnova to cross the Balkans. Instead, however, of choosing the Shipka Pass, he marched from Tirnova on the road to Slivno, and then a little beyond Elena turned to the south, crossing the Balkans on one of those small bridle-paths known only to the native Bulgarians The passage, owing to the difficulties of the country, was a very difficult one. A correspondent of the London *Times*, who accompanied the expedition, spoke of it as follows:

"Two passes, well known, lead through the mountains in this direction, the one by Gabrova, the other by Elena. We are attempting to pass between them along such a path as guides take a tourist who wishes to ascend a mountain where there is no road. Sometimes in a valley there is a good cart track for a mile or so, then the way lies along the bed of a stream; but two squadrons of Cossacks, and another of Cossacks turned into mounted sappers, have reached the top of the pass, and made such alterations as render it practicable for guns, practicable after a fashion, but very

GENERAL GOURKO.

THE ROAD TO THE SHIPKA PASS.

difficult. . . . . Yet all the while the Cossack improvised sappers are hard at work preparing the road for the artillery. It is a mere mountain path, leading partly across or along streams, partly around hill-sides, sometimes hanging many feet above the stream, and sloping dangerously toward it. General Rauch is there in front, and the men are doing their best. . . . . For the artillery, especially for the last battery, because the others had cut up the road, the day's work was terrible; nearly all the drivers were pressing their horses and laying on their whips with true Russian good-will, the gunners pushing and pulling. Never did horses work harder; yet the guns hung behind, for it is doubtful whether guns were ever taken along such roads before at such a pace."

On the 14th he reached Hainkoi on the southern slope of the Balkans Small detatchments of the enemy which were met here were repulsed, as well as on the following days at various other points. On the 17th the enemy was also driven from Kasanlik, and the village of Shipka, lying to the north, was taken after a short engagement. On the same day Prince Mirski, with the Orloff infantry regiment and the 30th Don Cossacks, attacked the Shipka Pass from the north, coming from Gabrova. The Turks were well intrenched here, with fourteen tabors of infantry and eight guns, and after having been driven from their more advanced positions at the point of the bayonet, they made, for a time, a desperate resistance, the Russians losing over two hundred dead and wounded. But fearing to be surrounded both from the north and the south, they withdrew on the 19th, leaving their artillery in the hands of the Russians. During his march in the valley of the Tundja, General Gourko had sent a cavalry detachment to the south, which cut the telegraph wires at Yeni Sagra. Detachments of Cossacks also made their appearance at Yamboli. Two days before the capture of the Shipka Pass, a detachment of troops under General Sherebkoff occupied Lovatz, which was of great importance in securing the right wing of the Balkan positions.

The Russians had gained possession of the line of the Yantra from Sistova to Gabrova, and had immediately prepared for the march over the Balkans. In order to secure their line, they must gain a considerable extent of territory on their right and left, and form for themselves a secure, broad basis of operations, which extending as far to the east as the Turkish line of Rustchuk, Rasgrad and Shumla, should include the river Lom in its scope, and should stretch westwardly over the Osma Valley to the river Vid. In the west, lay on the Osma the important towns of Nicopolis, Bulgareni, Lovatz, Trojan, Selvi, east of Trojan, Plevna further west on the river Vid. If they were masters of this territory extending from the Vid to the Lom, they would have a solid position against the quadrilateral, and any force which might come out from it would also be secure against attack from Widin, Nissa, and Sophia on the west, and would be able to guard their troops in the Balkans against an attempt to cut them off.

The first point of attack was Nicopolis. This is a very ancient and important fortress, and was the scene of the defeat of the French and Hungarian army by Sultan Bayazid, in 1396. It threat-ened Sistova and the right wing of the Russians, and its capture was indispensable to the success of a further advance. The move-ment had been made against it even before the successes of General Gourko in the Balkans, and the position, with its garrison of six thousand men, had surrendered to the Russians on the 15th. The correspondent of the New York *Herald* gives the following account of the operations previous to the surrender:

" A crossing at Nicopolis possesses many advantages over that at Sistova. The river's current is not as strong, and a number of small islands fronting Turnu-Magurelli are very favorably located for bridging purposes. In reality Nicopolis was the selected point for the original crossing of the Danube, but circumstances and the Turks forced the adoption of the Sistova line. The batteries at Turnu-Magurelli had reduced Nicopolis to ruins; but the two hills on which the town was built completely sheltered the Turkish forces from the Russian fire. Therefore, it became necessary to attack the town and position from the Bulgarian side of the river. For this purpose a considerable force of infantry was massed west of Sistova, and during the concentration these troops served to cover the crossing. When the two corps had established themselves in the direction of Biela and Tirnova the covering body was prepared to move on Nicopolis. But, in the meantime, the Turks were strengthening their position and preparing to defeat the clearly apparent object of their enemy. All the indications, therefore, pointed to a bloody struggle for the possession of Nicopolis, and, to speak truly, neither side seemed over-anxious to begin it. The threatened failure of the Sistova bridge and the frequent interruptions of traffic, necessitated by the repairs, forced the Russians to make the attack

"The extensive swamp and lake west of Sistova interfered considerably with the Russian advance, although it afforded a decided protection against Turkish attack from that side. The Cossacks had been skirmishing and scouting for more than two days in the direction of Plevna and Nicopolis, and their operations and activity masked the preparations of the attacking column very effectually. Finally the order for the Russian advance was given, and after an arduous march around the lake and toward Nicopolis, the contending forces came into collision. The Turks had taken the precaution to cover their position by double lines of pickets, supported, at intervals, by several companies of picked troops. This was to guard against the raids of the Cossacks, whose enterprise has impressed itself thoroughly upon the Turkish mind. These lines of pickets made what might be termed a formal show of resistance, and slowly retired on the main body. As soon as the Russians came within effective range of the Turkish position they were met by a severe artillery fire, which, however, did not check their advance, and to which they replied with a still more formidable fire. The Turks being posted on a commanding position had a considerable advantage, and, as the Russians approached, frightful gaps were made in their ranks by the Turkish artillery. With surprising valor, however, they continued to approach the heights, and as soon as they came within rifle range they opened a terrible fire on the Turks. For half an hour this musketry duel continued with unabated vigor. The Russians, in the meantime, developed their front, so as to approach their left in the direction of the Osma River. This was a movement which threatened the Turkish line of retreat to the southwestward and westward. About midday on Sunday the order for the assault was given, and the whole Russian line, supported by several batteries of artillery, advantageously posted, stormed the heights occupied by the Turks. During this awful climb, in the face of a deadly fire, the Russians suffered terribly; while the Turks, stubbornly defending their position, sustained equal losses. But the onset was so impetuous that the Turks could not withstand it and were driven headlong over the crest of the hills toward Nicopolis, followed by the Cossacks and detachments of light infantry "

The Russians, who were commanded by Baron Krüdener, fought

with great bravery, according to all accounts. The entire Turkish garrison, consisting of 6,000 men, with Hassan and Achmed Pashas, surrendered to the victors, together with two monitors and forty cannon.

The capture of Nicopolis gave to the Russian army, for the first time, a secure foothold on the right bank of the Danube. A bridge was not constructed at this point, but a regular communication with Turnu-Magurelli, on the Rumanian bank, was established by boats. The advance of the Russian columns which, since the beginning of July, and the occupation of the Yantra bridge at Biela, had been directed against the western front of the quadrilateral, and against the passes of the central Balkans, could now proceed more smoothly. Active preparations were made to take Rustchuk. The Twelfth and Thirteenth corps, under the command of the Czarevitch, were detailed to invest this fortress. In the middle of July the advance guard had reached the heights on the left bank of the Black Lom, and had repulsed several advances of the garrison under Eshreff Pasha. But as these troops were not deemed sufficient, the Eleventh division of the Eleventh corps and a part of the Eleventh cavalry division were added, so that at the close of July the army of the Czarevitch consisted of fully two and two-third corps, which enabled him to extend the crescent-shaped position of his lines south of Rustchuk, beyond Kadikoi to the railroad station, Vetova, thus interrupting the communication by rail between Rustchuk and Shumla. But even these forces did not suffice to complete the investment of Rustchuk from the land, for it was absolutely necessary to send several brigades up the Lom into the neighborhood of Osman Bazar, for the Turks had drawn a large number of the troops stationed at Varna and Shumla to Rasgrad, and had strongly fortified themselves at that place. The 50,000 men under Achmet Eyub Pasha, which were gathered at this point, formed the real army of operation, of which two brigades were advanced as far as Eski Djuma and Osman Bazar, while Turkish outposts extended as far as Yenikoi. The remainder of July was filled up with unimportant engagements of the outposts and a bombardment of Rustchuk from Giurgevo, frequently interrupted by long pauses.

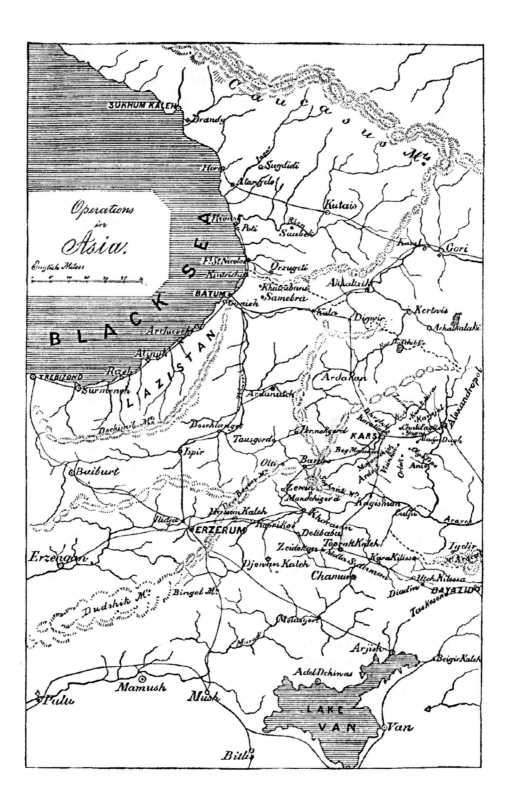

Operations
in
Asia.

English Miles

SUKHUM KALEH

Drandy

Horiu

Sugdidi

Alargelo

Kutais

CAUCASUS Mts

Isgr

Kwarel

Gori

Rion

Poti

Rion

Saabek

Osrugeti

Akhaltzilh

Kertvis

F. St. Nicolai

Kintrichi

BATUM

Khazubani

Samebra

Kula

Dignir

Arkalkalaki

Nat. Tchutchi

Onieh

BLACK SEA

Archaveh

Atinuk

LAZISTAN

Ardahan

TREBIZOND

Rize

Surmench

Ardanutch

Dachimil Mts

Boschlagget

Pennekgord

KARS

Beg Mainmen

Tausgord

Ispir

Oltis

Bardis

Baiburt

Baron Mt

Zewin

Mandchigerd

Kagisman

Hassan Kaleh

Ilidga

Khapriki

Khoracan

Delibaba

ERZERUM

Zeidekan

Toprak Kaleh

Kara Kilissa

Araxes

Iydir

Erzengan

Djenin Kaleh

Mela Siatimen

Chamur

Ulih Kilissa

Diadin

BAYAZID

Tas Kosen

Dudshik Mts

Bingol Mt

Molasgert

Mierd

Arjish

Beigir Kaleh

Adel Dchiwas

Pulu

Mamush

Mush

LAKE
VAN

Van

Bitlis

THE EMPEROR ALEXANDER II. IN THE NEVSKI PROSPEKT,
ST. PETERSBURG.

CHAPTER III.

THE RUSSIAN ADVANCE IN ARMENIA.

Sketch of the Field of the Armenian Campaign—Its History—First Advance of the Russians—Capture of Bayazid—Capture of Ardahan—Gen. Melikoff before Kars—Gen Tergukassoff at Zeidekan — The Turks everywhere Retreating before the Russians.

THE district which was the scene of operations in Asia is a country possessing considerable historical interest, and has been the scene of important expeditions and fierce wars during several thousand years. Extending from the Caucasus Mountains to Lake Van, and from the eastern boundary of Turkey to Erzerum, it includes the ancient Colchis, the objective point of the Argonautic Expedition, the first commercial enterprise mentioned in Grecian history, and the central part of the former kingdom of Armenia. The head-waters of the Euphrates and Araxes are within or near its borders ; and on its eastern edge, between Russian Erivan and Turkish Bayazid, almost directly in the line of march of the Russian left wing, stands the mountain called Ararat. The expeditions of Cyrus and Darius marched through Armenia when they went to give to the Scythians of the region between the Don and the Danube, the present Little Russia, an impression of the power of the Persian Empire. Later in Persian history, the famous retreat of the ten thousand Greeks, the story of which, related by its leader, is still one of the most cherished treasures of classical literature, was conducted by Xenophon after the disastrous defeat at Cunaxa, up the Tigris to the shores of Lake Van, whence it proceeded north-westwardly, most probably by way of the site of what is now Erzerum, which was then occupied by several wealthy villages—Hassan Kaleh, Zewin, Bardess, Olti, and Gymnias, supposed now to be Ardanutch—places whose names will appear frequently in the course of the present history—to Trebizond, on the Black Sea. The battles which decided the fate of Armenia during the wars of Alexander the Great, were fought around it, but not within it ; but the region

again appears as a field of battles during the wars of the Romans
with Mithridates, King of Pontus, when Tigranes, who had made
a considerable kingdom of the Greater Armenia, or Armenia east of
the Euphrates, provoked an invasion of the Romans, by giving support to their foe. Armenia remained independent, and upon the
rise of the Parthian Empire, became an object of contention
between that power and the Romans. The Emperor Trajan
took possession of the country A.D. 115, and made it a Roman province, but his successor, Hadrian, restored it to its sovereign and to
independence. The kingdom was overcome by Sapor, King of Persia, in the middle of the third century of the Christian Era, but recovered its independence under Tiridates, twenty-seven years afterward. It was made tributary to Persia on the death of this king,
A.D. 342, and became a Persian province a few years afterward. The
heroic and protracted resistance which was made by Artogerana, a
fortress situated near the head-waters of the Tigris, and the last
place in Armenia that surrendered to the Persian King, is a fitting
parallel to the famous defense which was made by Kars against the
siege by the Russians in 1854. Early in the fifth century the country was divided between the Persians and the Romans, upon the
conclusion of a truce between those nations. The Romans supported Arsaces, the successor of the regular line of sovereigns, as
king of their part. Upon the death of Arsaces, the district was reduced to the condition of a subject province. Thirty years afterward
the Persians substituted a provincial governor for the king whom
they had allowed to reign over their part of the territory, and the
kingdom of Armenia was extinguished after having enjoyed a precarious existence of more than five hundred and sixty years, during the
most of which time it had been a coveted object of contention between the two great rival powers of the world. In the eleventh
century Armenia, sharing the fate of Persia and the Asiatic possessions of the Eastern Empire, fell into the hands of the Turks. The
western part has remained bound with Turkey; the eastern part
formed a portion of the new Persian Empire till 1828, when all of
the Persian territory north of the Araxes was ceded to Russia.

The country is extremely rugged, being crossed by nearly parallel
mountain chains rising to from 8,000 to 12,000 or more feet in
height. The mountains contain difficult passes through which are
carried the few roads which the nature of the country allows to be
constructed, and of which the capacities for defense make them

dreaded by an invading force. The valleys are watered by the source of rivers which find their way into the Persian Gulf and the Black and Caspian Seas, and afford a soil which admits of excellent cultivation, extending often to a considerable height up the mountain. They are also the sites of numerous towns, many of which are quite important and flourishing. The climate is one of extremes. The winters, owing to the height of the mountains, are long and severe, while the heat during the short summer in many places rises to a point exceeding any temperature that is experienced in the United States. The snow, even in the southern parts of the district, remains on the mountain tops till July or August. The backwardness of the spring occasioned by the protracted stay of the large snow-masses, makes extensive military operations impracticable till late in the season. The earlier Russian campaign of 1877 was further impeded by unusually heavy masses of snow and severe rains, which made most of the roads nearly impassable. Then, when the summer comes, the heat and drought are so extreme as to weaken the strength of men not accustomed to the climate, and seriously impair the force of the army.

The headquarters of the Russian operations were at Tiflis, the capital of the province of Georgia, the political and military center of Transcaucasian Russia. This city is in communication with European Russia by means of a military road leading to the pass of Vladikavkas, about ninety miles north in the Caucasus Mountains, whence a connection exists by a railroad five hundred miles in length to Rostov on the river Don. This road might be entirely closed by an enemy at the pass of Vladikavkas, or Dariel, a magnificent gorge, which is described as resembling in some of its features the Yosemite Valley of California, over which the road passes at a height of eight thousand feet above the sea. Another road extends from Tiflis north-westwardly to Kutais in the Rion Valley, and along the coast by Sukhum-Kaleh to Anapa Kertch. The road between Tiflis and Kutais is a railway, which is continued to Poti, on the sea. This route, although it is well guarded, was impracticable in the present war, because it reaches no good harbors, and is exposed to the attacks of the Turkish fleets which have command of the eastern waters of the Black Sea, in such landing-places as are accessible to it, and because the region through which it passes is inhabited by the untrustworthy tribe of the Abkhasians.

Russian operations were attended with disadvantage, growing out of the superior marine facilities enjoyed by the Turks. Aside from their possessing a large excess of naval force over the Russians, the only good port near the theater of war—Batum—was in their hands Its harbor affords a secure anchorage for vessels of any draught of water; it can be reached by two routes from Tiflis, and would afford an easy route of communication by the valley of the Tchoruk River with the Russian posts in Turkish Armenia. Of the two posts belonging to Russia, Poti, at the mouth of the Rion River, is inaccessible to large vessels, and Sukhum-Kaleh, further north, is extremely unhealthy, and is cut off from the interior by hills and numerous streams. Hence the Russians attached importance to their operations against Batum, which were directed not more to capturing it for themselves than to preventing the Turks from using it to their annoyance.

Batum should have already belonged to Russia instead of to Turkey, and would have been given to it at the peace of Adrianople in 1828, but for a blunder of a clerk which has hardly a parallel in history. It was arranged in the preliminaries to the treaty that the Tchoruk River should be made the boundary between the two countries, and Batum thus be thrown into Russia; but the clerk who made the final draft of the treaty, by the mistake of a single letter, named the Tcholuk River, an insignificant stream, instead, and thus threw the boundary several miles north-west of Batum. When the error was discovered, it was too late to correct it.

The Turkish territory was defended by a system of four strong fortress towns, so arranged as to form what military writers call a quadrilateral. These were, Batum, already mentioned; Trebizond, an important port on the Black Sea, about 100 miles west of Batum; Kars, which is near the Russian boundary, facing the great Russian fortress at Alexandropol; and Erzerum, the capital of the province The space included between these forts gave room for the operations of a large army of defense, while of the two eastern forts, which the Russians would have to carry, one, Kars, was counted as among the strongest fortresses in the world, and the other, Batum, proved capable of resisting the strongest attacks which the Russians could make upon it during the whole summer of 1877. The other outlying forts, Ardahan and Bayazid, were considered as subsidiary to the greater forts, and of inferior importance. Ardahan was considered a work of superior strength, while Bayazid was so weak that it yielded readily to every serious attack that was made upon it.

THE GRAND DUKE MICHAEL.

CITADEL OF TIFLIS.

THE DEFILE OF DARIEL IN ARMENIA.

The Russian plan of campaign contemplated a simultaneous movement toward Erzerum, by three columns moving from near the northern and southern extremities and the center of the boundary-line between Russia and Turkey, while a fourth auxiliary column, under General Oklobjio, was stationed in the valley of the Rion River to watch Batum and co-operate in the movements which were to be undertaken against that port.

The force with which the operations were begun consisted of seven divisions of infantry, which had not yet been organized as a corps, but were banded together as the army of the Caucasus. It numbered, including the battalions which had to be left to keep watch over the native population of the Caucasus, 180,000 infantry and 45,000 cavalry; or, deducting these detachments, about 140,000 infantry and riflemen with their artillery, 12,000 cavalry, and 372 field-guns available for offensive operations. The force was strengthened by the levy of irregular mounted troops among the Caucasians, and by the addition of the Caucasian siege-batteries, with several battalions of artillery from the fortresses. The whole was under the command of the Grand Duke Michael, Governor of the Caucasus. The direction of the advance and operations in the field was intrusted to General Loris Melikoff. The center, under the personal command of General Melikoff, was posted at the fortress of Alexandropol (called Gumri by the Turks), close upon the border, about one hundred miles south-west, or one hundred and forty-four miles by road from Tiflis, with which city it is connected by telegraph. It consisted of the Caucasian Grenadiers and the Thirty-ninth division of infantry, the Caucasian dragoons, and the Terek Cossack division of four regiments and two mounted batteries, with volunteer cavalry, and numbered about 45,000 men.

The right wing, under the command of General Dewell, was stationed at the fortress of Akhalzikh, also near the boundary, about 156 miles north-west of Alexandropol, toward the Black Sea, about 100 miles due west, and 119 miles by road from Tiflis. A supporting and connecting detachment was placed at Fort Akhalkalaki, about half way between Akhalzikh and Alexandropol.

The left wing, called also the Erivan column, consisting of the Thirty-eighth division of infantry, with cavalry, under the command of General Tergukassoff, was assembled in front of the city of Erivan, which lies in the mountains south east of Alexandropol, and about 150 miles south-west of Tiflis.

14

The three columns presented a front of nearly 220 miles, facing the boundary-line, and were separated from each other by distances of about sixty-two miles and 156 miles respectively as well as by high mountains.

The Turkish line of defense covered the whole frontier from Bayazid to the Black Sea, but was removed some miles back from it. It extended from the port of Batum, on the Black Sea, to Ardahan, on the left bank of the river Kur, thence southward to Kars, after which it bent around, following the frontier to Bayazid. It depended, for its natural bulwark, upon the confused mass of rocky mountains with which the country is occupied. The second line of defense passed through Trebizond, on the Black Sea, Erzerum, and Van, but the troops destined to protect it were nearly all concentrated at Erzerum, so that they might be rapidly directed against the advancing Russians, should they break through the first lines.

The Turks had to occupy these lines and oppose the Russian advance, a force which was estimated at about 70,000 men, with 200 pieces of field-artillery. Of this force about 18,000 men were stationed at Kars and in front of that city; 7,000 men were stationed on the road from Erzerum to Bayazid; about 8,000 men were near Ardahan, on the road from Erzerum to Akhalzikh; about 20,000 men were at Batum, and about the same number were around Erzerum. The whole force was under the command of Ahmed Mukhtar Pasha.

Of the routes to be followed by the three advancing columns of the Russians, the shortest and least difficult was that given to the center. On the other hand, the advance might expect to encounter the mass of the Turkish army on this road, and to have its progress impeded also by the interposition of the important and remarkably strong fortress of Kars. The nature of the valley of Kars is, however, such as to permit an army to go around that fortress on either side, pressing forward, as the Russians actually did. Beyond Kars another obstacle presented itself in the range of the Soghanli Dagh, a line of hills rising about fourteen hundred feet above the level of the surrounding country, and nearly eight thousand feet above the sea, and stretching obliquely for a distance of thirty-seven miles between Kars and Erzerum. The two passes over this range are capable of an energetic and obstinate defense, and are seldom free from snow before the middle of July.

The route of the right wing from Akhalzikh by way of Ardahan and Olti to Erzerum, is a little longer (188 miles) than that followed by the center, and presents but little difficulty till the fortified city of Ardahan is reached. From this point the road to Erzerum is more difficult, but that to Kars is comparatively easy.

The third line of march, that pursued by the left wing, was the longest of the three. The principal obstacles to be apprehended were the citadel of Bayazid, which proved to be easily overcome, and the passes of the mountains between the Upper Euphrates and the Araxes, among which the first campaign, as it proved, was destined to receive its fatal blow. The road from Bayazid to Erzerum is a part of the great caravan road upon which the trade between Trebizond and Persia is conducted, and is one of the most important roads in the East.

The forward movement was begun by the three columns simultaneously, on the 24th of April. The center pressed forward directly toward Kars, thirty-eight miles from its starting-point at Alexandropol, with the purpose of investing that fortress and then advancing toward Erzerum, one hundred and seventy-five miles further southwest. The two wings were expected to assist in this movement, the right wing by disabling the fortress of Ardahan, and then by a flank movement from the north against the Turkish force opposed to the center, supporting that column in its effort to cross the Soghanli Dagh, the mountain range lying between Kars and Erzerum; while the left wing was to march from Erivan southward to Bayazid, and having carried that point, to turn toward the north-west and force its way to Erzerum.

Erzerum, the objective point of the campaign, is the capital of the province of the same name, and is the most important road-station in Turkish Armenia. It has a population variously estimated at between thirty thousand and fifty thousand; is situated in a mountainous country, on a plateau some seven-thousand feet above the level of the sea, at the point where all the roads from Constantinople to the east converge, and whence they again diverge as they continue their way eastward. It is, therefore, a town of considerable commercial importance. It is estimated that at least $1,500,000 worth of English goods find their way to this place every year. The city is described by travelers as presenting a beautiful and imposing appearance at a distance, but being squalid and filthy within. It is a prominent missionary station of the American Board. The old fortifications of Erzerum had been allowed to fall into decay till they had become substantially of no worth, but they had been renewed previous to the beginning of the Russian operations, so that at this time they made the town one of the most formidable positions in the whole Empire, and competent to resist a long attack before it could be forced to surrender.

The central column on the 28th of April reached Zaim, a village in the valley of the Kars Tchai, without having met any serious opposition. A reconnoitering force was sent forward under Major-General Prince Tchavtchavadze, which went around both sides of the fortifications of Kars and destroyed several miles of the telegraph line to Erzerum. On the next day the detachment encountered a column of eight Turkish battalions, and on the following day had another skirmish at Visinkoi, south-east of the fortifications of Kars. It was joined at that point by a division of Caucasian Grenadiers, which Gen. Melikoff in person had led up to its support by the way of Chaliph Oglu. Gen. Melikoff opened fire from his batteries upon the Turkish detachment which had taken up a position under cover of the advanced works of Kars, and disabled one of the enemy's guns. He returned on the 1st of May to his camp at Zaim, having lost during the artillery engagement one man killed and five wounded, and carrying with him more than one hundred prisoners. The enemy, leaving a strong garrison at Kars, retired to Bardess in the direction of Erzerum, in a position where they could hold the passes of the Soghanli Dagh.

Gen. Tergukassoff, with the left wing, appeared before Bayazid on the morning of the 30th of April. The town, which was deficiently fortified, was occupied by only about thirteen hundred male inhabitants, with a garrison of seventeen hundred soldiers, who, upon the approach of the Russian advance guard, fell back into the Ala Dagh Mountains, leaving behind a considerable supply of munitions. The town and citadel were occupied by the Russians. A scouting party, under Count Grabbe, was despatched from Culpi on the Araxes to Kagisman, where that river is crossed by the road leading from Kaia Kilissa to Kars, and there meeting, on the 6th of May, a regiment of dragoons sent down from Kars by Gen. Melikoff, opened a communication with the center.

A tentative attack was made upon the works of Kars on the 3d of May, which was repulsed by the Turks. The Russians had, however, decided that it would not be necessary for them to delay to capture this place, but that the purpose of neutralizing its efficiency as an obstacle to their advance could be gained by leaving behind a part of their force to invest it and subject it to a continued bombardment, while the rest of the column pushed forward.

Kars is a city of about twelve thousand inhabitants, lying in a bend of the Kars-Tchai or Kars River, which running to the north here, afterward turns to the north-east, then to the east, and finally to the south east, taking a nearly semicircular form, and empties into the Arpa Tchai at the boundary between Turkey and Russia. The city is surrounded with a double-walled line of fortifications, with five bastions. A citadel of stone several stories high, and accessible only from the city, stands upon a hill overlooking the town. The citadel is connected with the river by an underground passage of three hundred steps In addition to this, the position is guarded by nine other forts, with casemates and bomb-proofs, which are connected with each other by intermediate redoubts. One of these forts, which stands north-west of the city, on a steep bald summit, contained most of the provisions and ammunition stores, and overlooks all the surrounding buildings. Still higher are the forts Kara Dagh Tabia and Arab Tabia, standing on the Kara Dagh (Black Mountain), east of Kars, and supported by redoubts, which were regarded by Hussein Avni Pasha as the most formidable obstacles to the advance of the Russians in Asiatic Turkey, and are the actual key to the place. A line of forts or redoubts begins opposite the Kara Dagh across the river, and runs south-westwardly to opposite the citadel, including the forts Teesdale, Thompson, Zohrab, Churchhill, and Lake, the whole system being known as the Ingliz Tabias, or the English forts. Of these, Fort Lake is the strongest, and shares with Kara Dagh the importance of a key to the position. Nineteen hundred yards west of Fort Lake are the heights of Tahmasp, also supplied with a line of forts, which command Fort Lake with heavy guns. The Turkish army occupied an intrenched camp south-east of the city, protected at the extreme east by Fort Hafiz Pasha, facing the Kara Dagh forts on the opposite side of the road to Alexandropol

According to the local traditions, Kars was a city of some importance and the capital of a province during the reign of Tiridates, King of Armenia A D. 259. The citadel was built by the Sultan Murad III., of Turkey, in 1580, and was used by him in the wars with Persia, which resulted in the acquisition ten years later of Georgia and Tabriz. It was subjected to a formidable, but unsuccessful attack by Nadir, Shah of Persia in 1795. The remains of the Shah's encampment, which is said to have contained ninety thousand men, are still pointed out. The fortress was besieged by the Russians in 1807, when it withstood three successive attacks, but was taken by storm by the Russians in 1828, to be given up again two years afterward on the conclusion of the peace of Adrianople.

The town was captured a second time by the Russians during the Crimean war—in November, 1854, after a siege of more than five months, in which the garrison, led by Gen. Williams, of the British army, made one of the most desperate and brilliant defenses recorded in history. Even then, the fortifications proved superior to all the efforts of the Russians to reduce them by force, and the surrender of the place was induced only by the complete exhaustion of its stores and the starvation of its defenders. The city was restored to the Turks upon the conclusion of the Treaty of Paris. A large part of the fortifications which have made the position so formidable were constructed by the English engineers at this time, hence the name " Ingliz," or English, which is applied to some of the forts.

Kars is less than thirty miles distant from Alexandropol, and its minarets are visible from that place. The little semicircle of country included in the bend of the Kars Tchai and Arpa Tchai Rivers, which has for its diameter the line extending from Kars to Ani, deserves a special study. It includes the greater number of the points which were covered by the operations of Gen. Melikoff's center, between the time of the capture of Ardahan, May 17th, and the battle of the Aladja Dagh, October 15th, and which will be often mentioned in the course of this history. A clear understanding of their relative positions will contribute much to the comprehension of the different movements, particularly of the autumnal campaign.

A reconnoitering force of Russians under Major-General Sheremetieff was intercepted by a body of Turkish cavalry in the Valley of Bardyk, on the 8th of May, and obliged to cut its way through. Shortly after this, the Russian reconnoissances were extended to Kizil Kilissa, more than half-way from Kars to the Turkish position at Bardess. A hand-to-hand fight took place on the 16th of May between a Russian detachment under Major-General Komaroff and a force of one thousand Turkish dragoons, in which the Turks were repulsed, leaving sixty-four dead on the field, the Russians losing twenty-one killed and fifty nine wounded.

General Melikoff, leaving General Komaroff with a corps of

observation before Kars, had marched on the 12th of May with the major part of his force to the support of General Dewell and the right wing in the operations against Ardahan, taking a position at Tchevorhan, nine miles south-east of the fortress. General Dewell had already attended to the erection of batteries for the attack, a work of no easy character, for the heights on which they had to be placed were all commanded by the guns of the Turkish forts. General Melikoff, having built a bridge across the river Kur during the night between the 15th and 16th, opened fire upon the fortifications, the result of which was that all the Turkish guns were dismounted, their barracks were destroyed, and two of their outworks were captured. On the next day, May 17th, the fortress and town were captured by assault. General Melikoff, in his dispatch to the Grand Duke Michael, describing the character and extent of his victory, said: " The outworks of Ardahan, its fortifications, citadel, sixty guns, immense stores of provisions and ammunition, and the camp formerly occupied by fourteen lines of Turks, lie at the feet of the Czar. On May 17th the admirable fire of the artillery between three and six o'clock in the afternoon made a breach in the walls. At six o'clock the Erivan, Tiflis, and Baku regiments and the sappers advanced to the assault. The enemy could not withstand the onslaught and fled, leaving a great number dead. At nine o'clock our troops traversed the whole town and fortifications, the band playing the National Anthem."

The Russians reported their loss to be fifty-one killed and one hundred and eighty-four wounded. The loss of the Turks must have been very severe, as the Russian commander at Ardahan reported on the 21st of May that he had buried 1,184 men and was not yet done. The inhabitants of the town placed it at 3,000 men. The Turks, who numbered 10,000 men, retreated in different directions, a part of the garrison going toward Ardanutch, on the Tchoruk River, on the road to Batum, and a part toward Olti, on the road to Erzerum.

Hassan Sabri Pasha, the Turkish commander at Ardahan, was accused of having sold the place to the Russians for the sum of thirty thousand pounds sterling, and was arrested and held to trial. The case was referred, with a number of others, to a court martial which met at Constantinople on the 25th of August.

The capture of Ardahan was attended with important advantages to the Russians. With it the Turks lost their only fortress on the river Kur, and one of the essential links in the line of communication between their positions among the head-waters of the Kur and their coast-depot at Batum   Only through Ardahan could an expedition from Batum reach the flank of the Russian columns advancing toward Erzerum.   Since it had become a Russian fort, and the only crossing of the Kur was in Russian hands, the immunity of the north flank of their columns was assured; so that they would be able to employ more troops in the field, for a much smaller force would be needed to garrison the place than to besiege it.   It gave them, moreover, a fortified point of support for the continued advance of their right wing toward Erzerum, besides furnishing them with a considerable number of guns, which the Turks had left in the works, available for siege operations against Kars.

The purpose for which General Dewell's command had been organized as a separate column of the army of invasion was accomplished by the capture of Ardahan.   Its union with General Melikoff's center was the logical and necessary consequence of that success.   The union having been completed, the operations against Erzerum were resumed by the combined force.   General Melikoff returned to his headquarters at Zaim, where he was joined by General Dewell with the columns of the former right wing, while Ardahan and its environs were held by Major-General Komaroff. A detachment of General Dewell's force was sent in pursuit of the Turkish troops which had retreated on the road to Batum, and went as far as Ardanutch, where they found the enemy lying in their front at Artvin.   A body of cavalry, which was despatched upon the road to Erzerum, reached the neighborhood of Olti, about half way to the capital, without meeting resistance, but found that the enemy held that place.   A sortie was made from the garrison of Kars on the 25th of May, which resulted in an engagement at Magardslich, with the Cossack division under General Melikoff. A part of the Cossacks dismounted and fought well on foot.   The Turks were repulsed, leaving forty dead on the field, while the Russians lost only one man killed and six wounded.

On the 29th of May, General Melikoff, in making his final arrangements for the investment of Kars, arrived at Hadji Kalil, nine miles south-east of the city.   Here he learned that a body of four thousand Circassian cavalry, under Moussa Pasha, had come down the Soghanli and had encamped at Beg Mahmed, about nine

THE BATTLE OF TAHIR.

miles south-west of Kars. A surprise was planned against them, to be executed during the night. A division of cavalry, a regiment of foot, and sixteen guns were sent forward under Prince Tchavtchavadzo to Ardost. The enemy was attacked in his bivouac from three sides soon after midnight, and after a long conflict was put to flight. The Russians lost seven killed and thirty wounded, while the Circassians left on the field eighty-three dead and several trophies— guns, ammunition wagons, and standards—which fell into the hands of the Russians. This victory was regarded by the Russians as of considerable importance, inasmuch as it was a decisive repulse of the first offensive efforts of the Turks, and in effect destroyed the best part of the Turkish cavalry, which was already disproportionately weak. The Turks reported that the whole force was slaughtered, but this was an exaggeration, as most of the horsemen escaped. But it was not entirely false, for the body was really destroyed as a soldiery. According to subsequent reports from Erzerum, very few of the men returned to service, by far the greater part of them being scattered in flight or going back to their homes. Olti was occupied without resistance on the 8th of June.

On the 8th of May Lieutenant-General Tergukassoff, with the left wing of the Russian army of advance, or the Erivan column, as it was called, occupied Diadin, a town of seven thousand male inhabitants, mostly Mohammedan Kurds, about sixty, miles west of Bayazid, and on the 11th he reached the Armenian cloister of Surp Ohanes, or St. Johannes, where he established a. station of supplies and of support for his advance, which was sent out toward Kara Kilissa, at the crossing of the eastern branch of the Euphrates by the caravan road. A number of guerrilla bands of Kurds and Bashi-Bazouks had been assembled at Lake Van to harass the rear and flanks of the Russian force, and an expedition of cavalry was dispatched to suppress them. It penetrated to the lake and scattered the bands, one of the divisions having encountered a band at Ardish, on the north shore of the lake itself.

On the 4th of June General Tergukassoff advanced to Kara Kilissa, the Turks having fallen back to the mountain-pass of Toprak Kalch. On the 10th, he occupied Zeidekan, about eighty miles east of Erzerum, and the Turks retired to Koprikoi, about forty miles toward Erzerum.

CHAPTER IV.

THE RUSSIAN REVERSE IN ARMENIA.

The Situation in Armenia at the middle of June—Battle of Zeidekan—An unexpected change in the Fortunes of War—Defeat of General Tergukassoff at Delibaba and of General Mehkoff at Zewin—Retreat of the Russians—General Tergukassoff reaches Igdir, and marches to the relief of the Russian garrison at Bayazid—Horrible condition of that place—The Siege of Kars abandoned—The Russians again in Russian Territory

So far the advance of the Russians had been attended with uninterrupted success. It had not been rapid, for it had been impeded by the nature of the country, and by the necessity of taking or neutralizing the fortresses of Ardahan and Kars. The invading army, moreover, lacked a sufficiency of numbers to make it as efficient as it should be in marching into a hostile country. A considerable part of the force had to be detached to man the supporting posts along the lines of communication, to garrison Ardahan, and to maintain the investment of Kars, leaving the body which was destined to operate in the field none too large to cope with the Turkish army. Nevertheless, the Russian front had been pushed forward to near Kara Kilissa and Olti, beyond Kars. Cossack scouts had penetrated to Ispir, far beyond Olti and north-west of Erzerum, where their presence suggested danger to the communications between Erzerum and its supply-post of Trebizond, and the Russian lines of communication were well kept up. The Turks had been expected to make a desperate defense in the Soghanli Dagh, but so far had steadily retreated as the Russians moved forward. Their line had been drawn back from Ardahan, Kars, and Bayazid, to Olti, Zewin, and Kara Kilissa, and in the first days of June the headquarters of the center had been retired to Koprikoi, about forty miles east of Erzerum, the point of union of the roads leading from Kars through the Soghanli with the caravan road from Bayazid, while the left wing was stationed near Kisil Kilissa, and the right wing occupied the passes of Delibaba and Toprak Kaleh as its extreme outposts. Military critics thought that a speedy collapse of the Turkish resistance was assured, and it was generally and confidently expected that the campaign would result in the whole of Armenia falling into the hands of the Russians. The Russians anticipated this as the end of their advance, for they went prepared to organize civil administration in the conquered territory, and had actually established governments intended to be permanent in the districts which they had gained.

Mukhtar Pasha, finding that the Russians were not in great force at Olti, pushed forward his troops against their position there, in such a manner as to threaten to cut off the advanced guard of the right wing from the main body. The Russians, to avoid such a disaster, retreated to Pennek, and Olti was again occupied by the Turks on the 9th of June. The Russians concentrated their forces in greater strength around Kars, and the bombardment was for a few days conducted with extraordinary vigor.

Encouraged by his success at Olti, the Turkish Commander-in-chief ordered up three more battalions and six hundred cavalry to strengthen Mohammed Pasha at Delibaba, and ordered Mohammed, with seventeen battalions, two field batteries and one mountain battery, to drive the Russians of the left wing out of Zeidekan. These orders were carelessly executed, so that Mohammed Pasha reached the place of attack with less than his full force, to find the Russians prepared to attack him. The Russians were in a strong position on the heights of Tahir, above Zeidekan, having between them and the Turkish front a high ridge completely commanding the Turkish position, which was skirted by a deep ravine. This ridge and ravine afforded important points of advantage, the possession of which proved to be the turning point of the engagement. The Turks could have occupied them at the beginning of the battle, but Mohammed Pasha was convinced that the Russians were in small force, and neglected to improve his opportunities. Artillery skirmishes took place between the two armies on the 15th of June. The attack was opened by the Russians at five o'clock on the morning of June 16th, with a fire which increased in vigor and accuracy as the hours advanced, and which was received by the Turkish soldiers with steadiness and replied to with gallantry. At a quarter past nine the Russians, notwithstanding the brave resistance of the Turks, had by their overwhelming force of artillery, driven the Turkish guns out of action. By noon they were in possession of the ridge held by the Ottoman troops and of every gun they had, had turned their position and got around to their rear, and the Turkish army was routed. The Russians followed up the Turkish infantry, who had exhausted their ammunition, to the pass of Delibaba, capturing about one thousand prisoners, while another body of cavalry, with horse artillery, moving around by another road, effectually prevented all communication between Mukhtar Pasha and the remnants of the right wing, and captured a battalion and battery of Turks which were encamped on one of the streams.

The arrangements of the Turkish forces were, according to the correspondent of the London *Times*, faulty in the extreme. The army was suffering from an insufficiency of rations and a lack of supplies; was without medical staff or hospital arrangements, and was scantily furnished with ammunition. The officers were incompetent and careless, and despised the enemy, Mohammed Pasha, it is said, believing that the Russians would not dare to attack him. On the other hand, the same correspondent speaks in the highest terms of the bearing of the Turkish rank and file. "Untrained men," he says, "ignorant of the use of their weapons, and for the most part agriculturists, fresh from the plough, they were yet unused to the hard school of war. Cold and hungry, badly clad and badly shod, uncared-for and unnoticed, they stood their ground right nobly under a murderous fire from the sixteen sixteen-pounder Russian guns playing on their front under a hailstorm of rifle bullets from the battalions that had turned their flank, and it was not until their ammunition had failed, and the Cossacks were riding them down, that they turned and broke. . . . . The rank and file of the Turkish army are men of whom any nation might be proud." The Turkish loss is not stated. It was very heavy, and was aggravated by the disorder into which the whole line was thrown on its flight.

The Turks retreated to Delibaba, and the Russians took possession of the pass through which they had retired, and fortified it. Mukhtar Pasha telegraphed to Rashid Pasha, of his left wing, which was occupying the Olti road, to join him with nine of the twelve battalions forming that wing. He quitted his headquarters at Zewin on the night of the 17th, for Delibaba, to take command of the right wing in Perun. On the following day he received reinforcements by the arrival of Chalim Pasha, which raised the strength of his force to nineteen battalions, four cavalry regiments, and three batteries. The Russians, under General Tergukassoff, in the Delibaba Pass, who had been reinforced from the center, numbered 20,000 men, with five batteries. On the 20th the Turks began to move forward, and cavalry skirmishing between the outposts took place at Khaliage, near the entrance to the pass. On the 21st, Mukhtar

Pasha gave battle in the pass itself. The attack was begun at six o'clock in the morning, and the fighting lasted, with varying fortune, till eight o'clock in the evening, when the Turks bivouacked in positions slightly in advance of those held by them on the previous day. The Turkish commander at first dislodged the Russians from their positions, but they returned and drove away their assailants. Several charges of Russian infantry and cavalry followed, by which the Turkish front was, for a time, staggered, but the Turks finally rallied, and compelled the Russians to fall back with heavy loss.

The correspondent of the London *Standard*, who was with the Turkish army, gives the following graphic account of this day's engagement:

"On the morning of the 21st of June the battle began with an artillery fire on both sides, but soon Mukhtar Pasha proceeded to the attack The battalions from Erzerum and Erzengan, who counted many a gray head among their ranks, had the distinction granted to them of opening the attack. With indescribable heroism, though scarcely 1,400 strong, they advanced up the heights occupied by the Russians. Exposed to a perfect hailstorm of shells and musketry from the front and right flank of the enemy, they suffered frightful losses, but never for one moment wavered. Soon, however, it was perceived that the positions of the Turkish guns were very unfavorable for replying to the Russian cannon, and that they afforded a very insufficient protection against the enemy's fire directed toward the right flank. The two battalions which had suffered so severely were, therefore, withdrawn, while Mukhtar Pasha himself sought out fresh positions for the guns and superintended their transport. A brisk attack of cavalry, led by Shamyl Pasha, in the valley of the brook, covered the movements of the infantry and artillery. The latter, from their new positions, kept up a more effective fire than hitherto; they soon dismounted a Russian gun and covered a fresh attack of the infantry. Visibly the Turkish lines advanced, when suddenly the Russians rushed down from their mountains and again and again tried to storm the Turkish position. One after the other their attacks were repulsed; the Turks aimed splendidly, and the ranks of the storming parties were rapidly thinned. While this was going on, the cavalry regiments on both sides fought with varying success. At length night put an end to the combat. It was a fearful night. The number of the wounded on the Turkish side was very great, and of ambulances, etc., there

were next to none. An icy wind swept over the plateau; the men
had nothing to eat; for many miles around there was not a tree or a
shrub that might serve as fuel; and, what was worst of all, the artillery, which had, it is true, been almost constantly at work, complained of a want of ammunition. Not without anxiety did the
Marshal, as he told me himself only a few hours ago, look forward
to the morrow."

The battle was renewed on the next day with an attack by Mukhtar Pasha upon the Russians, who still occupied the eastern end of
the pass. The Russians replied with a violent attack, which was repulsed with great difficulty; but the battle soon turned against
them, and by the close of the day they had been driven from their
positions, and were in full retreat. The Turks pursued them as far
as Zeidekan, and thus regained all the positions which they had lost
in the battle of the 16th at that place. The fighting on the two
days lasted thirty-three hours, and cost the Turks 2,500 killed and
wounded, and the Russians a much larger number. According to
the correspondent of the London *Standard*, the Turkish force
actually participating in this battle numbered only six thousand
men.

Gen. Tergukassoff telegraphed respecting this engagement, that the
Russian column under his command " was attacked on the 21st near
Daiare by the Turks with twenty battalions, twelve guns, and 4,500
horse. The fighting lasted ten hours, and the Turks were eventually
repulsed, but the Russian losses were very considerable. The Russian
troops fought on a line of five versts with great gallantry against
overwhelming numbers. The Russian artillery was admirably
served. On the following day some skirmishes occurred, and
subsequently the Turks were allowed to collect the corpses of the
men in the Russian positions."

Gen. Heimann was despatched from the center to support Gen.
Tergukassoff and effect a junction with him if that were practicable;
and on the 20th of June, Gen. Melikoff left his camp at Mazra, before Kars, to follow him. The intention was to release General
Tergukassoff from his embarrassing position, inflict defeat upon
Mukhtar Pasha, and advance upon Erzerum if possible. General
Melikoff having overtaken Gen. Heimann, it was determined to
make a movement of the cavalry on the right flank of the enemy,
while the infantry should push along to Zewin.

On the 25th of June, Gen. Melikoff, with the Russian center

attacked the Turkish camp at Zewin This position was very strongly posted among the mountains of the Soghanli Dagh, near the point where the road from Erzerum to Kars crosses that range. It was surrounded by high mountains, and itself occupied a lower mountain, on the summit of which was a redoubt armed with four Krupp guns which formed its center. The Turkish force, of seven thousand infantry, supported by two cannon, was posted in sheltered trenches around the redoubt, and their reserves, three thousand men with two guns, were stationed on the higher mountains back of the camp. They were commanded by Ismail Pasha, the Kurd, Governor of Erzerum, assisted by Feizi Pasha. The Russians, with ten battalions of infantry and twenty-one guns, had taken a position during the night of the 24th on the mountain opposite the camp, which was higher and less steep than the one in its rear.

The battle began with a skirmish of cavalry, after which the Russian batteries opened fire upon the Turkish redoubt and its supporting infantry. "Fifteen Russian guns," says the correspondent of the London *Standard*, "fired incessantly at the little redoubt armed with four cannon, which commanded the whole field of battle from its excellent position, and within an hour over fifty shells fell in the redoubt, but the men never flinched for a moment." The Turkish fire, he adds, was quite equal to the Russians', at least four times superior to them in numbers; "and the artillery fight had absolutely no result." Soon after noon the Russians made an attempt to storm the redoubt. Their infantry were sent forward to climb the mountain under cover of an incessant fire from their batteries. The ascent was extremely steep. The Russians were met by an accurate fire from the redoubt and the Turkish infantry, which thinned their ranks fearfully, but steadily reinforced, they pressed on, returning to the advance after each successive repulse. At last their attacks on the center were slackened. An effort was made against the Turkish right wing, but it was continued but a little while, and by nightfall the Russians were in retreat.

The Russian official telegrams gave the following account of this engagement:

"On the 25th of June Gen. Loris Melikoff attacked the Turks in their fortified camp at Zewin, the fight lasting from two o'clock P.M. till night. Our troops dislodged the enemy from his advanced position, but to avoid the fire of the Turkish forts, returned to their own positions in the night. The valor of our troops was truly heroic; owing, however, to our numerical inferiority, we have suffered considerable loss. The enemy had twenty-three battalions in a strongly fortified position. We had three officers killed, twenty-four officers wounded, and 850 soldiers disabled."

The nominal commander of the Turkish forces, Kurd Ismail Pasha, took no active part in the engagement, but spent his time in his tent praying, while the operations which led to decisive victory were directed by his second, or assistant in command, General Kohlman, chief of staff to Mukhtar Pasha, a Hungarian officer, who was called Feizy Pasha by the Turks. "Not only," says the correspondent of the London *Times*, "did this gallant old officer superintend all arrangements, personally visiting every battalion and shelter-trench, but once or twice early in the day, when the Russians, pressing close up to the intrenchments, caused the Turks to waver, in one instance, indeed, to retire somewhat rapidly, he led them himself forward, revived their drooping spirits, inspired them with fresh courage, and so won the day for his adopted Government." The Russian forces, after the battle of Zewin, retreated to their camp before Kars.

The battles of Delibaba and Zewin, in which the Russian left and center successively suffered defeat, were decisive of the fate of the campaign in Armenia. The Russians made no further attempts at offensive operations, but devoted their attention to protecting their forces against further disaster, and withdrawing them to safer positions. Their failure was ascribed to the division of the force into too many bodies, neither of which was sufficient for effective operations, while all were exposed to the attack and defeat in detail which actually took place. Had not the Turks been nearly as weak as they were, they would have been now in a perilous position, and in danger of being cut up by attacks upon their flanks and rear. As it was, the Turks were in no condition to pursue them, and their armies, with the exception of the garrison at Bayazid, succeeded in retiring without suffering material damage.

The Russian official dispatches gave the following explanations of their defeats: "General Loris Melikoff having reached the Araxes Valley by way of Kars and Kagisman, was marching west in the direction of Erzerum, when the Turks occupying the fortified position of Zewin menaced his right flank. To prevent an attack in front and rear, General Melikoff, before proceeding further west, had to turn north and attack Zewin. The attempt failed, and General

CITY AND FORT KARS IN ARMENIA.

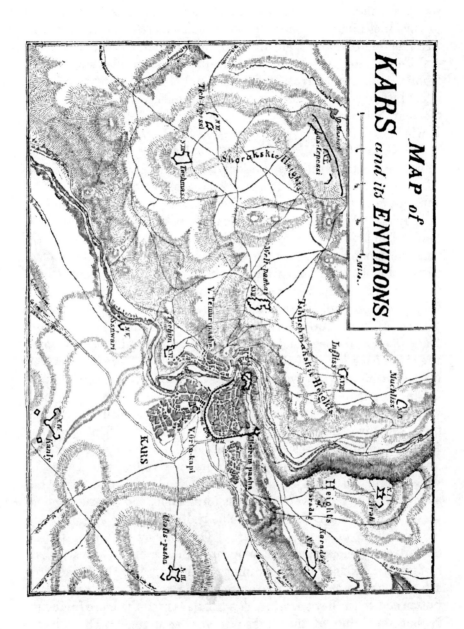

MAP of
KARS and its ENVIRONS.

½ Mile.

Melikoff fell back to the Araxes Valley, where he heard that the southern column under Lieutenant-General Tergukassoff, which was to have met him there previous to the joint march on Erzerum, was likewise defeated near Delibaba, and had retreated. Lieutenant-General Tergukassoff is seemingly determined to retrace his steps to the frontier and rescue Bayazid, while General Melikoff, according to the latest intelligence, intended to take up a position in the Araxes Valley and hold the road to Kars against the victorious force from Zewin."

The Grand Duke Michael arrived at Kars in the beginning of June, and established his headquarters with the investing force. The Russian camp before this fortress was situated north of the city, and on the east side of the Kars Tchai River, occupying a series of hills lying between Kars and Marza, about six or seven miles distant. The headquarters of the Grand Duke's staff were in advance, near the summit of a hill, at an elevation of six thousand feet above the level of the sea, from which every movement could be watched. Opposite the camp were two groups of lofty hills, separated by a deep gorge through which the river flows, and surmounted by three of the principal Turkish fortresses, Fort Arab in the center, Fort Kara Dagh at the left, and Fort Mukhlis at the right, on the opposite side of the gorge of the river. On the left of the town which lay behind Kara Dagh, was another fort, Hafiz Pasha, on low ground. On the left of the whole fortress a plain extended as far as the mountains, nearly two miles from the town. The grassy plain around the town was diversified by knolls, which afforded excellent positions for the Russian batteries and the concealment of troops. The Russians had seventy-four guns and mortars in position, the nearest of which were two miles from the fort. Of all the forts, Fort Arab and Fort Kara Dagh were the most formidable, and it was against these two that the Russian fire was chiefly directed. The siege afforded but few scenes of especial interest. The same events were repeated day after day, consisting of the opening of the fire by the Russians at five or six o'clock in the morning, the response by the Turks after a few hours, after which the cannonading was incessant till night put an end to the day's work. The Russians fired the more frequently, but the firing of the Turks was very accurate. "There is no doubt," said a newspaper correspondent who was in the Russian camp, "that the Turks have splendid guns, and that they know how to direct them."

15

The Russians made several attempts to carry particular positions by storm, which were always repulsed, and the garrison made sorties which were without result till Sunday, July 18th, when, the Russians having been weakened and partly disorganized by their recent defeats at Delibaba and Zewin, they reopened communications with Mukhtar Pasha. On the 4th of July, General Melikoff announced in a dispatch issued at Alexandropol that the siege of Kars had been suspended in order to place the besieging troops in a position to move with greater readiness against Mukhtar Pasha's advance, which had been pushed to within twenty miles of the city; that the siege artillery had been sent to Kuruk Dara and Alexandropol; the greater part of the cavalry had been concentrated at Chalifaghlie to protect communications, and the infantry had been stationed at Zaim.

On the following Sunday, July 8th, the Turkish force having been advanced to Wahiran Kaleh, eight miles south of Kars, Mukhtar Pasha, accompanied by Sir Arnold Kemball, the Commissioner of Observation appointed by the British Government to accompany the Turkish army, rode into the city and went over the batteries at Kara Dagh Tabia, where the bombardment had been heaviest, without being molested. The Russian headquarters were then at Zaim.

General Tergukassoff, after having been defeated in the battle of Delibaba, withdrew his forces in good order and began a retreat toward the Russian frontier. He was continuously followed by Ismail Pasha, and threatened on his left by Faik Pasha, who had collected a host of Kurds for the investment of the Russian garrison at Bayazid, but neither officer made any serious efforts to intercept his movement. An attack was made upon him at Kara Kilissa, and one of more importance at Ipek, which, however, had no effect in disarranging his plans. He afterward turned suddenly from the direct road, quite throwing his antagonists at bay, and proceeded to Igdir, in the Russian territory north of Bayazid. His march was delayed by the crowd of Christian fugitives who sought his protection flying from the Bashi-Bazouks and Kurds, who were swarming through the districts occupied by the Russians, and committing their characteristic outrages. Yet his movements were so rapid that the possibility of his arrival at Igdir at the time he was reported to have reached that place was doubted until a confirmatory dispatch was received. His stay at Igdir was short, for he only waited

long enough to lay in stores of provisions and war materials, and
hastened away to relieve the Russian garrison at Bayazid, which was
already beleaguered by a horde of 13,000 Turks and Kurds, and was
in destitution and distress. Bayazid had been captured from the
Turks at the beginning of the campaign, and had been left in charge
of a garrison, while General Tergukassoff advanced with the main
part of his column toward Erzerum. It was exposed to incursions
from the Kurds, who were swarming around Lake Van, and the
garrison had been cut off from the main army for about a month.
On the 19th of June, a part of the garrison, consisting of two battalions and about one thousand Cossacks, moved out of the post and
were attacked and defeated by the Turks. The Cossack cavalry, who
attempted to cover the retreat, were surrounded and compelled to surrender, after which, a dispute arising between some of the Cossacks
and the Kurds, they were massacred. The Turks held possession of
the town, while the garrison were confined to the citadel. Their situation was painful in the extreme. The defenses of the fort were
weak, the stores of provisions were nearly exhausted, and the men
were worn out by the constant watchfulness and efforts which they
were obliged to exert to avoid surprise by their powerful foe ; worst
of all, there was no water inside of the citadel, and they were
obliged to fetch it from outside the works in the face of the enemy.
General Tergukassoff, making a march of remarkable speed, reached
Bayazid on the 9th of July. After a cannonade of several hours,
the Russians made a fierce onslaught, advancing their whole line
with a well-directed and sustained fire, under which the Turks were
compelled to fall back. As soon as the regulars yielded, the Kurds
broke and fled in every direction, and the Russians marched into
the town. Several prisoners, four cannon, and a large quantity of
ammunition and provisions were captured. The town was in ruins,
and the atmosphere was so infected from dead bodies in a state of
decomposition—"a testimony of Turkish atrocities," the Russian
commander alleged—that he considered it impossible to prolong the
sojourn of his troops there. The garrison were in a deplorable condition, and physically unable to fight. The Turks were receiving
reinforcements, and General Tergukassoff wished to complete the
movement to join the main body of troops at Zaim ; therefore, having secured the safety of the garrison, he evacuated the citadel, and
it was immediately occupied by the Turks.

The statements of General Tergukassoff as to the condition in which he found the town are confirmed by the testimony of two British officers who visited the place after it was restored to the Turks. They represented that the whole town was in ruins, and filled with the bodies of Christian citizens whom the Turks had ruthlessly slaughtered, and that the Russian soldiers were employed for six days in burying the dead citizens.

The gallantry of General Tergukassoff was warmly commended by the correspondent of the London *Times,* who was with the Turkish army, who pronounced him the only Russian who had "shown any pretension to generalship." This writer characterized the manner in which he had handled his troops at Tahir, or Zeidekan, the stubborn resistance which he had offered at Delibaba, the incidents of his conduct during his retreat, and "finally his dashing flank march from Igdir to Bayazid, and the relief of that place in front of two Turkish corps, both superior to him in numbers," as stamping him as a general of the first class.

CHAPTER V.

THE BATTLES AROUND PLEVNA.

Change in the Fortunes of the Russians—Removal of Abdul Kerim—Appointment of Mehemet Ali to the Supreme Command—Plevna, its Situation—Arrival of Osman Pasha—Battle of July 19th—Defeat of the Russians—Osman Captures Lovatz—Battle of Karabunar—Retreat of General Gourko—Battle of Eski Sagra—Second Defeat of the Russians at Plevna, July 31st—Retreat of the Russians from the Lom—Operations in the Dobrudja—Bombardment of Kustendje—Struggles in the Shipka Pass—Battle of Karasan—Repulse of a Turkish Attack on Pelisat—Skobeleff Recaptures Lovatz—Battle of Kechlova—Third Defeat of the Russians before Plevna—Capture of the Grivitza Redoubt—Bravery of the Rumanian Troops.

OUR last chapter on the operations in Europe left General Gourko across the Balkans, and the Russians in possession of Nicopolis. Hitherto, all had gone most prosperously with the Russians. Their advance had been pushed without meeting any resistance that could delay or embarrass their movements, and it seemed very probable that they would soon have all of Bulgaria north of the Balkans in their possession. A sudden change now took place in their fortunes, in consequence of which they were compelled to withdraw from much of the country they had won, and to begin over again the hard work of the campaign.

At about this time, Abdul Kerim was removed from the command of the Turkish forces and sent to Constantinople to be courtmartialed, and Mehemet Ali, who had been transferred from Montenegro to the Danube, was appointed commander in his place. Osman Pasha, finding that he was too late to accomplish anything upon the Danube against the overwhelming numbers of the enemy, and judging that the Russians would attempt to follow the road leading from Sistova, Rustchuk, and Biela, toward Sophia, changed the direction of his march to one leading south-eastward, and taking with him the troops he had gathered from Widin and Nissa, occupied Plevna.

This point, which was destined henceforth to play a part of paramount importance in the campaign, had not before been recognized as possessing any great strategical advantages. Plevna was an open town of about eighteen thousand inhabitants, principally Bulgarians, situated on the southern side of the Grivitza River, one of the affluents of the Vid, a little less than four miles from the junction of the two streams. It is traversed by a small stream which; coming down from Bogot in the south, empties here into the Grivitza. Lying low in the valley, it is surrounded by a hilly, fertile, well-tilled district, with vineyards and cornfields on the ridges, and is an important market town for the region. Its location and the relations of its roads made it a point at which troops could be easily concentrated, which was what the Turks needed at this time in this part of their field of operations. From Plevna roads diverge in all directions, to Sistova and Rustchuk, to Nicopolis, to Biela, to Lovatz, to Sophia. The main road from Sistova to Sophia runs through the town and over one of the ridges to the east of it; and herein lay the strategical advantage of the place at this moment. Whoever held it in force commanded the flank of the Russian army, and was able to block their onward march. Osman Pasha, having occupied the place, and perceived its peculiar advantages in the present situation, immediately began to concentrate in it all the troops within his control, and to surround it with a system of strong works. The wisdom of his operation was justified by the fact that he had the main force of the Russian army engaged before Plevna for several months, and that however successful they might be elsewhere, they could make no permanent impression upon the integrity of the Turkish defense until they had carried this position.

The Russians, under Gen. Shilder-Shuldner, of Baron Krudener's corps, entered Plevna on the 19th of July, with the intention of driving the Turks out. The Russian general was negligent as to his precautions. He grossly underestimated the strength of the Turks, and having let his corps be weakened by sending one detachment to protect the bridge at Simnitza and another to transport the provisions taken at Nicopolis, and having left a garrison in that city, he set out with the remainder to attack Osman in his selected stronghold. Owing to the character of the topography of the place, the Russians were not able to perceive the full strength of the Turkish position until they were almost upon it. Consequently, they were surprised and thrown back with a heavy loss, given, according to the most careful estimates, at sixty-six officers and 2,771 men killed, wounded, or taken prisoners, or more than one-third of the whole force. Reinforcements came to the Russians on the next day, but their officers would not risk a renewal of the attack.

After this defeat it was necessary to strengthen Lovatz. It was done, but not sufficiently, for on July 26th Osman Pasha drove the Russians from the place after a severe fight. At the same time, Baron Krudener improved his own position considerably by withdrawing the garrison of Nicopolis, who were replaced by a Rumanian division under General Manu, the first Rumanian troops to cross the river, while he also received considerable reinforcements from the main army.

South of the Balkans, Suleiman Pasha, who had arrived from Montenegro with the greater part of his army, effected a junction with Rauf Pasha, and was appointed Commander-in-chief of the army of Rumelia, with 60,000 men under his command. On July 26th he was encountered by Gen. Gourko at Karabunar, south-west of Yeni Sagra, and having been defeated, retreated upon Adrianople. After the Russian disasters at Plevna, it was, however, deemed important that Gen. Gourko should secure the passes held by him, and for this purpose he was ordered back. He immediately retired to the Shipka Pass, followed closely by Suleiman Pasha, who inflicted a defeat upon him at Eski Sagra, on July 31st.

On July 30th, General Krudener, by order of the Grand Duke commanding, again attacked Plevna. His force, which had been doubled since his recent defeat, consisted of four infantry divisions, three cavalry brigades, and 170 guns, composed of his own, the Ninth army corps, with the exception of the Nineteenth infantry regiment, which had been sent to Nicopolis as garrison, the Thirtieth infantry division of the Fourth army corps, the Thirty-second infantry division, with four squadrons of cavalry of the Eleventh corps, and the brigade of Caucasian Cossacks of Gen. Skobeleff. Grand Duke Nicholas had, on July 21st, ordered the Thirtieth division of the Fourth corps, which had just crossed the Danube, to march to Plevna instead of to Tirnova, and to be placed at the disposal of General Krüdener. The Eleventh army corps, which was said to have reached Osman Bazar, and in that case would have formed the right wing of the army operating against Rasgrad-Shumla, was also ordered to send at once the Thirty-second division with four squadrons of cavalry to the Osma, to form the left wing of the force operating against Plevna. Prince Shachovsky, the commander of the corps, led this column in person, and reached the Osma after a six days' march. General Krüdener, to whom the chief command of the operations against Plevna had been entrusted, had originally concentrated his own corps at Bryslam, between Plevna and Nicopolis, and had afterward moved almost the entire corps to the south, taking a position up the road from Biela to Plevna, with his headquarters at Tirstenik, about eighteen miles east of Plevna, leaving only one brigade of the Ninth cavalry division, with some mounted batteries, at Bryslam to secure his right flank and the road to Nicopolis. The *Daily News* correspondent described the battle as follows:

"The night between the 30th and 31st was very wet, and troops did not begin to march forward before six, instead of four. The number of infantry combatants was actually about 32,000, with 160 field cannon and three brigades of cavalry. Baron Krüdener was on the right with the whole of the Thirty-first division in his fighting line, and three regiments of the Fifth division in reserve at Karajac Burgarsky. He was to attack in two columns, a brigade in each. On the left was Shachovsky, with a brigade of the Thirty-second division and a brigade of the Thirtieth division in fighting line. Another brigade of the Thirtieth division was in reserve at Pelisat. The Turkish position was convex, somewhat in horse-shoe shape, but more pointed. Baron Krüdener was to attack the Turkish left flank from Grivitza toward the river Vid. Shachovsky was to assail their right from Radiscvo, also toward the river Vid. On the left flank of the attack stood Skobeleff, with a brigade of Cossacks, a battalion of infantry, and a battery, to cope with the Turkish troops on the line from Plevna to Lovatz, and hindering them from interfering with the development of Shachovsky's attack. On the right flank stood Lascaroff, with two cavalry regiments to guard Krudener from a counter attack. The morning was gloomy, which the Russians regarded as a favorable omen. The troops cheered vigorously as they passed the General. Physically, there are no finer men in the world. In the pink of hard condition, and marching without packs, carrying only great-coat, haversack with rations, and ammunition, they seemed fit to go anywhere or do anything. Shachovsky's right column marched over Pelisat and Sgalievica. The left column headed straight for Radisevo. The artillery pushed forward from the first, and worked independently. Marching forward, we found the cavalry foreposts on the sky line above Pelisat,

ABDUL KERIM.

GENERAL SKOBELEFF.

and on the sloping downs the infantry deployed as they advanced, as the Russian practice is on open ground. The formation was in column of double companies, with rifle companies in front of each battalion. Krudener, on the right, opened the action at 9:30, bringing a battery into fire from the ridge on the Turkish earthwork above the village. At first it seemed as if the Turks were surprised. It was some time ere they replied, but then they did so vigorously, and gave quite as good as they got from Krudener. The objective of Prince Shachovsky, with whom I rode, was, in the first instance, Radisevo, and it behoved us, therefore, to bear away to the left. The village of Radisevo lies in a deep valley behind the southern wave or ridge of the Turkish position, and there is another ridge behind this valley. On that ridge our cannon, placed by Col. Bishovsky, chief of Prince Shachovsky's staff, was firing in line on the Turkish guns on the ridge beyond the valley with fine effect. The infantry went down into the valley under this covering fire, and I accompanied the column. We carried Radisevo with a trivial skirmish, for in the village there was only a handful of Bashi-Bazouks, who, standing their ground, were promptly bayonetted. The infantry remained under cover of the village. I returned up the slope to our batteries. These, firing with great rapidity and accuracy, soon compelled the Turkish cannon to quit the opposite height. During the last spurt of their firing, Prince Shachovsky rode along the rear of our batteries from the right to the left, under a fire which killed two horses in our little group. Our cannon, playing on the Turkish guns on the opposite ridge, quelled their fire after about half an hour's cannonade, and it was then for our batteries to cross the valley passing through Radisevo and come into action in the position vacated by the Turkish guns; and following them, our infantry also descended into the hollow, and lay down in the glades about the village and on the steep slope behind our guns in action."

The second period of the battle commenced at 2:30:

"Two brigades of infantry were in the Radisevo Valley, behind the guns of Gen. Tcherkoff's brigade—the Thirty-second division on the right, the First brigade of the Thirtieth division on the left. The leading battalions were ordered to rise up and advance over the ridge to attack. The order was hailed with glad cheers, for the infantrymen had been chafing at their inaction, and the battalions, with a swift, swinging step, streamed forward through the glen and up the steep slope behind, marching in company columns, the rifle companies leading. The artillery had heralded this movement with increased rapidity of fire, which was maintained to cover and aid the infantrymen when the latter had crossed the crest and were descending the slope and crossing the intervening valley to the assault of the Turkish position. Just before reaching the crest, the battalion deployed into line at the double, and crossed it in this formation, breaking to pass through the intervals between the guns. Presently, all along the face of the advancing infantrymen burst forth flaring volleys of musketry fire. The jagged lines spring onward through the maize fields, gradually assuming a concave shape. The Turkish position is neared. The roll of rifle fire is incessant, yet dominated by the fiercer and louder turmoil of the artillery above. The ammunition wagons gallop up to the cannon with fresh fuel for the fire. The guns redouble the energy of their firing. The crackle of the musketry fire rises into a 'sharp peal. The clamor of the hurrahs of the fighting men comes back to us on the breeze, making the blood tingle with the excitement of the fray. A village is blazing on the left. The fell fury of the battle has entered on its maddest paroxysm. The supports that had remained behind, lying just under the crest of the slope, are pushed forward over the brow of the hill. The wounded begin to trickle back over the ridge. We can see the dead and the more severely wounded lying where they fall on the stubbles and amid the maize. The living wave of fighting men is pouring over them ever on and on. The gallant gunners to the right and to the left of us stand to their work with a will. On the shell-swept ridge the Turkish cannon fire begins to waver. In that earthwork over against us more supports stream down with a louder cheer into the Russian fighting line. Suddenly the disconnected men are together. We can discern the officers signaling for the concentration by the waving of their swords. The distance is about one hundred yards. . There is a wild rush, headed by the Colonel of one of the regiments of the Thirty-second division. The Turks in the sheltered trench hold their ground, and fire steadily, and with terrible effect, into the advancing forces. The Colonel's horse goes down, but the Colonel is on his feet in a second, and, waving his sword, leads his men forward on foot. But only for a few paces. He staggers and falls. I heard afterward he was killed. We can hear the sound of wrath, half howl, half yell, with which his men, bayonets at the charge, rush to avenge him. They are over the parapet and shelter trench, and in among the Turks like an avalanche. Not many Turks get a chance to run away from the gleaming bayonets, swayed by muscular Russian arms. The outer edge of the first position is won. This time the Turks did not wait for the bayonet points, but with one final volley abandoned the work. We watched their huddled mass in the gardens and vineyard behind the position, cramming the narrow track between the trees to gain the shelter of their batteries in the rear of the second position. So fell the first position of the Turks. Krüdener was clearly jammed. The Turks were fighting furiously, and were in unexpected force on the broad central ridge of theirs as well as against Krüdener. The first position, in natural as in artificial strength, was child's play to the grim starkness of the second on that isolated mamelon there with the batteries on the swell behind it. But Shachovsky determined to go for it, and his troops were not the men to balk him. The first rush, however, was out of them. Many must have been blown They hung a good deal in the advance, exposing themselves recklessly, and falling fast, but not progressing with much speed. It is a dangerous time when troops sullenly stand still and doggedly fire when the stationary fit is on them. Shachovsky kept his finger well on the throbbing pulse of the battle. Just in the nick of time half his reserve brigades were thrown into the fight, while the other half took part in the attack on our left flank. The new blood tells at once. There is a move forward, and no more standing and craning over the fence. The Turks in the flank earthwork are reinforced. I can see some Russian officers on horseback standing coolly behind the bank of the vineyard that serves as a parapet, observing the addition to the Turkish force. They ride off and speedily return. I can hardly say how it all happens, but all of a sudden the white smoke spurts forth, and swarms of dark-clothed men are scrambling on. There is evidently a short, but sharp struggle. Then one sees a swarm of men flying across the green of the vineyard. But they don't go far, and prowl around the western and northern faces of the work, rendering its occupation very precarious. The Turkish cannon from behind drops shells into it with singular precision. As a matter of fact, the Russians occupied this, the second position of the Turks, but never held it. It was all but empty for a long time, and continuous fighting took place about its flanks. About six the Turks pressed forward a heavy mass of infantry for its recapture. Shachovsky took a bold step, sending two batteries down into the first position he had taken to keep them in check. But the Turks were not to be denied, and, in spite of the most determined fighting of the Russians, had reoccupied their second position before seven. The First brigade of the Thirty-fifth division had early inclined to the left, where the towers and houses of Plevna were visible. It was rash, for the brigade was exposing its right flank to the Turkish cannon astride of the ridge, but the goal of Plevna was a keen temptation. There was no thoroughfare, however. They would not give up, and they could not succeed. They charged again and again, and when they could charge no more from sheer fatigue, they stood and died, for they would not retire. The reserves came up, but only to swell the slaughter. And then the ammunition failed, for the carts had been left far behind, and all hope failed the most sanguine. Two companies of Russian infantry did indeed work round the right flank of the Turkish works and dodge into the town of Plevna, but it was like entering the mouth of hell. On the heights all round, the cannon smoke spurted out, and the vineyard in the rear of the town was alive with Turks. They left after a very short visit, and now all hope of success anywhere was dead, nor did a chance offer to make the best of defeat. Shachovsky had not a man left to cover the retreat. The Turks struck without stint. They had the upper-hand for once, and were determined to show that they knew how to make the most of it. They advanced in swarms through the dusk on their original first position, and captured three Russian cannon before the batteries could be withdrawn. The Turkish shells began once more to whistle over the ridge above Radisevo and fall into the village behind, now crammed with wounded. The streams of wounded wending their painful way over the ridge were incessant. The badly wounded mostly lay where they fell. Later, in the darkness, a baleful sort of Krankentraeger swarmed over the battle-field in the shape of Bashi-Bazouks, who spared not. Lingering there on the ridge till the moon rose, the staff could hear from down below on the still night air the cries of pain, the entreaties for mercy, and the yells of bloodthirsty fanatical triumph. It was indeed an hour to wring the sternest heart. We stayed there to learn, if it might be, what troops were coming out of the Valley of the Shadow of Death below. Were there, indeed, any at all to come? It did not seem to be the case. The Turks had our range before dark, and we could watch the flash of flame over against us, and then listen to the scream of the shell as it tore by us. The sound of rifle bullets, was incessant, and the escort and the retreating wounded were struck. A detachment at length began to come straggling up, but it will give an idea of the disorganization to say that when a company was told off to cover somewhat the wounded in Radisevo, it had to be made up of the men of several regiments."

The battle was now over, and the Russian defeat complete. The correspondent adds:

"About 9 o'clock the staff quitted the ridge, leaving it littered with groaning men, and moving gently lest we should tread on the prostrate wounded. We lost our way as we had lost our army. We could find no rest for the soles of our feet by reason of the alarms of the Bashi-Bazouks swarming in among the scattered and retiring Russians. At length, at one in the morning, having been in the saddle since six on the previous morning, we turned into a stubble-field, and making beds of the reaped grain, correspondent and Cossack alike rested under the stars. But we are not even then allowed to rest. Before four an alarm came that the Bashi-Bazouks were upon us, and we had to rouse and tramp away. The only protection of the chief of what in the morning was a fine army was now a handful of wearied Cossacks. About the Bashi-Bazouks there is worse to tell. At night they worked round into Radisevo, and, falling upon the wounded there, butchered them without mercy. Krüdener sent word in the morning that he had lost severely, and could make no headway, and had resolved to fall back on the line of the river Osma, which falls into the Danube near Nicopolis. There had been talk, his troops being fresh, of renewing the attack to-day (31st) with his co-operation, but it is a plain statement of fact that we have no troops to attack with. The most moderate estimate is that we have lost two regiments, say, 5,000 men, out of our three brigades, a ghastly number, beating Eylau or Friedland. This takes no account of Krüdener's losses. We, too, retire on the Osma River, above Bulgareni, and to the best of our weak strength, cover the bridge at Sistova. One can not, at this moment of hurried confusion, realize all the possible results of this stroke, so rashly courted. Not a Russian soldier stands between Tirnova and the victorious Turkish army in Lovatz and Plevna. Only a weak division of the Eleventh corps stands between Tirnova and the Shumla army. I look on Shachovsky's force as wrecked—as no longer for this campaign to be counted for a fighting integer. It is not ten days since the Thirtieth division crossed the Danube in the pride of superb condition. Now what of it is left is demoralized and shattered."

This description of the battle of Plevna was written by Mr. Archibald Forbes, of the London *Daily News*, who spent more than twenty hours in the saddle under fire. Riding with the retreating Russians, he wrote off-hand, his dispatch, which was considered by the London critics the most brilliant war dispatch ever sent to any newspaper. The Russian authorities paid Mr. Forbes the compliment of using his dispatch as the official account of the battle throughout the Empire.

Osman Pasha did not leave his position at Plevna after his victory. The effect which a pursuit, even to the Osma only, might have produced upon the Russians, was shown by the panic which was occasioned in their ranks by a report that the Turks were in their rear. The immediate consequence of their defeat was that the corps of Gen. Gourko, the important point of Tirnova, and even the connections in the rear of the army operating against Rasgrad-Shumla were threatened. It became necessary to withdraw the left wing of the latter force, so that in the beginning of August, the communications of the Turks between Rustchuk and Shumla were restored, and their field troops centered around Rustchuk advanced as far as Pisanzi on the Lom. The Russian headquarters, which had been for some time at Tirnova, were moved back to Biela on the 31st of July, and the Czar retired to Tsarevitza on the Danube. The mobilization of the Imperial Guards, consisting of three divisions of infantry and two of cavalry, and of several other bodies of troops, was ordered, and a ukase, dated July 22d, was promulgated for the mobilization of 185,467 men of the Opoltchenie or Landwehr.

In the Dobrudja, after the crossing of the Danube, the Russians had comparatively easy work. The opposition made by the Turks was very weak; everywhere they retreated before the advancing Russians without risking an engagement. The Russians continued their forward movement as far as Trajan's wall, occupying the cities of Kustendji, Medjidie, and Tchernavoda. Detachments of Cossacks penetrated even south of the wall, but were forced to retire before a body of Egyptians. Gen. Zimmermann, however, continued to hold the wall of Trajan, without assuming the offensive in any direction, merely concentrating his troops toward the Danube. On July 31st, a Turkish fleet, consisting of seven ships, appeared before Kustendji, and shelled the place for two hours, after which it anchored for a few days in the harbor, without making any attempt at landing. The few Cossacks stationed at the port remained quiet during the whole period of the presence of the ships.

After the battle of Plevna of July 30th and 31st, comparative quiet reigned for a time on the scene of action On August 7th, the Turks repulsed an attack of the Russians on Lovatz. Osman Pasha sent his cavalry on reconnoissances as far as Nicopolis. On their other front, that turned toward Rustchuk, Rasgrad, and Shumla, the Russians evacuated the whole country east of the Kara Lom or Black Lom, while their right wing was withdrawn from Osman Bazar to Kesrova on the road to Tirnova. The Russian position in the middle of August was virtually as follows: The right wing, consisting of three army corps, was situated with its front on the line of Plevna-Lovatz, on both banks of the Osma, leaning on the right on Nicopolis, which was garrisoned by the fourth Rumanian division. The center, consisting of one army corps, fronting toward the south and stationed upon the line Tirnova, Gabrova, and Elena, was expected to support General Gourko, who, returning from his dash across the Balkans, was fortifying himself in the Shipka Pass. The left wing, consisting of two army corps, fronted on the line of Shumla, Rasgrad, and Rustchuk, and was stationed along the Kara Lom. According to the most trustworthy reports, the Russians were opposed at this time by the following forces: Mehemet Ali Pasha, with 70,000 regulars and 30,000 irregulars, in and around Rasgrad, and 12,000 men at Osman Bazar; Suleiman Pasha, on the southern slope of the central Balkans, with 15,000 regulars and 5,000 irregulars; Osman Pasha, at Plevna and Lovatz, with 30,000 regulars and 10,000 irregulars, making altogether 127,000 men and 45,000 irregulars. In addition to these, Prince Hassan of Egypt had 15,000 men in the Dobrudja, north of Varna; Said Pasha had 25,000 men in Silistria and Turtukai; 14,000 men were stationed around Nissa and Sophia, and 12,000 men in and around Widin, and about 7,000 irregulars were distributed with the four last-named forces. Not including the army of Rustchuk, whose strength was unknown, the Turkish army in Bulgaria at this time amounted to about 193,000 men and 52,000 irregulars. But in the beginning of August some change had taken place in the disposition of these troops, as the forces in Nissa and Sophia had been directed to join Osman Pasha at Plevna. It seems more than doubtful, however, that these troops should have increased his force to 70,000 men, as he stated himself. The only reinforcements which the Turks received in Bulgaria during the month of August were several thousand regulars, transported by vessels from the Caucasus to Varna, and several thousand men (ten thousand, according to Turkish reports), which were sent from Philippopolis to Suleiman Pasha. The operations during August consisted mainly in a fierce struggle for the Shipka Pass. In turning their attention chiefly to this pass, and in leaving the task of storming it to their center only, while their right and left wings, both of them stronger than the center, were left idle, the Turks gave to the hard-pushed Russians what they needed more than all else, time. Every day gained brought the reinforcements nearer, which were on the march from Poland, the shores of the Black Sea, and from St. Petersburg. Even before the Shipka Pass was attacked, it seemed for a while as if Suleiman Pasha would cross the mountains to the east of it, while leaving a considerable force at Kasanlik. On the 15th, several Turkish detachments started from the village Hainkoi to cross the mountains by the Hainkoi Pass, the same pass which General Gourko had used. They were, however, stopped by the 39th infantry regiment, and left the pass on the 17th. The Russians had not expected to see the Shipka Pass attacked from the front. All the orders issued by the Grand Duke commander, clearly showed that he anticipated attacks from the Plevna-Lovatz position on the one hand, and from Rasgrad and Osman Bazar on the other, at the same time. Suleiman Pasha was expected, by turning the Shipka Pass on the east, to join hands with Mehemet Ali's army, advancing from Osman Bazar. It was reasonably supposed that by a simultaneous advance of the different Turkish forces north of the Balkans, the pass would fall into their hands without a great struggle. But the Turks disappointed all reasonable expectations, and while the two Turkish wings remained almost inactive, the center, under Suleiman Pasha, advanced to the attack of the Shipka Pass. After having occupied the village of Shipka on the 19th, he assailed the fortified positions to the north of it on the 21st. The Russians, not suspecting the intention of the enemy, had left but a small garrison in the pass, consisting of the Bulgarian Legion and an infantry regiment of the 9th division. The Russian position, however, was very strong. The correspondent of the London *Times* described it as follows:

" The Russian position is extremely strong —in fact, if it were

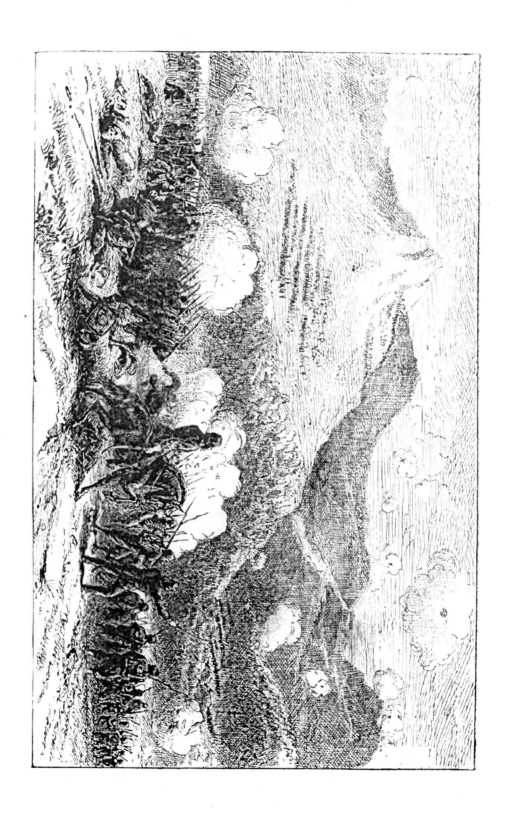

PRINCE HASSAN.

LIEUT.-GENERAL RADETSKY.

properly defended it might be held against overwhelming numbers. But the Russians have either not had time, or do not intend to hold the pass, for they have only fifteen guns in position, and these, I imagine, from the broken pieces of shell that I have seen, are ordinary field-pieces. The position of these guns is almost inaccessible from the southern side, or where the Turks are attacking, as one-half of them are placed on a kind of buttress of rock, commanding the road, and the remainder are divided into three small earthworks that enfilade the approach, to the base of this rock, and also sweep the broad glacis of green turf which flanks the road on both sides. For 500 yards on all sides of the Russian position there is no kind of shelter, and the only way in which these works can be carried is by assault."

The entire Russian force, in all probability, did not exceed 4,000 men. They nevertheless repulsed the numerous attacks of the Turks, made with great force and energy. On the same day Osman Pasha made a feint from Lovatz on Selvi, in order to prevent assistance being sent from that point to the pass. On the 22d the Turks took the Russians on the flank, so that on the 23d the brave garrison found itself in very close quarters, having been compelled to give up some of the ground held, and having suffered considerable loss. At this critical moment the Russians received considerable reinforcements, and General Radetzky himself hastened on from Tirnova to assume the command, so that on the evening of the 24th the Russians had regained all their lost positions. The losses on both sides were very great; but while Suleiman continued to send fresh troops to the front, the Russians also received considerable reinforcements from Tirnova on the 25th and the following days, so that although the struggle was renewed from time to time, General Radetzky, at the close of the month, was in complete possession of the pass. The correspondent of the London *Times* gives the following description of the Russian position and the operations in the pass:

"General Radetzky occupies the positions held so manfully during the twelve days in which the Moslem host dashed themselves so bravely, but fruitlessly against his intrenched lines. His advanced center holds Mount St. Nicholas, the highest point in the Shipka Pass; his right and left flanks rest upon two crests, which stand a little to the northward of that point. His line forms a very obtuse angle, the vertex of which is cut off by the central position at

16

Mount St. Nicholas. To his extreme right and left are ridges extending parallel to the Russian wings, and running northward nearly to the Gabrova road, the only line of communication of the Russian troops. The Turks, having vastly superior numbers, extended their flanks down these last-mentioned ridges, and nearly enveloped the Russian positions, so nearly accomplishing this result, that they swept the Gabrova road in many places with musketry fire. Nothing but absolute want of generalship on the part of the Turkish commander prevented this double flank movement being so extended as completely to cut off the Russians from both food and water before the arrival of General Radetzky with his timely reinforcements. When Radetzky came up on the 23d of August he at once charged the Turkish positions on his flanks, and carried them, in this way overcoming to a great extent the difficulty of providing his men with food and water. Between the two lines held by the opposing forces are deep valleys, which might almost be called ravines, and the Russian troops had to go up and down the steep sides of these ravines to reach their enemies.

"The Russians now hold the crest formerly occupied by the Turks on their right wing, while the latter have fallen back to the next ridge, where they keep up a desultory fire with the Russian pickets. In the rear of Mount St. Nicholas is a second peak about half a mile from it, which forms a second center, so to speak, both of them, however, running into the line of heights held by the two wings of the Russian army in the Shipka Pass. Strong batteries have been constructed upon all the Russian heights, and they are practically impregnable.

"A General officer told me to-day, that during the twelve days' operations in the Shipka Pass the Turks made one hundred and four distinct aggressive movements. From this some idea may be formed of the enormous losses which they must have suffered. They made every assault with the most desperate courage, and were compelled to move up precipitous hill-sides, defended on the summits by intrenchments."

The fighting throughout was of the most sanguinary character, the Russians particularly performing deeds of valor, which were described as truly wonderful by eye-witnesses. The correspondent of the London *News*, in describing the fighting, said:

"Occasionally, at some point the Russians would be hurled clean back out of the wood altogether. I could mark the Turks following them eagerly to its edge, lying down while pouring out a galling fire. The troops who were charged with making this front attack merely succeeded in preventing the Turkish efforts to work round to the Russian rear. It was therefore decided at noon to deliver a counter flank movement. Two battalions, executing this movement, had to advance under a tremendous fire from Turkish mountain guns. The fighting on the Turkish front and flank lasted for a full hour, but at last the Turks were seen withdrawing their battery of mountain guns near the right flank, which was a sure sign that danger menaced it if it stayed longer. Their left battery followed their example, which showed the Russians gained the ridge on the Turkish left also. There remained but the central peak of the Turkish positions. That carried, the ridge would be ours, and our right flank would be set free from the dangerous pressure on it."

Owing to the inactivity of Osman Pasha, who did not undertake anything beyond the feint on Selvi, General Radetzky was enabled to bring up nearly his entire army corps to the defense of the position, while the Second infantry division was ordered from the lower Yantra to the pass. This division went to Selvi, where it replaced the Ninth, which had hurried on to the scene of action. Mehemet Ali on the Rasgrad and Eski Djuma line did as little as Osman Pasha to assist Suleiman Pasha. There were indeed engagements, on August 22d, at Karakoi, on the Upper Kara Lom, and on August 23d, at Kisilar and Yaslar, between the troops of Mehemet Ali and the Thirteenth Russian army corps; but these actions were only casual ones, not forming parts of any preconcerted plan.

Rustchuk was bombarded during August from both sides, from Giurgevo and from the Bulgarian side of the river, but little impression was made. A weak movement from Rustchuk against Dolob, five miles from the fortress on the Lom, was easily repulsed by the Russians. The last days of August saw a resumption of hostilities along the entire line. On August 30th, both of the Turkish armies on either side of the Russians assumed the offensive. On the left wing of the Russian army, commanded by the Czarevitch, a battle was fought at Karasan, twenty-five miles north-west of Osman Bazar, which resulted in a victory for the Turks. Three Turkish divisions, including the Egyptian division under Prince Hassan, which had been ordered up from the Dobrudja, advanced on both banks of the Kara Lom and drove back the Russian troops, four thousand men with ten guns, after severe fighting, with heavy losses on both sides.

At the same time sorties of the garrison of Rustchuk compelled the Twelfth army corps to remain at the Lower Lom. The correspondent of the London *Times* gives the following description of the battle :

"Early this morning Nedjib Pasha advanced from Adakoi, near Rasgrad, with three brigades, two batteries of artillery, two squadrons of cavalry, and one brigade of infantry reserve. Mehemet Ali and Prince Hassan took up a position with their staff on a high hill immediately north of Yenikoi, which commands an uninterrupted view from Rasgrad to beyond Osman Bazar. The Russians from their batteries behind Sadana opened fire about nine o'clock on the advancing Turks. Nedjib steadily advanced, and entered the burning village of Sadana by half-past eleven o'clock. The retreating Russians were hotly pressed. They retired precipitately, to Karasan, where they made a vigorous stand. Savfet Pasha created a diversion by attacking Haidarkoi. The Russians had a battery of three guns to their right, near Haidarkoi. They made splendid practice at the advancing Turks and Egyptians, but these cleverly opened out and advanced to the right and left of the village in a really workmanlike style. The engagement now became general, and extended over some fifteen miles. A heavy and continued roll of fire of skirmishers was heard along all the ridges from Basisler to near Sadana. By four o'clock Karasan was in flames. The Russians gradually gave way, and the Turks redoubled the energy of their attack. At five o'clock the enemy were scampering out of Haidarkoi, and horses were trotting up to take the guns out of the battery. The Turkish battery was making splendid practice, and fired just as the guns were taken off. One gun was struck with the last shell. The Turks cheered, and dashed through the blazing village and away to the left to Popkoi like a pack of hounds. The Russian camps were hastily cleared out, two guns covering their retreat and making excellent practice. But the Turks and Egyptians still scampered over the ground in fine style. The Russians were now in full retreat in every direction, and by sunset the Turks had proved for the second time, not only capable of meeting the Russians in the open, but also of driving them from their strongly-intrenched positions."

On the Russian right wing, fronting toward Plevna, General Zotoff repulsed a Turkish attack on Pelisat on August 31st. The battle is described by the *Daily News* correspondent as follows:

"Osman Pasha's attack on the Russian positions at Pelisat and vicinity was one of the most hardly-fought battles of the war. The Turks, early in the fight, captured a Russian redoubt, one mile in front of Pelisat. In the course of one hour this redoubt was taken by the Turks, retaken by the Russians, and taken again by the Turks. The Russian left wing was driven back on Pelisat, in front of which trenches had been dug and were lined with troops. The Turks advanced as though determined to drive our left out of Pelisat and turn it. The Turks began to descend the hill in that direction, not with a rush, but leisurely, and without firing; not in masses or lines, but scattered and diffused. They came down about half way in this manner, the Russian artillery tearing up the groups all the time in the most savage manner. The Russian infantry fire, which had for the last five minutes been very heavy about Zgalince, now began to roll along the hill-crest in our direction, and the Turks, who were just coming into range, began to drop rapidly. The Turkish advance now veered to the left, and went at the Russian trenches on the crest of the hills between Pelisat and Zgalince with a shout, opening fire at the same time. The Turks descended into a little hollow and were lost to sight for a time, while the Russian trenches flamed and smoked, and a storm of balls was poured into the advancing Turks. This must have lasted fifteen or twenty minutes, during which time fearful loss of life must have occurred. Then we saw the Turks begin to withdraw, carrying off their wounded. The Turks had no sooner withdrawn from the Russian fire than they formed and advanced again. Many dead bodies of Turks were found within ten feet of the Russian trenches. The little slope, on the crest of which the trenches were situated, was literally covered with dead. I counted seven on a space of not more than ten feet square. The battle here was terrible, but the Turks were again repulsed. It will hardly be believed that they went at it again, and yet they did so. It seemed madness, because we could see that the Russian fire never slackened an instant, and that the Russian line never wavered, while reserves were waiting behind ready to fall in at the least sign of wavering. This scene of carnage was again repeated, but only lasted a moment. The Turks, completely broken, withdrew sullenly, firing, and carrying off their wounded and many of their dead. They fell back on the redoubt which they had first taken, apparently with the intention of holding it, but they were not allowed to remain long there.

Another attack on the Russian center had been equally as unsuccessful as that on the Russian trenches on the left. The Russians pursued the retreating Turks with a murderous fire. Then six companies went at them with bayonet and swept them out of the redoubt like a whirlwind. At four o'clock the Turks were in retreat everywhere, and the Russians occupied the whole of their first position, besides pursuing the Turks a short distance with cavalry. The Russians were about twenty thousand strong. Their loss is estimated at five hundred, and the Turkish loss at two thousand killed and wounded."

On September 3d, Gen. Skobeleff, by a brilliant stroke, recaptured Lovatz, which had been in Osman Pasha's hands for five weeks. The battle was described by eye-witnesses as very severe, and the losses on both sides were very great. The loss of Lovatz interrupted the direct communication between Osman Pasha and Suleiman Pasha, while it enabled the Russians gradually to surround Osman Pasha's position at Plevna, and to cut off all his communications.

On August 31st, Mehemet Ali's headquarters were at Yenikoi, on the Lom, while on the same day the Russians held the left bank of the river as far south as Gagova. Mehemet Ali quietly holding his positions on the Lom, concentrated all his forces on its right bank toward Yenikoi, while on the left bank the Thirteenth Russian corps was stationed on the line of Ablava and Kechlova, near Biela. The Twelfth corps remained before Rustchuk, on the Lower Lom. Some detachments of this corps had an engagement at Kadikoi with troops from Rustchuk, in which the Turks were forced to retreat. In the meantime, Mehemet Ali, remaining in his posts on the Lom, and without pursuing the advantage he had gained, ordered Achmet Eyub Pasha to advance from his position at Rasgrad. On Sept. 6th, Eyub Pasha attacked the Russian positions at Kechlova. The Turkish forces were greatly superior to the Russians in point of numbers and were constantly receiving accessions. The Russians fought with great bravery, but were finally compelled to retreat beyond the Lom. The correspondent of the London *Standard*, at Shumla, stated that the battle was a very fierce one, and lasted fully ten hours. On the 7th, the Turks took Kadikoi and forced the Russians to cross to the left bank of the Lom at this point also, so that the entire right bank was cleared of Russians. On the 8th, Mehemet Ali crossed the river with three divisions, and began to advance slowly toward the Yantra.

Osman Pasha, in the meanwhile, had transformed his position around Plevna into a fortress of unusual strength, against which single attacks were of no use, and which could only be reduced by a long and protracted siege The correspondent of the *Daily News*, in speaking of the situation, said: . " It is obvious that the fortifications have been much strengthened since the last battle. The longer one looks at the place, the more thoroughly does one feel the toughness of the Russian task. The position must be attacked as a whole and taken as a whole. If the northern ridge were taken and occupied, the position of the central swell would not be materially impaired. Suppose that a lodgment was effected on the central swell, that lodgment would be commanded by the northern ridge and the redoubts on the south of the town. All that is wanted to make the Turkish position virtually impregnable is the fortification of the ridge in front of Radisevo."

The Russians assigned to operate before Plevna had also not been idle, but had received considerable reinforcements, including three Rumanian divisions. The combined Russian and Rumanian forces were placed under the command of Prince Charles of Rumania.

A series of battles was begun around Plevna on the 7th of September, which lasted for a week, and were not exceeded in sanguinary character by any of the fierce conflicts which had taken place for the Shipka Pass. The Russians began the attack with a furious cannonade. This was kept up until the 11th, when the Russians proceeded to storm the Turkish positions. An idea of the fighting may be gained from the account of the correspondent of the *Daily News*, of the operations on the 8th:

" When the cannonade recommenced this morning it was not easy at first to recognize that the Russians had gained any advantage the day before. The parapet of the Grivitza redoubt had been a good deal jagged by Russian shells, but under cover of the night all its defects had been made good, and it looked as trim as if never a shot had been fired at it. But the Russians had, during the night, gained a large slice of ground in the direction of Grivitza, and a battery of siege guns had been built on an elevation within easy range of the redoubt. At sunrise that battery came into action in rear of the advanced battery, and sent its fire sweeping down into the redoubt, which could not reply to the siege battery, the range being too long ; so it pounded away at the field batteries on the ridge, but the practice was not good, and few casualties occurred. The Russian siege battery made admirable practice at the Grivitza redoubt, which is the key to the position, and instead of spreading their fire, the Russians should have concentrated upon it the whole weight of the bombardment. As it is, they may bombard it for a week and after all not succeed in taking it. The assault was intended to begin yesterday afternoon at 5 o'clock, but owing to delays the troops were not in position by the appointed time. Everywhere now the infantry is in position waiting for the word.

" Toward noon the Russian infantry pushed forward in skirmishing order, driving back the outlying Turks; the artillery followed and came into action at short range. The Turkish return fire, chiefly directed at the Russian first line of artillery, was very heavy, but little harm was done. Further on the left, to the crest of the range beyond Radisevo, which was one array of field batteries, the firing was very heavy, the Turkish shells doing great damage among the gunners, and falling behind among the infantry on the reverse slope and in Radisevo. At three o'clock the Russians advanced toward the Turkish positions, and continued to fire somewhat slackly. The fire must have reached into Plevna."

On the 9th, the Turks undertook a sortie against the Russian left wing, but were forced to retreat with considerable loss. The Rumanians then advanced close up to the redoubts of the enemy. In the evening the Russian siege batteries were brought into a more favorable position.

The morning of the 11th, the day intended for the assault, broke with rain, which settled down into a dense mist, through which objects were invisible at a distance of one hundred yards. The *Daily News* correspondent gives the following description of the battle, as witnessed by him from the heights in front of Radisevo :-

" About ten A.M. the fog lifted somewhat, and at that time the Grivitza redoubt was still alive, although its fire could not be called brisk. To our left, near the Lovatz and Plevna road, there were occasional intermittent bursts of infantry fire. Soon after ten o'clock occurred an ominous lull in the firing. Of this the Turks jauntily took advantage to come out from behind the parapets and stroll about the glacis with the utmost nonchalance. Then the fog came down again, veiling everything and hiding everything. At eleven precisely a furious musketry fire suddenly burst out on our left from the Russians pushing their way out of the gap through the passes of the Lovatz-Plevna road and against the redoubt on the summit of an iso-

RUSSIAN INFANTRY GOING INTO ACTION.

STORMING OF THE GRIVITZA REDOUBT BY THE ROUMANIANS.

lated mamelon, south-east of the town of Plevna. The Turks, so far as could be judged from the sound, seemed to be in great measure reserving their fire until the Russians came to close quarters with them, as everything was invisible at a distance of twenty yards. This also applies to their artillery fire, although the Russian batteries continued furiously to shell the Turkish positions.

"About noon the fog lifted somewhat, but fell again. During the interval the cannon in the Turkish second position could be seen firing hard in the direction of the hostile musketry fire. After the fog again fell, one thing became certain from the sound of the firing, that the infantry fighting had a tendency to retrograde from the Turkish front, moving further to the left and nearer to the fighting just above the western edge of the village of Radisevo. Exactly along the space held by Prince Shachovsky's staff as the foremost line on the night of the 30th of July, I found several batteries of Russian field artillery in steady action against the first and second Turkish position on the central swell, a little to the right and rear of the infantry still engaged in desultory fighting. The commander of a battery told us, with an assumption of indifference, that the fighting which was dying out was merely forepost work to clear the way for a grand assault against the redoubt on the isolated mamelon, which was to be made in the afternoon, but with a glass I could discern on the slopes leading up to the mamelon Russian dead and wounded lying about sadly thick. Successive bodies of Turks were streaming down the slope of the mamelon against the huddled mass of Russians, retiring seemingly on the shelter trenches athwart the mouth of the road ravine, and ascending the slopes to our immediate right. It was also clear that Gen. Skobeleff had attacked the redoubt and covered way due east from the isolated mamelon. Yet further to the left on the extreme westward of Radisevo ridge skirmishing was going on, but the Turks presented an obstinate front, and fired steadily from shelter trenches. This was at two o'clock, and for nearly two hours little forepost affairs of no consequence went on."

The operations in other parts of the field were described as follows by the London *Times :*

"At 12:50 P.M. one brigade of Gen. Zotoff's corps, supported by another, attacked the center redoubt on the south side, one and a half miles from Radisevo. The attack was repulsed by a rifle fire, after lasting ninety minutes. It was renewed again at 4 P.M. Twelve battalions of Russians advanced with the most splendid and devoted bravery, right up to the ditch, carrying scaling ladders. They surrounded the redoubt on three sides, and hung on to it magnificently. At 4:45 o'clock they were actually in the redoubt, but nothing mortal could face the fire from the repeating-rifles. They were destroyed by hundreds at a few paces. At 4:52 the survivors fell slowly back. The Rumanians at the same time, under the personal observation of the Emperor, three times assaulted the most salient central redoubt lower down than Grivitza, but were always beaten back. Their scaling-ladder parties were killed on the counterscarp of the ditch to the last officer and man. At 5 P.M. the assault had been repulsed along the whole line, and very few reserves remained in hand. News was brought the Czar at daybreak on Wednesday that at 7 o'clock on Tuesday evening two fresh Russian brigades had carried the redoubt where the Rumanians had been repulsed in the afternoon, and after sustaining a counter attack from the Turks, followed them up and took the next redoubt also.

"The first redoubt which was captured partially, commands the rest, and can, with a little spade-work, be converted into a means of approaching all the rest in turn. A great failure was therefore remedied at the eleventh hour. The Archangel regiment achieved the greatest feat. Col. Schmetler, an Aide-de-camp of the Emperor, was shot dead as he planted the colors on the parapet with his own hand. I estimated the forces engaged at about 57,000 on the Russo-Rumanian side, against from 50,000 to 70,000 Turks. The valor of the Russian troops is the only thing to be praised, as the attack was unskillfully directed, and the waste of life unnecessary. The Turks were very skillfully handled. They must have lost some men in their two sallies in the open; otherwise they were completely covered and lay close till the moment of assault."

From this report it appears that the Russians again committed the blunder which lost for them the first battle of Plevna, and the same charges were made as to the inefficiency of the leaders.

On the morning of the 12th, no further direct attacks were undertaken by the Russians, but a continuous bombardment of the fortifications as well as of the town was kept up. The Turks did not respond to this fire very strongly; but in the afternoon they undertook, on their part, a series of attacks on the Russian left wing, which threatened them in the rear. Five times Gen. Skobeleff repulsed these attacks, but at the sixth attack he was forced to evacuate the two redoubts on the Lovatz road captured the day before, so that only the redoubt at Grivitza remained in the hands of the Russians.

The correspondent of the London *Times*, in speaking of this position, said:

"On the evening of the 11th, after the Russians had failed three times in attempting to take the redoubt at the western extremity of the Plevna valley, Skobeleff succeeded in driving the Turks out of the double redoubt, and established himself in their place. This work is situated between the Sophia and Lovatz roads, and was captured by Skobeleff from the westward. He immediately asked for reinforcements, and continued to do so in vain until the evening of the 12th, when the shattered remains of a regiment which had suffered severely the day before, were sent to him. Shortly afterward two other battalions were sent, but this style of reinforcement was like a drop in the ocean; and the Turks becoming aware of the fact that Skobeleff had not been properly supported, made a detour round the hill and assaulted the redoubt with an overwhelming force of infantry. Five times they were hurled back by Skobeleff's men, but the sixth assault was too much for the overburdened garrison, and the Turks recaptured the redoubt and still continue to hold it."

The blunders committed by both armies were severely commented on by all eye-witnesses, all of whom agreed that bravely as the soldiers on both sides fought, the mistakes of their generals nullified all the advantages gained. The London *Times* said, on this subject, that "The blunders of both Turks and Russians in this campaign are unequaled in the history of warfare. A success by either side is certain to be followed by some suicidal attempt which more than neutralizes all that has been previously gained with heavy expenditure of blood."

The Rumanian troops, on this occasion, were under fire for the first time during the war.—Much-had been said against them, and it was generally expected that they would fail to deport themselves well while under fire. The result, however, proved the opposite to be the case. All who witnessed the terrible struggle for the Grivitza redoubt, which was held by the Rumanians, agree that they behaved with the utmost gallantry. The correspondent of the London *Times* speaks as follows of their conduct during the battle:

"The great redoubt was defended entirely by Rumanian infantry, who held the work with the most desperate courage and tenacity, receiving therefor the eulogies of the Russian Emperor and all the foreign spectators of their valor.'. . . . Should the Russians succeed in taking Plevna, they will owe no trivial part of their victory to the co-operation of their Rumanian allies."

The losses on both sides were very great. The Grand Duke Nicholas, in an official despatch, stated the Russian loss in killed and wounded to be 300 officers and 12,500 men, and the Rumanian loss at 60 officers and 3,000 men. The Turks did not lose as many men as the Russians, during the first days, as they were not so exposed, but during the attacks on the redoubts, their loss was reported to be fully equal to that of the Russians.

CHAPTER VI.

THE FALL OF PLEVNA.

Renewed fighting in the Shipka Pass—Defeat of Mehemet Ali at Tcherkovna—Mehemet Ali replaced by Suleiman in the Supreme Command—Formation of the Army of Orkhanie—Reinforcements and Ammunition for Plevna—Battle of Gorni Dabnik—Capture of Telis—Battle of Radomirze—The investment of Plevna complete—Capture of the Green Hill—Formation of the Army of Sophia—Capture of Teteven and Vratza—The Rumanians take Rahova—Capture of Pravetz and Etropol—Turks evacuate Orkhanie and retreat beyond the Balkans—Suleiman's advance on the Lom—Capture of Elena by the Turks—End of the Turkish Advance—The fall of Plevna.

SULEIMAN PASHA having nearly exhausted his forces in the last days of August in a vain struggle for the Shipka Pass, and the Eighth Russian army corps, under Gen. Radetzky, having maintained all its positions, the Turkish general spent the first few weeks of September in reorganizing his forces. He did not, however, receive reinforcements of any account. While Radetzky was completing his fortifications and his roads, Suleiman Pasha was actively engaged in constructing war batteries, and in bringing up heavy guns. The first half of the month, therefore, passed without any engagement of consequence, but was occupied with cannonades and skirmishes. But in the night, from the 16th to the 17th, the Turks suddenly attacked the Russians along the entire line. The correspondent of the London *Times*, writing on September 17th, described the attack as follows :

" At length the eventful day for which we have been so patiently waiting has arrived, and for once rumor proved correct, so far as that the attempt to capture the Russian positions would be by a night attack. For the last three days sure signs had been observable that some movement of importance was imminent, not the least of which being the provision made for the expected wounded, as to whom the English and Austrian ambulances appear to have worked a revolution with regard to their treatment in this army. Last night the preparations were complete, and at about ten o'clock eight battalions, numbering 3,000 men, marched noiselessly and passed headquarters to form the central attacking column, under

Salih Pasha, while an equal force, commanded by Veisel Pasha, ascended the western heights, and some 2,000 men were sent to the eastward, where Brigadier Redjib Pasha has for some time been established. The night was favorable. The assigned positions were taken without the enemy having the slightest intimation of anything unusual being about to occur. . . . . Shortly before four o'clock on Monday morning, the general, on whom devolved the duty of leading the attack on the center and chief position—Fort St. Nicholas, a huge rock which towers on high above the point where the Shipka road attains its greatest elevation—taking advantage of the darkness of the hour, quitted his well-selected cover, and advanced his men up the green slope at the base of the rock, and, proceeding further, was soon established upon its steep and rugged face without firing a shot. Arrived here, however, the alarm was quickly given, and the rock soon became alive with vivid flashes of rifle firing. This continued for the space of half an hour, at the expiration of which the fire became lessened, giving assurance that the position, formidable as it is, was won at the commencement of the attack. I was at headquarters on the plain, at the mouth of the Pass, when it was announced that a telegram had been received from the eastern battery that Fort St. Nicholas had actually been taken. The rapidity with which this seems to have been done astonished Suleiman Pasha, who was upon the point of telegraphing the welcome news to Constantinople, when he reflected upon it and made use of the wire to inquire if there could be any misconception. The answer was reassuring, and the cessation of the fire seemed to confirm the truth of the message. At this moment, however, the Turkish artillery opened upon the rearward portion of the fort, and this proved, unfortunately, that Suleiman's doubts were too well founded. His mortar batteries were firing heavily also, and the rattle of musketry became incessant. Dawn had just lifted the curtain of darkness, and every moment of increasing light extinguished, as it were, the flash of the rifle. Not alone in the center, but to the eastward and westward, the din of battle could now be heard, echoed and re-echoed in the mountain spaces where the combat was progressing. . . . . Arrived at last at the top, the exertion was amply repaid, and the reason of the error above referred to became easy to understand. Seen from the plain, the rock might readily be supposed just before daylight to have been captured, for its summit is, perhaps, a hundred yards deep, and is broken up into jagged and

storm-torn ravines. About half-way along is a cleft, and the Turkish troops could be seen firing with the utmost energy across at the
Russians, hidden under whatever cover there was to be met with
upon their side of it, while their own numerously intrenched men
were picking off their exposed assailants most mercilessly. The
eastern battery was pouring its shells in among the enfiladed
trenches, but their guns on the western side were unable to play
with so great effect on account of the closeness of the combatants to
each other. All this time I looked anxiously, but in vain, for the
attacks which it must have been intended that the battalions told off
for the purpose on either side should have long ago carried out.
Fighting was to be heard going on in the valleys covered from view
by the intervening ridges of the mountains, but this was of a desultory nature, and soon ceased almost entirely, and one's attention became rivetted by the events passing immediately before the eye.
The Turkish center was evidently admirably and bravely led by
Salih Pasha's second in command. He poured up his men with the
utmost rapidity, and their fire was as incessant as their exposure to
that of the enemy from their thickly-lined trenches was great. That
the Turkish fire was effective was shown by the sight of the wounded
who were being conveyed from the stoutly-defended side of the cleft.
The eastern battery was hotly replied to all the time by the Turkish
guns on the Shipka road, and their having fuse shells gave some
compensation for the losses which their side sustained from the correctness of aim of the Turkish artillerymen. The delay in the further advance of the Turkish center was becoming extraordinary, the
numbers opposed to it being very inferior numerically. No reserves
appeared to be sent forward on the Russian side. Something had
evidently gone out of gear, as the best-contrived plan will sometimes
do, and the fighting had endured, it must be remembered, since
dawn. About a quarter to-eleven, however, a startling change occurred. A dark mass of men was to be seen advancing from the
direction of Gabrova along the high-road through the pass. This
unlooked-for apparition quickly determined whatever hesitation the
gallant Turkish leader of the center might have entertained, for he saw
himself in danger of being surrounded by fresh masses of the enemy.
It proved to be some 1,600 Russian Chasseurs, who had been sent
forward as speedily as possible on the alarm of the attack arriving.
The order to retire was at once sounded, and down again came the
now disheartened troops, with the cup of victory dashed from their

lips. Fortunately, however, the enemy did not follow, and, as regards the reinforcements, they were even yet too far distant to attempt pursuit, excepting to a much less extent than could have been expected. Down the hill pell-mell the center men came, passing on their way their own side trenches nearest the rock. The troops which held the trenches in question deserve the highest praise for not having joined in the panic—for panic soon it became as the alarm spread among the now easily-excited soldiery. Had the Russians followed up their advantage and merely made a show of pursuit, the consequences must have been disastrous, as it is not by any means improbable that the army nearest the unfortunate center would have caught the contagion. Happily, the result was avoided, and the beaten soldier, who had been so near the goal, was able to rally his men, and kept every one from descending and spreading terror among the rest."

The Russian loss was stated at 31 officers and 1,000 soldiers killed and wounded, while, according to the Russian report, not less than 3,000 Turkish corpses covered the rocks on the hill. Everything now remained quiet up to the close of September. With the close of the month, Suleiman Pasha, who had taken Mehemet Ali's place, was replaced by Rauf Pasha.

The Czarevitch, after having abandoned the line of the Lom River in the beginning of September, not being pushed by Mehemet Ali, was enabled to occupy strong positions on the Yantra, where he could wait for reinforcements. On the 20th of September he occupied a line extending from Tcherkovna, about twelve miles southeast of Biela, to Pyrgos, on the Danube, presenting a front fully twenty-four miles long. His army, which had originally consisted of the Twelfth and Thirteenth corps, had been reinforced with parts of the Eleventh, and probably the entire Second corps. On the 21st of September Mehemet Ali attacked the Czarevitch on his extreme right at Tcherkovna, and here encountered his first check. The Russians were posted on both sides of a road connecting Tcherkovna, Verboka, and Cairkoi, partly on a ridge and partly on the slope of the heights which rise on the left bank of the Jordan, a small brook flowing into one of the tributaries of the Banicka Lom, which empties into the Kara Lom. The Turks were posted on the other side of the Jordan, occupying the heights on the right flank, at a distance of only three kilometres, or not quite two miles, from

THE BULGARIAN LEGION DEFENDING THE LUNETTE IN THE SHIPKA PASS.

A CAVALRY FIGHT NEAR PLEVNA

the Russian position. The battle is described as follows by the correspondent of the London *Times :*

" The favorable weather which has suddenly set in made it possible for Mehemet Ali to carry out the reconnoissance which it had been arranged to make yesterday of the Russian position near Tcherkovna, where the Russians had taken up a strong position in considerable force, with their main strength on the left wing. This was protected by a wood extending from the top to the middle of the declivity lining the left bank of the Jordan brook. The intervening ground is pretty steep, does not afford the slightest cover, and makes the task of attacking exceedingly difficult. The Turkish arrangements were made in such a way as to allow them to begin the advance at about twelve o'clock. Ten battalions of Hassan Pasha's corps were appointed to this task ; a brigade remained in reserve and never came into action at all. At one o'clock the Turkish batteries on both sides of the road to the north of Tcherkovna opened fire on the Russian intrenchments situated on the ridges to the south-east of Verboka. The Russians at once replied, at first with eight guns from that position. At about half-past one, eight more guns were moved up to the same heights, and then began a rather furious artillery engagement. At two o'clock a body of Russian infantry advanced, under cover of a wood, against the left wing of the Turks, but encountered only one battalion, which kept its ground till two other battalions, under the command of Riza Pasha, attacked the enemy's flank and drove them to a favorable position in the rear, where they made a stand. From the rear of the Russian infantry half a battery opened fire upon the Turkish troops, and this lasted about thirty minutes, when a Turkish battery, likewise from behind their own men, gave voice, and attracted the enemy's fire.

" After, however, the Russians had received strong reinforcements in that direction, the Turks, on their part, directed nine Egyptian battalions against the Russian right wing, but these did not enter into action. For this reason the Turkish left wing could not gain any ground. From the Turkish center and right wing then three battalions advanced, the center force, under the command of Sifat Pasha, against the heights to the east of Verboka, and the right wing against the wood to the north of the village. Then there gradually began a furious infantry battle, which grew in intensity, until at about six o'clock it reached its highest pitch. The center

17

column advanced as far as Verboka, and after having been ordered four times in vain to retire, had to be led out of the fire by the divisional commander in person. It was apparently not the intention of Mehemet Ali to gain ground in the center. Not less heroically did the battalions on the Turkish right wing fight. At half-past eight in the evening firing ceased, and the Turks returned to their former positions."

After this defeat, Mehemet Ali, on the 24th of September, began to retreat on his entire line beyond the Lom, and completely stopped the forward movement begun four weeks previously. He gave as a reason for this unexpected resolution that he had become convinced of the numerical superiority of his enemy. It was also known that he was seriously hindered in his operations by the continual disobedience to his orders displayed by his subordinates, Achmet Eyub Pasha and Prince Hassan of Egypt. This retreat was seized upon in Constantinople as a pretext for his removal, and while he was sent to the Servian frontier, Suleiman Pasha was appointed in his place. His want of success, however, was due more to the fact that the other commanders failed to co-operate with him, than to any fault of his own. Osman Pasha, instead of making use of the favorable opportunity presented to him after the second Russian defeat at Plevna to pursue the completely demoralized Russians to the Danube, remained quietly in Plevna, and permitted himself to be surrounded again. All later efforts of Mehemet Ali to approach him from Osman Bazar by way of Tirnova and to establish a communication with him, were left unnoticed by Osman Pasha. Suleiman, also, seemed to show but little inclination to render Mehemet Ali any aid. After the Russians had retreated from Rumelia to the Shipka Pass, Mehemet Ali had desired that Suleiman, after leaving a corps of observation before the Shipka Pass, should cross the Balkans with his army, and that having joined their forces, they should then defeat the Russian forces at the foot of the Balkans, and then establish communication with Osman. This plan seemed certainly to be the most correct and most feasible one. A decided Turkish success in Bulgaria would make a Russian advance in Rumelia impossible. Suleiman, however, instead of acting upon the plan of the commander-in-chief, undertook those attacks on the Russian positions in the Shipka Pass, in which he sacrificed fully 10,000 of the best Turkish troops, and which, according to the best military authorities, were entirely senseless.

In the middle of September a corps made up of troops from Widin, Sophia, and Nissa was gathering at Orkhanie, on the road from Sophia and Plevna, under the command of Shevket Pasha. Although Russian and Rumanian cavalry were on this road, Hifzi Pasha succeeded, on September 23d, in reaching Plevna with reinforcements amounting to 20 battalions, one regiment of cavalry and two batteries, in all 12,000 men, together with a large train of provisions. Later on, the Rumanian cavalry on the west began to be more active, and managed, at the close of September, to capture a train of ammunition of eighty wagons, while a detachment of Russian cavalry destroyed a provision train, capturing 1,000 head of cattle. The blockade on the west of Plevna was by no means as yet complete. This was proven by the fact that on October 10th Shevket Pasha again brought a train of provisions and ammunition safely into the town, and on the 11th had a conference with Osman Pasha there. In order to secure the road to Orkhanie, which is said to be one of the best roads in Turkey, Shevket Pasha's troops, about 12,000 strong, occupied its most important points and defiles, among them Gorni Dabnik, Telis, and Lukovitza.

As long as the investment of Plevna could not be effectually carried out on the west, and Osman Pasha therefore remained in connection with his friends in Orkhanie and Sophia, the Russians could not expect to reduce the post. The guards which arrived at the headquarters of the Czar, near Gorni Studen, were placed under the command of General Gourko, together with two other cavalry divisions and one infantry brigade, and this officer was then entrusted with the task of breaking the connection between Plevna and Orkhanie. On October 9th, the guards were about seven miles north-west of Lovatz. Owing to the bad condition of the roads they advanced very slowly, and did not take a position opposite to the positions of Hifzi at Gorni Dabnik and Telis until October 23d. The Russian cavalry west of Plevna during this period had a few skirmishes with the enemy, none of which were of any importance. On the morning of the 24th, General Gourko attacked Gorni Dabnik, and after a very fierce conflict, not only took the Turkish position, which was commanded by Hifzi Pasha, but also captured 3,000 prisoners, four guns, and a whole cavalry regiment. His own loss was stated at 2,500 men. Simultaneously with this attack a heavy cannonade was opened along the entire line east of Plevna, and demonstrations were made so as to give the impression of an intended assault, and prevent Osman Pasha sending assistance to Hifzi Pasha. Whatever the reason may have been, Osman did not attack Gourko, although the battle took place but nine miles from Plevna, and the Russian right flank was very much exposed. The Russians were repulsed at Telis on this day, but this place also surrendered four days later. On October 31st, Osman Pasha evacuated Dolni Dabnik, at the crossing of the Dabnitza creek and the road from Sophia to Plevna, and the Russians were enabled thereby to advance their lines seven miles closer to Plevna. Shevket Pasha, who was standing at Radomirze, retreated upon being informed of these events. On October 31st, he again advanced against Radomirze, but was defeated after a battle lasting several hours. From this time on the investment of Plevna was complete.

Osman Pasha had surrounded his position with a number of enclosed works and redoubts, so formidable as to forbid the attempt to capture them by assault, a fact which the Russians and Rumanians had learned to their cost during the battles of early September; and it only remained to maintain the investment till the Turkish army should be forced by necessity to surrender. The most important of these works was the Grivitza redoubt, constructed north of the village of Grivitza, which was captured by the Rumanians on the 30th of August. Southward of the Grivitza redoubt was the Radisevo redoubt, commanding the approaches from the southeastward and eastward on the south side of the Sophia-Sistova road. On the northern front of the position was Fort Bukova The following description of the Russian and Turkish works was given by a correspondent who was with the Russian army at a late period of the siege :

"Starting from a point on the Plevna-Biela road, about 1,000 yards west of Grivitza, we are on the other line of works and right under the guns of the three Turkish redoubts, connected by galleries and infantry trenches, defending the approach to Plevna by the *chaussée*, the only means of reaching the town from the east, northeast, or south-east, as the rivulet on the map running from Tutchenitza through Plevna courses through an impassable ravine, with perpendicular sides of rock. The line then runs south-west about a thousand yards west of Radisevo, and so on in the same direction until it reaches the ravine above mentioned. On the western side of this ravine we start from the point where the Lovatz road bends to the eastward, thence westward between Brestovatz and Kirshine to a point 2,000 yards from the Lovatz road; thence north-west between Blagivas and Oleagas to the river Vid. Crossing the Vid we go due north to a point in front and east of Etropol, thence north-east to the Vid, just beyond Oponetz, and from this place we pass north of Bukova, and south-easterly to the starting-point on the Grivitza *chaussée.* From the Grivitza ridge round to the position between Brestovatz and Kirshine the Russian lines are higher than the Turkish From this point to the Vid the latter are higher, but in a very slight degree, while from the Vid round to the Grivitza ridge again the Turkish intrenchments are generally more elevated. There are between twenty and twenty-five closed redoubts on the Moslem line, with innumerable rifle trenches, batteries, and covered ways. The allied lines have been gradually advanced nearer and nearer to those of the Turks, and with each advance a new line of intrenchments has been constructed, so that all the intervening spaces between the first and the present allied lines is bristling with parapets. There is no place on the line where close siege operations have been carried on, excepting at the Grivitza redoubt, where the Rumanians have sapped up to the neighboring Turkish earthwork. The lines are within close rifle range at other parts of the circum-vallation, and the gradual exhaustion of Osman Pasha's supplies is thus awaited. The line of circumvallation around Plevna is fully thirty miles in length, but the conformation of the ground is such that it is not necessary to have the divisions in actual contact at all points. The guns of the allies are mounted generally *en barbette;* those of the Turks are all in embrasures. The Rumanian earthworks present a more technically correct appearance than those of the Russians, the lines and slopes of the former conforming strictly to the drawings laid down in works on military engineering. Their parapets also have a much higher command than those of the Muscovites. Enough spade work has been done around Plevna to build many miles of railway embankment, and iron enough thrown away to furnish the rails."

On the 9th of November Skobeleff captured the Green Hills, a mountain south of Plevna, after having occupied Brestovatz on the 5th.

To the west of Plevna the Russians continued to advance rapidly. During the month of November Mehemet Ali collected an army at Sophia, which, together with the army stationed at Orkhanie, under Shakir Pasha, who had succeeded Shevket Pasha, seemed in the beginning to threaten the Russians, and to offer a chance for the relief of Plevna. The principal events, west of Plevna, during the month of November, were as follows:

On Nov. 1st, one brigade of the Third infantry division took the city of Teteven by storm. This city is situated about fifty miles south-west of Plevna, and is of considerable importance, as it is connected with Slatitza by a pass across the Balkans. On Nov. 9th, a detached cavalry corps, consisting of three regiments of guards, under the command of Gen. Leonoff, attacked and captured Vratza, situated on the road from Sophia to Rahova, and a place of considerable importance, in that it afforded facilities for threatening the communications of Sophia and Widin. An important advantage was gained on the Danube by the capture of Rahova by the Rumanians on Nov. 22d, after a battle reported to have continued for three days. But the main object of the Russian operations was to capture Orkhanie, and then make a demonstration against Sophia. In order to accomplish these objects it was necessary, in the first place, to take the two important positions of Pravetz and Etropol. For this purpose the Russians, on Nov. 21st and 22d, left Yablonitza, the furthest of their advanced points on the Plevna-Orkhanie road, in two columns, under Gen. Count Shuvaloff and Gen. Rauch, for Pravetz, which was taken on Nov. 23d. During the entire engagement the detachment at Vratza made a pretended demonstration against Orkhanie, and two Russian infantry divisions a similar one against Etropol, in order to keep the Turkish forces at those points engaged. Etropol was also taken on the 24th. These successes decreased still more the ability of Mehemet Ali to relieve Plevna. After the capture of Pravetz, the Turks abandoned Novatchin, Skrivena, and Orkhanie, and on the 29th they also evacuated Vraktchesh Gen. Ellis immediately started in pursuit, and on Dec. 1st, occupied strong positions in the mountains opposite to Arab Konak.

Before proceeding to describe the fall of Plevna, it will be well to see what Suleiman Pasha had done to relieve Osman Pasha. Suleiman's forces, composing the army of Shumla, and consisting almost entirely of trained veterans, was far better qualified to come to the relief of Osman, than the raw recruits of which, for the most part, the armies of Orkhanie and Sophia were composed. During the month of October, Suleiman kept entirely on the defensive, while his opponent, the Czarevitch, undertook several reconnoissances. During one of these, Prince Sergius of Leuchtenberg was killed, the only member of the Russian Imperial family that had fallen during the war. During the early part of November both armies on the Lom kept comparatively quiet. Finally, on Nov. 19th, Suleiman proceeded to take the offensive, and made a demonstration from Kadikoi against the extreme left of the Czarevitch's army. On the 19th, the troops stationed at Kadikoi crossed the Lom in three columns at, Bassarbova, Krasna, and Yovan Chiftlik. They forced the Russian outposts, standing at Pyrgos, to retreat, then destroyed Pyrgos, but were subsequently forced back beyond the Lom. On the 26th, Suleiman again crossed the Lom, near Kadikoi, and attacked the Russian positions at Metchka and Tirstenik, but was again repulsed on all points. Shortly after these events, Suleiman moved his headquarters to Osman Bazar, and gathered a considerable army. The strength of this force is not known, although its left wing, which was the strongest, was estimated by the Russians at from 30,000 to 40,000 men. The estimate may have been exaggerated, but the forces collected at this point were certainly of considerable strength. On Dec. 3d, the army of Suleiman began to advance in three columns. The left column, comprising the greater part of the force, advanced against Elena and Slataritza; the center marched from Osman Bazar on the main road against Kesrova, and the right wing moved from Sarnasuflar to Popkoi. The movements against Kesrova and Popkoi were of a demonstrative character only, and that against Popkoi in particular was conducted with a very weak force. The main column, under Fuad Pasha, on the morning of the 4th surprised the Russian advanced positions at Bebrova and Marian, and forced detachments which held them to retreat in much disorder. The reinforcements which were immediately sent from Elena, were unable to change the situation, and were also forced to retreat with considerable losses. The strength of the Turks and the disorder among the Russians seemed to be so great, that Prince Mirsky, the Russian commander, found himself unable to hold his positions, and had to evacuate even Elena. Three miles west of Elena, at Jakovitza, he made a stand, and gathered the remnants of his army. The Turks did not advance beyond Elena, although a column belonging to their left wing penetrated beyond Bebrova to Slataritza. On the 5th, the Turks kept up a cannonade, but did not attack the Russians directly, and Gen. Dellingshausen, commanding the Eleventh army corps, was enabled to bring up reinforcements. He arrived at Jakovitza on the morning of the 6th. Immediately upon his arrival the Turks proceeded to attack the position, but were repulsed. Suleiman did not repeat the attack, and desisted from his attempt to advance upon Tirnova, although he continued to hold Elena for a short time.

The operations against Plevna came to an end on December 10th, the one hundred and forty-fourth day after the first arrival of Osman Pasha, forty-five days after its complete investment, and two months after the arrival of the last supply train. On that day Osman Pasha attempted a sortie to the west, but after a fierce contest was forced to surrender. This final contest was described as follows by General Todleben, in his official report to the Grand Duke Nicholas, on the investment and capture of Plevna, as published in the *Invalide Russe:*

"Already, during the night, the patrols of cavalry reported a great concentration of Turkish troops upon the Vid. The attack of the Turks commenced about half-past seven in the morning. Our advanced line fell back before them. Major-General Daniloff, of the staff of the Emperor, and commanding the Third division of Grenadiers, ordered the Second battery of the Third brigade of artillery, which occupied the battery in position No. 3, to open fire, and the Tenth regiment of Grenadiers of Little Russia to march in the direction of Kopany-Moguila. The Second brigade, with its batteries, was also sent from Gorni Netropol.

"While these orders were being executed, there was already light enough to see the Turkish troops which had concentrated in front of us during the night, and which were followed by a train line of wagons of all kinds. The Turks, having opened fire from their guns planted upon the heights near the bridge, and along the Vid to some distance below the bridge, rapidly deployed their forces, taking advantage of the fog which covered the plain on both sides of the river, and of a long strip of high ground which was in front of the bridge, and which sheltered the numerous troops massed there during the night.

"The attack of the enemy upon the trenches occupied by the Third division of Grenadiers was characterized by an extraordinary impetuosity. Forward marched the thick lines of skirmishers, immediately followed by deployed battalions, behind which came the reserves. The artillery followed the skirmishers, advancing rapidly, stopping occasionally to throw us a shell, and then hastening to rejoin the skirmishers.

OSMAN PASHA.

THE BATTLE OF PLEVNA.

" In spite of the rapidity of the fire from our guns, and in spite of the fire of the infantry posted in the intrenchments, the Turks traversed in less than three-quarters of an hour the distance which separated them from our position, and reached our line of defense which was occupied near battery No. 3 by a portion of the troops of the Third division of Grenadiers. The enemy, penetrating into the interstices of the intrenchments, after having killed all those who were defending them, found but a few survivors, who, being too feeble to resist the attack, commenced to fall back. When the trenches of work No. 3 had been occupied by the enemy, and the greater portion of the men of the Second battery had been sabred at their guns, the survivors could only succeed in getting out of this earthwork two guns, carrying away the breech-screws of the six other pieces.

" Then, at half-past eight o'clock in the morning, the troops occupying the central position—the Second battalion, with the second and third companies of skirmishers—having lost a large number of men and many officers, commenced to fall back upon Kopany-Moguila, and upon the left lunette. The Third battery of the Third brigade of Grenadiers, artillery, which occupied work No. 4, was able to hold out some time longer, throwing grape upon the Turks ; but, finding themselves threatened by a flank movement upon the right, they abandoned the position, and were only able to carry away six guns, the horses of the two others having been killed.

" The Tenth regiment of Grenadiers of Little Russia, having arrived upon the field of battle while the regiment of Siberia was engaged with the enemy, was formed in companies and advanced by the interstice between lunette four and Kopany-Moguila. Having rallied the regiment of Siberia, the Little Russians checked the advance of the enemy, but this cost them heavy losses. In a few moments three commanders of battalions and one-half of the captains were placed *hors du combat*.

" The furious attack of the enemy became more and more threatening. The First brigade of the Third division of Grenadiers was exhausted by the efforts it made to defend the lunettes. Eight of our guns had fallen into the hands of the enemy, and the Second brigade of the Third division of Grenadiers had not yet arrived to the support of the First. It arrived, however, toward ten o'clock in the morning, and at the same moment the news was received that the Eighth regiment Grenadiers of Moscow and the Seventh of the Grenadiers of Samogitia, of the Second division of Grenadiers, were approaching the positions defended by the Third division. The arrival of these reinforcements secured for us a favorable issue of the struggle, and rendered it impossible for the enemy to succeed in his attempt to break through. A loud hurrah, which burst forth at about half-past ten o'clock, told us that the Second brigade of the Third division of Grenadiers had just attacked our trenches, which were then occupied by the Turks. Having dislodged the enemy from the two lunettes, the Grenadiers of Astrakhan and Phanagoria, sustained by those of Siberia and Little Russia, continued to advance rapidly, without paying any attention to the losses which they sustained by the murderous fire of the Turks, whom they dislodged and drove from the trenches at the point of the bayonet. Our guns, which had fallen into their hands, were retaken, and the Grenadiers of Astrakhan captured, in a hand-to-hand fight, seven Turkish guns and one standard. Two battalions of the Eighteenth regiment of Vologda operated upon the Turkish flank with the aid of a Rumanian battery. At the moment of the attack of the Second brigade of the Third division of Grenadiers, the Seventh regiment of Grenadiers of Samogitia, under the orders of Lieutenant-General Svetchine, commander of the Second division of Grenadiers, deployed in the interstice between Gorni and Dolni Netropol. Attacking the enemy with the bayonet, the Grenadiers of Samogitia chased the Turks from their intrenchments without firing a single shot, and having put them to flight, captured three guns.

"After having again occupied the advance lines, our troops halted for a moment. It was nearly noon when the Turks commenced slowly to retreat upon the Vid, while they continued to direct upon us a well-sustained fire. The guns taken from the Turks, not having been disabled by their artillerymen, were turned against them and served by infantry soldiers. At the same time all the batteries of the Third brigade of artillery, having been brought forward and placed in position upon the same line with our infantry, opened upon the enemy a terrible fire with case-shot, which changed the retreat of the Turks into a rout. They became massed into disordered groups near the bridge of the Vid pell-mell with the wagons, of which there were a great number upon the roadside. In the face of this complete disorganization of his army and his immense losses, Osman Pasha could no longer even think of renewing his attempt to pierce through, especially as the troops of the other sectors of investment had advanced, and as the arrival of the Sixteenth division of infantry made his complete defeat a certainty

"Soon our troops commenced the attack along the whole line. The division of General Daniloff advanced in front, sustained upon the left flank, in the neighborhood of Gorni Netropol, by the First brigade of the Fifth division of infantry, and upon the right by the Second brigade of the Second division of Grenadiers. The First brigade of the Second division of Grenadiers coming out of the trenches, proceeded. to turn the left flank of the Turks. Moreover, the Second battalion of the Fifth Grenadiers of Kiev, and a battalion of the Sixth Grenadiers of Taurida, were marched toward the Vid, which they forded to occupy the heights on the right bank. The Grenadiers having crossed the river, with the water up to their waists, scaled the heights of Blasevats, and threw themselves upon the redoubt which crowned those heights, and the garrison of which surrendered without firing a shot. The brigades of the Third division of the Guard, and of the Sixteenth division of infantry of the line, which were sent, according to the orders which I had given the day before, to support the corps of General Ganyetzky, did not participate in the battle.

"While the Second and Third divisions of Grenadiers heroically repulsed the attack of the whole Turkish army, the other troops of the army of investment, under the command of Lieutenant-Generals Zotoff, Baron Krüdener and Kataley, and Major-General Shnitnikoff and General Cernat, who commanded the Rumanian corps, advanced upon the Turkish fortifications fronting the east and south. The greater portion of these works had already been evacuated, and the troops occupied the town of Plevna in presence of your Imperial Highness.

"After having entered the-place, the troops, with your Imperial Highness at their head, received the order to continue to advance in the direction of the Vid, upon the rear of the enemy, and they concentrated little by little upon the heights to the west of Plevna, near the Sophia road.

"The Rumanian troops, with whom was his Highness Prince Charles, from that morning met with resistance at the redoubt of Oponetz, which the enemy still occupied. After a short struggle, the garrisons of these works threw down their arms, and the Rumanians captured their guns and 2,000 prisoners.

"Gen. Kataley having remained upon the right bank of the Vid with the remainder of the Third division of infantry of the Guard, perceiving the retreat of the Turks in the direction of the river, resolved to capture the redoubt facing the Volhynie mountain, in order to cut off all chances of retreat by the enemy upon the fortified camp. At 11:30 o'clock the Red redoubt was occupied without resistance, and soon afterward the redoubt of Mohammed Tobia surrendered after a short resistance. Toward one o'clock, after a short fusillade, the Black redoubt and that of the Sugarloaf were also taken. In these redoubts the soldiers of the Guard made prisoners of one Pasha, 120 officers, and 3,734 men, with four guns. On their side they had three men killed and fifteen wounded.

"Enclosed by superior forces, the Turks could no longer continue the fight, and consequently they sent a flag of truce, and the chief of the staff of the Turkish army, who presented himself to General Ganyetzky and told him that Osman Pasha was wounded, and desired to know the conditions of capitulation. Gen. Ganyetzky demanded an unconditional surrender of the entire army. Osman Pasha consented, and Gen. Ganyetzky went personally to his brave and wounded adversary.

"There surrendered during that memorable day of the 28th of November (December 10th, new style), 10 Pashas, 130 superior officers, 2,000 subaltern officers, 40,000 soldiers and gunners, and 1,200 cavalry. We took 77 guns and an immense quantity of munitions, especially cartridges. The enemy lost during the battle nearly 6,000 men.

"On our side the Second and Third divisions of Grenadiers suffered the following losses: Killed, two superior officers, seven subaltern officers, and 409 men; wounded, one general, three superior officers, 47 subaltern officers, and 1,263 men.

"The First brigade of the Fifth division of infantry had one officer and 47 men wounded.

Speaking of Osman's reception by the Russians, the *Daily News'* correspondent says:

"Grand Duke Nicholas rode up to Osman's carriage, and for some seconds the two chiefs gazed into each other's faces without the utterance of a word. Then the Grand Duke stretched out his hand, shook the hand of Osman heartily, and said: 'I compliment you on your defense of Plevna. It is one of the most splendid military feats in history.' Osman smiled sadly, rose painfully to his feet in spite of his wound, and said something which I could not hear He then reseated himself. The Russian officers all cried ' Bravo ! ' ' Bravo ! ' repeatedly, and all saluted respectfully. There was not one among them who did not gaze on the hero of Plevna with the greatest admiration and sympathy. Prince Charles of Rumania, who had arrived, rode up, and repeated, unwittingly, almost every word of the Grand Duke, and likewise shook hands with Osman, who again rose and bowed, this time in grim silence. He wore a loose blue cloak, with no apparent mark on it to designate his rank, and a red fez. He is a large, strongly-built man. The lower part of his face is covered with a short, black beard, without a streak of gray, and he has a large Roman nose and black eyes. ' It is a grand face,' exclaimed Colonel Gaillard, the French military attaché. ' I was almost afraid of seeing him, lest my expectation should be disappointed ; but he more than fulfills my ideal. It is the face of a great military chieftain.' Said young Skobeleff : ' I am glad to have seen him. Osman Ghazi he is, and Osman the victorious he will remain, in spite of his surrender.' "

Osman had certainly done all that could be required of him. Coming from a direction to which the Russians had neglected to pay any attention, he had occupied the town of Plevna almost before the Russians knew that he was on the way. He had inflicted three severe defeats upon the Russians, had changed an open town into a fortress, proving himself in this respect fully a match for Todleben, and had kept up communication for a long time with Sophia and Widin, whence he drew his supplies. It was not until the latter part of October, when the Russian Guards and Grenadiers arrived at the seat of war, that the Russians began to operate with success. Osman was now completely cut off from the outside world, and General Todleben's plan of reducing the garrison by starvation, could be carried into effect. It was Osman's work that the army of invasion was brought to a standstill for over four months. He had engaged an army three and four times as large as his own in a direction entirely aside of the main line of invasion, and thus gained for his Government time to raise new armies, and to complete the works of fortification. By his defense of Plevna he had raised the military reputation of Turkey, which had begun to wane in consequence of the continued Turkish reverses. He had also inflicted a loss upon the Russians and Rumanians, amounting to not less than 30,000 to 35,000 killed and wounded, the killed in all probability not amounting to less than 15,000.

The suffering among the Turks in Plevna was described as very great by all accounts. The special correspondent of the *Daily News*, with General Gourko, who visited Plevna immediately after its surrender, states that the awful misery and wretchedness found within the narrow limits of that place could not be pictured even by those who had become familiar with the varied incidents of the siege. Such ghastly horrors have hardly been paralleled since the days of the plague, in past centuries. When Osman Pasha attempted his sortie, he made no provision for the sick and wounded in the place, of whom there were thousands, and the Russians did not at first attend to them. It was not until the morning of the third day that something was done. The dead were then separated from the living, with which they were crowded in small, unventilated, pestilential rooms, and food was given to those who were still alive. Many, however, died while eating it, the effort being too great for their waning strength. The removal of the dead was at once commenced, and was still going on, but with most inadequate means, only three ox-carts and a score or so of men being employed. · The brutality with which the work was being performed is described as terrible to witness. The correspondent blames the Russians for being unprepared to deal with the sick and wounded, whom they knew beforehand they would find in Plevna, and says that a month before the place fell proper officers should have been appointed to prepare everything for the care of the surrendered troops. .

On December 11th, the day after the surrender of Plevna, the Czar paid a visit to the town, riding through the streets, and lunched in a small house, where Osman Pasha was presented to him. The scene is thus described by an eye-witness: "When Osman Pasha was brought before the Emperor, he was carried by a Cossack officer and one of his attendants. On passing through the yard to the house in which the Czar was lunching in Plevna, many of the staff who were breakfasting, rose from their tables and saluted the brave General, crying, 'Bravo! bravo! Osman.' The Pasha acknowledged the compliment by nodding and smiling." The Czar shook hands with the captive General, and told him that, in consideration of his brave defense of Plevna, he had given orders that his sword should be returned to him, and that he could wear it.

THE MEETING BETWEEN OSMAN PASHA, THE GRAND DUKE NICHOLAS,
AND PRINCE CHARLES OF RUMANIA.

OSMAN PASHA BROUGHT BEFORE THE CZAR AT PLEVNA.

CHAPTER VII.

THE SECOND CAMPAIGN IN ARMENIA.

A Summer's rest in Asia—Position of the Armies—The Russians again approach Kars —Battles of Kisil Tepe, Yagni, and Aladja Dagh—Retreat of Mukhtar Pasha—Advance of Gen. Tergukassoff on the Southern line—Battle of Deve Boyun, before Erzerum—Capture of Kars.

For several weeks after the retreat of the Russian armies from their advanced positions in Turkish Armenia, no events happened that changed the strategical situation. During July all of the Russian columns retired to near the positions from which they had set out in April, and there waited for reinforcements, from the boundary line between Russian and Turkish Territory to Orzugeti, near Poti and Fort St. Nicholas; Gen. Loris Melikoff in front of Alexandropol, and facing Kars and the army of Mukhtar Pasha; and Gen. Tergukassoff in the neighborhood of Igdir, where he confronted the Turkish right wing, which now held Bayazid. The enemy likewise did little to disturb the mid-summer quiet, their most noteworthy movement being an attempt to retake Ardahan, which Gen. Komaroff held fast against them. In the meantime they diligently improved the opportunity afforded them to re-provision Kars and strengthen the fortifications of Bayazid. Mukhtar Pasha established his headquarters at Sabatan, one of the ancient capitals of Armenia, while his army, numbering forty battalions, was encamped in fortified positions on the northern slopes of the Aladja Mountains, near Visinkoi. A few skirmishes took place between the centers in July. About the middle of the month the Russians crossed the frontier to a point near their old camp at Zaim, whence they attacked the Turks. Reinforcements began to arrive in the latter days of July, during which the Russians continued their reconnoissances in front of the Turkish positions, which, however, led to no important results. At the beginning of August, Gen. Melikoff moved his line around, so as to extend his left to near the ruins of Ani, another of the ancient capitals of the country, on the Arpa Tchai River, about twelve miles south-east of Kars, and threatened the Turkish right, while his center was established opposite the Turkish headquarters, and his right at Kurukdara, about six miles north of his center. The central camp at Bash Kadiklar was situated in the plain, near one of the roads from Kars to Alexandropol, and was the scene, in the Crimean war, of an important battle, in which the Russians defeated the considerably superior forces of the Turks. To the south and south-west of it lay the camp of Mukhtar Pasha, spread along the flanks of the mountains. Nearly half way to the Turkish position were three extinct craters, which were occupied by the Russian troops, and still closer to the mountains was another eminence, which had been strongly fortified by the Turks. One of the intervening hills was Kisil Tepe, which later in the month was the object of a hardly-contested battle. A reconnoissance in force was made by the Russians against Kars on the 18th of August, the object of the demonstration being, according to the Russian accounts, to divert attention from some contemplated movements of Gen. Tergukassoff. An engagement of several hours' duration took place, at the end of which the Russians withdrew, in accordance, as they professed, with their previously arranged plans. The fighting was renewed on the next day, and was sustained with spirit on both sides until dusk, when the Russians fell back in good order.

On the 25th of August the Turks made an attack on the Russians for the purpose of gaining possession of the heights of Kisil Tepe. This position was an important one to either army, standing directly in front of the Russian camp at Kadiklar, and forming an excellent point from which to direct offensive operations against the Turkish camp on the opposite side of it. Notwithstanding its value was well known, the Russians had had possession of it for a month without making any effort to fortify it. On the 24th of August, Gen. Melikoff's force was weakened by the dispatch of Gen. Dewell with a part of the command to the assistance of Gen. Tergukassoff, and in consequence the strength of the advance guard on Kisil Tepe was reduced. An artillery force was ordered to go to the support of the guard, but the artillerists delayed moving till morning. At about three o'clock on the morning of the 25th, a band of Circassian cavalry advanced up the hill, and were challenged by the Russian sentinels. This force, it was reported in the Russian camp, was commanded by a woman, the daughter of an Arab Sheik, who was killed in the battle. The Circassians, who had obtained the Russian watchword, answered correctly in Russian to the challenge of the sentinels. While the Russians were hesitating whether to fire, the Circassians opened their ranks and exposed a force of Turkish infantry and artillery which had been concealed, and at the same time an active fusillade was directed upon the guard. In half an hour the hill was in possession of the Turks, and they were putting their guns into position. At daybreak the Turks opened a sudden fire upon the Russian camp, to the great surprise of its occupants. Gen. Tchavtchavadze was sent to retake the hill; he was wounded, and Gen. Sheremetyeff took the command in his place. He was finally compelled to retire from a position of advantage that he had gained, when the whole army was led to the assault. The battle raged fiercely during the afternoon. The Turks made several efforts to take the Russian camp at Kurukdara, a few miles north of the point of battle, but were defeated on each occasion. The tents at this camp had, however, all been taken up, and everything had been made ready for immediate removal, which, fortunately for the Russians, did not become necessary. The Turks kept the hill which they had gained, but were not able to drive the Russians from any other of their positions. They claimed to have captured a considerable quantity of arms and ammunition. The Russians acknowledged a loss of 1,007 men. The affair was very creditable to the Turks, as it showed their ability to fight well on the offensive, and in the open country, as well as behind earthworks. On the day following the battle of Kisil Tepe, August 26th, the Grand Duke Michael arrived at the Russian camp and took command in person, leaving to Gen. Melikoff the execution of his orders. On the 30th of August the Turkish quarters were pushed forward close up to the positions which the Russians had occupied.

Gen. Tergukassoff, although he had received reinforcements which swelled his command to 25,000 men, remained during August in the position near Igdir, which he had taken immediately after his retreat from Armenia, where he for a long time kept himself on the defensive. His forces were so posted that he was able to command most of the important roads of the region, particularly those leading from Bayazid and Erivan to Alexandropol, and the roads which diverge eastwardly from the Erivan-Bayazid road and converge in this neighborhood. His army presented a line of about ten miles in length, intrenched upon the high plain of Igdir, with the Araxes River about a day's march in his rear, and lay close upon the northern foot of the boundary-hills between Russia and Turkey. His

18

adversary, Ismail Pasha, the Kurd, with about 47 battalions, 50 guns, and 12,000 irregular Kurdish cavalry, occupied positions opposite to him, also on Russian territory, grouped around the passes through which the roads from Bayazid and Diadin to Igdir cross the boundary-hills, while his reserves occupied the heights of Tchingili, close upon the border. The Turks made several attacks upon the Russian lines during August and September, which were not attended by any noteworthy results. An attack was made upon the whole Russian line on the 5th of August, which was continued in skirmishes for several days. The affair was followed by a slight change in the positions of both armies, Gen. Tergukassoff drawing back a part of his line, and Ismail making movements indicating an intention to concentrate his forces in the direction of the narrow defile of Mysye. The Turks resumed the offensive toward the end of the month, when a number of skirmishes took place, all in Russian territory, in which the assailants were generally defeated. An attack upon both the advance guard and the right wing of the Russians on the 18th of September, was defeated. Another attack was made on the 27th against the Russian right wing, commanded by Gen. Dewell

The impression was allowed to go out at the beginning of the second campaign by the Russians, that the Erivan column was about to resume the offensive in connection with that from Alexandropol, and the fact that Gen. Dewell had been sent down to join Gen. Tergukassoff, and had to be recalled after the battle of Kisil Tepe, strengthened this belief. If such a purpose was entertained by the Russians, it was given up after the battle of Kisil Tepe. The subsequent movements of that campaign indicate that it was not designed that Gen. Tergukassoff should advance at once, but that the purpose was to keep him at Igdir with a threatening force, so as to keep Ismail Pasha and his Kurds employed, and guard the left flank of the Alexandropol column from attack by them while it executed the real object of the campaign in the direct movement against Kars and the main army of Mukhtar Pasha. In harmony with this plan, a large part of Gen. Tergukassoff's force was withdrawn from him when it was needed to strengthen the Alexandropol column for the important work it was to perform in October. The persistent attacks of Ismail Pasha, which were nearly always made against Tergukassoff's right wing, had for their object to break his communication with Gen. Melikoff's division. Gen. Melikoff received the full complement of the reinforcements which he was expecting toward the end of September, and was ready by the 1st of October to begin offensive operations in earnest. The weather was still favorable, but the season was fast approaching when active operations could not be prosecuted. The contemplated movements must be begun without delay, if the Russians would secure any advantages in Armenia before the close of the year.

The Turkish line was stretched out to a length greatly out of proportion to the strength of its force. It extended from the Yagni hills on the Alexandropol-Kars road, south-eastwardly over the Aladja Dagh, twenty miles to the Arpa Tchai River, which at this point forms the boundary line between Turkey and Russia. A triangular group of posts stretched out six miles in front of the main line occupied the heights of Hadjiveli, Sabatan, and Kisil Tepe. The last of these points proved to be particularly exposed to the attacks of the Russians, demanded the services of a detachment of troops which could be of no advantage to the main work of defense, and in effect weakened the Turkish lines and increased their dangers This line was intended to cover all the ways by which Kars could be reached by the invading force. Its important points were the Yagni hills, the Olya Tepe, and the Aladja Dagh. The Yagni hills are the Little Yagni Tepe and the Yagni Tepe, standing on either side of the Alexandropol-Kars road, the first rising some seven or eight hundred feet above the surrounding hills, and about 6,760 feet above the sea, and the latter being much higher. These hills were occupied by the left of the Turks, and their possession gave the control of the road. The Olya Tepe lies between the Yagni hills and the Aladja Dagh, rising about one thousand feet above the neighboring hills, and, with the Great Yagni, covers the road to the important point of Visinkoi, which was the real key to the Turkish position. The Aladja-Dagh is a large range about eighteen miles south-east of Kars, its eastern declivities sloping down to the Arpa Tchai below Ani. Its northern slopes were dotted with the tents of Mukhtar Pasha's army. The Russians saw that if they could gain possession of the Yagni hills, they would not only completely disarrange the Turkish left wing, but would also be able to establish themselves in the valley through which the Visinkoi road runs, and be in a position whence they might hope to succeed in separating the right wing from Kars. It was accordingly decided to make a combined movement for the purpose of attacking these hills and flanking the Turkish right wing. It was arranged that while the right and center attacked the enemy in front, and forced its way through between the Great Yagni and Olya Tepe, another body should attempt an advance in the rear of the Aladja Dagh.

The attack was begun on Tuesday morning, the 2d of October, with an assault upon the Great Yagni The Turks seem to have been taken by surprise, and the battalion with which they held the hill was cut to pieces or captured after an obstinate resistance. The time during which this body engaged the attention of the Russians was well improved by the rest of the Turkish force in preparation to make a more effective resistance, so that the Russians found that they had still a day of hard fighting and even disaster before them. The Little Yagni was found to be so strongly fortified that an attempt to assault it was considered premature. Repeated assaults were made on either side, in which, while the Russians held the ground they had already obtained, they were not able to make any further advances. They fortified themselves in the positions they had occupied, and bivouacked at night on the Great Yagni A feint attack was made on the same day on the hill of Kisil Tepe, and was repulsed. The flank movement against the Turkish right, which was made in connection with these attacks, was undertaken with a force less than half of what had been contemplated in the original plan of the battle. Marching from the Arpa Tchai near Ani, the flanking force attempted to get between the Turks on the Aladja Dagh and Kars. The movement came very near succeeding, and the Russians had at one time actually put themselves in the desired position, where they were met by Hussein Hami Pasha with three brigades, and driven back to the Arpa Tchai. On Friday, the 5th of October, the Russians evacuated their positions at the Great Yagni, and fell back to Karajal, in the immediate vicinity of their old headquarters at Kurukdara. The losses of both parties in these three days' engagements were severe. The Turks acknowledged a loss of about 2,500 men.

The plan of the Russian operations was revealed by this movement and those which followed it, to be, not so much to defeat the Turks in pitched battles, as to take advantage of their exposed positions, annoy them at their weaker points, and involve them in daily engagements so as to wear their force away slowly, but surely, and reduce them to so weak a condition that ultimately they should find it impossible to offer further serious resistance They were helped by the exigencies of the Turks in Europe, which made it necessary to dispatch a part of Mukhtar Pasha's forces to the assistance of their hard-pressed armies in Bulgaria.

Mukhtar Pasha perceived that the holding of his more advanced and exposed positions was disadvantageous to him, and undertook to put his forces into a more compact shape. During the night of the 8th of October, he abandoned the Kisil Tepe and the other positions which he held in front of his main line, and readjusted his forces, so that on the next morning the Little Yagni hill was held by a brigade, and Visinkoi by a division, while the commander-in-chief, with the main army, consisting of thirty-three battalions, occupied the slopes of the Aladja Dagh above Kharkana, with a detached post on the Olya Tepe, connecting Visinkoi with the main camp. On the 9th, the Russians advanced, and occupied Kisil Tepe, Sabatan, Hadjiveli, and the eastern slopes of the Great Yagni. They made artillery attacks on the Turks during the next two days, resulting in severe losses on both sides. "The Turkish camp now (October 12th)," says an English correspondent who wrote from Erzerum a few days afterward, "had the appearance of being besieged; their whole front, extending from the Little Yagni to the Aladja Dagh, was defended by almost continuous shelter trenches, batteries being thrown up in the most favorable situations, while opposite them, in the plain below, lay the vast army of the Czar, outnumbering them two to one, and bringing four guns to bear on each piece the Turks could produce."

On Sunday, October 14th, the Russian left having been extended to the banks of the Arpa Tchai, beyond Ani, a division under Gen. Lazareff moved south of the Aladja Dagh, drove the Turks from the Orlok heights upon Visinkoi and Kars, and occupied Orlok, thus completely turning Mukhtar's right. On the morning of Monday, the 15th, a heavy cannonade was directed against Olya Tepe, which was the key to the Turkish position. In the afternoon Gen. Heimann, with about 10,000 infantry, carried Olya Tepe by assault, cutting the Turkish army in two.

While this was going on, the Little Yagni, held by Mehemet Pasha with ten battalions, four siege and six field pieces, was hotly contested. All day long the Russians endeavored to get a footing on the hill, but were thrown back. At night, however, the Turkish ammunition having failed, and the Russians having surrounded them, Mehemet Pasha, to avoid the necessity, which he foresaw would be forced upon him in the morning, of surrendering, abandoned his guns, having first dismounted them and removed the breech pieces, and cut his way through to Kars.

The defense of the Olya Tepe is described from the Turkish side as having been most gallant, but the losses of the four battalions upon which it fell were most severe. "The Russian artillery was as accurate as it was heavy, the shells, fitted with time fuses, bursting over the crest with terrible precision. Mukhtar, dreading the loss of this hill, the connecting link between Visinkoi and the Aladja Dagh, detached five battalions to its support. Three desperate attacks had been repulsed, and yet the garrison showed no signs of flinching. These five battalions moved out in column; one at last extended, and sending half a battalion to the right, the remaining half reached the top in safety, when the rest of the column moved slowly up. From some unexplained cause a panic seized these men, and they turned and broke, then re-formed, and slowly retired. Their conduct was simply inexplicable; an eye-witness assures me they never returned a shot to the heavy fire which the Russians poured into them, but marched slowly and sullenly off, utterly regardless of the hail of bullets rattling about them, knocking over man after man." The panic spread, "position after position was abandoned as soon as threatened, and a scene of the wildest confusion ensued, crowds of unarmed fugitives rushing wildly along the road to Kars, while others strove madly to reach the Aladja Dagh. Mukhtar Pasha showed the greatest gallantry, but his example, his orders, were of no avail. Officers were menaced by their men, and they soon joined in the general rout."

The three divisions constituting the Turkish right wing had in the meantime been surrounded and attacked, and driven from their fortified camp with great loss. Omer Pasha, with 2,000 cavalry, surrendered early in the day, and by eight o'clock in the evening of Monday, the remainder of this part of the army, with seven Pashas, thirty-two guns, and twenty battalions, had laid down their arms. The Russians claimed that during the whole battle they captured 18,000 men and 40 cannon, and gave their own loss at the Aladja Dagh at 1,441 men. Their loss in the other parts of the field was not stated. The Turks claimed that their battalions numbered only between three and four hundred men each, and that their loss, consequently, by the surrender of their left wing, was only about 9,000 men. With these men they lost also their ammunition and commissariat stores, camp bag-

THE DEFEAT OF THE TURKS BEFORE KARS

ACHMED MUKHTAR PASHA.

GENERAL MELIKOFF.

gage, animals, and hospitals. The Commander-in-chief escaped with difficulty to Kars.

Mukhtar Pasha succeeded in collecting a force of about 14,000 men, remnants of 40 battalions. With 4,000 men and five mountain guns he fell back to Bardess, and afterward to Koprikoi, leaving Hussein Hami Pasha, with 10,000 men, to defend Kars. This force was not considered sufficient to hold one-quarter of the defenses, and the commander acknowledged that the men were cowed and worn out, that he could not hope to hold the fortress unless succor should arrive soon, and that he feared that it would be carried at the first assault.

The uncertain fortunes of war are curiously illustrated by the fact that just previous to the opening of the campaign which led to this disastrous defeat of the Turks, Mukhtar Pasha, as well as his fellow-general, Osman Pasha, in Europe, had received from the Sultan, in acknowledgment of his services and victories in the summer campaign, the title of Ghazi, or the conqueror, the highest honor which can be given to a Turkish general, and one that is rarely conferred; and that on the morning of the day the Russian attack was began on his position, he held a review of troops, at which he distributed to the men who had most distinguished themselves in the battle at Kisil Tepe, the decorations which had been forwarded to them by the Sultan. He himself received, besides his proud title, a sword set with brilliants, a pair of handsome Arab chargers, and the cross of the first class of the Osmanlieh set in brilliants.

Koprikoi, the position to which Mukhtar Pasha retired after his defeat at Aladja Dagh, being situated at the junction of several roads, was formerly considered a position of importance for the defense of Erzerum, and was selected for the purpose by Sir Fenwick Williams in 1855; the remains of the earthworks which he threw up then still remain, and formed the foundation of the works which were used by the Turks. The value of the position has, however, diminished since the use of rifled arms has become general, since it is commanded by hills from which it is easily reached by long-range arms.

Ismail Pasha, on the 17th of October, after hearing of the defeat of Mukhtar Pasha at the Aladja Dagh, moved from his position near Igdir and marched to join the commander-in-chief on the road to Erzerum. He was followed by Gen. Tergukassoff, but was not seriously molested by him, and joined Mukhtar Pasha at Koprikoi on the 27th. The Russians were moving in force upon the Turkish position, and threatened to flank it. Mukhtar Pasha, finding that it was becoming untenable, burned his stores at Kara Kilissa, and began a retreat. The backward movement was executed in good order to Hassan Kaleh. The Turkish rear guard having halted at that place, the Russians came down upon it and effected a surprise, by means of which two Turkish battalions were taken prisoners. The correspondent of the London *Daily Telegraph* was among the captured, but he was released by Gen. Heimann, after having had everything except his horses stolen from him by the Cossacks. The Turks halted upon the heights of Deve Boyun, in front of Erzerum, and prepared to make a stand for the defense of their capital. Feizi Pasha—the Hungarian Gen. Kohlman—who had been left in command at Erzerum, had anticipated that this would be the result of the movements that were going on, and had already prepared to give the army a good position on the heights. He had drafted every able-bodied man in the city to work on the intrenchments, haul up guns, and man the batteries.

The Deve Boyun, or Camel's Neck, is the crest of a range of mountains some two thousand feet higher than the plain below, over which the road from Koprikoi passes about six miles east of Erzerum. It had been selected as a defensive position by Sir Fenwick Williams in 1855, and Hassan Pasha, the governor of the city, and Gen. Kohlman, had spent much labor upon it since July, 1877, in building earthworks, so that it was considered in a good condition to resist an attacking force

The Russians, Generals Heimann and Tergukassoff, having effected a junction, advanced against the left of the Turkish lines on the heights of Deve Boyun, on the morning of the 5th of November. The Turks awaited the assault in their intrenchments. The Russians came up, and were repulsed. They returned with repeated assaults, but were again and again repulsed, and finally retired at about eleven o'clock in the morning.

Soon after noon the attention of the Turks was directed to the appearance of a body of Russian cavalry manœuvering in the plain as if about to make an assault upon the Turkish center. The idea of a cavalry attack against such a position was preposterous, and the Turks were very much puzzled by the demonstration. It was a feint, designed to draw the Turks into an ambuscade. During the previous night the Russians had taken nearly all their infantry and noiselessly, in the darkness, posted them in the ravines and recesses of the hills. It was a movement that had to be executed with great skill, for the Turks could have defeated it in a very short time upon the slightest warning that it was going on, but no one among them had any knowledge of it. The cavalry came nearly up to the base of the hill, presenting an imposing aspect. They kept on till the Turkish general decided it was time to meet them, and dispatched eight battalions of infantry to attack them. Although the cavalry could plainly see the operations of the Turks, they paid no attention to them. The Turks went down the hill till they got within range of the Russians, and fired upon them Their shots began to take effect, when, says a correspondent who was an eye-witness of the engagement:

"In a moment everything is changed. From many places on the hill-sides, where but a moment ago there was nothing to be seen but the bare ground, start up dense files of Russian infantry. The hills are covered with them—their shouts echo from side to side. In an instant they are pouring fearful volleys at murderously short distances on both flanks of the unsuspecting, unprepared Turks. Too confident, too anxious to punish the over-daring of the Russian cavalry, Mukhtar's men have advanced so far down in the valley that there is no longer left the possibility of recovery. The narrowness of the road, the closeness of the overwhelming fire, the advantageous positions secured by the enemy—above all, the suddenness of the attack, unman and paralyze them."

Mukhtar Pasha, seeing the trap into which he had fallen, endeavored to retrieve his mistake. Placing himself at the head of two battalions, he threw himself into the advanced shelter-trenches, and tried to check the Russian movement. But it was too late The division under Ismail Pasha, the Kurd, turned and ran. Feizi Pasha endeavored to stop their flight, but in vain. They were completely panic-stricken, and ran every way, bewildered, and unable to make any resistance. The Russians advanced up the hill, reached the intrenchments as soon as the Turks themselves, and occupied the positions as fast as they reached them. The Turks were driven over the crest of the hill in utter confusion, abandoning everything, while the Russians pushed their advance with unabated vigor. All was done with amazing speed and ease. It was fully noon when the Russians gave the first warning of their presence, and at two o'clock in the afternoon the Turkish army was in full flight. Not a gun was fired at the Russians as they advanced up the hill, but the Turkish gunners cut the traces of their artillery, mounted their horses, and galloped away. The infantry struggled as well as they could, but they too had at last to join in the retreat.

The narrow roadway from Deve Boyun to Erzerum was blocked by a dense crowd of fugitives, who would have been annihilated, had not Feizi and Mehemet Pashas—both foreign officers, and no Turks—taken a stand with their brigades, and poured such a fire upon the advancing columns of the Russians as checked their pursuit. The demoralized soldiers, says another correspondent, who was also an eye-witness of the scene, entered Erzerum unpursued by the foe, who really might have followed them up and gained possession of the capital without striking another blow. All through the night the crowds of fugitives continued to pour into the city. Many merely passed through and deserted to their homes; others, worn out with fatigue, cold, and exposure, threw themselves down in the streets, and, in spite of the pouring rain which was falling, slept, with no cover but the clothes they had on. Feizi Pasha entered the place, having succeeded in drawing off his men unperceived; Mehemet Pasha, his fellow officer, had to fight his way back. The Russians advanced to the crest of the Deve Boyun, where they took up a strong position overlooking Erzerum, and began to throw up redoubts. A number of the Mohammedan citizens fled from the city during the evening.

On the 6th the head civil authorities of the town presented petitions to Mukhtar Pasha, asking him to surrender the place in order to avoid the destruction attendant upon an investment and bombardment. The General replied that he would have to apply to the Sultan for permission to carry out such a request. Immediately afterward a summons came from the Russians demanding a surrender. Mukhtar again replied that he must consult the Sultan, and asked for three days' grace to telegraph to Constantinople for instructions. He afterward answered the Russians that the Sultan had directed him to hold the place to the last man and the last cartridge, and he should do so. On the 7th, Gen. Heimann sent him word that three days' grace would be given him, after which the bombardment would begin. A council of war was held, at which several officers of the city, members of the Chamber of Deputies, priests, and Mohammedan residents attended, and it was resolved to defend the place to the last extremity. The Russians had, in the meantime, erected works commanding the road from the Deve Boyun and the whole town.

On the next two days public criers went about the streets announcing that inhabitants wishing to leave the city must do so before the hour fixed for the bombardment to begin.

On Monday, Nov. 9th, the Russians made an attack on another of the Turkish fortified positions around Erzerum, Fort Azizie, situated south-east of the town. The Turks were surprised for the moment, and the Russians gained a temporary occupation of the position; but the Turks soon rallied, and turning upon their assailants, attacked them with vigor, and drove them out at the point of the bayonet, after a hard hand-to-hand contest. The Russians retreated to the Deve Boyun, closely followed by the Turks, leaving a large number of killed and wounded in the intrenchments, but carrying off, as they claimed, a considerable number of Turks as prisoners.

The Russians now proceeded to prepare for the investment of Erzerum, beginning with the strengthening of their intrenchments on the Deve Boyun, and gradually extending their lines around the north of the city. Before the close of the month the snow had fallen to the depth of three feet on the mountains. The Russians held their posts on the Deve Boyun while their troops were quartered in the neighboring villages, and improved the favorable weather that was given them, in movements looking to the cutting of the communications with the city.

While Generals Heimann and Tergukassoff were occupied with their preparations for the siege of Erzerum, Gen. Melikoff, with the Grand Duke Michael, was pressing the investment of Kars. An attack upon the fortifications, with the view of carrying them by assault, was arranged for the 14th of November. It rained heavily at that time, and the attack had to be postponed. Frosty weather set in on the 16th, and it was decided to make the attack on the 17th. It curiously happened that no newspaper correspondents were present at the battle, so that the only accounts of it, from eye-witnesses, that have been published, are given by members of the Russian army. The troops were divided into five columns, the whole being under the command of Gen. Lazareff. The night was calm and frosty, cloudless, and with a full moon. The troops advanced noiselessly, in a silence that was broken only by the occasional firing from the siege batteries, continued as it had been all day. "Before us," says one of the Russian correspondents, "lay the plain, stretching away forward to the lowest of the enemy's works, but we could nowhere detect the storming columns, so silently did they advance." The account is continued by another Russian correspondent:

"Shortly after nine o'clock were heard a few musket-shots, which showed that the outposts were reached. Then thundered the cannon, and the fight began. The storming columns met with such a terrific fire that nothing was heard but a continuous roll of big guns and musketry. All the forts were suddenly, as it were, girded about with a belt of fire, in some places with several belts one above the other. The Kara Dagh heights were literally covered with flame, and looked like a great bonfire. Every soldier of the garrison fired hundreds of shots. All the big guns, it seems, were in action. From a distance it appeared impossible to remain for a moment under such a fire, but through it silently, without firing, unwaveringly, advanced the storming columns. When near the fortifications they rushed forward with a 'hurrah.' The artillery fire ceases. Our soldiers jump over the 'wolf-holes' down into the ditch and begin to scale the parapets. The storming ladders, twenty-one feet in length, are too short, but the brave fellows climb and clamber all the same, clinging to each other, digging their bayonets into the parapet, giving each other a lift, and ever forward. Now they are on the top; the gates are blown open with dynamite; Fort Kanly the Terrible can no longer resist. Count Grabbe is in front with his volunteers, and falls with two bullets in his breast. After him comes Colonel Belinski, at the head of the regiment, and he, too, falls under bullets and bayonets. But that does not stop the forward movement. The garrison wavers, takes to flight, and our troops enter. Kanly is ours; and those of the defenders who shut themselves up in the casemates are obliged to capitulate. Soon fall, in like manner, Suvarri and Hafiz. An advance is then made on the citadel. At all points the Turks offer a desperate resistance. Toward morning the Kutais regiment takes the Kara Dagh and Arab Tabia, and soon afterward the citadel falls into our hands."

As soon as the Kara Dagh and Arab Tabia were taken, the Turks determined to abandon the town. They went out, about eight o'clock on the morning of the 18th, toward Olti and Erzerum. They were fired upon by the artillery of Gen. Roop's forces, which were stationed in this direction, and were intercepted by a body of cavalry sent in pursuit of them, and surrendered. The number of prisoners was 12,000.

The correctness of this account is attested by the concurrence of witnesses, and by all the known circumstances, but it still remains a remarkable fact, hard to be explained, how twenty-four Russian battalions could march in five columns on a perfectly clear moonlight, winter night over the level space of two and one-half miles, which intervened between their positions and the forts, without being observed by a single Turkish sentinel. The movement was one of great audacity on the part of the Russians, and its success shows extreme negligence on the part of the Turks. The Turks charged treachery upon one of their Pashas, but he could hardly have infected all the sentinels of all the forts

A grand religious service was held in the Russian camp on the 20th in honor of the victory, and the Grand Duke conveyed to the officers and soldiers the thanks of the Emperor and Commander-in-chief for their gallantry.

The whole interest of the war in Asia after the capture of Kars centered around Erzerum, where, however, the depth of the snow and the severity of the weather forbade all continuous active movements. While the Russians were strengthening their lines of investment as the weather permitted them to adjust their positions, the Turks were endeavoring to collect forces and preparing to offer as obstinate a defense as possible. Feizi Pasha was stationed at Baiburt, where he was to endeavor to organize the mountaineers of Lazistan into regiments. Kurd Ismail Pasha was dispatched to Erzengan, where large stores of provisions had been concentrated from the market towns of Asia Minor, and announced his intention of returning shortly at the head of 40,000 men. A communication with provision-trains was kept up with this place, so that at the beginning of December a sufficient supply was said to exist in Erzerum to enable the place to stand a six months' siege. Nevertheless, the poorer inhabitants were already suffering great privations on account of the famine price of food. Mukhtar Pasha declared that he had no thought of surrendering, but that his sole idea was to hold out as long as possible, giving his lieutenants time to organize a fresh army, with which he would begin operations again in the spring. Still, he was forced to confess that not only were his present forces numerically weak, but their moral condition was bad, and that he had only four battalions which he could trust in action. He had, however, entire confidence in the towns-people, and believed that with their aid he would be able to repel any assaults made upon the city. Much sickness was prevailing both at Erzerum and at Kars. The hospitals at the former place were filled with soldiers, so that the Governor of the town was obliged to appropriate eighty additional houses to hospital uses.

, On the 11th of December, the British Consul, Mr. Zohrab, received orders to leave Erzerum, and take with him the archives of the Consulate. His departure was felt to be a great loss by the citizens of the place, for he had made himself useful and beloved by many acts of kindness and humanity. Among other acts, he had organized a committee, composed of Mohammedans and Christians, to inquire into and alleviate all cases of distress among the poor of the city, and had rendered valuable aid to all sanitary agents and to strangers who visited the place. A few days after the departure of the British Consul, a movement was made threatening the city from the north, but it failed. The Russian lines were pushed further forward, and the place was almost invested on the 25th.

At the close of December, Mukhtar Pasha, in obedience to orders from his Government, retired from Erzerum, leaving Ismail Kurd Pasha as commander of the troops in his place. The reason of the removal of Mukhtar was not given. It was reported on the one hand that he was recalled to account for the disasters which the Turkish forces had suffered in Armenia under his command, while other reports assumed that he would be assigned to a command in Europe. He was, actually, after his arrival in Constantinople, placed in command of a body of the troops which were stationed in the works at Tchataldja for the defense of the capital. The change of commanders was not to the advantage of the Turkish cause at Erzerum. Mukhtar Pasha, though not a brilliant general, nor one of extraordinary ability, had proved himself throughout the campaign a faithful, competent officer; had gained the confidence of his followers and the respect of his enemies. He had been in turns a victor and a sufferer by defeat, without stain upon his honor; and he was believed to be clear of complicity with the atrocities committed by the Kurds, which, like those of the Bashi-Bazouks in Europe, disgraced the Turkish cause in Asia. His successor was a bigoted Mussulman, a man who was accustomed to spend his time in prayers, while he left the duties of planning and acting to his lieutenants, who had entered the campaign without reputation for generalship, and had acquired none in its course. The Russians

THE RUSSIANS STORMING KARS.—Nov. 18th, 1877.

THE LAST SHOT IN THE DEFENCE OF KARS.

had so well invested the city at the time of Mukhtar's recall that it was reported that he had to escape from the city in disguise as one of the suite of a European Consul there; that he was stopped by the Cossacks, and was only let go on the Consul producing his credentials.

Ilidja was occupied by the Russians during the first week in January, and the investment of Erzerum was complete   The Russians had, by the middle of the month, concentrated about 20,000 men on the plains, and occupied a space of forty-two miles, stretching from Hinsk, on the north, as far as Pirnakabar, on the west.   On the 12th of January, a Turkish officer, bearing a white flag, passed through the Russian lines, entered Erzerum, and delivered to Ismail Pasha a telegram from Constantinople, announcing the opening of negotiations for a suspension of hostilities.   The Russians, nevertheless, continued to concentrate their troops.   The close investment of the city was continued without material changes, or the happening of any striking event, until the signing of the preliminaries of peace.

A Russian commission had been at work in anticipation of securing a permanent acquisition of territory in Asia, at the conclusion of the war, for the organization of the conquered parts of Armenia, and finished its labors early in February.   The male population of the territory, including the not yet conquered districts of Erzerum, Van, and Batum, was found to amount to 610,744, including 180,188 Armenians, 207,049 Kurds, 189,250 Turks, 25,098 Kistl-bashas, and 2,000 Tartars.   The commission provided for the division of Armenia into two governments, and the six districts of Tchaldir, Bayazid, Van, Mush, Erivan, and Kars, from the whole of which it was anticipated the Government would receive a net revenue of 3,000,000 rubles.

CHAPTER VIII.

THE OPERATIONS BEFORE BATUM AND IN THE CAUCASUS.

Batum—Its Importance as a Port—The Russians Undertake its Investment—The Turkish Expedition to Sukhum Kaleh, and their Effort to Excite an Insurrection of the Caucasian Tribes—Insignificant Results of the Movement.

WHILE the Russians were pushing their main campaign in Armenia, important subsidiary movements were prosecuted by both sides on the coast of the Black Sea and in the Caucasus. The Russians were attempting offensive operations against Batum, the most important port held by the Turks in this region, and the only really good port on the coast, and the Turks were directing expeditions to points on the Caucasian shores further north, to stir up and assist insurrections among the Mohammedan tribes, with a view to the destruction of the Russian line of communication over the Caucasus Mountains.

The shores of the Black Sea, between the Turkish fortified ports of Batum and Trebizond, a distance of about one hundred and twelve miles, are destitute of roads, rocky, and impassable. The ground rises in a distance of a little more than twenty miles from the coast into the Barchel Mountains. As the Turks were masters of the sea, they might have inflicted great damage upon the Russians by harassing their right wing and cutting its communications, if they had had good points from which to send detachments of troops against them. The only point, however, offering a practicable basis for such operations was Batum, which presented a combination of advantages for military movements against the line of Russian invasion. It has an excellent and convenient harbor, is connected by good roads with Tiflis and Akhaltzikh, the base of the Russian right wing, and communicates directly with the country to the south, by the river Tchoruk, which is navigable to Artvin, and by a road running up the valley of the river. The Turks actually made much use of Batum as a station for their troops and a rendezvous for their fleets, whence expeditions were fitted and sent against the

Caucasian coasts, and they kept there a force of between eighteen and twenty-four thousand men. It was important to the Russians that they should either capture this port, or keep its garrison so engaged that it would not be able to operate against General Melikoff's right wing

The duty of taking care of Batum was assigned to the Rion corps, Gen. Oklobjio commanding. On the 11th of May, this officer, having established himself in the position of Mucha Estate, made an attack upon the heights of Tchatzubani, on the left bank of the river Kintrisi, a river which empties into the sea just south of the boundary line. A severe fight ensued, in which the Russians failed to carry the point they aimed at, although they claimed to have maintained the positions they had assumed, with a loss of 128 killed and wounded. The Turks represented the affair as a great victory for them, and rated the Russian loss at 4,000. An attack was next attempted upon Batum from the sea. The Russian steamer "Constantine" left Sebastopol on the 12th of May with four torpedo boats, which were sent forward into the harbor to be attached to the Turkish ships and destroy them. The movements of the torpedo boats were observed from the shore, the alarm was given, and the boats had to be withdrawn without accomplishing their object. The fighting on the land side was renewed on the 23d, and again on the 28th, when the Turks were driven from the heights of Sameba, on the left bank of the Kintrisi. An expedition was dispatched up the river and secured the submission of the inhabitants, the roads were repaired, and Russian batteries were established at Sameba. The situation was not materially changed for several weeks, although new movements were attempted and skirmishes took place nearly every day till the latter part of June, when a new commander, Dervish Pasha, was appointed for the Turkish forces, and greater energy was infused into their movements. On the 23d of June, the new commander reported that he had compelled the Russians to withdraw their batteries, and retreat, with a loss of 1,500 killed and wounded. The heights of Sameba and Khatzubani were recaptured by the Turks, and the Grand Duke Michael announced about the 1st of July that General Oklobjio had found it advisable "to concentrate his forces in a more advantageous position." Gen. Oklobjio withdrew his headquarters to Mucha Estate, in the vicinity of the frontier. The engagements which ended in this result were fought with great gallantry on both sides, the Russians defending the positions which they successively lost, with brave persistency, and losing many high officers in the conflicts, while the Turks suffered such losses that they were not able to follow up their victory with that degree of energy which they had hoped to exhibit.

During the interval between the two campaigns in Armenia, the forces of Gen. Oklobjio were stationed in the small district lying between the boundary of Turkey and Russia and Orzugeti, near Poti and Fort St. Nicholas. No new operations were undertaken in this field for several months. Ardanutch, which had already been taken and abandoned by the Russians, was again taken by a detachment under Gen. Komaroff, who was co-operating with Gen. Oklobjio, on the 17th of November. The bombardment of Batum was resumed early in November. On the night of the 27th of the same month, Dervish Pasha, the Turkish commander, suddenly abandoned his position at Khatzubani, leaving in it merely an insignificant force, and the post was occupied on the following day by the Russians, who, after driving out the small remaining garrison, found themselves in possession of the Ottoman camp with huts for 10,000 men, and some stores of provision and ammunition. In the latter part of December, the Russians were continuing an intermittent fire upon the Turkish lines without effect. The situation continued without material change till the end of January. Gen. Oklobjio did not make any progress against the intrenchments of Dervish Pasha. The co-operating column of Gen. Komaroff at Ardanutch, on the 13th and 22d, defeated a division of the enemy which stood between him and Batum at Artvin. The Russian steamer "Constantine" approached the Turkish fleet at Batum on the 26th and sent out a torpedo-boat, which succeeded in blowing up one of the vessels. The remaining vessels of the fleet then took on board a part of the garrison of the fortress, with Dervish Pasha, to transport them to Constantinople. Learning this, Gen. Oklobjio undertook to storm the Turkish positions on the 30th, but was driven back after he had crossed the Kintrisi River, with considerable loss.

The Turks, in forming their plans at the beginning of the campaign, had placed considerable dependence on the expectation that an insurrection would be excited among the Mohammedan tribes of the Caucasus. Taking it for granted that the sympathies of these people would be with them as Moslems, and that they were discontented under Russian rule, they hoped to promote an insurrection, and make it so formidable that the attention of the Russians and a considerable part of their armies would be diverted from the active prosecution of the invasion. Besides, as the only lines of communication between the Russian army of the Caucasus and the European bases of supply traversed the Caucasian country, and were beset with difficult mountain passes and narrow defiles, they anticipated that if a general insurrection could be excited they would be able so to embarrass the Russians as, possibly, entirely to defeat their movements and break up their campaign. A revolt in the Terek district would seriously impede the operations of the railroad from Tiflis to Rostov, and would, in case the insurgents should be able to control the Pass of Vladikavkas, entirely blockade it. A general movement of the tribes along the Black Sea, aided by the naval superiority of the Turks in its waters, would make the coast road—the only other means of communication available to the Russians—impracticable. This road, running along the narrow levels between the spurs of the mountains and the sea-shore, and intersected by numerous difficult rivers and mountain streams, is exposed through much of its length to the direct fire of men-of-war, as well as to attacks from hostile bodies posted on the hills or valleys above. The country is one in which an insurrection would be extremely difficult, even impracticable, to deal with, being thickly wooded, and the only roads being bridle-paths, which do not exist on any map, but are perfectly well known to the natives. It was in this region that the Turks made, at the very beginning of the war, and continued for many months, a deliberate and energetic effort to kindle an insurrection of the whole people. Signs of revolt also appeared in other parts of the Caucasus, and a rising took place among the Tchetchentzes, immediately after the declaration of war, in consequence of which a state of siege had been proclaimed in the Terek province.

Admiral Hassan Pasha sailed from Batum, near the end of April, with a squadron of five vessels. Proceeding along the coast the fleet cannonaded some of the Russian forts near the mouth of the Rion River, and on the 12th of May reached Fort Godauty, and landed there about one thousand Circassians, who were joined by a portion of the inhabitants of the district. On the 14th the squadron reached Sukhum-Kaleh, a town of about sixteen hundred inhabitants, on the north-eastern coast of the Black Sea, the only port, though a

poor one, of the Caucasus north of Poti, and in the midst of the
Abkhasian country. The first bombardment of the fortifications
was followed by an attempt to land, which was defeated with considerable loss to the assailants. The bombardment was continued
till the town and fort were nearly destroyed, when the position was
stormed and captured, the Russians retreating. The Russians attempted to retake the place on the 18th, but were repulsed. The
spirit of revolt spread quite rapidly among the Abkhasians for a
short time after the Turkish movement was begun. One of the
sons of Shamyl, Ghazi Mehmed Pasha, went with the Turks to join
the rising tribes, under the expectation that his name would arouse
a great excitement among them. His influence was thwarted, however, by the adherence of his brother to the Russians, as an officer
in their army, who also was sent to the Caucasus to encourage the
loyalty of the tribes. The Turks prosecuted their movements with
such energy, that by the first of June they had the control of the
shore of the whole Abkhasian coast. A council of war held at Constantinople resolved to treat the movements in this region as of
paramount importance, and decided to send reinforcements to assist
them, and a large quantity of rifles to distribute among the tribes.
Fazli Pasha was sent out with a force of ten thousand men. The
Russian counter movements were prompt; the revolt in the Terek
district was quickly put down; measures were immediately taken
to prevent the Abkhasian revolt from extending into the interior
from the sea-coast. The district was put under the command of
General Alkhasoff, and troops were thrown into it from the region
of the Kuban and the east, and the insurrectionary movement was
confined to an unimportant stretch of the coast, extending, according
to the admissions of the Turks, not more than forty miles into the
interior. The Turks continued their attacks at various points along
the sea-coast, where the Russians did not consider it worth while,
since it was useless, in view of the advantages which the enemy enjoyed from their naval superiority, to offer them any serious opposition. The control of the interior was still entirely with the Russians, who had also set limits to the revolt both in the north and
the south. At the beginning of July they claimed that the insurrection was virtually suppressed, while the Turks still held the
positions which they had captured, and the whole Caucasian population were still very uneasy. The Russian statements, however,
received a striking confirmation less than a month later, when the

Turkish Government resolved to abandon the Caucasian expedition, to evacuate the captured positions on the Abkhasian coast, and to remove to Turkish territory all of the population who had compromised themselves with their Government by taking part in the insurrection. Admiral Hobart Pasha, the commander of the Turkish fleet in the Black Sea, was commissioned to superintend the transportation of the refugees. The Abkhasians eagerly availed themselves of the offer of the Turks to remove them, and came in throngs from all directions to the points of embarkation, and the vessels were employed for several days in conveying them and their cattle to Trebizond. The number who sought to emigrate was given at fifty thousand, with one hundred and fifty thousand head of cattle. By the end of August all who presented themselves for removal had been taken away, only four hundred having, according to the Turkish accounts, fallen into the hands of the Russians. Sukhum-Kaleh was finally abandoned by the Turks on the first of September, after an unprofitable occupancy by them of about four months, and was entered by the Russians under General Alkhasoff on the same day. A general proclamation was issued by the Russians summoning the insurgent Abkhasians to submit and lay down their arms, under severe penalties in the event of their refusal. A number of those who had participated in the insurrection were exiled to Siberia.

Notwithstanding the manifest failure of the attempts of the Turks to excite a general insurrection, the whole region of the Caucasus was in a disturbed condition during the whole period of the summer campaign. An insurrection broke out in Daghestan, in the eastern side of the province, in June, where a raid was made by Turkish irregulars, and they succeeded in destroying parts of the Tiflis Railway, and the insurgents received the assistance of a number of young Circassian officers, who had-been trained in the Russian military schools. A second insurrection broke out in the Terek district in July, in consequence of which it was considered necessary to hold a force in reserve to support the troops regularly stationed there.

Another revolt broke out in the central districts of Daghestan in September, and gradually extended. Bodies of the insurgents, represented to number about 4,000, were met by the Russians on the 30th of September and the 3d of October, and were defeated. The revolt was completely suppressed by the middle of December.

These outbreaks caused the Russians some trouble in the earlier campaign, and required the detachment of considerable bodies of troops to meet them. After the failure of the first Armenian campaign, engineers were dispatched to explore the routes by the Caspian Sea, with a view to the construction of new roads for their transportation of supplies that should avoid the passes of the Caucasus. A few weeks later, the slowness of the Russians to move in opening their second campaign, was excused by the statement that their forces had been weakened by the necessity of detailing detachments to assist the troops in the Caucasus. Very little was heard of the insurrections after the second campaign was fairly opened.

DERVISH PASHA.

MAHMOUD DAMAD PASHA.

HOBART PASHA.

HASSAN PASHA.

CHAPTER IX.

ON TO CONSTANTINOPLE.

The Close of the Campaign on the Lom—Servia enters upon the Scene of War—Capture of Ak Palanka and Pirot by the Servians—Gourko Crosses the Etropol Balkan—Battles of Taskesen and Kamarli—Capture of Sophia, the Trojan Pass, the Shipka Pass, and Philippopolis—Suleiman Pasha Defeated and Forced into the Rhodope Mountains—Capture of Adrianople—Suleiman's March to the Sea—The Russians Occupy Tcholuk and Tchataldja, and Push their Lines along the North Shore of the Sea of Marmora—Final Operations of the Servians—Surrender of Widin—The Czarevitch Occupies Rasgrad, Osman Bazar, and Rustchuk—Gen Zimmermann Assumes the Offensive—Capture of Bazardjik.

SULEIMAN PASHA undertook, on December 12th, another attack on the extreme left of the Czarevitch's army stationed at Metchka and Tirstenik. The Twelfth army corps, under the Grand Duke Vladimir, was stationed here. Suleiman attacked these positions five times, and was proceeding to the sixth attack when the Russians received reinforcements from the Thirteenth corps and forced him to retreat. His losses during this retreat were considerable, amounting, according to the best estimates, to at least 2,000 men. Two days later, on the 14th, he withdrew his troops from Elena, and on the 15th the extreme right of the Czarevitch's army had again occupied this place and Slataritza. This put an end to all operations on the Lom on the part of the Turks.

The fall of Plevna was the occasion of the re-entrance of Servia into the war. This principality, which had received such easy terms from Turkey, when it concluded the treaty of peace in February, had been the scene of considerable political excitement throughout the year. A strong party had clamored loudly for renewing the war, and on several occasions it had seemed as if Servia would again take the field. When the Russians entered Rumania, Prince Milan paid a visit to the Czar at Ployeshti, where he met with a very friendly reception, although it was reported at the time that he was advised by the Russians not to resume hostilities against Turkey. Now, when Plevna had fallen, and the Turkish power seemed to have been effectually broken, Prince Milan embraced the opportunity again to declare war In his declaration, issued on December 12th, after denouncing Turkish cruelty and barbarity, he continued:

"Although Servia behaves toward Turkey most honorably, the Porte begins preparing new perils for our country, besides concocting secret conspiracies against our internal security. The Ottoman Foreign Minister threatens us openly with innumerable kinds of injury, without being formally at war with Servia. Servians! When the Porte assumes against us such a threatening tone, at a moment when it is pressed by an army of the strongest power, it is evident that we can not permit the occasion to pass by without trying once more to secure our future. The struggle with our foe of many centuries was not finished with last year's war; it would be inglorious, unprofitable for us doing peaceable work, not to try within the boundaries of our strength to remove threatening dangers for the Servian nation and not to fulfill our national task. . . . . Great works, like the one undertaken by us last year, can not remain half accomplished. . . . . If last year the enemy had superior forces to bring against the Servian principality, to-day entering the field we find on our side the victorious Russian army, our heroic Montenegrin brethren, our brave Rumanian neighbors. We take up arms to-day for the holy national Christian cause. . . . . Let us now fulfill the great national task which the old heroes of Takova so gloriously began, and which we renewed last year. Let us move forward alongside of the victorious banner of the Czar, the Liberator, with Christian faith in God Almighty, the Protector of right, and success is sure, in the name of the liberator of our oppressed brethren; our country's welfare, Servia's independence, and its heroic people. It is God's will."

The Servians had at this time four armies ready to take the field—those on the Drina, on the Javor, on the Morava, and on the Timok Rivers. While the army of the Drina was intended for defensive purposes only, the armies of the Morava, and of the Timok, occupied Mramor, Ak Palanka, and Pirot, invested Nissa, and proceeded toward Sophia. Nissa surrendered on January 10, 1878, when the Servians took 8,000 prisoners, 90 cannon, and 12,000 guns.

We left Gen. Gourko in the latter part of November on the heights of the Baba Konak Pass. The Turkish army occupied at this time a position at the south end of this pass at Arab Konak and

Kamarli, and here repulsed several artillery and infantry attacks made by Gen. Gourko during the early part of December. The surrender of Plevna enabled the Russians to send considerable reinforcements to Gourko.

On December 28th he crossed the Etropol Balkan, a feat which was attended with great suffering and loss of life to the Russians, and then advanced upon Sophia. Several changes had taken place at this point during December. Mehemet Ali had been removed from the command, and Shakir Pasha appointed in his place, and the latter officer was also removed within a week to make place for Nedjib Pasha. On December 30th and 31st, Gourko defeated the Turks in two severe battles at Taskesen and Kamarli. The Turks were completely routed and scattered, a small body forcing its way to Slatitza, while the greater part of the remainder were taken prisoners. This victory opened the way for the Russians to Sophia, which they occupied on January 3d without meeting with any resistance. Further east, Gen. Dandeville, commanding the 3d cavalry division of the Guards, had occupied Slatitza on January 2d, and advanced as far as Kosnitza, where the Prohod Pass leads into the valley of the Derbent River. This pass, however, could not be taken as long as the Trojan Pass, leading from Trojan into this valley, was in the hands of the Turks. The Trojan Pass was finally taken on January 7th, by General Karzoff, under the greatest difficulties, a large number of his men perishing from the cold. On the 8th, Gen. Radetzky, commanding in the Shipka Pass, attacked the Turkish positions in that pass so suddenly that he captured the entire Turkish army under Ressel Pasha. In his telegram to the Czar, who had returned to St. Petersburg after the fall of Plevna, the Grand Duke Nicholas said:

"I am happy to congratulate your Majesty upon a brilliant victory gained this day. Gen. Radetzky has, after desperate fighting, captured the whole Turkish army defending the Shipka Pass, consisting of 41 battalions, 10 batteries, and one regiment of cavalry. Prince Mirsky has occupied Kasanlik. Gen. Skobeleff holds Shipka."

This estimate of the Turkish army was in all probability exaggerated. The latest estimates received of the strength of the Moslem forces defending the southern end of the Shipka Pass placed the number at 10,000. This victory gave the entire line of the Balkans, from Servia to the line of Osman Bazar to Selvi, into the hands of the Russians, and enabled them to move their reinforcements direct from Sistova to Tirnova, and thence across the Balkans to Rumelia. In Rumelia, Suleiman, who had moved the greater part of his troops from the Lom across the Balkans after the surrender of Plevna, had gathered a considerable army at Adrianople. In the first days of January, Suleiman was put in command of the forces at Philippopolis, and Mehemet Ali was for a second time during the war appointed to the supreme command.

Gen. Gourko, after having taken Sophia, left the place in the hands of a garrison, and pushed on with the greater part of his army toward Philippopolis. He met with but very little resistance until he had passed Tartar Bazardjik, when a little beyond this city he encountered, on January 14th, the first serious opposition. The fighting was continued during the following days, the contending forces continually approaching Philippopolis, and on the 16th, Gourko entered this town. On the same day he was joined here by Skobeleff's cavalry, which had been sent him by Gen. Radetzky. On the 16th, Gen. Strukoff, who had been sent out by General Radetzky, occupied Hermànli, and then continued to advance upon Adrianople, where he expected to join Gourko's army. During this time, the left wing of the Russian army was advancing on Adrianople, having occupied, also on the 16th, Slivno, Kasan, and Yamboli. One regiment of this column had left the main column at Slivno, and marched upon Karnabad on the Black Sea.

After Gen. Gourko had entered Philippopolis, he sent his right wing, under Count Shuvaloff, against Dermendere, where Fuad Pasha had occupied a strong position; his left wing, under Gen. Dandeville, was to cross the Maritza at Yeni Mahala, advance against Stanimaki, and threaten the Turkish line of retreat; his extreme left was to advance on the road to Adrianople with the three-fold object of pursuing the Turks, who had retreated in this direction, of blocking the direct road to Constantinople, and of effecting a junction with Radetzky's troops advancing on Adrianople. In a series of fierce engagements, extending to the 18th, Suleiman's army was forced into the Rhodope Mountains, while a smaller part effected its retreat to Adrianople. This city was evacuated on the 19th, and on the following day Gen. Strukoff, commanding the advance guard of Radetzky's army, took possession of it. Adrianople, which, up to the capture of Constantinople in 1453, was the capital of the Turks, and which even in the 17th century was the residence of the Sultans Mohammed IV. and Solyman II., is to-day nothing but an immense collection of wooden huts. The streets are filthy and narrow, and it is only with great difficulty that one can ascend to the higher quarters of the city. But few of the great buildings of former times have been preserved. Among these few there are besides, several caravanseries, which, however, have been diverted from their original purpose, and now serve as warehouses, three large mosques, which are situated in close proximity to each other in the middle of the city. The oldest of these, established by Murad I., is not accessible to the unfaithful, as it is the receptacle of the Kaaba relics brought home by pilgrims to Mecca. Near to the "Muradyeh," is the "mosque of the three minarets," so-called because each of these minarets differ in shape, height, and style from the other. The third mosque, that of Selim II , is a magnificent building. It is the masterpiece of the great Ottoman builder, Sinan, who made it the finest house of worship in Turkey.

Suleiman, after a most disastrous retreat through the Rhodope Mountains, and after lying encamped for over a week on the sea-shore, was embarked with his entire army at Kavala for Constantinople. The correspondent of the London *Times* gives the following description of the condition of the army : " The army was found in a miserable plight ; no tents, nor the slightest shelter for the men even at night The poor fellows were stretched along the beach, seeking as best they could to keep themselves alive upon the scanty ration of a biscuit a day. Suleiman's headquarters were established in a ruined fort, a considerable distance from the shore, and here he was found by the Commodore, intent, it would seem, only upon his own escape, without one thought of the devoted army which had been reduced to such miserable straits through his incapacity and obstinacy, to call it by no worse a name. If ever a man was hated and detested, Suleiman Pasha is by all those who have lately served under his command. He is roundly accused of being the cause of all their disasters ; not a single voice in the army is heard in his favor, and charges of cruelty, neglect, and a criminal waste of opportunities are laid to his door, which, if substantiated in the case of a General in another country, would lead to his death by order of court-martial. . . . . The true story of this disastrous retreat will, perhaps, never be known ; a few of the details which I have gathered here suffice to brand Suleiman as a traitorous and cruel coward, who recklessly exposed the lives of his best men in the jealous desire to rid himself of generals who were his more than rivals in renown. Suleiman deserted his sick and wounded, and lost all his guns; and among other worse acts of which he is accused, is that of having burned a hospital at Philippopolis containing one hundred and eighty wounded."

The Russians continued to advance steadily on their whole line toward Constantinople, and occupied the most important positions on their way without meeting with any opposition.

Negotiations for an armistice were begun soon after the fall of Adrianople, and were brought to a successful conclusion on January 31st. During the whole of the negotiations the Russians continued their advance upon Constantinople When the armistice was concluded they had advanced as far as Tchorlu, within a short distance of Tchataldja, which were the central and most important points of the defenses of the capital. Tchataldja had been fortified during 1877, under the direction of Blum Pasha, a Prussian by birth, who had erected fifteen strong redoubts at this point. A considerable army had been gathered here under the command of Mukhtar Pasha. Even the armistice did not check the Russians in their career, as will be seen from the following telegrams from Mr. Layard to Earl Derby.

On February 5th he telegraphed: "Although armistice has been concluded, the Russians are pushing on to Constantinople. Notwithstanding the protest of the Turkish commander, the Turkish troops were compelled by General Strukoff to evacuate Silivria last night, and the protest of the Turkish commander was refused. The Russian General declared that according to his orders it was absolutely necessary that he should occupy Tchataldja to-day" And on the following day he telegraphed: "The Russians have occupied Tchataldja in considerable force. The Russian General insisted upon the abandonment, by the Turks, of the Tchekmedje lines as one of the conditions of the armistice, and the Turks have been compelled altogether to retire from them, leaving Constantinople quite undefended." The Russians continued to move their troops through Tchorlu, Tchataldja, and then along the coast of the Sea of Marmora to Eregli and Rodosto. On February 24th, San Stefano, a suburb of Constantinople, situated on the Sea of Marmora, and but ten miles from the capital, was occupied by the Russians. On the Bosporus they advanced as far as Bujukdere, but did not enter this town.

The Servians endeavored to secure, while hostilities were still in progress, as much of Old Servia as possible One column, that of the Javor, operated along the southern border, occupying most of the important points up to Novi Varosh, while another column, starting from Nissa, proceeded southward, and occupied Vranya and Prishtina. The Servians were, however, not very well received in Old Servia, the inhabitants of which are, for the most part, Bulgarians, and do not entertain very friendly feelings for the Servians. A correspondent describes the manner in which the Servians proceeded in towns conquered by them, as follows :

" Wherever Servian troops and officials appear, the inhabitants of the villages and towns are called together to be sworn in collectively as Servian subjects. Their *modus procedendi* deserves particular attention. As soon as a village has been taken, the Servian commander orders the inhabitants to appear in the town hall. Here they are received by the priest in full vestments, with the cross and the Bible in his hands, who announces to them, in very few words, that the Servian Prince Milan Obrenovitch IV. has set out to liberate the ancestral lands of the Servians from foreign rule. All the inhabitants of these lands would be from this time on citizens of Servia, enjoying equal rights, and it was expected that they would be loyal subjects of the Prince. They should, therefore, now take the oath of allegiance. After this ceremony had been gone through with, the priest kissed all the new Servians, while the military commandant embraced only the notables. The community then offered their presents, consisting chiefly of provisions, while the commandant gave to the elder a handful of ducats, which were regarded as a present of the new ruler." Widin, which had been invested by a force consisting of Rumanians and Servians, surrendered on Feb. 23d. The Ottomans marched out with arms and baggage before the Rumanian army, which then entered the fortress. _The town had suffered much from the bombardment. The Christian and Rumanian inhabitants, numbering, with the fugitives from Plevna and the environs of Widin, not fewer than 70,000, gave the victors an enthusiastic reception. A few days before the armistice was concluded a deputation of leading inhabitants begged the governor to put a stop to useless conflict.

After Suleiman Pasha had left Bulgaria with the greater part of his army, the remainder gradually retreated on the one hand to Rustchuk, and on the other to Shumla. On Jan. 24th, the Czarevitch finally crossed the Lom, occupied Osman Bazar on the 27th, and

Rasgrad on the 28th, and then proceeded to invest Rustchuk and Shumla.   Rustchuk was evacuated by the Turks on February 20th.

Gen. Zimmermann, in the Dobrudja, after advancing as far as Trajan's Wall up to the middle of June, stopped there, and kept entirely on the defensive, with the exception of an occasional cavalry reconnoissance in the direction of Varna.   On Jan. 20, 1878, after a period of inactivity of over six months, he suddenly left his position at Medjidie and advanced against Bazardjik, where a force of about 10,000 were stationed.   On the 22d, the Russian advance guard engaged the Turkish outposts at Cair Harman, and occupied this place.   On the 26th, after a short engagement, Bazardjik itself was taken.   The Turkish army, composed mainly of the Egyptian contingent, escaped to Varna.

A TURKISH BATTERY OVERTAKEN BY A STORM IN THE BALKANS.

A CAVALRY FIGHT DURING SULEIMAN'S RETREAT.

CHAPTER X.

MONTENEGRO AND THE GREEK PROVINCES.

Negotiations between Turkey and Montenegro broken off—The Turkish Armies Operating against Montenegro — The Montenegrin Forces—Operations in the South—Ali Saib Repulsed—Suleiman Captures Kristatch, the Duga Pass, and Relieves Nicsic—Incapacity of the Montenegrin Leaders— Suleiman Captures Ostrok, and marches through Montenegro to join Ali Saib in the South — Suleiman and his Army sent to Rumelia — Prince Nicholas takes Nicsic and other Points in the Herzegovina—Cessation of Hostilities—The Montenegrins Capture Spizza and Antivari—Operations against Scutari interrupted by the Armistice—Operations in the Greek Provinces and in Crete—Short participation of Greece in the War.

IMMEDIATELY upon the departure of the Montenegrin delegates from Constantinople, April 13th, Prince Nicholas addressed a note to the powers, in which he accused the Turks of having broken off negotiations because Montenegro demanded that refugees from Herzegovina should be restored to their homes and the Kutchi prisoners liberated. The Prince declared that alone, without allies, but relying on the abnegation of his subjects, he would; as in former times, desperately defend his territory against superior forces, hoping that if he were defeated, Christian Europe would save the women and the children.

At the same time the Montenegrins again began blockading Nicsic, which had been regularly provisioned during the negotiations, and also showed considerable activity at various other points. But the Turkish army, owing to disease within its ranks, did not resume hostilities until the beginning of June.—At that time a forward movement was made by the Turks from three different sides. On the southern border, Ali Saib advanced from Spuz up the valley of the Zeta with 30,000 men. In Herzegovina Suleiman Pasha was advancing with 10,000 men, while Mehemet Ali Pasha, who commanded the troops in Rascia, was to advance from the north-east with 53,000 men. But while the latter commander was to act on his own responsibility, the other two generals were to advance, the one from the north and the other from the south, and after joining their forces at Danilograd, proceed to conquer the country. Opposed

(379)

to these forces the Montenegrins had about 25,000 men at the northern end of Duga Pass. Vukovitch invested Kristatch and the fort Goransko. Another part of the northern corps of the Montenegrins was at Presyeka and Osdrenitchi and invested Nicsic. A third part was gathered around Kolashin to oppose Mehemet Ali. In the south the main corps was stationed at Martinitza under the command of Petrovitch. The most difficult work was that allotted to Suleiman Pasha, whose main object was necessarily to relieve and provision first Kristatch and Goransko, and then Nicsic, and afterward march on to join Ali Saib. The distance from Nicsic to Spuz is twenty miles, while the width of Montenegro on this line is but fifteen miles. From the boundary to Danilograd, Suleiman Pasha had but twelve miles, and Ali Saib about four miles to march, so that if the two Turkish generals had once reached the boundary, they ought to have met within one day, provided they did not encounter any opposition.

In the south, Ali Saib, after a few engagements, advanced, on June 6th, from Spuz against the main position of Petrovitch at Martinitza, but was repulsed after a long and severe engagement, and retreated to Spuz. From here he attempted, on the 7th, to march up the valley of the Moratcha, and to attack Petrovitch's flank, but finding him prepared, again retreated to Turkish territory. Petrovitch now took the offensive, and in the following days drove Ali Saib beyond Spuz, before which place he then encamped without formally investing it. He continued, however, to bombard Spuz, and to hold Ali Saib in check until the middle of June, when the events in the north made it impossible for him to retain this position.

In the north, Suleiman divided his troops into two columns, and marched them against Goransko and Kristatch, at the entrance to the Duga Pass. At the latter point the corps of Gen. Vukovitch had erected fortifications, which the Turks attacked. At first they were repulsed, but afterward succeeded in forcing Gen. Vukovitch to retire to his second line of defense. The engagement was very sanguinary, the loss of the Turks being over 3,000 men, while that of the Montenegrins was also very large.

At Goransko the Montenegrins were more successful. General Sotchitza repulsed the Turks under Ali Pasha, who then retreated to Muratovizza. The third Turkish column, which invaded Montenegro in the district of Vassovitch, the extreme north-eastern corner of the principality, under the command of Mehemet Ali, was chiefly intended to harass the Montenegrins, and draw their attention from the other points.

The first task of Suleiman Pasha, after dislodging the Montenegrins from Kristatch, was to relieve the garrison and provision the fort of Goransko, or Piva, as the Turks call it. With a view to this, he made a demonstration in the direction of Presyeka, whither the Montenegrins had retired, and strengthened the column under Ali Pasha, likewise making for Goransko. Thus reinforced, the column advanced and provisioned the fort.

Suleiman Pasha then again took up his operations against Nicsic. After two days' fighting, lasting almost from morning till night, he dislodged the Montenegrins from their positions in the Duga Pass, and forced them to retire to Lakovo, toward Banyani. The Montenegrin force arrayed against Nicsic also left the plain, and Prince Nicholas transferred his headquarters from Planinitza, near Nicsic, back to Ostrok, on the heights in Montenegrin territory. The battle was very severe, and cost thousands of men on both sides. Nicsic was soon after relieved.

The battle of Kristatch proved the incapacity of Gen. Vukovitch as a military leader. Both armies were exhausted after the battle, and that of Suleiman Pasha had no communication. The Montenegrins lost no positions, and might have maintained Kristatch against any further direct attack, or by following up the battle by an attack in full force with the six fresh battalions received a day or two later, might have forced Suleiman Pasha back on Gatchko, he being less able to sustain a renewal of the struggle than the Montenegrins. The interval of inaction which followed sufficiently proves this. In falling back on Presyeka, Vukovitch acted under exaggerated impressions of the strength of the Turkish force and apprehensions which had no proper basis. At Presyeka he made the graver mistake of spreading his army along a thin line of four miles, the battalions being often without any means of intercommunication or supports, and concealed from one another, and in great part from their commander, by dense forests, owing to which he could not follow the operations. Some battalions received no orders at all. During the fighting which preceded the revictualling of Nicsic, the Turkish attack was concentrated on the right wing, two battalions of which, after a desperate fight of two hours, partly hand-to-hand, were driven in, and there being no supports, the rest of the wing was cut off and obliged to fall back. For two days many of the men had no food.

20

What made the blunder worse was that Vukovitch had decided not to oppose the further advance of Suleiman Pasha before the attack was made; but, instead of immediately removing his troops and providing for the defense of Planinitza, the Montenegrin General waited till the Turks had entered Nicsic, when he was compelled to make a circuitous march of two days to reach the Prince, while the Turks, having rested two days, were in front of Planinitza, before a sufficient Montenegrin force had arrived to fortify and hold it. The defense of this strong position being thus impracticable, Prince Nicholas fell back, followed by the Turks.

Suleiman Pasha continued to advance very slowly, the road being obstinately contested by the Montenegrins. But, bravely as the Montenegrin soldiers fought, the utter incapacity of their leaders lost for them all the advantages gained by their bravery. It was a matter of great wonder at the time that the Russians did not provide Prince Nicholas with capable officers. For, although according to consular reports, in the middle of June, Suleiman Pasha had 22,000 regulars and from 5,000 to 8,000 irregulars, against whom the Prince could only oppose 8,000 to 10,000, and the entire Turkish forces operating against Montenegro amounted to 60,000 men, the odds were no greater than those against which the Montenegrins had frequently successfully contended.

On June 17th, Suleiman Pasha attacked Ostrok. This place, at which Prince Nicholas had taken up his headquarters, is a convent, built in a spacious cavern on the side of a cliff, which rises 400 feet above it. It was always the great stronghold and powder magazine of the Montenegrins, and is considered nearly impregnable, having been defended in 1768 by thirty men against 30,000 Turks. The convent was burned on June 20th. The fighting continued until the evening of the 21st. On the 22d, the Montenegrins remained quiet, and the Turks, improving this opportunity, gathered their forces on the heights between Ostrok and Gradatz. On the 23d, the Turks continued their march to the south, gaining but little ground, and continually harassed by Montenegrin detachments. Petrovitch, on June 22d, left his positions before Spuz in order to advance against Suleiman Pasha. Ali Saib, leaving his main force at Spuz, sent only an advanced guard after him. On June 23d, Suleiman Pasha began to descend from the heights of Ostrok into the valley of Gradatz, being continually attacked even by detachments from Petrovitch's main body. On the 24th, his advanced guard finally met detachments of Ali Saib's troops at Gradatz. During the eight days, from June 17th to 24th, he had advanced at the most nine miles, and had lost, according to his own statements, 631 dead and 864 wounded; altogether, 1,495 men out of about 12,000 combatants. The loss of the Montenegrins is not known, but it can not have been nearly as much as that of the Turks. On the other hand, it is generally believed that Suleiman Pasha lost many more men than he stated, and in fact than he could have known. The proposed march to Cettigne was now abandoned after the experience gained, and the two Pashas gathered their troops in the plains of Spuz and Podgoritza, and set to work to prepare them for embarkation at Antivari, to go to a more important seat of war.

Mehemet Ali undertook but one expedition. He sent his Bashi-Bazouks into the north-eastern part of Montenegro, where they devastated the country in a manner peculiar to them.

After the departure of the Turkish troops, Prince Nicholas again took the offensive and invested Nicsic. On July 22d and 23d several outlying works of this city were taken, and on September 8th, Nicsic itself surrendered, after a Turkish corps under Hafiz Pasha, which had been sent to relieve it, had been defeated. The fall of Nicsic was followed by that of Presyeka on the 16th, of Bilek on the 17th, and of the four forts in the Duga Pass on the 18th of September. Montenegro thus came into possession of a part of Herzegovina, on whose final maintenance the Montenegrins could count all the more readily, as their conquests were only in the interior, and as Austria therefore did not raise any objections to their holding them. For over a month there was now a cessation of hostilities, during which the Montenegrin troops were dismissed to their homes for the ostensible object of gathering their crops. The few regular Turkish troops which had remained behind, were stationed in Northern Albania, under Ali Saib. In the beginning of November, the Montenegrins again resumed operations, stormed several of the outlying works of Antivari on the 12th; captured the fortress of Spizza on the 16th; and having taken the town of Antivari shortly afterward, proceeded to a siege of the citadel. It was expected that Ali Saib, who was at Scutari, would come to the relief of the garrison, as he was ordered to do by the Sultan. But he declared himself unable to perform this task, and the Montenegrins forced a surrender of the citadel on the 10th of January. The garrison at the time of the surrender consisted of 1,500 men under the command of Saban Bey and Selim Bey, while the civil population of the town numbered 2,600. The Montenegrins found here large quantities of arms and ammunition, comprising eighty barrels of powder, fifteen large cannon, and many small arms, all of which they could make good use of. As the Montenegrins were short of provisions, they were forced to dismiss the prisoners, the majority of whom were Albanians from the neighboring towns, to their homes. On January 19th, the Montenegrins attacked the fortified heights above Dulcigno, and carried them after a long and bloody fight, notwithstanding the severe firing which they suffered from a Turkish iron-clad in the road. One whole battalion of Turkish regulars were taken prisoners. The same evening the town was stormed, and the garrison of the citadel, including several hundred Bashi-Bazouks, being driven out, took refuge on board the fleet. The Montenegrins then proceeded to invest Scutari. For this purpose they planted batteries commanding the river Boyana, thus cutting off the place from the sea, and successively occupied all the Turkish inland fortresses on the Lake of Scutari. Another Montenegrin force occupied the line of the Sieveno River, effecting an interruption of communications between Podgoritza and Scutari. They were, however, prevented from proceeding any further against Scutari by the conclusion of the armistice.

The Greek provinces of Turkey, comprising Thessaly, Epirus, and the island of Crete, were the scene of great excitement during the war of 1877-'78. In Crete the National Assembly demanded reforms of the Turkish Government, which were, however, not granted. The island, on the contrary, was completely blockaded by the Turkish fleet, while irregular troops were stationed at various points, ready to suppress any attempt at a rising. A revolutionary committee had established itself in the interior of the mountains, which were inaccessible to the Turkish troops, and gathered around itself large numbers of the discontented inhabitants. In February, 1878, the revolutionary government proclaimed their annexation to Greece. In Thessaly the condition of the people was a truly miserable one. Large bodies of irregular troops, together with bands of robbers, plundered the country, and the Turkish authorities were represented as unable and unwilling to protect the population. A body of insurgents under a leader named Kastakis established itself in the mountains. No actions of any importance occurred, however, until on February 2, 1878, the Greek army crossed the frontier. The action of the Greek Government in permitting this step was explained by the following official declaration, published on Feb. 1st:

"The Hellenic Government, moved by the sufferings in the Greek provinces of Turkey, has given orders for an army of 12,000 men to cross the frontier to-morrow morning, and occupy Thessaly, Epirus, and Macedonia, for the purpose of maintaining public order and preventing massacres of Christians"

On the following morning, a corps of 10,000 Greek troops and many thousand volunteers, under the command of General Soutzo, crossed the frontier into Thessaly. The Turkish troops, on the approach of the Greek army, delivered up the keys of their barracks to the Greek commander, and withdrew to Domoco. The insurgents, who co-operated with the Greeks, occupied Rendina. The Turks lost no time in threatening their new adversary on his most vulnerable side—the sea. The Turkish fleet under Hobart Pasha was ordered to the Piræus, and the news of its approach caused a great panic in the Greek capital and throughout the kingdom, more especially as there were only 500 troops in Athens, and only a small English gunboat in the Piræus. The Government, however, at the request of the representatives of the powers, recalled its troops soon afterward. On February 14th, M. Kumunduros, the Minister President, stated in the Chamber of Deputies, that the powers, having represented to Greece that if she continued her course of action alone, after the armistice was signed, she would forfeit their protection, but if she suspended her military action, she might be assured of their support, the Government thought it was their duty to recall the army. This step caused much popular indignation among the Greeks, which was considerably augmented when great numbers of Christians from the villages in Thessaly evacuated by the Hellenic troops sought refuge in Greece, in consequence of the murders and savage aggression which were-committed by the Bashi-Bazouks. The insurrection continued after the withdrawal of the Greek troops, although no actions of any importance occurred.

CHAPTER XI.

NAVAL OPERATIONS.

Russian Fleet on the Black Sea—Russian Fortifications on the Black Sea—Expedition of the "Constantine"—Destruction of Turkish vessels—Expedition to the mouths of the Danube—Capture of a Turkish Mail Steamer with a valuable cargo—Torpedoes—Their use in the present War.

AT the beginning of the war the Russian forces in the Black Sea consisted of two monitors, called "Popoffkas," four medium-sized screw corvettes, twelve smaller steamers, and an unknown number of smaller vessels for transport and packet service. As will be seen from this statement, Russia did not have a single man-of-war on the Black Sea, her whole force in its waters being intended for defensive purposes only. The twelve steamers mentioned above had been bought from the Russian Society for steam navigation and commerce, and with the exception of three, which had been built recently, were all old vessels. The schooners and packet boats, among which was included the Imperial pleasure yacht "Livadia," were small screw steamers of wood or iron, carrying two four-pounders each. These vessels were not formed into squadrons; they were assigned to duty more with a view of aiding the local coast defense. The most important points of this are the fortifications in the bay of Kherson, consisting of the two opposite forts of Oksakoff and Kieburn. Between Oksakoff and Odessa, the coast is inaccessible; from the latter point to Akkerman, it is defended by strong fortifications, while the shore is lined with torpedoes. The weakest point between Nikolayeff and Odessa is the peninsula of Perekop, where there is an old wall which was erected by the Tartars, at the time of their rule over the Crimea, and which greatly resembles Trajan's Wall in the Dobrudja. It was formerly used as a defense against invasions, and at the beginning of the war of 1877 was again intended to serve this purpose. The entire south side of the Crimea is strongly fortified; earthworks have been erected at Sebastopol. Temporary fortifications have also been erected at

Sudak, near Feodosia. The entrance to the Sea of Asov is closed by the works of Kertch, which consist of the batteries of Yeni Kaleh, and the forts on the western point of the opposite peninsula of Taman.

The activity of the Russian fleet on the Black Sea gave proof of great daring and bravery on the part of the Russian seamen. Even the first undertaking showed that they were not willing to relinquish all aggressive movements and to confine themselves to a defense of the coast. On the evening of May 12th, the steamer "Constantine" left Sebastopol for Batum; after having proceeded for some distance, it stopped, and sent out four torpedo-boats, which succeeded in applying a torpedo under a Turkish frigate. The torpedo did not ignite, and the alarm which was given compelled the Russian boats to seek safety in flight. On the morning of the 15th, the "Constantine" arrived with two of the torpedo-boats in Sebastopol, while the two others succeeded in reaching the harbor of Poti. An engagement which the Russian steamer "Vesta" had with a Turkish iron-clad at Kustendje on July 23d, resulted less fortunately for the Russians. The engagement lasted five hours, during which the rudder of the "Vesta" was destroyed, while she received two damaging holes in the hull. It was owing only to the fact that a Russian bomb exploded in the turret of the monitor, that the latter desisted from continuing the engagement, and that the Russian steamer could return to Sebastopol. On July 21st, the steamer "Argonaut" had reconnoitered the Kilia mouth of the Danube, and had encountered three Turkish iron-clads and ten merchantmen. A short engagement ensued, and in the evening the "Argonaut" returned safely to Oksakoff.

The expeditions undertaken by the steamers "Elborus" and "Constantine," from July 30th to August 4th, were of greater importance than the previous expeditions, as showing the assurance with which the Russians went to work in these undertakings. The "Elborus" returned from a cruise to the coasts of Rumelia and Anatolia after having sunk a Turkish brig. The "Constantine" had, in the night from August 3d to 4th, advanced as far as the entrance of the Bosporus, and at Kilia, near the European side of the strait, blew up by means of torpedoes a Turkish sailing vessel laden with grain, and destroyed three other Turkish vessels carrying petroleum. On August 8th, a flotilla consisting of five larger vessels and four torpedo-sloops set out from Odessa under the protection of the two Popoffkas, the

steamer " Vladimir," and two torpedo-cutters, to which were afterward added the steamers " Elborus " and " Argonaut " and the yacht
" Livadia," and after a successful voyage, reached the Kilia mouth of
the Danube, which it entered under the very eyes of a fleet of Turkish iron-clads stationed at the Sulina mouth. The object of this
successful expedition was to reinforce the Russian fleet in the Lower
Danube, and to supply it with the material for torpedoes

On October 8th, another Russian flotilla, consisting of floating
batteries and armored gun-boats, attacked the Turkish men-of-war
lying before Sulina, and not only forced the entrance into the
Danube. but also compelled the Turkish vessels to retreat to Varna,
where Hassan Pasha was stationed with several iron-clads.

The only other action of importance on the Black Sea was the
capture of the mail-steamer " Mersine " by two Russian vessels. The
" Mersine," which is described as a fine ship, and which had been
but newly repaired, had on board a very valuable cargo, a large
quantity of silver ore, on its way to the mint at Constantinople.
There were also on board all the private papers and effects of Mukhtar Pasha; all the Government dispatches and orders which had
been received from time to time, and it was by the merest chance
that Mukhtar himself was not on the vessel. Beyond an occasional
bombardment of Russian towns on the Black Sea by Hobart Pasha's
squadron, nothing of any importance occurred up to the conclusion
of the armistice.

The Russians had a powerful weapon for their naval operations
in the torpedoes which they employed. These instruments, as used
in naval warfare, are of two kinds, stationary or defensive, and locomotive or offensive. The stationary torpedoes are sunk and
arranged so as to keep at a fixed distance below the surface of the
water. They are usually ignited by electric action. They were used
by the Russians to great advantage during the Crimean war, while
during the present war, it was said that the shores of the Black Sea
were lined with them. The knowledge of which fact was probably
the cause of the reluctance of the Porte to countenance the project
of attacking the Russian towns on the Black Sea, which Hobart
Pasha is understood to have urged.

While the stationary torpedo was not called into use during the war
of 1877 to 1878, the locomotive torpedo played a prominent part.
The Turkish monitor destroyed on the Danube was attacked by torpedo-boats, while an unsuccessful attempt against other Turkish ves-

RUSSIAN TORPEDO BOATS ENGAGING THE BATTERIES NEAR SILISTRIA.

A RUSSIAN BATTERY.

sels was made by a boat carrying a torpedo affixed to a long pole. At the extremity of the pole is fixed a metal case, made water-tight, containing a sufficient charge of gunpowder or other explosive, while from a battery on board electric wires are stretched along the pole to the fuse of the machine. At the right moment the pole is launched forward, and at the same time thrust beneath the water. Upon the torpedo's touching the object, the operator in the boat presses down the key, the electric circuit is closed, and the charge exploded.

Various methods to protect vessels from torpedoes have been tried. Hobart Pasha surrounded his vessels off the mouth of the river Danube with a circle of boats and connecting-chains, and thereby secured them against a resolute attack. Crinoline frames have also been used, by which the locomotive torpedo is arrested before striking the vessel, while English authorities recommend a flexible wire matting, which, yielding when struck, checks gradually and not suddenly the force of the explosive engine.

The "fish," or "Whitehead torpedo," invented only recently by Mr. Whitehead, an English gentleman, is a cigar-shaped hull of iron or steel, containing a powerful charge, and a small locomotive engine worked by compressed air. When used, it is thrust out through a tube from the ship's side, and the engine being set in motion, it proceeds for several hundred yards beneath the surface, at a speed said to be as high as twenty miles an hour, till it strikes the vessel aimed at, when it explodes by concussion. These torpedoes have given eminent satisfaction, and a number of them were ordered by the Russians.

CHAPTER XII.

DIPLOMATIC HISTORY OF THE WAR.

How the Declaration of War was received in Europe—England and Austria—Correspondence between the British and Russian Governments—Mr Gladstone's Resolutions—The British Fleet in Besika Bay—The Vote of Credit in the British Parliament—Agitations in Austria-Hungary—The War Feeling in Servia—Prince Milan's Visit to the Czar—The Excitement in Greece—The Mouths of the Danube—The Salonica Murderers.

THE declaration of war intensified the anxiety which prevailed throughout Europe. The efforts which the powers had strenuously made during the past two years to preserve peace and prevent a rising of the Eastern Question, were defeated; and this dreaded question, with all of its contingencies and unknown perils, was again before the world, and would have to be met without evasion. A course of events was begun, of which no statesmanship could see the end, and which no power, perhaps not even all the nations combined, would be able to control. Of all the powers, Austria and England were most concerned; for they foresaw that in case of Russian victory, which all agreed must be the possible ending of the war, interests which they held near and precious would be put in doubt, and harm would ultimately come to the integrity of their dominions or to their prestige, and the greatest uneasiness prevailed in these countries, both in government circles and among the people, during the whole course of the war, despite the official proclamations of neutrality which were promptly issued, and despite the often-repeated declarations of their ministers of adhesion to the attitude of neutrality which they had assumed in the beginning. These declarations, however, were never absolute, but were always qualified by the reservation that the policy of neutrality would be observed only as long as British or Austrian interests were not endangered; and they received a curious commentary in the movements which were quietly instituted under the eye of the Government, in England at least, looking to preparation to be ready for action when the time for decision should come. In Austria, the Hungarian party, and in England, the extreme wing of the Conservative party, urged active demonstrations against the Turks; and their efforts were barely kept in check by the more prudent policy of the Viennese Cabinet and the sturdy opposition of the English Liberals to every act which could bear the appearance of favoring the continuance of Turkish oppression of Christian peoples.

The first expression of the British Government upon the questions at issue after the declaration of war was given in a communication of Earl Derby, Secretary of State for Foreign Affairs, to Lord Loftus, British Ambassador at St. Petersburg, communicating the reply of the Government to the Russian circular announcing the commencement of hostilities. The dispatch stated that her Majesty's Government had received the announcement made by the Russian Government with deep regret, and could not accept the statements and conclusions with which Prince Gortchakoff had accompanied it, as justifying the resolutions taken. "The protocol," the dispatch continued, "to which her Majesty's Government, at the instance of that of Russia, recently became parties, required from the Sultan no fresh guarantees for the reform of his administration. With a view of enabling Russia the better to abstain from isolated action, it affirmed the interest taken in common by the powers in the condition of the Christian populations of Turkey. It went on to declare that the powers would watch carefully the manner in which the promises of the Ottoman Government were carried into effect; and that should their hopes be once more disappointed, they reserved to themselves the right to consider in common the means which they might deem best fitted to secure the well-being of the Christian populations and the interests of the general peace.

"To these declarations of the intentions of the powers, the consent of the Porte was not asked or required The Porte, no doubt, has thought fit—unfortunately, in the opinion of her Majesty's Government—to protest against the expressions in question as implying an encroachment on the Sultan's sovereignty and independence. But while so doing, and while declaring that they can not consider the protocol as having any binding character on Turkey, the Turkish Government have again affirmed their intention of carrying into execution the reforms already promised.

"Her Majesty's Government can not therefore admit, as is contended by Prince Gortchakoff, that the answer of the Porte removed all hope of deference on its part to the wishes and advice of Europe, and all security for the application of the suggested reforms. Nor are they of opinion that the terms of the note necessarily precluded the possibility of the conclusion of peace with Montenegro, or of the arrangement of mutual disarmament. Her Majesty's Government still believes that, with patience and moderation on both sides, these objects might not have improbably been attained.

"Prince Gortchakoff, however, asserts that all opening is now closed for attempts at conciliation; that the Emperor has resolved to undertake the task of obtaining, by coercion, that which the unanimous efforts of all the powers have failed to obtain from the Porte by persuasion; and he expresses his Imperial Majesty's conviction that this step is in accordance with the sentiments and interests of Europe.

"It can not be expected that her Majesty's Government should agree in this view. They have not concealed their feeling that the presence of large Russian forces on the frontiers of Turkey, menacing its safety, rendering disarmament impossible, and exciting a feeling of apprehension and fanaticism among the Mussulman population, constituted a material obstacle to internal pacification and reform. They can not believe that the entrance of those armies on Turkish soil will alleviate the difficulty or improve the condition of the Christian population throughout the Sultan's dominions.

"But the course on which the Russian Government has entered involves graver and more serious considerations. It is in contravention of the stipulation of the Treaty of Paris of March 30, 1856, by which Russia and the other signatory powers engaged, each on its own part, to respect the independence and the territorial integrity of the Ottoman Empire. In the Conference of London of 1871, at the close of which the above stipulation, with others, was again confirmed, the Russian Plenipotentiary, in common with those of the other powers, signed a declaration, affirming it to be 'an essential principle of the law of nations that no power can liberate itself from the engagements of a treaty, nor modify the stipulations thereof, unless with the consent of the contracting parties by means of an amicable arrangement.'

"In taking action against Turkey on his own part, and having recourse to arms without further consultation with his allies, the Emperor of Russia has separated himself from the European concert hitherto maintained, and has at the same time departed from the rule to which he himself had solemnly recorded his consent.

"It is impossible to foresee the consequences of such an act. Her Majesty's Government would willingly have refrained from making any observations in regard to it; but, as Prince Gortchakoff seems to assume, in a declaration addressed to all the Governments of Europe, that Russia is acting in the interest of Great Britain and that of the other powers, they feel bound to state, in a manner equally formal and public, that the decision of the Russian Government is not one which can have their concurrence or approval."

To this note the Russian Government made no formal reply; but a statement was published by the Russian news agency, which was considered as its informal reply. This dispatch remarked that there would be no Russian rejoinder, for "to send one would be to carry on a controversy, when it was a question of making history." England's apprehensions of future complications were, so far as Russia was concerned, utterly unfounded; but the powers which seriously desired to re-establish an understanding and a guarantee of general peace must seek a new basis more in conformity with circumstances, without further dwelling on mistaken views of past results, which are the best refutation of the English dispatch.

As respects the Treaty of 1871, appealed to in this dispatch, it might be asked if the Porte was not the first to break the engagement of the preceding Treaty of 1856. If the English Cabinet maintained that the Porte was not bound by it, then that treaty would only have served to guarantee the Porte's entire impunity. All the documents of that period proved, on the contrary, that the Christian powers did not mean to defend a *régime* oppressive for Christians. They simply decided against the exclusive protection of Russia. They substituted for it the common protection of Europe. The rights and duties attaching thereto they have often exercised.

The article cited instances of intervention which had taken place since the treaty went into effect, such as the Andrassy note, the Berlin memorandum, and others, and added:

"Results have proved that these platonic interventions led to nothing. If the English Cabinet regards the Treaty of 1856 as important, that interpretation will hardly be accepted by Europe, or even by the English nation, especially not by the Russian Government or nation. In the interest of this treaty the common action and pressure of Europe should have been exerted. Russia has done everything for this purpose. Her efforts were fruitless. It only remained for Russia to execute alone the duty which the other cabinets, agreeing with her in principle, hesitated to assume in practice. The Imperial Cabinet is justified in affirming that it is acting in conformity with the sentiments and interests of Europe. The English Cabinet can not extricate itself from this dilemma except by proclaiming that England is the first Mussulman power in the world, and that she consequently wishes for the maintenance of Turkish dominion over Christians, even at the cost of their extermination. We hold the English nation in too great esteem to believe it would sanction such a policy."

On the 6th of May Earl Derby addressed to Count Shuvaloff, the Russian Ambassador, who was about leaving for St. Petersburg, a note on the position of England toward the belligerents. After stating that the British Government had from the first warned the Turkish Government that it must not look to them for assistance, and that they were determined to carry impartially into effect the policy thus announced, so long as Turkish interests alone were involved, the note continued :

" Should the war now in progress unfortunately spread, interests may be imperilled which they (the British Government) are equally bound and determined to defend ; and it is desirable that they should make it clear, as far as at the outset can be done, what the most prominent of those interests are. Foremost among them is the necessity of keeping open, uninjured and uninterrupted, the communication between Europe and the East by the Suez Canal. An attempt to blockade or otherwise to interfere with the canal or its approaches, would be regarded by them as a menace to India, and as a grave injury to the commerce of the world. On both these grounds any such step—which they hope and fully believe there is no intention on the part of either belligerent to take—would be inconsistent with the maintenance by them of passive neutrality."

Speaking of the ultimate fate of Constantinople, the note continued :

" The vast importance of Constantinople, whether in a military, a political, or commercial point of view, is too well understood to require explanation. It is, therefore, scarcely necessary to point out that her Majesty's Government are not prepared to witness with indifference the passing into other hands than those of its present possessors, of a capital holding so peculiar and important a position.

The existing arrangements made under European sanction, which regulate the navigation of the Bosporus and Dardanelles, appear to them wise and salutary, and there would be, in their judgment, serious objections to their alteration in any material particular."

Other points were referred to in the note as involving interests which the course of the war might show it to be necessary to protect, the principal of which was the Persian Gulf. These statements were intended to indicate the limits within which the British Government hoped that the war might be restrained, or, at least, the limits which, so far as the present circumstances would permit the formation of a definite opinion, would confine its policy of abstention and neutrality.

The Russian Government replied to this note May 18th, expressing an appreciation of the "frankness of explanations the object of which was to clear up the misunderstandings between the two Governments," and continuing with an exposition, "in the same frankness and with the same clearness," of its own views, both upon the points mentioned by Lord Derby, and upon those which touched the interests which the Czar on his side considered it his duty to protect. On the points named in Earl Derby's dispatch, the note said: "The Imperial Cabinet will neither blockade, nor interrupt, nor in any way menace the navigation of the Suez Canal. I consider the canal an international work, important to the commerce of the whole world, which should remain free from every attack. Egypt is a part of the Ottoman Empire, and its contingents figure in the Turkish army. Russia might, therefore, consider herself as at war with Egypt. Nevertheless, the Imperial Cabinet does not overlook either the European interests engaged in the country, or those of England in particular. They will not bring Egypt within the radius of her operations. As far as concerns Constantinople, without being able to prejudge the course or issue of the war, the Imperial Cabinet repeats that the acquisition of that capital is excluded from the views of his Majesty the Emperor. They recognize that in any case the future of Constantinople is a question of common interest, which can not be settled otherwise than by a general understanding, and that if the possession of that city were to be put in question, it could not be allowed to belong to any of the European powers. As regards the Straits, although their two shores belong to the same sovereign, they form the only outlet of two great seas, in which all the world has interests. It is, therefore, important, in the interests of peace and of the general balance of power, that this question should be settled by a common agreement on equitable and efficiently guaranteed bases." As to British interests in the Persian Gulf and the route to India, the Imperial Government declared that it would not extend the war further than was required by the clearly declared purpose for which the Emperor had been obliged to take up arms, and would regard British interests so long as England should remain neutral. It expected, in turn, that the English Government would equally regard the interests which Russia sought to promote in the war, and for which it was making great sacrifices; which interests involved the necessity of putting an end to the deplorable condition of the Christians under Turkish rule, and to the periodical crises which it provoked. This object could not be attained till the Christian populations of Turkey are placed in a situation in which their existence and their security shall be effectively guaranteed against the intolerable abuses of the Turkish administration. This interest, vital for Russia, was in contradiction to none of the interests of Europe, which suffered, in its turn, from the precarious condition of the East. The Imperial Cabinet had desired to pursue its object with the concurrence of the powers; but, obliged to pursue it alone, his Imperial Majesty was resolved not to lay down arms till he had completely, securely, effectively realized it.

On the 30th of April Mr. Gladstone gave notice in the House of Commons of the introduction of five resolutions recording the dissatisfaction of the House at the conduct of the Ottoman Government regarding the dispatch of the British Government on the Bulgarian atrocities; declaring that until such conduct should be essentially changed and substantial guarantees for future good government given, the Porte would have lost all claim to the moral and material support of the British Crown; advising that British influence be used to secure local liberties and practical self-government for the disturbed provinces, so as to secure them from oppression without imposing on them any other foreign dominion; advising that it should also be addressed to promoting the concert of the European Powers in exacting from the Porte, by their united authority, such changes as might be effectual for the purposes of humanity, for defense against intrigue, and for securing the peace of Europe; and asking that an address to the crown embodying the substance of the resolutions might be prepared and presented. The

QUEEN VICTORIA.

GLADSTONE.

debate on the resolutions began on the 7th of May, and was continued during the week till the 14th, when the first one was rejected by a vote of 354 to 223, after which the others were withdrawn. Mr. Gladstone failed to receive the full support of his Liberal colleagues on this occasion, a meeting of the Liberal members having resolved that in view of the overshadowing importance of British interests in the East, it would not be advisable to go as far in their declarations of hostility to Turkey as he would have them. He was, nevertheless, supported by an influential portion of the press, and had a large and devoted following among the people. Among others who gave expressions of their sympathy with his views, was the brilliant historian and pamphleteer, Thomas Carlyle, who said in a letter published in the London *Times:*

"As to 'British interests,' there is none visible or conceivable to me, except taking strict charge of our route to India by the Suez and Egypt; and, for the rest, resolutely steering altogether clear of any copartnery with the Turk in regard to this or any other 'British interest' whatever. It should be felt by England as a real ignominy to be connected with such a Turk at all. Nay, if we still had, as, in fact, all ought to have, a wish to save him from perdition and annihilation in God's world, the one future for him that has any hope in it is even now that of being conquered by the Russians and gradually schooled and drilled into a peaceable attempt at learning to be himself governed. The newspaper outcry against Russia is no more respectable to me than the howling of Bedlam, proceeding, as it does, from the deepest ignorance, egotism, and paltry national jealousy."

The British Mediterranean squadron returned to Besika Bay on the 3d of July, after an absence from that port of about six months. This station, which has been frequently mentioned in connection with the later transactions of Great Britain with the Porte, is a small bay in the coast of Asia Minor nearly opposite the island of Tenedos, and under the plains of the Troad It is very near the entrance to the Dardanelles, and is the nearest harbor to Constantinople which an armed vessel can approach without entering the straits and thereby violating the Treaty of Paris. The fleet had been ordered to the Bay in 1876, and kept there for several months during the hostile operations of the year, for the purpose, as was generally believed at the time, of signifying to the Czar that he would have to count with England in case of any aggression upon

21

the Sultan's rights—or, as was stated by Earl Derby some time afterward, to protect the Europeans and the native Christians of Constantinople in case of any outbreak of Mussulman fanaticism. When Lord Salisbury arrived at Constantinople at the time of the conference, in December, 1876, he found that the Turks were possessed with a fixed idea that, do what they might, England would never allow them to be attacked; and the fleet was withdrawn at that time, and transferred to the Piræus (the harbor of Athens) at his request, not so much, as it was said, to mark the displeasure of the British Government at the obstinacy of the Turks, as to convey to them, by unmistakable signs, that they had nothing to expect from England in case they should be involved in a war with Russia. The return of the fleet at this time was regarded as designed to convey an intimation to Russia that England would not quietly see it proceed too far in its aggressions. Considerable reinforcements were sent to the squadron during the following weeks, while large numbers of troops were concentrated at Malta, and the impression grew that England was preparing to take a part in the war. In the face of these active preparations the ministers declared in both Houses of Parliament that their intentions were still peaceful, and stated that the fleet had been ordered to return to Besika Bay for convenience of communication with the Government at home, and the Ambassador at Constantinople, and in no way with the intention of making a menace, and that the movements of troops had been ordered simply because it had been found desirable, in view of the disturbed condition of Europe, to bring up the garrisons in the Mediterranean to their full strength. On the 10th of August, just before the prorogation of Parliament, the Chancellor of the Exchequer declined to say whether the Government would regard the temporary occupation of Constantinople by the Russians as so far inconsistent with British interests as to disturb the friendly relations of Great Britain with Russia. On the next day, in reply to a request made by Mr. Fawcett for a pledge from the Government, that if during the recess, they felt it necessary to depart from their attitude of neutrality, they would call Parliament together before taking any decisive step, the Chancellor said that the Government were fully aware of their constitutional obligations, and determined to act up to them.

The new session of Parliament for 1878 was called to meet on the 17th of January, three weeks before the usual time of opening the session. Russian success had become an established fact, and the friends of Turkey were known to be in great anxiety. Speculation was rife concerning the objects of the Ministry in hastening the session, and apprehensions were expressed by many members of the anti-Turkish party that they would commit the country to some act that would compromise it with Russia, and ask Parliament, in the heat of the temporary excitement, to sanction it. The Queen stated in her speech that, in view of the successes of the Russian arms in Europe and Asia, the Turkish Government had sought her friendly offices in the interests of peace; that she had exercised them; that through them communications had taken place between the Governments of Russia and Turkey, and that a favorable conclusion was hoped for. Nevertheless, should hostilities unfortunately be prolonged, some unexpected occurrence might render it necessary for the Government to adopt measures of precaution, and the liberality of Parliament was appealed to, to supply the means which might be required for that purpose. The Ministry asked a supplemental vote of credit of £6,000,000 for military and naval services. The measure was opposed by a fraction of the Liberals, but the rapid advance of the Russians toward Constantinople had had the effect of consolidating the public opinion of the country in favor of giving the Government a firm support, and placing it in a position to assume a vigorous attitude, if necessary, and the vote was passed in the House of Commons on the 8th of February, by the decisive vote of 328 to 124.

A Ministerial Council, held at Constantinople on the 10th of June, to consider the case of the Suez Canal, decided not to consider it as wholly neutral, but to reserve a full right over this part of the territory of the Empire not less than over any other, and particularly the right of preventing Russian ships from using the artificial water-way. It agreed, however, by stationing a naval force at the entrance of the canal, to insure the freedom of navigation, and prevent the canal from becoming the theater of any conflict.

The declarations of the Austro-Hungarian Government were more reserved than those of Great Britain. It seemed to be acting under hesitating councils, and to be watching the course of events before deciding what position to assume. The Ministers made identical replies to interpellations in both the Chambers at Vienna and Pesth, on the 4th of May, to the effect that the Government was not tied by any kind of engagement, but had reserved the fullest freedom of action, and that "Austria-Hungary maintains an attitude of benevolent interest in the Christian subjects of the Porte, and, while observing strict neutrality, reserves the right to protect its own interests, or intervene with efforts for the cessation or localizing of the conflict. The Ministers recognize the Empire's intimate connection with, and interest in, the affairs of European Turkey, but deem a resort to warlike measures for their protection unnecessary, in view of the attitude of the other powers and the cordial support the Government can command from the representatives of the people whenever action becomes necessary." The Slavic and Magyar populations, however, gave full expression to their sympathies— the former for Russia and the latter for Turkey—and the Empire was kept in a state of agitation during the whole period of the continuance of hostilities. The Magyars sought, by interpellations in the Chambers, to commit the Government, and by pamphlets and speeches to commit the people, to an attitude of definite hostility to Russia. The Croats, on the other hand, took advantage of a visit of the Archduke Albert to Agram, in May, to make a demonstration of sympathy with Russia, and the Czechic National Party in Bohemia entered into communication with the Pan-Slavists; but their enthusiasm was unexpectedly dampened when Aksakoff, the Pan-Slavic leader, invited them to leave the Roman Catholic and unite with the Greek Church. After this, the Archbishop of Prague forbade the clergy participating in the Slavic demonstrations.

The influence of the Austrian Government upon the course of Russia was again perceived when, just after the Russian troops had crossed the Danube, the Czar declined to accept the active assistance of Rumania. On the 26th of June, Mr. Tisza, President of the Hungarian Council, had declared that the monarchy was resolved not to tolerate the seizure of a neighboring territory by a foreign power, and had answered attacks which had been made upon the Government by stating that the army was completely equipped and ready to undertake a campaign, and that the Government could, for that reason, calmly and securely look events in the face, knowing that it was at liberty to act according to its judgment, and prepared to act as soon as occasion should arise. One month later, the fact was learned that Russia had accepted the co-operation of the Rumanian troops; the introduction of a Russian civil administration into Bulgaria was held to signify an intention to occupy the province permanently; and rumors began to prevail that Servia would after all enter the contest. A Cabinet Council was held at Vienna, at which the subjects of mobilizing several divisions of the army, and of occupying Bosnia and Herzegovina, were discussed. No resolution was taken, but Count Andrassy was invested with full powers. A few days afterward, the Emperors of Austria and Germany met in consultation at Ischl. The interview was said to have been one of formalities and courtesies, in which a few questions respecting the trade relations of the two countries were spoken of, but nothing of importance was said concerning the Eastern Question; but it was followed by a marked change in the tone of the Austrian journals—a sudden subsidence of the excitement under which they had discussed the events of the day. The time and circumstances of the interview, and the quiet in Austria which followed it, all gave color to the impression which prevailed, that a concert existed between Austria and Germany—an impression which was confirmed by events which happened later. The semi-official papers of Berlin and Vienna professed to regard the interview as a demonstration of the continued existence of the alliance of the three Emperors.

Servia had just come out from a disastrous war with Turkey, at the conclusion of which it had secured terms of peace, which were, considering the relative situation of the belligerents, unexampled in their liberality. A sense of propriety and prudence, under these circumstances, should have counseled the observance of a scrupulous neutrality; but the same party which had forced the principality into a war in 1876, began its agitations as soon as the Russian declaration of war was issued, to plunge it into the new struggle. Similar measures of pressure were brought to bear to those which were applied successfully in 1876. Bills were posted on the walls of Belgrade threatening Prince Milan with-dethronement if he did not renew hostilities. The Government was forced, in view of this pressure, as well as by the possibility that a contingency might arise which would make some action necessary, to adopt measures of precaution and preparation Still, the Ministers insisted that their intention was to preserve peace. Servia was fortunately prevented, by influences other than those originating within its own borders—influences which even its war-party could not ignore—from participating in the war at this stage.

In the latter part of May, the intention of Prince Milan was made known to seek an interview with the Czar. The news caused profound dissatisfaction in the Cabinet at Vienna, which objected, for reasons connected with the internal peace of the Empire, to Servia taking any part in the war. The feelings of the Austrian Government were promptly communicated to the Czar and Prince Milan. There were sufficient obstacles of etiquette in the way of the Prince's making the proposed visit before the objections of Austria were made known ; these added to them. In the first place, it was difficult for a vassal of the Sultan to visit the armed enemy of the latter without giving offense to his suzerain ; in the second place, the Prince, who could by no means claim an equality or even an approach to it, in rank with the Czar, could not visit him without having first gained his permission, and this proved not easily obtained. These difficulties were, however, removed by skillful diplomacy, and on the 12th of June the Servian Premier announced to the agents of the Foreign Powers at Belgrade that the Prince, with three of his generals, would visit the Czar at Ployeshti, explaining also that his Highness had notified the Porte of his intended step in such a way as it was hoped would prevent any misunderstanding or irritation. At the same time that the Prince received permission to visit the Czar, the announcement was made that Russia had intimated, far more positively than it had done before, that it was its will that Servia should keep aloof from the war. The visit of Milan was made the means of removing any doubts which Servia might still have had of what was expected of it. The Prince was received kindly, although the interview was confined, so far as the world has learned, to formalities, and he returned to Servia apparently well satisfied. At the opening of the Skupstchina, on the 1st day of July, he expressed the belief that the sacrifices made by Servia in the war against Turkey had not been in vain. When, after consulting with the great national Skupstchina, he had concluded a peace with the Porte, he had told his people that the care of the Christians of the East was now in more vigorous hands than those of Servia, and the war could be interrupted without peril to the cause which had drawn the country into it. Events had quickly confirmed his words, and the victorious standards of the Czar-liberator, at the head of his heroic army, were waving not far from the boundary. During his visit to Ployeshti, he had received satisfactory assurances from the Czar, who had promised him that he would always have a regard for Servian interests. The Skupstchina should proceed with the greatest caution, as the interests of Servia would be imperilled by every wrong step.

New signs of warlike activity were manifested in Servia during September. A ministerial council was held during the first week of the month, presided over by Prince Milan, the result of which was reported to be a resolution to engage in the war. No declaration of war was made as yet, but renewed energy was exercised in preparation. An order was issued by the Minister of War on the 5th, commanding all militia-men of the first class to be at their depots on the 13th, while those of the second class should hold themselves in readiness to march. This threatening attitude of the principality called out remonstrances from the diplomatic corps, the English and German agents pointing out that if Servia took up arms against the Porte, the guaranteeing powers would be placed in a difficult position, and dwelling with stress on the gravity of the consequences which would ensue to Servia itself in the event of defeat, since the Turks would not be inclined to treat its vassal with the same indulgence as it had exercised in 1876.

An interview took place between the Chancellors of Austria and Germany, Count Andrassy and Prince Bismarck, at Salzburg, on the 19th of September, the character and results of which were not made public. A few days afterward the Austrian and Hungarian Premiers made important declarations in their respective chambers. Mr. Tisza, in the Hungarian Chamber, on the 27th, stated that there was no reason to change the policy of neutrality, to which it was due at this time that the interests of the monarchy were not threatened in any way by the European complications. He did not believe that this policy was contrary to the wishes of the Hungarian people, and he declared the charge that the neutrality had been observed in a manner favorable to Russia, unfounded. What the Government desired was to protect the interests of the country, in a peaceable manner as long as possible, but to protect them at all hazards. If Servia should break the peace, Austro-Hungary would not prevent Turkey from proceeding against it. The triple alliance imposed no particular obligations upon the powers concerned, either in the Eastern or in any other question. The whole of this so-called alliance consisted in this, that the three Emperors and their Governments agreed, in the interest of European peace, to come to an understanding on any question that might arise. This understanding had prevailed for several years—since 1873; and even at this time the fact that the war had not become a European one must, in part at least, be attributed to the friendly relations of the three powers. The fact that one of these three Governments, against the opinion of the two others, had begun a war, created no obligation concerning the Eastern Question as regarded either of these two other powers, and none certainly as regarded the Austro-Hungarian Government. "On our side," M. Tisza added, "it has been declared from the beginning that, whatever the issue of the war may be, nothing shall be done of which we disapprove."

In the latter part of September a secret project for helping the Turks was discovered in Transylvania, that part of the Austro-Hungarian monarchy lying furthest east, and bordering on Rumania. Its object was reported to be the formation of a Hungarian legion of five thousand men, who were to meet at a certain point in the mountains forming the frontier between the two countries, with a view of making an irruption into Rumania. Several hundred stands of arms, with a considerable quantity of ammunition and other articles, were seized in various places close to the Rumanian frontier. Many arrests were made, and a large number of prominent Hungarians were implicated in the affair. Among them was General Klapka, a distinguished participant in the revolution of 1848, who, however, denied all complicity in the plot, and declared that he would have discountenanced the formation of a Hungarian legion had he known of it, because he considered that it would be useless to Turkey, and could only result in divisions among the Hungarians.

A note was sent by the Turkish to the Servian Government, about the beginning of October, demanding explanations regarding its purpose in arming and in entering into negotiations with Russia and Rumania, and more particularly regarding the presence of the Russian Consul-General at Belgrade, who had arrived there during September. The Porte declared it would be obliged to send a special commissioner to Belgrade, to inquire whether its sovereign rights were not being tampered with. In answer to this note, M. Christitch, the Servian Envoy at Constantinople, on October 30th communicated a dispatch to the effect that the attitude of Servia did not justify the complaints of the Porte; that its military measures were designed solely to protect its frontier; and that Servia hoped for the maintenance of good relations with Turkey.

Prince Milan made an address to the troops in Belgrade on the 2d of December, in which he thanked the army for the exertions it had made in the war of 1876, which war had led to the Turko-Russian struggle, and would lead to the liberation of the Christians in the Turkish Empire; pointed out that the chance for Servia was now much better than it had been in the previous year, for the country was better prepared and had the support of a powerful ally; and assured the troops that he himself would share in the fatigues of the campaign. This speech removed all the doubts which may have previously existed as to the intentions of the Government to enter into the war, and no surprise was felt when the declaration of war was published on Dec. 14th.

In Greece, the Russian declaration of war called forth, on May 6th, an anti-Turkish demonstration. A number of students, numbering from 1,500 to 2,000, proceeded to the house of the Prime Minister, calling for an immediate declaration of war. The minister answered that circumstances did not make war necessary, and recommended calmness and prudence. A similar demonstration occurred on May 28th, when a crowd, estimated at from 5,000 to 10,000 persons, filled the square before the palace and demanded from the king strong and warlike measures. The crowd, however, soon dispersed when the king told them that he still had the welfare of the nation at heart. These popular demonstrations found a response when the chamber assembled on May 26th. The ministry under Deligeorgis was forced to resign, and several new cabinets were formed successively, to fall to pieces almost immediately, until finally a coalition ministry was organized under Admiral Canaris, one of the revolutionary heroes of Greece. The appointment of this ministry was received with mistrust in Constantinople, so that Savfet Pasha, the Turkish Minister of Foreign Affairs, thought it advisable to question the Greek Ambassador with regard to the intentions of the new cabinet. The Ambassador, denying all hostile intentions, assured the Porte that the armaments undertaken by Greece were for defensive purposes only. With regard to the fear entertained by the Porte, that Greece would favor a rising in Thessaly, he declared that his Government would under all circumstances act openly, and should it decide upon war, it would be an open war. The new ministry nevertheless actively pushed forward the completion of the armaments. The standing army was filled up to its full complement of 27,000, and was stationed in four large fortified camps. At the same time bodies of volunteers were formed, which contained, besides native Greeks, a large number of Greek subjects of Turkey.

A difficulty arose in the latter part of June which threatened, for a time, to bring Greece and Turkey into actual collision. The Greek Government, on the 28th of the month, seized a quantity of ammunition at Corfu while it was on board an Austro-Hungarian steamer in transit to Turkey. The Austrian Government promptly protested against the proceeding; the Turkish Government also protested, and threatened to send a vessel to Corfu to demand a return of the arms. The Greek Government endeavored to explain its action by professing that it had been taken to defend the neutrality of the island, but was not able to maintain its position. The trouble was finally adjusted by shipping the ammunition on board a neutral vessel to Trieste, to be detained there till the end of the war. In the beginning of July a proclamation of the Central Revolutionary Committee of Athens was circulated in Epirus and Thessaly, calling upon the Greeks to rise for independence, and assuring them of the help of " 80,000 warriors " from Greece itself. The fruits of this appeal appeared later in the war when the provinces in which it was circulated actually revolted, and induced the kingdom of Greece to a step which came near involving it in serious embarrassments. On the 12th of September, the Greek Government, having been called upon by Earl Derby, at the request of the Porte, to give a pledge that it would not make war against Turkey, replied that it would not renounce its privileges as an independent State by making such a pledge, and that the condition and danger of Hellenism in Turkey rendered it now more than ever necessary that the nation should have that liberty of action which was essential to independence.

The hostile attitude of Greece caused Server Pasha, the Turkish Minister of Foreign Affairs, to send a note, in the beginning of October, to the Turkish Ambassador in London. This note was submitted to Lord Derby, who acquainted the Greek Government with its contents, adding that Greece would do better to turn her attention to her internal development, and to the removal of the financial difficulties under which she was laboring. The Turkish note formulated five complaints. First, that the warlike preparations made for some months past by the Greek Government, and the dispatch of numerous detachments of troops to the camps along the frontier, are calculated to disturb the friendly relations between Turkey and Greece. Secondly, the enlistment of numerous Greek volunteers in Turkey, openly carried on by agents, adds to the difficulties of the Imperial Government. Thirdly, ever since the beginning of the present war, the Greek press, which claims to represent the views of the Government, has preached a crusade against Turkey, which was not only tolerated, but apparently inspired by the Greek Government. Fourth, revolutionary committees existing for years in Greece, have now organized agencies in the Turkish provinces. These committees show the greatest activity in the frontier districts, and are plainly patronized by the Greek Government. Fifth, the revolutionary agitation of the committees not seeming sufficient, armed bands are organized in Greece and thrown into Epirus and Thessaly, without in the least being prevented by the Hellenic authorities. In answer to this note, M. Tricoupi sent a note to the Greek Chargé d'Affaires in London, contesting the accuracy of these statements and making Turkey alone responsible for all. "If Turkey," the note said, "has any cause of complaint, she ought not to address herself to England, but directly to Greece."

The popular excitement in favor of war continued to increase as the progress of the Russian arms became more decided, but the Government maintained a practical neutrality till, almost simultaneously with the conclusion of the armistice, it was induced to send its troops across the border, only to repent of its action immediately, and retrace its ill-considered step at the earliest possible moment.

During the month of July, the Russians closed the Sulina mouth of the Danube by sinking vessels and then throwing rocks and sand on them, thus making the Sulina channel impassable for large vessels. This course produced considerable dissatisfaction, particularly in England This caused Prince Gortchakoff to issue a special note early in August, in which he promised that all obstructions placed in the river would be removed at the close of the war. With regard to the British complaints, he said that after the Czar had promised not to attack Egypt, he might have assumed that the British Government would do their utmost to prevent the Khedive from participating in the war. In the recent fighting in the Balkans, however, the Russians had found themselves opposed to Egyptian troops. If England, therefore, did not desire to see its Egyptian interests imperilled, it should use its influence with the Khedive to restrain him from steps which Russia might be forced to resent.

The murder of the French and German Consuls at Salonica, in 1876, led to a joint action of the French and German Governments in September, 1877. Strange to say, the men concerned in the assassination of the Consuls, who, upon the representations of the two powers, had been sentenced to imprisonment, were suddenly released after having served a little over half a year. This led to notes of remonstrance from the two powers as stated. But before these notes were delivered, the Porte had sent orders to Salonica that the men should be put back into prison. Their release furnished a curious specimen of the fashion in which a Turkish official occasionally understands his duty. The prisoners, who had been kept at Widin, had to be removed, and at the time of the bombardment, were taken back to Salonica, where the Governor, on the plea that he had not been told what he was to do with them, first set them free, and then telegraphed for instructions. It perhaps never occurred to him that it might be as well to telegraph to his Government before taking steps which would scarcely be very palatable to Germany and France, and was certainly not consistent with the usual course of justice.

CHAPTER XIII.

INNER HISTORY OF TURKEY DURING THE WAR.

The Feeling at Constantinople at the Beginning of the War—Discontent over the Management of Affairs by the Government—The Holy War and the Flag of the Prophet—The Turkish Parliament—Ministerial Changes—The Sultan still talking of Reforms—Rise and Growth of the Party of Peace—The Second Session of Parliament—The Government Censured—Boldness and Independence of the Deputies—The Sultan Dissolves the Chamber with Signs of Displeasure—Further Ministerial Changes—How the Porte Supported the War.

IT was clear from the very beginning of the war that the Porte would have to make use of all its resources in order to carry it on successfully. The opinion which had gained some currency abroad, that the Christians at the capital would either favor the Russian attack, or would affect neutrality, or at most give the Government only a half-hearted support, were not confirmed; and the declaration of war produced an apparent unity of sentiment among all classes of the population of Constantinople, of whatever religion, in favor of maintaining the integrity of the Empire to the last. In the Chamber of Deputies, several Christian members protested against the pretext put forward by Russia, that it had declared war for the protection of the Christian population of the Empire, and are said to have averred that they did not desire the protection of Russia, and that the Christian subjects of the Sultan were ready to take part in the defense of the country. The Greek Patriarch provided a form of prayer to be used in the churches for the Sultan and for the success of his Majesty's arms in the war; and the Armenian Patriarchs gave his Majesty assurances of their sympathy and the support of their people. A decree was issued in May making the Christian population liable to the conscription equally with others who had been long held to service in the army, and was received by the Christians without any signs of dissatisfaction. The duty and privilege of serving in the army were extended not only to the Christians. The non-Mussulman youth of the capital, who had from ancient times enjoyed exemption from military duty, were also brought under liability, and other measures were adopted showing

(413)

a design to render the whole manhood of the country available, if necessary, for its defense. A measure was sanctioned for the issue of a forced loan of five million Turkish pounds, and an effort was made to raise an additional loan in England.

It was foreseen in the Cabinet of the Sultan that the war might probably result in a conflict that would involve the very existence of the Empire and of Mussulman rule, and that it was, therefore, important to appeal to the piety of the believers, and to excite their devotion, by impressing them that their faith was at stake, and by surrounding the cause with all the prestige it could command; yet it would not be well to arouse their religious zeal to too great an extent lest conflicts be produced between the Mussulman and the Christian population, and embarrassments engendered with the other Christian powers.

On the 25th of April, or the day after the declaration of war, the Sultan addressed the Turkish army, saying: "The fatherland is in danger. It is my duty to take in my hand the banner of the Caliphate and go into the midst of my soldiers—to sacrifice, if necessary, my life for the independence of the Empire and the honor and life of our women and children."

The important question was submitted to the Sheik-ul-Islam, the Mohammedan high-priest, whose decisions on Mohammedan law are final, whether a Holy war should be declared. A Jehad, or Holy war, is a momentous affair for a Mussulman, and involves the gravest duties. It is declared against a nation which is an enemy of Islam, and sometimes against a prince who issues a decree directly contradicting the statutes of the Koran. It may be declared if the smallest precept of the Koran is in danger. When it is declared, it becomes a religious point of honor with the Mohammedan to approve himself as an Islamite, with arms in his hand; the Prince must place himself at the head of the faithful and lead them; all the faithful who are over thirteen years of age must take the sword and go to battle, while those who are not able to go must perform the work for their brethren in the field, and support them; and the leader of the fighting faithful may appropriate all the property of the nation, even that belonging to the mosques, to the prosecution of the war. As a reward for their participation, the faithful who engage in the Holy war, may take and keep whatever valuables they may find in the land of the enemy, and those among them who fall in battle are promised an immediate entrance into Paradise as Jehid, or martyrs. If they return victorious, they bear the title of Ghazi, or victors, while their sons may call themselves Ghazi Zade, or the sons of the victors, and they have a right to demand a pension from the State. According to the original idea, the Jehad, when once declared, must not cease till the enemy is wholly overthrown, or, if he is an unbeliever, is converted to Islam, although a brief armistice was tolerated. The numerous treaties which Turkey has been obliged to make with Christian States have, however, made this regulation a dead letter. The question concerning the Holy war was submitted, and the answer was returned in the following form:

"*Question:* If, after the Commander of the Faithful—whose Caliphate may God prolong to the day of the judgment—has concluded a solemn treaty with the ruler of an unbelieving country, the Sovereign of such country makes unendurable and unacceptable demands which lessen the glory of Islam and degrade the Mohammedan nation, and, in order to impose these demands upon Mussulmans, insultingly makes preparations for war, transgresses the boundaries of Mohammedan States and devastates the same, and thus breaks the solemn treaty: in such a case, as soon as it is plain that the Mussulmans possess the necessary strength and resources for the contest, and that the contest on behalf of the Faith is meritorious, is it the duty of the Protector of the Faith, the Sultan of the Mussulmans— to whom may the Almighty God grant victory—to send the conquering troops of Islam against that country, and, in confidence in God the Supreme Ruler, to undertake the War of Faith for the glory of Islam against the said country and people? It is an answer that is sought.

"*Answer:* Yes, God knows that it is so.

"Thus writes the poor Hassan Kairullah, unto whom may God be merciful!"

Assurances were published that the declaration of the Holy war was not aimed against the Christian subjects of the Porte, but only against the common enemy of all Turks, the Russians. In the latter part of July, the powers having made remonstrances against the adoption of measures likely to excite the Mussulmans against the Christians, a charge by the Sheik-ul-Islam was read in the mosques recommending calmness and resignation, and the avoidance of all acts of hostility toward Christians. At about the same time that the question concerning the Holy war was submitted to him, the Sheik-ul-

Islam was asked whether the Sultan could at that stage of the war assume the title of Ghazi, or conqueror. He replied that it would be better to wait till the war was closed, and the unbelievers were fully vanquished. A state of siege was proclaimed shortly afterward.

The question of raising the banner of the Caliphate was again raised in July, and the fact brought out a remonstrance from the powers against the adoption of measures which would further inflame the fanaticism of the Mussulmans, and increase the danger of the powers having to interfere to prevent an indiscriminate war upon Christians. This banner, the flag of the Prophet, is one of the most sacred objects to the Moslem, and the unfurling of it is the most solemn and the final act of instituting the Holy war. It is also called "the Heavenly Standard," and in the Turkish language Bairak. Its color is green, and it is believed to have been the banner of the Prophet Mohammed, delivered to him by the angel Gabriel, through the medium of Ayesha, as an indubitable token of victory over their enemies. It was formerly laid up in the Treasury of the Sultan of Constantinople, but is now kept in the mosque at Eyoob, where the new Sultans on the day of their coronation gird on the sabre of the Caliphate. In case of any serious struggle, a religious duty compels the Sultan to give orders to the "Mollahs," or Mohammedan clergy, to display the Prophet's standard before the people and army, and proclaim "Al-Jehad," or the Holy war, by exhorting the Moslems to be faithful to their religion and defend their kingdom. "This is the Prophet's banner," the Sheik-ul-Islam exclaims; "this is the standard of the Caliphate; it is set up before you and displayed over your heads, oh, true believers, to announce to you that your religion is threatened, your Caliphate in danger, and your life, wives, children, and property exposed to be the prey of your cruel enemies! Any Moslem, therefore, who refuses to take his arms and follow this holy Bairak is an infidel, and must, therefore, suffer condemnation."

It has always been held in extreme respect, and the unfurling of it has been efficient to settle all questions as to the duty of obedience, except in one instance, happening in 1658, when an insurrectionary chieftain turned his back to it, and continued his resistance. It has been shown many times that the so-called flag of the Prophet was not the genuine flag used by Mohammed, which was black, but without disturbing the faith of the Mussulmans in its sanctity. The most generally accepted account of the origin of this particular flag is that when the Prophet was dying, Ayesha, his favorite wife, tore down the green *purdah* from the door of the death chamber, and, giving it to the assembled chiefs, bade them make it the flag of future victory. The Moslems, therefore, call this green banner "Bairak-un-nabi," as being used as the standard of the kingdom and the religion of Mohammed.

Discontent arose early in Parliament and among the people over the inefficiency of the proceedings of the Government, which reached a culmination after the capture of Ardahan, in Armenia. It was generally understood that the Sultan, as is nearly always the case at the Turkish court, was governed by a small faction of adherents who were styled the Palace clique, and who looked upon all measures that were proposed more with an eye to their personal designs and their advancement, than to the good of the country. The Chambers were brought into frequent conflict with Redif Pasha, the Minister of War, and Mahmond Damad, the Sultan's brother-in-law, who was considered the real controller of the councils of the Government. Even before actual hostilities began, the tardiness of the Serdar Ekrem in going to the seat of war, became the subject of remark and comment in the Assembly, and opportunities for animadversion arose often enough afterward, and were not lost. Complaints from the army reaching the members of the Assembly, gave them excuses for exposing mismanagement and incapacity, and the system of favoritism and nepotism which continued to flourish. The Chambers were visited on the 25th of May by a deputation of Softas, or theological students in the mosques, making demands for changes in the administration and the methods of carrying on the Government. The opportunity was embraced by some of the deputies to make direct attacks upon the Seraskier, Redif Pasha, as Minister of War, and to speak plainly of the incapacity of the Cabinet, asking that men of-well-known and approved capacity should be elevated to power. These demonstrations and expressions were understood at the time to be made in contemplation of the recall of Midhat Pasha, and it was believed that this minister was actually about to be reinstated in his former position. If the Sultan ever had such an intention, it was defeated by the machinations of Midhat's enemies, who had the ear of his Majesty through Mahmoud Damad, and retained their influence over him throughout the war. A few days after the visit of the Softas to the Chambers, the Government announced the discovery of a conspiracy which aimed at

22

the deposition of the Sultan and the removal of the whole reigning dynasty. Several of the Softas who had participated in the demonstration were arrested, and five of them were banished. At the beginning of July, Redif Pasha was ordered to join the Commander-in-chief at Shumla, ostensibly to inquire into the causes of the inactivity of the army, but really, it was currently thought, to get him away from the capital. At about the same time the ministers were ordered to sleep in Stamboul, so as to be able to meet together in council, should an emergency arise.

The Parliament, having fulfilled its constitutional duty of being in session for three months, was adjourned, by order of the Sultan, on the 28th of June. It had not accomplished much, although it had perhaps done all that could have been expected of a body so novel to the country and to its theory of government, but it had shown vigor and activity in discussion, and a public spirit and boldness in the expression of opinions, that were decidedly creditable to it as a body and to its members. A correspondent of the New York *Tribune,* writing from its sessions, thus describes its distinctive traits :

" The Assembly is doing much more in the way of independent discussion than was expected, but the division between Moslems and Christians is probably going to prevent any serious advantage arising from the institution of Parliament. Nevertheless, it is pleasant to find men who can stand up in the Assembly and tell the Government that its law of the press may more fitly be entitled a penal code, and who can rally about them a majority sufficient to vote down the obnoxious clauses of the law, one after the other. It is pleasant, also, in this country, where so long a silence has been enforced, to see a man get up and face the Finance Minister in the Assembly, and charge home upon his employés corruption, and carry the whole Assembly with him in the charge ; or to see another man oppose the greed and selfishness of the Pashas, who call upon the people to support the treasury in this war crisis, and give nothing from their own luxury."

The correspondent likened the appearance of the Assembly to that of a school-room, with straight rows of desks and benches, " exactly modeled after the American school desks of fifteen years ago," running across the room, while the members were so like school boys under the rule of the teacher, who sat upon the platform in the front, that there seemed nothing incongruous in the arrangement. The President exercised his functions with decision and tenacity, so that it required great nerve to insist on the yeas and nays after he had said that a measure had been adopted by the House. " And even after a hard-fought battle and victory, the President is sure to bring up the defeated bill again, with the remark that the Ministry have made explanations in committee, and the committee has now a report to make, the result being that the bill is reported upon favorably by the committee and adopted without a ballot, before any slow-moving intellect has risen to the height of calling for the yeas and nays again."

The excitement and dissatisfaction at Constantinople were still further increased after the passage of the Balkans by Gen Gourko, and both the Commander-in-chief and the Ministry fell victims to the general discontent. Savfet Pasha was replaced as Minister of Foreign Affairs by Aarifi Pasha, and Mahmoud Damad became Minister of War, in place of Redif Pasha. The same " Palace clique" remained in power, but with a new face turned toward the public. The newspapers called attention to the fact that the enemy were at the gates of Constantinople, and urged the inhabitants to constitute volunteer battalions; and the works on the fortifications were carried on with great activity. Ten days later, Aarifi Pasha retired from the Ministry of Foreign Affairs, and was succeeded by Server Pasha. The recall of Midhat Pasha was still talked of, but Mahmoud Damad, who ruled the Court, would not permit his rival to return.

Early in August, the Porte conveyed an intimation to the powers, through a confidential interview between the President of the Council of State with Count Zichy, the Austrian Ambassador, that "the Ottoman Government, in spite of late successes in arms, was firmly convinced that the war was really a misfortune for the whole world, that it would lead to no real result on either side, and that the Sultan would be happy to see it end in a peace honorable to both belligerents. If Russia only demanded autonomy for Bulgaria under several Christian governors, the Porte would agree to make peace." A very guarded intimation had been made shortly before by the Russian journal *Golos*, that Russia was ready to enter into negotiations for peace, and that the terms of Russia would not be found oppressive; yet no steps seem to have been made to bring the parties together, and the war was allowed to go on. During August, a new loan for £5,000,000 nominal was put upon the mar-

ket, the mobilization of the landsturm in Rumelia and Anatolia
was ordered, for which all the population should be enrolled, with
the intention of forming a camp of 70,000 men for the defense of
the capital, and a new forced loan was commanded. Near the close
of the month, Mahmoud Damad was removed from the office of
Minister of War, because he was supposed to be responsible, by
having ordered the movement which led to it, for the reckless sacrifice of life in the attempt of Suleiman Pasha to recover the Shipka
Pass. He was succeeded by Mustapha Pasha, and Savfet Pasha
was appointed Minister of Justice in place of Hassim Pasha, who
was nominated President of the Senate.

On the 5th of October, the Sultan, on the occasion of his ceremonial visit to the mosque, reviewed a body of the local militia,
and made an address to them, in which he expressed the hope that
after the conclusion of a glorious peace they would show the same
aptitude and zeal that they had exhibited in devotion to the defense
of the country, in assisting him "to carry through the reforms on
which the prosperity of the country and the welfare of the people
depend." This was favorably received, as an assurance that the
Sultan had still at heart the reforms in which he had embarked
when he was interrupted by the war. A few days afterward, the
Sultan received two members of the British Parliament, when he
expressed himself extremely desirous of carrying out the reforms
and improvements he had begun, but regretted that he had prejudices of long standing to deal with, and that it was impossible,
without danger, to proceed otherwise than gradually; but he was
fully resolved to form a basis for further reforms. He was specially
anxious for such measures as would insure the equality of all his
subjects. The Parliament would, of course, require time to develop
itself, and to show real, practical results; but, nevertheless, he felt
quite sure that the freedom of discussion permitted to the members,
and the publication of their speeches and of the measures they
passed, would gradually accustom the people to take a more active
interest than now in the affairs of the Empire. He hoped that,
eventually, the laws would be firmly administered, and the promised
reforms resolutely carried out.

Reports of the existence of a peace party at Constantinople,
strong enough to attract attention, and of the existence of political
conspiracy, seeking the restoration of Murad as Sultan, were followed in November by notices of the meeting of Ministerial Coun-

cils, at which the determination to continue the war seemed as
strong as ever.   After the fall of Kars, Mahmoud Damad, who was
supposed to be in sympathy with the movement for peace, was
removed from the direction of military affairs, the war council was
abolished, full powers were conferred on the Seraskier, Mustapha
Pasha, and a new resolution seemed to have been taken to carry on
the war with energy.   Two weeks later, Mustapha was removed,
and Rauf Pasha was appointed Minister of War in his place.   This
was considered to indicate a restoration of the ascendency of Mahmoud Damad.   The ascendency of the pacific policy in the councils
of the Government seemed clear enough about the middle of December, when the Turkish Government addressed a circular to the
powers, suggesting mediation; but a week later, when the Sultan
reviewed a large force of infantry about to proceed to the seat of
war, the war party appeared to be predominant.   These vacillations
were very natural in the desperate condition of affairs which existed
at the time, when to yield, after the terrible succession of defeats
which the Turkish armies had suffered, seemed to involve the surrender of the larger part of the Empire in Europe, a part of that in
Asia, and all of Ottoman pride.   Yet, without armies, without
money, without friends, almost without fortified positions, and with
the Russians pressing all around, what was to be done?   All doubts
were finally set at rest on the 8th of January, when the Sultan, the
Ministerial Council, and the Parliament united in asking for an
armistice.

The Parliament met in its second session, December 13th.   In
the speech from the throne, the Sultan, after referring to the events
of the year, and the extension of the liability to military service to
the Christians, spoke of the new Constitution, and the reforms
which he had undertaken, in regard to which he said : " The salvation of the Empire depends entirely upon the complete and sincere
carrying out of the Constitution.   Our greatest wish has been to see
all classes of our subjects enjoy the benefits of a complete equality
and our country profit by the progress of modern civilization ; the
reform introduced into the finances, the fulfillment of all our engagements, the distribution, in accordance with the principles of political economy, of the taxes and dues ; the collection of the revenue
in such a manner as not to injure the interests of the population ;
the revision of our judicial system in conformity with the requirements of the time, in order to insure the impartial administration of

justice by our tribunals; the reform respecting the property of the Vakufs with a view to facilitate the acquisition of landed property; the formation of communes, and the specification of their powers as an essential basis for the administrative fabric; and lastly, the reorganization of the Gendarmerie. But the war has postponed the fulfillment of these wishes. Furthermore, the calamities of the war have exceeded all limits; a numerous population, non-combatant and inoffensive women and children, whose life and honor ought according to the usages of war to have been respected, have been subjected to cruel treatment, revolting to humanity. I am pleased to hope that in the future nothing will prevent the truth in that respect from coming to light. We believe that we have given you a manifest proof of our firm intention to persist in the path of progress, by directing our attention to internal reforms, even at a time when the Government is engaged in a great war. It is by means of complete liberty of discussion that one can arrive at the truth in legislative and political questions, and thus protect the public interest. The Constitution renders this a duty on your part, and I do not think I have to give you any other order or encouragement in this respect."

The members of the Chamber in discussing the address spoke very plainly about the inefficiency which had been shown by the officers charged with the conduct of the war; and the house decided on the 2d of January, by a vote of fifty to thirty, to retain, in the reply to the address of the throne, a passage averring that the Government had not done its duty. A considerable advance in the independence and apparent capacity of the deputies was observed at the present session. A division of parties began to appear; the opposition were remarkably bold in their denunciations of the faction in power, some of them not sparing the Sultan himself. It was a subject of especial remark that among those who had rendered themselves conspicuous were men from the provinces—from Smyrna, Janina, Aleppo, Syria, Anatolia, and Adrianople—and not from the capital; "and yet they displayed an amount of political insight which could scarcely have been expected of them." At a later stage in the proceedings the ministers were called personally into the Chamber and made to give an account of their administration in answer to searching questions.

These proceedings were very unacceptable to the ruling faction in the Turkish cabinet, which used every exertion to induce the Sultan to get rid of the too free-spoken deputies. The Sultan accordingly ordered the dissolution of the Parliament on the 20th of February, and directed that certain of the deputies who had played a prominent part in exposing the abuses of the administration should be sent back to their homes.

An important change in the Ottoman Government took place about the 5th of February, when the office of Grand Vizier was abolished, and a new Ministry was organized under European forms and designations, the constitution of which was as follows:

"Ahmed Vefik Effendi, President of the Council of Ministers and Minister of the Interior; Server Pasha, Minister of Foreign Affairs; Rauf Pasha, Minister of War; Said Pasha, Minister of Marine; Kiani Pasha, Minister of Finance; Namyk Pasha, Grand Master of the Artillery: Ohannes Tchamith Effendi, Minister of Public Works and Commerce; and Savfet Pasha, President of the Council of State."

This measure was understood to indicate a further step in carrying out the reforms which had been promised.

The question was often suggested during the war, how Turkey, confessedly bankrupt at the beginning of the operations, could find means for carrying them on so long and so well. Notwithstanding the total destitution of money, the armies were kept in good condition and tolerably well supplied until a part of the force was disabled by the severities of winter and the rest was destroyed by capture. The explanation is found in the fact that the Turkish army and officers had learned to do without money. Official salaries were seldom paid till from five to fifteen months after they were due; they were liable to charges amounting to about twenty-five per cent. of their nominal value, and were further reduced fifty per cent. on the 12th of July. Thus the Government was not, in fact, paying salaries to its officers, and the army was expected to live off the country, without need for money. As the Government was not pretending to pay its foreign debt, and the army was taking care of itself, all of its actual income was available for the purchase of such supplies as it needed from abroad, which had to be paid for in cash. This method of management would answer so long as the weather was pleasant, but the need of the army for a better method of provision became imperative when winter closed, and the pressure of necessity became one of the forces to compel a surrender.

CHAPTER XIV.

ARMISTICE AND PEACE.

Early Measures relating to Peace—What Russia would have Demanded in June, 1877—
German Prognostications—Growth of the Peace Party in Turkey—The Porte issues a
Circular Appeal to the Powers for Mediation—The Powers Decline to Interfere, but
England brings about a direct Negotiation between the Belligerents—Turkish Com-
missioners appointed, with full powers to Treat—The Armistice and the Conditions
of Peace—The Treaty Signed and Ratified—Its Conditions.

THE war had hardly begun before speculations were set afloat in
both official and unofficial circles concerning the terms upon which
peace might be made. Rumors were in circulation in the Russian
army, in Berlin, and in Vienna, in the latter part of May, relative
to the possibility of a peace being negotiated even before the Russians should cross the Danube. The existence of a peace party at
Constantinople was assumed even at that early date, and the Grand
Vizier, Edhem Pasha, was mentioned as a functionary who maintained intimate relations with the Court of Berlin, and through
whom overtures of mediation might be made by Germany. It was
suggested that the fall of Ardahan and the retreat of the Turks on
Erzerum, together with the impression made upon the Sultan by
the menacing attitude of the Chambers and the population of the
capital, had already furnished an opportunity for German mediation;
and it was intimated that the Sultan would not be unwilling to
listen to overtures for a settlement, as affording means by which he
could escape from the embarrassing situation in which he was placed
at that time. The semi-official *Journal de St. Petersburg* dismissed
these rumors by saying that diplomacy had better not pronounce in
favor of any definite plan for the termination of the war until
decisive events had occurred on the battle-field. The terms of peace,
it said, must depend upon the course of the war.

Russian diplomacy in private, however, was doing at almost that
very time what its organ before the public advised should not be
done; for before the sheet which contained these words had had

(424)

time to become an old newspaper, Count Shuvaloff, Russian Ambassador to England, held a confidential interview with Earl Derby in London on the 8th of June, at which he explained to him the terms which Russia would exact under different conditions of success of its arms, and among them included almost the identical terms which it did exact after its complete success in January, 1878. Egypt and the Suez Canal would be left alone, as Prince Gortchakoff had promised; Constantinople would not be occupied permanently; a new settlement of the regulations for the Straits would be demanded of the powers; it was not for the interest of Russia to trouble England in its Indian possessions, or, consequently, in its communications with them. If the Porte should sue for peace before the Russian armies crossed the Balkans, the Emperor would agree not to pass that line. In this case the terms of peace would be the autonomy of Bulgaria as a vassal province under the guarantee of Europe, the Turkish troops and officials to be removed from it, the fortresses to be disarmed and razed, and self-government to be established within it, with a national militia; the powers to agree to assure to that part of Bulgaria which is to the south of the Balkans, as well as to the other Christian provinces of Turkey, the best possible guarantees for a regular administration. Montenegro and Servia should receive an increase of territory, to be determined upon by common agreement, and Bosnia and Herzegovina should be provided with such institutions as should be judged compatible with their internal state and calculated to guarantee them a good indigenous administration.

It was admitted to be right to give Austria-Hungary a preponderating voice in the future organization of these provinces. Russia would, however, reserve the right of stipulating for certain special advantages as compensation for the costs of war, which would not exceed the restoration of the portion of Bessarabia ceded in 1856 and the cession of Batum, with adjacent territory. In this case, Rumania could be compensated by the proclamation of its independence, or by the annexation of a portion of the Dobrudja, and Austria-Hungary would not be opposed in seeking its own security and compensation for the extension of Russia by adding to its dominions territory in Bosnia and partly in Herzegovina. If the Turkish Government should refuse to accept these terms, Russia would be obliged to pursue the war until the Porte was compelled to agree to peace, and in this case the terms of the Imperial Cabinet might be altered. These views were communicated to the British Government, not to be used to influence the Porte in favor of peace, for there was no probability that it would accept them till it had learned by experience how weak it was, but that the neutrality of England might be insured by giving it some actual evidence of the moderation of Russia's demands. A minute of these propositions was communicated to Count Andrassy and Prince Bismarck, as representatives of the Austrian and German Governments. At a subsequent interview, the Russian Ambassador informed Earl Derby that his Government had decided that the separation of Bulgaria into two provinces would be impracticable, for "local information proved that Bulgaria must remain a single province, otherwise the most laborious and intelligent part of the Bulgarian population, and notably that which had most suffered from Turkish maladministration, would remain excluded from the autonomous institutions," and that the proposed terms of peace would be modified in accordance with this view. Earl Derby furnished Mr. Layard, the British Minister at Constantinople, with a report of Count Shuvaloff's declarations, leaving it to his discretion whether or not he should communicate the Russian propositions to the Ottoman Government. Mr. Layard decided that it would be useless to try to induce the Porte to consider such terms; and the fact that such communications had taken place remained a secret in the four Cabinets till February, 1878, when the matter was made public in a British Parliamentary document.

While the conversations of Count Shuvaloff and Earl Derby were going on, the Berlin Ministerial *Post*, said, June 9th, that the announced determination of the Russian Government to annex nothing resolved itself into the intention to govern and direct all. Were Russia to annex Bulgaria, Austria would lay her hand on Bosnia and Servia; Greece and England would protect their interests by similar measures; Rumania would be accorded a fresh guarantee; while Armenia, if embodied with the Russian Empire, might bring on a rupture with Great Britain. To avoid these unpleasant results, the Russian Government had resolved to maintain the integrity of Turkey, but so to remodel Turkey as to place it under the absolute control of the St. Petersburg authorities. The plan was favored by the vacillating conduct of the British Cabinet, disposing Turkey to settle with Russia, no matter how much the interests of the other powers might be injured by the act.

The development of a sentiment in favor of peace in Constantinople began to be noticed a little later. The Sultan and his advisers were disheartened by the rapid advance of the Russians toward the Balkans, the incapacity of their generals, and the want of men and money, and notes were sent to the representatives of the powers calling attention to the danger threatened to Europe by the Russian advance. Subsequently the generals reported the military situation and prospects improved, and public sentiment became more warlike. The intimation of the Sultan to the Austrian Ambassador, at the beginning of August, that he was willing to make peace on the basis of the Andrassy note, came at about the same time that the Russian papers were representing the readiness of their Government to enter into negotiations, but no advantage was taken of a coincidence which seemed to afford a rare opportunity to stop the further progress of the war.

The party of peace at Constantinople evidently grew stronger during the fall, and exercised a perceptible influence over the deliberations of the Cabinet long before its intentions were declared; and new weight was added to its force as reverse after reverse fell upon the Turkish arms. On the 12th of December, the Porte issued a circular appeal to the powers, in which, after referring to the origin of the war with a profession that it had not provoked it, but had done everything to avoid it, and after reciting the measures of reform which it had voluntarily instituted for the whole Empire, it said: "If any doubt could still survive as to the religious fulfillment of the new Constitution and of the reforms that we have promised in the Conference of Constantinople, this doubt should disappear in the presence of the formal and solemn declaration of the sincerity of our resolutions. We proffer in this regard a guarantee of which we invite Europe to take note. The true and only cause of hinderances which might slacken our efforts in this path would be found in the continuation of a state of war. Such a situation is not only disastrous with reference to reforms, but equally calamitous in regard to the general prosperity of the country." Recalling the fact that the desire for conquest had been expressly disavowed by Russia, the circular inquired, with what object, then, should the armies prolong desolation and ruin for their respective countries? and concluded: "We, on our part, think that the moment has come when both belligerents might accept peace without forfeit to their dignity, and when Europe might usefully interpose its good offices. As for the

Imperial Government, it is ready to ask this, not that the country has reached the end of its resources. There are no sacrifices which the entire Ottoman nation is not willing to face to maintain the independence and integrity of the Fatherland. But the duty of the Imperial Government is to avert, if possible, any further effusion of blood It is, therefore, in the name of humanity that we make this appeal to the sentiments of justice in the Great Powers, and that we hope they will be inclined to receive our advances favorably."

The note was generally regarded by the powers as affording an insufficient basis for mediation. Germany refused to act upon it. Austria could not recognize in it a direct appeal for mediation, but regarded it as only an indirect effort to ascertain the dispositions of the powers. The British Cabinet, while acknowledging that it scarcely afforded the basis of a successful mediation, thought it might serve as a starting-point for mediation, and should be confidentially, if not officially, communicated to the Russian Government, but finally answered that it could not undertake to mediate, the views of the other powers on the subject being too divergent. The Italian and French Governments did not wish to take the initiative. So the appeal was not communicated to the Russian Government. The English Cabinet, however, upon the invitation of the Sultan, undertook to ask the Russian Government confidentially on what terms it would consent to make peace. The Russian Government replied that the decisions and acts of the Imperial policy were still guided by the two paramount considerations of putting an end to the constantly recurring disturbances, and avoiding complications by respecting the interests of third parties, but that all intervention would be refused. If the Turks desired an armistice, they must apply directly to the Russian Commander-in-chief, and the terms of peace must be discussed between the belligerents alone.

The English Government advised the Porte to treat with the Russians on their own terms. Server Pasha and Namyk Pasha were appointed, January 13th, to go to the Russian headquarters at Kasanlik and negotiate with the Grand Duke Nicholas for an armistice, and concerning the preliminaries of peace. The plenipotentaries reached Kasanlik, and the negotiations were begun on the 20th. On the 23d, the Turkish Government telegraphed to the plenipotentiaries giving them its orders and full powers to accept whatever terms the Russians offered. So eager did the Government seem to put an end to its troubles that it was said that the Grand Vizier could not admit that any delay or procrastination in the matter, on the part of the Turkish plenipotentiaries, was possible. The progress of the negotiations were inexplicably delayed from day to day, although the Russians knew well what they were to demand, and the Turks were ready to grant anything that was asked of them, so that it was the 31st of January before the armistice and the preliminaries of peace were signed, and the 8th of February before they were officially published. In the meantime, the place of the negotiations was changed, by the continued advance of the Russian armies, to Adrianople, the most important place in Turkey after Constantinople. As communicated by Mr. Layard to the British Government, the armistice contained ten articles. It was concluded between Russia, Servia, Rumania, and Turkey, and was given by Mr. Layard as follows:

" 1. A notice of three days must be given before a resumption of hostilities takes place. The armistice is to be communicated to Montenegro by Russia.

" 2. Restoration of the guns and territory taken after the signature.

" 3. Gives the details of line of demarkation and neutral zone for Turkey, Russia, and Servia, placing in Russian hands almost all of Bulgaria, Rumelia, and Thrace up to the lines of Constantinople and Gallipoli. Fortifications are not to be retained on the neutral territory, and no new ones are to be raised there. A joint commission will determine the line of demarkation for Servia and Montenegro. The Russians to occupy Burgas and Midia, on the Black Sea, in order to obtain supplies, but no war material.

" 4. Armies beyond the line of demarkation to be withdrawn within three days of signature of armistice.

" 5. The Turks may remove arms, etc., to places and by routes defined, on evacuating the fortifications mentioned in Article 3. If they can not be removed, an inventory of them is to be taken The evacuation is to be complete within seven days after the receipt of orders by the commanders.

" 6. Sulina is to be evacuated within three days by the Turkish troops and ships of war, unless prevented by ice. The Russians will remove the obstacles in the Danube, and will superintend the navigation of the river.

" 7. The railways to continue to work under certain conditions.

" 8. Turkish authorities to remain in certain places.

" 9. Black Sea blockade to be raised

" 10. Wounded Turkish soldiers to remain under the care of Russia."

The armistice commenced at 7 P.M. on the 31st of January.

The Russian and Turkish commanders on the spot were authorized to settle matters relating to the armistice in Armenia.

The preliminaries of peace, as published in the *Journal of St. Petersburg* on the 8th of February, were :

" If the Turks demand peace or an armistice at the outposts, his Imperial Highness the Commander-in-chief shall inform them that hostilities can not be suspended unless the following bases shall have been previously accepted :

" 1. Bulgaria, within the limits determined by the majority of the population of Bulgaria, which limits shall in no case be less than those indicated by the Constantinople Conference, shall be formed into an autonomous tributary principality, with a national Christian Government and a native militia. The Ottoman army shall no longer remain there, except at certain points to be settled by mutual agreement.

" 2. The independence of Montenegro shall be recognized. An increase of territory, equal to that which the fortune of war has placed in its hands, shall be secured to it. The definite frontier shall be arranged hereafter.

" 3. The independence of Rumania and Servia shall be recognized. An adequate territorial indemnity shall be secured to the first, and a rectification of frontier to the second.

" 4. Bosnia and Herzegovina shall be granted an autonomous administration, with adequate guarantees. Analogous reforms shall be introduced into the other Christian provinces of Turkey in Europe.

" 5. The Porte shall undertake to indemnify Russia for the expenses of the war and the losses which she has had to bear. The nature of this indemnity, whether pecuniary, territorial, or otherwise, shall be settled hereafter. His Majesty the Sultan shall come to an understanding with his Majesty the Emperor of Russia for the protection of the rights and interests of Russia in the Straits of the Bosporus and the Dardanelles.

" As proof of the acceptance of these essential bases, Ottoman plenipotentiaries shall proceed immediately to Odessa or Sebastopol, to negotiate there preliminaries of peace with the Russian plenipotentiaries. As soon as the acceptance of these preliminary conditions shall be officially notified to the Commanders-in-chief of the Imperial armies, armistice conditions shall be negotiated at the two theaters of war, and hostilities may be provisionally suspended. The two Commanders-in-chief shall have power to complete the above conditions by indicating certain strategical points and fortresses as a material guarantee of the acceptance of our armistice conditions by the Sublime Porte and of its entrance on the path of peace negotiations."

The conditions, it was explained, had been drawn up before the rapid advance of the Russians south of the Balkans. The altered position of affairs rendered it unnecessary for the plenipotentiaries to go to Odessa or Sebastopol to carry on the negotiations for peace, which would now take place at Adrianople.

The negotiations for the final adjustment of the terms of peace proceeded slowly, as they were interrupted by the occurrence of differences on many points of detail, in which the Turkish plenipotentiaries asked concessions of the Russians. Among the questions which gave rise to discussion were the extent that should be given the new principality of Bulgaria, the amount of the indemnity that should be paid by Turkey, some points concerning the surrender of Turkish iron-clads to Russia, and the demand for the removal of the Mohammedan officers and troops from Bulgaria. A clause hypothecating the Egyptian tribute and certain other revenues as security for the indemnity to be paid to Russia, was objected to as infringing upon the vested rights of foreign creditors. Modifications were granted on most of these points. In the meantime, although an armistice existed in name, it was effective to prevent active movements of the Turks only, for the Russians continued to advance steadily, while the Turks offered no resistance, nor apparently any protest, till the Russian headquarters were established at San Stefano, within ten miles of Constantinople, and, in fact, a suburb of the capital, and the negotiations were carried on during the last days at that place. The preliminary treaty was finally signed on the 2d of March, and the fact was announced to the soldiers at San Stefano on the following day (Sunday). The plenipotentiaries immediately entered upon the discussion of the details of the several points of the treaty which had been agreed to *en bloc* or as a whole. On the 7th of March, Rauf Pasha was appointed to accompany Gen. Ignatieff to St. Petersburg to exchange the ratifications of the treaty. The ratifications were exchanged ten days afterward, March 17th, and the treaty itself was published on the 21st of March. Its principal provisions are as follows :*

The opening articles relate to Montenegro, Servia, Rumania, and Bulgaria. Montenegro and Servia are declared independent. Montenegro is given Antivari, and Servia is given Nissa, the valley of the Drina, and Little Zvornik. The questions between Montenegro and the Porte are to be settled through Austria and Russia. The Mohammedans of Servia are allowed to retain their personal property. A Turkish-Servian Commission shall determine within two years questions respecting real estate, and within three years those respecting the property of the State and of the Church (Vakuf). Rumania is made independent. The question concerning a war indemnity shall be arranged by a special treaty between Rumania and Turkey. Rumanian subjects shall have the same rights in Turkey as those of other powers. The final boundaries of Bulgaria shall be determined by a Russo-Turkish Commission previous to the evacuation of Rumelia, and shall follow the following lines : On the west the New and Old Servian frontiers ; the boundary line starts from Vranya, crosses the Kara Dagh Mountain, the Kara Drina River, the Grammos Mountain, passes by Kastoria and around Salonica, and follows the river Karasu as far as Yenidje, on the Ægean Sea; south-west of Kavala the boundary runs along the coast to Dedeagatch, thence northward as far as Tchirmen. It winds round Adrianople at a distance of two and a half hours' march, passes through Kirk Kilissa, joins Luleh Burgas, and reaches in a straight line to Hekim Tabiassi, on the Euxine. It runs along the coast as far as Mangalia, includes Varna, bears off to the west, and terminates at Rassova on the Danube.

The Prince of Bulgaria shall be chosen by a free vote of the people, confirmed by the Porte, and approved by the powers. No member of any dynasty of the Great Powers shall be eligible. The National Assembly shall be convoked at Tirnova or Philippopolis, to consider the future organization of the country, which shall be analogous to that of the Danubian principalities as established in 1830, which shall be arranged before the choice of the prince, under the superintendence of a Russian, and in the presence of a Turkish commissioner. The introduction of the new government shall be intrusted for two years to a Russian commissioner. After one year,

---

* The text of the treaty is given in Appendix II.

the plenipotentiaries of other powers may participate, if it is considered necessary. The Turkish army having left Bulgaria, all the fortresses shall be razed at the cost of the communities. Till a national militia can be formed, Bulgaria shall be occupied for two years by the Russians, with six divisions of infantry and two divisions of cavalry, in all 50,000 men, which shall be maintained at the cost of the Bulgarians. The amount of tribute to be paid by Bulgaria shall be settled by Turkey, Russia, and the other powers. Bulgaria shall assume the obligations of Turkey in reference to the Rustchuk-Varna Railroad Company, after an agreement has been reached between the Porte, Bulgaria, and the company. Arrangements concerning the other railway lines are reserved.

The Porte shall have the right to construct a road for the transport of troops and war material to the provinces lying beyond Bulgaria. This road will go from Salonica up the valley of the Vardar and to Pristina. The regulation of postal and telegraphic connections shall be intrusted to a special commission.

The same provisions are made in respect to the rights of Mohammedans possessing property in Bulgaria as are applied to Servia.

The Danubian fortresses shall be razed ; the building of forts on the Danube and its navigation by vessels of war are forbidden. Only customs and police vessels are permitted. The privileges of the International Danube Commission are continued in force. The Porte shall re-establish the navigation of the Sulina mouth, and allow indemnification for private losses.

Reforms shall immediately be introduced into Bosnia and the Herzegovina, the same as were demanded at the first sitting of the Conference at Constantinople, with the assent of Austria and Russia. Arrears of taxes are not to be claimed. The revenue until 1880 is to be applied to indemnify the sufferers by the insurrection, and to provide for local needs.

The application of the ordinance of 1868 is renewed to Crete. Similar ordinances shall be made for Epirus, Thessaly, and other parts of European Turkey. A special commission shall arrange the particulars of this ordinance, which shall be submitted to the approval of the Porte, and applied under the supervision of Russia.

Armenia shall be given reforms according to local needs, and shall be protected against the Kurds and Circassians. A complete and general amnesty shall be declared.

The Porte shall take into earnest consideration the views of the

23

mediatory powers in regard to the possession of the city of Khotur, and shall carry out the work of the demarkation of the Turco-Persian boundaries

The indemnity to be paid by Turkey to Russia is fixed at 1,410 millions of rubles, of which 900 millions shall be charged to the costs of the war, 400 millions to the account of damages to trade, 100 millions to the insurrection in the Caucasus, 10 millions for the damages to Russian subjects and. property in Turkey.

In consideration of the stringent financial condition of the Turkish Empire, and in accordance with the desire of the Sultan, the Czar of Russia is satisfied to be offered in payment, together with the sanjak of Tultcha (which may be exchanged for Bessarabia), Ardahan, Kars, Bayazid, and the Armenian territory to the Soghanli Dagh.

Turkey undertakes to settle, in a conciliatory spirit, all actions between Russian and Turkish subjects, and to execute immediately all legal judgments already delivered.

The privileges of the monks of Mount Athos are preserved to them.

The return of the Russian troops from Turkish territory shall be completed within three months. A part of the troops shall be embarked at the ports of the Black Sea and the Sea of Marmora, and at Trebizond.

The Russians shall administer the Turkish territory till the return of their troops.

The Porte promises not to proceed against Ottoman subjects who have had relations with the Russians.

A discharge of prisoners shall take place after the ratification of the treaty.

Ratifications shall take place within not more than fourteen days. The formal conclusion of peace is reserved, but in any case these preliminaries shall be binding for Russia and Turkey.

According to an estimate based upon returns made some time before the recent war, which makes the total population of the new Bulgaria 3,822,000, the inhabitants of the principality are classified as 2,372,000 Bulgarians, 819,000 Turks and Tartars, 220,000 Albanians, 101,000 Greeks, 65,000 Circassians, and 15,000 Rumanians, besides gypsies, Jews, and others.

The accession of territory to Servia is equal to 4,100 square miles, with 246,000 inhabitants, of whom 92,000 are Mohammedans. That part of the new territory which lies around Nissa is inhabited by Bulgarians; further west Albanians extend up to the frontiers of Old Servia; and many of the inhabitants of the remainder of the new territory, though Servians or Bosnians, are Mohammedans Servia, as newly constituted, will have an area of 18,590 square miles, with 1,598,522 inhabitants, among whom are 150,000 Bulgarians, 160,000 Rumanians, and 92,000 Mohammedans.

Montenegro is increased by the districts of Gatchko and Nicsic in the north; Spuz and Podgoritza in the east; and a seaboard on the Adriatic. These territories have an extent of 1,450 square miles, with 45,000 inhabitants, of whom 15,000 are Mohammedans and about 10,000 Albanians. The principality will now have 3,150 square miles, with 241,000 inhabitants.

The Dobrudja, or the sanjak of Tultcha, which is ceded to Russia, to be exchanged for Bessarabia, comprises 4,990 square miles, and has 194,000 inhabitants, of whom 109,000 are Mohammedans. The part of Bessarabia for which it is proposed to exchange it has 4,700 square miles and 18,000 inhabitants.

The whole amount of the cessions made by Turkey is 74,580 square miles, with 4,306,000 inhabitants, of whom 933,000 are Turks and 1,646,000 are Mohammedans. The political divisions of what has hitherto been known as Turkey in Europe, will, in future, be according to this estimate, as follows:

		Area in Square miles.	Population	Mohammedans.
Independent	Rumania............	46,798	4,850,000	. . . ..
	Dobrudja (Russia).	4,990	194,000	109,000
	Servia...	18,590	1,598,522	92,500
	Montenegro	3,150	241,000	15,000
Tributary....	Bulgaria................. .	64,040	3,822,000	1,430,000
Turkish.	Metropolitan Provinces .	5,470	991,000	584,000
	Greek Provinces.........	19,950	1,274,000	336,000
	Albania.	24,820	1,693,000	1,065,000
	Bosnia	29,950	1,122,000	576,000
	Crete............	8,320	275,000	40,000
		158,080	9,661,000	4,247,500

Turkey in Europe has been reduced to 83,510 square miles, and 5,355,000 inhabitants, of whom 2,601,000 are Mohammedans. Of the inhabitants, 1,645,000 are Albanians, 1,142,000 are Servians (Bosnians and Croats), 1,359,000 are Greeks, but only 834,500 are Turks.

In Asia, Turkey has surrendered about 10,000 square miles, with 270,000 inhabitants, and there remain to her 714,000 square miles, and about 16,000,000 inhabitants, of whom less than 7,000,000 are Turks.

THE HANGING OF CHRISTIANS BY THE TURKS IN THE STREETS
OF PHILIPPOPOLIS.

HEADS OF RUSSIAN WOUNDED.

CHAPTER ·XV.

THE ATROCITIES OF THE WAR.

The Expectation that Outrages would be Committed—It was not Disappointed—The Kurds in Southern Armenia—American Missionaries in Danger—The Massacre at Bayazid—No one Punished for it—Charges of Outrages by Russians in Armenia—They are not Confirmed—Statements of English Witnesses on the Conduct of the Russians—Gen Melikoff's Statement—Proclamation by Mukhtar Pasha Enforcing Principles of Humanity—Russian Severities in Abkhasia—The Rivalry of Massacres in Bulgaria—Attacks on Neutral Property and Hospitals at Widin and Rustchuk—The Manufacture of Atrocities—Official Statements by the Turks against Russians and Bulgarians—The Mob at Nicopolis—The Bulgarians at Offandlik—Destruction at Sistova—Wounded Women and Children at Rasgrad and Shumla—Bulgarian Excesses at Eski Sagra—The Turks Recapture the Town and Obliterate it—The Russians Exculpated from the Charge of Committing Outrages upon Non-combatants—What the Turks Ascribed to the Russians—Testimony of Mr. Archibald Forbes—Report of Lieut.-Col Wellesley—How the Bulgarians Regarded the Case—A few Bright Spots in the Picture—Turkish Atrocities far in Excess of Anything which the Bulgarians did—Destruction of Yeni Sagra—Trial and Punishment of the Bulgarians—Wholesale Executions—Remonstrances of Foreign Governments—Cruelty of Turkish Soldiers toward Armed Foes—The Geshoffs—Destitution in the Ravaged Districts—Movements for Relief—Conduct of the Montenegrins.

THE remembrance of the hideous deeds which were perpetrated by the Turkish irregular troops in Bulgaria, in the summer of 1876, gave reasonable grounds for the expectation that the far more important campaigns of 1877 would be distinguished by the enactment of similar scenes on a more extended scale, even though the perpetration of outrages in a more atrocious degree were not possible. The conduct of the Turks in the matter of the Bulgarian outrages had given no reason to hope that either their Government or their officers would exert any serious efforts to repress the cruelties of their barbarous adherents. The few executions which the administration in Bulgaria had made a show of making of obscure murderers, inspired no confidence in the determination of the Porte to stop barbarous acts by its soldiery, while high officers, who had abetted outrages, escaped arrest. Shevket Pasha, their commander in Bulgaria, whose duty it had been to put an end to the outrages while they

(439)

were in progress, but had made no effort to do so, not only remained in favor, but after a brief retirement was again brought forward and intrusted with responsible commands during the campaign of 1877. The truth was, the Turkish Government could not afford to adopt a determined course toward its irregulars. It was fighting for existence, with a scarcity of means and men, and depended largely upon these wild adventurers to keep the ranks of its armies full. Severe discipline against them would have involved the danger of alienating them from their fidelity, and perhaps have provoked them to desertion or mutiny. It was not expected, on the other hand, that the course of the Russians would be humane, according to the views that prevail among the more cultivated nations of the West. The Russian Government itself is not humane; its most liberal measures have been characterized in their execution by a severity and disregard of personal rights, repugnant to modern ideas; and it has, within a few years, carried into effect measures that were intolerant in themselves, in a manner that may be characterized as barbarous. The peasants, of whom its regular forces are composed, have enjoyed no education in the humanities, and its irregular troops are hardly less unruly and rash and cruel than the Bashi-Bazouks and Kurds of the Turks. The world was ready to hear, without surprise, of at least extreme carelessness or indifference with regard to the laws of war on the part of the Russian soldiers, and the exercise of severity by their officers.

The worst apprehensions were justified in the event. The long list of murders, burnings, and devastations committed on both sides during the campaign of 1877, finds a parallel—if it does find it—only in the accounts of the slaughters and spoliations that accompanied the campaigns of such barbarian "scourges of the human race" as Tamerlane and Genghis Khan. The first accounts of depredations came from Lower Armenia, in the country around Lake Van. While the Turkish armies were concentrated around Erzerum, to resist the advancing armies of Generals Tergukassoff and Melikoff, the Kurds flocked up from the south, and did their own will in the region. They were organized into bodies of troops and placed under the general command of Faik and Ismail Pashas, but were not restrained, and soon the district of Bashkalleh, comprising some twenty Christian villages, was deserted in consequence of their depredations. The inhabitants fled, many of them escaping to Persia, where they arrived in a starving condition. The missionaries of the American Board, which has an important station at Van, were compelled to place their families, for safety, upon an island in the lake. One of the missionaries, having received a sunstroke, had to be taken to the town for medical aid, and the party who had him in charge would have been dispatched incontinently by the Kurds, had not the Pasha, a friend of the missionaries, given them the protection of a strong guard. The Christian charges of the missionaries were subjected to the grossest treatment; their crops were carried away, their cattle killed, their villages burned, their women and even their children violated Ten Christians who fled for safety into the church at Utch Kilissa, were murdered. The region of Bitlis, where the missionaries have another station, was reduced to anarchy by the presence of the Kurds, so that the inhabitants of the city were able to remain in their own houses only by keeping armed and demonstrating their ability to defend themselves. After the defeat of the Russians at Delibaba, the irregulars swarmed into the Alashgerd district, where they are said to have massacred the populations of whole villages, and to have compelled three thousand Christian families to seek the protection of Gen. Tergukassoff's army, which was afforded them, although the Russians themselves were harassed in their retreat by the enemy, and were hastening to reach their own territory.

The culmination of Kurdish atrocities took place at Bayazid, where, after the engagement of the 19th of June, when nine hundred Cossack cavalry surrendered and were immediately murdered, the Kurds rushed into the town and literally put it to the sword. "The scene that ensued," says a correspondent of the London *Times*, who wrote from the Turkish camp near Kars, "was one of unparalleled horror. The town contained 165 Christian families, and all of the men, women, and children were ruthlessly put to the sword. A Turkish officer who visited the town a few days subsequently states that there was not a single inhabitant left; all had fled, and, including the Russian prisoners, upwards of 2,400 people had been killed. In every house he entered, small groups of dead were lying shockingly mutilated, and in the most revolting and indecent positions. Captain M'Calmont, who visited the place shortly after the Russian relief, states that it is entirely deserted, and a mere heap of ruins; also, that soldiers were employed for six days in burying the dead, the number of whom it was impossible to estimate. On hearing of this massacre, Mukhtar Pasha at once sent down orders to have the Kurds disbanded and disarmed, and their

ringleaders shot. They, however, anticipated the first of these instructions by throwing down their arms and deserting *en masse* on
the approach of Tergukassoff's column on the 10th of July." In
one church 200 bodies were found, and scarcely a house existed in
which there were not two or more corpses. Faik Pasha, a Lieutenant-General, at the head of six battalions of soldiers, "never moved
a file into the town to check these bloodthirsty scoundrels in their
work of slaughter."

Sir Arnold Kemball, the British Commissioner at the headquarters of the Turkish Commander-in-chief, on hearing of the massacre,
immediately sent Captain M'Calmont as a messenger to Ismail
Pasha, the commandant of the regular troops in the district of Bayazid, to represent to him the horror which the news of the affair
would excite in the civilized world, and the injury which would accrue to Turkey in consequence of the perpetration of such acts, and
to impress upon him the necessity of adequately punishing the leaders in the outrage. He made similar representations to Mukhtar
Pasha, the Turkish Commander-in-chief, who expressed his full concurrence in the demand for the punishment of the Bayazid criminals,
and promised to suspend Faik Pasha, the commander of the Kurds, and
have him brought before a court-martial for not preventing the outrage.
Faik Pasha was continued in command, notwithstanding this promise. A court-martial was indeed cons ituted later in the season for
his trial, along with other offending Turkish officers; but he was
arraigned, not for the inhumanities which he had permitted, but for
inefficiency in not having prevented the relief of Bayazid by Gen.
Tergukassoff. The Sheik Ulaledin, the reputed instigator of the
massacre, was in September still in the camp of Kurd Ismail Pasha,
"an honored guest." It was stated in August that 10,000 Christians
had escaped into Persian territory.

The difficulties experienced by the Turkish generals in dealing
with these offenders of the "Irregulars," are illustrated by the result
of the execution of a Circassian by Mukhtar Pasha a few days before the Bayazid massacre, for shooting a villager, whose lamb he
had stolen. The chief of the band to which the criminal belonged
threatened that if he were hanged, he would retire to his home with
his whole tribe, and the body of 1,100 men did actually desert on the
day after the execution.

The Turks, in their turn, freely charged the Russians with violations of the laws of war during their campaign in Armenia. The

principal accusations were summed up in a circular which was addressed by the Turkish Minister of Foreign Affairs to the representatives of the Porte abroad, which recited that the Russians had carried off all the property of the Sheik Evlia Yusuf, near Bayazid, and made all his family prisoners; that they had summoned a party of Kurds, including five or six chiefs, to the palace of the Armenian bishop near Utch Kilissa, and had there massacred them; that Toprak Kaleh and several villages, in fact all of the villages through which the Russians passed in their retreat, had been destroyed; that a great number of the inhabitants of these localities, Mussulmans and Christians, had been maltreated and carried off; that all the property of twelve tribes had been seized by the enemy; that two notables of tribes in a village of Kara Kilissa and forty old men, with women and children, who had taken refuge in the mountains, with a number of other inoffensive persons, had fallen into the hands of the Russians, and been put to death one after another; and that some Mussulmans of one of the towns who had made their submission to the Russians, had been sent to Siberia, and the remainder, without distinction of age or sex, had been ruthlessly massacred. During the siege of Kars, on the 5th of July, the Turkish commandant at Kars sent a messenger under a flag of truce to the Russian lines on some matter connected with hospital duty; according to one account to claim some dead and wounded on the field, according to another to warn the Russians that they were firing into the hospital. The flag was not respected, but the Russians directed their fire upon the messenger and killed him.

The accusations against the Russian officers, so far as they charge the perpetration of outrages in Armenia, were not substantiated. Most of them were contradicted by the representatives of the British Government and the English press who were attached to the Turkish army. The cases specified in the Turkish official statement, even if they were correctly described in the report, can not be classed in the same category as the massacre at Bayazid, or the depredations committed by the Kurds around Van and Bitlis, and in the plain of Alashgerd. That the Russians committed any real atrocities is specifically and unequivocally denied by Englishmen of high station, whose positions guaranteed their general impartiality, and whose association with the Turks made it impossible that they could be in collusion or sympathy with the Russians. The single act of firing on the flag of truce at Kars was clearly established; but the fact appears in connection with the evidence in this case, that a few days before that event, the Turks had killed a Russian doctor who carried the Geneva cross above his head and wore a white badge on his arm, and that a Turkish sergeant had gone about Kars boasting that "he had killed the Russian doctor by cutting off his head as he would that of a sheep." For the rest, an English telegram from Kars at the beginning of August stated that the stories were utterly untrue; that the Russians throughout had behaved well; and that the Turkish regulars had also behaved well, but the irregulars, Kurds and Circassians had been guilty of atrocities past belief, despite the most laudable efforts of Mukhtar Pasha to restrain them. A correspondent wrote from the headquarters of the Fourth Turkish army corps, Camp Kirk Bunar, July 6th: "I have now for the last week been following in the wake of the retiring Russian army, and can see no traces nor hear any reports of any such misdeeds. On the contrary, they appear to have behaved with the greatest moderation, and paid for everything they consumed. It is true that there is a great scarcity of grain in the villages through which they passed, but this is accounted for by their large force of cavalry requiring enormous supplies of this commodity. Fowls, sheep, goats, and cattle are as plentiful in the district recently occupied by the Russians as in that in rear of the late Turkish positions. And while all over the Passin plain there were signs of misrule and piratical violence, and loud complaints of outrages perpetrated on the Christian populations, outrages of which it is not well to speak, here all is peace and plenty." In another letter the same correspondent again makes special mention of the quantities of live stock and poultry throughout the district which the Russians had occupied, and adds: "The corn is now full in ear, and shows plainly that the Russian troops carefully avoided trampling down the crops, while the abundance of rouble notes, for which the villagers refuse to take less than their full value, is sufficient evidence that Loris Melikoff's army possesses sufficient discipline to respect the property of harmless villagers, and that his men pay for all they take. Very different is the sight when we approach Christian villages. These are considered fair fields for pillage by the irregular horsemen of the Turkish army, and I regret to say that these disgraceful proceedings are not checked in any way by the officers of the army."

Near the spot where these letters were written was the village of Beg Mehmed, where the Russians had inflicted the great surprise upon four thousand Circassian cavalry on the 29th of May. A part of the Circassians had returned to the village "when the coast was clear," and accusing the Christian inhabitants of having given information to the enemy, massacred thirty-one men in cold blood. When the correspondent with the army passed through the village, "the place was completely deserted, doors of granaries burst open, the contents spilt over the road," and the soldiers were busy gathering the grain and straw and whatever they could lay their hands upon.

The British Consul at Erzerum, reported officially to Lord Derby that the conduct of the Russian troops toward the inhabitants had been humane and just, alike to Mussulmans and Christians. Severity, he admitted, had sometimes been employed, but only when villagers had provoked it by trying to escape from the villages after having been told that by remaining in their homes and attending to their labors they would be protected and cared for. The Consul further stated that he had read with surprise the protest entered by the Porte against the Russians for atrocities committed in Asia Minor, and was inclined to believe that the Turks desired to publish as atrocities the hanging and shooting, by order of Russian commanders, of several Kurds who were executed for committing the worst of crimes.

A correspondent of the London *Times*, writing from Erzerum on the 31st of August, stated that he had been unable to get any confirmation of Ismail Pasha's reports of Russian atrocities in the Alashgerd plain. Both Mohammedans and Armenians maintained that they had been treated with consideration and kindness by Tergukassoff's column, and that it was not until after the Russians had fallen back from Zeidekan, that they were exposed to the cruelties spoken of by Ismail Kurd Pasha, and that "these acts were one and all committed by Kurds, and not by Russians."

The Russian side of the case was represented in the following language in a statement made by Gen. Melikoff to a correspondent early in July:

"Warfare here is very different from what it is in Europe. Among our enemy we have, no doubt, many who are thoroughly civilized. But there are also Kurds and Bashi-Bazouks, and, as a general rule, we can not trust to the humanity of our foes. Now, this has crippled my actions very materially. Had we been at war with civilized people, I would have written a letter to inform the authorities that I had left so many hundred wounded in such and such a village, and requested that their persons should be respected. But here it would be madness to trust to them in that way, and so I was obliged to retreat. Otherwise, I assure you, I should have advanced, and by this time would have been before Erzerum. In this way the Turks have a great advantage over us, which is totally one-sided; for we, on the contrary, take as great care of Turkish wounded prisoners as of our own men. For example, at Ardahan we found an hospital with 800 Turks. They were totally destitute of medical appliances; and although my stores of bandages and medicines were insufficient for my own uses, I gave orders that everything should be divided impartially between the two nationalities. So that you see we are always fighting at a disadvantage, even when we are equal in numbers."

After his victories in the summer, Mukhtar Pasha issued a proclamation to the soldiers and irregulars of the army operating on the frontiers of Van and Bayazid, in anticipation of their crossing the frontiers, on the subject of the behavior they ought to practice toward the enemy and the people of the country. He expected every one "to comport himself with mildness toward the oppressed inhabitants of the country of Erivan" (the Russian province), and exhorted the soldiers, in conformity to their "good sentiments and traditional generosity," "to abstain from every act having for its object to satisfy the passions." He instructed them that they should never causelessly take the life of a human being; should take care never to cause any injury to those who should ask mercy at their hands, to prisoners, or to deserters, unless they should commit acts which would render their destruction necessary, but should conduct the wounded among them to the hospitals; that they should respect the property, the honor, and the houses of the inhabitants; should abstain from every blameable action which is forbidden by the Holy law and the rules of generosity, and from every kind of disorder— as the setting on fire and destruction of stations, of straw and hay— and should be careful not to exceed the bounds of the law in carrying off booty. By their obeying these exhortations, he hoped their names would embellish the future history of Caucasia, and that by teaching with good examples civilization and humanity, they would "bring the torch of justice into those regions now covered with darkness."

Accusations that the Russians had perpetrated acts of severity in repressing the Abkhasian insurrection, were made in a document which was published in July, under the signature of a Turkish chief of staff, the essential points of which may be summarized as follows: That the Russians had burnt all the villages in the country; that they had fired upon the hospitals established at Otchemtchiri; that they had left the Turkish dead unburied, and eventually burnt them; and that they had no prisoners, having killed all the wounded whom they took. The truth of these charges was admitted by implication. They were not denied, but were explained. The villages were burnt; as to the firing upon the hospitals, it was suggested that the proper steps had not been taken to make the position of the hospitals known to the Russians; the Turkish dead lay between the two armies on the other side of a river from the Russians; they were not buried by either side, and, becoming offensive, the Russians placed dry wood over the corpses, and they were burned; and, lastly, it was the rule to take no Abkhasians prisoners, but to shoot or bayonet them as rebels.

Mr. Layard, the British Minister at Constantinople, wrote to the British Foreign Office, July 10th, that the accounts of the shocking treatment by the Russian authorities and troops of many villages in Circassia, on the approach of the Turkish forces, came from so many independent sources, that their general truth could scarcely be called in question. It does not appear, however, that these offenses were of a nature different from those specified above, which come under the head rather of barbarous severities to rebellious subjects than of wanton atrocities.

The war in Europe was accompanied during the summer of 1877 by a series of massacres and-reprisals in which the scenes of 1876 were re-enacted by Moslems on one side, and Bulgarians on the other, till the fairest parts of Bulgaria south of the Balkans were made an uninhabited waste. Charges of disregard of the laws of war and of the sanctity of hospitals and the property of neutrals were also brought, in several instances, against the Russians and their allies with such directness and force of testimony that they could not be escaped.

On the 27th of May, the Rumanian batteries at Kalafat directed their fire at the principal Turkish hospital in Widin, although its position was pointed out by the flag of the Red Crescent. Several sick and wounded soldiers were killed or injured. During the bombardment of Rustchuk, in the latter part of June, the Russian batteries were aimed directly upon the French and English Consulates, the latter of which was destroyed, and upon the hospitals. When the attack was begun on the British Consulate, the Consul thought that the Russians did not see his flag, and put up a larger one, but the building was a wreck in half an hour afterward, and all of the furniture was broken up. This was continued for two or three days. The actuality of the damage done to neutral property is attested by pictures which were taken of the destroyed buildings and published in the illustrated papers. The Turks, in return, made a vigorous fire upon Giurgevo, and destroyed the town, not sparing the hospitals.

From the beginning of July, stories of atrocities committed in Bulgaria by the followers of either side—now by Christians on Mohammedans, now by Mohammedans on Christians—were narrated with great volubility, and filled all the papers. Many of them were sheer fabrications or enormous exaggerations. It was stated, on undoubted authority, that the manufacture of reports of atrocities had become a distinct business within the lines of both parties, and the stories were palmed off upon whatever correspondents could be induced to send them, or were forged and sent off in the names of correspondents without their knowledge. Many of these stories were taken up by the English newspapers and repeated and commented upon without discrimination or extenuation, for partisan purposes. But after ample allowance is made for the tales that failed to be substantiated, or were disproved, the record of fully authenticated instances of wanton destruction and murder must constitute one of the darkest chapters in the history of savage lust and vengeance. The first accusations were brought against the Russians and Bulgarians; and it is proved by an accumulation of indisputable testimony that the Bulgarians took advantage of the presence and protection of the Russian troops while they occupied the country south of the Balkans to make reprisals on their Mussulman neighbors for the insults they had had to endure from them, and to avenge themselves for the massacres of 1876.

An official statement made by the Turkish Minister of Foreign Affairs on the 22d of July, recited, as established facts, that a mosque where the inhabitants of the village of Tiamsikoi had taken refuge upon the occupation of Tirnova by the Russians and Bulgarians was burned, with all of the refugees within it; and that twelve unarmed Mussulmans, inhabitants of the village of Soukoulan, near

Eski Sagra, having surrendered to the Russians, seven of them were massacred with axes by the Bulgarians, and three others by the Cossacks; and added the result of an estimate which had been made as exact as possible of the number of houses destroyed by fire, and of the Mussulman inhabitants killed by the Russians and Bulgarians in the villages which, to the date of the dispatch, had suffered by the invasion, as follows:

"*First*—At Batak, a village exclusively Mohammedan, in the district of Sistova, 100 houses were burned; 200 men and 300 women perished; total, 500 victims. It is believed that seven inhabitants survived.

"*Second*—At Balovan, a Mussulman village in the district of Tirnova, 250 houses were burned; 700 men and 1,200 women perished—in all, 1,900 victims. One person only, it is believed, escaped from the massacre.

"*Third*—At Caba-Bonnas, 100 houses were burned; 200 men and 300 women perished; total, 500 victims. Two persons escaped alive.

"*Fourth*—At Kestambol, 150 houses were burned; 300 men and 600 women perished; total, 900 victims.

"*Fifth*—At Chems, a mixed village, 60 Mussulman houses were destroyed; 120 men and 200 women perished; total, 320 victims. One person only escaped.

"*Sixth*—At Tundja, a mixed village, 100 houses were destroyed; 250 men and 400 women perished; total, 650 victims. Only three survivors."

A statement followed, asserting that 820 houses had been set on fire in seven villages, which had been abandoned by the inhabitants before the enemy's arrival. On the 24th, the Governor-General of the vilayet of the Danube telegraphed that on the preceding Sunday some Russians and Bulgarians had massacred every inhabitant, except three women and two men, of the village of Yenikoi, eight hours distant from Osman Bazar, and that they had killed five persons in the village of Kost, nine hours distant from the same city. Another official circular asserted that the Russians and Bulgarians had burned all the men and a part of the women of the village of Herste; that seventy Mussulmans and the Imam of Dalioka had been shut up by the Bulgarians and Cossacks in a granary, and burned; forty other Mussulmans of the same village had been massacred, the women outraged, and the greater part of them then led, with their children, to the outskirts of the village, and assassinated; and that, after all the Mussulmans of Eski Sagra, Kasanlik, and the neighboring villages had been disarmed, the Bulgarians, having their arms, massacred 400 Mussulmans of Maglis, in the district of Kasanlik. Other official circulars described numerous outrages, which were alleged to have been committed by Bulgarians in the district of Kasanlik, and that they had disarmed all the Mussulmans of a number of villages in the neighborhood of Kasanlik, and, "after shutting them all up—men, women, and children—in a mosque, they tied them together by the arms, by means of their belts, and then stabbed them to death." Later dispatches, issued from time to time, gave accounts of murders and pillaging at Tirnova, Sistova, and numerous other places, which had been occupied by the Russians.

A large number of the Turkish stories of outrages, said to have been committed by their adversaries, stand unproved; many of them appear to be exaggerations of acts of heated violence; some of them have been contradicted and disproved; but many of them have been circumstantially confirmed. A correspondent of the *Neue Freie Presse* of Vienna, a journal friendly to the Russians, describes the massacre at Batak, which is mentioned in the Turkish official dispatches, as having occurred just after a street fight, in which the Bulgarian inhabitants were driven out by the Moslems. Half an hour afterward, the Cossacks entered the town, and began an onslaught on the Turkish population. According to the testimony of eye-witnesses, who escaped the massacre, even the Bulgarian women urged on the slaughter, and took part in it. This Batak is not the village where the massacre of 1876 occurred, but is in another district. The same correspondent described the Bulgarian women at Diskot as leading the mob of murderers, collecting the bodies of the murdered Turkish women and girls, and piling them in front of the house of the Mudir, and dancing upon them.

Upon the capture of Nicopolis, the mob rushed through the streets, murdering all the men who resisted, and committing barbarities on the women and children. In one quarter of the city, where the more fanatical Moslems dwelt, not a house·was left without damage, and hardly a citizen could be found who had not been maltreated. On the day following the capture, the town was plundered.

A correspondent of the London *Times* visited the village of

Offandlik, near Kasanlik, and saw evidences that a massacre had been committed, in the shape of the body of a beautiful young woman, who had been murdered and cast away, and in the remains of women and children which had been thrown into a well. The people who remained in the place said that the Bulgarians, with a few Cossacks, had visited the place after the retreat of the regular Russian army, had taken the men outside of the village and shot them, had collected the women and children in one of the large houses, where they outraged them repeatedly, and had "continued pillaging and burning, and occasionally killing anybody they found." On his way back to the Turkish camp, the correspondent "came across upward of 120 dead Turks, who had all been massacred by bayonet or sword, or shot suddenly. They were lying in groups, in one place forty, in another fifty, and two or three smaller parties." Among them were one woman and several old men.

The work of destruction at Sistova after its capture was thoroughly done. The correspondent of the London *Times* wrote: "When I entered the Turkish quarter of the town (which has been deserted) I found that the pillagers had been there. Turkish books and manuscripts littered the streets; the Moslem houses and shops were minus doors and windows, and their interiors were empty. I visited a mosque, and found little Bulgarian children gathering firewood from the mass of splinters and woodwork which covered the floor. Upon inquiry, I found that the Russian soldiers and Bulgarian residents were about equally responsible for these 'vandalisms.'" The correspondent of the New York *Times*, who also visited the place, gave a further description of the desolation: -

"I have been all through the original Turkish quarter, where the Pasha's Konak and the palace of a wealthy Osmanli, with its high walls and grated windows, have been occupied by the Russian authorities. Every other house lies open to inspection, for the Bulgarians finished the work of destruction commenced by the Muscovite soldiery. It was natural enough, too; the latter came in with their blood up from the fight, and the rayahs, as liberated slaves, sought to vent their fury upon their former masters. The negroes did it at San Domingo, and there is no negro fresh from the shores of the Congo whom I would insult by comparing him socially or intellectually with a home-bred Bulgarian. There were some horrid scenes, they tell me, in Sistova on the morrow of the assault, and for

24

days after, and Turks were hunted out of their hiding-places and shot down like dogs, and rape and murder and pillage, and every foul deed which lust and brutality could imagine, was perpetrated, under the eyes of the Russian officers, until there was nothing left wherewith to reproach the Osmanli for last summer's atrocities, except, it may be, the number of the victims. When human victims were wanting to their vengeance they wreaked it upon inanimate things; every house, from cellar to roof, has been gutted; chimney-places and walls have been demolished, floors torn up in search of concealed treasure. Handfuls of wool, bundles of rags of every sort and color, the accumulations of generations of Osmanli for the stuffing of their traditional divans, are scattered about the rooms like a thick carpet, or lie in heaps in the streets and gardens, where even the fruit trees have been chopped and hacked simply because they were once dear to the Moslem."

On the 17th of July seventeen victims were collected in the hospital at Rasgrad, all bearing evidence of wounds inflicted by Russian soldiery. The correspondent who saw them, and who tells the story, says that with what degree of thoroughness the injuries upon these poor people were inflicted, "may be gathered from the fact that the seventeen victims showed a total of thirty-six wounds. Of these, for example, a little girl of six years bore four. It would, therefore, appear that the murderers went to work in cold blood, and were not content with killing or wounding at the first stroke. These seventeen victims of Russian barbarity belonged to a band of fugitives from Ablava, who, on the 30th of June, were hurrying away to Rustchuk in a train of forty wagons, having received intimation of the atrocities which the advancing Russians were perpetrating in other places. The hostile horsemen had overtaken the fugitives on their way, and straightway began the human slaughter. Thirty-five poor people were killed on the spot, and the seventeen wounded creatures here are part of those who escaped with a little remnant of life." The wounds were from sabre strokes, lance-thrusts, and pistol shots.

At about the same time the hospital at Shumla contained forty wounded persons, among whom were old women and children, and even sucking babes, one of the last bearing six wounds. On the 21st of July, the Turkish Minister of Foreign Affairs published officially a statement, which had been drawn up and signed by all the newspaper correspondents at Shumla, embracing the representatives of seventeen leading papers of Germany, Austria, Hungary, France, England, Scotland, and the United States, reciting that "they declare that they have with their own eyes seen and have interrogated, both at Rasgrad and at Shumla, women, children, and old men wounded by lance and sword-thrusts, not to speak of injuries from firearms, which might be attributed to the accidents of legitimate war. These victims give horrible accounts of the treatment the Russian troops, and sometimes even the Bulgarians, inflict on the fugitive Mussulmans. According to their declarations the entire Mussulman population of several villages have been massacred. Every day there are fresh arrivals of wounded. The undersigned declare that women and children are the most numerous among the victims, and that they bear lance wounds "

According to a report made by Lieut.-Col. Wellesley, British Military Attaché at the Russian headquarters, the Russian officers accounted for the condition of these creatures by stating that some Russian cavalry had come across what they considered to be a Turkish convoy leaving Rustchuk, and summoned it to surrender. The Turks replied by firing on the cavalry, and women and children might easily have been wounded in the skirmish which ensued, for the supposed convoy proved to be a caravan of Turkish peasants leaving Rustchuk with their household goods. The Emperor had given orders to have the affair investigated.

One of the correspondents who signed the circular at Shumla, afterward caused it to be published that one of the wounded women had confessed to him, that the attack upon them was made by Bulgarians, not by Cossacks, but that they had been told to say that it was by the latter.

The occupation of Eski Sagra by the Russians on the 22d of July was hailed by the Bulgarian population with wild enthusiasm. They took the management of affairs into their own hands, organized a provincial government, and proceeded forthwith to make reprisals on the Turks for all the wrongs they had suffered during centuries of misgovernment. A court-martial was instituted, before which obnoxious Turks were tried and condemned. Six were hanged and four shot in one day, and executions followed on the succeeding days, until, it is said, "At last the Turks were taken out of the city and killed by any Bulgarian who chose to do so, without form or trial," until the slaughter was stopped by an order prohibiting summary executions. The sale of food to the Turks was prohibited, and the houses and shops of the Moslems were pillaged by the rabble. This state of affairs continued for eleven days, during which, according to the Turkish accounts, 1,100 Mussulmans were put to death, till the attack was made on the Russian positions before the town on the 31st of July, when panic and confusion set in among the Bulgarian citizens. The utmost terror took the place of the exultation which they had felt, and the whole population, or all who could get away, fled incontinently from the city. The Bulgarian volunteers who were fighting in the lines outside, having orders to defend the town, bravely resisted the advance of the Turks, falling back step by step, and continued to fight in the streets until they were overpowered. The Turkish citizens did not wait till their army had entered the place, but anticipating that event, came out from their hiding-places and proceeded to attack the Bulgarian houses. Pillaging and massacre prevailed through the day and night. All Bulgarian men were killed at sight, while as a rule, women and children were spared. On the next day, Suleiman Pasha, the Turkish commander, ordered all the Moslems and Jews to leave the place, taking with them their property. He then set fire to the town, and it was completely destroyed.

Nearly all of the outrages committed on the Russian side were perpetrated by Bulgarians. Some of them, as in the case of the women in the hospitals at Rasgrad and Shumla, were traced apparently, but not conclusively, to the Russian cavalry and Cossacks. There seem to be a few plausible grounds for the assertion which was made, that the Russians countenanced, if they did not encourage, the pillaging which took place in some of the larger towns, as at Sistova and Eski Sagra. The Russian higher officers disclaimed all responsibility for the more atrocious acts of massacre and mutilation, and professed on all occasions an anxiety to repress them, and to inflict rigorous punishment upon any of their soldiery, against whom acts contrary to the usages of civilized war could be proved.

The Turks had a theory upon which they made the Russians responsible for all, even the worst acts, even when they were committed, as were several of the massacres, by Bulgarians, far from their lines. They charged that the whole process of instigating riot, pillage, and massacre was conducted systematically by the Russians, after a regularly formed plan. On the arrival of a column into a village, notice would be given that the safety of the Mussulman population would be guaranteed. As soon as the headquarters of the commanding officer were established, the Mussulman inhabitants, consisting chiefly of women and children—for all the able-bodied men were in the army—would be gathered in a distant quarter, under guard, while the houses were searched for concealed arms and stowaways. Then the regular troops would be withdrawn, the commanders washing their hands of future consequences, and a few hours afterward, the massacres by Cossacks and Bulgarians would commence. The foreigners and newspaper correspondents having been all the time with the regular force, would see nothing of the disorderly proceedings which followed the withdrawal of the troops, and would neither be able to bear witness to them nor to contradict the Russian denials, but would always be able to say that the Russian regular troops were not guilty of disorders.

Admitting that the Russian treatment of hostile populations was severe, and that their prisoners were not as well cared for as they might have been under better circumstances of provision and transportation, the fact remains that a careful examination of all the incidents of the war has failed to bring home to them a single substantiated instance of atrocity against them, and hardly one of cruelty which may not find some sort of an excuse in the circumstances of the case. The character which is given of their treatment of the Turks, by correspondents in Asia, is confirmed by the accounts of correspondents in Europe. Except as to the case of the wounded women at Rasgrad and Shumla, no charge of outrage made against the Cossacks has been substantiated with proof sufficient to give it even probability. Mr. Archibald Forbes, who accompanied the Russians in their campaigns north of the Balkans, as correspondent of the London *Daily News*, published in the *Nineteenth Century* for November, 1877, a careful review of the question of atrocities, in which he strenuously denied that the Russian soldiery were ever guilty of them. "On soul and conscience," he said, "I believe the allegations thereof to be utterly false. Of all events which occurred south of the Balkans, I have merely hearsay knowledge. 'Atrocities' in plenty were, however, charged against the Russians north of the Balkans, and respecting these I can speak from a wide range of personal experience. The Turks resident in the towns and villages of Bulgaria were peremptorily enjoined, by commands from Constantinople, to quit their homes and retire before the advancing Russians. In the great majority of cases they did so, and their evacuation was accomplished before the first Russian reached the vicinage of their abodes. This was so at Sistova, at Batak, and at many other places where murder and rapine were systematically and lyingly averred against the Russian soldiers. The Turks who anywhere chose to remain were unmolested, without exception, so far as I know. . . . . Constantly accompanying Cossacks and other Russian cavalry in reconnoissances in front of the Rustchuk army, I never noticed any disposition to be cruel. I do not aver, remember, that atrocities were not committed on fugitive Turks; but not by the Russians. North of the Balkans, at least, Cossack lances and Russian sabres wrought no barbarity on defenseless men, women, and children."

The views of Mr. Forbes on this subject are corroborated by a report which Lieutenant-Colonel Wellesley, a special attaché of the British Government at the Russian headquarters in Bulgaria, made to Earl Derby on the 6th of August, to the effect that the result of his inquiries among Russians and Englishmen, had led him " to the honest and firm conclusion, that the statements of Russian cruelties are entirely without foundation." Yet he believed that the present war was one in which little quarter was given or expected on either side. He had heard of incendiarism and plunder by Bulgarians, but believed that the Russians tried to check them, and he had known cases where Turkish peasants had actually applied for a Cossack guard to protect them from Bulgarian attack.

The Bulgarian population, usually so peaceful and submissive that it had become a reproach to them, seem to have been excited to frenzy by the presence of the Russians among them, and the belief that they were finally delivered from the Mohammedan oppression under which they had suffered. In their simplicity and ignorance they thought the conquest of the country from the Turks was finally effected as soon as the Russian lines had reached their homes, and all that they had to do was to possess and exercise their newly-gained liberties. They were too short-sighted to comprehend that it was possible for the tide of battle to turn, the Russians be driven away, and the Turks be restored to mastery over them. With the ardor that is characteristic of such peoples, under similar circumstances, they gave themselves up to unrestrained, because unaccustomed, license; with only the single thought of the wrongs they had suffered from the Turks, they set out to take vengeance, and make to themselves restitution for them. They sincerely thought that in pillaging the Turkish homes, they were only getting back what was their own, for they were accustomed to reply, when spoken to on the subject,

MADAME CAMARA AND A WOUNDED CHILD.

WOUNDED TURKS RETURNING FROM THE BATTLE OF KASANLIK.

that all that the Turks had, had been stolen or wrested from them, and that they were fairly entitled to the whole of it.

The dark story of Bulgarian excesses is relieved by a few acts showing the assertion of the spirit of justice amid the temptations to rapine and revenge. At Tirnova, the people took a pride in trying to show that they were superior in civilization to the Turks. Their behavior to the Turks was good, and the pillaging soon ceased. A committee was formed under the Archimandrite to watch over Turkish property, and special constables were appointed from among the young men of the town to help them in this work. A mixed commission of seven Bulgarians and three Turks was appointed at Kasanlik, who, sitting on the same bench together, harmoniously and impartially adjudged the cases which were brought before them solely in the interests of good order. The executions which took place in that city were in accordance with sentences inflicted by this commission. The missionaries of the American Board at Eski Sagra remained in the city through the whole conflict; during its occupation by the Russians and its recapture by the Turks; befriended the suffering of both sides, and received the respect and protection of both. At one time they gave shelter to some Turks who were fleeing from the Bulgarian mob, and fed some of their Moslem neighbors while the edict against selling food to Mussulmans was in force. When it came the turn of the Turk to pillage and destroy, these Moslems formed a guard around the missionaries, defended them against an attack by the Circassians, and finally induced the governor of the city to provide them with a guard of regular soldiers. At Sistova the Kadi, who was the only Turk that remained in the town, was treated with respect, and his house was not molested.

The worst atrocities charged against Bulgarians were eclipsed, in magnitude and heinousness, as well as in number, by the excesses in which the Turks indulged. Terrible as are the stories which are told of their march of devastation through Lower Bulgaria or Rumelia, there is no lack of proof of the worst charges that are laid against them. The total destruction of Eski Sagra, which has been already recorded, is but a specimen of the fate which overtook many of the once flourishing cities and villages of the country of the rose gardens. On the 14th of July, a band of Bashi-Bazouks entered the town of Yeni Sagra and warned the Moslem population that the Russians were within a short distance. The Moslems all fled, and some of them reaching Constantinople the next day, reported that the Russians were driving out and massacring the people, although no evidence has been produced that any Russians were actually near the place. The Bashi-Bazouks camped during the night near the railway station, and on the next day entered the town, plundered the bazars, set fire to the place, and began a scene of slaughter which lasted twenty-four hours. How many were killed can not be exactly ascertained, for they were left to lie where they fell, in their private gardens, in their houses, in the fields, and of those who fled it is not known how many succeeded in escaping. The place was visited three days after the massacre by an English correspondent, accompanied by an officer of the English Diplomatic service, whose search showed that not a single house or shop had escaped pillage. "It seems incredible," the correspondent says, "how they could have ransacked the place so completely in so short a time." The writer, after giving a description in detail of the murdered bodies and hideous sights that he saw, all of which formed conclusive evidence to him that there had been "a foul massacre of Bulgarians at Yeni Sagra," closed his account by stating that he had not mentioned a thing that he had not personally seen, and that he could substantiate every detail by witnesses of undoubted integrity.

Kavarna is a town on the Black Sea, near Varna, inhabited by four or five hundred families, mostly Greeks, of more than usual intelligence. In addition to its regular population, many of the inhabitants of the surrounding country had come into it for refuge against depredations. The Circassians attacked the town on the 21st of July, and were met by a vigorous resistance. A proposition was made to the inhabitants to give a ransom of sixty thousand piasters or abandon the place, in consideration of which they should be spared. While this was under discussion, a part of the Circassians entered the town and began a course of plunder and murder which continued for more than twelve hours. The Turkish Governor at Varna was appealed to while the massacre was going on, to send a force to save the people, and promised to do so, but at the same time attempted to excuse the massacre by saying that the Christians at Kavarna ought to have quitted their homes rather than repel the aggression by force of arms. Two vessels with troops were sent, which reached the place too late, the Christians assert, to stop the massacre. The Turkish official report claims that the vessels arrived in good time, that no such extensive massacres occurred as were reported, and that the whole number of persons killed among the plunderers, the troops, and the inhabitants, was only thirty. The Greek estimate of the number of victims was several hundred. The women and children and wounded, numbering in all, according to the Turkish official report, two thousand five hundred, were taken care of on the Turkish war vessels.

Sopot and Carlova were beautiful towns of about 10,000 and 20,000 inhabitants respectively, finely situated in a country of abundant pasturage, and inhabited by a thrifty and well-to-do population. Every building stood in a well-kept garden, and the gardens, as well as the whole towns, were watered by means of artificial canals leading down from the mountain streams. At Carlova was the center of the native cloth manufacturing of the country. The Russians came into Sopot, accompanied by Bulgarians, and disarmed the Mussulman population, a few of whom were killed in street rows. Then the Russians retired and the Turks returned, bringing with them Bashi-Bazouks and Circassians, and the customary indiscriminate slaughter of the inhabitants was set up. The commander of the plundering force ordered them to desist from their wicked work, whereupon, it is said, they turned against him and locked him up. Having done all the damage possible at Sopot, the irregulars went to Carlova, which was saved from complete destruction by the arrival of regular troops, but not till a great many of the inhabitants had been killed. The whole district in which these towns were situated was visited, a few weeks after the massacres, by an English committee of relief, who bore provisions and aid to the desolated inhabitants. They reported that a fearful degree of suffering existed in consequence of the destruction which had been effected. At a village near Carlova was a camp of ten thousand Turkish refugees, who had no means of support whatever, and would again have none after the supplies given them by the committee were exhausted. One of the commission wrote to the New York *Times* of Carlova, that except that the houses were all standing, "the place was hardly worth calling a town any longer. There were no men left in it, and there was not a house or shop which had not been utterly wrecked within." The women showed the blood-stains on the walls and floors which marked the spot of the murder of their male relatives. The attention of another of the party was attracted to the faces of a number of children at the wooden bars of a window carefully fastened against intruders.

"At our inquiry if anybody was within, given in Turkish, the spaces between the bars became instantly blank. Calling up our dragoman, who spoke Bulgarian, we told him to speak gently, and the little noses reappeared. 'How many of you are there?' we inquired. 'Ten,' was the faint reply, in a childish treble. 'How long have you been shut up here?' 'Nearly forty days.' 'But why do you stay in there?' 'Oh, do not ask us! they are killing everybody. Where is our father?'—from a dozen little throats at once"

The father of these children, as well as the husband of a woman who made anxious inquiry respecting his fate, had probably been taken to Philippopolis and hung. "The desolation of desolation," says one of the members of this commission, "was reached at Sopot. I am used to the phrases, 'razed to the ground,' 'utterly destroyed,' 'savagery,' and 'utter vandalism,' but what is there left to give the reader a faint idea of what has happened to Sopot? Scarcely one stone adheres to another. How men unhelped by the devil could have done the mere mechanical part of the work is a mystery. With scarcely an exception that we could make out, every Bulgarian house has been reduced to a heap of stones, bricks, and tiles." Another of the commission says that several of the houses at this place were left standing, but describes Kalofer, another town in the immediate neighborhood, as an "utterly and irretrievably complete ruin," "without a single roof remaining or a single whole wall left standing." Six hundred and forty Bulgarian women and children were found in a state of starvation at Sopot. Such are the accounts given by members of a committee which was organized to give relief, not to Bulgarian, but to Turkish sufferers. Both the members of the committee and the suffering women, spoke in high terms of the conduct of the Turkish regulars, who, one of the women said, had been as brothers to them.

Similar descriptions were given by men who visited the country and saw for themselves the things of which they tell—of village after village, " actually by the hundred," as one writer has it, till the reiteration of horrors and the use of the most expressive terms to denote utter devastation and fiendish atrocity becomes monotonous. The country people and the witnesses themselves became so accustomed to scenes of outrage that, to use the language of one of the latter, " What had shocked one's nerves a few weeks before, was now looked upon almost with indifference."

The Turkish Government inflicted rigorous punishment upon all the men who were implicated in the outrages committed by Bulgarians. A series of executions, which may be well characterized as wholesale, followed the recovery of the territory south of the Balkans from Russia ; and the policy of severity was continued even after the circumstances of the political and military situation had ceased to justify it It was even carried into undisturbed districts where no revolt had been attempted, so that, it was said, no Bulgarian Christian, however innocent, was safe. A reign of terror prevailed through all the country from Adrianople to the Balkans, and the " Terror in Bulgaria " became the name by which the situation throughout the province was designated. A correspondent wrote from Adrianople near the end of August, of executions going on at the rate of thirty in one day, and stating that the spectacle had grown so familiar on the streets that a hanging excited " no more popular attention than would be created by the merest trifle of street interest in London and New York." A few days after this the statement was made in a private letter from the same place, that the most substantial and respectable men were selected there, and their property was confiscated ; that eighty of the chief inhabitants of Carlova had been hanged there, they being those whose consciousness of innocence had kept them from running away. Some of the incidents connected with the executions showed a peculiar heartlessness and indifference to public opinion on the part of the officers.

Ahmed Vefik Pasha, one of the most intelligent and cultivated of the Turkish statesmen, and a man of literary reputation, was appointed Governor of Adrianople late in August, and hopes were entertained that his administration would be signalized by a relaxation of the severity of Turkish justice. The executions were, however, continued, but with more order and greater regard for the forms of law. The German Ambassador spoke to the Sultan in September about the excessive number of the executions, and the length of time they had continued, and was answered that the insurgents had been tried and sentenced by duly appointed and capable officers, and that only those were executed who had been guilty of offenses against the common law.

A petition was presented to the Sultan in August, signed by three thousand Bulgarians, including the Archbishop and Bishops of Adrianople, imploring the clemency of his Majesty, and promising to remain in future faithful subjects of the Porte

The stories of these many violations of the usages of war and of the canons of humanity attracted the attention of the Governments of Europe. The correspondence which ensued upon the subject gave the Turkish Government an opportunity to make its excuses for the sad condition which was acknowledged to exist, and gave publicity to the results of such inquiry as it was possible for foreign agents to make as to the location of the responsibility for the atrocities. On the 10th of July, Mr. Layard, the British Ambassador, reported to his Government that the Sultan and his ministers had expressed the fear that when the cruel treatment to which the Mussulman populations had been exposed became known, it would be very difficult to repress the feelings of indignation and revenge which it would cause among their fellow-believers. In regard to the reports of Turkish misdeeds, Mr. Layard believed that the Turkish Government had been obliged to withdraw its troops and police from the provinces to strengthen its forces in the field, and the Circassians, Tartars, Kurds, and other wild tribes had taken advantage of this state of things to plunder and rob. On the 25th of July, in sending a number of stories of outrage, he desired it to be clearly understood that he in no way vouched for their truth, and thought that many of them were greatly exaggerated. Partisan prejudice on both sides rendered it impossible to get trustworthy accounts. On the 1st of August, he wrote that lawlessness was encouraged by the state of anarchy into which the country had been thrown in consequence of the war, and that the measures taken by the Porte to remove the inhabitants and cattle of certain districts had added to the evil. The German Government, in the latter part of August, moved by official reports made to it of Turkish cruelties to the Russian wounded and prisoners, addressed a note to the Porte, reminding it of the provisions of the Geneva Convention. Other powers, Austria and Italy, were invited to co-operate with the German Government in its representations, and did so, assuring the Porte, however, in their notes, that their course was not taken in any spirit hostile to Turkey, but solely in the interests of humanity. These powers also professed their readiness to address a similar protest to the Russian Government against any proved violation of the convention by that nation. A few days afterward, the British Government was notified by the Turkish Grand Vizier that orders had been given for the distribution among the Turkish troops of a Turkish translation of the Geneva Convention, in order that the violation of some of its rules, which was alleged to have taken place, and which it was admitted might in some instances have occurred through ignorance of the convention, might not be repeated. The Grand Vizier gave assurances that he would issue instructions that every possible measure should be taken to prevent excesses on the part of the Circassians and other irregular troops.

The weight of evidence tends to exculpate the Turkish Government from the charge of deliberately countenancing the outrages that were complained of. It was a party to the Geneva Convention, and intended in good faith, in its feeble way, to adhere to its provisions, but the same intrinsic weakness which infects every department of its administration deprived it and its regular officers in the field of all power of restraining the excesses of its irregular troops. The regular Turkish soldiery are likewise exculpated by general testimony from all connection with outrages upon unarmed populations. The officers are almost universally spoken of as gentlemen, observing the usages and acknowledging the obligations of civilization, and the soldiers as, in the main, kind-hearted and humane; and instances were not infrequent in which the poor Bulgarians, suffering under the infliction of a Bashi-Bazouk or Circassian raid, appealed confidently to the regulars for protection, and received it. The cruelty of the Turkish soldiery to their armed foes whom they had disabled or taken prisoners is well-established. The dead bodies of Russian soldiers were found in large numbers on numerous battle-fields, as at the Shipka Pass, at Telis, where an engagement took place on the 24th of October, stripped and mutilated; and not a few instances are related in which the disabled Russians taken prisoners were left unattended to rather than kept to be in the way and to consume the scanty stores of provisions of the Turkish commissariat.

The case of the Geshoffs, Manchester merchants at Philippopolis, excited much interest in England Though native Bulgarians, they were accomplished gentlemen, of the best social and financial standing at home and abroad. They had been educated at an English college, and were said to be in speech and ideas, "as British" as if they had been born "and brought up in England." They were arrested in August, ostensibly upon a charge that a man just before his execution had denounced them by name as guilty of treason.

The British Vice-Consul at Philippopolis was instructed not to interfere for them. Their case was, however, taken up by the American Legation. An appointment as Vice-Consul of the United States was secured for one of them, but the Turkish Government refused to recognize it, because it was made after they had been arrested. A day was appointed for their execution in September, but the act was delayed. The intercessions of their foreign friends were finally of effect, for orders were given in November to treat themselves and their families kindly; they were afterward taken to Constantinople.

A terrible amount of destitution was produced throughout the country in consequence of the rivalry of murder and destruction that prevailed. In Bulgarian and Mohammedan districts alike, whole stretches of country, with the villages they had once contained, were converted into a complete waste. The people who escaped massacre fled to the large towns for refuge, or were picked up by the regular soldiery and gathered into camps, where they suffered great privations, being destitute of food and clothing, and wholly dependent for the means of existence upon such aid as was sent them from abroad. Mr. Layard, in a dispatch to the British Foreign Office, dated August 21st, described the number of fugitives as daily increasing. They were "wandering over the face of the country in the most terrible misery, having saved nothing, scarcely even their clothes." Disease was appearing among them, and when the cold weather set in, their sufferings would be dreadful and the loss of life great. Mr. Young, of the Red Cross Association, had found, in one spot, without shelter and food, about 2,000 Mussulman women and children, many of whom were wounded. Another agent had reported crowds of these fugitives in East Bulgaria, bivouacking over the country, having found 15,000 families at Eski-Djuma alone, in the utmost want. Some five thousand were at Rodesto, nearly 13,000 at Adrianople, some seven or eight thousand at Philippopolis, many thousand at Constantinople, while vessels or trains were constantly running with hundreds more at different points. There was scarcely a town in the east of Rumelia, Mr. Layard said, which was not crowded with fugitives, and the total number could not be estimated.

Subscriptions were taken and organizations formed in the more fortunate commercial towns and abroad for the relief of the destitute. The Turks, in the country and at Constantinople, co-operated in these efforts, " making no distinction between Mohammedans and Christians." The Sultan opened one of his palaces to the fugitives, and many of them were received into private houses at Constantinople.

Charges were made that the Montenegrins were cruel to the prisoners whom they captured, and murdered them They had a basis of truth, in that during the four hundred years that Montenegro has been at war with Turkey, it had been the policy of the Montenegrins to surround themselves with all the horrors as to their enemies that they could create, in part compensation for the disparity in numbers between them and the Turks. In accordance with this policy, it had been their custom to take no prisoners, but to behead all the Turks whom they captured. This custom has been greatly mitigated under the influence of an improved civilization, so that during the recent wars the Montenegrins have generally taken prisoners and treated them as did other civilized people. Still there were many who indulged the old practice, and much that was alleged regarding the murder of prisoners was admitted to be true. Nevertheless, hundreds of Turkish prisoners were kept in the country, in perfect security to themselves and with good feeling prevailing between them and the people, and were well cared for. It was the boast of the Montenegrins that they never harmed a woman or a child of their enemies.

CHAPTER XVI.

THE PHILANTHROPY OF THE WAR.

Progress of Humane Principles—The Geneva Convention—The Russian Soldiers Aid Societies—The Empress and Ladies of Rank—The Turkish Aid Societies—The British Aid Societies—Queen Victoria—Lady Strangford—Baroness Burdett-Coutts—American Societies—Union of Nations for the Relief of Distress.

AMONG the worst of the evils of war in olden times was the suffering which was inflicted upon the sick and wounded of the armies. Not only was the treatment which a disabled prisoner would receive at the hands of the enemy a matter of great doubt, but the provisions existing within the armies for the care of their own sick and wounded were extremely defective. The intensity of this evil has been greatly mitigated with the advance of civilization and the growth of comity among nations; and the subject of improving the provisions for the care and comfort of invalid soldiery, and for insuring their security in the hands of an enemy, have received especial attention within the last twenty-five years. The manner of life of an army, and the circumstances under which war is necessarily conducted, make the best provisions that can be devised terribly inadequate. The resources of the army administration and of the Governments behind it have generally been found wholly insufficient to meet the cases to which they were to be applied; and it has been found convenient in all nations, as the ideas of the amount of attention which should be given to this branch of the service have been enlarged, to supplement the official work with the resources of private benevolence. The later wars have seen the whole people of the belligerent nations interesting themselves in various ways in measures to prepare and forward to the field of action all articles and provisions which could be of use in saving suffering and promoting the comfort of the soldiers, and in dispatching agents to attend to their wants. The Sanitary and Christian Commissions in the United States during the civil war

LOADING AN AMBULANCE.

DEATH OF AZIZ PASHA

A TURKISH SURGEON AND FIELD EQUIPAGE.

showed how efficient this voluntary work might be made. The spirit which impels to such effort has so spread that during the Russo-Turkish war the Sanitary and Aid Societies received sympathy and help from all the leading nations of civilization.

The most important step which has ever been taken to relieve suffering and establish humanity in war, was in the adoption of the Geneva Convention, a code providing for the neutrality of hospitals and the care of the wounded in 1864. It was suggested by Henry Dunant, who, having witnessed the sad suffering on the battle-field of Solferino, devoted himself to the search of a remedy against the recurrence of similar scenes. Representatives of several European Governments met at Geneva, upon the invitation of the Swiss Government, and adopted regulations providing that the places where wounds were dressed and the hospitals should be regarded as neutral; further, that all persons engaged in the care of the sick should be free from molestation as long as they were attending to their duties of taking up or attending to the wounded on the battle-field, and that when this work was over, they should be allowed to return in safety to their own lines. Houses in which wounded were placed should be spared from the allotment of troops and the exaction of contributions, and the inhabitants of the country should be invited to participate in the care of the wounded, and assured of respect to their neutrality while doing so. A flag bearing a red cross to accompany the national flag was established as the sign by which the neutral places and buildings should be covered, and persons engaged in the humane work were required to distinguish themselves by wearing a white band with the red cross upon their arms. Several additional articles were adopted in 1868, and the provisions of the Convention were extended to cover warfare by sea. All the principal States of Europe, including Russia and Turkey, have accepted the provisions of the Convention, and it was generally regarded and enforced among the regular troops in the wars of 1876 and 1877. The Turks substituted on their neutral flags a red crescent for the red cross of the Christian nations, in deference to their religion, of which the crescent is the symbol, as the cross is of the Christian religion.

In 1874, delegates from all the European powers met at Brussels on the proposition of the Emperor Alexander of Russia, with the intention of extending the principles of the Geneva Convention to the population of belligerent countries, to the organization of volunteers and reserve troops, and even to the arms and missiles employed, but the negotiations brought no results.

The sanitary wants of the Montenegrins and Servians during their wars of 1876 were carefully attended to by their Russian sympathizers. Large amounts of supplies were raised in Russia, and sent to the seat of war under the auspices of the Slavic committees, and German and Russian doctors were employed to attend to the sick and wounded. Spacious hospitals were established in Montenegro and near the scenes of the Herzegovinian insurrection. In the districts of Herzegovina and Bosnia, remote from these hospitals, however, the fate of the wounded insurgents was a hard one, as no provisions whatever existed for their care. The arrangements of the Montenegrins and Servians themselves, as well as of the Turks, were very defective. The Servian service was, however, much improved during the course of the campaign under the care of Baron Mundy, an Austrian officer and Professor of Military Sanitary Science in the University of Vienna, who came to Belgrade at the end of July, 1876, and took charge of this branch of the work.

During the war of 1877, the belligerents did much in the line of sanitary measures. Public and private letters from Russia declared the Empress and the Russian ladies were as diligent in efforts to relieve the sick and wounded of the army, as the Emperor in preparations to carry on the war.

At the opening of hostilities, the Red Cross Society was installed in a building near Fort Nicholas. There everything that human ingenuity could suggest or invent for the sick and wounded, was at hand, ready to be forwarded as soon as needed.

The officers of the Russian Red Cross Society were women of high rank, Madame Narishkina, born the Princess of Kourakini, Countess Shuvaloff—all ladies of fortune—working as if life depended on their success. From mansion to cottage the work went on the whole day long; ladies offered their jewels, and they were rich in jewels; funds rolled in from all sides, the peasants urging the acceptance of their mites.

When the battles began, from every direction the report came that the Russians treated their Turkish prisoners with kindness. Among the prisoners at one time were four Turkish and two German doctors. The Turkish doctors were released, and the two Germans put in charge of the Turks, with the same pay the Porte offered.

The Russian troops carried the Bulgarian children of Eski Sagra, Yeni Sagra, and Kasanlik, some on gun-carriages and some in their arms, to save them from the Turks; others drove along a cow to feed the little ones with milk, and at Shipka they prepared a big cauldron of soup, which was ladled out and given to the starving fugitives.

On the Shipka Pass, in spite of the horrible mutilations of Russian prisoners by the Turks, Turkish prisoners in the hands of Russians were spared, and their wounds carefully attended to. At first the Turks looked afraid; they could not believe the Russians less barbarous than themselves. On a certain day, a cart drove up with two wounded Bashi-Bazouks. The Grand Duke at once gave orders to have them furnished with bread and wine from his own quarters, and as there was no room in the hospitals, they were sent to a neighboring village. Hundreds of fugitives were met who were loud in praise of Russian kindness. All who could travel had free passes to their homes, and were furnished with five days' provisions.

The field and transfer hospitals were located at Simnitza, Fratesti, and Turnu-Magurelli; the latter was described as "one vast hospital," but was very unfavorably located in a district abounding in marshes and stagnant pools. The Government hospitals were very imperfect concerns, on account of the incompetency and inexperience of their attendants, and their ignorance of sanitary science and the elements of practical military surgery, although they were earnest and faithful enough. The amateur establishments and volunteer ambulances were pronounced better than Government provisions. Near the town were the buildings of the Red Cross of Rumania, directed by Dr. Severance; on the public square the hospital of Independence, able to receive but fifty patients, and presided over by Mademoiselle Marie Rossetti; further on, the tents of the ladies of Jassy, superintended by the Princesses Nathalie, Soutzo, and Ghika. Next was the Government Military Hospital, and then the admirable ambulance of the Jews of Moldavia. Mademoiselle Rossetti, assisted by the wives of the Ministers of War and Justice, secured the services of two leading physicians of the capital, also half a dozen young men who had just completed their medical studies in Paris. The hospital at Gorni-Studen, one of the best, could accommodate 2,000 patients, yet one week's fighting gave 10,000 wounded.

According to a foreign medical officer who visited them officially, the Rumanian field hospitals were very defective. He wrote of them:

"There is an insufficiency of surgeons, who are generally incompetent from want of experience, and utterly deficient in executive ability, in the Rumanian field hospitals. Every one is either ignorant of the first principles of field hygiene, or culpably negligent in not enforcing proper police regulations. Dirt, disorder, and confusion everywhere; order nowhere. There is material enough, if properly administered, for the immediate wants of 250 to 300 wounded, but from first to last I have met with but two men who knew or did their duty. No one can form an idea of the sufferings of the wounded, for whom there is no other conveyance from the field to the rear than bullock carts without springs, and the stretchers are reeking with filth. Excuses may be made for much of this, from the fact that the Rumanians have had no experience in warfare, are deficient in means, and have been forced into a fight for which they are to-day unprepared. The parties charged with the execution meet the exigencies of the moment with doubt and indecision, where the safety of the soldier demands promptness and decision." The Russian field hospitals were not much better, except as regarded the surgeons, who were more numerous, and some of whom were men of talent and experience.

The chief center of the Russian organization for the relief of sick and wounded, was at Kiev, on the Dnieper. Here was the regular military hospital and the second Red Cross Society, with Prince Demidoff at its head.

At Kolrocheni, opposite the Prince's summer palace, was the large hospital, capable of receiving one thousand patients, and near it a number of frame buildings to supplement its accommodations. The nurses merited and received great commendation. The soldiers called them the little sisters, as they went quietly about, dressed in neat, brown serge, with long, white aprons, the red cross embroidered on the breast, and white handkerchiefs pinned over their heads, giving medicines, showing pictures, reading, or pouring out a cup of tea.

Nine Russian cities pledged themselves to construct and support hospitals which should contain 1,280 beds.

Among the noteworthy generosities of patriotic Russians, that of a village blacksmith, in Southern Russia, deserves praise. He offered to shoe, free of charge, all cavalry horses that passed his door, and as Cossacks were daily passing through the village, his gift was no mean one. A merchant of Odessa gave 250,000 cigars and cigarettes, and

another, 400,000, to the sick and wounded. A merchant of Voronez
gave ten tons of tobacco to the army, and another sent liberal supplies of food and luxuries to five thousand Cossacks who were encamped near Rustchuk.

Turning to Turkey, we find she had not been idle in philanthropy;
she had her Red Crescent Society, which did noble work. The Sultan
took great interest in the work of the societies, and offered a room in
the palace as a meeting-place for the committee, in order that they
might be under his special protection. He examined the models of
ambulance wagons, and rejected one with only two wheels, saying
if he were wounded he would wish to be carried in a vehicle with
four wheels, and he did not see why any soldier in his army should
not be treated as well as himself.

The Sultan himself subscribed £2,500 to the Red Crescent Society;
his Turkish subjects, following his lead, contributed more than
£16,000. Sub-committees were formed in all the principal towns of
the provinces. These committees were composed of representatives
of the Ottoman Bank and the medical officers of health. They prepared and distributed large supplies of stores, also country wagons
with mattresses, and a surgeon for each army. Besides large hospitals at Rustchuk and Varna, they fitted up one at Anatolie Kavak,
on the Bosporus, and another on the Dardanelles. A very favorable
account was given of the hospital at Varna by a correspondent of the
Edinburgh *Scotsman* who visited it. It was under the management
of the Stafford House Committee. "The building," says the correspondent, " is the most appropriate that could have been chosen in
this desirable locality. It is of stone, has plenty of windows, and its
ventilation has been improved by wooden shafts (with partitions to
facilitate up and down draught) passing through the roof. I was
gratified to remark that there was no display of luxury. On the
contrary, the utmost frugality prevails. The resident surgeon's
room, on the left of the entrance, is uncarpeted, and its sole furniture
consists of a small deal table, a truckle bed covered with a rough
horsecloth, and a most penurious-looking washstand. Opposite is the
operating room, and behind is the pharmacy, well-stocked with
drugs, most of which, for want of time, had to be procured from
Constantinople. Passing on, we come to a spacious kitchen with
the usual native kitchen-range for charcoal fires, and a large wash-
house provided with every requisite. There are two wards, one containing thirty-five beds and the other fourteen. The first is unex-

ceptionable.   It is quite a pleasure to get out of the sun into its cool, pure atmosphere.   The beds are ranged on raised floors on each side of an earthen path, and their dainty white coverlets look quite tempting to one who has been obliged, as I have, to camp out or sleep on the filthy floors of native coffee-houses in the interior. Beside each bed is a small table, furnished with a decanter and glasses."   The hospital contained another ward, and a loft with stores and an abundance of all fixtures and appliances, disinfectants, and arrangements for ventilation.

At Kars there were nine doctors with the army; at Ardahan, five; one with the battalion of Molla Suleiman, and eleven in the hospital at Erzerum.   In the Scutari hospital, the doctors visiting it found 1,300 sick and wounded Turks and two Russian prisoners, all well attended.   Much difficulty was felt in caring for the wounded Turks on account of their aversion to amputation.   Most of them preferred to die whole to living mutilated.   Their surgeons sympathized with this feeling, which had a religious foundation, so that in many of the purely Turkish hospitals numerous deaths occurred in cases in which life could have been saved with proper attention or under European surgeons.   Much of the neglect which was charged against the Turkish management arose from their doctrine of fatality, and from their superstitious objections to maiming the body.   The Turkish soldiers, however, proved hardy patients, and many of them recovered under circumstances in which death would have seemed certain to a European.

At Smyrna, where 1,500 Bulgarian refugees arrived, the authorities did all in their power to relieve their distress.   At Constantinople, the Sultan placed one of his palaces (Beylerbey) at the disposal of the authorities for the reception of fugitives of all classes, and ordered that other buildings should be prepared for their accommodation. Many were taken into private houses, and some Turks, with Ahmed Vefik Pasha, exerted themselves to procure clothing for them before cold weather set in.   The throngs of fugitives severely taxed the resources of the authorities to supply their needs, and although all the available buildings were given up for their accommodation, and much aid was afforded by private munificence, so great were their numbers and so destitute was their condition that a vast amount of suffering was inevitable.   A similar state of affairs existed at Adrianople, where 2,500 fugitives were congregated in August, and the garrison and 2,000 wounded soldiers had to be cared for.   A correspondent wrote from this place August 8th : " The wounded soldiers are being far better attended than I could have expected. Great difficulty was at first entertained of being able to have them, but that is now not so much felt as the want of surgeons. The military hospital, which I visited yesterday and found clean and well-ventilated, contains about 600 men. The civil hospital some two hundred more ; while the rest are distributed about the town in what are called boujeklik, or large wooden buildings for storing silk cocoons, which seem designed by Providence for hospitals, so admirably suited are they to this purpose. Besides this, to their credit it must be recorded, the Sisters of the Assumption have undertaken to house and nurse between sixty and seventy wounded soldiers at some houses in different suburbs."

While the war was stained with the horrible atrocities which we have related in another place, and the Turkish officers sometimes, as did Osman Pasha at Plevna, excusing himself under the plea of necessity, allowed their prisoners to be exposed to suffering and almost certain death, the Turkish regular officers and soldiers generally showed the traits of civilized humanity in their bearing toward their wounded enemies. In one instance, a Russian soldier said, " My mate was wounded ; two Turks found him, washed his wound and bandaged it, then put him on his way. They wanted to take away his rifle, but when he declared his life would not be safe without it, they allowed him to keep it and charged him to keep out of the way of the Circassians, as they might do him harm." At Shumla, the Turkish officers placed fezzes and Turkish cloaks on Russian wounded lying on the field, to prevent their irregulars murdering them during the night.

Next to the belligerents, England did much in the line of relief. The English Minister, Mr. Layard, and his wife, took great interest in the sanitary work. The English efforts were directed through two leading societies. The Stafford House Committee worked all through the Servian war, but during the Russo-Turkish war confined itself, till the middle of June, to sending out stores to be administered by Ahmed Vefik Pasha, President of the House of Representatives. It then appointed a special commissioner, under whom surgeons were engaged in England and assigned to fields of duty in Europe and Asia, and local surgeons, principally Greek and Armenian, were employed. A wagon transport line was organized for communication with the Balkans, and the head of the Yamboli Tirnova Railway; stores were forwarded to Erzerum, and numerous hospitals were established at suitable places. The society entered into relations with the Red Cresent, the National Ottoman Society for the Relief of the Sick and Wounded, under which it received protection and enjoyed all the privileges of the Geneva Convention. The British National Society for aid to Sick and Wounded, dispatched a ship with surgeons, who were sent where their services were most needed. Some of its surgeons rendered valuable services during the earlier operations south of the Balkans, and their attentions to the poor wounded women and children are described as having been incessant, "while they sacrificed every thought of personal comfort and rest to alleviate their sufferings." All of the societies, as well as the ladies' committees, worked together, with the sole object of relieving suffering, regardless of creed or nationality, and sinking everything like petty competition among themselves.

In Therapia, a place of fashionable resort, and where the English Minister's palace is, the ladies, mostly English residents, won much praise for their admirable work for the soldiers, contributing large sums of money, preparing bandages, beds, sheets, and all such necessaries, and uniting their work with other aid societies in the vicinity.

Mr. and Mrs. Layard were invited to dinner by the Sultan, who received them with great distinction at his table. Mrs. Layard was presented by his Majesty with a magnificent set of diamonds, in recognition of the generous offerings of the English people for the Turkish wounded. In August, Mr. Layard received from the Baroness Burdett-Coutts, who represented the contributors to the Turkish Relief Fund, £4,000, to relieve Turkish women and children, and afterward £200 for suffering soldiers.

At Adrianople the Stafford House Committee made great exertions, opening two military hospitals for two hundred and sixty patients, and in one day dressing the wounds of one hundred and eighty soldiers. One surgeon took charge of fugitive women and children who were Turks, Bulgarians, and Jews

The Central Bulgarian Relief Committee, Sir H. Eliot, President, sent £300 for Bulgarian relief, and offered to supply medicines to any surgeon who would give his services to the work, and funds to provide food for urgent need.

Queen Victoria and the Princess Beatrice spent much time making lint for the wounded of both sides, and forwarded a large number of bandages to Mrs. Layard for distribution.

Two of the physicians sent out at the expense of Lord Blantyre, Drs. Casson and Featherstonehaugh, were able to show, under their charge, a well-ordered hospital, and through the liberality of Mrs. Layard, Lady Kemball, and other English ladies in Constantinople, they were able to provide themselves with many comforts unknown in Turkish hospitals. They worked nobly among the wounded, greatly aided by American missionaries.

At Adrianople a small hospital was organized and conducted by an English lady, Mrs. Camara; she was the only person of her position who dared remain in the city. Hearing of the dreadful massacre, she opened a large house for Turkish women and children, wounded or not wounded, receiving rations from Government for them.

A Greek gentleman gave some large silk cocoon stores to be used as hospitals for wounded women and children. It was stated the fugitives in Adrianople numbered twenty-five thousand five hundred, besides soldiers The military hospitals contained six hundred men, the civil hospital two hundred, and the wooden buildings were filled also. In the suburbs the Sisters of the Assumption offered to house and nurse sixty or seventy wounded soldiers.

A large supply of stores was forwarded to Erzerum under Lieut. M. Drummond, R. N. All stores and supplies were handed over to the Red Crescent Society, which took the expense of working them.

Sometimes the Turkish officials were jealous of foreign interference, and would not allow members of the Soldiers' Aid Societies to carry out their work, but in many places the English surgeons were met with gratitude and co-operation.

Much good work was done at Adrianople, Philippopolis, Eski Sagra, Kasanlik, and Shipka. Even when ordered to return, the English surgeons gave into the hands of the chief Turkish surgeon the medicines, bandages, stretchers, soups, and appliances they brought. What civilized nations call Turkish cruelty, the Turk counts far-sighted wisdom. When the doctors wished to amputate limbs, the Pashas told them they had special orders to prevent it. "If they die now they will go to Paradise; if you save their lives the Sultan will have to pay them a pension for forty years, and Turkey is not rich enough to afford that." Mr. Layard, the British Ambassador, when he made an appeal to England for aid, said, "The Turkish Government is doing its best, but its action is almost paralyzed by the magnitude of the misery it has to deal with."

At Bucharest the English opened hospitals, and received for them ample stores. The Rumanian hospitals were finely fitted up, and the patients well attended. The Hospital of the Princess of Rumania had fifty-six patients, all bad cases, selected by her Highness on account of the severity of their wounds. The Princess attended the wounded in person, clad in common working dress, and cheered the poor fellows by kind words and attention. General Richter, the President of the Russian Red Cross Society, sent messages of thanks to the English people and their societies for their generous sympathy and aid to Russian wounded.

. In September large funds were sent from England to Mr. Layard for distribution among the Turkish sufferers by the war. The Turkish Government placed one hundred and forty wagons, six pack horses, and an escort of ten horsemen, at the disposal of those who took in charge the sanitary and relief measures. The poor Bulgarian and Turkish sufferers were exceedingly grateful, saying, "Our children shall always call English people blessed." The four military hospitals at Eski Djuma were most complete with the help of the English societies.

Lady Strangford's name is a synonym for benevolence. She is a member of a rich and noble family in England, her husband having been once British Ambassador to Turkey, but she left her home to organize the Red Cross service in that country. She was employed during the whole year in equipping hospitals and training others for the care of the wounded. Among the principal of the hospitals which she established was the one at Sophia, where she organized a corps of women and trained them, simply to show the Turks how to do.

The Baroness Burdett-Coutts was very active and efficient in her exertions for the relief of sufferers, and received a public acknowledgment from the Sultan.

The extent which the organization of the benevolent work reached as the war advanced is shown by a letter written from Constantinople in October, which, speaking of the Red Crescent Society, says:

"It is astonishing what amount of money and hospital articles it has sent out to Turkey, the ambulances it has built, the many surgeons it has in its employ, and the great number of disciplined agents it has under its orders.

"Every steamer from England brings stores of preserved meats, of liquors, of lint, and material for the transport of the wounded, such as spring-beds, ambulances, etc. Every division of the Turkish army has some of the Red Crescent personnel with complete field-apparatus, stationed near it when in camp and following it when it marches to battle. Yesterday six baggage vans of the society, with ambulance furnishings, went up to Philippopolis by the Adrianople Railway. Before she left here for the seat of hostilities, Lady Strangford had hospital accommodations provided at the royal palaces according to the Red Cross system and under its superintendence The palaces of Beylerbey and Tcheragan, two of the finest imperial residences on the Bosporus, are now turned into hospitals, and they, as well as the great barracks at Scutari and on the heights of Bellevue, are crammed with patients under treatment. The headquarters of Lady Strangford are at Adrianople, where a vast hospital has been prepared, which now holds within its walls over two thousand. From this point she is enabled to communicate with the temporary and permanent hospitals in the rear of the armies and on the line of the roads to the Balkans and Servia. You can form an idea of the amount of suffering needing relief when I say that the battles in the Shipka Pass alone furnished over two thousand patients in two weeks."

In New York two American Societies were organized, the Society of the Red Cross, to aid Russians, and the Society of the Crescent and the Cross, to aid both Russians and Turks. The Red Cross Society was given up. The Cross and Crescent held a ball which yielded $600, and with other moneys contributed, $10,000 was raised; half of the sum was sent to Constantinople and half to St. Petersburg, through the American Legations at the two cities. Mrs. Marshal O. Roberts gave a musical reception at her house, the proceeds of which went for the benefit of the sufferers in the Eastern war. The American missionaries in Turkey were often mentioned as giving valuable aid to those who suffered in the war.

The French people exhibited their sympathy with the enterprises for relief by the organization of numerous societies in the various parts of the republic to aid it.

The Jews of Europe and the United States took a warm interest in the philanthropic work, particularly in behalf of their co-religionists, large numbers of whom were exposed to much suffering.

Committees were formed in all their principal societies, and liberal contributions and supplies of stores and provisions were made and forwarded from all quarters.

Thus this war, which was marked in some points by atrocities of unusual heinousness, showing to what excesses the unrestrained passions of man may lead him, brought about in other points the co-operation of all nations in works of humanity and for the relief of distress. The cruelties of the belligerents and the outrages committed by their irresponsible followers are another lesson against the evils of war. The union of mankind in works of relief, and the extent of the relief and provisions which were afforded and distributed without distinction or prejudice, the combination of different races and religions for common humanity which was exhibited, mark an important step in the progress of civilization and humane principles, which may be referred to in future times as one of the most creditable characteristics of the century.

MURAD V.

ALEXANDER,

HEIR APPARENT TO THE RUSSIAN THRONE.

CHAPTER XVII.

THE ACTORS IN THE CONTEST.

Interest in the Personalities of the War—Sovereigns : The Czar and the Imperial Family of Russia—Sultans Abdul Hamid, Abdul Aziz, and Murad V.—Ismail Pasha, Prince Charles I , Prince Milan IV , Prince Nicholas, the Emperors William and Francis Joseph, Queen Victoria, President MacMahon, King Humbert—Statesmen : Prince Gortchakoff, Gen. Ignatieff, Count Shuvaloff, Prince Bismarck, Count Andrassy, Earl Beaconsfield, Earl Derby, Mr Layard, Lord Loftus, Sir H. Elliot—Midhat, Edhem, Savfet, Aarifi, Server, Hussein Avni, Redif, Mahmoud Damad and Ahmed Vefik, Pashas—Ohannes Tchamith—Russian Generals · Nepokoitchitzky, Todleben, Radetzky, Zimmermann, Baron Krüdener, Gourko, Skobeleff, Shilder-Shuldner, Prince Shachovsky, Dragomiroff, Prince Imeretinski, Tchernayeff, Loris Melikoff, Tergukassoff, Dewell, Heimann, Oklobjio—Turkish Generals : Abdul Kerim, Mehemet Ali, Suleiman, Osman, Hobart, Mukhtar, Ghazi Mehemed, Feizi, Yaver, Shevket, Rauf, Fuad, Dervish, Pashas.

THE troubles in Turkey and its dependencies have now engaged a large share of the attention of the Governments and people of the principal States of Europe for three years. The negotiations and actions relating to them have brought into prominence as participants many men, some of whose names were before familiar to the public, while of others little or nothing was known, in the United States at least, till they were mentioned in the current dispatches. The personal interest is always strong in matters of history, and the course of events is often largely shaped by personal character and motives. For these reasons, and because the knowledge of personal character and motives is often of material assistance in explaining why certain turns are given to public affairs, it seems appropriate to give sketches of the lives and characters of the most prominent actors in the war, and its discussions, so far at least as they relate to those points. The sketches that follow are begun with accounts of the ruling families of the nationalities which were immediately engaged in the war, after which notices are given of the rulers of the States which participated in its discussions, then of the leading statesmen of the several nations, and of the Generals of the Russian and Turkish armies.

Alexander II., the Autocrat of Russia, is one of the best known monarchs of our age. When he acceded to the throne, Russia had long been one of the great powers of the globe; during his reign, which has now extended over more than twenty years, it has considerably grown in extent, increased in population, and advanced in civilization. At the present time the power of Russia is greater than it has been at any previous period of its history, and according to all appearances, it has not yet reached its climax. Alexander was born April 29 (old style, 17), 1818, and succeeded his father, the Emperor Nicholas, March 2, 1855. According to the wish of his father, who had been surnamed the Iron Czar, his education, like that of all the Russian princes, was to have an essentially military character, but Alexander's disposition was found not to be warlike, and under the guidance of gifted teachers, especially the poet Shukovski, the development of his mind received a quite different direction. Even during the reign of Nicholas he was anxious to keep as much as possible aloof from the war department, and to become thoroughly initiated into the administrative and diplomatic affairs of the Empire. He was repeatedly intrusted, during the absence of Nicholas from Russia, with the responsible duties of Regent of the Empire, and in 1848 he was sent by his father on a special mission to Berlin, Vienna, and other European capitals. As he ascended the throne in the midst of the Crimean war, he could not well change at once the policy of his father, but as soon as peace had been concluded, March 10, 1856, he hastened to Moscow to proclaim to the country and to the world the reformatory ideas which were to characterize his reign, and which aimed chiefly at a development of all the material and intellectual resources of his country. Rarely has the beginning of a new reign been hailed by a large people with greater enthusiasm. The Imperial promise that, " by the combined efforts of the Government and the people," the public administration should be improved, and that justice and mercy should reign in the courts of law, was received as an indication that the Emperor contemplated to substitute for the autocratic form of government an approach toward the freer and more civilized institutions of Central and Western Europe. Many acts in the first years of Alexander's reign appeared as a vigorous inauguration of a reformatory policy. Several ministers published reports on their departments which officially acquainted the entire people with facts which formerly had been treated as State secrets. The number of students at the Russian universities was no longer restricted; the difficulty of obtaining passports for traveling abroad was removed; the rigor of the press laws was relaxed; and the numerous newspapers and periodicals which were founded were allowed to publish crushing philippics against administrative tyranny, and the habitual peculations of the officials. An enthusiastic and even fantastic expectation of sweeping reforms and a radical regeneration of the Empire, and an impetuous desire to aid in the introduction of the new era, and to profit by it, spread through all classes of the population. When a law was issued for the creation of limited liability companies, no less than forty-seven companies of this kind were formed in the space of two years, with a combined capital of 358 millions of rubles, a fact full of significance, if we consider that from the founding of the first joint stock company in 1799 down to 1853, or during an entire half century previous to the commencement of the present reign, only twenty-six companies had been formed, and their united capital amounted only to 32 millions of rubles. The construction of a vast net of railways which were to traverse the Empire in all directions was planned and begun immediately after the accession of Alexander. Preparatory steps were also taken for a reorganization of the army, and the introduction of a system of public education comprising all degrees, from the lowest primary school to the university. But all these reforms were eclipsed by the abolition of serfage, a glorious act, which makes Alexander the second founder of Russia's greatness, and will assign to his reign a conspicuous place in the history of civilization. While these and other acts have gained for Alexander the deserved encomiums of the civilized world, he has justly been blamed for the barbaric severity with which his Government suppressed the Polish insurrection in 1863. Two attempts against the life of the Emperor, which were made in 1866 and 1867, the one in St. Petersburg by a member of the Russian sect of the Socialists, the other during a visit to Paris by a fanatical Pole, greatly diminished his reformatory zeal. The leaders of the anti-reformatory party made Alexander believe that the natural tendency of the reforms was the spreading of wild, communistic theories, and of a spirit of general insubordination and anarchy, and they must have made a deep impression upon the Emperor's mind, for it is a fact generally conceded by modern writers on Russia, that the policy of the Russian Government from that time has been less progressive. This is especially

apparent in the determined opposition which the Government made
to the many and urgent demands for the introduction of a constitutional form of government. In some departments, however, the
work of progress has steadily been going on. The army was a
second time thoroughly reorganized, and improvements highly commendable were made in the department of education, supplying
Russia with a national system of schools which is superior to that of
many older countries of Europe, and promises to elevate the people
ere long to a level with the best educated nations of the globe.
Alexander has generally shown himself of a mild, humane disposition, without being subject to a weak sentimentalism. Having the
good fortune of finding at the beginning of his reign a statesman
of eminent ability, Prince Gortchakoff, he has with unwavering
confidence intrusted to his Chancellor during his entire reign the
supreme direction of the Russian foreign policy. There are not
many traces of the Emperor demanding compliance with favorite
views of his own. Only in regard to the maintenance of the most
intimate relations with Germany has he on many occasions given
so emphatic utterance to his personal feelings that they may be supposed to have guided the foreign policy of the Empire.

The Emperor was married in 1841 to Maria, daughter of the
Grand Duke Ludwig II. of Hesse, and his domestic life is believed
to have been very happy. His oldest son, Nicholas, was born in
1843, and died in 1865, having shortly before been betrothed to
Princess Dagmar of Denmark, daughter of King Christian IX. and
sister of the Princess of Wales and of the King of Greece After
the death of Nicholas, Princess Dagmar married the second son of
the Emperor Alexander, who is now heir-apparent to the throne, or,
as he is called in Russia, Czarevitch. The offspring of this union
are two sons and one daughter—Grand Duke Nicholas, born May
18, 1868, and Grand Duke George, born May 10, 1871, and Grand
Duchess Xenia, born April 18, 1875. The Czarevitch has given
but few indications of his future policy; he is generally represented
as not sharing altogether his father's views as to the continuance of
intimate relations between Russia and Germany, and of being in
much more outspoken sympathy with the most advanced section
of the Pan-Slavists. He is Adjutant-General of the Emperor, General of the Infantry and of the Cavalry, Commanding General of the
Guard, and Hetman of all the Cossack troops.

Besides the Czarevitch, the Emperor has four sons, namely :

1. Grand Duke Vladimir, born April 22, 1847, and married August 27, 1874, to the Duchess Maria of Mecklenburg; 2. Grand Duke Alexis, born January 14, 1850, and well-known by his travels in the United States; 3. Grand Duke Sergius, born May 11, 1857; and 4. Grand Duke Paul, born October 3, 1860. The only daughter of the Emperor, Grand Duchess Maria, born October 17, 1853, was married January 23, 1874, to Alfred, Duke of Edinburgh, the second son of Queen Victoria of England, and heir-apparent to the throne of Saxe Coburg-Gotha.

The Emperor has three brothers, the Grand Dukes Constantine, Nicholas, and Michael. The elder, Constantine, born September 21, 1827, is Grand Admiral of the Russian navy and President of the Imperial Council. He was married September 11, 1848, to Alexandra, daughter of the late Duke Joseph of Saxe Altenburg, and has from this marriage four sons and two daughters. One of his daughters, Olga, is married to the King of Greece. Grand Duke Constantine takes a special interest in the affairs of the Church of Russia, and warmly patronizes the Society for Ecclesiastical Enlightenment, which endeavors to cultivate a better acquaintance with the churches of Central and Western Europe, and thereby to raise the Russian Church to a higher level.

The second brother, Grand Duke Nicholas, born August 8, 1831, holds the most influential position in the Russian army. He bears the title of a General of Engineers and Adjutant-General, and is President of the Supreme Council for the organization and instruction of the army. Having early shown a predilection for military studies, he received in his youth the most careful instruction in military science, and since his promotion to the high position he now holds, he had given his undivided attention to a thorough reorganization of the Russian army. On the approach of the present war, the Grand Duke proposed to the Emperor that the State should take charge of all the families which might be deprived by the war of their supporters. The request was granted by the Emperor, and has of course gained for the Grand Duke an immense popularity with the Russian army. He was appointed Commander-in-chief of the European army, and his departure for the South, on December 1, 1876, was made the occasion for a most enthusiastic ovation.

The youngest brother of the Emperor, Grand Duke Michael, was appointed Commander-in-chief of the army of operations in Asia. Grand Duke Michael was born on October 25, 1832, and received a

26

military education similar to that of his brothers Like them, he has long been invested with the highest military dignities. He is General of the Artillery, Quartermaster-General, Imperial Adjutant-General, and chief of eight Russian and several foreign regiments. He has been married since August 28, 1857, with Princess Caecilia of Baden (now called Olga Feodorovna), and has six children, five sons, Nicholas, Michael, George, Alexander, and Sergius, and one daughter, Anastasia. On February 26, 1873, the Grand Duke was appointed Governor-General of the Caucasus, an office with which the chief command of the troops is connected. The residence of the Grand Duke and his family in Tiflis has impressed upon this Asiatic city the character of European civilization. Though always very active in the discharge of his military duties, the Grand Duke has taken a special interest in promoting European civilization in the Asiatic dominions of Russia, and is regarded as a patron of science and art. When the telegraphic dispatch from Kishenev, which ordered him to cross the Turkish frontier, was received in Tiflis, the Grand Duke was already on his way to Alexandropol. The order was sent after him, and as everything had been fully prepared, could be immediately carried out. The Grand Duke was accompanied to the army by his eldest son Nicholas, born in 1859, and, therefore, now nineteen years of age.

The only sister of the Emperor, Grand Duchess Olga, born September 11, 1822, is married to the King of Würtemberg.

When the war against Turkey had been declared, the Czar, the Czarevitch, and all the adult members of the Imperial family, joined the advancing armies, the chief commanders of which, as has already been stated, were the two brothers of the Emperor.

Abdul Hamid II., the present ruler of Turkey, is the second son of the late Sultan, Abdul Medjid, and the thirty-fourth Sultan of the Ottoman Empire. He was born Sept. 22, 1842, and succeeded his brother, Murad V, August 31, 1876. Little was known of him up to the time when the revolutionary movements in Constantinople unexpectedly elevated him to the throne. His mother having died young, he was adopted by the second wife of his father, herself childless, who is very wealthy, and has made him heir to all her property It is said that his initiation into the depravities of harem life was unusually early and complete, but that his vigorous constitution withstood the excesses that undermined his brother's health. His education, like that of his brother Murad, was partly conducted by Edhem Pasha, who, in February, 1877, was appointed by him Grand Vizier. In 1867, he, with his brother Murad, accompanied his uncle, Sultan Abdul-Aziz, to the Paris Exhibition, and from this journey he derived a great fondness for the study of geography, which has ever since constituted his favorite pastime. Although he has always shown himself a staunch adherent of the Mohammedan creed, and was, therefore, supposed to sympathize as Sultan with the " Old Turkish " rather than the " Young Turkish " party, he has introduced French customs and demeanor into the daily life of those by whom he is intimately surrounded. Before he was called to the throne, he resided with his wife and two children, a boy of six years and a girl of three years, in a small palace which he had inherited from his father. Abdul-Hamid has been placed upon the throne during the greatest crisis through which the Ottoman Empire has yet passed. Though supposed to sympathize with the Old Turks, he followed during the first months of his reign the wise counsels of Turkey's greatest statesman, Midhat Pasha ; and while intimidated by the urgent demands of the Constantinople Conference, even gave his assent to Midhat Pasha's bold draft of a Turkish Constitution. But only a few weeks later the sudden discharge, from the most despicable motives, of Midhat Pasha, gave to the world an unmistakable proof of the utter incapacity and worthlessness of the young Sultan. His conduct throughout the war has confirmed the unfavorable opinion which has quite generally been formed of his character. While the Russian Czar, his sons, brothers, and nephews, are taking an active part in the campaign, and on many occasions have personally shared the dangers and privations of the war, Abdul-Hamid has not left his harem for a single day, and what has become known of his words and deeds, has only exerted a chilling influence upon the demoralized Turkish army. When, therefore, a report spread in July, 1877, that Abdul-Hamid, being tired of the cares of government, intended to resign in favor of his cousin, Izzedin Pasha, the eldest son of Abdul Aziz, it found ready credence.

Abdul Aziz, who ruled over the Ottoman Empire when the insurrection of 1875 began, was the thirty-second Sultan. He was born Feb. 9, 1830, and succeeded his brother, Abdul Medjid, June 25, 1861. His early life and the first years of his reign awakened a general hope that he would inaugurate an era of reform, and possibly regenerate the decaying Empire. These hopes were, however, doomed to disappointment, and the Empire during his reign rapidly advanced on the road to ruin and dissolution. Turkey had at this time many statesmen of more than ordinary ability, who were anxious to arrest the progressive decay of the Empire, and to place the country on a level with the civilized nations of Europe and America. But their advice was not heeded; and the Sultan, indifferent about the financial ruin of the country, and the dangers which threatened its very existence, wasted the greater part of the loans by which some of his ministers hoped to restore the national credit, for the most trivial purposes. The feeble hold which the Ottoman Porte had had for some time of its Christian dependencies, was still further weakened by still further concessions which were extorted by the Rumanians and Servians. In Rumania, the election of Prince Charles of Hohenzollern secured the permanent conversion of this country from an elective into a hereditary monarchy, and was an important approach toward its entire independence. In Servia, the Turkish garrison had to be withdrawn from the fortress of Belgrade, and complete political autonomy to be granted. The ruler of Egypt, Ismail Pasha, succeeded in obtaining the higher title of Khedive, nearly all the prerogatives of an independent sovereign and a change of the law of succession in Egypt, so as to make it conform to that prevailing in all the Christian States of Europe. When the insurrection in Herzegovina, in 1875, involved the Empire in new and immediate dangers, the Sultan, although only forty-five years of age, bore in his body and mind the marks of utter senile infirmity. The insatiable avarice which prompted him to appropriate, even in the most imperilled condition of the country, all the money that could be raised for personal purposes, would have hastened the downfall of the Empire, had not two of the greatest Turkish statesmen, Hussein Avni Pasha and Midhat Pasha, brought his reign to a sudden end, by proclaiming Murad V, the son of the late Sultan Abdul Medjid, and nephew of Abdul Aziz, and by forcibly dethroning Abdul Aziz. The dethroned Sultan survived his fate only for a few weeks, and his sudden death was declared by the testimony of a number of physicians to have been caused by suicide.

Sultan Murad V., the eldest son of the late Sultan Abdul Medjid, and elder brother of the present Sultan, Abdul Hamid, occupied the throne of the Ottoman Empire for a few weeks only. He was born September 21, 1840, and was educated together with his brother, Abdul Hamid. During their stay in France, Murad gave himself up to dissipations which seriously undermined his health. Having returned to Constantinople, he continued his excesses, and shattered his entire system by intemperate habits. After the accession of his uncle, Abdul Aziz, to the throne in 1861, he was treated very harshly, and shut out from all public affairs, as his uncle was anxious to change the law of succession, and to leave the throne to his own son, Izzedin, in the place of Murad, who, according to the Turkish law, was the heir-apparent, because he was the next oldest male member of the Imperial family born in the Imperial harem. Upon the dethronement of his uncle by a palace revolution, on May 30, 1876, Murad was called to the throne, and—the first instance in Turkish history—was proclaimed as "Emperor by the grace of God and the will of the nation." Soon, however, it became evident that the condition, both of his mind and his bodily health, made him utterly unfit for being the head of the State in these troubled times. In consequence, his brother, Abdul Hamid, was appointed Regent on July 29th, and on August 31st, Murad was dethroned, and Abdul Hamid proclaimed Sultan in his place. According to a letter from a person of rank in the Turkish capital, published in the London *Times* of June 15th, Murad looked upon his brother as a usurper, and declared that some day he would have to ask an account of him. He also declared himself strongly in favor of peace, as the country had the misfortune of no longer possessing a good administration. The letter in the *Times* produced a great sensation, and the Turkish Government deemed it necessary to publish an official denial of all the assertions contained in it.

Ismail Pasha, the ruler of Egypt, is the second son of the great warrior, Ibrahim Pasha, and grandson of Mehemet Ali, the first Viceroy of Egypt. He was born in 1830, and received his education in Paris He acceded to the Government of Egypt in 1863, after the death of his uncle, Said Pasha. His reign abounds in important events. The opening of the Suez Canal in 1869, which was attended by the Empress of France, the Emperor of Austria, the Crown Prince of Prussia, and the representatives of the principal newspapers in Europe and America, foreshadowed a new era of power and independence for a country which had been so famous in the history of the ancient world. Ismail had contemplated from the beginning of his reign the severance of all connection with Turkey, and though want of sympathy of the great powers of Europe with this project caused him to desist from an open war of independence, he has gradually obtained important concessions from the Porte. By conferring upon him the higher title of Khedive, and by changing the law of succession so as to make it, in accordance with the laws obtaining in Christian Europe, hereditary in the direct line of Ismail, the Porte herself smoothed the way for the future independence of Egypt. A still more efficient preparation for this event may be found in the annexation of large tracts of land west and south of Egypt, especially of the entire kingdom of Darfoor. Even now the Khedive of Egypt rules over a country which, in point of extent, is the seventh among the large countries of the globe, and none of the others certainly has a better prospect of further territorial progress under an energetic ruler. By the convocation of an assembly of notables, a beginning was made in 1866 of introducing parliamentary government. Numerous Europeans and Americans were employed in the civil and military service of Egypt, and promoted to the highest offices, and it can hardly be doubted that the Khedive would have succeeded in establishing the entire independence of Egypt, had it not been for the utterly disordered condition of his finances. It has been a matter of surprise that the embarrassed position of Turkey in 1877 did not induce the Khedive to declare his own independence; that he even, the only one of the vassals of Turkey, came to the aid of the Sultan by sending an auxiliary force to the seat of war. But it must be remembered that the Khedive can not change his relations to Turkey without having the support, or at least the sympathy, of England, and that England at present finds it her interest to patronize Turkey.

Prince Charles I. of Rumania, the second son of Prince Charles Anthony of Hohenzollern, was born April 20, 1839. His father was a sovereign prince of Germany, until 1849, when he ceded the sovereignty over the little principality of Hohenzollern-Sigmaringen to the kindred royal house of Prussia. His son Charles was, in April, 1866, elected, almost unanimously, Prince of Rumania by a popular vote of the country. The election was accepted by the young Prince after a short hesitation, and on May 22d, he entered the capital of the country, Bucharest, where he was enthusiastically received by the people. The task of Prince Charles was extremely difficult, for the condition of the people was in many respects wretched. Hardly anything had been done for the education of the people; the state of the finances was most deplorable, and the bitter strife of opposing political parties appeared to make a stable government almost impossible. It is generally conceded that the principality has made great progress during the reign of Prince Charles The education and financial condition of the country have greatly improved, and the aim which all the political parties of Rumania have invariably kept in view, has steadily been approached. The Prince of Rumania, in common with the unanimous opinion of the leaders of all the political parties, has always conformed the foreign policy of the principality to this aim. Since the beginning of the troubles in 1875, he has alternately been ready to join the insurrection against the Porte, or to proclaim his neutrality, according as the interest of the principality appeared to demand it. After the declaration of war by Russia, the long-awaited time for proclaiming the independence of Rumania appeared to have come. Rumania declared war against Turkey, and Prince Charles thus became the first sovereign of an independent Rumanian State.

Milan IV. Obrenovitch, Prince of Servia, was born Sept. 18, 1854, and is the fourth Prince of Servia from the house Obrenovitch. His father died soon after his birth, and his mother, a Wallachian Princess, after conducting his education for some time herself, sent him to Paris, into the institution of Professor Huet. He remained there until the fourteenth year of his age, when he was elected Prince of Servia, to succeed his assassinated grand uncle, Michael III. A regency consisting of three distinguished statesmen carried on the Government in his name until August 22, 1872, when Milan assumed himself the reins of government. An immense crowd, greater than had ever been seen there before, assembled in Belgrade to witness the coronation festivities. On this, as on every subsequent occasion, the people of Servia did not conceal their ardent hope that the young Prince would succeed in wholly severing the connection of Servia with Turkey, and re-establish an independent Servian Empire. The insurrection of the oppressed Christians in Bosnia in 1875, appeared to afford the right opportunity for the realization of these hopes. In 1876, Servia declared war against Turkey, and the Servian army, which was commanded by the Russian General Tchernayeff, proclaimed Milan King of Servia ; but the disapprobation of this step by the great powers of Europe, compelled Milan to decline the offered dignity, and even the proclamation of the independence of Servia. The Servian war ended in a complete victory of the Turks, and the confidence of a large portion of the Servian people in Milan was consequently shaken. There were rumors of conspiracies against Milan, aiming at either placing Prince Karageorgevitch, the representative of a rival family, and the reputed author of the assassination of Prince Michael III., upon the Servian throne, or of uniting Servia with Montenegro under the rule of Prince Nicholas of the latter country. The treaty of peace which concluded the war between Russia and Turkey recognized the independence of Servia, and thus made Prince Milan the first sovereign of the restored Servian State.

Prince Nicholas of Montenegro is one of the most popular and idolized princes of the present age. He was born on September 25, 1841, and received his first instruction at Cettigne, under the personal inspection of his predecessor, Prince Danilo. Subsequently, he continued his studies in Trieste, and in 1855 Danilo sent him to Paris, where he entered the military academy. In the spring after the assassination of Prince Danilo, he was proclaimed Prince of Montenegro In the autumn of 1860 he married the beautiful daughter of the Waywode Vukovitch, Milena, by whom he has one son, Danilo, born in 1871, and six daughters. The assassinated Prince Michael of Servia was godfather to the first three children, and the Emperor Alexander to the others. Nicholas has made several journeys through Europe, and has been received with marked distinction at the Courts of Austria, Germany, Russia, and Italy. In Russia he was even treated as a member of the Imperial family. Prince Nicholas is a very accomplished scholar. He speaks the Servian, French, Italian, German, and Russian languages, and has distinguished himself as a poet. The best known among his poems, "*Onamo, Onamo, sa brda ona,*" (Yonder, yonder, behind that Mountain), is full of patriotic fire, and expresses the longing of the Servian nationality for deliverance and reunion. It has become a favorite song of the Servian race, not only in Montenegro, but in Servia, Bosnia, and the Servian provinces of Austria. Prince Nicholas is greatly beloved by his own people. He takes part in all the pleasures of his subjects, mixing in the athletic sports, casting the stone, pitching quoits, laughing, frolicking, quizzing; one morning firing at a mark, another sitting as umpire in a quoit match of his guard, passing the evenings at games of dexterity with his staff and his guests, in all cases taking his part of the consequences of the game in perfect good humor, and from his sheer herculean physical force always getting the best in the rough games. "I have seen him weep," writes a correspondent, "in the midst of all his guards as a poor old mother came with the cap of her only son (killed at Rogami) in her hand, to salute her

WILHELM, EMPEROR OF GERMANY.

THE EMPEROR OF AUSTRIA.

Prince in the high-street, not to ask for charity, but for sympathy. He turned to me to tell me her story, but he could hardly speak for emotion."

The Emperor William of Germany has risen during the last twelve years from the position of the head of the smallest of the so-called Great Powers to be the leading sovereign of Europe. He gained the first step toward the increase of his kingdom in 1866, when he wrested from Austria the supremacy of influence in Germany, and made Prussia the head of the North German Confederation. The war with France in 1870–'71 was followed by the union of the German States for national purposes into the German Empire, and the proclamation of William as Emperor. This position, combined with the prestige which he won through the excellence of his civil administration and the skillful handling of the German armies, has given him and his State an influence which no other power has yet ventured to question. He has been for many years the confidential friend and trusted adviser of the Czar of Russia, who is his nephew. As a member of the Tri-Imperial Alliance, he has had much to do with the consultations and discussions which have taken place in regard to Eastern affairs, and is credited with having often used his influence to smooth away the differences that have arisen between Russia and her rivals—Austria and Great Britain. The ties of relationship and personal friendship have caused him to sympathize with the Czar, and so to manage his mediations as to disarrange as little as possible the plans of the Russians.

The Emperor Francis Joseph of Austria-Hungary, although he represents the State which, next to the belligerents, has the most direct and intense interest in the settlement of the questions of the war, has taken but little active part in the movements relating to it. A weak sovereign of a State that is in a decline, his reign has been unfortunate. He came into power after the close of the revolutionary movements of 1848, when his uncle, the Emperor Ferdinand, having been proved incompetent to meet requirements of his position, abdicated, to give way to a younger man, who, it was hoped, would be able to meet the new situation with greater vigor. He brought only common abilities to face duties which required extraordinary ones. A few years after his accession, he was obliged to give up some of the best provinces of the Empire in Italy; the war with Prussia in 1866 resulted in depriving Austria of its influence

in Germany.　Austria was then obliged, in order to preserve
its existence, to arrange a compromise and divide its sovereignty
with the strongest of its disaffected nationalities, the Hungarians;
and it has since been distracted by the conflicting claims of its other
rival nationalities.　The Emperor has taken but little part in the
adjustment of these troubles, but has left them all, as well as the
negotiations with relation to Turkish affairs, involving matters
relating immediately to the internal condition of the Empire, wholly
to his chancellors.　He is supposed to be rather more in sympathy
with the German party, which is not strongly hostile to Russia, than
with the Hungarian party, which is intensely Turkish and anti-
Russian.

The Queen of England has less actual influence over the public
affairs of the nation than the head of any existing State.　Hence,
the views of Queen Victoria are really of less importance than those
of her ministers, of the members of Parliament, upon whom the
ministers depend for official existence, or even than those of prominent citizens.　The Queen is personally allied to the German
Emperor by the marriage of one of her daughters, and with the
Czar by the marriage of her second son, and might be expected to
be influenced somewhat by the consideration of these facts; on the
other hand, she can not forget that the integrity of her new title of
Empress of India is thought by many leaders of the dominant
party of her nation to be seriously imperilled by the success of the
Russians and the defeat of the Turks.　Prince Albert, the late husband of the Queen, was a strong friend of Turkey during the
Crimean war; and her Majesty, so far as she has expressed herself,
has been supposed to incline to the same side.

Marshal Marie-Edme-Patrice-Maurice de MacMahon, Duke of
Magenta, and President of the French Republic, is of Irish descent,
and was born in 1808.　He entered the military service of France
in 1825, and has served his country in many important military and
official positions.　He distinguished himself during the Crimean
war in the storming of the Malakoff at Sebastopol on the 8th of
September, 1855.　He served with success in the Italian campaign
of 1859, where he received his ducal title.　He was appointed
Governor of Algeria in 1862, but his administration was a failure.
He was a prominent commander of French troops in the war with
Prussia in 1870, in which he suffered several defeats, culminating
in the surrender of the army and the collapse of the French power

at Sedan on the 2d of September. He was wounded in the action at this place, and was obliged to retire from command, so that he escaped the mortification of personally signing the capitulation. He afterward successfully conducted the siege of Paris against the Commune. He was elected President of the Republic to succeed M. Thiers on his resignation in May, 1873. In November of the same year the term of his office as President was definitely fixed at seven years. The French Government was represented during the negotiations of 1875 and 1876, and was one of the signataries of the Andrassy note and the Berlin memorandum. During the most of 1877, the attention of President MacMahon and the French people was engrossed with the settlement of questions of internal politics, and no interference was attempted in Eastern affairs. President MacMahon is devoted to the interests of France, and his views on Eastern topics are governed wholly by the consideration of those interests. Relating chiefly to Syria, the interests have not been directly affected by anything that has yet taken place.

The present King of Italy, having been upon the throne only a few weeks, has had very little to do, officially, with the discussions to which Turkish affairs have given rise. He became king in January, 1878, upon the death of his father, King Victor Emmanuel. The late king, as King of Sardinia, participated in the Crimean war as the ally of France, Great Britain, and Turkey, against Russia. In the recent controversy, he gave his signature to the Andrassy note and the Berlin memorandum, but afterward, when Russia and Turkey went to war, committed his Government to a policy of unconditioned neutrality. The visit made by Signor Crispi in the fall of 1877 to the continental courts was supposed to be semi-official in its character, and to involve the presentation of the views of the King upon the Eastern as well as upon other questions; but nothing is publicly known of its nature further than that Crispi proposed an enlargement of Greece and the formation of a Slavic confederacy. King Humbert was trained in a period of iconoclastic revolution and of the advancement of liberal ideas. He is regarded as even more progressive and liberal than his father, whose reforms were so radical, vigorous, and bold as to astonish the whole world. He is strongly attached by personal friendship to the Crown Prince of Germany, and his views and policy with reference to the affairs of the East may be in a considerable degree affected by his sympathy with Germany. In his address at the opening of the Italian

Parliament, March 7th, he stated that he had unhesitatingly assented to the Conference of the powers, desiring to secure a durable peace for Europe, and expressed the belief that the impartiality of his government would give greater value to its counsels, while the recent history of the country would afford "a convincing argument for supporting the solutions most in conformity with justice and the rights of humanity." The views of King Humbert with regard to the final settlement are liable to be affected by the desires and movements of Austria. That Empire still possesses some Italian cities and provinces in which the Italian population is in the majority or considerable. Humbert would therefore be disposed to join any anti-Austrian combination, or if any of the Turkish territory were annexed to that Empire, to demand compensation for Italy in the cession of some of the Italian possessions of Austria.

The Chancellor of Russia, Prince Alexander Michailovitch Gortchakoff, is universally recognized as one of the greatest statesmen of the nineteenth century. He was born on July 16, 1798, and was appointed Russian Minister a few weeks before the conclusion of the Treaty of Paris, April 29, 1856. Both in point of age and of duration of office he excels all other statesmen in Europe. He is seventeen years older than Prince Bismarck, and twenty-five years older than Count Andrassy, and was intrusted with the heavy responsibility of steering the politics of one of the great world-empires six years before Bismarck, and fifteen years before Andrassy. Soon after entering upon his office, he defined his political programme by the celebrated word, "*La Russie se recueille*" (Russia collects herself), and during twenty-one years he has aimed with singular steadiness of purpose at carrying through this programme, and at accomplishing the work in which his country had failed during the Crimean war. The chief features of this policy were the greatest possible reserve in all international complications and the introduction of such reforms as would tend toward developing the immense resources of the Empire. Thus Russia is indebted to him for the long peace she has enjoyed since the Paris Treaty of 1856, and for reforms like the abolition of serfdom, two thorough reorganizations of the army, and the construction of an extensive railroad net. The abolition of serfdom in particular was not merely a philanthropic measure, but, by preparing a universal liability to military service, it was still more intended, by the sagacious statesman, as a means of strengthening the military power of the Empire. During the war between Austria and France, in 1859, Russia observed a complete neutrality. She had no sympathy with either of the belligerent powers, one of which, France, had been, during the Crimean war, her open enemy, while the other had "surprised her by ingratitudes." A few years later Gortchakoff had an opportunity to give a conspicuous proof of his statesmanship. Some of the European powers showed a disposition to meddle with the Polish question, and Austria, France, and England addressed identical notes to Russia. The answer of Gortchakoff to these notes was so firm and energetic that it put an immediate end to the diplomatic complications. Austria had even to bear with the blunt remark that it would do better to check the dangerous tendencies in its Polish provinces by measures appropriate both for its own interests and for its international relations. This defiant attitude toward Austria was maintained for several years, and Gortchakoff, on one occasion, gave vent to his anti-Austrian feelings by the contemptuous remark: "Austria is not a State, it is only a Government." On the other hand, Gortchakoff established the most intimate relations between Russia and Prussia. Though not taking an active part in the Franco-German war of 1870, the Russian Government made an unreserved display of its sympathy with Prussia, and thereby made it impossible for Austria to avail herself of the troubles of Prussia. This friendly relation continued without the slightest disturbance until and through the great Eastern war, and proved of great advantage to Russia. Only four days after the capitulation of Metz, Gortchakoff wrote the celebrated circular dispatch concerning the Pontus question, in which he informed the surprised statesmen of Europe that Russia could no longer abide by that article of the Paris Treaty which excluded the Russian flag from the Black Sea. The Cabinets of Vienna and London were very reluctant to consent to this unauthorized and one-sided repeal of an article of an international treaty; but France being powerless, and Germany on the side of Russia, they saw that further opposition on their part would be resultless, and yielded to the demand of Russia. In 1872, Gortchakoff differed from all the European Courts by refusing to acknowledge the Spanish Government of Marshal Serrano, and the views expressed by him on the probable short-livedness of that Government were soon proved to be correct by the course of events. More recently he was reported to have said that he did not mean to be extinguished like a light. He has risked the boldest step of his long diplomatic career, and while the opinions of the civilized world on the justness of this step widely differ, the consummate skill with which it has been taken and carried through, has elicited admiration on all sides. The very numerous notes and circulars which have been issued by Prince Gortchakoff during his long diplomatic career are counted among the most remarkable productions of modern diplomacy. One of the most notable documents, in a literary point of view, is a letter addressed in 1876 to Count Shuvaloff, in which he ironically criticised the "political mythology" which still tries to palm off the "old woman's story" (*vieillerie*) of the testament of Peter the Great for authentic history.

By far the ablest among the diplomatic agents of Russia at foreign Courts is General Nicholas Paulovitch Ignatieff, the Russian Ambassador at Constantinople from 1864 to the beginning of the Eastern war. He not only outshone in Constantinople all the Ambassadors of other powers, but he is undoubtedly one of the great diplomatists of the nineteenth century, and public opinion has long designated him as the only Russian statesman who will be able to fill the place of the aged Gortchakoff when it shall become vacant. Ignatieff was born in 1832, and is descended from a family which belongs to the numerous lower nobility of Russia, and which has given to the State a number of high dignitaries. He was educated for the army at one of the military academies, and became a Colonel at the early age of twenty-four. While connected as a military attaché with the Russian embassies in London and Paris, he greatly distinguished himself at the conclusion of peace between Russia and the Western Powers. In recognition of these services, his Government appointed him in 1858 Major-General. The signal success with which his first diplomatic activity had met, induced him to devote himself wholly to this career. He conceived the plan of enlarging the territory and consolidating the power of Russia in Asia, while in European questions the programme of Gortchakoff to recover gradually and to wait was consistently carried out. The wonderful increase of the Russian dominions in Asia during the last twenty-five years is chiefly the work of Ignatieff. In 1858 a treaty was concluded between Russia and China, by which the Amoor country, a territory as large as Italy, and abounding in rich harbors, was ceded to Russia. At first the Governor of Eastern Siberia was credited with this remarkable feat of Russian strategy which surprised all Europe, but subsequently it became known that Ignatieff was the real author of it. After concluding favorable commercial treaties with Bokhara and Khiva, Ignatieff was, in 1859, appointed Russian Ambassador in Peking, where during the four years of his stay he achieved wonders of diplomatic success. He inspired the Chinese with the belief that in Russia they would find a friend against England and France, and while the two latter powers extorted, by a bloody and expensive war, some commercial advantages, Ignatieff obtained the cession of a large territory of the extent of France, and the right of free trade along the entire frontier. The Chinese ambassadorship was, however, regarded by him as a stepping-stone for the great mission of his life, and to that end he acquired so perfect a knowledge of the Turkish language that subsequently at Constantinople he was the only one among the foreign ambassadors who could treat with the Sultan without any interpreter. During the Polish insurrection he was, for a short time, recalled to assist Prince Gortchakoff with his advice, being appointed at the same time Adjutant-General of the Emperor, and Director of the Asiatic Department in St. Petersburg. On July 26, 1864, Ignatieff was appointed Extraordinary Ambassador and Minister Plenipotentiary at Constantinople. His labors in this position fill some of the most interesting pages of the history of the last decade. He knew how to make Russia dreaded by all Turkish statesmen, some of whom even became his pliant tools. By showing an outspoken sympathy with the Pan-Slavist movement, he gradually accustomed the Slavic Christians of Turkey, the Turks, and the whole of Europe, to regard Russia in the light of a natural protector of the Slavs of Turkey. When he entered upon his office in Constantinople, Turkey appeared to be gaining slowly, but steadily, in strength. When the war was declared in 1877, it was said, with much truth, that by the machinations of Ignatieff the Turkish Empire had been undermined. He is described as being about the middle height, thin in person, with the strongly-marked Slavonic type of thick lips, broad face, long, thin mustache, and small, piercing gray eyes, through which, at times, passes a glare of ferocity. His wife takes a very active part in her husband's affairs, and it is said that not only no dispatches ever left Constantinople for St. Petersburg without first having been submitted to her approval, but that she has been the initiator of many of the General's most successful political inspirations.

Next to Gortchakoff and Ignatieff, Count Peter Andreyevitch Shuvaloff is regarded as the most noted Russian diplomatist. He is the scion of one of the oldest and most celebrated families of Russian nobility, and was born in 1828 at St. Petersburg, where his father was administrator of the Imperial palaces. Like Ignatieff, he received a military education, and was rapidly promoted to the highest rank, though, like Ignatieff, he never took an active part in any Russian campaign. In his early life he had little practical experience in diplomacy, as he was only for some time connected as military attaché to the Russian Embassy in Paris. In 1865, he was appointed Governor-General of the Baltic provinces. One year later, a plot against the life of the Czar, which the chief of the secret police was unable to discover, led to the elevation of Count Shuvaloff to this office, for which, on a former occasion, he had shown a special aptitude. He had scarcely been twenty-four hours in office, when he had fully cleared up the mystery of the plot, and found out that the perpetrator of the attempt was not, as had at first been believed, a Pole, but an adherent of the sect of Russian socialists which is known by the name of Nihilists. For eight years he remained at the head of this very influential, but also very burdensome office, and so great was the power wielded by him that the people gave him the nickname of Peter IV. When, finally, regard for his health compelled him, in 1873, to resign, he was intrusted with an extraordinary diplomatic mission to the English Court. He was instructed to calm the excitement of the English over the advance of the Russians in Central Asia. He was supposed to be specially fitted for this mission, as, in direct opposition to Ignatieff, he was regarded as a decided adherent of a peace policy and of the development of the resources of the Empire, and as unfavorable to the acquisition of any new territories. He had never manifested any sympathy with the Pan-Slavists, but was looked upon as their opponent. By promising, in the name of Russia, that Russian troops would not advance beyond the Oxus, and that Afghanistan would be respected as inviolable territory, he succeeded in re-establishing friendly relations between Russia and England. In order to strengthen the good understanding between the two Courts, he brought about a marriage between Maria, the only daughter of the Russian Emperor, and the second son of Queen Victoria, Alfred, Duke of Edinburgh, and heir-apparent to the German Duchy of Saxe-Coburg-Gotha The Czar rewarded these services by appointing Shuvaloff, in October, 1874, as Envoy at the British Court, in the place of the aged Brunnow, who retired. Since the beginning of the present complications in the East, he has

BISMARCK.

DISRAELI.

been less successful Diplomatic marriages have generally proved' to have little or no influence on the policy of the great European Court, and the one between the Duke of Edinburgh and the Russian Grand Duchess proved no exception. The Tory Cabinet openly took sides with the Turks, and all that Shuvaloff could hope to accomplish was to prevent English sympathy with Turkey from drifting into an open war with Russia. Like few Russian statesmen, Count Shuvaloff enjoys the special confidence of the Czar, a signal proof of which was given to him when he was instructed to solve the *mésalliance* between the Grand Duke Alexis and Miss Shukoosky.

Prince Carl Otto Von Bismarck-Schoenhausen, the Chancellor of the German Empire, has won the reputation of being the ablest of living statesmen. His astuteness and obstinacy, complementing the patriotic ambition of his master, the Emperor William, have contributed much to the success which has attended the scheme for uniting and establishing the power of the German Empire. He has represented his nation in the principal negotiations which have taken place in relation to the war, with the same skill and ability which he has exhibited in other fields of political and diplomatic activity. His movements and utterances have been anxiously watched by all the other parties interested in the struggle, both because they were those of the one statesman who thoroughly understood himself and his policy, and because they were supposed to indicate the designs of that power which could at any time turn the balance of the scale.

Count Julius Andrassy, Chancellor of the Austrian Empire, is a Hungarian, the son of the distinguished scientific and social economist, Count Charles Andrassy. He entered public life as a member of the Diet from his native town in 1847; gave all his influence to the Hungarian revolution in 1848; was an agent for the revolutionists to the Porte in 1849; and was in exile in France and England after the defeat of the revolution until he was enabled, by the amnesty of 1857, to return to his native country. He was elected to the Hungarian Diet in 1860; on the reorganization of the Austrian Empire, in 1867, he was appointed Prime Minister of Hungary, and was unanimously elected from Pesth to the Hungarian Chamber of Representatives in 1869. He succeeded Count Von Beust—the ablest Minister Austria has had since Metternich—as Minister of Foreign Affairs in 1871. He has had a prominent

27

share in all the negotiations which have taken place respecting Eastern affairs, and has had his name inseparably associated with them through the authorship of the famous "Andrassy Note" of 1875, which first combined, in a single paper, a formal statement of the grievances of the Christian populations of European Turkey, with the united demand of the powers that effectual measures be taken to redress them. His position during 1877 was one of great delicacy, but he conducted himself with much skill under the pressure of discordant counsels, preserved the neutrality of the Empire, maintained its honor, and escaped reproach.

Earl Beaconsfield, the Premier of the British Cabinet, was born Benjamin Disraeli in 1805. He acquired distinction as an author at an early age. He was first elected to the House of Commons in 1841; was Chancellor of the Exchequer under three administrations of the late Lord Derby, and was Premier during 1868. He was again appointed Premier on the final resignation of Mr. Gladstone in 1874, and has continued in that position to the present time. His wife was made Viscountess of Beaconsfield in 1868, and he himself was made Earl Beaconsfield in 1876. His course in the discussions of the Eastern Question has been signalized by a strong partisanship for the Turks, and has invoked the bitter criticisms of the Liberal party. The fact that he is of Jewish origin, has been used by the more extreme Liberal partisans as the basis of insinuations that his policy has been governed by a stronger regard for the welfare of the Jews than of the Christians.

Earl Derby, British Secretary of State for Foreign Affairs, was born in 1826, and was first elected to the House of Commons in 1848, shortly after his graduation from Trinity College, Cambridge. He had an honorable career in the House of Commons and in several public offices, in which he was known as Mr. Henry Stanley, till he succeeded to the Earldom of Derby in 1869. In 1874, Mr. Disraeli made him Secretary of State for Foreign Affairs. In this capacity, he has had charge of the diplomatic correspondence with foreign Governments, and his name has been frequently mentioned and appealed to in the discussion of British interests. He has steadfastly upheld the attitude of neutrality which was assumed by his Government at the beginning of the war, and has been regarded as a moderate, but not positive friend of Turkey. He has headed the party in the Cabinet which has opposed and counteracted the tendency of the Premier to commit the country to some embarrassing position.

As is generally the case with men who stand between two opposite factions, his course has not given satisfaction to either party. He has gained great literary distinction by his most successful translation of Homer.

The Right Honorable Austin Henry Layard, British Minister to the Sublime Porte, was born in 1817. Yielding to scholarly tastes, he started on an extensive course of travels in 1839, embracing, among other countries, a large part of the Turkish Empire, and studied the Arabic and Persian languages. He gained much distinction by his excavations and discoveries among the ruins of Nineveh, which were begun in 1845, and by his efforts to introduce the results of Assyrian studies to the public. He has filled various diplomatic stations connected with Eastern politics, and as a member of Parliament has given much attention to questions of a similar character. He was a close observer on the field of the Crimean war, and afterward spent some time in India during the mutiny of 1857–'58, endeavoring to ascertain its cause. He was a member of Mr. Gladstone's Cabinet for about a year, after which he was appointed Minister to Spain in 1869. He succeeded Sir Henry Elliot as Ambassador to the Sublime Porte at the beginning of 1877. His correspondence with his Government shows him to be strongly Turkish in his sympathies.

Lord Augustus Loftus, British Minister at St. Petersburg, was born in 1817, and has been employed in the diplomatic service of his Government since 1837. He was appointed to the Court of St. Petersburg in 1871.

Sir Henry Elliot, late British Ambassador to the Sublime Porte, was born in 1817, and has been engaged in the service of the Foreign Office since 1840. He was appointed Ambassador to Turkey in 1867, and retired from that office soon after the Conference of December, 1876.

The greatest among the living statesmen of Turkey is undoubtedly Midhat Pasha, the father of the new Turkish Constitution. He was born in 1822, at Constantinople, where his father was a kadi. His employment in the public service began at the early age of twelve; and when only nineteen years old he accompanied Faik Effendi to Syria as his secretary. After occupying, in succession, a number of different positions, he was sent during the Crimean war to put down brigandage on the eastern coast of Rumania, an errand which he accomplished with complete success. A like success attended him in 1857, when he was sent to pacify Bulgaria, and to inquire into the conduct of the ex-governors of Rustchuk and Widin. He afterward obtained a short leave of absence, during which he visited London, Paris, and the other capitals of Europe, and made himself thoroughly familiar with the institutions and civilization of some of the leading European States. In 1860 he was made a Pasha, with the rank of a Vizier, being named Governor of Nissa, to which were subsequently added the districts of Uskub and Prisrend. In 1865 he was appointed Governor-General of the eyalet of the Danube (Bulgaria), and in 1869 Governor-General of the eyalet of Bagdad. He subsequently became a member and President of the Council of Justice, and was for a short time Grand Vizier. On his resumption of the Presidency of the Council, he brought about the dethronement of Abdul Aziz, and shortly afterward escaped from the assassin of Hussein Avni Pasha. Midhat Pasha remained President of the Council of State during the reign of Murad V., and retained this position after the fall of Murad, during the first months of the reign of the present Sultan, Abdul Hamid. On June 1, 1876, Midhat published the draft of a Constitution which he proposed to introduce as the fundamental law of the Empire This document produced a great sensation throughout Europe, and Midhat prides himself upon it as the great achievement of his eventful life. He had been known in Constantinople for five or six years as the advocate of a constitutional form of government, and his position on this subject had been several times the cause of his fall. When finally the approval of the plan by Abdul Hamid had been secured, the promulgation itself was postponed by the Servian war. After Midhat Pasha, on Dec. 21, 1876, had again become Grand Vizier, he hastened to promulgate the Constitution on Dec 23d, as an offset against the demands of the Constantinople Conference, which he was unwilling to accept. The character of Midhat was a guarantee to his own countrymen and to the civilized world, that the Constitution was not intended by him as a blind for misleading the European statesmen, who were unanimous in demanding a reform of the Turkish administration, but as the real beginning of a new era in Turkish history. He began to carry out its principles with unflinching energy. His orders had a military ring. They never contained the time-honored phrase, "And may God's grace incline your heart to obey this order," but by sharp, clear commands he endeavored to convince the officials that he was in earnest in demanding prompt obedience. A clerk in the Porte who did not know how to write, and who had obtained a $2,000 clerkship for presenting a pretty Circassian slave to a former minister, was summarily dismissed. Midhat showed the same firmness in his relations to the Sultan. Abdul Hamid wished to overdraw his allowance, and the Minister of Finance, Galib Pasha, hesitated, but Midhat resolutely declared that the Sultan must observe the new laws and keep his finances within the prescribed limits, and when Galib Pasha, nevertheless, yielded to repeated demands, and sent the Sultan several millions of dollars, he was immediately removed from his office by Midhat. This firmness soon led to the fall of the Grand Vizier. The Sultan, who, like so many of his predecessors, showed a greater concern about his private finances than about the dangerous crisis of the Empire, listened to the insinuations of his brother-in-law, Mahmoud Damad Pasha, who hated Midhat from simple jealousy, and succeeded in creating a jealousy toward him in the mind of the Sultan. On February 5th the great statesman was summoned into the presence of the Sultan to be deposed. The circumstances attending the fall of Midhat are a curious illustration of the rottenness of Turkish administration. A steamer was in waiting with steam up, and Midhat Pasha had hardly arrived at the palace when soldiers appeared, and he was rather ostentatiously arrested and sent out to the steamer without being allowed to go to his house again. Even the money necessary to defray his expenses on landing in Italy was given to him at the palace, because he insisted on returning to his house for a little pocket-money. Before it was known among the people that Midhat Pasha had fallen, the steamer which took him to Brindisi was already out at sea. In England, where Midhat took up his residence, he received marked proofs of esteem. He observed great reserve in his remarks on the condition of Turkey, but expressed his firm conviction that already a national sentiment was showing itself in which Christians and Jews, as well as Mohammedans, took part. The greatness of the loss which Turkey suffered by his exile has been forcibly demonstrated by the disgraceful inefficiency of the Turkish Government during the war. All classes of the population became more and more impatient in the demand for his return, and no doubt was entertained that the Sultan would find himself compelled by the pressure of the people to recall the exiled statesman, who was now regarded as the only man who could save the country.

Midhat Pasha is the chief representative of the so-called Young Turkish party, which, while anxious to preserve the integrity of the Ottoman Empire, desires to regenerate it by introducing the institutions of Western Europe. While Grand Vizier, he earnestly enjoined upon the governments of the provinces to promote a good understanding between the different religions and races, and was indefatigable in encouraging every germ of progress, whether among Mohammedans or among Christians. For counteracting and thwarting the machinations of Ignatieff, he may be said to have done more than all the other Turkish statesmen together. Among the many examples which are related of the energy he displayed in this respect, an incident in his administration of Bulgaria is of special interest. Having carefully watched the secret movements of the Pan-Slavists in Bulgaria, he had several of the chief agitators, whom he thought to be Russian emissaries, arrested. Ignatieff at once interceded in behalf of the prisoners, and the timid Grand Vizier of that time, Ali Pasha, instructed Midhat by telegraph not to proceed any further against them, but to send a full report of their case to Constantinople. Midhat laconically replied by telegraph, " To-day, two culprits convicted, sentenced, and executed. Report will be sent." The threatening remonstrances of Ignatieff induced the Grand Vizier to send a second more urgent telegram, to which Midhat, with undisturbed laconism, replied: " Two other culprits sentenced and executed. Report follows by mail." Frightened at the rage of Ignatieff, Ali Pasha telegraphed to Midhat, "I forbid you to take any other step, upon penalty of deposition and severe punishment. I expect telegraphic report." To which Midhat replied, " Report sent by courier; the explanation will be found satisfactory. Quiet has been restored. The four last culprits will be executed immediately." During its whole history, the Turkish Empire has had few, if any, statesmen so enlightened and so energetic as Midhat Pasha ; but the number of his intelligent followers among the Young Turks has been small. Midhat Pasha converses fluently in French, but does not speak English at all. He is of middle height ; his short beard and whiskers are quite gray, although he is only fifty-five years of age He dresses in the European style, except that he wears a red fez. He impresses those with whom he converses as an eager and active man, full of good humor, but as a man also of the most determined resolution.

Edhem Pasha, who, in February, 1877, succeeded Midhat Pasha

as Grand Vizier, is less known than his predecessor. He was born in 1823 at Chio, of Circassian parents. While still a boy he was sold as a slave to the well-known Turkish statesman, Khosrev Pasha, in whose house at Constantinople he for some time performed servile duties. His master, who soon perceived the extraordinary ability of his young slave, not only gave him his liberty, but sent him, together with four other Circassian boys, to be educated in Paris. Here he remained at school from 1832 to 1835, and then at the request of his patron, studied mining for four years, during which period he traveled in France, Germany, and Switzerland. He returned to Constantinople in 1839, and was at once appointed a captain on the general staff. In this capacity he was chiefly employed in topographical work, and showed such skill that he was rapidly advanced to the rank of colonel. In 1849, he was appointed aide-de-camp to the Sultan, and after being promoted to the rank of general, he successively became chamberlain of the Sultan's palace and member of the Council of State. After the dismissal of Ali Pasha, Edhem became Minister of Foreign Affairs, and he subsequently represented his country at various European Courts, including that of Berlin, whence he was called at the close of 1876 to take the post of second Plenipotentiary of the Porte at the Conference. While chamberlain of the Sultan's palace, Edhem instructed Abdul Medjid in the French language, and became the tutor of the Sultan's children, in particular of Murad and Abdul Hamid. Like Midhat, he is an outspoken opponent of the Russian claims, but at the same time he is represented as a stauncher advocate of all the Mohammedan interests.

Savfet Pasha, the Minister of Foreign Affairs, was born in 1816. He belongs to the oldest school of Turkish statesmen. He was introduced into the diplomatic career by Ali Pasha, and became the friend of Reshid and Fuad Pashas. He entered the service of the Government at an early age, and was at first employed as a translator. Subsequently he was for some time translator of the Sultan Abdul Medjid, and later he was an influential member of the Council of the Empire. During the Crimean war he was commissary of the Danubian principalities, and in 1858 he presided over the commission which had to revise the affairs of Moldavia and Wallachia. In 1865 and 1866, Savfet represented the Sublime Porte at the Court of the Tuileries, where he was held in high esteem. After his return from Paris, he became in succession Minister of Commerce and Public Works, Minister of Justice, Minister of Public Instruction, and several times Minister of Foreign Affairs. He specially distinguished himself as a Minister of Public Instruction by founding the lyceum of Galata Serai, the university and the archæological museum of Constantinople, and a number of gratuitous schools in the capital as well as in the provinces. As Turkish Minister of Foreign Affairs, he had to preside over the International Conference of Constantinople, which met in December, 1876, for the purpose of finding, if possible, a peaceable solution of the Eastern Question. Upon him also devolved the more difficult task of declining, in the name of the Porte, nearly all the propositions emanating from the Conference as irreconcilable with the dignity of the country. The circular by which Savfet Pasha, in February, 1877, communicated to the diplomatic agents of Turkey the news of the proclamation of the new Turkish Constitution, produced considerable sensation. While in this remarkable document he laid, on the one hand, great stress upon the active part which the Sheik-ul-Islam himself had taken in drawing up the Constitution, he called, on the other hand, attention to the fact that the new Constitution was based upon the principles of freedom and equality that are found in the most liberal constitutions of Europe, and that it could therefore be expected to satisfy fully the wants of those provinces which had of late attracted the special attention of Europe

Aarifi Pasha, who succeeded Savfet Pasha as Turkish Minister of Foreign Affairs in July, 1877, is a fine scholar, being acquainted with the French and German languages, and is considered an able statesman. He was interpreter to the late Sultan Abdul Medjid; was appointed Ambassador to Austria in 1872; was recalled in 1873; was made Minister of Foreign Affairs in 1874, and Minister of Education and Justice in 1876; was again appointed Ambassador to Vienna in 1877, but was recalled in July of that year to succeed Savfet Pasha as Minister of Foreign Affairs, but was himself removed within ten days. He gained a literary reputation by translating Michaud's "History of the Crusades."

Server Pasha, one of the negotiators of the Treaty of Peace, has had considerable experience in public affairs, and especially in the Foreign department, of which he was Under-Secretary of State during the last years of Ali Pasha's life. Upon the latter's death, Server became Foreign Minister in Mahmoud Nedim's first cabinet, and subsequently went as Ambassador to Paris. In the last days

SAVFET PASHA.

A TURKISH SOLDIER PRAYING BY THE GRAVE OF A COMRADE.

of July, 1877, he succeeded Aarifi Pasha as Minister of Foreign Affairs, and in January, 1878, was sent to the Russian headquarters to negotiate the Treaty of Peace.

Hussein Avni Pasha, who, with Midhat Pasha, took a leading part in the dethronement of Abdul Aziz and the elevation to the throne of Murad V., was born in 1819 in the sanjak of Sparta. He was graduated from the military school in Constantinople in 1842, distinguished himself in the Crimean war, and was, in 1856, the Turkish delegate to the commission which was appointed to regulate the Persian frontier. Soon after, he was appointed director of the military school of Constantinople, and chief of the general staff of the army. In the war with Montenegro he was commander of a division, and after the insurrection in Candia he was appointed to the chief command of the Turkish troops in that island. He early gained the entire confidence of the two great statesmen who directed the affairs of the Empire during the first years of the reign of Abdul Aziz, Fuad Pasha and Ali Pasha—especially of the former. In 1869, he was appointed Minister of War, which position he held until the death of Ali Pasha, in 1871, when he was removed by Mahmoud Nedim Pasha, the new Grand Vizier, who even sent him into exile on a charge of misappropriation of public moneys. When Midhat Pasha became Grand Vizier, in 1872, he was permitted to return, and, under Essad Pasha, he became Minister of the Navy, and afterward of War. In 1874, he reached the goal of his ambition, the Grand Vizierate, but in this position he was unsuccessful, and when he was dismissed, in 1875, the Empire was in a much more wretched condition than when he entered upon his office. The position of a Governor-General of Smyrna, to which he was appointed, he soon resigned, in order to visit France and England. In July, 1875, he was called back to Constantinople, as the Grand Vizier, Essad Pasha, had urged upon the Sultan the necessity of calling the ablest statesman of the Empire into the Ministry. Soon after his arrival, in August, the new Ministry was formed, under Mahmoud Nedim Pasha. Hussein received the Department of War, while his enemy, Midhat Pasha, became Minister of Justice. In consequence of an irreconcilable difference of opinion between him and the Grand Vizier, as to the policy to be pursued, he was removed from his seat in the Cabinet in October, 1875, and appointed Governor-General of Brussa. The overthrow of the administration of Mahmoud Nedim Pasha, on May 11th,

and the appointment of Mehemed Rushdi as Grand Vizier, led to
his reappointment as Seraskier, or Minister of War. In order to
secure his reappointment, he found it necessary to ally himself with
the party of the Young Turkey, though he had never sympathized
with them before. The affiliation with this party also compelled
him, after becoming Minister of War, to take part in the movement
for dethroning Abdul Aziz, although the chief leader of this movement was his great enemy, Midhat Pasha. He was even the principal actor in the proclamation of Murad V., the new Sultan. As
he was known to be decidedly opposed to Midhat's plan to give
to Turkey a Constitution, the breach between the two statesmen
would undoubtedly soon have widened; but only a few weeks
after the dethronement of Abdul Aziz, Hussein was assassinated by
Hassan Bey, the adjutant of the oldest son of Abdul Aziz.

' Redif Pasha, the Turkish Minister of War in 1877, was long
commander of the Sixth corps, and subsequently became chief of
the Imperial Guard of Constantinople. He distinguished himself
in the Syria campaigns, and gained the reputation of being, next to
Abdul Kerim, one of the ablest generals of the Turkish army.
When it was deemed necessary that Abdul Kerim, who had been
designated to be the successor of the assassinated Hussein Avni
Pasha as Minister of War, should go to the front, and assume the
chief command of the European army, Redif Pasha was selected as
his successor in the Cabinet.

· Mahmoud Damad Pasha, Palace-Marshal, and a brother-in-law of
the Sultan, is best known as the person who brought about the fall
of Midhat Pasha. This he did by creating a jealousy in the mind
of the Sultan, to whom he has constant access, against his Minister.
He is a son of Fethi Ahmed Pasha, who was a brother-in-law of
the Sultan Abdul Medjid, and director of the Artillery and Fortification Bureau. ·He was for several years President of a section of
the State Council, and was in 1872 appointed to the Ministry of
Commerce, an office in which he proved so incapable, and blun-
dered so much, as to bring down all the foreign ambassadors against
him, and caused the Russian Embassy to declare that Russia would
not regard the Turkish trade laws so long as the administration
of them was in his hands. He was removed from this office, but
was reappointed to it in 1875, and again in 1876, by Sultan Murad
V. Sultan Abdul Hamid—whose sister, the Princess Jemile, he
married in 1858—appointed him to the same office in the artillery

department which his father held. His peculiar relationship with the Sultan, combined with his capacities for intrigue, has given him a position of great influence at the Court, and he has been regarded as the real director of the affairs of the Turkish Empire, so far as they were directed from the capital, during 1877.

The President of the first Turkish Chamber of Deputies, Ahmed Vefik Pasha, is regarded as the greatest Turkish scholar of the present time. There are few names more popularly known in Constantinople than that of the "Recluse of the Hissar," as he has been called, and there is no official man in Turkey who has been more often and longer in disgrace. In turns Ambassador in Persia, member of Council of State, Minister of Public Instruction, Ambassador in Paris, and again member of the Council of State, and more than once candidate for the office of Grand Vizier, he has always ended by going back to his Yali in Hissar, to dig and plant in his garden on the hill-side, and to indulge in his taste for reading and study. His friends and the popular voice attribute his ill success to his integrity. His adversaries complain of him as an intractable, quarrelsome man, and as an enthusiast, sincere, but quite impracticable. But there is no difference between friends and adversaries in recognizing the purity of his character and the grasp of his mind. He has always been known as an uncompromising adversary of foreign interference, for which he was erroneously set down as a fanatical "Old Turk." Ahmed Vefik Pasha speaks and writes English and French with facility, has considerable acquaintance with the classics, and is well versed in many branches of science. His high principle and unbending character have gained him much respect among his countrymen, and his love of justice has passed into a proverb. Among his writings is a translation into Turkish of Molière's plays. He was also among the representatives of Turkey at the Orientalists Congress at St. Petersburg.

Ohannes Tchamith Effendi, who, in February, 1877, was appointed Minister of Commerce and Agriculture, belongs to one of the most respected of the Armeno-Catholic families of Constantinople. He is considered one of the most capable and industrious of the public functionaries of the Porte. He speaks and writes French with remarkable facility, has some reputation as a historian and political economist, and has published a book in the Turkish language on logic.

The history of the last great wars in Europe has called the attention of the world to an appreciation of the importance which ingeni-

'ous plans of a campaign has for the issue of the war. As these plans are the work of the staff, the heavy responsibility of the chiefs of the staff and the great part they have in the results of the war, comes to be better understood. The chief of the Russian army on the Danube, Arthur Adamovitch Nepokoitchitzky, is looked upon as one of the most gifted Russian generals now living, and sometimes even been designated by his admirers as the Russian Moltke. He was born on Dec. 8, 1813, and is the son of a marshal of the nobility in the Government of Minsk. He began his military career in 1832 as officer in a body-guard regiment. The first campaigns in which he took part were those against the people of the Caucasus, in which he greatly distinguished himself, and won the special favor of the Czar. When the Russians, in 1849, invaded Hungary, he was appointed General, and justified the great expectations which were entertained with regard to him, by the occupation of Kronstadt and Hermannstadt and the great victory of Temesvar, which was followed by the entire submission of the Magyars. During the war between the Russians and the Turks in 1853, and in the following years, he not only sustained his military reputation, but greatly added to it by many brilliant exploits. His name is honorably connected with the passage of the Pruth by the Russian troops, with the advance of the Russians against the Turkish fortifications on the Danube, near Braila, with the capture of the town of Matchin, and with the siege of Silistria, when Nepokoitchitzky, while reconnoitering in the neighborhood of the fortress, repulsed a desperate sortie of the Turks. Subsequently he fought in the Crimea against the allied armies of England, France, and Turkey. In 1859 he was appointed President of the War Codification Committee, and in 1868 he was promoted to the rank of General of the Infantry.

Todleben, General Franz Eduard, Chief of the Russian Engineer Corps, and one of the most distinguished engineers in the world, was born in 1818, at Mitau, and entered the engineer corps in 1838. He gained the distinction which he deservedly enjoys by the planning and construction of the fortifications of Sebastopol, which he made confessedly one of the strongest fortresses in the world. The length and determination of the resistance which the Russians were enabled to offer from this position to the assaults and siege attacks of the allied forces engaged against them in the Crimean war, were made possible by the sufficiency and excellence of the works which he built. Since 1860, he has held the position of technical aide to

the Grand Duke Nicholas His principal services in the present
war were rendered in connection with the planning and execution
of the siege works around Plevna.

Radetzky, General Feodor Feodorovitch, commander of the main
division of the Russian army of the Danube, was born in July, 1820,
at Kazan, of a family who are distantly related to the Austrian
Marshal Radetzky. Having completed his studies at the Engineers'
and General Staff Academies, he was assigned to a command of engineers at Warsaw in 1839, and afterward in Grusia. The greater
part of his military life has been spent in the Caucasus, where he
distinguished himself in several brilliant actions and successful campaigns. He was appointed a Major-General in 1860, and a Lieutenant-General in 1868. In 1876 he was appointed to the command
of the Eighth army corps, with which he effected the crossing of the
Danube at Simnitza, in June, 1877, five days after Zimmermann had
crossed the same river at Braila, and participated with great credit
in the battles of the Shipka Pass.

Zimmermann, General Apollo Ernestovitch, the commander of the
corps of the Lower Danube, or the "Dobrudja Corps," at the beginning of the war, is of German descent, and was born in Livonia in
1825. He first entered the military service of the King of Wurtem-
berg. Having finished his studies at the Military Academy, he was
attached to the Russian General Staff, and was assigned to duty in
the Governments of Archangel and Olonitz. He took active part in
the Hungarian campaign of 1849, and served in the Caucasus from
1851 to 1854, where he was promoted to be a Lieutenant-Colonel.
In the Crimean war, he had, at first, the command of one of the
corps which were operating in Asia, was called to the Crimea at a
later period, where he was attached to the garrison of Sebastopol till
that post was captured, and was wounded during the bombardment.
In 1860, having become a Colonel, he participated in the campaign
against Khokand, and was made a Major-General. He took part in
the suppression of the Polish insurrection in 1862, and was made a
Lieutenant-General in 1868, and was assigned the command of the
corps with which he effected the crossing of the Danube at Braila
in the night of the 21st and 22d of June, it being the first division
of the Russian army which entered the European territory of
Turkey.

Krüdener, General Baron Nicholas Paulovitch, "the hero of Nicopolis," as he was called early in the war, is the oldest of the Russians

in the field. He was born in 1811 in Esthonia. Having studied in the School of Engineers and the Imperial Military Academy, he entered the General Staff in 1836. He was made a Major-General in 1859, and as commander of the Volhynian Life Guards, he took part in the suppression of the Polish insurrection of 1862. He was appointed in 1876 to the command of the corps which he led in the war of 1877. Success attended him at the beginning of the war. His capture of Nicopolis on the 15th of July, with 6,000 men and two Pashas as prisoners, was a brilliant achievement, and brought him praise; but the fame he thus gained was dissipated by the disaster which he suffered at the second battle of Plevna, on the 30th of July, when he was driven back with the loss of 7,000 men He afterward excused himself for his failure by showing that he had made the attack under the express orders of the Commander-in-chief. He said that he had estimated the forces of Osman Pasha at 50,000 men, and had so reported it to headquarters, but was told that the Turks had only 27,000 men, and ordered to go on and attack the position. The result was what he had foreseen and tried to avoid.

Gourko, General Joseph Vladimirovitch, the daring Russian cavalry chief, was born of an old Russian family in November, 1828. He was appointed a cornet in the Life Guard-Hussars in 1846, afterward went through the course of the School of the General Staff, and was appointed a Captain in 1852 in a regiment with which he served through the whole Crimean war. He was promoted in succession to be Captain of Horse, Commander of the Imperial Squadron in the regiment of the Czar, in 1860 Wing-Adjutant of the Czar, and in 1861 Colonel. In 1862 he was appointed a member of the commission on the emancipation of the serfs, a cause which he actively promoted. He was advanced to the rank of Lieutenant-General, and made commander of the Second division of the cavalry-guard in 1876. He engaged in the campaign in Bulgaria in advance of his division, having been placed at the head of an "advance-guard corps," whose duty it was to press forward before the army, without regard to the operations of the main force, as far and as fast as possible, and spread alarm through the Turkish population. He performed this duty with great energy. On the 27th of June he was still on the Danube; ten days later he had captured Tirnova, the old capital of Bulgaria, and found the way open to the Balkans; on the 14th of July he had, to the surprise of all who were observing the movements of the war, passed the Balkans, accomplishing in one week what former Generals had thought themselves entitled to credit for doing in two years. He continued to advance into the heart of the mountain region, with wonderful moral effect upon Europe and Turkey, till the exigencies of the Russian army compelled his recall. His special corps was dissolved, and he returned to his old command to get it in readiness to take part in the ensuing campaigns. For his services in penetrating the Balkans, he was made an Adjutant-General. Gen. Gourko's reputation increased as the war advanced, and when it closed, it was considered that he had shown himself the bravest and most skillful of all the Russian generals

Skobeleff, Michael Demetrivitch, although an officer of most distinguished service, is the youngest General, not only in the Russian, but also of all the European armies, having been born in 1845, and being now consequently only thirty-two years of age. He became an officer in the Russian army in 1863, and has performed his principal services in Central Asia. He was the most active and efficient leader in the campaign against the Khanate of Khokand, which resulted in the conquest of the country in 1875, and its annexation to the Russian Empire. He received the appointment of a General in recompense for services in this campaign. After the submission of the Khan of Khokand had been secured, he led the expedition which, in the summer of 1876, cleared the valley of Ferghana of the adherents of the pretenders, Abdurrahman and Pulad, and secured peace to the whole of the new acquisition. He served as military Governor and Commander-in-chief of the Province of Ferghana, as the late Khanate of Khokand was called after its annexation to Russia, till March, 1877, when he was ordered to join the Grand Duke Nicholas, commander of the Russian troops in Europe. His name has been mentioned repeatedly since the entrance of the Russian army into Turkish territory, and always with honor, as that of a daring, brilliant, and generally successful officer. At Simnitza, he led a reconnoitering squad of ten Cossacks which crossed the Danube to reconnoiter the opposite shore on the evening before the general crossing by the main force was to take place. At the second battle of Plevna, July 30th, he made the final attack on the Turkish position to cover the retreat of Prince Shachovsky after the day was lost. He was named as "the hero of the day" in the Russian official bulletins of the battle of Lovatz, September 3d, which was largely through his services the first success, after many reverses, which the Russians had gained for more than six weeks. He also acquitted himself with credit in the battles at Plevna, September 11th and 12th, the loss of which on the latter day, after a success on the former day, was ascribed by English correspondents to his not having been properly supported. The Russian papers find fault with General Skobeleff as being too much addicted to the "American method" of fighting, and too reckless of the lives of his men. He is described as "a tall, handsome man, with a lithe, slender, active figure, a clear blue eye, a large, prominent, well-shaped nose, and a face young enough for a second-lieutenant." At the end of the war, General Skobeleff had gained universal admiration as one of the most gallant of the Russian generals.

Shildner-Shuldner, General Jurij Ivanovitch, the Russian officer who suffered the repulse at the first battle of Plevna, was born in 1816, of a noble family of the Government of Vitebsk. He was trained in the "Nobles' Regiment" of that day, the present Constantine Military School, and was afterward appointed instructor in the regulations of the service to the late and the present Czarevitch. After serving for twenty years as commander of the battalion of infantry instruction, he was appointed in 1860 to the command of a regiment in Poland, and was actively engaged in the suppression of the insurrection. He was made a Major-General and chief of a military district in Poland in 1864, and a Lieutenant-General in 1873. In the present war, a part of his division, which was attached to General Krudener's corps, had to sustain the first shock of Osman Pasha's force at Plevna on the 20th of July. It was driven back with the loss of 2,771 men, or one-third of its strength, and the disaster led to the loss of the day and the failure of the first Russian campaign in Bulgaria.

Shachovsky, Prince Alexis Ivanovitch, the commander of the Russian left wing at the second battle of Plevna, was born in 1812, and is a lineal descendant of Rurik, the founder and first sovereign of the Russian nation. He entered the military service in 1837, but did not become an officer till 1842, and it was not till after he had served for twelve years in the Caucasus that he became a Colonel. He was not engaged in the Crimean war. He was made a Major-General in the suite of the Czar in 1860, and a Lieutenant-General in 1868. In 1876 he was assigned to the command of the 11th army corps. His corps was completely cut up at the second battle of Plevna, July 30th, and was afterward dissolved. He still remained nominally a corps commander, but was without a command.

General Dragomiroff, a Russian officer who was wounded in the Shipka Pass, was born in 1830 in the Government of Tchernigov, and entered the active army from the military school as an officer in 1849. He accompanied the Sardinian army as a Russian military plenipotentiary during the Italian war of 1849 till the battle of Solferino. He afterward served as Professor of Tactics at the Nicholas Academy from 1860 to 1869, during which period he spent two months with the Prussian army during the Austro-Prussian war of 1866 as a military attaché, and embodied the results of his observations there in a special report to his Government. In 1868, he was made a Major-General and chief of staff of the military district of Kiev, in 1872 a Major-General of the suite of the Czar, and in 1873, commander of the 14th division.

Imeretinski, Prince Alexander Constantinovitch, a young Russian General of promise, is of an Asiatic princely stock, being a descendant of the kings of Imeretia, the ancient Colchis. His father bore the title of Czarevitch of Imeretia. He was born in 1837, and received his first training in the Page-corps When eighteen years old, he entered the military service as an ensign. He served in the Caucasus from 1856 to 1859, when he returned to Russia and completed his military education. He joined the general staff as a Captain in 1862; took part in the suppression of the Polish insurrection, and for his services in that campaign was promoted to the rank of Colonel and Adjutant in the Imperial suite. In 1869, he was made Major-General and chief of staff of the Warsaw military district. He was not engaged in the field at the beginning of the campaign of 1877, but was assigned to the command of a division of the reinforcements which were sent down to the army of the Danube in August. He had the good fortune to be associated with General Skobeleff in the capture of Lovatz on the 4th of September, and to have his name made known with honor in connection with this event through all Europe. It is well-said in regard to his service on this occasion, that it is no great achievement to defeat 7,000 of the enemy with 20,000 men; but it is something to know when to bring the 20,000 against the 7,000, and to do it at the right time. Prince Imeretinski was also associated with General Skobeleff in his success at Plevna on the 11th, and his defeat at the same place on the 12th of September.

One of the most enthusiastic Panslavists among the Russian generals is Michel Gregoryevitch Tchernayeff, to whom the Government of Servia in 1876 intrusted the chief command of the Servian army. He was born in 1828, and is descended from a family belonging to the old Russian nobility. After finishing his studies in the military academy of Nicolayev, he was in 1853 attached to the corps of infantry which began the military operations on the Danube. From that time Tchernayeff took an active part in all the Russian campaigns on the Danube near Sebastopol, in the Caucasus, and in Central Asia. His advancement in the army was very rapid, and in 1864, at the age of only thirty, he attained the rank of Major-General. In the following year he was appointed Governor-General of the province of Toorkistan, which had been conquered by him for Russia. On June 20, 1876, he was placed on the retired list, and soon after he offered his services to the Servian Government, which intrusted to him the chief command of the army.

Loris-Melikoff, General Michael Tarielovitch, commander of the Russian army of operations in Armenia, is an Armenian by descent, the son of a Grusian gentleman, a merchant of Tiflis, where he was born January 1, 1826. He received his military education at St. Petersburg, and entered the army in 1843. Four years later he became adjutant of Prince Voronzoff, military governor of the Caucasus. He took part with honor in the campaign against the Tchetchentzes in 1847; he was engaged as a Major in the campaign against Shamyl in 1851, and, at the head of one thousand Cossacks, inflicted a severe defeat upon that chieftain. He distinguished himself during the Crimean war in the campaigns around Kars, and was appointed governor of that fortress after its capture in 1855. He was made a Lieutenant-General in 1863, and a General of Cavalry in 1875. He speaks fluently Turkish, Persian, Armenian, and Grusian. A few months before the declaration of war, he entered into communications with the Kurds and Karapaches in order to engage them on the Russian side, with a slight degree of success. He spoke with them in their native language, and showed himself quite familiar with their usages and views. In order to show his confidence in them, he took a number of their chiefs into his body-guard. It is said that these wild sons of the country never abused the trust he reposed in them.

Tergukassoff, General Arsas Artemyevitch, commander of the

"Erivan Corps" of the Russian army of invasion in Armenia, was born in 1819, the son of an Armenian priest, in the Government of Tiflis He was appointed an ensign in the Engineer corps in 1837, and has served continuously since 1841 in the Caucasus. He was made a General in 1865, and a Lieutenant-General and commander of a division of infantry in 1876. He has so far proved himself the most capable of the Russian commanders in Asia.

Dewell, General Feodor Danilovitch, commander of a division in the army of the Caucasus, was born in 1818, received his education in the higher school of engineers (now the Nicholas Engineer-school), and entered the service in the cuirassiers of the body-guard of the Czarevitch. He was transferred to the sapper-battalion of the army of the Caucasus in 1842, and has since that time served continuously in the Caucasus. He distinguished himself frequently in the wars against the mountaineers, gained a wide and honorable fame, and made himself formidable to the enemies of Russia by his deeds of heroic bravery. In 1856, he was a colonel of engineers in Kars, which the Russians had then captured from the Turks. Afterward he was commander of the regiment of infantry which had the honor of capturing the Circassian chieftain Shamyl. He was made a Major-General in 1865 and a Lieutenant-General in 1876. At the opening of the war in 1877 he was assigned to the command of the column of the army of invasion which had to march from Akhaltzikh to Ardahan. In capturing the latter city, he achieved the second notable Russian success of the campaign.

Heimann, General Basili Alexandrovitch, of the Russian army of the Caucasus, an officer who distinguished himself in the capture of Ardahan in May, 1877, was born at Grodno in 1823. He is of German descent. He entered the Nizhni Novgorod regiment as a "Younker" in 1839, and was transferred in 1842 to the Army of the Caucasus, with which he has ever since been connected. He became an officer in 1844, and in the next year distinguished himself in several brilliant engagements with the hostile Caucasian tribes, in one of which he was wounded and narrowly escaped being taken prisoner. He was in active service during all the campaigns till the Caucasian war was ended by the surrender of Shamyl in 1859, when he had risen to be a Colonel. In 1863 he escorted Prince Albert of Prussia during his journey through the Caucasus, for which service the Prince recommended him to the Czar, and he received the appointment of Major-General. In 1872 he was appointed Lieutenant-General and commander of a division, in which capacity he served under General Loris-Melikoff in the campaign of 1877 in Armenia. For his services at Ardahan, he received the gift of an elegant golden sword adorned with brilliants. He was less fortunate at Zewin, where his division, supported by the forces brought by General Melikoff to his assistance, suffered a crushing defeat from the Turks.

Oklobjio, General Ivan Dimitrievitch, commander of the "Rion corps" of the Russian army of the Caucasus, is, according to some accounts, a Dalmatian, according to others, a Montenegrin. He was born in 1821, received his earlier training in the Austrian Military Institutes, and afterward completed a course, with honor, in the faculty of law of the University of Padua. He entered the Russian military service in 1846 as a Second Lieutenant in the Yàgers of Prince Voronzoff, which was then in the Caucasus. He was engaged in the war against the Caucasians, but was present at the siege of Silistria in 1854. He was wounded several times during his Caucasian campaigns; and in a battle with the Turks in 1853, he became entirely deaf in one ear, and had his head so disfigured that with the consent of the Czar he afterward wore a cap instead of a helmet. He is a good fighting soldier, but he is not regarded in Russia as having very high military talent.

Abdul Kerim Pasha, who was appointed Serdar Ekrem or Generalissimo of the Turkish army in the beginning of the war, was for a long time looked upon as the ablest of the Turkish generals. He is a Turk of the old school, and his subordinates are fond of extolling the straightforwardness of his character. He was born in 1807, and received his military education in Vienna, where he went as a young officer. He has ever since retained a great predilection for the German language, which he speaks tolerably well, and especially for German newspapers and military works, which he reads regularly. He has held the rank of Mushir for more than twenty-five years. He served at first in Mesopotamia, near Diarbekr, and Erzerum. In the Crimean war he commanded the Anatolian army near Erzerum and Kars, but as the statesmen in Constantinople withheld from him the necessary supplies, he could not be successful. He took part in the campaign against Montenegro under Omer Pasha (1862), and during the Cretan insurrection he commanded the corps of observation in Thessaly. After that he was a minister on several occasions, either Minister of the Police or Minister of War. The latter position he held upon the outbreak of the war with Russia. In the war with Servia he held the chief command of the Turkish army, and upon the outbreak of the war with Russia, resigned his position as Minister of War in order to assume the supreme command of the Turkish forces in Europe. After the successful and rapid advance of the Russians beyond the Balkans he was removed on July 23, 1877, and was sent to the island of Lemnos. He is to be tried by a court-martial after the conclusion of peace. The immediate instigator of his removal was Prince Hassan of Egypt, who, having come to the conclusion that Abdul Kerim was following no definite plan, complained to the Sultan. Namyk Pasha was sent to investigate the charges made, and when he corroborated Prince Hassan's statements, Abdul Kerim was removed from the command.

Mehemet Ali Pasha, the Commander-in-chief of the Turkish forces in Bulgaria after the removal of Abdul Kerim Pasha, is a Prussian, having been born in Magdeburg, November 18, 1827. His original name was Julius Detriot, and his father was a staff-trumpeter in a regiment of Brandenburg The boy was placed in a house of business at Magdeburg, but becoming dissatisfied with the dull routine of his life there, ran away, when in his fifteenth year, and embarked as ship-boy on board a merchant vessel at Rostok, which was about to sail for the Levant. The youth was no better satisfied with life on the ship than he had been with that of the business-house. One day, while the vessel on which he had shipped was lying in the Bosporus, he observed a caique, conveying a Turkish officer. He jumped overboard, and swam toward the caique. The officer, who proved to be Ali Pasha, afterward Grand Vizier, heard his story, became interested in him, and took him under his protection. At the very outset of his career in Ali Pasha's household, he expressed his intention of changing his religion, but was advised to reflect before taking such a step. The Chaplain of the Prussian Embassy was even called in to remonstrate with him against this step, but he persisted, and was at length admitted to the new religion, with the new name of Mehemet Ali. Two years later he was sent to the military school, where he distinguished himself as one of the foremost scholars. Having completed the course of the school in 1853, he was offered a position as assistant in the institution, but declined it, preferring a more active life in the campaigns of the Crimean

war. He received a commission as Lieutenant, and went to the field
on the Danube, where he first came under fire at Silistria. In 1857,
he was a Captain at Shumla, came under the notice of Omer Pasha,
and was appointed to a position on his staff, in which capacity he
served through the Crimean war, and later in campaigns in Montenegro, Arabia, and Bosnia. He became a Colonel in 1863, and a
General, with the title of Pasha, in 1865 He served with distinction
during the insurrection in Crete, and again on the Montenegrin
frontier. In 1873, he was appointed to the chief command of the
forces in Thessaly, with the duty of suppressing brigandage, which
he discharged with great ability and creditable success. Toward the
close of 1875, he was appointed commander at Novi Bazar, in
Bosnia, and was afterward engaged in operations in Servia. While
his abilities have been well-known and acknowledged, he was, until
he was appointed to the chief commandership in 1877, kept back in
secondary places, under the jealous and foolish policy of the Turkish
politicians, which leads them to prefer, even for the most important
posts, a second-rate native Mussulman to a first-rate officer of foreign
birth. After commanding the forces in Bulgaria for a few weeks,
he was superseded by Suleiman Pasha.

Suleiman Pasha, who attracted considerable attention by the impetuosity displayed by him in the operations against Montenegro
and in the Shipka Pass, was born in 1838, in a small town of
Thrace. Like his father, he devoted himself to religious pursuits.
He received his education in some of the best medressehs of Constantinople, and pursued his studies with such diligence that the
Ulemas gave him the title of Hafuz—expounder of the Koran.
The Crimean war found him in the army, where he rose to be adjutant to Omer Pasha. Upon the conclusion of peace, he entered the
military school of Constantinople, left it in 1860, and in 1862 took
part in the campaign against Montenegro. When the insurrection
broke out in Crete, he went there as the commander of a battalion
in the Imperial Guards, and displayed such bravery that he was
given the command of a division, although he only held the rank
of Major. Even here he showed a predilection for operating
wherever the most difficulties presented themselves. Upon his
return to Constantinople, he was appointed professor in the military
school, was sent to Yemen when the revolt broke out there, and returned with the rank of Colonel. A year later, he was a Brigadier-
General and sub-director of the War School, and when, a few months

later, Ghalib Pasha died, Suleiman was appointed its first director in his place. This position he held uninterruptedly until the outbreak of the Servian war in 1876. In this position he did much to reorganize the entire system of military instruction. In the Servian war of 1876, he commanded the First division of the army of Nissa, with the rank of Ferik, or Lieutenant-General. During the short interval of peace that followed, he was a member of the commission that drew up the Turkish Constitution. In 1877, he was appointed Mushir, or Field-Marshal, and was assigned to the command in the Herzegovina. The campaign against Montenegro forms the most brilliant episode of his life. "For the first time in the history of Turkey," the Turkish papers said, "did Turkish troops set foot on the heights of Ostrok." He was afterward appointed to the command of the forces in Rumelia, and was then ordered to replace Mehemet Ali on the Lom. After the fall of Plevna, he again went to Rumelia, where he was completely defeated by Gen Gourko. He was said to have been unpopular, both with his soldiers and officers, on account of the strictness of his discipline. It is said, also, that he was very jealous of his fellow-officers, so that he does not like to co-operate with them. He is described as being, in appearance, much more like an Englishman or a North German than a Turk, being tall and well-grown, with light blue eyes, and a flowing red beard, exceedingly particular in his dress, and fond of displaying all the pomp and ceremonial of his station.

Osman Pasha, the defender of Plevna, attracted public attention to a greater degree than any of the other Turkish generals who participated in the war. His defense of Plevna ranks among the most brilliant operations of the kind, while, by his selection and fortification of this place, he displayed an ingenuity and skill which gave to him a high rank among great generals. When he gained his first successes at Plevna, and his identity was in doubt, it was stated at one time that he was Marshal Bazaine, the defender of Metz, and again that he was an American officer by the name of Crawford; but both of these stories are without foundation. Osman Pasha is a full-blooded Turk, having been born in Tokat, in Asia Minor, in 1836 He began his studies under the care of his brother, the late Hussein Effendi, Professor of Arabic in the Preparatory School at Constantinople. He studied at the military school, where he distinguished himself by his excellent scholarship, and whence he came out the first in standing, at the final examinations, as a Lieutenant.

He entered the army in 1853, and at the beginning of the Crimean war was appointed a staff officer, and sent to Shumla. After the close of the Crimean campaigns, he entered the Imperial Guard at Constantinople as a Captain, and was shortly afterward promoted to be commandant of a battalion of the Imperial Guard. With his battalion, he was sent to Crete, to assist in suppressing the insurrection which had broken out in that island. He was present in every movement of the campaign, and returned to the capital a Colonel. He was subsequently appointed Brigadier-General, General of Division, and Chief of Staff of the Fourth army corps, in which capacity he commanded a division at Widin. In reward for his eminent services in the war against Servia, he was raised to the rank of Mushir, or Marshal. In every position in which he has been placed, Osman Pasha has distinguished himself by his ability and efficiency.

Among the many foreigners who have entered the Turkish service, none probably has deserved so well of the decaying Empire as the English Captain Augustus Charles Hobart, now called Hobart Pasha, the Admiral of the Turkish fleet. Hobart Pasha is the third son of the Earl of Buckinghamshire, and was born April 1, 1822. He entered the British navy in 1835, distinguished himself in the Crimean war, and rose to the rank of Captain. Thirsting for an adventurous life, Captain Hobart quitted the active service in the English navy, which, however, continued his name in the list of retired officers. During the civil war in the United States, he commanded a swift blockade runner, the "Don," which cruised along the coast of North Carolina, and kept up maritime communications with the Southern States in spite of the Federal blockading squadron. He assumed the name of Captain Roberts, and under this name subsequently published an account of his experience, but during the war very few people knew the daring dealer in contraband as the son of the Earl of Buckinghamshire. A few years later, Admiral Farragut met Captain Hobart in London, and in the course of conversation remarked that he had great trouble with one English blockade runner named Roberts, and that he had always regretted his inability to overhaul him. When assured that Capt. Hobart and Capt. Roberts were one and the same person, the Admiral was very much amused. In the account which Hobart himself gave of his experience as a blockade runner, he stated that he made about £1,000 on each venture, and that he learned by his success that no coast of much extent

GENERAL TODLEBEN.

SULEIMAN PASHA.

could be successfully blockaded. In 1867, he was invited by the Turkish Government, which had just awakened to the urgent necessity of reorganizing its demoralized navy, to assume the difficult task. Great pecuniary inducements and the dignity which belongs to the rank of a Pasha were tendered to him, and he concluded to accept this offer. The English admiralty was greatly displeased with this step, and warned him that by entering the Turkish service he would forfeit his professional rights at home. Captain Hobart's first commission in the Turkish navy was that of Rear-Admiral. During the Cretan insurrection he was commander of the fleet which was to enforce the blockade of Crete against the Greeks. He was completely successful in this attempt, and even compelled the Government of Greece to surrender the transport "Enosis," which had taken Greek volunteers to Turkey. In reward for these services, the Turkish Government appointed Hobart Pasha, in the latter days of 1869, Vice-Admiral, and early in the following March he was made an Admiral, and Inspector-General of the entire Turkish navy. When the English admiralty asked for explanation of the active part he had taken in the suppression of the Cretan insurrection, Hobart prayed that if his name should be taken from the active list, he might remain as a retired officer. The request, however, was not complied with, and on March 19, 1868, his name was removed altogether. Not long afterward he applied for a reinstatement, and the subject was postponed. In 1869, a Liberal Ministry was installed, and the request was renewed, only to be promptly refused. In 1874, however, a Conservative Ministry having succeeded the Liberal one, Captain Hobart renewed his appeal, reciting in eloquent phrases the disgrace attending his dismissal, and reminding the Ministry of the encomiums he had earned by organizing the Turkish navy. The Earl of Derby supported this application "as a matter of Imperial policy," considering it to be of material advantage that Admiral Hobart Pasha should occupy the position he held in Turkey. The Lords of the Admiralty, therefore, consented to allow the Hon. Augustus Hobart to be reinstated in his former rank as a Captain in the Royal Navy, placing him on the retired list, with the half pay, £400 a year, and with the opportunity of rising by seniority to the rank of Retired Admiral. At the beginning of the war of 1877, Hobart Pasha attracted attention by his bold and successful exploit of running down the Danube, past the Russian batteries, with the Turkish dispatch-boat "Rethymo."

Achmed Mukhtar Pasha, the Commander-in-chief of the Turkish

troops in Asia Minor, is believed to be a son of the late Sultan Abdul-Aziz. He is one of the few pupils of the Constantinople Military School who are famous for military acquirements at home, and successively rose to be a Professor and Governor of the institution in which he was educated. He is still a young man, but his advancement in the Turkish army has been very rapid. He began his military career in 1862, as an officer of the general staff in the war against Montenegro. Later he fought in Yemen, Arabia, under the command of Redif Pasha, against the rebellious Bedouins, and during this campaign he attained the rank of a Brigadier-General. When Redif Pasha was recalled to Constantinople, Mukhtar Pasha became *Vali* (governor) of Yemen and commander of the troops of this vilayet, with the rank of a Vizier. From Yemen he was recalled in order to be appointed Governor-General of Bosnia and Herzegovina, where Dervish Pasha had been entirely unsuccessful in his efforts to subdue the insurrection. At first he gained a few successes, but his defeat in the Duga Pass seriously injured his military reputation. Against the small number of the Montenegrins he was equally unsuccessful. To the chief command of the Asiatic army he was appointed at the special request of the Minister of War, Redif Pasha, who refused to assume this position because he feared that a protracted absence from Constantinople would be equivalent to a loss of his power and influence. The opening of the Asiatic campaign strengthened the widespread mistrust in Mukhtar's military ability, and the loss of Ardahan was followed by a general clamor for his removal. Mukhtar Pasha has a kindly expression, and large, dark Oriental eyes.

Ghazi Mehmed, Chief of the Circassian Free Corps in Asia, is a son of the celebrated Circassian chieftain Shamyl, the leader of the Circassians in their last war against Russia. He was taken a prisoner with his father by the Russians, and was brought up under the supervision of the Court of St. Petersburg. His brother entered the Russian army, but he would not accustom himself to European relations, and used every opportunity to form for himself connections with the East. With the permission of the Czar he went to Constantinople ; thence he entered into communication with the Circassians of Upper Armenia who lived under Turkish rule. Upon the outbreak of the war in 1877 he avowed himself a Mussulman, and an enemy of Russia, raised a free-corps, and was sent by the Porte to Trebizond. He accompanied the Turkish expedition to

Sukhum Kaleh and Abkhasia, and exerted himself actively to excite a general insurrection of the Mohammedan tribes. He bears a striking resemblance to his father.

Feizi Pasha, Chief of Staff to Mukhtar Pasha, and the most accomplished and skillful of the Turkish generals in Asia, is a Hungarian by birth, whose proper name is Kohlman. He came to Turkey about thirty years ago, and owes his Pashalic to the late Sultan Abdul-Aziz, who was struck by his behavior at a sham fight a few years ago, and promoted him. He won renown in the defense of Kars, under Sir Fenwick Williams, in 1855. In the present war, he is credited with the completion of the defensive works around Batum, Ardahan, Kars, and Erzerum; with the able management as nominally second, though really chief in command, at the battle of Zewin, by means of which that engagement resulted in a grand Turkish victory; and by his preparation of the Deve Boyun in front of Erzerum for occupation by the retreating Turkish army, and his gallant conduct in the engagement of the 5th of November on that hill. Owing to the Turkish jealousy of foreign officers, he has been kept in a secondary position, much below that which his merits should have commanded for him, and was retired to one still more subordinate during the interval between the summer and fall campaigns. The success of Mukhtar Pasha during the summer campaign is believed to have been mostly owing to his counsels, and the belief is confirmed by the fact that after his retirement Mukhtar's good fortune deserted him. Feizi Pasha has not become wholly a Turk, for he retains many European ways in his family life.

Nedjib Pasha, also called Medjid Pasha, is about forty years old. He is a Turk by birth, but a European by education and by his mode of living. Contrary to the customs of his race, he married a Christian lady of Banialuka, in Bosnia, and since then has always lived in accordance with the manners of Western civilization. He was educated in the military school of Brussels, and spent several years in France, England, and Italy. In 1875 he commanded a brigade in the Herzegovina under Dervish Pasha. Returning to Constantinople in the early part of 1876, he joined in the conspiracy to overthrow Abdul Aziz, and was promoted by Murad V. to the rank of Lieutenant-General. During the war with Servia, he was Chief of Staff to Abdul Kerim, and upon the outbreak of the present war was appointed to the command of the First division of the Army of the Danube, with which he inflicted several defeats on the Russians.

Yaver Pasha, a Circassian by birth, is a graduate of the Military School of Constantinople, and is considered to be the most accomplished infantry commander in the Turkish army. He particularly signalized himself at the head of the chasseurs in the sorties which marked the siege of Silistria in 1854 He was appointed Minister of War by Abdul Aziz in 1871, and acquitted himself of his functions with rare honesty and zeal. After the passage of the Danube by the Russians, he was sent to aid in directing the defensive operations on the Turkish side of the Danube. Yaver Pasha is one of the handsomest men living, and, like his Circassian compatriots, is brave and adventurous even to rashness. He is noted for the singular mildness of his disposition, and his unwillingness to prosecute recalcitrant giaurs, without which he would probably long since have been appointed to the command in chief of one of the armies of the Empire.

Shevket Pasha is the Turkish officer who is charged with the responsibility for the outrages which were committed in Bulgaria in 1876. He had the command of the forces whose members committed the outrages, and should have prevented them, but made no effort to do so. It is told of him that three years ago he was a lieutenant, serving in the Herzegovina under Edhem Pasha. His commander, having a taste for drawing, sometimes made portraits of his officers, which he would send to Constantinople for the entertainment of the Sultan. Among these portraits was that of Shevket Pasha. Abdul Aziz, being struck with its appearance, directed the picture to be placed in his private gallery, and each time that he passed before it ordered the promotion of the original to a higher rank. Shevket Pasha's complicity with the Bulgarian outrages did not lose him the favor of the Porte. He was removed to a more obscure field of action for a short time, but was brought back to Bulgaria during the summer of 1877, and placed in a higher position than he had before occupied.

Rauf Pasha, who occupied various positions during the war, was born in 1838. He was nominally Minister of the Navy, but since July, 1877, he was employed on the seat of war. He served as Minister of War for a short time in October, 1877, and was appointed to the same office in the reorganized Cabinet of February 5, 1878.

Fuad Pasha is considered the best cavalry general of the Turkish army. He is a Circassian by birth, but was brought up in Constantinople, and received an excellent education. He has brought his cavalry division to a high standard of perfection. He commanded the right wing of Suleiman's army, which made the advance on Elena in the beginning of December, and with it captured that town on the 4th.

Dervish Pasha, the commander of the Turkish forces at Batum, is a Bulgarian by birth, who has apostatized from Christianity to Islamism, and was born in 1817. He first became known in a campaign in the Cassan Dagh against the Kurds. He was appointed War Minister in 1873, and afterward became Minister of the Marine. At a later period he was assigned to the command of the forces in Albania, with which he conducted, in 1876, an unsuccessful and disastrous campaign against Montenegro. He was superseded in his command by Mehemet Ali, and was shortly afterward, after the massacre of the 6th of May, 1876, appointed Governor of Salonica. In June, 1877, he was transferred from this position to assume the command at Batum, and the direction of operations in Northern Anatolia. His campaigns in this district were very successful, he having, in July, 1877, compelled the Russians to abandon, one after another, the important positions which they had occupied around Batum, and to retire to the frontier.

THIRD BOOK.

THE
EASTERN QUESTION AT THE CLOSE OF THE WAR —AN OUTLOOK INTO THE FUTURE.

THIRD BOOK.

THE
EASTERN QUESTION AT THE CLOSE OF THE WAR
—AN OUTLOOK INTO THE FUTURE.

CHAPTER I.

THE DOOM OF TURKEY.

The Turkish Power in Europe destroyed by the War—The Turks can not retain their hold upon the Autonomous Provinces—Discontent sure to spread to the other Provinces—How Bulgaria separates the Capital from the Provinces—Probable Destiny of Bosnia and the Greek Provinces—What will become of the Turks—Principles of Decay essential in the Turkish System — The Koran a Barrier to all Progress — The Mohammedan System in Conflict with Popular Government—The Turk can not be Europeanized — Fatalism—Low Condition of Education in Turkey —Amusing Illustrations—The Turkish Language an Obstacle to Scientific Instruction—Christian Schools—They tend to build up the Christian Nationalities at the Expense of the Turkish System — Debasing Effect of Polygamy — The Conscription depleting the Country of its Moslem Youth—Sanitary Deficiencies—Decline of Turkish Population—Growing Importance and Influence of the Christians—Decadence of the Turkish Official Aristocracy—Condition of Asia Minor—Account by a French Traveler—Picture by an American Missionary—Testimony of other Authors to the Ruin of the Country—The African Dependencies of Turkey—Egypt, Tunis, Tripoli —Frailty of the Tenure by which they are held—The Bedouins—The Ultimate Fate of Turkey

THE war of 1877–'78, although it has not expelled the Turks from Europe, has destroyed their power there forever. It has inflicted a greater blow upon their dominion than was given by the achievement of the independence of Greece, and the erection into semi-independence of Servia and Rumania. It has made the independence of the last two States complete, and has established in their former position of semi-independence, a new principality—Bulgaria—which, having equal natural advantages and a population equally enterprising and capable, has before it a promise of a career of at least ás rapid advance toward full independence as they enjoyed at the time of the conclusion of the peace of Paris. It is a district which already contained the most prosperous agricultural and manufacturing industries in the Empire, and which only needed a good government and the steady protection of its people, to become its richest and happiest province. However much diplomatists may seek in their treaties and their agreements with each other to restrain the natural course of events in order to preserve the balance of power in Europe, however much they may quarrel over some particular provisions of the treaty of peace, and however much they may endeavor, in order to serve their own ends or defeat their rivals, to preserve the integrity of what is left of European Turkey, the Turks have ceased to control its nationalities; and the semblance of control which is yet allowed to remain to them can not be permanent, but must pass away. The Treaty of Paris, with its provisions carefully framed to perpetuate the power of Turkey as it was, and render attempts to assail it impossible, has been gradually worn away by the friction of national and religious rights, till it was discovered to be ready to collapse under a determined assault as suddenly as the Turkish power collapsed after the surrender of Plevna; and any new instrument which may be framed by the powers will as surely be worn away under a similar friction, and become void. The Turks found it extremely difficult to manage their Christian provinces under their old system of appointing Turkish and Mohammedan administrators over them; they will find it impossible to do so after the provinces have been given governors of their own people and have become accustomed to having the administration of their affairs lodged in their own hands. Bulgaria, with autonomy, and fortified with the preparations for self-government, which it has already been able to make under the most adverse circumstances, will soon find means to rid itself of the last remnant of Turkish power. It has already, as we shall show further along, won a harder fight against the Fanariote Greeks, and popular ignorance, and lassitude than the one now before it is likely to be; and it has the example of Servia and Rumania to encourage it. The happy fate which has now befallen it, with the inspiration of ever-successful Montenegro, can only serve to increase the discontent in the other provinces, one of which, Bosnia, may be regarded as the birth-place of the late war, while the others are inhabited chiefly by Greeks, who are among the most enterprising of peoples, are always determined to possess as

good gifts as their neighbors enjoy, and are quite as averse to foreign rule as are any Slavic nationalties.

A glance at the map will show how great is the loss in territory
to Turkey by the recent changes. A careful examination of the
map of the distribution of the races and religions of Turkey, which
is given in this work, will make it manifest that this is far from being the most serious of the breaches that have been made in its
power. The new autonomous principality of Bulgaria takes more
than one-third of what is left of the European part of the Empire
after Servia and Rumania are removed from direct Turkish rule;
and this part includes nearly all the compact settlements of Turks.
The Turks, it will be noticed, are congregated in the largest masses
in the Dobrudja and North-eastern Bulgaria, which are lost to Turkey, and in the vilayet of Adrianople, where the greater part of
them fall within Bulgaria. To Turkey fall only the smaller settlements in the south-west sandwiched between compact masses of
Greeks and Bulgarians, those around Constantinople, and the scattered Turkish settlements between the capital and the Bulgarian
part of the vilayet of Adrianople. The rest of the territory is inhabited entirely by Greeks, Albanians, or Servians. This is not all.
The new Bulgaria splits the European Empire completely in two.
Leaving a very small territory around Constantinople, it wholly cuts
off Epirus, Thessaly, Macedonia, and Albania from land communication, and leaves Bosnia practically inaccessible and quite at the
mercy of Servia and Montenegro. The situation and extent of the
principality deprive the Turks of every means of counteracting the
gravitation of their Greek provinces toward Greece, and render it
almost certain that Bosnia will be pressed into union with Servia or
the new Slavic nation which may be formed in Austria-Hungary, or
absorbed in the Austrian Empire. Even if the Turks were the
most civilized and influential of the nationalities on the Balkan
peninsula, it would be difficult for them to retain their sovereignty there. As the opposite is the case; as they are the least civilized, the least active, and the least liked, a long continuance of their
rule seems impossible; and as we have seen, the situation and conformation of the Bulgarian principality can only act to hasten the
time of their removal   It is generally hazardous and unwise to predict the future of any nation; there are so many circumstances that
may suddenly change the aspect of its affairs; and the possibility
must always be taken into account that great reforms may be in-

stituted to arrest a downward tendency, and the occurrence of great crises may operate to awaken the slumbering energies of the people and excite a revival of their national life; but it is certain that there is very much in the condition and character of the Turks which makes the reduction of their Empire to very small limits, or even their total destruction, highly probable.

The principle of decay is contained in the very foundation of the Turkish system. The whole political and social fabric of a Mohammedan State is built upon the Koran. The Koran is not only the religious book, or Bible; it is also, and as much, the law book and the school book for every true Mussulman. It is regarded as containing everything that is necessary as a rule of life in the individual or the State. Whatever is not in the Koran, is held to be useless if it does not disagree with it—false, if it is inconsistent with it; in either case is liable to be rejected. While we may admit that the gift of the Koran, imperfect as it was, was a boon to the barbarous peoples upon whom it was at first conferred, in that it imposed restraints upon those who had acknowledged none before, and principles upon those who had known no principle. the gift was also a harmful one, in that it fixed a mark beyond which improvement would not be permitted to go, and would not be possible. " The great evils of the old Oriental system," says Mr. E. A. Freeman, in his " History and Conquests of the Saracens," " were despotism, polygamy, absence of law. None of these has Mohammedanism removed. It has, indeed, partially alleviated them, but, by the very fact of alleviating, it has sanctioned and stereotyped them." These few words contain, as in a nut-shell, the whole story of Turkish misrule, and of the failure of attempts at reform, and the evils under which the Empire is suffering at this day

By the law and doctrine of the Koran, the State is regarded as a theocracy. Its theory is, that the State exists by the direct will of God; that it is governed in His service, and in accordance with His foreordained decrees, and it leaves no place for the inclusion of the good and prosperity of the people and the consultation of their desires, which are now fundamental features of the Constitution of most Western Governments. It also precludes the introduction of any genuine and general system of consulting the will of the people in directing the Government, for that would be at once to set up another authority in contradiction to the one by which the head of the State holds his right to rule. On this point, Mr. Freeman again says: "The legitimate Mohammedan despot either claims to be himself the Caliph, or representative of the Prophet, or to act as the lieutenant of one who does. . . . . His will is, indeed, bridled by the precepts of the Koran and the expositions of its commentators, but the existence of this check effectually precludes the existence of any other; consequently, Mohammedanism has done really little or nothing for the political improvement of the Eastern world. No Mohammedan nation has attained, or ever can attain, to Constitutional freedom, while the same man is Pope and Cæsar, while the same volume is Bible and statute book; there is no choice but despotism or anarchy. The individual Caliph, or Sultan, may be got rid of when his yoke has became insupportable; but the institution of an irresponsible Caliph, or Sultan, can only be got rid of when the creed of Mohammed is got rid of also." This, although it was written twenty years ago, presents as accurate a picture of the Turkish nation in 1877 as if it had been said in the full light of the dethronement of two Sultans in the same year, and of the failure of the effort to satisfy the complaints of the people by the introduction of Constitutional government.

The Mohammedan system in Turkey at last finds itself in full conflict with the demand of the age for government by the people, for the people—a demand which has revolutionized every other State in Europe except Russia. It can not make a genuine submission to the demand without ceasing to be itself. No compromise is possible. A complete surrender must be made by one side or the other. In the light of the history of the last thirty years, it is impossible to doubt which side will prevail.

The theocratic system was well-adapted for the purposes which the earlier Mohammedan leaders had to carry out, and was undoubtedly a real source of strength while those purposes were prosecuted. The mission of early Mohammedanism was to overcome the nations, and convert them to the faith revealed to the Prophet. It made an army of the believers, who were kept constantly at war, going forward from one conquest to another. All their wars were holy wars. The teachings of the Koran were skillfully adapted to inflame their fanatic zeal, to make them brave, enduring, inflexible, devoted. It forbade them the enjoyments of a settled life, and gave them those which appertained to the camp. It took from them what made the present life agreeable, and promised them instead the richest

rewards in the life to come, for self-denying devotion. To destroy
what few of the attractions of home-life the Orientals knew, the
Koran was made to speak everywhere slightingly of woman. As
the pursuits of knowledge and art were not compatible with the
warlike condition, painting and sculpture were condemned as inventions of the devil, music and poetry as trifling. Hatred was instilled
against unbelievers who refused to be converted, who were further
made lawful subjects for murder or spoil. The reservation that the
conquered infidels should be permitted to purchase immunity by the
payment of a ransom, while it did not abate the zeal of the faithful,
inflamed their cupidity. Lastly, the doctrine of fatality, teaching
that all events are predestinated by God, and are inevitable, was
invented to make the soldiers reckless and insensible to danger.
"Thus," says Dr. Carl Grubler, in his "Mohammedanism, Panslavism, and Byzantism," "was everything taken away from the
believer, and nothing left to him but the duties to obey, to fight,
and to die. Mohammedanism is an iron-hearted, narrow, and strict
soldiers'-religion."

While the Mohammedans continued to lead a soldier-life, these
regulations had their fullest sway, and were a real bond of union
among them and a source of strength They were, however, un-
fitted for any other life. When the tribes ceased to war, and began
to settle, they were no longer active, or could act only in a perverted
manner; and the whole system, of which they were an essential
part, was subject to a decay, which has become more manifest as
time has removed the nation further from the conditions to which
they were adapted.

In the present century they have operated among the most powerful agencies for undermining the political and social life of the
Ottomans. They can not originate a progressive civilization, but they
may and do operate as a block to the introduction of any other civilization. As Mr. Freeman has well expressed it: "A Mohammedan native
accepts a certain amount of truth, receives a certain amount of civilization, practices a certain amount of toleration. But all these are so
many obstacles to the acceptance of truth, civilization, and toleration in their perfect shape. The Moslem has just enough of all on
which to rest and pride himself, and no longer feels his own deficiencies." As the principles of Mohammedanism are opposed to all
the ideas on which European culture rests, they forbid the successful introduction of such culture among the Turks while they remain

Mohámmedan. It is impossible to conceive of a nation as free or enlightened according to Western views of freedom and enlightenment, whose ruler, though he be a fool or an idiot as well as a debauchee, is invested with sanctity; which has no family life, which despises art and attaches no value to knowledge, and whose fatalism forbids all kinds of enterprise and every earnest, persistent effort to improve its condition, and which despises its neighbors in their strength while it cherishes its weaknesses with pride. It is therefore just what might have been expected from the nature of things that every effort to engraft European principles upon Moslem life has either totally failed, or has resulted in the creation of a ridiculous travesty. The French traveler, M. Auguste Choisy, after having carefully observed the Turks at home, both in Constantinople and in Asia, remarks that it is a mistake to believe that their capital has become a European city. "The Old Turk may wear the garments of reform, but he has only changed his clothes, and this same Turk who dresses as you do and speaks your words, no more shares your feelings, your tastes, or your ideas, than a contemporary of Solyman or Mohammed II." Another writer compares Ottoman culture to a building which has been begun at the roof without a proper foundation, and Turkey clothed in European garments to a pretentious peasant girl who has dressed herself in fine feathers and gloves, while she knows nothing about stockings and pocket-handkerchiefs. The views of these writers are corroborated by the general testimony of writers on Turkey and correspondents from the chief towns of the Empire.

The doctrine of fatalism has proved a rigid barrier to progress, and has prevented the development of everything like energy or enterprise. It teaches that as everything has been foreordained of God, nothing can be avoided, nothing can be hastened; then why struggle, why plan, why build for the future? Let everything go; it is God's will. In rare consistency with his professed faith, the Turk does let everything go. Indolence is a universal characteristic of the race Indifference to ruin and the progress of destructive agencies prevails everywhere. Foresight is rarely found. The peasant tills enough ground to afford him probably a bare living, and if the crops fail, he dies of hunger. The result in either event is accepted as the decree of fate. This doctrine, which was good, as we have shown, in war time, and in which lies in part the secret of the wonderful bravery and endurance of the Turkish soldiers, becomes a fatal one under other circumstances. One can not doubt, says Mr. Freeman, that it "had a wonderful effect in animating the spirits of the first Saracens; but its ultimate effect has been pernicious to the last degree. When the first heat of enthusiasm is over, this same doctrine leads to quite opposite results. It becomes a mere excuse for stupid and listless idleness; submission to the divine will is held to render all human exertion superfluous. Nothing in the world is so energetic as a Mohammedan nation in its youth; nothing is so utterly feeble as a Mohammedan nation in its old age."

The blighting influences of the Koran are strikingly exemplified in the low condition of education in Turkey. A liberal, thorough education is incompatible with the principles of Islam. The Koran is the universal text-book; it is the only text-book in most of the schools; and is the standard in all the people's schools, to which the teaching must conform. It is full of errors on matters of fact, but they must be taught without attempting to correct them, for it is impious to contradict what is in the Holy Book. More often, however, the teaching amounts to nothing. The instruction is quite mechanical, and consists chiefly in learning to read the characters, to recite the phrases of the Koran in an approved style, and to write a fair hand. As the book is in the Arabic language, which the children never comprehend and the teacher seldom understands, no ideas whatever are conveyed. A pupil may learn to repeat the whole Koran by heart without being able to give, or comprehending himself, the meaning of a single text. Further than this he may learn what principles of Moslem duty and outward behavior the fanatic teacher may be able to impart, prominent among which is contempt for all unbelievers. In some schools instruction is given in the four primary rules of arithmetic and in geography; but in the latter branch the teacher has to guard carefully against affording too much information, lest he come in conflict with the extremely absurd doctrines of the Koran respecting the shape and extent of the earth and the structure of the universe. Better schools have been provided in a few places; but they are only special schools, to which a limited number of privileged persons have access, and are, in no sense, popular schools, and can not contribute materially to the general education of the country. The Government has been compelled, by the pressure of the necessity of educating competent officers, to establish a number of schools of a high order to which foreign teachers have been called, but these are exceptional institutions, and stand out in striking contrast with the character of the national schools. No general improvement in the standard of education is likely to be made while the mosques remain the centers of the higher instruction and the national schools are subordinated to Mohammedanism; for real instruction would destroy the authority of the Church. A ministry of instruction has been in existence since 1847, and has made some efforts to raise the standard of education, but has accomplished nothing worthy of remark beyond securing a registry of scholars. The most earnest desires of the enlightened men, who have sought to introduce better systems into the schools, have been baffled by the conservative and bigoted prejudices of men from whom, judging by the positions they held, better things might have been expected. Some amusing anecdotes, illustrating this fact, are given in the book "Stamboul and Modern Turkdom."

The Department of Instruction, several years ago, appointed a commission to prepare a series of text-books on Ancient, Mediæval, and Modern History. The preparation of the works was given to a Christian, who, in due time, submitted the work on Ancient History to the inspection of his Mohammedan fellow commissioners. It was rejected, because it told of a certain Cyrus, who had been King of Persia, of whom the Mohammedan histories made no mention. When he was referred to the mentions of Cyrus made in the Bible, and existing on inscribed monuments standing within the territory of Turkey, the Mussulman president of the commission declared the Bible records had been falsified by the Jews and Christians, and the monumental inscriptions were an invention, and he would have none of this Cyrus. The History has not since been heard of. At another time the Sultan ordered a translation of a certain historical work made for the use of the schools. The Minister of Instruction objected to the book, when it was submitted to him, because it failed to relate that Abraham was condemned to be burned by Nimrod, as was related in some of the Mohammedan fables, and, because in giving the story of the building of Solomon's temple, it omitted to tell that the temple was built by Genii at Solomon's command. "I think,' said the Minister, "that such a book is not fit for our schools, and that we had better use the 'Lives of the Saints' instead of it." The book was printed, because the Sultan had ordered it, but it has never been introduced into the schools.

The office of a court-astrologer is still maintained at the capital. The present incumbent was, till the middle of March, 1877, Presi-

dent of the Council of Instruction, and was afterward a Senator
It is his business to calculate the lucky hours and moments for
Court festivals, and to publish an almanac every year with general
instructions of a similar character. The distinguished astronomer, Dr.
Peters, whose more recent discoveries have reflected enduring honor
on American science, visited Constantinople in 1850, with recom-
mendations from A. Von Humboldt and other distinguished scholars,
but was dismissed, it is said, because he could not compete with this
functionary. A disastrous explosion took place in the arsenal on the
day that he was introduced by the Prussian Ambassador to the
Grand Vizier, Reshid Pasha. "This Frankish astronomer," said
the Grand Vizier, "either knew beforehand that this event would
take place, and in that case he is a great villain; or he did not know
it, in which case he is an ignorant fellow; we can not have anything
to do with him anyhow."*

Other obstacles are offered to the progress of modern knowledge
by the character of the Turkish written language, which is ill adapted
to the inculcation of new ideas. The characters are syllabic, each
one representing combinations of consonanted sounds, without
reference to the vowels. The same combination of characters may
represent several words of widely different meanings, which can not
well be distinguished without knowledge of the context, or some
previous general knowledge of the subject. Such a system is, in the
nature of things, useless for teaching subjects totally foreign to the
genius of the people.

While the Mohammedan Turks are thus without education, or the
means of acquiring it, the situation of the Christian populations is
far different. Servia has established an efficient system of schools
according to the modern standard; Rumania is but little behind it
in the creation of educational advantages; and in all the Turkish
provinces of Europe the Christians have been very active, and have
accomplished wonderful things considering the disadvantages under
which they have labored. The Greeks have been particularly energetic in this enterprise, having established good schools even before
the Greek Revolution, and having now multiplied them in every
part of the Empire, where they are numerous. The Catholic Armenians, sending their young men to European institutions to be
educated, have raised themselves to a rank among the most intelli-

* "Stambul und das Moderne Türkenthum " Leipsic, 1877

gent communities of the Empire.   The Gregorian Armenians, and
the Jews, have also made a great advance within the last ten years.
The revival of education among the Bulgarians is noticed in another
place.   Numerous schools, high-schools and colleges, quite equal in
their plans and methods to the best European standards for similar
schools, are maintained by both Roman Catholic and Protestant
missionaries in Europe, Asia Minor, and Armenia.   All of these
movements are, it is true, for the advantage of Turkey, but it is the
advantage of non-Mohammedan Turkey that they promote; and
just in the measure that they build up the character and strengthen
the intelligence of this part of the people, in the same measure do
they threaten ruin to the Mussulman system.

The superiority of the non-Mussulman schools has not escaped
the attention of the more intelligent Turks.   The *Bassiret*, a leading newspaper of Constantinople, published an article on the subject
in 1873, which, after complimenting the Greeks and Armenians on
their enterprise in maintaining schools and the quality of their instruction, cited in illustration of the latter that the pupils of one of
these schools could readily compute problems and bank accounts
involving millions with the utmost accuracy, while a Mussulman
tradesman could not calculate a transaction of ten piasters without
the help of his beans.   It admitted that in the face of this difference
in knowledge, the Turks would not be able to compete with the
Greeks and Armenians, and proposed as a remedy for such a contingency, that the Government should institute an inspection of the
Greek and Armenian schools, in order, of course, though the purpose was not avowed, to reduce them to the level of the Turkish
schools.

Polygamy is one of the most active causes for Turkish decline.
It is not peculiar to the Turkish people, nor even to Mohammedans,
but has existed among the Asiatic peoples from the earliest period of
their history.   Even before the time of Mohammed, it had become so
interwoven with the national and social life of many of those nations as to have become one of the central principles around which
their institutions were formed.   Mohammed could not have abolished
it if he had tried; he could hardly have controlled it.   He regulated
it, but was far from establishing it.   It was only a coincidence that
the nations in which his faith took root were polygamous nations;
but it is one of the results of this coincidence that the most conspicuously polygamous nations of the present are the Mohammedan

ones. Polygamy and the vices which it generates will leave more or less disastrous effects, both moral and physical, upon the soundest and best organized constitutions.   These effects will be less manifest upon an active, energetic race, whose life is all out of doors, and who are engaged in constant aggression, as were the Turks of old, because they are neutralized by the predominance of the habits and influences which go to build up manly strength.   But they show themselves immediately among a people who have settled down to sedentary life, and have thereby fully exposed themselves to all enervating and destructive influences; and with such people they show themselves with steadily-increasing force.   While the nomadic Turks and the Bedouins are still hardy and aggressive, their lazier and more comfortable neighbors among the wealthier classes of Turkey and Persia have nearly reached the end of their manly race. Polygamy has the mark of barbarism in its origin.   The American political catch-word, which describes it as a twin relic of barbarism with slavery, is full of truth.   Polygamy is a real symbol of slavery, for wherever it prevails in the East, the woman is bought, and may be the slave of the man until he raises her to the condition of wife-hood.   In many Mohammedan countries, as in Circassia before it fell into the hands of the Russians, the training of girls was regarded merely as preparing them for the market, in anticipation of the day when they were to be sought by some rich lord, or taken to some capital to be delivered to the highest bidder.   The whole system of the harem is opposed to the idea of a spiritual relation between man and wife, which is the foundation of marriage in Western countries, and reduces the relation to a sensual one, established simply for the gratification of lust and the propagation of offspring.

Some of the most direct evil results flow from this view of the relation.   It gives prominence to the play of the animal qualities, and depresses, in a corresponding degree, the moral and æsthetic qualities.   With blunted spiritual conceptions, the polygamist gives himself up to a course of indulgences which exhaust his constitution. He transmits his weakness to his children, who also inherit, in an aggravated degree, the propensities whose cultivation has caused it, and thus the degradation is accelerated from generation to genera-tion until the race is exhausted and dies out.   The evil is intensified by the custom of early marriages, under which the Turkish youth are often permitted to begin the process which undermines their constitutions when hardly more than mere children.   It is a characteristic of Turkish history that few of the great families endure for more than a few generations, but that they have to be replaced from the more vigorous ranks.

The moral effects of polygamy are as plain and direct as the physical. The man does not know how to bestow an exclusive love; the woman has no hope of receiving such love. The opportunity for the culture of the nobler faculties, which is one of the richest gifts of Western marriages, is hopelessly lost to both. Home life there is none. The life of the harem is idle and listless. The wife is one of several who are rivals, and whose rivalry leads them all to nurse the less noble faculties at the expense of the nobler ones, and to substitute craft and tricks for true affection and faithful wifeliness. She is liable at any time to be supplanted by a new favorite. Divorce is easy; accomplished almost with a word. No inducement is offered for training women for a higher life, for no opportunity is given them to enter such a life. Hence the education of women is not thought to be of much importance. The mother becomes such without having received the slightest qualification for training her children, and the children emerge into youth without having received any discipline or preparation to adapt them to a manly calling. Thus that period which in Europe is regarded as most precious, and is employed in instilling the principles in which the future conduct is to be based, and for laying the foundation of a solid education, is in Turkey spent in vacuity or under the evil influences of harem-attendants. The effects of polygamy reach far beyond the families in which it is an individual feature. While the proportion of the sexes remains even approximately equal, unusual marital privileges can not be accorded to one man without reducing, in a corresponding degree, the privileges of his fellows. Hence it must always be that a large part of the male population are forever deprived of the hope of marriage; and this part is likely to be of the most robust, for it will be of the poorer people, whose ranks have been least subjected to the debasing influences of the practice. The practice of importing wives from abroad hardly lessens the evil, for the newly-bought women go to swell the already well-supplied harems, and not to the households of the enforced bachelors. A steady decrease of population is directly incurred by this condition. Since a monogamous household ordinarily furnishes the State with four children, the harem ought to afford four times as many children as it has wives; but no such rule prevails. Generally, the larger the harem, the smaller, relatively, is the number of the children. The late Sultan, Abdul Medjid, with five hundred wives and concubines, had only thirteen children, and his brother, with half as many in his harem, had five children.

The severe jealousy with which women are guarded in the East, and the restrictions which are imposed on them, leading to the adoption of practices which are regarded by civilized nations with abhorrence, must be accredited to the necessities of the institution of polygamy. The disabilities which it imposes extend even to the Christian women of Asiatic Turkey, who are compelled, by the force of custom and Mohammedan ideas, to submit to regulations which are foreign to the teachings of their faith.

The damaging effects of polygamy upon the constitution are directly exemplified in the feebleness and mortality of the Turkish children. The proportion of children who are diseased from their birth is extraordinarily large; extraordinarily large also is the proportion of early deaths. Sixty per cent. of the children in the Turkish districts die before they are five years old. The practices which operate to cause the death of children or to prevent their birth prevail in Turkish families to an alarming extent. The Koran does not prohibit abortion, and the Turkish laws which aim to prevent it, are ineffective, partly on account of their indefiniteness, partly through the complicity of the officers upon whom their execution depends in the offense, but most of all by reason of the privileges of the harem, which make an investigation substantially impossible. The author of "Stamboul and Modern Turkdom" says that "what appears in Christian societies only as an isolated offense, is in Islam a social custom, and abortion has assumed, among the Turkish population, such colossal proportions that the Government, alarmed at the desolating consequences of the evil, has for many years endeavored in vain to find an efficient remedy for it." The same author quotes an estimate from a Turkish newspaper, to the effect that about four thousand cases of abortion occur in Constantinople every year, in which the result is fatal to ninety-five per cent. of the children and two-thirds of the mothers.

The Koran limited the number of a Mussulman's wives to four, and affixed other regulations to marriage which still remain in the text, but have been so modified by interpretations and new conditions as to be of little effect. Practically, the number of a Moslem's wives and concubines is limited by his ability to support them. Wealthy Turks have as many as they want, while the poorer ones have to be contented with one apiece, or none. The degree of enervation and demoralization corresponds very closely with the size of the harem. The Turks of the wealthy classes are thoroughly indolent and sensual, while those of the lower classes are more sober and robust. The poorer Turks have saved the Ottoman race from the exhaustion with which it has long been threatened. As the higher families have died out, their places have been filled from the ranks. Every position and function in the Empire short of the Sultanate has been filled repeatedly by men of the masses, who have brought to the offices the virility which higher-born officers could not supply. The Imperial family, whose polygamy has been most excessive, has nearly run out, so that it is widely recognized that there is not a person of ordinary capacity among the heirs to the throne. Mahmoud II. was the last of the Sultans who was a man of respectable ability, and it has been asserted, with much show of truth, that the removal of the effete reigning family will be an essential condition precedent to the taking of any measures to be effective for the regeneration of the Turkish State.

Another cause which is ever active to weaken the hold of the ruling race in Turkey, is the conscription for the army, which has been confined to the Mohammedan part of the population. It removes the Turkish youth at the most vigorous period of their life, while it leaves the Christians secure in their homes, to follow their ordinary callings and raise their families. It is a cause which in the manner of its operation is peculiar to Turkey, for in all other countries the armies are recruited from the whole population; while here, the very wars which the nation is obliged to wage for its existence, contribute the more rapidly to its destruction by giving the hostile elements within its own borders unusual opportunities to increase at the expense of its vital forces. It is only within a little more than the last year that the Government has been obliged to supply a waste that had become otherwise irreparable, to make provision for the general enlistment of Christians in its armies.

The total want of knowledge of sanitary science, and the consequent lack of intelligent sanitary regulations, must be counted among the notable factors that contribute to the depletion of the country. Intelligent physicians are scarce; the people know nothing of the laws of health; and the best sanitary regulations, whenever they are attempted, are easily evaded through the corruptibility of the officers. The country is consequently exposed, almost without defense, to the ravages of all forms of disease, and experience has taught often, that it is impossible to stay the progress of an epidemic when it has been introduced into a Turkish city, till it has run its course The Empire has been repeatedly devastated by plague and cholera, and is no better defended against them now than it was in the most primitive times.

The testimonies to the steady decline of the Turkish population are so numerous that the repetition of them would be tedious. The fact is obvious and generally admitted. The author of the book "Stamboul and Modern Turkdom" says that the fact that the population is diminishing at an increasing rate, can not be denied, although it has been contradicted. The steady recession of the Ottoman element before the Greeks and Bulgarians in Rumelia, is said to be incontestible. The officers of the railroads have noticed that the Turkish towns are declining, and Bulgarians are taking the place of the former Moslem inhabitants. The ruined minarets of deserted mosques in such towns as Nissa, Widin, Lom, Florentine, Rustchuk, and others, are pointed to as evidence that the Mohammedan population is dying out ; and although there is as yet no important place in Old Servia, Bosnia, and Bulgaria, in which Islam is not represented by at least a few adherents, the number of such is constantly becoming less.* While the Turkish households in these provinces seldom contain more than two children each, Greek and Slavic families often have from five to ten children. The *Bassiret*, the organ of the Old Turkish party in Constantinople, said, in April, 1875, in an article on this subject : "The decrease of the population is visible, and has already reached such proportions that not only the defensive strength and taxable resources of the country, but also the credit of the State abroad, yes, even its existence, is threatened."

The Mussulmans recede before the non-Mussulmans wherever the two come in contact. All of the enterprise, all of the progressive force that exist in the Empire are the results of Christian or Jewish energy. Even before the Greek Revolution, the commercial and naval fleets of Turkey were manned by Greeks and commanded by Greek officers. The maritime commerce of the East is still controlled by Greeks, and all the important trade of the commercial

---

* *Die heutige Türken*, (The Turkey of To-day). By Fr. Von Hellwald and L. C. Beck, Leipzig

ports is managed by Greek and Armenian merchants The experience of the French traveler, Choisy, who went to Constantinople from Trieste in a ship of Turkish nationality, but manned by Greek and Dalmatian sailors, is the rule at most Turkish ports. The Christian populations are most numerous all' along the sea-coasts, wherever any enterprise exists or any progress is visible. This is most conspicuously true of the towns of the Macedonian and Thracian coasts, but the non-Musulmans are also a power at Alexandria and even at Constantinople, while Smyrna and Beyrut have come largely under foreign influences, and several recent writers speak of the whole west coast of Asia Minor as steadily undergoing a Grecianizing process. In Napoleon Bonaparte's time the Sultan Mahmoud II., when asked to make an unacceptable peace with Russia, boasted that Rumelia alone could furnish him enough troops with which to give an answer to seven kings. It is doubtful if Rumelia now, under the depopulation of the Turkish race and the growth of European strength could afford enough troops to put down a determined insurrection of its own Greeks and Bulgarians. The city of Brussa, the very home of the Turks, the original capital of the nation, the place to which the Sultan will flee if he is ever driven from Constantinople, is, according to M. Choisy, only half Turkish. Its industries, its spinning establishments and looms, which are quite important, " are in the hands of Europeans, chiefly English." Throughout the Empire, all those things which point to progress, which give strength, which promise a future, are in the hands of races opposed to Islam, while the Moslems possess the traits and influences which lead to decay and ultimate extinction.

Even the chief offices of the Empire are no longer controlled by Turks. Says the author of "Stamboul and Modern Turkdom": " While the level of the intellectual cultivation of the Turks was sinking deeper from year to year, the force necessary for the administration of the State was likewise in constant depreciation, so that the Government had to avail itself of European vigor, and recruit the personality of its offices from among the Christian populations ; and thus the number of Christian officers has increased every year since Sultan Abdul Medjid." The design was at first to employ such persons in routine work, without giving them positions of responsibility and influence ; but this has been abandoned under the pressure of necessity. Now, there are a large number of Christian officers employed in every ministry ; and in some bureau, as in

30

those of Customs and Foreign Affairs, the Christians have numerically half the appointments, and an overwhelming majority of those which require capacity. In all the provinces' where the Christians form a considerable fraction of the population, are Christian higher officers. Within ten years an Armenian has been Minister of Public Works; in 1877 an Armenian was Minister of Trade; Greek under-secretaries were employed in the Ministries of Foreign Affairs and Instruction, an Armenian in the Ministry of Justice; the under-Governors in Crete and Epirus, and the Governor-General of the Archipelago, were Greeks; and the Governors of the Lebanon since 1860 have been Catholics. The same work from which we have just quoted proceeds, in illustration of the growing sterility of the Turkish official aristocracy, to show how, with only a few exceptions, those persons in high positions who have distinguished themselves by their intelligence, talents, and capacity, are not of the "Stamboul race," as follows: "The father of Ahmed Vefik Pasha was a Jew converted to Islam, his mother a Greek; Grand Vizier Edhem Pasha is a Greek, who fell into the hands of the Turks when a boy, at the catastrophe of Scio in 1822; Subhi Pasha is of Morean or Peloponnessian stock, and is the son of a Greek woman; Munif Effendi, Minister of Instruction, is an Arab from Aintab; the deceased Grand Vizier, Mehemed Pasha, was of Cypriote descent; the ex-Grand Vizier, Mehemed Rushdi Pasha, was from Sinope; Midhat Pasha, from Widin; the family of the Khedive of Egypt from Kavala in Macedonia.

A book has been published in Constantinople since the beginning of the present-year, called "The Cause of the Misfortunes,"* which gives, from a Turkish point of view, a sad picture of the condition of the Empire and its decay within the last twenty years. The author, Ahmed Midhat Effendi, is attached to the Young Turkish party. He was too young at the time the leaders of the party were sent into exile in 1867, to receive the attention of the Government, but when Midhat Pasha succeeded Mahmoud Nedim Pasha as Grand Vizier, in 1872, he started a paper, the first number of which contained an article prescribing what the new Grand Vizier ought to do to retrieve the errors of his predecessor, which was expressed in so pointed a style that the journal was promptly suppressed. He is

---

* Uess-i Inkylab; first part; from the Crimean war to the accession of Sultan Abdul Hamid II. By Ahmed Midhat Effendi; Constantinople, 1295—A.D. 1878.

now principal editor of the *Takwim-i Wakaje*, or State Gazette. He regards the rule of Abdul Aziz as having been extremely disastrous to Turkey, and the period as having been one of decided decline, and makes some startling exposures of the demoralization which prevailed in different departments of the public service. The Sultan himself was, in temperament and in regard to all points of ceremonial, a typical Oriental despot, a representative of a class of characters which it was thought had disappeared under the contact of European influences, even from Turkey. He allowed no relaxation in his presence or as toward him of the honors amounting to devotion, which were due to him as Caliph of Islam and Padishah of the Ottoman Empire. Every one who approached him was required to bow to the ground forty times; no one was permitted to look him in the face. He would not allow any one but himself to be called Aziz; and if he had to sign the appointment or removal of an officer who was named Aziz, he would have the name changed in the decree to Izzet or something else. All documents, even those which related to the most insignificant affairs, must be profuse in expression of praises of him, and the invocation of blessings upon him, otherwise they would receive no attention. An example of the quality of the administration of affairs during this period is given in the recital of the fact that when the bonds for the consolidated loan were printed in Paris, a considerable number of them were issued bearing duplicates of the same number. The matter could not be concealed, and the officers charged with the printing were arrested. No further steps were taken to punish them, and the only inconvenience they ever suffered was that they were subjected to a short sequestration in their houses.

The futility of any hopes that may be entertained that the regeneration of the Turks can be accomplished through any efforts of their own, is exemplified by the narrow-minded views and the bigoted partisanship of this work, which, written by one of the most active members of the party of reform to ascertain and define the causes of the evils with which the Empire is afflicted, might be expected to embody their most advanced views respecting the future of their nation. Yet the work, while it is full of high-sounding phrases respecting the freedom and equality of all the people, without distinction of faith, abounds also in expressions and peculiarities of phraseology which show that no substantial significance is intended by these beautiful words, and that the Young Turks still intend to look upon their Christian fellow-citizens as blemishes on an otherwise beautiful body, and to give them nothing real if they can help it. It lauds polygamy as the most glorious privilege of Islam, and while it condemns the trade in negro slaves, it upholds the traffic in white girls for Moslem harems as one of the precious treasures and a palladium of the Empire. If this is the best programme that the men of new ideas have to propose for their country, how little have we to expect from those who still avow their attachment to all the old ways.

The best examples from which to judge the condition and character of the Ottomans may be drawn from Asia Minor, where they still live in their purity, and are isolated from foreign contact. There they have not been contaminated by modern ideas, have not been affected in any way by the pressure and competition of Europeans, which has forced an unnatural and spasmodic semblance of activity upon the Turks at Constantinople. Whatever traits they may show in that country are the fruits of their own nature and the workings of their system, which have been going on for six hundred years without being hastened or hindered by any external influences. Several accounts have been recently given of this region by travelers and residents, all of which corroborate each other. Among them is a very interesting picture by a French engineer, M. Auguste Choisy, who traveled through Asia Minor to study the ruins with which it is dotted, contained in his book "L'Asie Mineure et les Turks en 1875" (Asia Minor and the Turks in 1875). We have every reason to consider his observations impartial, for his errand had no reference to politics or religion, and the French, not having for many years taken any active part in the discussions of the Eastern Question, are not warped by the partisan prepossessions which infect the views of the English, Germans, and Russians His account is a sad one of ruin, desolation, indolence, thriftlessness, and poverty. The country, which was formerly one of the most prosperous and flourishing in the world, is wholly destitute of roads; trade hardly exists, and what little there is, is prosecuted by barter; and the people are given up to lassitude and indifference, try to mend nothing, and accept misfortune, decay, and ruin as part of the natural course of events which it is useless to oppose The evidences of a diminishing population prevail widely. Where a few years ago were prosperous cities, are now to be seen only clusters of miserable huts; offices are venal, the administration of justice is corrupt. An important lawsuit was the topic of conver-

sation at one of the khans, or inns, where the traveler stopped, and
the drift of the inquiries was as to which of the parties would be
able to give the most bakshish. "It is a business to be a witness,
a speculation to be a judge." The people view such spoliations as
a matter of course, and give their bakshish without complaining.
In a district that was infested with robbers, to M. Choisy's inquiry
why the people did not call for military assistance, the answer was
returned that it was enough for them to have the robbers to deal with
without being also exposed to plunder by the soldiery. At another
place the people were suffering from a scarcity of fuel, while only a
few miles away wood was abundant. This would have been remedied in any country enjoying respectable facilities for trade and
moderately passable roads, but here—and the same is the case in
nearly every part of the Turkish Empire—every mountain ridge
forms an impassable barrier, on one side of which famine may prevail, with no means of relieving it out of the abundance which may
be existing on the other side. The Turks are characterized by this
author as thoroughly indifferent beings, who vegetate from day to
day in perfect carelessness, bring all manner of evil upon themselves by their negligence, and then when the culmination of the
misfortunes they have induced comes upon them, will exclaim, "It
is the will of Allah, so it is written." They comprehend nothing
of the thirst for knowledge, the spirit of progress, the struggles for
improvement characteristic of the Western people, and have no
appreciation of the value of time, but will delay and dally, though
an emergency of life may be pending. They may be stirred up to
exertions, and made to work with great activity and pains for a
short time, but such spells are spasmodic with them and anomalous,
and are soon over, when they subside into their former indolence.
They are ready to make promises, and even to plan enterprises, but
their promises go unfulfilled and their enterprises are never carried
out, because their normal apathy overcomes them again before anything is done.

Another picture, quite similar in its outlines, is given by the Rev.
Dr. Edward Rigg, a well-known missionary of the American Board
at Sivas, in Asia Minor, in an article upon this especial subject,
which he contributed to the *Presbyterian Quarterly and Prince-
ton Review* for July, 1876. No foreigner probably has had a better
opportunity to make himself acquainted with the internal condition
of this part of the Empire, for Dr. Rigg has lived at Sivas for many

years, engaged in an occupation which brings him into friendly contact with all classes of the people. He describes, first, the material interests of the country as in a state of decay. This was illustrated in fact by the absolute prostration of that part of the land which had been recently visited by famine at the time his article was written, and which the mismanagement of the official administration rather aggravated than remedied. Trade, he says, is prostrate. Every one is in debt, so universally and so much, that it has become, in a measure, the habit to regard debt as a natural condition. The obligations bearing twelve per cent. interest, most of the people stagger for life under the oppressive burden, have no hope of relieving themselves from it, and generally never think of trying to do so. The system of fixed prices is unknown outside of the capital. An absolute want of confidence prevails in all business transactions. Deceit and falsehood are current everywhere to such an extent that every one is a habitual liar; artfulness is taught even in the family, and the detection of a falsehood involves only the shame of having managed so awkwardly as to be found out. Nothing is ever committed to writing if it can possibly be avoided, and ignorance of the first principles of mercantile science characterizes the entire people.

Indolence and unskillfulness mark all agricultural and industrial operations. The old crooked stick is still used to stir the ground instead of the plow; threshing-machines have been introduced, but find no favor, the people preferring to follow the old way of treading out the grain with oxen, even though a better way may be within their reach. The crops are still confined to the one or two kinds of grain that have been cultivated from time immemorial, and farmers limit their tillage to the fields their fathers dug; while the climate and soil would permit the addition of a great variety of productions to the crops, and rich fields are within the reach of almost every one, which he could easily add to his cultivated estate and till, if he would. While mineral resources of unknown extent and variety exist, no effort is made to develop them. Iron is brought from Europe at great expense for transportation, to be worked up in a blacksmith-shop which may be standing right over an iron mine. A fine mine of copper exists at Harpoot, from which the ore is hauled two hundred miles to Forcat to be smelted, because the furnace happens to be there, and no one has thought to put up a furnace at Harpoot, although no reason exists why it should not be done.

This inertness among the people is promoted by the incapacity and weakness of the Government. The reforms which the Sultans have promised seem not to have reached Asia Minor at all, and the attempts of the Government at reform and retrenchment, says Dr. Rigg, "would be ludicrous in the extreme were it not for the melancholy light which they cast on the threatening chasm, on whose brink the country stands." The most hopeless weakness and corruption are shown in the local and provincial governments. Justice is never administered simply for justice's sake. "It is impossible to convey to the mind of any one who has not actually seen it, any idea of the utter prostitution of the very name of government in the provincial towns, or the bold effrontery with which the highest officers will shift their ground from one untenable falsehood to another in dodging the performance of the plainest duties." The incapacity of the officers was strikingly exemplified in the case of the famine already referred to. At first the existence of famine was denied, in the face of the multitudes that were perishing; then, when denial could no longer avail, the time was spent in making out a formal statement of the case, and haggling about the manner in which the aid given should be distributed. When aid was at last sent to the country from foreign lands, those who sent and distributed it, instead of being thanked, were charged with bad motives and called hard names by the jealous officials. Even the mixed tribunals of Mohammedans and Christians which the Government has introduced, afford no practical relief from misgovernment, for even the Christian members of them "are, almost without exception, induced by cupidity, fear, lack of self-respect, and general unfitness for self-government, to retain their seats and salaries by yielding passive assent to all the machinations of their Turkish associates, and with closed eyes and placid countenances, affix their seals to all papers offered them."

The contemplation of social and religious conditions yields a similar disheartening result. "Habits transmitted from a nomadic, tent-dwelling ancestry, cause the people to dwell huddled together in narrow quarters, where filth, disease, and vice grow uncontrollable. Poverty and ignorance so rivet the chains of those habits, that even improved circumstances in these respects fail to correct them. The present age undoubtedly sees a wonderful waking up and reaching forth toward education; but even this is only a small movement as compared with the mass of the people."

Dr. Rigg ascribes the origin of all those evils to the creed of Mohammed, which has demoralized· even the Christians of the country by teaching them to lie and cheat under the guise of righteously evading oppression and tyranny. It is, he says, the source of every woe, which palsies every effort at reform throughout the Empire, and forbids the hope of Turkey ever taking its stand among the civilized nations.

These accounts are confirmed by the testimony of other travelers who have recently visited Turkey. The German Baron Von Schweiger-Lerchenfeld, in his book, "Unter dem Halbmonde" (Under the Crescent), published in 1876, which embodies the results of his personal observations in many provinces, describes the condition of affairs everywhere prevailing as giving testimony of "frightful certainty" of the rapid decay of the Empire, of general stagnation, of the total demoralization of the Government and all of its organs, of the absolute unfitness of the ruling race. Mr. James Bryce, who has recently published an account of his travels through Causasia to Mount Ararat, and his return by way of Poti, on the Black Sea, and steamer, says of the Turkish Pontic coasts[*]: "There is hardly a sail on the sea, hardly a village on the shores, hardly a road by which commerce can pass into the interior. You ask the cause, and receive from every one the same answer: misgovernment, or, rather, no government; the existence of a power which does nothing for its subjects, but stands in the way when there is a chance of their doing something for themselves."

Capt. Burnaby, the author of that popular book, "A Ride to Khiva," and no friend to the Russians, has lately traveled through Asiatic Turkey, and published an account of his observations in a book entitled "A Ride Through Asia Minor." In this work, he says that the vast resources of the country are almost entirely neglected. There are mines, and no one works them; there are soils where almost every product wanted by civilized man might be grown in abundance, but nobody cultivates them. There are no means of communication between place and place. The taxation is very heavy; the Courts of law, if not closed to the Christians, are yet of little protection to them; the Government does little or nothing for the people, and what may be squeezed out of

---

[*] Transcaucasia and Ararat. London, 1877.

the provinces is sent to Constantinople; but the Government is not oppressively tyrannical.

The attachment of the African dependencies to Turkey has been weakened, till it is now only of the most slender character. Formerly, the direct rule of the Empire extended over the whole northern coast of Africa, except the States of Fez and Morocco; now, Algiers has become a French province, Egypt and Tunis have cast off all but a nominal allegiance, and the only parts of the once extensive Turkish dominions which remain wholly loyal are Fezzan and Tripoli. Egypt, the most important dependency of the whole Empire, has been almost completely withdrawn, except in name, from Turkish dominion, and is at present halting between independence and subjection to British influences. Twice, during the present century, the integrity—almost the existence—of the Empire was threatened by the rebellion of the Viceroy, Mehemet Ali. The present Viceroy has been able to gain from the Sultan the title of Khedive, or hereditary Prince, and has, by a special decree from the Porte, had the order of succession changed in favor of his eldest son, as against the claims of his brother, who is the regular heir under the Mohammedan law. He is ambitious for independence, and has pursued a policy looking toward it during his whole reign. While he still continues to pay a tribute to the Porte, and has responded with a contingent to its call for troops, he has been engaged in great national enterprises, and in wars for conquest, without reference to his suzerain. With extensive works of internal improvement, with manufacturing establishments scattered all over the land, with Courts after the European model sitting at Cairo and Alexandria, he has advanced considerably toward providing the machinery and some of the requisites for an independent administration and a self-existing State. His great conquests in the interior of Africa have given his territories the dimensions of a great State. Thus Egypt has grown, at the expense of the authority of the Sovereign Empire, and is watching for a favorable moment to throw off its allegiance entirely. Nevertheless, Egypt is in no condition for independence. The fatal diseases of Mohammedanism have impaired its vitality, and, while it has experienced a marvelous development in some points, it has been subjected to corresponding exhaustion in others. The domestic enterprises of the Khedive have imposed fearful burdens upon the people, who can not endure the weight of taxation and labor that are laid upon them, and his wars are depleting the country of its best men, of whom it has not too many to spare. The same enterprises have imposed a debt upon the State far beyond its ability to sustain it, in consideration of which the Suez Canal has substantially passed into the hands of the English, and nearly all the productive resources of the country have been mortgaged to English and French creditors. The improvements remain to Egypt, and the spirit of enterprise which has been awakened—which will be kept up by foreign speculators—but all of its available resources are in foreign hands. The English look upon Egypt as, next to India, their nearest special interest, and are determined to have a potent voice in the decision of its fate. Whether Turkey keeps a part of its European provinces, or loses them all, Egypt is destined soon to pass out of its hands. Its most probable fate will be to become an English protectorate.

The Porte will not be able to retain Tunis long after it shall have lost Egypt. The relation of this dependency, which is at present, except as to the payment of a tribute and the furnishing of a small contingent in war, chiefly nominal, is not likely to be maintained long after the Porte has been seriously weakened and the more powerful intervening State has fallen away.

Tripoli is still governed by a Viceroy appointed immediately by the Porte, and who is as subject to the orders of the central Government as one of its provincial officers at Constantinople. It is a small State, in respect to population, and will count for very little in any question affecting the destinies of the Empire.

The Bedouins of Syria and Mesopotamia and the settled Arabs of Northern and Western Arabia form a large proportion of the Turkish subjects in Asia. They are held to their allegiance by the tradition of the Sultan's great power. When this tradition is broken by a decisive defeat, they will be no longer to be depended upon. The Bedouins dream already, it is said, of a great Bedouin Empire, which is to be set up in Syria after the Turks have been defeated by the Russians, and the Russians have in turn been driven away by the Bedouin hosts.* In the Sherif of Mecca they have a prince of the family of Mohammed, which the Sultan is not, who can set up claims to their allegiance superior to those of the Sultan.

---

* Rev. Dr. D. H. Jessup, Missionary at Beyrut, in *Foreign Missionary* (Presbyterian Board of Missions) for April, 1877.

The review of the condition of the Turkish Empire in the light of the events which are now taking place, clearly indicates that all of the European provinces will, at no distant period, be converted into European, Christian States; that Constantinople will again become a European city; that the African dependencies will pass into the condition either of independent States or of European dependencies; that Armenia will become Russian; that the Arabs will fall away soon after Turkey has been sensibly weakened and attempt an independent sovereignty of their own; and that the Turks will be driven to their home in Asia Minor, where, hemmed in on one side by the Russians, and on another by the future owners of Syria, and crowded by the enterprising Greeks on the sea-coast, they will live out what remains to them of national life, an insignificant State, without power to molest any one seriously and exposed to a process of gradual wearing away by the pressure and friction of the enterprising States which will surround them.

The London *Times* recently expressed the opinion that the result of the war, by causing the Turks to give up their hostile European Provinces, while they receive a tribute from them, and by concentrating the Mussulmans around Constantinople and in Asia Minor, will be to enable them to " create a new Ottoman power ten times stronger than if it were spread over a vast, badly-organized, and hostile territory. This might be the case were the Turks capable of becoming a progressive nation, or of being regenerated. The facts which we have cited show, however, that all the essential qualities of the Turkish character and religion, and the features which are at the roots of their life and social condition, are against any such transformation taking place. While they remain Turks they must continue to go down; and the revival of their race can be effected only at the expense of casting away everything that distinguishes them from other races.

CHAPTER II.

THE NEW STATES OF THE BALKAN PENINSULA.

I. BULGARIANS AND GREEKS.

The Nationalities that are to Rule Turkey—The Bulgarians, Greeks, Rumanians, Servians—Latent Traits of the Bulgarians—The Ancient Bulgarians—Relations of Bulgaria and the East Roman Empire—The Bogomils—The Second Bulgarian Kingdom; its Culmination and its Speedy Fall—Four Centuries and a half of Oppression and Darkness—The most Wretched People in Europe at the Beginning of this Century—The Marvelous Awakening and Speedy Advance—The First Printed Bulgarian Book—Beginning of a Movement for Education—The First Popular Schools—What has been Accomplished in Fifty Years—Newspapers—Books—School-books and Literary Works—The Ecclesiastical Struggle and the Victory of the Bulgarians—The Capacity of the People Proved—Opinions of Intelligent Travelers—Kanitz and Von Hellwald—They are Destined to Become a Leading Nation of the Earth—The Claims of the Greeks—Their Noble Ancestry—What the World Owes to Greek Learning—The Greeks the Ancient Settlers of Turkey—The Modern Greeks not Hellenized Slavs—The West Responsible for the Conquest of the Greeks—Tenacity of the Grecian Character—Greece During and Since the Revolution—Reasonableness of the Demands of Greece for Territorial Expansion—Attitude of Greece in 1876-'77—Advance into Thessaly in February, 1878—A Mistake—The Adjustment of Grecian Interests more Practicable than in case of any other Nationality of Turkey—Attitude of the Greeks toward the Slavs—Foreign Views on the Expansion of Greece—Earl Derby's Expression.

WHEN Turkish rule has come to an end, other nationalities will soon supplant the Turks in the possession and places of influence and as the predominant races of the country which they inhabit. The principal difficulty in the settlement of the Eastern Question so far has been to determine who should take the place of the Moslems as the rulers of their European provinces. This difficulty is now likely to be removed in time, in a natural way, and by the operation of natural forces which will eventually work out their own solution, whether the powers are willing to agree to it or not. The treaty of peace has already put the Balkan peninsula into the hands of the nationalities, which form the masses of its population. The question that now remains to be solved is not whether or even how soon these nationalities will come into complete possession of their inheritance, but how it shall be divided among them. A study of the map of nationalities and religions will give the reader a fair idea of the general course that must be followed by the lines of division;

(572)

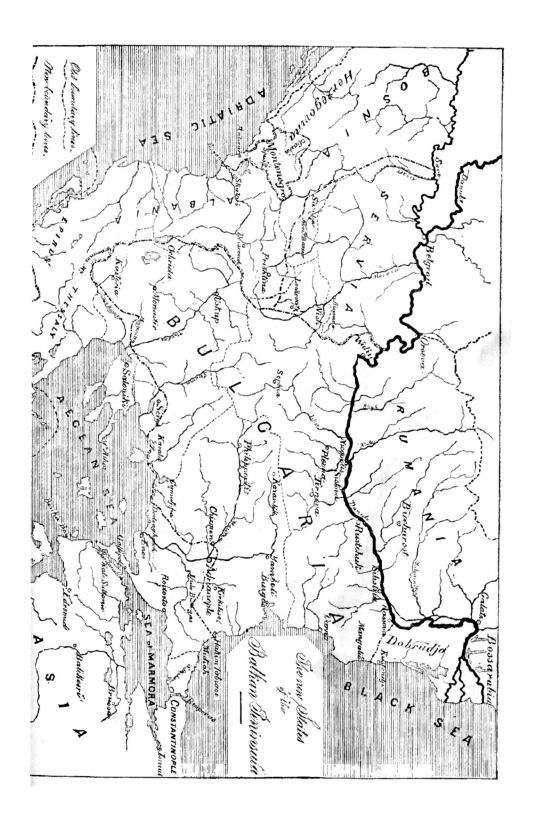

UP A TREE.

a course which, except as to the Turks, has been fairly regarded in adjusting the boundaries of the new Bulgaria.

An objection which has always, heretofore been opposed with force against the division of Turkey among its nationalities and their erection into separate powers, has been that they were, and would continue to be for a long time, too weak and too backward in the arts of civilization to be self-sustaining States, and would necessarily, therefore, exist in dependence upon some strong power and be its puppets; and that this power, whatever it might be, would be more dangerous to the peace of Europe than Turkey had been. The new States themselves only can give the answer to this objection by developing and exhibiting their capacity for independent government. We may even now form an estimate of the extent to which they may be able to do this, and of the speed with which they are likely to accomplish it, by a study of the character of the nationalities, and of the account which they have given, and are giving, of themselves. This we may do by an examination of what they achieved in the past, before the Turks crushed them, and of the efforts which they have put forth in our own day for their national generation.

Four nationalities compete to share the control of the Balkan peninsula—the Bulgarians, the Greeks, the Servians, and the Rumanians. The Bulgarians and Servians belong to the Slavic race; the Greeks and Rumanians form each a distinct race. The desires of the Bulgarians and Greeks for territorial autonomy and independence could be satisfied without interfering with the interests of any European States. The claims of the Rumanians and Servians, on the other hand, involve the readjustment of boundaries, would require, if they were fully conceded, a considerable reduction of the territories of the Austrian Empire, and would threaten a dissolution of the Empire itself, with the overthrow of Magyar supremacy in the South.

The new principality of Bulgaria, as established by the treaty of San Stefano, will include more than half of the territory of European Turkey, aside from Servia and Rumania, and will contain about 74,400 square miles, an extent about equal to that of the States of Ohio and Indiana, and from 5,000,000 to 5,500,000 inhabitants. Of the rest of Turkey, 59,500 square miles are in Bosnia, Albania, and the Grecian provinces, and 8,500 square miles around Constantinople.

The Bulgarian boundaries have been skillfully stretched out by the Russian diplomats, so as to include nearly every part of the country in which there is any considerable proportion of Bulgarians, and have been fixed in the South, often in disregard of the claims of the Greek nationality, so as to embrace an ample stretch of coast and commodious harbor privileges on the Ægean Sea. The Bulgarians constitute about four-fifths of the population in the western part of the territory; the Turks are settled in nearly equal numbers with the Bulgarians in the eastern part; three-fifths of the people in the Macedonian districts are of Albanian or Illyrian origin, and parts of the sea-coast are wholly settled by Greeks.

The Bulgarians appear in the present times under unfavorable lights, and show to superficial observers but little promise of the brilliant future which their friends predict is in store for them. The majority of travelers give very unfavorable accounts of them, and only a few have had the penetration to discover, or the courage to declare, that under the mask of stolid stupidity, indolence, and half barbarism which Turkish oppression and Greek repression have caused them to wear for centuries, are hidden traits and faculties, which, if given a fair opportunity to develop themselves, would shortly place them among the foremost of the Slavic races. The Bulgarian peasants did much, it is true, during the war, by the atrocities of which they were guilty, to discredit themselves and to lend an air of confirmation to the most that has been said against them. Those acts, however, in all their wickedness, were in reality the natural workings of a reaction against the long oppressions under which they had suffered with a patience which has itself helped to condemn them; and were the symptoms of a morbid condition for which the Bulgarian nation had itself already applied the remedies, and from which it would probably have freed itself in a few years if there had been no war.

That this nation has in it the elements out of which it may yet work a noble development of itself, is made probable against all appearances, by the recollection of the character of the ancestry whom it boasts, and is confirmed by the view of the measures which the people have already taken to improve their condition. The ancient Bulgarians were a conquering people. They came down from the North like the other barbarian races which revolutionized Europe during the first thousand years of the Christian era, and were, by all accounts, the peers of the best of them. Having established themselves in the region which they made their kingdom, their stock became intermingled with Slavic blood till they became in effect a Slavic race, but more warlike and more fierce than the other Slavs. The nation constituted an important and powerful kingdom for about three hundred years, till in the earlier part of the eleventh century it fell under the dominion of the Emperors at Constantinople. During this period it was converted to Christianity, in the latter part of the ninth century; and some literary activity was developed among the priests, who translated the Bible and a few of the classical authors into the Old Slavonic tongue, while the language of the people, the real Bulgarian language, had not yet been reduced to writing. At one time, the kingdom having been divided, the Emperor Nicephorus called in the Russians to help him conquer the eastern part to the Danube The conquest having been achieved, the Russians settled upon the Balkans and turned their arms against the Empire. The Emperor called upon the Bulgarians to help him, and the Russians were expelled. The western kingdom maintained its independent existence for forty years after the eastern one was subjected, in constant war with the Empire. At one time fifteen thousand Bulgarians are said to have been taken prisoners and blinded by the Greeks, except that about a hundred were left with one eye to lead their fellows back to their homes. The shock of the sight of his mutilated heroes killed the King, Samuel, and the whole kingdom then fell into the hands of the Greeks. The story of this atrocity is still told among the Bulgarian people, and helps to keep up the hatred of the Greeks, which is one of the distinctive features of their national life.

Previous to this time the country had fallen largely under the influence of the Bogomils, a heretical sect corresponding to the Cathari and Albigenses of Western Europe. Their doctrines were well suited to the disposition of the people. They set store upon a certain degree of education; and the popular language of the Bulgarians being still unwritten, the Bogomils applied an alphabet to it, adapted it to literary uses, and gave the people the first books that they could comprehend. These books consisted principally of Biblical and classical stories, and stories from the "Arabian Nights," translated and modified so as to suit the popular tastes, with a few original works. The translations found their way into the neighboring countries, and through them, it is said, the Bosnians, Croats, Wallachs, and Russians received their first knowledge of the productions of ancient Eastern literature.

The kingdom of Bulgaria again became independent in 1186. Under the Czar Joannes II., from 1218 to 1241, its boundaries touched the three seas, the Adriatic, the Ægean, and the Black Seas, and its capital, Tirnova, was distinguished for its wealth and splendor. The virtues and independent spirit of the people had, however, been weakened by the unhealthy influences of foreign rule and association, and the State was distracted by the unintermitting quarrels between the adherents of the Orthodox Church and the Bogomils, often rising to bloody conflicts, in which one party or the other would not infrequently call in aid from abroad. Under the influence of this demoralization and dissension the State rapidly declined after the death of Joannes, until, after the defeat of the Servians in the battle of Kosovo, in 1389, it fell an easy prey to the Turkish conquerors.

A barbarism which endured more than four centuries, and has as yet only begun to disappear, now settled upon the people. The Boyars embraced Mohammedanism to save their estates; the Bogomils were likewise won over to Islam through the influence of a heretical Mohammedan sect which had some sympathy with them in doctrine. With the Boyars, the people lost their leaders; with the Bogomils they lost the bond which had held them in fellowship. Their Church was made subject to the Patriarchate of Constantinople, and was delivered in effect to the control of the Fanariote Greeks (or the Greeks of Constantinople, called Fanariote after the quarter (Fanar) of the city which they inhabited), who were enemies of their nationality. "Seldom, in the course of history," says a recent writer,* "have one people acted toward another more execrably than did the Greeks in Turkey to their Bulgarian fellow-believers." They obtained concessions of privileges from the Porte, and used them in every possible way for the repression of the Bulgarian nationality. The priestly offices were filled by Greeks or renegade Bulgarians, or were made matters of bargain and sale, so that the author from whom we have already quoted is impelled to say, with a semblance of truth, that although "many unworthy priestly castes have ruled on the earth, none have been more so than the Greek priests of the Bulgarians Their unscrupulousness, their greediness, can not be described in words." They made a determined attack upon all the motives of the national spirit, endeavored to de-

---

* R. C. Franzos, in the *Allgemeine Zeitung*, October, 1877.

stroy all the books and manuscripts which existed either in the Old Slavonic or in the popular tongue, and established a system of oppression and plunder, which carried on even into the present century, left the Bulgarians little else than their bare life, but utterly failed to destroy their national feeling.

The collections of the songs of the people current during this period which have been recently published bear evidences of the feelings which they entertained toward both their Turkish and Grecian oppressors, in many printed allusions to them and to the indignities which the people had to endure from them. Some of the braver men, refusing to submit to these oppressions, took refuge in the mountains, where they were known as Haiducs, and whence they kept up an unceasing guerrilla warfare against Turks and Greeks. They have been called robbers, but as they were accustomed to discriminate between friends and enemies, and always spared and often protected their own people, they are better entitled to be ranked with the heroic defenders of Montenegro.

At the beginning of the present century, no people in Europe were in a more wretched condition than the Bulgarians. Their nationality was regarded as a stigma. The people in the towns were Grecianized; and whenever any one rose to a position in which he had an ambition to appear respectable and figure in society, it was the fashion for him to give his name a Greek form. The native language was regarded as a barbaric tongue, and its use was confined to countrymen and dwellers in small towns. Nothing was written in it, even the commercial and private correspondence being carried on in Greek, or if the Bulgarian language was used, it was written in Greek characters. The services of the churches were performed exclusively in Greek. A Russian traveler, Gregorovitch, who visited Ochrida, the ancient seat of the Bulgarian Church, could not find there any one who could read Slavic.

The people who remained true to their nationality were isolated from each other; they had no means of knowing how large a proportion of the population they formed, or how their countrymen who lived outside of their own neighborhood felt. Deprived of civilizing influences they necessarily sunk lower. The priests, upon whom alone. they could depend for instruction, were either hostile or ignorant. like themselves. In many districts the people grew up without any knowledge of religion or worship, and became the victims of error. and brutalizing influences.

31

The awakening from this condition has been marvelous, almost miraculous; the results that have followed it have been rapid and extensive almost without example.

A Bulgarian priest at Mount Athos, in 1762, composed a small Sloveno-Bulgarian History, of which several copies were made and circulated. Stoico Vladislavoff, who afterward became Sopronius, Bishop of Braca, saw one of the copies, and was induced to devote himself to the cultivation of his mother-tongue. He translated a number of popular works from the Greek, and in 1806 published a book of Bulgarian Prayers, which was the first book ever printed in the modern Bulgarian language. The Greek war of independence, the revolt of the Hetarists in Wallachia, and the invasion of the country by the Russians in the war of 1828, all contributed their share toward rousing the national spirit.

There were a few Bulgarian merchants and bankers at Bucharest, originating from the lower classes, who were not ashamed of their nationality, but were pained at the low esteem in which it was held. They decided to do what they could to improve it. They formed a society whose double object was to send Bulgarian youth to Vienna to be instructed, and to arouse a thirst for education among their countrymen at home. The association was well provided with means, and brought forth noticeable fruits in a short time. Its young students returned from school thoroughly imbued with national ideas. A Bulgarian primer containing reading lessons and pictures of an instructive character had been published in 1824. Some of the students supplemented it with works of a more advanced character, and others returned to their homes as teachers. The production of other books followed, in all of which adaptation to the need of the people for instruction was the first quality sought. It is remarkable and creditable to the character of the Bulgarians, and is, perhaps, one of the secrets of the success that has attended their literary and educational efforts, that the first books which appeared, besides school-books, were grammars, dictionaries, cyclopedias, and histories. "We must not," said one of the leaders of this period, "write what will merely please, we must write what is useful. Schools! by that sign only can we conquer!" The first people's school was opened at Gabrova in 1835. The Fanariote priests opposed it. and tried to induce the Pasha to forbid it, but he replied, "Learning is no sin." The second school was opened at Sistova in 1836, the third at Koprovitchtica in 1837. Fifty-three primary schools had been established in 1845, besides the Central Lyceum at Philippopolis. In 1873 there were in the province of Philippopolis, with a total Bulgarian Christian population of 390,000 souls, three hundred and seventy high, preparatory, elementary, and girls' schools, with 402 teachers, and 13,885 boys and 2,615 girls as pupils. Instruction is given free of cost, in all the branches of an ordinary common school education. Statistics are not accessible for the other provinces.

The growth of Bulgarian journalism corresponds fairly with the development of the schools. The first Bulgarian periodical was a monthly, started in 1844, at Smyrna; the first political journal was published at Leipzig in 1846. A daily paper was founded at Constantinople in 1849, which was for ten years the principal organ of the people, and fought bravely for them in the battle against the Greek ecclesiasticism. In 1876, fifty-one newspapers in the Bulgarian language had been started. Many of them had only a brief existence, but fourteen of them remained in 1875, including four political journals in Constantinople, official papers at Rustchuk, Salonica, and Adrianople, two literary, one theological, and three technical papers, and the political organ of the emigrants at Bucharest. All but the political journals have been suspended since the war begun. The larger journals were well edited, with matter chosen to suit the tastes of their readers, who formed, as a whole, an interested and appreciative class; they were very patriotic, and exerted a great influence.

Literary works other than school-books began to appear about 1840. In 1876, about five hundred such works had been published, some of them in editions numbering three or four thousand copies. About half the number are translations, among which are mentioned the poems of Bulwer and Byron, a part of Shakespeare, English governess-stories, sensational novels, German and French classical works, Russian and Polish books. The original works are lyric poems, describing the popular life or deeds from the national history, or reflecting the national aspirations, and generally of a character promising a hopeful future for this kind of literary effort, and dramas, of which about forty have been published since 1870 A few novels have been published, the best known of which are the stories of Karaveloff and the historical novels of Bishop Drumoff; history is represented by four writers of reputation, and philological research by the works of three authors.

Considering what is the condition of the country, the Bulgarian authors enjoy a large clientage and are liberally supported. The people have a taste for reading, and gratify it; and the Bulgarian patriot, it is said, considers it a sacred duty to buy books.

The turning-point in the national development of the Bulgarians was reached when they gained from the Porte, against the strenuous opposition of the Fanariote Greeks and of all the Fanariote influences, the freedom of their Church. The struggle which ended in this result was a long and severe one, and was well fitted to test the capacity for endurance of many a people who stand higher in the world's estimation. That the Bulgarians achieved so complete a victory as they have done, is not the least of the evidences which they have given of their capacity to constitute an independent and strong State. It was perceived, at the beginning of the efforts for improvement, that the most earnest and wisely-directed exertions of patriotic endeavor would fail to accomplish the object that was sought, while the Church was ruled by a hostile, anti-Bulgarian hierarchy, and the people were under the influence, in their homes and their closest relations, of a priesthood who would employ every means in their power to baffle the aims of the reformers. Accordingly, the emancipation of the Church was made one of the most essential and important objects of the new movement. In 1833, the people of Samokov and Skopie asked for the appointment of Bulgarian bishops, instead of the unworthy Greeks who had been removed from their sees, but other Greeks were sent them in their stead. In 1840, a Bulgarian, who had been appointed Bishop of Widin, died while he was gone to Constantinople, it is said, of poison. Ten years later, the attention of the Government was directed to the Bulgarian grievance by means of an insurrection which broke out near Widin, and the Patriarch was requested to consecrate a Bulgarian bishop. He consecrated one, but left him without a diocese. When the Porte called a National Assembly to consider the question of reforms in 1858, the ecclesiastics took care that no Bulgarians should obtain seats in the body, and the demand of the people for a voice in the appointment of their ecclesiastics was denied, because the Church, the ecclesiastics answered, recognized no difference of nationalities. At one time during the struggle, the Bulgarians sought a union with the Roman Catholic Church. The union was very nearly effected, by the help of Napoleon III. of France, in 1854, when England and Russia interfered, and stopped the negotiations. A general movement was instituted against the Fanariote ecclesiastics in 1860. The bishops were driven out from several cities, native bishops were provisionally appointed in their places, the Bulgarian language was introduced into the schools, and the Bulgarian congregation at Constantinople showed its approval of the revolutionary acts by refusing to recognize the election of a new Patriarch, which took place at about that time. The prayer for the Patriarch ceased to be repeated in the churches, his name was hooted at when it was mentioned, and the name of the Sultan was substituted in its place. The Government sought to gain from the Patriarch concessions to the demands of the people, but assent was twice refused to its propositions. It then acted on its own account, and a firman was granted on the 28th of February, 1870, constituting the Bulgarian Church an independent Exarchate. A pastoral letter, full of extravagant, but sincere, expressions of gratitude to the Sultan, announced the victory to the people. Bishop Anthrin, of Widin, was chosen Exarch in 1872. His journey to Constantinople to be consecrated was like a triumphal march.

Some authors have ascribed to Russia a larger share in the regeneration of Bulgaria than it deserves. The contributions of Russia to this work have been indirect, and have been given chiefly in the shape of the presence of military forces, and in such encouragement as the Panslavist agitations may have afforded in the awakening in the hearts of despondent Bulgarians the hope that their people might participate in the regeneration of the Slavic races, and in inspiring them with the motive to prepare themselves for the bright destiny that was painted for them. The Russians, during the campaign of 1828, made fair promises to the Bulgarians of the aid and support which they would give them, which were rudely broken when the peace of Adrianople was concluded, a few weeks afterward, without making any provisions for them. The Bulgarians were deceived by these promises into compromising themselves, by engaging in movements for resistance to the Turks, only to be told by Gen. Diebitch that he could do nothing of what he had undertaken to do for them, and to discover that they would have to settle with the Turks in the best way they could. So, again, they were misled by the persuasions of Russian agitators into the insurrectionary attempts of 1876, and, by the appearance of a Russian army, into the disastrous outbreaks of 1877, to repent of their mistakes in mourning and suffering. All the active, real work of their regeneration has been done by themselves, and Franzos asserts that not a single Great Russian has had any direct part in it.

The value of the service which Russia has rendered the Bulgarians in delivering them from Turkish despotism can not be overestimated. It is the first real service that, with all its pretensions, it has ever performed for them. The best conclusion it can now make of its work will be to leave them alone to work out their own development in their own way and through their own resources. That Russian influence will not be beneficial to the best interests of the Bulgarians is shown by the history of past dealings of Russia with them, which have been marked by manifestations of a policy to denationalize Bulgaria, to discourage the national features of its literature, and to make the people Russian. This was exemplified several years ago, when the Russians, having induced a colony of Bulgarians to settle in Bessarabia, suppressed the use of their language in the schools, substituting the Russian language for it, and forbade the publication of a Bulgarian newspaper. The restrictions upon the national life of the settlers were not removed till the colony, by the operation of the Treaty of Paris, passed under the rule of Rumania, when the Bulgarian language was restored. The jealousy of the powers, which is ever watchful to prevent the extension of direct Russian power, and the strength of the newly-awakened national feelings of the Bulgarians, are probably too strong to permit such a policy being attempted with any hope of success in the new principality.

A great impulse was given to the material progress of Bulgaria under the administration of Midhat Pasha. During this brief and exceptional period of good government, the province enjoyed such order as it had never known before, improvements were made, enterprise was stimulated, industries were established, and a promise of prosperity appeared which was unexampled in the history of European Turkey. This improvement was quickened by the growth of the rejuvenated national spirit, and was aided by the settled habits of the people, who are almost universally spoken of as industrious and thrifty, with no inclination to drunkenness or wasteful vices, and prudent in their investments; so that the province became the richest and the most productive of revenues of any of the European possessions of Turkey. The succeeding administrations, although they were misconducted after the old fashion, did not deprive the people of the advantages they had gained, or abate their progress, so that it was said that the Russian soldiers were astonished when they entered the country they were called upon to deliver, to find that its people were better off, in many respects, than they were in their own homes.

The Bulgarians have proved themselves worthy of the advantages they have gained. That they have fairly won their literary culture is shown by the number of their newspapers and books, which would not be published if they did not find readers and purchasers, not less than by the prosperity of their schools. In the schools they bear the most favorable reputation. The Protestant missionaries describe them as their best scholars, and as a people of extraordinary natural abilities. Kanitz speaks in the highest terms of their desire for education and practical sense, as shown by the fact that they will seek knowledge, without religious prejudice, wherever it may be got. He found those who had been instructed abroad to be people of unusual intelligence. He considers them superior to the Servians in qualifications for engineering and the industrial arts. Their rose-gardens in Rumelia, from which the attar of roses of the world's markets is derived, are among the most profitable agricultural fields of that province; their industrial villages in the Balkans were among the most prosperous as well as the most beautiful towns of the Empire. Two of them, which have been destroyed by the Turks, Carlova and Sopot, are described by a war correspondent as places which each member of a company who visited them after their destruction declared he would have chosen as a residence next after his own home. Kanitz says that we must look among them for the future industrial population of Turkey. Von Hellwald and Beck, in their "Die Heutige Türkei" (The Turkey of To-day), say that they are "the most intelligent, and in a literary sense, the most cultivated people of European Turkey, in whose spiritual development they are certainly destined to take a great part."

A people who can be described in such language, who are capable of manifesting such energy, and of doing so much for themselves as our record shows, can not be consigned to an ignoble future. The qualities they have developed, the advances they have made, indicate that with freedom they would become one of the leading nations of the East. Their progress has been suddenly and rudely interrupted, their country made desolate by war, and they have been put back materially many years. Their national aspirations, their desire for improvements, and their spirit of progress, however, remain to them, and will command consideration in whatever adjustment may be made bearing on the future of the Empire.

The Greeks constitute the most vigorous, the most enterprising, and the most cultivated nationality of the Turkish Empire, and must always command a first place in the consideration of questions relating to its future. They claim a hearing by reason of their numbers, influence, and social standing; by reason of their progressive spirit; of the obligations which the Great Powers have incurred toward the kingdom of Greece, and of what they are capable of doing for the regeneration and civilization of the decaying Turkish provinces. They can also appeal to history, can call to mind the obligations which civilization owes to their race, and can show that they are the rightful heirs to the greater part of the provinces which the Turk has so wretchedly misgoverned since the Western Powers permitted him to subjugate them.

No nationality in the world has a prouder record than the ancestors of the Greeks. Civilization and liberty grew up among them and flourished to a degree that has never been excelled in any other nation till the present century. No equals have ever been found to their best works of literature and art. They originated the training and the methods of study which have given the impulse to all modern progress in learning and discovery; so that there is hardly a good gift which the world enjoys to-day to which they have not directly or indirectly contributed. They transmitted their civilization and learning to the Romans, and the Romans distributed it over their world. While Western Europe lost its knowledge in the Middle Ages, the Greeks preserved theirs at Constantinople; and the scattering of Greeks over Europe consequent upon the conquests of the Turks, is mentioned by the historians as one of the prime motives to the revival of learning in the fifteenth and sixteenth centuries.

The Greeks were the first civilized people who settled in the European parts of Turkey; and they are the first civilized people who lived within the historical period in a part of its Asiatic territory. Their first exploration of the Black Sea and opening of it to navigation, lies back of history in the mythological period. Constantinople was a Greek city, known as Byzantium, hundreds of years before Constantine rebuilt it and renamed it, having been founded in the seventh century before Christ. The western provinces of European Turkey are called in current books and writings by the names Thessaly, Epirus, and Macedonia, which were given them by their early Greek inhabitants. In most of these ancient Greek possessions the people of that nationality still form the major part of the population, and are the leaders of enterprise. A German author, Fallmerayer, has undertaken to show that the modern Greeks are not the genuine descendants of the ancient people, but are of a mixed Illyrian and Slavic stock, who have settled in the Grecian countries and become Hellenized. His view is contradicted by all the features of modern Greek life, which resemble in a striking degree those of the ancient Greeks, and give the most positive testimony in favor of the theory of a direct legitimate descent. It is true that some parts of the Grecian countries have been largely colonized by Slavs, and that traces of their settlement have been left in some of the local names and in a few Slavic traits which survive. But, even in these instances, it is the Greeks who have absorbed the Slavs. The type is predominantly Greek, and the Slavic features which have been retained are only those survivals of casual peculiarities which seem always to remain when one people have been for a long time associated with another, as historical mementoes of the contact.

The West owes a reparation to the Greeks and to Christianity for allowing them to be driven out of Constantinople. The Turks might have been repelled and driven back into Asia on several occasions had the Western States combined to assist the Emperors; but the selfish interests and religious jealousies of professedly Christian States kept them aloof, and they coldly witnessed the expulsion of their fellow-believers and the planting of an anti-Christian standard in what had been the stronghold of the faith. So strongly did religious differences make themselves felt, that Greek merchants visiting the Latin countries, were accustomed, it is said, to disguise themselves as Turks in order to secure for themselves better treatment than they could have received as Eastern Christians. The piratical expeditions which were fitted out by the Christian knights of those days against the infidel, found their most profitable victims in the Greek towns, which were regarded as legitimate spoil because they belonged to the country of the enemy. On the other hand, Greeks, as Christians, had to suffer in Mohammedan countries for the indignities which the Moors endured in Spain.*

---

* W. E. Gladstone, the "Hellenic Factor."

The Greeks, in common with the other conquered peoples, suffered severely by the exaction of the tribute of children out of which the Janissaries were formed, which depleted their manly vitality to the lowest degree compatible with continued existence. When the tribute ceased, the people being allowed to enjoy their natural increase, immediately began to gain in strength and determination.

The Greeks exhibited the qualities of a brave manhood in an eminent degree in their Revolution. "It was," says Finlay, who has written its history, "a revolution of the people, in which they exhibited a tenacity and valor not less than that of the American colonists in their famous revolt." Mr. Gladstone describes the revolutionists as of "a race, to whom as yet, except in the Black Mountain (or Montenegro), no equals in valor have appeared among the enslaved populations of the East." The people fought alone, too, for they had but few leaders and only the assistance of individuals from abroad.

The people of Greece have done remarkably well since they gained their independence, especially when we consider how small is the State in which they have to work, and remember that it has been only about fifteen years since they have had a Government that has been able to give them any real help. The cause of good government has advanced steadily, having been promoted rather than hindered by the peaceful revolutions of 1843 and 1862; respect for the laws is becoming the habit of the people, and the kingdom enjoys a steady growth of population and wealth, the population having increased from 650,000 in 1834 to 1,238,000 in 1870, and the revenue from $1,375,000 in 1833 to $3,849,000 in 1873.

Equally great has been the spiritual advancement of the Greeks. The effort to restore the spirit of the past, to cultivate its literature and revive its language, has been responded to in a manner that shows that the people appreciate their high ancestry, and intend to try to make themselves worthy of it. Strenuous efforts have been made for the advancement of education, not only within the Kingdom itself, but in all the Grecian districts of the Turkish Empire. While, in 1830, there were within the Kingdom only seventy-one schools, with 6,721 scholars, there were, in 1874, 1,227 primary schools, with 81,449 scholars, besides nearly 200 secondary schools, a university at Athens, and several theological schools which are under the special care of the clergy. The numerous schools, both primary and higher schools, established by the Greeks in Mace-

donia, Thessaly, and Epirus—at all points where there is a considerable Greek population—are mentioned favorably by travelers, and
are generally spoken of as among the best schools in the Empire.
Seminaries for teachers, furnishing instruction quite equal to that
given in the best normal schools of Europe, have recently been
established in Macedonia, whose pupils are already teaching in the
elementary schools of the provinces, greatly to the improvement of
the standard of education among them. The result is that the
Greeks in the Turkish provinces, as well as in the Kingdom, are
far advanced in literary culture beyond any of their Slavic neighbors, and are already well prepared to maintain an independent
sovereignty.

The energies of the Greek nation are cramped by the smallness
of its territory, which is not large enough to give it either the population or the revenues of a really sovereign State. The reasonableness of its demands for expansion is generally conceded, but, as
they would involve an entire readjustment of the Eastern Question,
it has heretofore been impracticable to grant them. Since such a
readjustment has been forced by the course of events, it will not be
possible to evade answering them, whatever efforts may be exerted
by some of the powers to preserve the Turkish boundaries as the
treaty of San Stefano arranged them. They can be answered with
less embarrassment than those of any other nationality. The districts that Greece may claim are clearly marked out, and there is
little occasion for dispute as to the precise boundaries. Thessaly,
Epirus, and Southern Macedonia and the islands—the predominantly
Greek districts of Turkey—are removed from the rivalry of the
Great Powers, which makes it so difficult to gratify the full desires
of Bosnia, Servia, Rumania, and Bulgaria. No power could present any claim or interest adverse to the complete fulfillment of the
wishes of Greece.

The expanded Kingdom would be extended over a people who
desire its rule, and would prefer it to any other. They participated
in the Revolution, and were disappointed when they were shut out
from the State to which it gave birth. They have been interested
in the progress of the country, have sympathized with every movement which concerned it, and have shared its intellectual advancement.

The Greeks watched the wars of 1876 and 1877 with interest and
sympathy, without taking active part in them. They were re-

strained by a sense of the intrinsic weakness of their State, and discouraged by the advice of the friendly powers, particularly of England. Nevertheless, the Government was active in preparation, so as to be in a condition to take advantage of any opportunity which might arise for action with safety, and the people in the provinces kept bands under organization, ready to break out into insurrection at an auspicious moment. A camp of instruction was established at Thebes, under the immediate supervision of the King. The committee at Athens, formed in 1867 to assist the insurgents in Crete, was expanded into the "Pan-Hellenic Committee," and sent emissaries into all parts of Turkey, to prepare their countrymen for a general rising, and superintended the organization of skeleton bands in all the provinces, to serve as the nucleus of an effective force, to be filled up when the signal for the contemplated rising should be given. It was intended in 1876 that the rising should take place as soon as the Servians should gain any considerable victory over the Turks, and the Servians were given assurances to that effect, but their defeat prevented the fulfillment of this intention.

Although the Grecian people continued agitated during the whole of the war, it was not till the close of January, 1878, that the Government decided upon any action. Then, moved by the pressure of popular clamor, and the peril to which the Thessalian insurrectionists were exposed from the barbarity of the Turkish irregulars, it sent its troops over the border, to discover immediately that it had committed a great mistake, since the conclusion of the armistice with Russia had left the Turks free to send their whole force against the offending State. The Government then appealed to the representatives of the powers for an assurance of protection, which was given, with the promise that the Greek question would be submitted to the conference of the powers about to be assembled.

The Slavic population in these provinces who would prefer some other Government than a Greek one, is comparatively small. The Greeks number in all European Turkey about 1,120,000 souls, or thirteen per cent. of the whole population ; but in the Greek provinces, in the parts of Southern Rumelia which are excluded from the new Bulgaria, and in the islands of the Archipelago, they include nearly all the inhabitants, so that their valid claim includes all that is left of European Turkey south of Albania and the boundaries of the new Bulgaria. They are also fast occupying the seaports and coasts of Asia Minor, from which the Turks are steadily retiring before their steady increase; and no doubt can exist that a vigorous Greek kingdom in Europe would soon find a legitimate field of expansion in replanting the wastes of those once wealthy regions, furnishing an enterprising population of tradesmen and farmers to replace the indolent and imbecile Turks, substituting good government for Ottoman misrule, and restoring to civilization those provinces of the East which the ancient Greeks covered with the splendor of their best achievements in literature and the arts. The Greeks have a capacity for assimilating and absorbing other peoples, which has been approved in hundreds of instances in the course of their history, and which is now manifesting itself upon the Slavic peoples wherever the two races come in contact in Turkey. The Greek language is spreading at the expense of other languages, as in Albania and in some of the Slavic districts, where it is extensively spoken. The Greeks are able also to exert a great influence through their power in the Greek Church, which embraces all the nationalities of Eastern Europe, the Patriarch and all the heads of the Church at Constantinople, having always been and still being of Grecian nationality. The fierceness of the ecclesiastical struggle which lately prevailed in Bulgaria affords the strongest possible testimony to the aggressiveness of the Grecian character, its tenacity in pursuing its purposes, and the difficulty with which its influence is overcome. All of these qualities will serve them well in moulding the people into a compact political and social organization.

The hostility which is alleged to exist between the Greeks and Slavs is more apparent than real. Their interests are diverse, but not opposed. Each seeks the freedom of its own nationality, but has no possible interest in opposing the success of the other; only naturally, neither is willing that either should prevail at the expense of the other. The attitude of the Greeks toward the Servian nation in its last struggle for independence was clearly defined and defended by Mr. Contostavlos, the Grecian Minister of Foreign Affairs, in an address which he delivered in the National Chamber of Deputies in November, 1876. He said that the Greeks had no hostility to that people, since they, like the Servians, were Christian, and their whole people were formerly, as some of them were still, subject, like the Servians, to the Ottoman yoke and liable to the same oppressions; but the question was not one of sympathy, but of action, and in this the policy of good sense rather than that of sentiment ought to be followed.

The justice of the Grecian claims is generally recognized. Even those who are most exclusively devoted to the advancement of Slavic interests do not dispute them. While not much attention has apparently been given them officially, they have been quite widely discussed in an informal manner, and have received favorable attention.

Signor Crispi, President of the Italian Chamber of Deputies, visited several of the Continental capitals during October, 1877, on what was generally supposed to be a semi-official mission on behalf of his Government. At Pesth, he declared to a number of deputies that Italy was not willing that Russia should solve the Eastern Question alone, but thought that in case of a Russian victory the powers should join in the settlement. In such an event, he would propose the formation of a confederation of the South Slavic countries and the extension of Greece to the Balkans as an adjustment that would prevent a renewal of the war.

The expansion of Greece would doubtless be supported with real enthusiasm by a large proportion of the English people, who have always manifested a strong sympathy with the struggles of the gallant nation, and consider themselves in a certain sense its natural protectors. Mr. Gladstone is a prominent advocate of the plan, and presented a strong argument in favor of it in November, 1876, in his article on "The Hellenic Factor in the Eastern Problem," from which we have quoted several facts. A foretaste of the spirit with which the people at large would receive the official agitation of the question was given in the loud applause with which a large audience at Bristol greeted the Liberal leader, Mr. Forster, in November, 1877, when referring to the announcements of Earl Derby and Earl Beaconsfield that "Her Majesty's Government is not prepared to witness with indifference the passage into other hands than those of its present possessors of a capital holding so peculiar and commanding a position as Constantinople." He said: "Well, no Englishman could view it with indifference. If the war should end with the defeat of the Turks, I should not look with indifference, but with very great pleasure, on the possession of Constantinople by the Greeks."

When, on the occasion of the awkward situation occasioned by the advance of the Grecian troops into Thessaly simultaneously with the conclusion of the armistice, a deputation of Greek residents in London waited on Earl Derby on the 5th of February, his lordship said that his sympathies had always been with the Greek race, and read in illustration of his position a dispatch of July 6, 1877, which declared that England always looked to the welfare of Greece. He further said that he would endeavor to obtain guarantees for the good government of Turkey's Hellenic provinces, and would endeavor at the conference to prevent the predominance of Slavs over Greeks.

The incorporation of the Greek provinces into an independent State would be an act of justice which Europe owes in a certain sense; would give respectable dimensions and stability, without making it formidable to a kingdom which is now insignificant; would contribute immensely to the material prosperity of the provinces affected, and to the advancement of civilization in the East; would furnish one of the easiest and safest solutions of the problem of the disposition of Constantinople, and is practicable and open to no reasonable objection.

CHAPTER III.

The Dacia of the Romans—Character of the Ancient Dacians—The Roman Conquest and Colonization—Withdrawal of the Romans—Successive Tribes of Northern Barbarians Occupy the Country—The Bulgarians and the East Roman Empire—The Kingdoms of Wallachia and Moldavia—They become Tributary, and finally Subject to Turkey—They become semi-independent and are afterward united as Rumania—The Rumanians and the Romans—The Wallachian, or Rumanian Language—The Culture of the Language—Wallachia in 1835—Count Von Moltke's Impressions—Marks of Improvement and Progress—Agriculture and Manufactures—Jealousy of Foreigners—The Nationalities in Rumania—Distribution of the Rumanians in Surrounding Countries—The Mistakes which the Rumanians have committed—The Better Qualities of the People—The Hopeful Prospects of the Country—The Servian Nationality—Its Numbers and Distribution—Education in Servia and Montenegro—Unity of Language—The Communal Organization of Servian Society—The National Movement and the Omladina—Capacity of the Servians to form a nation.

THE country of the Rumanians was known to the ancients as Dacia. It first came under notice in the time of Alexander the Great, who made war upon the Getae, the dwellers on the banks of the Danube. Gibbon describes the Dacians of five centuries afterward as "the most warlike of men, who during the reign of Domitian had insulted with impunity the majesty of Rome." The treaty which this Emperor was obliged to conclude with them, A.D. 81, is distinguished as marking the first occasion on which "Imperial Rome consented to purchase peace of an enemy." The Emperor Trajan conquered the country after a war of five years, in which "Decebalus, the Dacian King, approved himself a rival not unworthy" of his antagonist, and made it a Roman province, A.D. 107. It remained for one hundred and sixty-seven years a prosperous Roman colony. The Imperial rule was beneficial here as everywhere. The people were incorporated into Roman citizenship; they affiliated with the Roman settlers. The soldiers built roads and bridges and public works, and the country was happier than it ever had been before or ever has been since. The Roman dominion, though short, made a wonderfully deep impression on the manners

(594)

and customs of the people and their language, which has never been effaced.

The Goths appeared in the country in the third century, and at length became so numerous and troublesome that the Emperor Aurelian withdrew his legions and gave up the province. A part of the settlers emigrated to adjoining provinces, a part remained. First the Visigoths held it, then the Ostrogoths; the latter were replaced by the A'lani and Huns, then by the Avari, then by the Bulgarians, during whose rule, A.D. 861, Christianity was introduced by Methodius. From the time of the conquest of the Bulgarian kingdom by the Emperor Vasili in 1018, till 1186, the country formed a part of the East-Roman Empire. The second Bulgarian kingdom, founded in the latter year, included Rumania during a part of its existence. An independent kingdom was founded in Wallachia in 1241. Another kingdom was founded in Moldavia in 1354. The Wallachian kingdom became tributary to Turkey in 1391, and was made a Turkish province in 1688, governed at first by native Hospodars, but after 1716 by Fanariote (so the Greeks of Constantinople were called) Greek governors named by the Porte. Stephen VI., the Great, of Moldavia (1456–1504), was a prince of considerable distinction. He repelled the Tartars who invaded the land for the first time, waged war against the Hungarians and Poles, conquered Bukowina and Wallachia to the borders of Servia, but was unfortunate in a war against the Turks. His son, Bogdan II. (1504–1526), acknowledged the suzerainty of the Turkish Sultan, and Moldavia has, since his reign, been a vassal-State of Turkey, and shared the fate of its fellow province, Wallachia. During the last one hundred years, Rumania has been a battle-ground between Turkey and Russia and Austria. Its provinces have been occupied by the armies of all three powers, and have been prominent subjects of the negotiations between them. Austria has gained Bukowina, Russia the districts east of the Pruth from Moldavia. The Treaty of Paris, in 1856, gave to Moldavia and Wallachia the condition of semi-independence under the suzerainty of the Porte and the protection of the powers, under which they achieved a union in 1859, despite the objection of the Sultan, into the principality of Rumania, and from which the united principality, supported by the moral force of a Russian alliance, rose to independence in May, 1877.

It would be hard to define exactly what the Rumanians are. Judging from their history, they are among the most mixed of

32

races. Their country has been occupied, since the Romans left it, by a half-dozen barbarous tribes, ending with the Slavs, most of which came more numerously than the Romans, and some of which held it much longer than they did. Yet during all their fluctuations it has been the pride of the people to call themselves Romans—Rumani—and to speak a Roman language. Their most marked features are Roman, and of all modern languages the Italian is most like theirs. In this persistence to the Roman type, they present a curious contrast to the Bulgarians, so tenacious in other respects of their national life, for while the Bulgarians became Slavic under Slavic influences, they have escaped foreign impressions.

Some writers have urged that the Wallachian or Rumanian language is a Slavic tongue, and have been able to cite a considerable number of Slavic words in support of their view. It likewise contains German, and Greek, and Magyar, and other words of foreign origin. It could hardly fail to present many evidences of admixture, after such a number of different races have occupied the country. The body of the language is, however, unquestionably Latin, and its resemblance to the Italian can hardly fail to strike one who is acquainted with the latter at the first sight. Its alphabet, however, is of Slavic origin. It was reduced to writing in the fifteenth century, and given the characters called Cyrillic, because they were invented by Cyril, which are similar to those of the modern Russian. The Cyrillic alphabet continued in use until 1847, when it gave way to an alphabet composed entirely of Roman characters. The Slavic language was encouraged by the clergy during the period of Slavic predominance, but in 1643 Prince George Rakoczky ordered the archbishop to preach to the Rumanians in their own language. Greek became the fashionable language under the Greek governors appointed by the Porte, while the Rumanian continued to be spoken by the people, and has only supplanted the Greek among the higher classes within the present century. The first Rumanian books appeared about the middle of the seventeenth century, in the shape of translations of the Church books and sacred writings. The growth of the native literature has been slow, and has been exhibited principally in the field of lyric poetry.

A movement for the restoration of the ancient speech was begun in 1815, and has been prosecuted with vigor. The change from the Cyrillic to the Roman alphabet has not been entirely settled yet, so that the spelling is still quite uncertain. Many foreign terms have been cast out and replaced by words chosen from the ancient Latin or modern Italian. The Rumanian Academy was established in 1871 for the purpose of regulating the language and settling the orthography. It is preparing a grammar and a dictionary which will become the standards of the nation, and proposes as the result of its efforts to restore in its purity a speech which those who use it boast is the oldest of the languages now spoken, which were derived originally and directly from that of the Romans.

The Rumanians are passionately fond of poetry, and their list of writers of songs and romances is quite numerous. The language, being soft and musical, is well adapted to the lighter styles of verse. They have but little as yet to show in prose or in works of learning, but offer the names of three prominent historians and two grammatists, besides several writers who have translated works from other languages. For dramatic works they are likewise indebted to translations. Their three principal journals are published at Bucharest, Jassy, and Galatz.

Count Von Moltke, the great German General, traveled through Wallachia in 1835, and recorded a very unfavorable impression of the condition of the country. It had then been only partly extricated from Turkish despotism, having been for five years under a kind of double dependence upon Turkey and Russia, and the Count regarded it particularly with reference to its prospects for future development. The appearance of the land, he said, bore fearful evidence of a long servitude. The cities lay half in ruins, or were of earthen houses, the villages were hidden in the valleys as if the people had sought protection in poverty and concealment, and were without gardens, fruit trees, or churches, and "one might say without houses, for the latter are sunk in the ground and covered only with a roof of boughs." One might, at that time, travel whole days without seeing a farmstead, a mill, an inn, an avenue, a bridge, or a castle. The land was destitute of trees; the Boyars lived in the towns, where were all the churches, of which the rural parts of the country had none. The Wallachs had a fine appearance, but the Turkish yoke had completely debased them, and accustomed to make the least suffice for themselves, they knew nothing of the wants of other nations, dreaded want less than labor, the constraint of civilization more than the misery of barbarism. "From the present generation," said Von Moltke, "little is to be expected."

To-day finds the country with an awakened national spirit, enjoying a government under a wise Prince of one of the ablest houses of Europe, whose effectiveness is well shown by the honorable record which its soldiers made for themselves before Plevna. The people, their more enlightened leaders at least, are occupied with schemes for the improvement of the country, for the spread of education, the encouragement of literature, the development of national industries, and the construction of works of improvement.

Education has made considerable progress within twenty years, but much remains to be done. The law contemplates a school in every town of more than fifty families. The provision of the schools, though still deficient, is likely to become ample in a short time under the operation of the compulsory law which was passed in 1864. Some of the higher schools are of excellent character, but the tendency to superficiality and the preference of the showy to the substantial, which many of the private schools exhibit, displays one of the weak points of the people, a point which is still further displayed in the devotion to Parisian fashions and gayeties, and the copying of the frivolities of Parisian life, which are among the most marked characteristics of their capitals.

Rumania is predominantly an agricultural country. It enjoys a climate and a soil favorable to the most profitable culture, but has neither the capital nor the adaptability of its people to engage largely in manufactures. The Rumanians do not incline to industrial arts. They leave common trades to foreigners and gypsies, and themselves, when educated, seek the learned professions, which are consequently, especially that of the law, overcrowded. The Government has made efforts to build up and encourage manufacturing enterprises, with only a small degree of success, and this branch of national growth has been, so far, marked rather by what has been tried and failed than by what has been accomplished. The railroad enterprises which had been undertaken suffered a great shock by the defalcation of Dr. Strousberg, but they have been continued, and the country is now better supplied with railroads than any other part of the Turkish dominions.

One of the drawbacks to the progress of the people is their jealousy of foreigners. It is shown in their laws, which exclude foreigners from all official and public functions, and make naturalization difficult. It is particularly shown in the persecutions to which the Jews are exposed, and which occupy the multitude to such an extent that a native of the country told Carl Braun, the traveler, that the Jewish Question was the only one the populace really cared about. A country which is wholly dependent upon foreigners and their capital for the development of industrial enterprises can not expect to receive the benefits which it requires and should derive from them while it is thus intolerant of them.

More than four-fifths (4,293,000 out of 5,073,000) of the population are Rumanians. They are called Wallachs by the Germans, but themselves acknowledge no name but the one, *Rumani*, that points out their Roman origin. Next to them are the Jews, 400,000, whom they hate, because, as one of the national newspapers says, they do not cease to be a caste and become one with the people of the country. Next in order are Gypsies (200,000), Russians and Slavs, Austrians, Hungarians, and a dozen other nationalities, numbering each less than ten thousand. A peculiar feature in the distribution of the population for a Turkish country is the small number of Turks, who, together with the Tartars, do not number more than 2,700; and it is remarked that the Turks have never ventured to make a settlement in any large numbers north of the Danube. By religions, 4,529,000 belong to the Greek Church, 114,200 to the Roman Catholic Church, and 13,800 are Protestants. But the Rumanians are not all in the present Rumania. They are diffused over the whole of the former Dacia, occupy half the Austrian province of Bukowina, where they number more than two hundred thousand, form more than half (1,206,900) the population of Transylvania, and number more than a million in Hungary proper, more than 2,685,600 in all Austria and Hungary, and are largely represented in the Dobrudja and in other parts of Turkey. They also form a large proportion of the population of Russian Bessarabia.

Rumania thus has the population of a considerable State. It is not an unhomogeneous population when compared with that of Austria and Hungary, although it contains diverse and some antagonistic elements, for the Rumanians so outnumber all the others as to be able to have their way with but little friction. It has also an established government, which has created many of the agencies and some of the resources of an independent State; and it was substantially independent before the war began.

The Rumanians believe, the same as the Slavs and the Greeks believe of their nationalities, that the future of the East belongs to them. It can not be said that the prospect of their realizing this belief is as good as those of some of their neighbors. · With the same opportunities, they have not made as much progress as the Servians. They have not equalled the Bulgarians in stolid tenacity of purpose, and have fallen short of the preference that that people have displayed for the solid in education over the superficial; and they have not the activity and versatility of the Greeks. They have made mistakes at the start of the race, which Carl Braun has described by comparing them to one who prefers the appearance to the reality, or to one who adorns the top of a pyramid, instead of repairing its base. This writer, criticising their course and tendencies with some severity, says that efforts should begin at the bottom, rather than at the top; that they should be less political and more administrative and for amelioration; that the State should hold itself not exclusive, but receptive, of foreigners; that it should be concerned more for the Sergeant than for the General, for the village schoolmaster than for the academical teacher; should not seek the acquisition of territory, but, first of all, the improvement of the circumstances of· the interior; should not indulge in a vain pursuit after the grandeur of the Romans and the wit of the French, but should cultivate public spirit and rural industry.

It would not be fair, however, to apply to the people of the whole country these descriptions of the fashionable life of the capitals, whose vain notions and 'faults have been gained mostly through the limited intercourse which they have held with Western society, of which, like most copyists, they have imitated the most frivolous features, omitting the solid traits and the refinements. The moral tone of Bucharest was higher than it is before this took place. The traits of the national character, says a recent writer, have become gradually effaced among the residents of the capital, and "the Bucharest dandies are in no sense representatives of the Rumanian people." The true representatives are to be found among the highlanders of the Carpathians, "who continue to adhere to the ancestral worship and traditions, and who are probably capable of indefinite development.". "At present, the character of the peasants is in an embryo condition. Its prominent features are a disinclination to exertion and a dislike to cold water. . . . . ·Their want of energy and of ambition are attributable, to a great extent, to the untoward circumstances in which they have found themselves for generations. The change of masters—within forty years Wallachia has had seventy Princes—has not relieved the peasant from the burdens imposed upon him, not merely by the invading foreigner, but also by the upper classes of his own country. He plods on in a hopeless kind of fashion, for he is liable at any time to have his wretched belongings seized, and he is aware that the benefits of his labor will, in any case, be reaped by others."*

A fair judgment of the prospects of the country, weighing both sides, is given by Carl Braun in his "Turkish Journey,"† who says: "It is a country of extraordinary richness, to whose growth and development nothing is wanting but the provision of the necessary capital, and the requisite number of industrious and intelligent men. Both, capital and men, will be furnished when Rumania— and the time when this is done can be determined by itself—enters the family of European States and peoples as a full member. For this, it must be understood that the State shall assure the freest possible circulation of men and goods, shall give up its idiosyncrasies against foreigners as an offering to the genius of culture and civilization, and shall take part in international rivalries and the division of labor. The native population is gifted, and adapted to culture down to the lowest grades, but it needs the spur of competition and the firm support of a general, gratuitous, compulsory popular education of a solid character." Rudolf Henke, who is the author of a special work on Rumania,‡ the first that has appeared, says: "Rumania is a land of the future, which will be able to reach its full bloom as soon as the hinderances which now stand in its way are removed. From a small, obscure beginning, it has advanced to be a respectable State of the middle rank, and, averaging its qualities, stands, in respect to size, population, finances, and civilization, as about the twelfth or fourteenth- of the twenty-three States of Europe. In spite of its having been till now a vassal-State of Turkey, it has reached the same grade of culture, if it has not attained a higher one, as Spain, Portugal, and Greece, to say nothing of Turkey, and but little lower than Italy, Russia, and the non-German provinces of Austria." This picture is somewhat over-colored, but it represents the view of a man who has probably given the·

---

* *Pall Mall Gazette* Review of Florence K. Berger's "Winter in the City of Pleasure." March, 1877.

† "Eine Türkische Reise," von Carl Braun. Weisbaden, Stuttgart, 1876.

‡ "Rumänien; Land und Volk, etc." Geschildert von Rudolf Henke. Leipsic, 1877.

condition of the country more special attention than any other author.

The mind of the people, and especially of the young men, has suffered, in the abnormal condition of the country, for the lack or healthy stimulus. Full independence will introduce national objects and motives for political activity, giving serious objects to be sought, and positions of honor and responsibility to be struggled for, and a regeneration of the nation and a development and strengthening of the better qualities of the people can hardly fail to take place under its influence.

The principality has much to expect from its chief, who, a near relative of the Emperor of Germany, and trained in the traditions and usages of a princely house which is distinguished for its far-sighted intelligence and administrative ability, has devoted himself to the interests of the country, and will spare no labors to remedy its defects and increase its advantages and resources. The much that he has already done in reforms and measures for consolidating the character and strength of the nation, warrant the belief that he will accomplish much more now that he is relieved of the impediment of vassalage to a barbarian master. Under his skillful guidance, the people, encouraged by their newly-won liberty, and who are earnestly seeking a genuine national development, may be expected to adopt an enlightened course, and start upon the career which nature has indicated that they should adopt. While Bulgaria promises to excel in manufactures and special industries, and Greece in trade, Rumania is marked to become a great farming State, while the intellectual tendencies and æsthetic tastes of the people promise for them a national character not unlike that of the French.

The Servians constitute nearly the entire populations of the principalities of Montenegro and Servia, as well as of the Turkish provinces of Bosnia and Herzegovina. Thus the whole north-west of European Turkey is inhabited by people speaking one language, though politically they are designated by different names. Crossing the northern and north-western frontier of Turkey, we find large portions of Austrian territory occupied by the same people. They constitute 95 per cent. of the population in the former kingdom of Croatia and Slavonia; 90 per cent. in Dalmatia, and 80 per cent. in the former military frontier. Thus the Servian language is spoken by a compact population, numbering more than 6,000,000 persons, and occupying a territory of about 69,000 square miles, or of an extent equalling the aggregate area of the States of New York, New Jersey, Connecticut, Rhode Island, and Massachusetts. If we add to this the land of the nearly kindred tribes of the Slovens (also called Sloventzi or Winds), who are the predominating race in the Austrian crownland of Carniola, and in large portions of Styria, Carinthia, and the Littoral, and who are in profound sympathy with the movements among the Servians and the Croatians, we obtain for this people an aggregate area of nearly 80,000 square miles, and a population of about seven and one-half millions. For more than a thousand years they are known to have lived in the countries which they still hold. They have been unsuccessful in their struggles against the more powerful and more progressive nations by which they are surrounded; the independence of their national Empire has been destroyed by the Turks, Magyars, and Germany; they have hardly been touched by the wonderful progress of civilization and literature which marks the last century of the history of Central and Western Europe; and some portion of their territory belongs to the most illiterate countries of Europe. But in spite of their ignorance, and in spite of all oppressions, they have clung, with wonderful tenacity, to their language. The Austrians, and more recently the Hungarians, have tried to Germanize and Magyarize the Servian tribes of the Austrian Empire by giving them better schools and a higher class of literature; but these efforts, while awakening among them a thirst for literary culture, have, at the same time, greatly strengthened their devotion to their own native language and their desire to develop a national literature. The revolutionary year, 1848, greatly favored their national tendencies. The Government of Vienna, for a time, needed the aid of the Croatians against the Hungarians, and deemed it wise policy to favor as much as possible the aspirations of the Croatian nationalists.

In Turkey, the Servian race has been greatly benefited by the actual independence which the principality of Servia has been able to re-establish. The Government of this little country has shown a laudable zeal for promoting education and endeavoring to raise it to a level with the most advanced countries. Fifty years ago, Servia had no public primary school. Now a complete system of public education has been established, and for its management a special Ministry of Education has been organized. Education is compulsory, and is free to all, in the highest as well as in the lowest schools. In 1874, there were 517 public schools, with 23,278 pupils. In comparison with the other States of Europe, this result is still very unsatisfactory, for it shows that Servia has, as yet, only 17 pupils to every 1,000 inhabitants, while Switzerland has 155, and the German Empire, 153, and it is still inferior to every Christian country of Europe except Russia, which has only 14 pupils to 1,000 inhabitants. But the enforcement of the compulsory attendance law can hardly fail soon to raise it higher in the scale of European nations. In 1830, the first gymnasium was established, and now the principality has two complete gymnasia and five progymnasia, with an aggregate attendance of 2,000 students. The course of the Servian gymnasia embraces seven classes, which are instructed in religion, the Servian, Latin, French, and German languages, history, geography, mathemathics, natural history, physics, drawing, and gymnastic exercises. A normal school has been in successful operation since 1872. The high-school in Belgrade contains three faculties, and has about 200 students. The little principality of Montenegro has of late made similar efforts to organize a complete system of public instruction. Bosnia and Herzegovina have hitherto been in a most deplorable condition, but they may now be expected to enter into a lively com petition with the people of Servia and Montenegro, with whom they are so intimately connected by the strongest bonds of affinity and sympathy.

The Servians of all the different denominations in Austria and Turkey—Servians, Bosnians, Herzegovinians, Montenegrins, Croatians, Slavonians, Dalmatians, Slovenes—are only now awakening to the full significance of the fact, that the common language they speak makes them joint members of one nationality. Like many other nationalities, they have been, and still are, divided by religious differences. Almost the entire population of the principalities of Servia and Montenegro, the majority of Bosnia and Herzegovina, belong to the Greek Church, while the Austrian Servians are more equally divided between the Greek and Roman Catholic Church. A considerable number of the Bosnians are also Roman Catholics, and a large portion of the wealthier classes of Bosnians have even become Mohammedans. The Servians of the Greek Church, like the other Slavs of that faith, have been drawn more and more into close relations with Russia, while those of the Roman Catholic Church have begun to show a stronger dislike to Russia than to Turkey. The Catholic Bosnians kept aloof from the insurrectionary movements of 1876, and it was reported that several young priests who had betrayed some sympathy with the national cause, had been sent out of the country by their superiors. The Mohammedans, whose social prerogatives are so closely interwoven with the Turkish rule, are of course the most fanatical opponents of any aspiration for the independence and political progress of the Servian nationality. But even these Mohammedans have preserved the use of their Servian language to the present day. Yea, being the richest class in the Servian nationality, they speak their language with a greater purity than the Christians of Bosnia.

The social organization among the Servians is peculiar. It was originally based in all Slavic nations upon the principle of the Community, as is strikingly exemplified in one form by the Russian Mir. The same principle in another shape underlies the Zadruga, or household association of the Southern Slavs, which, as we have described it in a previous chapter, is the characteristic family organization of the Servians. The organization has undergone modifications and a decline among the Austrian Slavs, and has been compelled by the stress of circumstances to give way to a form of individual life among the Montenegrins, and in the towns, and it has been assailed by recent legislation, but it still prevails among the agricultural population of Servia. The several families who form the household, who may be supposed to have already some bond of connection, as blood relationship or inherited association, are united into free associations, which bear different names in the different countries, and in which each member subordinates his private interests to that of the community, without being absorbed in it. A head is chosen by the community, who is a president, not a ruler, but whose consent is required for undertakings of more than ordinary importance. The people are strongly-attached to this communal organization, and many of their proverbs show how entirely it has become a part of their ideal of life. "In Herzegovina, it is claimed that poverty never arrives until after the dissolution of the communities." "Nothing can be more beautiful," says Yankovitch and Gruitch, in their "Les Slaves du Sud," "than to live in a Servian family, nothing more interesting than to see and be acquainted with it. Thirty, sixty persons live together and labor in common. That mass obeys a single will, concentrated in its head. But it obeys with pleasure and with confidence, for the members of the household are not there by any constraint; the only bond which holds them is a moral tie, since they know that they are rendering obedience to a

wisdom which is furthest sighted of them all;" and these authors
add to their praise of the institution: "The Servian people are free
from absurd notions. There has never been a proletariat among us."
The dissolution of the community is always looked upon as a
calamity.*

The fact that all the Servian tribes speak one language, and the
hope that they may all co-operate in the building up of one common
national literature, have given a powerful impulse to the idea of
establishing as close a union as circumstances will allow, of all the
people speaking the Servian language. Youthful enthusiasts have
even intoxicated themselves with the dream of the restoration of a
Servian Empire, which, from the extent of its area and the number
of its population, might fill a respectable place among the States of
Europe, being in both respects superior to Sweden, Norway, Denmark, Belgium, Portugal, and Switzerland. This idea has found
zealous and enthusiastic leaders in the Young Servians studying at the
European Universities, who, from a study of the modern history of Europe, have imbibed a belief in a reconstruction of the map of Europe
on the basis of the nationality principle. They mean to profit by the
wonderful success of the sagacious Italian and German statesmen,
who, by a skillful use of this principle, have consolidated the dis-
jointed members of powerful nations into great Empires. The young
Servian enthusiasts who hope to follow in the footsteps of Cavour and
Bismarck have their center in a society called *Omladina*, the primary
and ostensible project of which is to cultivate Servian literature,
while it regards as its remoter and final goal, the foundation of a
general Servian Empire. The influence of this society is easily
traceable in the spirit of the young Servian literature, and in the
management of all the Servian institutions of learning The issue
of the war has greatly strengthened the hopes of the Servian nationalists. The power of the Turks to arrest the steady rise of the Servian people and to prevent the resurrection of a Servian Empire, has
been broken. Servia, Montenegro, Bosnia, and Herzegovina will
co-operate in smoothing the road for a future union. What direction this road will take, may as yet be unknown, but we can not wonder if enthusiastic Servians now more firmly believe than ever, that
the aspirations of a large nation will, in the course of time, call forth

* Countess Dora D'Istria, article on "The condition of women among the Southern
Slavs," in the *Penn Monthly* for January, 1878.

the ingenious statesman who will reintroduce it as a sovereign member into the family of civilized nations. It is certainly a significant fact, that in Hungary the Catholic and Greek Servians are now fully united in the struggle for maintaining the national character of their schools, and in cultivating a common literature, and the leaders of the national movement firmly hope, that as soon as the Mohammedan Bosnians clearly see the impossibility of expecting any further aid from the decrepit Turks, they may be found as ready to fall in with the national movement as their forefathers were in adopting the Islam.

The Servian nation includes the people who, after the Greeks, have made the greatest advancement in civilization and the improvement of their country of any of the populations of the Ottoman Empire. It also includes, in the Bosnians, those who are most backward. It is represented in the Montenegrins by the bravest people in the world. It has been more steadily faithful than any of the other subject peoples of Turkey, to the traditions of its former national life. The Montenegrins have never been subdued; the people of the principality of Servia have kept up a continual disturbance against Turkish rule, have advanced steadily toward independence since the beginning of this century, have let no consideration prevent their striking for it whenever they had opportunity, and have at last gained it; and the Bosnians, notwithstanding the influence the Mussulman begs may have tried to exert over their countrymen, have always been unruly and started the insurrection which led to the important results the world is now witnessing. These facts, constituting prominent features in the history of the race, furnish a sufficient answer to the question, whether the Servians are fit to maintain an independent existence. The training in the subordination of their own will and interests to those of the community which they have received under the institution of the Zadruga, admirably qualifies them to become thoroughly loyal to any Government of their choice, and public-spirited citizens.

The importance and influence of the new Servia will depend largely upon the extent which is given to it. The present State, even if it include all that the Servians now claim, is too small to admit of the best national development. If it should be given all the Servians of Turkey, it would form a State equal to any of the others to be set up on the Balkan peninsula. If it should acquire the kindred tribes of Austria, it would constitute a mighty Empire. The discussion of these alternatives involves the consideration of questions in which other important States have a strong interest; and if it should be brought up in form may produce another complication of the Eastern Question which will be hardly less difficult to resolve than that which attends the disposition of the remains of Turkey.

Another nationality of the Balkan peninsula, the Albanian, has not been prominent in the recent discussions, and has made no concerted manifestation of its desires. It is distinct in its origin from all other nationalities by which it is surrounded, and belongs to the oldest Aryan race of Eastern Europe, its Illyrian ancestors having antedated the Greeks in their settlement. Although the Albanians have been preserved distinct through all the revolutions of the past, and have at times made themselves conspicuous, they seem now, by means of the difference of religions, and the introduction of foreign languages and influence, to be gradually losing their national bonds, and to be showing a tendency to affiliate with the people around them. A large portion of them are now using the Greek language; and in many other ways the effects of Grecian and Italian associations appear to be modifying their habits. Their most probable destiny is not to become a separate State, but to be attached to some of the other States. A portion of them may unite their fortunes with the Greeks, with whom they have already had much to do, and among whose most famous heroes appear such Albanian names as Bozzaris and Canaris. The annexation of a part of Albania to Italy has also been mentioned as one of the possible results of the changes now going on; and the Montenegrins will always be ready to appropriate a share of the territory on the north, a part of which they still covet.

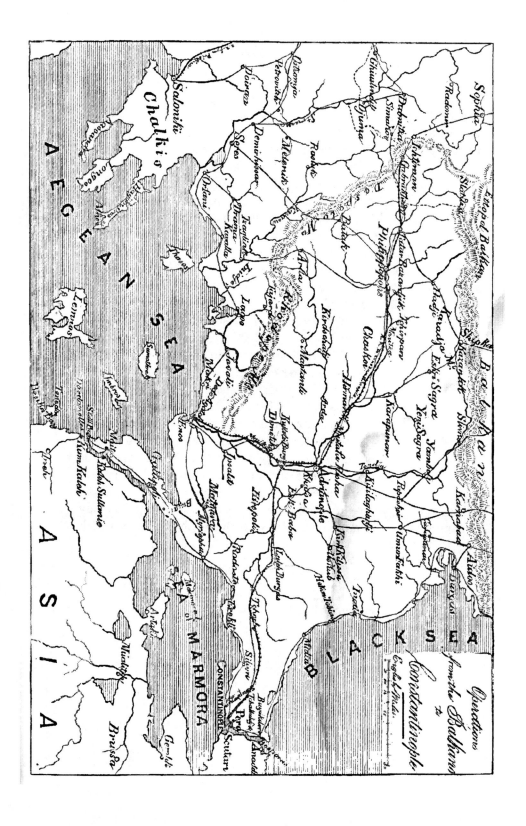

MARSHAL MACMAHON, PRESIDENT OF FRANCE.

CHAPTER IV.

PANSLAVIC HOPES AND TENDENCIES.

The Result of the War encouraging the Panslavists—Original Object of the Slavophile Party of Russia—Opposition to the Reforms introduced by Peter the Great—They sought to expel European Civilization and introduce a new Civilization of Russian, or Orthodox Slavic Development—Personal History of the Founders and Builders of the Party—The Aksakoffs, father and sons—Their Social Circle at Moscow—Literary Efforts of the Elder Aksakoff in behalf of the Cause—Stephanovitch Chomiakoff, the real Founder of the Party—His Travels and the Views he acquired—The Kireyevskis—Influence of these three over the Aksakoffs—Constantine Aksakoff's Eccentric Protests against French Fashions—He revives Obsolete Customs—The Group propose the Russian Mir, or Village Commune, as the Basis of the new Organization of Society—Ivan Aksakoff and his Journal—Katkoff and the Party of Young Russia—Panslavic Movements in Austria—The Slavic Committees of Russia—Their work in the Herzegovinian Insurrection—A Pro-Servian Excitement stirred Up—The Government drawn into the Movement—The Czar commits Himself at Moscow—Silence imposed during the Constantinople Conference—Activity resumed—Prince Tcherkassky—Aksakoff declares the Union in accord with the Czar—Slavic Meeting at Warsaw

THE result of the war has radically changed the position of the two Slavic nationalities of Turkey. Formerly crushed by an alien despotism and the victims of relentless efforts to quench all their national feelings and baffle their national efforts, they are now dominant and the possessors of a beautiful, promising country, offering substantial advantages for promoting their material, intellectual, and social growth. The hand of the oppressor being removed and they enjoying the good wishes of the world, they have now every motive and encouragement to work out their own advancement; they have also the additional encouragement that their efforts will be watched with a peculiar interest by a family of kindred peoples who have made their cause their own, and who see in their triumph the presage of a glorious triumph for the race to which they belong. The victory now achieved can not fail to give a powerful impulse to the aspirations of the whole Slavic race. These aspirations will lend further force to the operations of the powerful party which aims to elevate the Slavic subjects of all non-Slavic Governments to the same commanding position as has been gained for them in Turkey, and will in their turn be stimulated by

its efforts. The Panslavists have been referred to before in this
work; but as they are now likely to be more active and prominent
than ever, and as their designs are of a character that threatens the
peace of one of the most powerful States of Europe, and are likely
to present another extremely difficult question for diplomatists to
solve, it becomes proper to inquire what they are doing, and what is
their aim.

The name of Panslavism is applied in general to the movement which has been in progress for several years under the
auspices of an active band of agitators for the national union or the
independence and alliance of all the Slavic peoples who now live
under different Governments. It affects to disregard all claims of
those Governments, if they are non-Slavic, to the allegiance of their
subjects; makes light of national prejudices, and even hopes to
overcome the obstacles presented by differences in religion, which
are more formidable. The movement is chiefly the growth of the
nineteenth century; it received a strong stimulus through the efforts
of the Slovak Johann Kollar to promote a literary union of the
Slavs, which was warmly received by the Czechs, and was first introduced prominently to the world at the Slavic Congress which was
held at Prague in 1848.

It has, however, received its strongest support from the Russian
party known as the Slavophiles, and is now most prominently
represented and most urgently advanced by them. This party,
which originated naturally in the reaction against the changes which
were forced upon the nation rather than introduced into it by Peter
the Great, and against the ascendency of foreigners, foreign ways
and views, and foreign influence in the councils of the nation, corresponds closely with the party which exists in nearly all nations to
cultivate the predominantly national feeling and keep alive the affection for national customs, literature, and peculiarities; but it is more
pronounced in its views and measures in Russia than in most other
European countries, because Russian conditions, customs, and society
differ more greatly from those of Western nations than those of the
latter differ among each other, and because the process of assimilation begun by Peter the Great has hardly yet worked below the
surface in a very limited circle of Russian life.

This party, which has existed since the last century, was active
during the reign of the Czar Nicholas, but as under the military
system of that Emperor no scope was allowed for political discussion,

it had to confine its operations to literary efforts. The close of the Crimean war, with disaster to Russia, caused a new field to be opened to it, which was made all the more available by the preference of the new Czar Alexander for political over military methods and measures, and by the character of the measures which he undertook. It co-operated heartily in the emancipation of the serfs, and found in the proceedings which were taken for the Russianization of the Baltic (German) provinces the development of a policy exactly agreeing in principle with the line of action which it had marked out for itself. During the war of 1877, it held itself ready to take advantage of either event, of disaster or victory to the Russian arms In case Russia were defeated, and the nation had "to retire upon itself," new concessions would have to be made to popular demands, as had been done after the Crimean war. It would support the demands, and secure concessions which would promote the objects of its existence: In case of victory, it would have abundant opportunities for action and the exercise of its influence in the discussions that would follow in regard to the relations of the freed South Slavic nationalities.

Traces of the power and activity of the sentiment on which the Slavophile party is founded—that of reaction against the reforms of Peter the Great—may be found throughout the history of the eighteenth century, although they do not appear in such close connection as to constitute a visible chain of events. The quiet, but constant and formidable opposition of the sects of the "Old Believers" to the State Church; the Strelitz insurrections; the Dolgoruki conspiracy of 1730; the expulsion of German statesmen and marshals under the Empress Elizabeth; the intrigues of Lomonosoff against the German members of the St. Petersburg Academy of Sciences; the Pugatsheff outbreak; the removal of Barclay and Benningsen from the chief command of the army in 1812; the Dekabrist insurrection of 1825, which bore in some respects against West-European ideas, may all be referred to as forerunners of the great revolution which has spread during the last forty years in the bosom of Russian cultivated society, and has come to light under the reign of Alexander II. This revolution is not the work of any particular men, nor the result of a deliberate plan, but is the product of a combination of circumstances. There are a few men, however, who have been more prominently identified with the movement, and have contributed conspicuously to give shape and

33

direction to the thoughts and acts of their compatriots, whose character and history it is necessary to know in order to understand thoroughly the aims and mode of action of the party. For the account of these men and the history of the growth of the movement, we are indebted to a carefully prepared sketch published in the *Allgemeine Zeitung* in 1877. In nearly all countries, the popular sentiment finds its best expression and representation in the popular romantic poetry, from which it often receives also its strongest guidance. It is so in Russia; and the Slavophile party has been largely built up around and by means of the literature of this school, and has found its most influential directors in the ranks of the men who cultivate this literature.

Among the men most prominently known in connection with this party are the three Aksakoffs, the father and two sons. The elder Aksakoff, Sergius Timofeyevitch, was one of the well-to-do nobles of the middle class, and was born at Ufa in 1791, to the possession of important estates in the Government of Orenburg. He held an appointment on the Land Commission of 1804, and was employed at a later date in the Bureau of the Censorship. In all his public positions he was distinguished for capacity and independence of thought. Like all active Russians of his time, he fell under the influence of the French and German literature of the eighteenth century, and by their help raised himself above the crudeness of his ancestors. He translated some of the representative works of French literature, wrote for the paper of the party of reform, took part in the discussions of the day with those who advocated an advanced training, and in all of these engagements combined a patriotic, Russian tone of thought with irrepressible enthusiasm for cosmopolitan culture. His saloon was for many years the rendezvous of writers, poets, and publicists of the most diversified views, whose influence was manifested very perceptibly upon the sons, who grew up in the presence of such meetings, as well as upon the father himself.

These sons, of whom Constantine was born in 1817, and his brother Ivan was a few years younger, had been students at the High School in Moscow, where they had come in contact with the philosophy of the Germans Hegel and Schelling, and had become inspired with the mystic romanticism which was at that time making the circuit of the world. Controversies arose in time among the band to which the brothers were attached, respecting the relation of knowledge to faith, and of nationality to humanity, which resulted in bitterness and a separation into two groups. The Aksakoffs and their friends, Chomiakoff, Yuri Samarin, Peter and Ivan Kireyevski, formed a compact circle, out of which, in course of time, grew the Slavophile party. The watchword of this party was return to the Russian folk-life as it was before Peter the Great; in the name of which they demanded a departure from the heathenish western culture introduced by the great reformer, the study of the theology of the Slavic and Byzantine fathers, a transference of the political balance to the rural population who were uncontaminated by the false Western learning, and the destruction of all foreign, particularly German, influences. These objects were decidedly contrary to the views which had been held by the elder Aksakoff and his associates; nevertheless, the zeal and decision of the sons quite carried the father away, and he became an active participant in their movements. His home became a meeting-place for the followers of the school, and he himself hastened to spread the views he had newly adopted by means of his writings. At the request of his sons, he composed poetical descriptions of the impressions of his childhood-life, in the time of Catherine II. on the banks of the Ufa, in a region then newly won from the Kirghiz, far from any possible influences of European culture. These sketches, which were published in book-form as "Russian Family Chronicles," made a great impression, all in favor of the new party, are a standard work with the party, and rank among the most precious pieces of Russian literature. Sergius Timofeyevitch died in May, 1859.

The original impulse of the movement which led to the formation of the new party had been given by Alexis Stephanovitch Chomiakoff. He was the son of a wealthy Muscovite, and was born in the city of Moscow in 1804. He had spent his youth in a regiment of the horse-guards, had participated in the Turkish campaigns of 1828 and 1829, had afterward traveled through the greater part of Europe, and then returned when thirty years old to his native city. His travels had been made during a time of general reaction and depression, and had given him a bad impression of the condition of the Western nations. He reached the conviction that the civilization of these lands, which was the expression of the Roman Catholic Church, the Roman law, and feudalism, had passed its zenith and was in a decline, and about to yield to a new one originating with the orthodox Slavic and Russian races. To the rationalism, the

alienation, and the spiritual pride of the West, he opposed the
trusting humility of the Russian nationality and the assumed inward
life of the Oriental ecclesiasticism, to the senility and weariness of
Roman and German Europe the unbroken youthfulness of the Slavic
race, from which he expected a new birth of the whole of that quarter of the world. This miracle was to be worked out by a return
to the primitive Christianity of the Eastern Church. Together with
his associates he engaged in the study of the Byzantine fathers, whom
he considered an inexhaustible fountain of wisdom. His first writings were of a purely theological nature, and sought to show that
Roman Catholicism and Protestantism were inwardly hollow, and
had become unfit to give intellectual and spiritual standing to Western life, and that a religious renewal was needed to deliver European civilization from destruction.

A further development was given these ideas by Ivan Kireyevski,
a brilliant journalist, who entered with zest into discussions of the
destructive influence of the reforms which Peter the Great and his
German helpers had introduced into the country, alleging that they
were destroying what remained of the old popular freedom, were
estranging the higher classes from the masses of the nation, were
substituting officialism for self-government, and were carrying Russia into the danger of being involved in the bankruptcy with which
West-European life was threatened.

The propagation of these views, which Chomiakoff, Ivan Kireyevski, and his brother Peter made the work of their life, was at first
conducted by social means, and was confined to a select circle of the
higher society of Moscow. Chomiakoff had great conversational
powers, and a skill in argument and repartee which made him popular even with those who opposed his views, and as he was also in
high esteem as a poet, he occupied a prominent position in the
ancient capital; so his views had acquired more or less of currency,
even before they attracted the attention of the academical circle in
which the Aksakoff sons and their companions moved. Constantine Aksakoff embraced his views, and immediately went to advocating them and carrying them into execution, so far as his personal
habits were concerned, with the recklessness and ardor of youth.
He threw away his fashionable hat on the public street, at the remark of a friend, who suggested, during an evening-walk, that the
wearing of French fashions was the sign of a shameful dependence
on the West, and at the same time took a vow, which he kept liter-

ally, that he would thereafter wear clothes peculiar to his country. After that he wore, whether in the street or in the parlor, the sleeveless jacket and high boots of the peasants. To the astonishment of all who heard him, he expressed to the venerable Prince Galitzin, the Governor-General of the province, the wish that he might live to see the day when his Highness would not be ashamed of the dress of the Russian people. The use of the French language was avoided by himself and his friends; he transformed the appearance and furnishing of his father's house; he sought to restore the characters used in writing before the time of Peter, and made use of every occasion to illustrate his doctrines practically, by forming connections with the people of the lower classes, even going with Peter Kireyevski, one Easter Monday, to the doors of one of the churches, to engage in the disputations there between the Orthodox and Old Believers' sects, according to a custom which had been disused for a hundred years by people of the upper classes.

Two journals, the *Moskwityanin* and the *Mujuk*, were established to advocate the views of the new party. Particular importance was attached by the writers of the party to the reviving of the relations of the Russians with the Slavic peoples outside of Russia, and to the study of the profane and ecclesiastical history of their country. They were never wearied with depicting ideals of the conditions existing before Peter, of denouncing his reforms as an apostasy from the holy traditions of the fathers, of repelling the intrigues of the hated Germans against freedom, and of painting in glowing colors the future of the Slavic world restored to its pristine purity, and prevailing over the ruins of the Roman-German civilization.

At a later date, they indicated the undivided community of the Russian village-system (the Mir) as the fundamental principle of Russian life, and devised the doctrine that Russia was destined to be called, with the help of the new form of civilization peculiar to itself, to deliver the world, free all the bound on earth, and usher in the Slavic millennium. They likewise dwelt on the importance of restoring the old popular usage of the Artel, a kind of trades-union or guild, and on the deep significance of the sectarian life of the Old Believers as a genuine popular protest against the ecclesiastical pretensions and foreign influence of Peter, and aimed, finally, to remove all traces of the reforms which had been introduced during the last one hundred and fifty years. " The Petersburg period of

our history," said one of their articles, "has brought Russia out of
the simplicity of its national development, and has introduced it to a
State-life in which its own people have no part. But while the higher
classes have devoted themselves to the service of the Western idols,
the people have remained true to their native sanctuaries; this people must be established again in the soil of which it has been robbed,
and be made again the peculiar agents of our development if we
would be made whole. This can take place only if we return to
the foundations of our culture which have been deserted. Single
acquisitions of West-European civilization may have their value for
us, but we must completely and forever reject the false fundamental
principle of that civilization. That false principle is that of indi-
vidualism." The article further held up the Russian community as
the proper contradiction and denial of that principle, and praised it
as resting on the genuine Christian principle of humility and self-
denial.

Chomiakoff and Constantine Aksakoff died in 1860—the Kireyevski
brothers and Dimitri Valuyeff had died a few months before them—
making, with the elder Aksakoff, six of the founders of the party
who had died within a few years. Of those who were left, the most
prominent were A. Kosheleff and Yuri Samarin. With them were
associated Ivan Aksakoff, Constantine's younger brother, Prince
Tcheikassky, the Aide during the war of the Grand Duke Nicholas
and Civil Governor of Bulgaria, Lamanski, the elder Pogodin, and
Danilevski. Ivan Aksakoff established a weekly journal, the *Dien*
(the Day), toward the end of 1861, which he committed to the principle last advocated by his brother, of the adoption of the village
commune as the corner-stone of the Russian political life. He also
accepted some points of the programme of the Western Liberals (or
those of St. Petersburg), and urged them with such skill and force
that his journal soon surpassed its contemporaries in warmth and
force of advocacy. By the spring of 1862, the Slavophile organ had
come to be regarded as one of the most progressive journals of the
whole Russian press, and the fact was consigned to oblivion that the
founders of its policy had been regarded by their "Europeanized"
opponents as reactionists and champions of the old Russian political
and ecclesiastical systems; in fact, the political demands of Ivan
Aksakoff and his friends differed only in name from the liberal
measures sought by the Young Russian party. What was asked for
at St. Petersburg, in the name of the nineteenth century, was urged

at Moscow as the inevitable accompaniment of the adoption of orthodox and national principles. Western phrases were employed at St. Petersburg, Old Russian expressions at Moscow, to cover what, when analyzed, were found to be substantially the same specific objects. That the *Dien* laid especial stress upon the connection of Russia with the other Slavic nations, that it appeared more hostile to the Germans than other journals, that it advocated the general extension of the world-delivering communal tenure of property and the consequent abolition of rank, were deemed particular merits by the excited writers of both capitals; even its Churchly zeal caused no shock, for in this it urged primarily the deliverance of the lower spiritual orders from the dominion of the arrogant bishops and monks. The higher clergy or monks were looked upon as Grecian, not Russian—an importation from Constantinople—and, therefore, as proper objects for the animadversion of a Slavophile organ

The insurrection which broke out in Poland and Lithuania was a source of embarrassment to the Slavophiles and their organs. It was difficult to find a way of dealing with it which would not involve the violation of some of their principles. The Government party need not hesitate to suppress the insurrection; the Western Radicals, not being troubled with Old Russian doctrines, could give their sympathies, without question, to a people struggling for some of the principles of self-government; but to the Slavophiles was presented the spectacle of a Slavic people, with whom they should sympathize, struggling to preserve, among other things, the supremacy of the Roman Catholic faith, which it was one of their main objects to put down. On the one hand, Russia had no right to constrain the Polish people, and the Roman Catholics of Old Poland could never be true citizens of an Orthodox Russia; on the other hand, the freedom of the Poles would involve the Polanization and conversion to Roman Catholicism of the White Russians and Lithuanians, who would be subjected to their influence.

The solution of this dilemma was given by the Moscow *Gazette*, a journal which had been recently founded by Katkoff and Leontieff. It demanded a stern suppression of the rebellion, and the forcible deliverance of Lithuania and White Russia from Polish and Roman Catholic influences. The Slavophiles fell in with this line of policy, and proposed, in addition, the extirpation of the Roman Catholic Church, and the forcible subjection of the two provinces to Orthodox ecclesiastical supremacy and a communal division of the lands.

From this time, an accord was established between the Slavophiles and the party of Russian centralization, which was led by Katkoff, and represented by his Moscow *Gazette*. The parties differed as to some points of policy: thus, Katkoff advocated the Russianization of the Polish Roman Catholic Church, rather than its abolition; he had entertained European views on questions of property and instruction, and had no thought of the extension of the communal system; but those differences have not prevented their working harmoniously together under the pressure of questions demanding more immediate attention. On the question of the Baltic provinces, which followed that of Poland and Lithuania, both parties were perfectly agreed. The same measures which the Centralists demanded, in the name of the unity of the State, were urged by the Slavophiles, as called for by reason of the Slavic origin of the Lettish people, and the conversion of a few thousand of them to the Greek Church. Both agreed, also, that the Prussian victories of 1866 were fraught with danger to Russia, and that the only sure allies the country could have should be sought in the United States.

Aksakoff has gradually gained in influence within the United party. The Moscow *Gazette* began to lose in popularity, on account of its advocacy of the classical system of education, which was out of favor, and for other reasons; then Aksakoff, established a new journal, the *Moskwa*, in 1867, and took a stand for the policy of protection; finally, by his marriage with a lady of the Imperial Court, he obtained a prominent position in society, in Court circles, and in close relations with the Czarevitch. Leontieff died in 1875, and Katkoff, suffered by bad health; so that he lost much of his former activity. All of these events worked for the interest of Aksakoff. Finally, on the death of Pogodin, the Slavic committee at Moscow made him their President, and the Chief of a widely-ramified and highly influential society, which, under his direction, has exercised an influence over the course of Russian foreign policy far exceeding anything that he had ever ventured to anticipate.

The Slavic committees of Moscow and St. Petersburg, whose organization has now been repeated in numerous provincial cities, originated in 1857. The Curator of the High School at Moscow, Counselor Bachmetieff, in that year founded a society, for promoting the education of the Slavic people of other countries (especially of Ruthenian Galicia and Bulgaria), which should have for its purpose to furnish the means for pursuing academic studies, to supply books and other educational requisites to destitute Slavic communities, and promote the study of Slavic history and literature. The society became very popular, so popular that the Grand Duke Constantine and other people of prominence were induced to join it Political objects were not thought of at first, but, after a time, Pogodin took the place of Bachmetieff as the head of the committee at Moscow; Lamanski gained the control of the committee at St. Petersburg; the breaking out of the Polish insurrection turned attention to political affairs; political aims quite overshadowed the original objects of the society, and it was turned into an agency for the propagation of Panslavism. The attention of the committees was not directed to the Turkish, but rather to the Eastern-Austrian Slavic lands, particularly to Bohemia and the Ruthenian part of Galicia, where the national feeling has been very active since 1863. A lively business has been done in circulating Russian books, newspapers, church-furnishings, and pictures in these countries, in which numerous young priests, teachers, writers, and officers have assisted.

The principal objects sought by the committees were to effect an organization for the spread of a Russian propaganda in the Slavic foreign States, the establishment and maintenance of steady relations between the Northern and Southern leaders, and to make it possible to work in any given case with machinery already adjusted and in efficient operation.

Only two non-Slavic States in Europe, Prussia and Austria, now have any considerable proportion of Slavs among their subjects. They are, therefore, the particular States whose interests are unfavorably affected by the Panslavic movement. They are, however, affected in very different degrees. Those of Prussia are hardly affected at all, at present the kingdom finding security against Panslavic agitations in two facts. First, it is the interest of the Czar, as the whole course of the war has shown, to cultivate the friendship and support of the Emperor of Germany, who is also King of Prussia, and for that reason he would not tolerate any action originating within his own dominions or inspired from there which would give the Emperor any apprehension, or cause him to suspect his own good faith; second, the Slavic subjects of Prussia are chiefly Poles, who as Roman Catholics have no sympathy for the Greek Church, but an aversion toward it, and who on account of national grudges hate Russia, and everything that is Russian, with the utmost intensity. Austria, on the other hand, has a very large Slavic population, a considerable portion of which is attached to the Greek Church, and is already affected with Panslavistic ideas. The Slavophiles have a promising field for their propagandism among these people, and have already made themselves dangerous to the peace of the Empire.

The Czechs of Austria, notwithstanding the predominance of Roman Catholics among them, have for many years exhibited a warm interest in the Panslavistic movements, hoping by their aid to achieve their own independence. They have caused the Government considerable anxiety by their persistence in seeking autonomy and their refusal to acknowledge that they had any common concern in public affairs with the other nationality. Within the last year, the Roman Catholic priests have taken alarm at some of the religious aspects of the movement, and have forbidden their flocks to participate in the demonstrations, but the warning has been given too late to permit the expectation that it will be effective to restrain an agitation which has become so extensive and gained so much momentum as that for Bohemian autonomy.

A report made in 1878, by Mr. Grünwald, an administrative officer of the county of Sohler, in Hungary, makes a formidable exhibition of the progress which Panslavism has made in ten counties of Northern Hungary, where is gathered a population of 1,800,000 Slavic inhabitants, consisting partly of Greek-Church Ruthenians and partly of Roman Catholic Slovaks. Aided by the similarity of faith, language, and liturgy, the Russian propaganda has made extensive progress, and gained a firm foothold among the Ruthenians. The churches and schools are liberally pensioned by the Russians, and their designs are therefore materially assisted by the priests and teachers. The Hungarian Government has endeavored to counteract the evils produced by this condition, by exercising its authority in the appointment of the bishops, but its bishops find their positions the reverse of easy, and their authority very restricted.

The priests and teachers are also the leaders of the agitation among the Slovaks. Of 703 Roman Catholic priests in the ten counties which form the subject of the report, 268 belonged to the Panslavic party, and 99 of the 178 Lutheran pastors; and they were of the extreme wing of the party, the Lutherans being particularly zealous. A Slavic national casino and a Slavic printing-office have been established at the capital of the county of Thurocz; the Panslavists appear to be masters of the place, and the postmaster is an agent of the Panslavic committee, and was reported to exercise his functions in such a manner as to keep the movements of the Government officials constantly under the inspection of their propaganda. Numerous attractive papers are published by the committee, some of which were distributed gratuitously, and two gymnasia were described as " real hatching-places of Panslavism." The story that Russian money is circulated liberally in Hungary is pronounced to be no creation of the fancy, for the books of the postmaster before spoken of contain accounts of monthly remittances from Russia. This report gives the confirmation of an official declaration to the boasts which the Panslavists have made of the extent of their operations in the Austrian Empire, and to the progress which their cause has made among the people. What has taken place in the ten counties of Northern Hungary has been going on, with such differences in methods and degree as circumstances would produce, in other centers of Slavic population in the Austrian Empire, till the whole political structure of the State is exposed to a constant danger of a breaking out of a contention of race interests.

The Slavic committees of Russia were secretly very active during the Bosnian and Herzegovinian insurrections, and were in reality their main support during the winter of 1875 and 1876, and until war was declared by Servia and Montenegro. Seeing that Herzegovina, both on account of the character of the country and by reason of its nearness to Montenegro, offered the most promising field of operations, they gave their principal assistance to the insurrectionists in that district. Their deputies were stationed at Ragusa and Cettigne in the latter part of 1875, when the movements of the insurgents had come to a stand-still, and the insurrection broke out very soon afterward, although it was in the middle of the winter, with renewed violence. The rendezvous of the plotters was at the house of Colonel Monteverde, afterward chief of staff to General Tchernayeff in Servia, at Ragusa; their funds were distributed through the banking-house of the Messrs. Boscovitch, at Ragusa, and the most effective agent of the committees was Mr. Jonin, Russian Consul-General at the same place. The money with which the insurrection was supported was collected under the guise of taking care of the poor rayahs and fugitives in Dalmatia, Montenegro, and Servia, and the wounded; but the real destination of the money may be judged from the remark made by M. Vassiltchikoff, Director of the Hospital at Cettigne, to the writer from whom we derive the history of this proceeding:* "In order to tend the wounded, one must first procure them to tend. That will cost us half our money; the other half we will scrupulously employ in healing them."

Ivan Aksakoff was appointed Chief of the committee at Moscow, in place of Pogodin, in the spring of 1876. The declaration of war against Turkey by Servia and Montenegro, three months later, gave the Slavophiles an opportunity for actual work that they had never enjoyed before. That the Czar and numerous high officers, including the Chief of Police, were abroad, was a favorable circumstance for them. They appreciated the situation, and took advantage of it; and during the summer of 1876, the two committees spread their nets over the whole Empire, and soon had all Russia entangled in their meshes. They gave the initiation to the numerous festivals and charitable associations by which the interest of the nation in the Servian war was awakened and kept up, life was infused into the volunteer movement, sanitary supplies were collected for Belgrade and provisions for Bosnia. In consequence of this activity, the Czar was met, when he returned from Germany, with a cry for war which he could not well ignore. The agents of the committee stationed at Belgrade, Moscow, and St. Petersburg, superintended at the former place the distribution of the collected gifts, and at the other places looked out for a continuance of the supply. The recruiting and fitting out of volunteers was attended to in Russia, the assignment of the recruits and the adjustment of their relations with the native officers, in Servia, all under the auspices of the society.

The press was engaged in the service of the committees. Provision was made for the furnishing of correspondence and articles in behalf of the movement; the interest of the clergy, of prominent women, young men, and young women, was engaged, and sympathy with the cause of the Servian brothers was made popular in all grades of society, and, above all, fashionable. Men of good military standing were enlisted among the volunteers; women of the rank of the Princess Shachovsky engaged in work for the care of the sick;

---

* *Macmillan's Magazine*, November, 1877. This writer professes to write from personal observations and acquaintance.

counselors interested themselves in the conduct of the sanitary
trains ; excursions, fairs, concerts were projected in all parts of the
Empire, and returned liberal sums to the treasury of the society ;
the contribution-box was presented at every dinner and large meeting ; the cause was introduced at every church service and festival
and school-meeting ; the officers of the Government observed the
activity with respect to the volunteers, without showing anxiety,
believing that it afforded a safety-valve for the unquiet spirits of
the Empire. It proved, however, to be the source of complications,
for, at the very height of its activity, the Government was compelled,
by the collapse of the war and the critical situation of the volunteers,
to come out from its position in the background and take the lead
of the movement.

In the circles around the Czar and the central offices, opinions
were greatly divided. The women, the younger officers, and the
priests made no secret of their enthusiasm for the Servian cause ;
the higher dignitaries, the men of the counting-houses, the Germans,
and the Conservatives of the old school held aloof from it. They
made use of the defeat of the Servian army, of Tchernayeff's unauthorized proclamation of a Servian kingdom, and of other events
of the war, which involved danger to Russian honor, as arguments
with which, nursing the Czar's aversion to all things that savored of
conspiracy or disorder, they hoped to prevent his giving sympathy to
the movement. The war party maintained that the nation had
already gone too far in the support of the Bosnian and Servian complaints, to stop without harm to Russian influence in foreign
diplomacy. A strong word from the Czar and a significant flourish
of the sword would be potent to compel the Porte to make unconditional concessions, would lead to a triumph of Imperial influence,
and would serve to restrain the excesses of the national movement.
There was force in the views of both parties, and the Czar sought a
middle course, when on the 11th of November, 1876, he made that
address at Moscow, in which, after condemning the course of Servia
in the severest and most unequivocal language, he declared that
Russia must fulfill the pledges to the Slavic peoples which Servia
had made. The order for the mobilization of the army was issued,
which all Europe regarded as foreshadowing a declaration of war,
and at the same time enlistments for Servia were forbidden, the
returning volunteers were received with tokens of displeasure at the
course they had taken; Tchernayeff was forbidden to return to

Russia for some time, and the agitations, which had been publicly permitted for five months, were suddenly quieted. The pro-Servian enthusiasm of the past summer was afterward mentioned in courtly circles, with a shrug of the shoulders and a smile, as a " folly."

Aksakoff and his associates showed themselves equal to the difficulties of the situation. They received warnings and notices from the Press-administration, that during the course of the conference at Constantinople, communications concerning the agitations in favor of war, and particularly publications of the transactions of the Slavic committees, were forbidden. They well understood the change that had taken place in the views and decisions of the Sovereign; but they did not deviate from the policy which they had hitherto followed with so much advantage.

They construed the speech of the Czar into a promise to answer the wishes of the people, and bring them to a true fulfillment. Aksakoff, with great skill in sophistical interpretation, declared that the divine Czar had done no more than give legal expression to the voice of his people, and had expressed the firm determination of Russia to continue on the road it had already traveled. Only short-sighted fools could doubt what the Government would eventually do, and what it owed in respect to external affairs. As soon as the first indignation of the Government had passed away, the committee silently resumed its interrupted labors. What could not be spoken in public places was said, without hesitation, in the conversation of parlors. Pains were taken to secure an acceptable comprehension of the situation, and to combat the " unjust judgment" which had overtaken the Servian champions and their comrades, in consequence of a single mishap. The course of events at Constantinople worked admirably into their hands by seeming to confirm all that they had said about the duplicity of Western diplomacy and the obstinacy of the Porte, so that they even gained ground among their former opponents. It became known in the beginning of December that the attention of his Majesty had been directed to Prince Tcherkassky, Aksakoff's most trusted associate, with a view of making use of his administrative ability. A little while afterward, the Prince visited the headquarters of the active army at Kishenev, and his friends at Moscow and St. Petersburg felt that he had gained his end. His appointment as civil aide to the future Commander-in-chief of Bulgaria spoke volumes, and care was taken that the news, and its significance, should be spread into the quarters where the best use could be made of it.

When, at the beginning of the new year, the conference had proved a failure, and it was evident that the policy of the Government would be changed, but before the censorial prohibition had been removed, the Moscow *Gazette* published an address which Aksakoff had made at a meeting of the Moscow committee. This address denounced the attempt to effect a diplomatic mediation between Russia and the West as treachery, and reproached the wavering counselors of the Czar that "they were wandering in darkness, that they had taken the false lights of European ideas as their guide, were wandering in diplomacy, and had accepted, without rebuking them, affronts which had brought blushes to the face of the mortified nation. The blood of our slain brothers," he continued, " is not yet avenged, but is treated, as if it were the blood of Hottentots, with shame and scorn." After a strong exhortation to resistance against the " treachery which has spun its webs in Russia," he closed with the assertion that "we have behind us the people, before us the words which the Czar has spoken from the heights of the Kremlin." The number of the Moscow *Gazette* which contained this speech was confiscated. But thousands of copies of the speech escaped the censorship, and were circulated all over the Empire.

Two months later Aksakoff made another speech before the committee. He was able to announce the complete and public triumph of the cause to which he had unequivocally devoted himself in the darkest hour. War was declared, the Slavic committee had been converted, with the approval of the sovereign, into a Slavic Benevolent Union, to which its President was able to announce that the time for mere private activity was over, that the labors which had been begun by the committee could now be continued in the full light of day, and that his Majesty the Czar had been pleased to intrust to the civil aid of the commander-in-chief the duty of keeping up a direct intercourse with the Union. A delegate of the Union would accompany his Highness to the scene of the war, and he, the President, would take care that the great work should be maintained at the height of the standard of its national significance

An enthusiastic meeting of the Russian Club at Warsaw, on the 23d of May, 1877, was addressed by Professor Nikitsky, Professor of Russian History at the University of Warsaw, who spoke of Slavism as the new factor which had appeared on the historical scene. Slavic solidarity had now come forth as a colossal power, controlling millions. The Slavs appeared before the eyes of astonished Europe as one family, animated with one thought, one feeling, one will. The whole Slavic world, with Prague at its head, encompassed the holy Russia, which had gained, so to speak, millions of new sons. It had undertaken a new historical labor—the freeing of the Slavs—and had inscribed "the Slavic cause" upon its banners. Another speaker said that the Sagas related that in the old times three brothers, Czech, Lech, and Rus, had come from the Danube to the North and separated; "God grant that they may meet again on the Danube." Speeches harmonious with the others were made with reference to the Slavs in Germany and Bohemia.

On the 8th of November, 1877, Aksakoff made a noteworthy address before the Slavic committee at Moscow, in which he regarded the war from a national Russian point of view, and paid as little regard to the interests and aspirations of the West of Europe as to those of Turkey. He ascribed the poor success which had attended the Russian operations in the war to the errors of the leaders of the nation, or the "elder brothers," who had committed "the deadly sin which is the root of all our social evils; the sin of forgetting Russian nationality." The processes of the organic life of the people could be perceived only by a few, who had raised themselves by thought and education above the ordinary level. The Russian common people had little historic knowledge and no abstract conceptions about the mission of Russia in the Slavonic world; but they had historical instinct, and they clearly perceived one thing, that the war was caused neither by the caprice of an autocratic Czar nor by unintelligible political considerations. Free from all ambition and all desire of military glory, they accepted the war as a moral duty imposed by Providence. "The Russian nation," he said, "looks upon this war, not as the outcome of the absolute will of the Czar, but as its own cause—a sacred, inevitable work; a war for the Orthodox religion and the whole Slavic brotherhood. The popular movement of 1876 made the war inevitable. That which the national conscience pronounced to be an undoubted moral duty was at the same time the historical mission of Russia as the head and representative of the Orthodox and Slavic world, which has not yet been entirely created, and awaits its future development in history. All the importance of Russia in the world is based on her national and religious individuality, which has grown up from her internal strength and her spiritual elements, differing entirely from the elements of Western Europe; it depends, in a word, on her Orthodoxy and her Slavism. Russia will never be able to attain her complete development until she brings about the victory of these spiritual elements in their original dwelling-places, or, at least, until she restores to complete legal equality the peoples related to her by blood and feeling. If Russia does not liberate the Orthodox East from the Turkish yoke and from the physical and intellectual encroachments of the West, she will become an organism with a defective circulation, condemned to remain forever a cripple. The war was therefore as much an imperative necessity for her as the defense of her own existence, or as the natural progress of her development, of her growth, as the stream of her historical shaping. . . . . Diplomacy, that genuine figure of want of character and of national indifferentism with an unfeeling heart, which shuns men, began its activity in favor of the enemies of Russia and wholly against us. Europe was quick to believe the report of the unwillingness and unreadiness of Russia to make war, and stretched us upon the rack of diplomatic concessions. Turkey is fighting to the death for her religion and her race, while our diplomatists and conservatives tell us that the war is only one for humanity and civilization, not one for religion and race. But if it is not a war for religion and race, it is an absurdity. Though conservatives may be horrified at the ideas of Slavism and Orthodoxy, it is in those ideas that our strength lies, and they alone can lead us to victory. Any misunderstanding on this point is dangerous. Away with the senseless and colorless device of the interests of Europe! 'Russia could not retreat or stop,' though all Europe should place itself as a wall in our path. Retreat would be treachery toward the suffering Slavs, treason to an historical mission, and the beginning of death. Let us accept new burdens and make new sacrifices. The historical path of the nation has been and is still surrounded and obstructed by many obstacles and many trials; but with the help of God it has overcome them in the past, is overcoming them in the present, and will overcome them in the future."

34

CHAPTER V.

THE PERIL OF AUSTRIA.

The immediate Concern of Austria in the Integrity of Turkey—Austro-Hungarian Interests alone Regarded—The Heterogeneous and Discordant Populations of the Empire-Kingdom—Decline of Austrian Predominance in Germany—The Compromise with Hungary—Troubles arising out of the Diversities of National and Race Interests—The Czechs and the Poles—Discontent of the non-Magyar Nationalities of Hungary—Centrifugal Tendencies in the Empire and Kingdom—Hostile Designs of the Panslavists—The Magyars Friends of Turkey and Enemies of Russia—Any Change in the Eastern Situation Dangerous to Austria—Hungary—Views of Hungarian Statesmen—Gen Klapka—Louis Kossuth—Jealousy of the Visit of Signor Crispi, and his Proposition for a Confederation of Slavic States and the Enlargement of Greece—Pro-Russian Influences at the Court of Vienna

WE have alluded, in the two preceding chapters, to the manner in which the tranquillity of the Austrian Empire is imperilled by the national aspirations of Rumania and Servia on the one hand, and by the agitations of the Panslavists on the other. It is the opinion of those who are best acquainted with the affairs of Eastern Europe, that the internal condition of this Empire will give rise to the next complications which will occur in the East after the questions relating to Turkey are settled ; nay, more, that the settlement of the Turkish-Question will have an immediate and important influence upon the aspect of those affairs. In view of all these facts, it seems necessary for an adequate understanding of the bearings of the Eastern Question, and the position of affairs in reference to it, to give a more particular account of the relations of Austria to the late dependencies of Turkey, of the manner in which they are affected by the adjustments now going on, and of the views of prominent statesmen of the Empire on the subject

The Austro-Hungarian Monarchy is more immediately and deeply concerned in affairs relating to Turkey, and the adjustment of the Eastern Question, than any other State. Even England and Russia must give place to it in the extent to which their interests are involved, for their interests in Turkey are external, and relate, at the most, to colonial matters and the routes of trade ; while, with Austria, the internal social conditions, and the integrity of the most essential parts of the Empire, are affected by whatever takes place in the European provinces of Turkey. The Empire is so surrounded by Russian and Turkish territory, and has so many populations which are affiliated by race, religion, or language, or all of them, with contiguous populations in those States, that no movement can take place in either which will not be reflected in some of the provinces of Austria and Hungary.

So closely and predominantly are the Austro-Hungarian interests interwoven with the Russo-Turkish issues that the minds of the statesmen of the Empire, in considering the Eastern Question, are occupied with them to the exclusion of all the other questions of popular and national rights, of religious privileges, and of humanity, with which the discussions in all other countries are diversified. These questions are important, they admit, and deserve consideration by those whose position permits them to regard them, but they can only look to their own preservation. The text of all the official Austrian and Hungarian declarations since the complications began which led to the war, has been the same. The Imperial-royal Government (imperial as to Austria, royal as to Hungary) must be controlled in its course, not by the consideration of Turkish interests, or of Slavic interests, or of Christian interests, but of Austro-Hungarian interests. These interests were thought to demand the full maintenance of the territorial integrity of Turkey, but for quite different reasons from those which actuated English statesmen in seeking the same end.

Austria is, with the exception of Russia, the most heterogeneous as to its population, of all the European States; but while in Russia one race has an overwhelming preponderance, Austria enjoys no such advantage. In its population several races of opposite sympathies are nearly evenly balanced. Besides Austria proper, and the provinces which have been cut off from other kingdoms, the Empire-Kingdom embodies the remains of such once important kingdoms as Bohemia, a part of Poland, and Hungary. The people of these kingdoms have no sympathy with each other, and one of them, Hungary, is worse divided against itself than is the Empire as a whole.

The Austrian Empire began in effect to go to pieces in 1859, when it lost its Italian provinces. Until 1866, Austria considered itself a German State, and the leader of Germany. The victories of Prussia in that year forced it to retire from active participation in German affairs, and to endeavor to build itself up as an East-European State. Its first step, and a wise one, was to reconcile the Hungarians. Through the "Ausgleich" or compromise, of which the Baron Von Beust was the principal author, it restored to Hungary, in 1867, the substance of its former constitutional privileges, recognizing it as an integral and at the same time independent part of the monarchy, of which the Emperor of Austria was separately crowned the king, with a distinct title. The kingdom was given a separate Diet and a special ministry of its own, a representation in the General Imperial Ministry, and a joint board of the two divisions of the Empire was constituted to meet annually and arrange certain matters common to both. In the division of the Empire, Croatia, Transylvania, Slavonia, and the military frontier were attached to Hungary, and Croatia was given a local autonomy. The other provinces were attached to Austria, or the Cis-Leithan division, as it is sometimes called. The result of this arrangement was to convert the Hungarians from discontented subjects to strong supporters of the Empire. The Croatians have seemed on the whole satisfied with it; but the Czechs, or Bohemians and Moravians, and the Poles, have never accepted it, but have been made only more eager to secure like privileges for themselves. Cis-Leithean Austria contains in round numbers about 7,000,000 Germans, 5,000,000 Czechs, 2,500,000 each of Poles and Ruthenians, 2,000,000 Slovenians, 587,500 Italians (mostly in the Tyrol and Dalmatia), 207,900 Rumanians in Bukowina; Hungary contains about 5,500,000 Magyars, 2,000,000 each of Germans and Czechs, 2,500,000 Rumanians in Transylvania, and about an equal number of Croats and Servians. As a whole, the Empire contains 9,000,000 Germans, 5,700,000 Magyars, 16,258,300 Slavs of all names, 2,700,000 Rumanians, and Italians, who though they number less than 600,000, form a province. All of these people but the Magyars and Germans have sympathies averse to the present system of government.

The diversity of nationalities is the primary cause of all the losses which the Empire has suffered, and is the source of all the intestine commotions which still afflict it. The Czechs in Bohemia have stood in firm opposition to the Government ever since the compromise with Hungary was effected, and have agitated actively for a like recognition of their nationality. They remember the glories of the ancient kingdom of Bohemia, and express indignation that it has been extinguished and put under the hands of Germans and Magyars, and have many times refused to be represented in the Reichsrath. In 1873, the Austrian Government, fearing that the Slavic factionists might manage to secure so large a representation in the Reichsrath as to endanger the Constitution, secured an amendment to the electoral law providing for the election of deputies immediately by the people instead of through the provincial Diets, which were so imbued with hostility to the Government that it was felt they could not be trusted. In the next year, the Czechs presented to the Emperor, on the occasion of his visiting Bohemia, petitions for the decentralization of the Empire and the restoration of Bohemian autonomy, some of which were so strongly worded that it was deemed prudent not to take public notice of them. The Galicians, or Poles, manifest a similar spirit, but in a less demonstrative manner. Their immediate aim is to secure the autonomy of their province, and use the advantage thus gained to form a nucleus around which to rebuild a Polish Empire. They have an intense hostility toward Russia.

The discontent in Hungary is also very great. A convention of Croats, Slavonians, Rumanians, Slovaks, and Ruthenians, which was held at Temesvar in 1868, adopted a programme favoring a confederation according to nationalities, protested against the union of Transylvania with Hungary, and adopted a resolution approving the efforts to upset the compromise of 1867, because its provisions were fatal to the national rights of the non-Magyar races. The Rumanians also held a separate conference, the resolutions of which advocated abstention from the elections because the claims of the Rumanian nation had been disregarded by the Reichstag at Pesth.

The Slávs of both divisions of the Empire, notwithstanding their disagreement in many respects, have all united in demanding the recognition of their several idioms as the language of instruction in the districts where they prevail; the Croatians, Servians, and Slovens, as well as all the other tribes of Austria, have now a complete system of national instruction, embracing elementary schools for every town and village; a large number of gymnasia, progymnasia, real and special schools. A complete university has been established at Agram, which has been organized after the model of the German universities. Compulsory school laws have been adopted in Austria proper and Hungary, the effect of which will be to raise the Slavic peoples to the level of the more advanced Teutonic nations, at least so far as the universality of education is concerned. The educational system will also, so long as the Slavic languages are recognized, contribute to the strengthening of their national feelings, and enlarge their capacity and opportunity to make them manifest.

The security of the Empire and kingdom is thus endangered by centrifugal tendencies which are powerful in every part. In case it should be divided, there would be but little difficulty in deciding upon the fate of its component nationalities. The Germans desire to have a part again in the affairs of the German Empire, and to be one with the great German people, and are already not a little dissatisfied that they are set off away in the East with a number of nationalities with which they have no common interest. If they were sure they could continue to rule the nation, the case might be different, but they are not sure of it. They have had to divide their powers with the Hungarians, only to see other nationalities coming up to claim their share in the division. They labor under the constant apprehension that they will sometime become only a unit among the other constituents of the State, and this apprehension keeps them desirous of asserting their German relationship while there is yet time. The Czechs and Poles, as we have seen, aspire to a separate existence, or a predominant influence. The Rumanians hope to be made a part of the Rumanian nation. The Croats and Servians in the Banat and the military frontier dream of becoming part of the renewed Servia and of seeing united Servia and Bosnia with themselves formed into a Servian or Croatian Empire. South Tyrol and Trieste are gravitating to Italy. Over all the Slavic nationalities, moreover, hovers the great Panslavic scheme threatening to absorb them and unite them in a grand Slavic Empire, which Russian agents are industriously propagating throughout the country. Some of the Slavs, it is true, are averse to this plan in the exact form in which the Russian agents urge it, because it is allied with the Greek Church, while they are Roman Catholic, and it interferes with their desire to restore their own kingdoms, but they are, nevertheless, seeking a Slavic independence, and are always ready to assail the Austrian and Hungarian régimes.

We have shown in the previous chapter how the general aims and policy of the Panslavists are detrimental to the integrity of the Austrian Empire, and have cited examples of the character and extent of their operations among its Slavic populations. The fact of their entertaining a settled design of dismembering this Empire,

as the State which stands most in the way of the realization of their
schemes, is confessed and made prominent in the work on "The
Military Strength of Russia," published by the Russian General
Rostislav Fadaieff, a Panslavist, in 1869. According to his remarkably frank exposition of the designs of his party, it is the duty
of Russia not only to extend its territory in Europe, but also to
make allies of the kindred tribes and peoples of the Orthodox faith
outside of the Empire, and confirm their attachment by the closest
relations. One State, Austria, is an obstacle to the consummation
of this object. Austria, therefore, must be considered Russia's
natural, nearest, and most dangerous enemy. The condition of
enmity exists especially in respect to the Eastern Question, which,
according to General Fadaieff, is a living question for Austria as well
as for Russia, except that it affects them in an opposite direction.
General Fadaieff then delineates the strategical and political situation
of Austria in reference to the Eastern Question, showing how easily
and sensibly Austria could affect the Russian interests, and concludes
that there is but one means of opposing this wicked power. Russia
must take in hand, with decisive will, the cause of all the Slavs and
all the Orthodox. "The Greeks and the Rumanians are not necessary for Russia, but they are dear and welcome, because they are of
the Orthodox faith. The Polish Question will be ours, if we make
it a Slavic Question. We must make the Poles realize that they
are a Slavic people. We must proceed, in a similar manner, toward
the other Slavic peoples. Russia must arouse in them the conviction that their national leaders have their support and reserves there,
that every Slav has there his home." Fadaieff's scheme of reconstruction of the Slavic nationalities contemplated the autonomy of
the States, which should, however, constitute together a single Empire as before the world, and place the conduct of international and
military affairs in the hands of the great Slavic Czar, their common
head, while their own particular rulers should belong to branches of
the same family. The first step toward the attainment of this object should be the restoration, within ten years, of Ismail on the
Lower Danube and of East Galicia. The later proceedings of the
Panslavic leaders form a striking commentary upon the sincerity
of these declarations, and do not tend to diminish the alarm that
the Austrians feel in the face of them.

A total dissolution of the Austrian Empire would leave the
Magyars in a sad state, for they would be scattered all over Hun-

gary among the other nationalities, and deprived of the power of maintaining their existence as a State.

The apprehension of such a dissolution is real and active among the Austro-Hungarian statesmen, and has guided and governed their Eastern policy for a long time. The Magyars are, moreover, bitter enemies of the Russians and warm friends of the Turks, for reasons peculiarly their own. They are affiliated by race with the Turks, being Turanians of a related stock, and having come, centuries before the Turks appeared, from nearly the same part of the world which was the birth-place of the latter. They remember also how Russia helped to crush their national movement by force in 1848, and how, after it was crushed, Turkey received and befriended their exiled patriots. For a similar reason they are cool toward the Croatians, because the Croatian ban Jellachich and Croatian soldiers were the principal instrument of its own military force which Austria used to suppress their rebellion.

No change can be made in the relations of the European dependencies of Turkey that does not seem to be fraught with great dangers to Austria-Hungary. If Russia annexes any of them, its power will be strengthened to the weakening of Austria, and a fearful impulse will be given to the Panslavic movement. If they are made independent, or are formed into a confederation, the non-German and non-Magyar provinces of Austria and Hungary will be incited to demand to be joined to them or to be made autonomous States. A proposition to give one of them to Austria, such as has been suggested as a possible means of allaying Austrian jealousy, is mentioned with expressions of dread, because it will only add another Slavic nationality to a State which is already burdened with too many such incongruous elements. The Magyars especially deprecate such a scheme, because they are already in a minority in Hungary, and its operation would be to increase the numerical superiority of the dissatisfied races.

The effect which the establishment of the autonomy of Bosnia and Herzegovina would probably have upon the tranquillity of the adjoining Austrian and Hungarian provinces is set forth, in entire harmony with these views, by an English writer, whose article appeared while the negotiations respecting the fate of the Turkish provinces were still the subject of an active discussion. He said, in the London *Spectator* of February 23, 1878:

"The principal Slav provinces of Austria border on Bosnia and

Herzegovina; the population is a difficult one to govern, especially that portion which possesses a quasi-Italian element, and it must be admitted that Austria has been fairly successful. To give an auto-nomical form of government to the two Turkish provinces, to make them practically independent, with an amount of freedom such as it is politic as well as necessary to give to Bulgaria, would no doubt result in an unmixed benefit to the populations; but it would un-questionably raise a very strong feeling in Croatia and Dalmatia, which would no doubt spread into the adjacent provinces, and put a strong disturbing force into the hands of Italy. From my knowledge of the peoples of these countries, loyal as they are now to the Aus-trian Crown, I do not believe they would long remain so; and con-stituted as the Empire of Austria is, occasion would never be want-ing for the creation of disturbances which would shake the monarchy itself, if, indeed, any lengthened continuance of them did not dis-solve it. We should, in fact, be only closing the Eastern Question to open an Austrian-Slavonic Question."

Thus the Austro-Hungarian nation is placed in a position in which it is liable at any day to have to face the question of what excuse it has for continuing to exist.

Although the Government has refrained from making official ex-pressions bearing directly upon these points, utterances and acts are not wanting to show that it has had them in view, while the indi-vidual expressions of the journals and of the leading men upon the subject, especially in Hungary, have been very free. Semi-official communications were published in the Hungarian papers in May, 1877, which were intended to appease the agitation for a war with Russia. They conveyed the assurance that the Government would, under no circumstances whatever, approve the union of Servia, Bos-nia, and Herzegovina into a separate State under an Austrian Arch-duke, "as such an arrangement would not afford any guarantee to Hungary against the prejudicial influence likely to be exercised by such a State upon Hungarian interests," and gave, as among the points of Count Andrassy's programme: "The position of Ru-mania is to be regulated only in accordance with our interests. Ser-via is not to annex anything. No large Slavic State is to be estab-lished in South-eastern Europe. A Russian protectorate over the Danubian territories is out of the question." The apprehension was often expressed, that if the destruction of the Turkish Empire were allowed, Austria-Hungary would be the next object of attack, and it would soon share the fate of its Ottoman neighbor. Gen. Klapka made a speech at an important public meeting in Pressburg, on the 13th of August, 1877, in which he said that the conviction had been reached in Hungary that if Russia succeeded in the East, the turn of Hungary would come next. What can we substitute, he asked, for the Turks after they shall have been driven out of Europe? "Is there a single people in European Turkey which would be in a condition to display one-tenth of the force with which the Turks have defended their cause? But if, contrary to our hopes and wishes, Turkey is overcome by Russia, we should ask, what will be the consequence to Hungary and the Austro-Hungarian monarchy? . . . . After Servia, Rumania, Montenegro, and Bosnia are brought completely under Russian control, and are made to do whatever Russia orders them, and Bulgaria has shared their fate, Russia will be lord of European Turkey and will command the mouths of the Danube. If Constantinople is made a free city, it will only be to fall finally into the pocket of Russia. But can we hope that these people, after they have been enabled to gratify their morbid aspirations—Rumania for a great Daco-Rumanian kingdom, and Servia for a great Servian kingdom—will be satisfied with the country freed from Turkey, and will not seek to possess Rumania, all the Rumanians, and Servia, the so-called Voyvodina, Batschca, and Slavonia? While if Turkey prevails, it is plain that these people will pursue their development in other and peaceful ways, and Turkey itself will remain our true friend, possessing a power in our favor, the worth of which has been displayed even just now on twenty battle-fields."

A few days afterward, Louis Kossuth addressed a letter to a public meeting, in which he advocated efforts to prevent a Russian conquest, urging that, if they were not made, the Czar would be regarded as the great Panslavist leader; that the aspirations of Panslavism to rule the world would be grouped around the Czarism; that this would be the star to lead the way of the movement, its lord to command it, its Messiah, for whose call it would wait; its God, whom it would worship, and that out of Panslavism would be developed Pan-Czarism; but that, if the Czar were sent home without a victory, the charm would be broken, and the Panslavist aspirations would lose their spur. Then the different Slavic nations would seek their salvation, not in the culture of Czarism, which only leads to Russification, and into the fetters of slavery and brutality, but in the upholding and elevation of their own individuality. This, he said, is the way that leads to the gain of freedom where it does not yet exist, to the upholding and development of it where it is already possessed. The sympathy and help of the Hungarian people would be with the nationalities in seeking such a career. In a subsequent letter, this statesman—one of the bitterest enemies of Austria—declared that the life-interests of Hungary lay with that Empire, and advised his countrymen to defend it to the last drop of their blood. The integrity of Turkey, he averred, must be maintained, at all events, against Russia, the greatest enemy of Europe. He praised his countrymen for having rejected with indignation the immoral and improvident thought of consenting to a division of Turkey with Russia, and predicted that, "if St. Petersburg and Vienna should divide the fragments of Turkey between them, in less than twenty-five years Russia and Germany and Italy would combine to divide Austria and Hungary among themselves." M. Kossuth repeated these views, at greater length, but without presenting any new points of importance, in an article which he published in the *Contemporary Review* for December, 1877.

The visit of Signor Crispi, the President of the Italian Chamber of Deputies (afterward made Minister of the Interior), to Vienna and Pesth, in October, 1877, was regarded with jealousy by the press of both States. It was suspected that he came to sound the Imperial Government as to whether it would be willing to permit Italy to receive a slice of Turkish territory on the Adriatic, and those journals let it be immediately understood that no such acquisition of territory would be tolerated. They saw in it the first step toward the loss of Dalmatia and the Italian city of Fiume, now belonging to Hungary. The suggestion for a confederation of the Slavic States, and the extension of Greece to the Balkans, which Crispi threw out at a banquet of Deputies at Pesth, was criticised with much disfavor. Such a confederation, it was agreed, was, throughout, against the interests of Hungary, and responded only to the wishes of Russia.

These unfavorable expressions were justified in part by the fact that Mazzini, the distinguished Italian Republican, had expressed the opinion, in his essays on the Eastern Question, written between 1857 and 1871, that the maintenance of the Austro-Hungarian and Ottoman Empires, in their present state, was an impossibility, and that their place would be taken by four Slavic States or Confederations, and that, when Austria fell, the Southern Tyrol and Istria would naturally become a part of Italy.

The course of the Government was apparently controlled by a determination to adhere to the Tri-Imperial Alliance as long as possible—at least, until an Austrian or Hungarian interest was put in imminent danger. A party at the Court of Vienna was often spoken of, which was understood to be under German influences, and to be favorable to a co-operation with Russia in its attack upon the Porte; and it was accredited with having been able to persuade the Government to such an extent that it inclined to seek a policy between the one indicated and that which was advocated by the Magyar leaders. Although the personal feelings of the Emperor were in actual sympathy with those of the Germans, and although the Government reposed great confidence in the advice of the German Emperor and his Chancellor during all the trying scenes of the war, its course does not appear to have been changed under any of the conflicting influences which were brought to bear against it, but to have been pursued in adherence to the neutrality which was announced at the beginning of the war.

An official expression of regard for other interests than those of the Empire, was made at the opening of the Chambers on the 10th of December, when Count Andrassy declared that he was opposed to the idea that, in compliance with external prejudices, the Christian populations of Turkey should be under Turkish rule. This was regarded by some partisans as a concession to the German party at the Court. It was, more probably, a concession to the plainest principles of humanity, which even an Austrian Chancellor, with the fate of the precarious fabric of an unhomogeneous State in his hands, could not always evade.

The Government made a cautious expression of opinion respecting the bearing of the peace preliminaries proposed by Russia and accepted by Turkey, when on the 19th of February, 1878, the Austrian Minister-President in the Reichstag, and the Hungarian Minister-President in the Diet, stated, in answer to questions, that among the stipulations were some which could not be brought into harmony with the interests of the Austro-Hungarian Monarchy. This remark did not apply to those stipulations meant to improve the condition of the Christian populations of Turkey, which Austria-Hungary always had at heart as much as any other power, but to those which might produce changes in the relative position of the European powers in the East. The Government, however, hoped that it would be possible to smooth over these difficulties, and that a solution would be effected which would lead to a lasting peace, as satisfying all interested. But, in all circumstances, the Government would regard it as its main task to protect the interests of the monarchy in every respect and in every direction. The efforts of the Russian diplomats in their intercourse with Austria were for some time after this directed to the devising of measures to conciliate the Austrian interests and remove their objections to the substantial consummation of the Russian scheme.

CHAPTER VI.

ENGLAND AND RUSSIA.

Fear of Russia entertained by the Powers—Early advances of Russia toward Constanti-
nople—Frederick the Great on the Threatening Power of Russia—Will of Peter the
Great—British Interests in the East—Russia and England Rivals in Asia—Russian
Conquest Dangerous to the British Tenure of India—Kashgar and Russia—Afghan-
istan, its Importance to British Interests—Russian Influence in Persia—The Blunder-
ing Diplomacy of the English Government Condemned—Position of the English
Parties on the Question—Counter-arguments of the anti-Russians and the anti-
Turks—Views of the British Cabinet and Conservative Statesmen—The Positions
assumed by the Liberal Statesmen—Moderated tone of the English Journals—Why
England and Russia should not Quarrel—They are the Destined Rulers of Asia—What
Benefits they have Conferred upon it—What they may yet Accomplish for its Civiliza-
tion and Prosperity.

THE increase of territory and population which accrues to Russia
by the peace of San Stefano is not as great as the increase in prestige and in indirect influence. The actual increase in territory and
population is in fact small, comprising only that part of the Dobrudja
which it is proposed to exchange for Rumanian Bessarabia and a
small territory in Armenia; but the increase in prestige and influence is very great. It amounts to the conquest of the chief Mussulman power, the power to which most of the other Mohammedan
nations of the world looked up as their head, and to the establishment
of a new State touching both the Mediterranean and Black Seas, over
which no pains will be spared to make Russian influence supreme
It establishes a permanent terror among the Mohammedan nations
of Asia, which already had reason enough to fear Russia, and plants
a thorn in the flesh of all the Mediterranean powers. Most of the
European Governments have seemed to feel these facts keenly; and
even the German Government, which has been regarded as the supporter of Russia to a certain extent, has repeatedly shown that it
was not indifferent to the sudden exaltation its neighbor had received, and has more than once intimated that there might be a
limit, beyond which it would not allow it to go without a protest.

The jealousy and fear which the rival powers entertain of Russia are not of recent growth. They have been felt and expressed by the rulers of different nations ever since the Muscovite State became important enough to attract the attention of its neighbors. They have increased as its dominions have been extended on every side, have been fed by every new addition to the territory of the Czars, and have been intensified in the States which have successively been victims of Russia whenever some of their fair provinces have been torn from them. The tendencies of Russia toward Constantinople and the East have been noticed since the very foundatian of the republic of Novgorod. A Hungarian writer, Mr. Benjamin Von Kallay, in a pamphlet recently published in Pesth, recalls the facts, hitherto hardly noticed, that an expedition of the comrades of Rurik descended the Dnieper to the Black Sea in the year 866, and devastated the country around Constantinople; that a second expedition under Oleg, attacked Constantinople from the land and the sea in 905, the land force having marched through Bessarabia, Rumania, and Bulgaria, and over the Balkans, and that three other attempts were made against the Eastern capital during the tenth and eleventh centuries, and while it was still in the hands of the Christian Emperors. The series of expeditions was afterward interrupted by the dominance of the Tartars in the present territory of Russia, but the efforts against Constantinople were resumed as soon as the Tartars had been overcome, and Russia had gained liberty to follow its destiny.

The German Ambassador in Washington, Kurd Von Schlozer, has shown in an article published in the New York *Belletristisches Journal* of March 29th, that Frederick the Great of Prussia expressed his apprehension of the danger which would accrue from the growth and ambition of Russia without reserve. In 1769, after he had formed an alliance with the Empress Catharine, he wrote, "Prussia has reason to fear that its ally, become too powerful, may seek some time to impose laws upon it, as it has done to Poland;" and he wrote to Prince Henry at about the same time: "It (Russia) is a terrible power, which in the course of half a century will make all Europe tremble. Offspring of the Hunns and Gepidæ which destroyed the Eastern Empire, they will be able in a little, while to attack the West, and cause the Austrians to grieve and repent that in their mistaken policy they have called this barbarous nation into Germany and taught it the art of war. . . . At present,

I see no remedy for them, except in forming in the future a league of the great sovereigns to oppose the dangerous torrent."

The Emperor Napoleon I. also had a keen appreciation of the dangers of Russian aggressions, and made the destruction of Russian power a prominent object in his campaigns. To him was attributed the prediction, which has often been quoted, that in fifty years Europe would be either Republican or Cossack. The document called the will of Peter the Great, although it has been proved a forgery, was for some time regarded as genuine, and had a perceptible effect in stimulating the fear inspired by Russia. It was supposed to represent the plans of the great Czar for the future extension of the power and influence of the Empire and the eventual conquest of Europe, and to have been left by him as a guide for his successors to follow. The affectation of carelessness which was given to its style, so as to make it appear more like a memorandum than an elaborate document, and the mention of events which occurred after the death of Peter so that they should seem to be developments of the policy it outlined, contributed to give it currency. The document is so frequently referred to in the literature relating to the Eastern Question that we give in an appendix a full account of its history

The advances of Russia toward the East have appeared more prominent, and have attracted a greater degree of attention within the last half century than the dangers to the West. In the East, Russia is brought into direct conflict especially with two of the powers, Austria and England. We have shown in a previous chapter the nature and extent of the bearing which Russian movements in Turkey have upon the condition of the Austrian Empire. Great Britain, also, as a leading commercial nation is greatly concerned in all that takes place in the Eastern Mediterranean, especially in all that relates to the trade of the coasts and the freedom of navigation; as a Christian State holding large Mohammedan populations under its rule, it is vitally interested in all that affects the relations of the Christian and Mohammedan nations; and as the owner of large territories in Asia, toward which the Russian conquests are steadily advancing, it watches all the movements of Russia and all indications of its policy for the future with a most intense anxiety, which is aggravated by the fact, that these two powers, the greatest on the earth, and the only powers which can approach each other in extent and resources, are stretching their efforts to reach the same points, and are rivals for dominion and prestige in a sense and to a degree which surpass all other rivalry among existing nations. Thus, the action of Russia, whether it relate to Central and Eastern Asia or to Turkey, is scrutinized in England with suspicion, as involving a menace in either case; and the combination and complication of interests are such, that anxiety concerning one aggravates that concerning the other. Since Russia is always making some movement regarding Turkey or the East, the relations of the two countries are always in a critical condition. The discussion of "British Interests" has been among the more prominent features of the war and the negotiations which have taken place concerning it; the existence of those interests forms one of the most formidable and permanent obstacles to the satisfactory settlement of the Eastern Question; and the jealousies and conflicting motives of England and Russia occupied the largest share of the world's attention immediately after the conclusion of the peace of San Stefano. For these reasons, an explanation of the character of the British interests and of the relations into which they have been brought with the transactions and issues of the war is necessary to an adequate understanding of the situation and the course which events are taking.

Russia and England are opposed to each other on all questions relating to the East, because they are rivals for trade and dominion in the East. The trade relations of both powers in Asia have been built up with great expense and are nourished with great care. Dominion is sought by both powers, not, as they profess, on its own account, for both are already embarrassed by the extent of their territories and the lack of homogeneousness of their peoples, but as an incident of trade and a necessary means of protecting commercial relations that are already established. The political and commercial relations of either nation are so connected with every part of the land of Asia, that hardly a question can arise with reference to any part of the continent that will not in some way affect the interests of one or the other of them, and often bring them into conflict. As the acquisitions of both powers have been extended within the present century, the boundaries of their territories have steadily approached each other, until now a comparatively narrow neutral zone stands between them, and the time is looked forward to as possibly not far distant when the pioneer armies of the two States shall meet to dispute about the boundary line. In anticipa-

35

tion of this period, a brisk diplomatic war has been carried on for several years between the envoys of the two powers in the States intervening between Russian Asia and British India, with the object of gaining the precedence of influence and advantageous position.

It is chiefly by reason of these circumstances that the Eastern Question has acquired so much greater importance for England and Russia at this time than it had even during the Crimean war. For it is since the Crimean war that the Russian Empire has been stretched so far toward the East that its continued advance can be regarded as involving a definite threat to the integrity of the British Empire; and what was then only a vague question of general influence and of events which might take place in a distant future, has become for England an intensely practical problem of the safety of its Indian Empire. The question is all the more momentous for England because its tenure of India is in reality very frail. Its two hundred thousand or more of colonists in India are only as a drop in the bucket, by the side of the two hundred and forty-five millions of the native and Mohammedan population; and all the armies it could pour into the country would be insufficient to repress an insurrection of the inhabitants, supported by such able and skilled leaders as they possess of both races. The British had a foretaste of the difficulties they would encounter in case of such an insurrection in the mutiny of 1857, and have since then constantly given their best attention to the provision of measures that would render it impossible for an insurrection to gain headway. The best of such measures would be futile if a powerful neighbor were on the frontier, ready, for the sake of promoting its own interests, to stir up discontent and give assistance to a revolt. Russia, it is feared, might become such a neighbor.

The Chinese Empire has been sorely disturbed during the last twenty years by insurrections among the Mohammedan populations of its western provinces, who are of a kindred race with the Turks, and the Russians have not scrupled to take advantage of these movements to further their own purposes. The Sungarians of Northern Mongolia having risen and expelled the Chinese from the land of Ili and Kuldsha, the Russians came in and occupied the territory, signifying their intention to hold it until the Chinese should be in a condition again to extend their authority over it. With this occupation they came into the immediate neighborhood of the new Mohammedan State of Kashgar, which the adventurous chieftain Yakub

Beg had erected since 1864 within the boundaries of another Chinese province. They were thus brought into a suggestive proximity to the North-western Indian States, with which the British in India had been accustomed to cultivate the closest relations next to incorporating them into their own dominions. Yakub Beg was at first suspicious of the Russians, who also did not show themselves well inclined toward him. He sought a British alliance, and gave the British ample opportunity to cement a friendship with him, and gain an ally who would have been valuable to prevent the Russians approaching nearer to them in one direction. The British were slow in responding to the overtures of the Kashgarian prince, and when, at last, they sent Sir Douglas Forsyth to Kashgar in 1870, they qualified his embassy with such restrictions that it had but little practical result. The Russians, in the meantime, had begun to feel their way into the good graces of Yakub Beg, and at length concluded treaties with him which gave them an advantageous position for influence, and such commercial facilities as conferred upon them in effect the monopoly of the trade of the country. The result of these maneuvers was irritating to the English, and while they did not fail to award the full meed of blame to their own agents for the failure of their blundering diplomacy, their jealousy and suspicion of Russia were increased. The Chinese Government dispatched a formidable army to restore its authority over the revolted province ; the recent death of Yakub Beg—who was a Turkoman of rare genius —deprived the State of its chief defense, and exposed it to a speedy occupation by the Chinese ; but it is not yet safe to say that Russia will not make its power felt in the province.

Within the last fifteen years, Russia has acquired a dominion in Central Asia as large as the Austro-Hungarian monarchy, the Empire of Germany, and the kingdom of Belgium combined, and has found lines of trade which extend away into the western provinces of the Chinese Empire, and almost to the borders of British India itself Its manufacturers and merchants control the markets through most of this vast region. Its goods come into competition with those of English make at several points, and have crowded them out from some. It is fixing the settlement of its new territories, establishing civilization, replacing the nomadic and predatory occupations of its former inhabitants with steady industries and enlightened enterprises, and is preparing the deserts to become the seats of prosperous States ; but in doing all this it is strengthening itself effectually at points where it might come in the way of its rival. During the whole course of its conquests in Central Asia, the Russian Government has repeatedly given assurances that it meant no aggression; that it was obliged to take up arms to protect its merchants from the depredations of the Turkomans; but hardly a year has passed without its adding new soil to its domains, or posting its troops at some position in advance. Their first movements against the predatory tribes, on the Sea of Aral and the Syr Darya River, being avowedly for the repression of actual robbery and lawless violence, excited little alarm, for they clearly had a case in their favor. The Russians were even permitted to chastise the Khans of Khokand and Bokhara without exciting remark, for these barbarous despots had been guilty of acts which justly called for vengeance. As they began to exercise an influence in the internal affairs of these States, and to take steps which looked like reducing them to a condition of vassalage, inquiry was awakened as to their ultimate designs Prince Gortchakoff, in 1864, issued a dispatch to the powers, which was designed to quiet apprehensions, showing that the extension of the Russian territory had been made under the pressure of imperious necessity, and giving assurances that they would not be continued. Nevertheless, circumstances pressed to new annexations. The Khan of Khiva was reduced in 1873, only a small strip of territory being left in his possession, and the Khan of Khokand was conquered, and his whole territory made a Russian province in 1876. The Russian armies exacted the submission of the tribes as far as the borders of Kashgaria, and detachments of their troops made their way into districts not far distant from the frontiers of Persia and Afghanistan.

The disposition of Afghanistan has a very important bearing upon the security of British India. The territory of that State is strategically of great value both to the British and to their rivals, for through it lead the passes by which an army can be conducted from Central Asia to India. The country is practically impregnable to a hostile force, as the British learned to their cost many years ago, so that whoever possesses it, or can gain the friendship of its rulers and people, may have things in his own way, and, in effect, command the gates of India. The English have realized this fact for a long time, and have endeavored to acquire such a footing in the country as would make them safe. First they tried war, but when their armies had been nearly annihilated in the Khyber Pass, after having achieved some successes over the Afghans, they became convinced that a forcible conquest was impossible. They then adopted a peaceful policy, concluded a treaty with the Amir, Dost Mohammed, and kept him in good humor by the payment of subsidies as long as he lived. Upon his death, in 1863, a civil war for the succession broke out among his three sons, in which the English did not take sides, waiting to see which would prevail. The war ended in 1868 in victory for Shere Ali, the present Amir of Cabool, and the English recognized him, and granted him a large annual pension. Subsequently, the Amir quarreled with his son, Yakub Khan, and counted on the support of the English. He did not receive it. A breach was made between him and the English, of which the Russians took advantage Their envoy was publicly received at Cabool in 1876, and the British envoy was treated with coolness. During 1877, the subject of declaring a holy war against England was seriously considered in Afghanistan.

While these events were taking place in Central Asia and Afghanistan, negotiations were conducted for a short time between Great Britain and Russia for the permanent adjustment of their frontier interests and the prevention of future conflicts, by fixing limits beyond which either power should not go. The English proposed to make a neutral zone of Afghanistan, whose integrity and independence both powers should respect. The proposition was favorably received at St. Petersburg, but when it came to perfect the arrangement, a difficulty was met in determining what should be regarded as the exact limits of the territory of Afghanistan. The English could give no guarantees that the Afghans would respect the Russian domain, and the Russians, in the absence of such guarantees, were not inclined to commit themselves to regard Afghanistan as inviolable. The negotiations have, therefore, been so far without result, but the hope that some such settlement may be effected, has not been given up, and it is recognized as desirable by both parties.

The English administration having failed to make a trustworthy ally of the Amir of Cabool, turned its attention to his neighbor on the south, the Khan of Kelat, in Beloochistan. Friendly relations had existed with this chieftain for about twenty years, when they were broken off during the Vice-Royalty of Lord Lytton, in India. After an interruption of about three years, an effort was begun in 1876 to restore a good understanding, which has resulted in the conclusion of a treaty between the Indian Government and Kelat, which, in return for the pledge of support and the payment of an annual subsidy, accords to the English a number of valuable privileges, including the right to construct internal improvements in the country, to build forts, and to occupy prominent points with troops. Under this arrangement, a detachment of troops has been placed at Quettah, close upon the Afghan frontier, and the place has been put in communication with the world by a telegraph line through the Bolan Pass.

At present the Russians are understood to have their eyes fixed upon Merv, an 'important trading post in South-eastern Turkistan, about equally distant from the Afghan and Persian boundary-lines, and an easy march from Herat, in Afghanistan.

In all their operations in these quarters, the Russians count on the friendliness of Persia, at whose court they have gained a predominant influence at the expense of England, and with which their Government has commercial, postal, and political alliances. Russia is, in fact, in a position to compel Persia to act substantially as it desires, having already established itself as a formidable neighbor along or near its northern frontiers, both east and west of the Caspian Sea, and being able to threaten an immediate occupation of Tabriz, its northern capital, at any time. Already, Russia has exercised its influence in an important transaction to the discomfiture of English interests, in having induced the Shah to annul the concessions which he had made to Baron Reuter, of franchises for building railways in his dominions, and grant the privilege to another company. Under the franchise thus snatched from England, it is proposed to build a road which shall be extended eventually through Kurdistan to Bagdad, whereby Russia will gain access, if the plan is ever carried out, from a direction whence it was least expected, to the weakest part of the Turkish Empire, and will cut Asia in two with a Russian belt completely separating the eastern from the western part of the continent.

The bearing of the Russian advances on British interests in the East, is clearly set forth in Mr. Rawlinson's "The British in Asia," published in 1875, which carefully reviews the question in all its points. Speaking of the movements of the Russians which seemed to indicate a purpose to advance toward Merv, he says that they evidently mean mischief. "Political objects of high import could alone justify the movement. These objects necessarily point to Herat, which would lie at the mercy of a European power holding Merv, and whence India would be seriously threatened." Herat, adds Mr. Rawlinson, "possesses natural advantages of quite an exceptional proportion. It is the frontier town between Persia and India. It is connected by high-roads with the capitals of all the surrounding countries, ... lying in an admirable climate, and is situated in the midst of one of the most fertile and populous valleys of Asia. Above all, the city itself is surrounded by earthworks of the most colossal character, dating from prehistoric times, which might be improved and rendered very strong. Russia in possession of Herat would hold a grip on India, would command the military resources of Persia and Afghanistan, and would oblige the English to increase their frontier army by at least twenty thousand fresh men." In another place the same author speaks of Herat as "the pivot of the whole Eastern Question," the key to India. The importance which the British have attached in the past to the freedom of this fortress-town is shown by the fact that their Government sent an expedition to the Persian Gulf in 1838, in order, by effecting a diversion, to compel the Persians to raise the siege of Herat, and later, when the Persian troops occupied the place in 1856, went to war with the Shah to compel their withdrawal.

English writers acknowledge that Russia has gained advantages over their statesmen in negotiations, both with the Asiatics and with the British Government itself, and blame the blundering and halting diplomacy which has permitted such a result. Captain Burnaby, of the British Horse-Guards, represents, in his entertaining book, "A Ride to Khiva," that he found the subject talked about by the Tartars and Turkomans of Khiva, and relates a conversation which he had with the Khan of Khiva, in which that chief spoke of the Russian advances in the East, and seemed to be a little surprised that the English regarded them with so much unconcern. "Well," said his Highness, "the Russians will now advance to Kashgar, then to Bokhara and Balkh, and so on to Merv and Herat; you will have to fight some day, whether your Government likes it or not."

A writer in the Pall Mall *Gazette*, speaking of the alienation of the Amir Shere Ali of Afghanistan from the English and his inclination toward the Russians, accounted for them by stating that it was well-known that that prince had plainly said that the English would never, under any circumstances, stretch out a hand to help him in time of difficulty; that, in spite of the guns and money which they had given, he had never been able to conclude any definite alliance with them on which he could rely. They had abandoned Khiva and Bokhara, though "they had talked big about them," and they would leave Yakub Beg of Kashgar to his fate to be crushed out between the Russians and the Chinese, although they had concluded treaties with him, and had dispatched to him two missions. The Amir, in short, in order to save himself from absorption by that which he conceived to be the stronger of the two real powers in Asia, intended to make terms with Russia as against England.

An American writer, Mr. Eugene Schuyler, who has given careful attention to the subject, and whose book on "Turkistan" presents one of the fairest and most complete histories of the Russian advances in Central Asia, characterizes the attitude of England toward Russia, with regard to the points at issue, as "hardly a dignified one" "There are constant questions, protests, demands for explanations, and even threats—at least in the newspapers and in Parliament—but nothing ever is done." "It would seem wiser and more dignified," he adds, "instead of subjecting the Russian Foreign Office to constant petty annoyances, to allow the Russians plainly to understand what limits they could not pass in their onward movement. A state of mutual suspicion bodes no good to the relations of any Governments." *

The Eastern relations of England and Russia had a great influence upon the policy of the British Government and the attitude of English parties during the war. Questions bearing upon them formed the topic of most of the discussions with reference to the position which the country should maintain toward the belligerents. When the Liberals sought to rivet public attention upon the distressed condition of the Christian populations of Turkey, or demanded an imperative expression of opinion by the people and the Government against the atrocities committed by the Turkish irregular troops upon Christian non-combatants, the Conservatives would make no other answer than that it would never do to encourage Russia in a proceeding which might dismember Turkey, place Constantinople in the hands of rivals, or interfere with the communications of the English with their Asiatic possessions. The division of opinion with reference to the question ran very close upon the division lines of the parties. The Conservatives, who were represented by the majority of the Ministry and controlled the Govern-

---

* Schuyler's "Turkistan," ii., 269

ment, held it to be the supreme duty to checkmate Russia. The Government maintained an attitude of watchful observation, aiming to be always ready to interfere whenever any practical British interest seemed to be put in danger. The Liberals—of whom Mr. Gladstone and Lord Hartington were the most prominent—were active, without intermission, to prevent any encouragement being held out to Turkey to continue to refuse what they held to be the just demands of Russia and the Christian populations for guarantees for the permanent improvement of the condition of the latter.

In presenting their views on the merits of the case, the organs of the Conservatives represented that the condition of the Christian populations was only a pretext under which Russia concealed the purpose to carry on a war of aggrandizement. They pointed to the belief which prevailed, to a considerable extent, in other countries than England, and was supported by some plausible evidence, that much of the prevailing discontent was fictitious, and that the manifestations of it, under cover of which the war was made, were, in the first place, instigated by Russian intrigue, and afterward kept up by the influence of Russian agents in Bulgaria and Bosnia, and even in Servia and Montenegro. Some went further, and expressed the opinion that the warlike movements had been encouraged, not only by powers in sympathy with Russia, who expected to derive ulterior advantages from it, but also by other and jealous powers, who anticipated a precipitation of general European questions, in the settlement of which they would make some gain. Therefore, they urged, England must aim to avoid unknown dangers in store.

When in the early summer campaigns it appeared certain that Russia would make a speedy conquest of Armenia, the anti-Russian party endeavored to excite alarm respecting the practical advantages Russia would derive from its victory. It would gain, they said, a rich country, with valuable harbors in the Black Sea, and a friendly Christian population, so situated as to intercept all commercial intercourse between Turkey and Persia and Central Asia; would acquire an immense prestige, inasmuch as the capture and retention of the great Turkish strongholds would " be the occasion of amazement, consternation, and fear, from the head-waters of the Euphrates to the Red Sea, from the Mediterranean to the confines of China;" would cut off a portion of English trade with Asia, bind Persia in tighter bonds, and confirm its adverse disposition toward the English and the Turks, render the construction of the Euphrates

Valley Railway and the opening of a new and friendly route to India by way of the Persian Gulf problematical, and by causing the influence of the English to wither, would insensibly, but surely prejudicially, affect all their relations with the East. Then, having consolidated its Armenian conquests, improved and developed the country, it would, when a new generation of soldiers had grown up, achieve the comparatively easy conquest of Asia Minor, and while it need not disturb the Turks at Constantinople, would permanently cut them off from Syria and Arabia, from Persia and the Tigris Valley.

This view of the future was alarming enough, and had the merit of novelty at the time, for attention had till now been principally directed to the prospects and dangers of Russian conquests in Europe, and the capture of Constantinople, and had made comparatively little account of what was going on in Asia. The view was supported by the appearance of a translation of a pamphlet by the Austrian Baron Kuhn Von Kuhnenfeld, written in 1858, and first published in 1869, which gave a similar forecast of the probable progress of Russia. This author ascribed the Russian movements to the desire of securing a seaboard which would give to the Empire greater facilities than could be afforded by a few Black Sea ports, or even by the possession of the whole of an inland confined sea, like the Black Sea; in effect, to secure a Mediterranean or an Ocean seaboard, or both. He predicted that it would operate through Asia, where it would come into conflict with Turkey, with Persia, and in the end, directly or indirectly with England. Europe would be far off, not directly concerned, and would not be likely to interfere Having moved against Khiva and Bokhara, just as Russia has done, it would annex separate districts of Armenia, seize Persian provinces, bring its full weight to bear upon the Euphrates and Tigris districts and the whole of Persia; once in possession of Armenia, Syria and Asia Minor would of necessity fall to it, and thus it would advance on one side to the whole eastern coast of the Mediterranean, and on the other to the Persian Gulf.

A similar course of reasoning was presented by Mr. Layard, British Minister at Constantinople, in a dispatch to the British Foreign Office, dated May 30, 1877. He urged that whatever the designs of Russia might be as to the European provinces, their execution would be modified or prevented by the opposing interests of Europe, but that no such restraint would be offered against them in Asia. Then, after sketching the probable course of Russian conquest through Armenia and Asia Minor, and the Euphrates Valley, he referred to a suspicion which existed that Russia had already made secret offers to Persia to assist her in acquiring the province of Bagdad in exchange for Ghilan and Mazanderan, believing that it rested on grounds of intrinsic probability, inasmuch as the desire of Persia to possess the province of Bagdad and the shrines of the prophets and martyrs was of very ancient date, and was shared by the whole Persian people, while the possession of the entire coast of the Caspian Sea, and the direct road through a rich and well-inhabited country to Herat and Afghanistan, and ultimately to India, was a matter of vast political importance to Russia. "The possession, by Persia, of the province of Bagdad," the dispatch continued, "would be, as far as England is concerned, its possession by Russia. It must not be forgotten that the possession of Armenia by Russia as regards any designs that she may have upon India, supposing her to entertain them, would be very different from that of any part of Turkistan or Central Asia. In Armenia and the north of Persia she would have a hardy and abundant population, affording her excellent materials for a large army, ready at any time to advance upon our Indian frontier, and resting upon a convenient and sure base of operations, in direct communication, by the Caspian Sea and by Batum, with the heart of the Russian Empire. The moral effect of the conquest of Armenia and the annexation of Ghilan and Mazanderan by Russia upon our Mohammedan subjects, and upon the populations of Central Asia, can not be overlooked by a statesman who attaches any value to the retention of India as part of the British Empire."

When the collapse of the first Bulgarian and Armenian campaigns revealed the weakness and inefficiency of the Russian military organization, the anti-Turkish party were able to reply to these dismal forebodings that the idea that had been entertained of Russian power was a delusion. If, after all its bluster of preparation, and with all the aids it had invoked to its cause, it had not been able to make any headway against an effete and disorganized nation like the Turks, but had been ignominiously thrown back at every point, then it could have no military strength, and could be no match for a well-organized and drilled and effectively-administered nation like England While the probability, even the certainty, that the Russians would eventually come victors out of the war, was admitted, it was held that the victory would not indicate that Russia was any stronger than it now appeared to be, but only that it had greater powers of endurance than Turkey, and would be only the victory of an intrinsically weak nation over a still weaker one.

In reply to this, it was urged that military success was not all that was to be feared from Russia, but that it had a faculty of conquering by diplomacy. Once give it a position of advantage, it would extend its power by negotiation, if not by arms, and as effectively as even with the best successes of arms. The Russian diplomatic transactions during the insurrections in the European provinces, and before the outbreak of the war, had been extraordinary successes, and had almost resulted in the dismemberment of the Turkish Empire, without its being necessary to strike a blow directly. Similar results had attended their negotiations elsewhere, and the inference was justified, that " whenever the conclusion of the war with Turkey leaves them opportunity and leisure, the Russians will find no field so promising as the countries between their own provinces and India."*

The Liberal party considered the subject from a ·very different point of view from that of the Conservatives. They regarded chiefly the duty of England, as a Christian State and the leader of civilization, to seek an amelioration of the wrongs which the Christian populations of Turkey were suffering from their enforced degradation, from misgovernment, from the failure of the Turkish promises to amend their condition, and from such recent horrible incidents as the atrocities in Bulgaria. They believed that the Turkish Government owed its continued existence in Europe largely to British power and influence, and that it leaned upon England as a prop to support it in refusing even the reasonable demands of the powers for guarantees of reforms. They thought that their country was disgraced by tolerating the continuance of abuses for so long a time, and that it would be infamous to tolerate them longer; and they advocated, not participation in the war, but that the Government, informing Turkey that it should not have British support in any contingency, should admonish it effectually to grant the reforms demanded, with guarantees, and remove all pretext for war and Russian encroachment. They believed that if such a demand had been made in the beginning, the Turkish Government,

---

* *Pall Mall Budget*, September 18, 1877

seeing that its case was hopeless, would have granted it; whereas, the British Government, by its drifting policy, had allowed the Turks to delude themselves with vague hopes that England would sometime interfere for them, and had thus encouraged them to be obstinate, and was, therefore, indirectly responsible for the war. The question of trade routes and Eastern Asian relations was not insignificant, but should, in this case, be subordinated to that of duty, which was paramount. They even represented that a correct settlement of the latter question would remove many of the difficulties in the way of the satisfactory adjustment of the other one.

If England, they urged, had firmly, consistently, and honestly supported Russia in its reasonable demands, it would have had influence to prevent unreasonable ones being made. It would have had a measure of control on all the subsequent proceedings so long as it adhered steadfastly and sincerely to the right. If, when Turkey proved contumacious, if such a thing could be supposed, in view of the moral force which a firm attitude would have borne, England had gone forward with Russia to war, or had held entirely aloof from Turkey, it would have been able to restrain the war, to tell Russia when its conquests should stop, and to have a potential voice in fixing the adjustments to be made upon the conclusion of peace. In that case it would have been in a position to secure, without serious embarrassment or controversy, the advantages it desired, its trade routes and relations, and, most likely, a permanent adjustment of all rivalries and conflicting relations in the East. All of these advantages had been thrown away by imbecility and halting diplomacy, just as the alliances of the Eastern Asiatic Princes had been lost by similar means. The jealousy of Russia had been aroused, Turkey was dissatisfied, and the views of England would count for nothing when the time for settlement came.

The Liberals made less of the danger to trade, and Eastern influence involved in a Russian occupation of Armenia and Asia Minor, than did the men of the opposite party. Since the Suez Canal had passed into English hands, the overland routes had lost much of their importance. Let them guard Egypt and the integrity of this route, without reference to Turkey, and British commerce might risk the possession of the Black Sea and the eastern coasts by Russia. On the last point they were not widely separated from the Conservatives, who, foreseeing that the Russian occupation of Armenia was probably only a question of time, advised that especial attention should be immediately given toward securing the interests at Suez.

The view entertained by the British Cabinet of the manner in which English interests might be affected by the policy of the Russians and the success of their arms as against Turkey, was indicated in the dispatch sent by Earl Derby to Prince Gortchakoff on the 6th of May, 1877, just after the beginning of the war, when the unobstructed navigation of the Suez Canal, respect for the integrity of Egypt, the freedom of Constantinople from occupation by other than its present possessors, the maintenance of the existing regulations concerning the navigation of the Bosporus and Dardanelles, and the British interests in the Persian Gulf, were mentioned as points which the Government was determined to defend. The reply of Prince Gortchakoff to the dispatch, while it disclaimed any intention on the part of Russia at striking immediately at any of the interests named by Earl Derby, was so hedged about with conditions and reservations, that it gave no real assurance that in the course of the war some excuse would not be found for putting some of these objects in peril.

Six months after Earl Derby's note was written, at the Lord Mayor's banquet in London, November 9th, Earl Beaconsfield, the Premier, repeated the points which the Foreign Secretary had stated, in almost the same words. Her Majesty's Government, he said, had declared their policy at the outset of the war. It was not a policy framed for the occasion, and merely because war had been declared, but was one which had been deeply considered, it was unanimously adopted, and had been unanimously maintained. It was the policy of conditioned neutrality, of a neutrality which must cease if British interests were menaced. The Premier combatted the idea that Turkey was an effete State, not able to be independent, which was contradicted, he said, by the bravery and achievements of the half million of warriors it had put into the field.

The Liberal statesmen gave free expression to their views on every suitable occasion. The words of Mr. Gladstone, in particular, were remarkably strong, whether in his public speeches or in the articles which he gave to the public through the Press. Speaking in the House of Commons on the 14th of May, he said that the war might even now be ended within a fortnight if England would consent to restore the European concert, and pointed out what a disgrace it would be to England if the liberty of the Christians were secured by an agreement between Turkey and Russia alone. Speaking to the Exeter Liberal Association on the 13th of July, he lamented that England had not been the means of avoiding the war, as it might have been, if it had promoted the concert of Europe instead of checking it, if it had contemplated vigorous action instead of idle words. He had no doubt that if the Government had twelve months, or even nine or six months before declared to Turkey that Europe was in earnest and must not be trifled with, the Christians would have been relieved " by a process perfectly safe and effectual," and peace would have been preserved. He was very sorry to say that there were many indications "of a disposition to raise vain alarms about British interests, which are in no danger at all. Let us," he said, "on the other hand, preach the doctrine of British duties. Let us recollect what was the undimmed brilliancy of British honor; let us remember that this question of the East is not for us a new question; that it is through us that Turkey now enjoys the power she has been so grievously and scandalously misusing, that it is our duty to endeavor to redress the mischief that we may unconsciously have done."

Mr. John Bright, in a speech at Bradford on the 25th of July, said that England was utterly alone in Europe with respect to the closing of the Bosporus and to any question of danger as connected with the closing of the Suez Canal. Among other nations the English demands were felt to be unreasonable and arrogant, and he confessed that he sometimes felt that the English were in danger of a European combination against them, and that they would find themselves "not triumphant, but baffled."

Lord Hartington, the recognized Parliamentary leader of the Liberals, speaking at Glasgow, Scotland, on the 6th of November, said that to see in the Eastern Question nothing whatever except the question of the security of the route to India, was a totally one-sided and totally inadequate view of the case, because it altogether set aside what was, after all, of the greatest interest to England in the matter, the preservation of peace. The Government had boasted that the policy which they were pursuing was a selfish policy. He was not going to say that a selfish policy was necessarily a wrong one for a British Minister to pursue, but he would maintain that if a Government pursued a selfish policy, it ought to be not only selfish, but intelligent. A policy which looked entirely to British interests, omitting all consideration of the interest of other States, was not intelligent; because, however naturally English people might take this view, it was impossible to expect it would be taken by other nations.

Lord Northbrook, a former Viceroy of India, made a decided speech at Winchester on the 9th of November, in which he utterly condemned the idea that Russia could be dangerous to the British dominion in India. It had fallen to his lot, he said, in 1853, when the English were at war with Russia, to be one of those who were directed to inquire whether Russia could affect the British in India, or they could injure Russia in Central Asia. They came to the conclusion that the idea of a Russian attack on India was "perfectly futile." The danger was "a mere bugbear." If this was true in 1853, it was much more true now, for the British were much stronger in India than in 1853, the European army having been tripled, and the triangular railway completed. The extension of Russia in Central Asia, he said, was a natural process, like their own extension in India, and was attended on the whole with benefit, a point which was illustrated by the suppression, under Russian pressure, of the atrocious slave trade carried on by the Turkoman tribes. These remarks had the more force, since the policy which Lord Northbrook had pursued as Viceroy in India, as well as that which Lord Lawrence, another very successful Viceroy, had followed, had been in accordance with the views expressed in them.

Mr. Forster gave a novel view of the case, and one wholly contradictory of the fears which the Conservatives had urged that news of Russian victories would rouse all the East against British rule, when he pointed out in his speech at Bristol in November, that the defeat of Europe in Asia by a Mohammedan power would be at least as threatening to British rule in Asia as the occupation of Erzerum by Russia.

These views, so firmly and ably expressed by men for whom all Englishmen had a sincere respect, had an assuring effect upon the minds of the people at large, and were reflected in a modified tone of the more thoughtful Conservative speakers, and in the appearance of articles calculated to assuage apprehension in journals whose affiliations would have justified the expectations of declarations from them of the most alarming character.

The *Saturday Review*, a journal which speaks to the more cultivated class of English Conservatives, and is read by all the world, in its issue of the 10th of November, when the Russian conquest of

Armenia had become a foregone conclusion, brought forward several considerations as tending to show that the result would not be as injurious to British interests as had been apprehended. It said: "With the exception of Batum, all Eastern Armenia is virtually in the possession of the conquerors, and the acquisition may be permanently retained if it is thought advisable. None of the Continental Powers have any motive for objecting to the extension of Russian dominion in Asia, and the alarm which has been expressed by some English writers is not a little fanciful. The possession of the upper valley of a river offers no especial facilities for the acquisition of the territory further down. If the Russians hereafter wish to conquer Bagdad, or the plains between the Euphrates and the Tigris, it will matter little whether their base of operations is Alexandropol or Kars. It is not altogether desirable that Russia should occupy the nearest land passage to India, but no practicable route exists at present through the Valley of the Euphrates; and, in other respects, there is as little strategic connection between Armenia and India as between the Pyrenees and Poland. Englishmen may, for the present, regard with equanimity a Russian annexation, which they are in any case powerless to prevent."

A parallel view, from a stand-point outside of England, was given in the *Allgemeine Zeitung*, one of the leading papers of Germany, of the 25th of October. It showed that English interests in Armenia were really very insignificant; that the preponderance of their interests in South-eastern Turkey lay in the extreme corner of the Empire, as at Bagdad and Bozra, and a few other points around the Persian Gulf and along the Persian frontier; and that no English statesman had ever shown, or could show, what was the connection between these points and Armenia or any of the neglected Black Sea ports, for no such connection existed. Moreover, British interests had, within ten years, been drawn toward the line between the Nile and the Syro-Phœnician coasts and the Persian Gulf, while those of Russia were identical with the ancient trade-routes from the Black Sea through Armenia to Northern Persia. These two lines run parallel only in theory. Between them lay the whole Turkish Empire, and all the differences in productions, wants, material and spiritual conditions of the North and the South. The danger to English interests in Armenia was mostly imaginary, for the English had no important interests there. They had no trade through Erzerum or Armenia to India. Of the three hundred

36

steamers which entered the port of Trebizond annually, one-third were Russian and only five bore the English flag; and of the one thousand vessels which called at three other ports on the same coast, only seven were English In fact, England had had no relations with this region for ten years.

Even some of the Conservative statesmen, and men who had relations with the Government, took occasion sometimes to speak, deprecating agitation. Sir Stafford Northcote, on the 24th of January, 1877, said, at a Conservative meeting, that the Government had no unworthy jealousy of Russia, and to say that they had ever abstained from anything that they thought would be useful and right, because of such a feeling, was distinctly false, and great harm had been done by the propagation of the idea that they were guided by it.

The Marquis of Salisbury, Secretary of State for India, who was the special representative of the British Government at the Conference of the powers at Constantinople, in December, 1876, at a banquet held on the 11th of June, made light of the fears that the Russian advance would involve danger to India, and set out against them the picture of a friend of his, who, he assumed, lived at the Cape of Good Hope, that the same advances were a serious menace to South Africa.

Earl Derby was visited on the 28th of November, 1877, by a deputation of three societies, seeking active interference in favor of Turkey. He replied that he could not, for his own part, think that the true line of communication between England and India lay through the Euphrates Valley. He believed that, so long as they had the Suez Canal uninterrupted and unimpeded, they had a communication sufficient for all purposes. Some one having suggested that the Suez Canal would be endangered if the Russians should get Trebizond, he answered that that was difficult of proof, and he should have to suspend his judgment upon the point. He thought there was no immediate danger of the Afghans being joined, in case of a revolt, by the Mohammedan population of India. No such co-operation had been given in the war of twenty-five years ago, and he thought it would not be given now.

As the year drew to a close, a plain division appeared in the Cabinet, Earl Beaconsfield leading the party which favored the assumption of a hostile attitude toward Russia, and Earl Derby and those who agreed with him advocating a continued neutrality and the preservation of peace. This division grew more marked as the certainty of the Russian triumph became more apparent; it continued to widen as the discussions over the attitude which the Government should pursue, in view of the behavior of Russia with reference to the questions involved in its treaty of peace with Turkey, grew more animated, and resulted in the resignation of Earl Derby as Secretary of State for Foreign Affairs on the 28th of March, 1878.

The danger of collision between England and Russia is remote and contingent, and could be easily avoided if the two nations would put aside their jealousy. Those Englishmen who entertain a morbid fear of a conflict mistake a possibility for a probability, and are contributing more than any other cause by their passionate expressions to increase the danger of it arising. The two nations have no occasion to contend in Asia. Each has more territory than it desires, and feels burdened by the extent and responsibility of its dominions; and each has work enough to employ it a century in developing the resources and assimilating the peoples of its acquisitions. Both States affirm, with truth, that they have been driven to successive conquests by the necessity of preserving peace on their borders, and of protecting vested interests; and it follows, that when they shall have extended their dominions so as to join, they will have no occasion to quarrel; for they will have assured the preservation of peace and the protection of vested interests throughout the continent.

The occupation of the whole of Central Asia by Great Britain and Russia would be of vast benefit to the countries immediately concerned, and would constitute a strong impulse to civilization. Good has followed every conquest that either country has made in these regions. British rule has been a great blessing to India. It has brought that vast and populous country into the family of civilized nations; has delivered its inhabitants from a host of petty tyrannies; has freed them from the slavery of brutal customs and degrading superstitions, furnishing them instead the opportunity to improve their manhood; has developed the resources of the country, filling it with railroads and all modern inventions; has stimulated enterprise and built up commerce, and infused life and promoted growth where everything was still and in decay. It is just, though severe, and Hindoos and Mohammedans acknowledge its excellence, while they complain of it as a foreign domination. Every neighboring State to which it is extended feels an immediate benefit from it, and the adjoining barbarous principalities which have not yet received it are taught by what they can observe of its fruits, that there are desirable gifts in the way of law and arts which they have not reached. The world has also learned much that is valuable from India, for which it is indebted largely to British agency in making accessible the treasuries of knowledge which the Empire contains.

In a similar manner Russia, however much we may deprecate the application of its despotic theories of government to civilized European States, has conferred incalculable good on the barbarous hordes of Central Asia by subjugating them. It has substituted law and order where arbitrary caprice, violence, and robbery prevailed. For the first time in their history, the Turkomans know what it is to be governed under an established system, with fixed rules, based upon principles which regard the rights of persons and property. Profitable industries and a settled life are being introduced into districts which were formerly ravaged every year by predatory nomads. Colonies are being planted to till the waste places and make the desert fruitful. Railroads and telegraphs are built; plans are on foot for restoring the rivers and canals for irrigation, and measures are contemplated which have in view the conversion of lands which only anarchy has made barren into productive countries. The fact appears through all the works of the few persons who have visited Turkistan, that the Turkomans, while they profess to hate the Russians, appreciate the better order and the promise of future prosperity which they have given them.

The destinies of Asia seem to have fallen into the hands of these two powers. While they both have so much that they can accomplish for the good of mankind and their own glory in their own especial fields it would be criminal for them to quarrel. While the field of action is so large for each, there is no need that they should quarrel. Those men are the wisest and the nearest to the truth who point out that there is no real occasion for collision between them. If their statesmen shall be able to agree upon a line of division which shall limit the march of the one to the East, of the other to the West, and then go to work in good faith, each to build up their own Empire, peace would be assured, civilization extended, and the world at large as well as the people of Asia would receive incalculable benefit. The best statesmen of Russia and England look to this as the end of all their negotiations and suspicions. No good reason exists why it should not be reached very soon.

CHAPTER VII.

THE NATIONALITY PRINCIPLE AND THE FINAL ISSUE OF THE EASTERN QUESTION.

The End of the War brings New Complications—New Conflicting Interests—How shall they be Settled ?—The Influences which Control the Adjustment of State Lines—Dynastic Considerations—The Principle of Nationalities—Its History—Italian and German Unity—The Nationality Principle in Austria—Its Application to European Turkey—Indications that it will gain Strength—It affords the Best Guide to a Final Adjustment.

THE ending of the war has not brought a settlement of the Eastern Question, but has only caused it to be presented in a new aspect, hardly less formidable than those with which the world has hitherto been bewildered. The arrangements of the Treaty of San Stefano are only a first step in a road which promises to be full of difficulties and complications, to engage the attention of the peoples and powers of Europe, and involve them in future misunderstandings, and perhaps wars The Turks have at last been so nearly driven out of Europe, that it has become evident to all that their final expulsion is only a question of time, and their Empire, which only four hundred years ago was the terror of the civilized world, has been put back to a position of inferiority and doomed to a certain gradual extinction. New States have been set up to take a part of its place in Europe, and the candidates are claiming the rest of the portion to be divided out in a few years if not now. This, which has been accomplished, although it is much, is only the beginning of the trouble. To extend the use of that which has been a favorite figure among the European diplomatists, the sick man is dead ; next begins the quarrelling over his will.

We have described in the previous chapters the most important of the conflicting interests and jealousies which impede the permanent settlement of the affairs of the Balkan peninsula. They are partly intrinsic and essential, but some of them are of outside origin, and their relation to Turkey is only one of their incidents. This, how-

(663)

ever, does not prevent their being very formidable subjects for consideration. The intrinsic and essential interests concern the welfare and relations of the Christian peoples of European Turkey. The four different nationalities to whom the Balkan peninsula seems chiefly to belong, rub against each other at several points, and are so mixed at their boundaries that it is hard to tell, for some distance, on either side of the line, where one begins and the other ends. The Bulgarians and the Servians overlap each other through a considerable district, so that in the adjustment of their respective territories, which has been made by the Treaty of San Stefano, either nation is aggrieved that a part of the territory which it believes should be given to it, is allotted to the other. The Russians, moreover, have provided so liberally for Bulgaria, as to have given it considerable possessions along the sea-coast which were regarded as more properly belonging to the Greeks. These difficulties, however, which are of not uncommon occurrence among peoples which occupy adjoining territories, would be simple and comparatively easy of settlement, were they not complicated by the outside difficulties which engage the attention of the nations who are to decide upon the adjustment to a much larger degree than the wishes of the provinces. Prominent among these are the jealousy and fear of Russia, which have been aggravated by the easy disposition it has made of Turkey, and by the determination it has manifested to go on in its own course regardless of the protests of its neighbors. Russia is regarded, particularly by Austria, as the embodiment of Panslavism, and Panslavism is looked upon as a greedy monster, which is going to swallow everything that is Slavic, and a good deal that is not Slavic, if only a trifle of Slavic is mixed with it, and whose progress is sure to produce other Eastern complications indefinitely. As it is threatened on one side by Russia and Panslavism, so Austria is threatened on the other side by the progress of two of the new States—Rumania, whose peoples are affiliated with those of its provinces of Bukowina and Transylvania, and Servia, whose people and its own south Slavs have long dreamed of union and independence together. The contest between England and Russia for dominion in the East, if it comes to blows, is likely to be one of portentous magnitude and of indefinite duration. Both powers are too large and their interests are too extensive, for either to yield without an exhausting struggle. The particular point on which the attention of these two nations is now centered—Constantinople —has been the pivot upon which all the Eastern troubles have, till very recently, hinged ; it is too important a point to be trusted in the hands of any strong power. It has been left with Turkey because Turkey being weak could do no harm with it, and leaving it there saved the trouble of providing a new disposition for it. Europe will not quietly see England and Russia disposing of Constantinople alone ; and the war, or the negotiations, for its control can hardly fail to involve the whole world, and lead to incalculable perplexities. Thus the final issue is uncertain, and as far from settlement as ever It, in fact, admits of no lasting settlement, unless some just, equitable, and impartial basis can be found on which all nations can be forced to agree, as a principle, by a reference to which all the points shall be decided.

The history of the nineteenth century gives some valuable instruction respecting the character and strength of the agencies which are likely to be chiefly instrumental in shaping the future of the Eastern complication, and furnishes also a clue to the principle to which the ultimate settlement will have to conform. The century has been marked by the predominance of two great and often opposing influences operating to control the boundaries and relations of States, one of which, although it seemed all-powerful during the first years of the century, has had to yield to the other wherever the two have come in conflict, and seems now to be gradually being supplanted by the other. The' first of these influences is that of dynastic considerations, under the weight of which the great powers combined to adjust and preserve a balance of control on the continent in such a manner as it was thought would secure their own strength and growth, regardless of the interests of the smaller States and of all other considerations, and would protect them against real or fancied dangers which might arise from the increase of any of them singly, from the rise of new States, or from new combinations of other States. The dynastic considerations have so far, as we have seen in the preceding chapters, been the commanding influences which have prevented the solution of the Eastern Question, and under which Turkey has been upheld as a power so long after it had lost its capacity to maintain a real self-existence. Under the influence of these considerations, Europe was parceled out, by the treaties of 1815, among a certain number of ruling families, in total disregard of natural boundary lines or of the rights of the people, in such a manner that of a few selected dynasties none should be strong enough to become a terror to any of the others. Thus, it was imagined, the occurrence of new disturbances among the States and the rise of new complications could be postponed for an indefinite period.

This arrangement, which the diplomats of the Great Powers of the time thought was to be their lasting monument, has been thoroughly destroyed within the last thirty years, by the operation of various causes, the chief of which is the second influence we have mentioned—that of the principle of nationalities. This principle impels the dismembered portions of peoples having the same origin and speaking the same language, who have had at some time a common history, and have certain interests in common, to seek each other out, affiliate with each other, and form a political union under a central government. Under its operation, the map of Europe has undergone important changes since the revolutions of 1848, in connection with which its first marked manifestations were made. It is still a living force, and is destined to produce still further changes in the relations of States. It has been successfully applied to the reorganization of two of the most important countries of Europe—Italy and Germany. Italy was disorganized by the overthrow of the Roman Empire, and had been broken into a number of weak commonwealths ever since. The contentions of its rival States and factions had become a European scandal. Its people were despised, and were accredited with all the vices, and hardly any of the virtues. It was reparceled by the Treaty of Vienna into a number of petty States, some of which were contemptible in dimensions, and placed under the control of as many sovereigns, most of whom were also contemptible, and despots besides, and were branches and tools of the house of Austria. Besides the Pope, only one of all the princes which were provided for it was an Italian. This was the king of Sardinia. The contrast of the Italy of 1848 with the peninsula which had shone with the glories of ancient Rome was terrible; and the idea that the country could be regenerated was regarded as impossible, and the aspirations of the people for national unity, which then began to be heard, were considered fit subjects for ridicule. The sneer, "Italy is a geographical expression," was often repeated, in a tone indicating that the country could never hope to be again anything else. The revolutionary efforts of 1848 gave voice to a call of the people for Italian unity. The call was echoed by the one Italian prince of the peninsula, the king of Sardinia, and was supported by the arm and enthusiasm of

Garibaldi, and the sagacious counsel of Cavour. Each worked in his own way for the realization of the idea, and with equal effect, Garibaldi inspiring the people, the king extending the welcome protection of the State over them, the minister devising constitutional provisions. The Austrians were driven from most of Lombardy in 1859; four States of the center entered the Union in 1860. Garibaldi won Sicily in the same year; Venice and Verona were gained from Austria in 1866, and the last remaining part of the peninsula was recovered, and Victor Emmanuel was proclaimed King of all Italy at its eternal capital in 1870. Under the operation of the principle of nationality, this country, which was hopelessly divided, despised, and a reproach, within the memory of young men has become a compact nation, enjoying popular self-government, and is now one of the freest and most progressive States of civilization, and one of the acknowledged Great Powers of Europe.

The German Empire had ceased to be a solid State two hundred years ago. Under the increase of Prussia, and the growing rivalry between that kingdom and Austria, the nation suffered from divisions and lost in strength. During the wars of Napoleon, the name of the Empire disappeared. It was succeeded by the German Confederation, then by the Zollverein (or Customs Union), neither of which had any strong bond of connection, or were able to make the German name felt abroad as it had been felt during the whole of the middle ages. Germany was so happy as to escape the decadence of Italy, for its people always preserved their intellectual eminence, and never let go the traditions of their fatherland, but it was wholly without influence. Austria and Prussia were known as bitter rivals, whose conflicts always defeated national aspirations; besides these powers, were numerous smaller States, some of which were very insignificant, and all of which, despite their wealth and high civilization, counted for nothing in the world's politics. An effort was made, during the revolutions of 1848, to bring the thirty-nine States into a closer union, but it was defeated by an adverse combination of circumstances, partly of home, partly of foreign origin. The national principle, however, was strong, and would prevail over all obstacles. It was first manifested effectively in the war which resulted in incorporating the German provinces of Denmark with the Confederation, in 1864. Then Austria and Prussia quarreled in 1866, and the war which ensued resulted in the exclusion of Austria, and the establishment of Prussia as the leading State of Germany. Prussia united the Northern States with itself into the North German Confederation, and began the building up of a solid Germany. The war with France led to the adhesion of the Southern States to this confederation, and the restoration of the German name to a position of influence. King William, the victorious, was crowned at the capital of France Emperor of Germany, on the 18th of January, 1871, and the new Empire at once assumed the acknowledged position of the first power in actual strength and influence on the earth. The annexation of Alsace and Lorraine to Germany, which was one of the incidents of this great event, is another triumph of the nationality principle, inasmuch as it was the restoration to their normal national relations of two German provinces which had long been held by France.

Besides Italy and Germany, the two European countries which have been most conspicuously agitated by the question of nationalities are Austria and Turkey. Nearly all the troubles which Austria suffers, and has suffered since 1848, may be ascribed to the working of this question. It was at the bottom of the Hungarian Revolution in 1848. The Magyars sought the recognition of their nationality, and its elevation to influence in Hungary. They were opposed by the Slavs, who wished to be recognized in the same districts, and by the Germans, who were not then willing to divide their power. The Compromise of 1867 was a recognition of the national claims of the Magyars, and gave peace to the nation on that quarter. It, however, did not satisfy the Slavs, but rather increased their urgency for recognition, to which the Government yielded by making partial concessions to the Croats. Besides these nationalities, the Czechs, the Poles, the Servians, the Lithuanians, and the Rumanians, all form distinct and sometimes opposing communities, whose appetite for recognition has been whetted by what has been done for their neighbors. As Austria has already lost its Italian provinces and its influence in Germany, by the agitation of this question, so it is likely to lose other of its populations, unless it can devise some means of satisfying them all without loosing them from the State—a problem which may fitly tax the resources of the ablest minds and the most fertile in expedients.

Of the aspirations of the four nationalities in Turkey, those of one—the Bulgarians—have been the most fully met. They have, in fact, got more than they had reason to expect. The fact can not fail, however, to excite the desires of the others to the highest pitch, one of which, the Greek, has as yet obtained nothing, but sees a part of what it claimed given to its rival, the Bulgarians. The Greeks, and the Servians of Bosnia and Herzegovina, are still dissatisfied, and—the Greeks, at least—will never give up the struggle till they have gained what they are convinced, now more firmly than ever, is their right.

The more education advances among these struggling nationalities, the more will the masses begin to participate actively in their efforts for the realization of their national hopes. Those who have the management of educational affairs, will take care, as the regenerators of Bulgaria have done, and as the Greeks are doing, that the instruction given is national in spirit and influence. The literature of all the nationalities, which already, even in the present condition of general ignorance, forms a strong bond between them, is thoroughly impregnated with the national aspirations, and will strengthen the movement for national autonomy just in proportion as the masses of the people are able to read and digest it. As Homer was the bond of the ancient Greeks, as German literature has been a tower of strength in cementing the unity of the German race, as Dante in the middle ages planted, and Manzoni and Gioberti in modern times revived and stimulated the Italian sentiment for unity, and as literature has proved a powerful weapon with the Panslavists, so are the poets and story-tellers of Rumania and Servia and Bulgaria and Modern Greece—and they are not few—cultivating and diffusing and strengthening similar sentiments among the people to whom they speak. Thus the cohesive force of these nationalities is constantly tending to become stronger; and how tenacious a nationality can be, under the most adverse circumstances, is exemplified in the case of the Poles, upon whom even the alluring temptations of Panslavism have as yet exerted no influence.

None of the nationalities of Turkey or Austria can furnish the constituents for a new Empire on the basis of nationality equal to a united Italy or a united Germany. None of them has a population to compare with that of Italy or of Germany. The Poles number about 11,000,000; the Rumanians, 8,000,000; the Servians, 7,500,000; the Czechs, 7,000,000; the Bulgarians, 5,000,000; while Italy has a population of 26,800,000 and Germany one of 42,727,000. Those nationalities which are destined to see their aspirations fulfilled will owe their deliverance or extension, like Bulgaria, to the protection or co-operation of one of the larger powers, acting more for selfish interests than for the fulfillment of any abstract principle. But as the popular sympathy of the Italians with the Government of Sardinia aided in the foundation of the Kingdom of Italy; as Prussia needed the co-operation of the movement for nationality among the Germans for the establishment of the German Empire; and as the national aspirations of the Christian populations of European Turkey have played a prominent part in the overthrow of Turkish rule in Europe—so the aspirations of the nationalities, which still remain dismembered for union and restoration, may be expected to form an important factor in the transformation of South-eastern Europe; that is to say, in the solution of the Eastern Questions, which are hereafter to be brought to the surface.

In view of the great uncertainty which even the leading statesmen of Europe feel with regard to the future of the Eastern Question, and in view of the constant shifting of the aspect of affairs and arising of new complications, it would be foolish, as well as useless, to risk any definite prediction as to the final solution of the problem. It is, however, safe to predict that the course of the question will always be influenced by the workings of the principle of nationality, combined with dynastic considerations, chiefly of Russia, Austria, and England. Russia and the Panslavists will continue to press for a solution in the interest of the Slavic nations and Russian preponderance; Austria, while it can not long ignore the rights of its Slavs and possibly of its Rumanians, will seek to postpone a solution, or to make such a compromise of its interests, as it has done in the case of the Magyars and Croats, as will cause the least possible disturbance to the integrity and quiet of its own dominions; while England may find it the best policy, in order to keep or wrest Constantinople from the Russians and make it as nearly neutral as between the Great Powers as possible, to take up the cause of the Greeks and secure for them what remains of Southern European Turkey. A permanent solution can not be hoped for until the rights of all the nationalities are fully acknowledged and as fairly adjusted as the complex circumstances of the case will permit.

The principle of nationalities is the one which gives, in the organization of States, the fullest gratification to the desires and aspirations of the people, and the freest development to their growth and opportunity for the exercise of their energies. Its application inflicts no fundamental wrongs upon the people, for it unites those who have the most reason to wish to be united, and who are most readily attached to each other, and separates them from those who are alien to them in origin and sympathies. Under its operation, the spectacle can no longer be presented of a large people united in political association with those they permanently hate, or of a race possessing manly capacity crushed and oppressed by another of less or only equal civilization, under whose rule it has been forced, and which governs it only to drain its vital forces for the increase of its own strength. It will damage only the artificial constructions of States which have been formed in disregard of it, and whose continued existence as despotisms over subject provinces is a reproach to liberty and a barrier to the progress of civilization; and will discommode only those dynasties of rulers who, imagining that mankind were made for the emolument and glorification of their houses, have partitioned the earth to suit their own convenience and ambitions.

The arrangement of States according to the principle of nationalities can not be, nor is it likely to be, hastily done. The application of the principle presupposes a condition of civilization and intelligence on the part of the people who are to enjoy the benefit of it, sufficient to enable them to manage their own affairs so that they shall become useful factors in civilization, and their possession of strength enough to maintain their national existence under all ordinary contingencies. A people who from any cause are intrinsically weak, must make terms with some more vigorous power, and abide under its protection. One which persists in keeping in the way of advancement, or remains inert and degraded, must expect to remain subordinate, and submit to the influence of whatever State takes it in hand, till it proves its capacity to maintain itself; and it need not expect to emerge from that condition until it asserts itself and forces the recognition of its unity and independence, as the Italians and Germans have done, and the Christian peoples of Turkey are doing.

The tendency in all the European States is for the people to lay more stress upon the principle of nationality, and for Governments to pay more deference to it. The process which has been so conspicuously manifested in a few of the States, is going on in many of the others, perhaps unconsciously, where it is hardly suspected. Every year witnesses new concessions to popular rights which involve some features of this principle. It is intimately associated with the doctrine of popular self-government, and with the American doctrine of local sovereignty.

The future changes in the arrangement of the States of Europe may be expected to be made in conformity with this principle, as it is extended and becomes more generally acknowledged. They are not likely to be all violent, or be made more frequently, or on a larger scale, than they are now; possibly, their operation will be slower than the operation of such changes has been for a thousand years in the past. For as the world becomes more civilized, and constitutional governments become more free, people become better contented with their lot, and less anxious to agitate for changes which are even reasonable. Even this situation, however, implies a recognition of the principle of nationality, for the operation of constitutional freedom is to give it scope within the State instead of compelling it to seek a field for its exercise without. The changes that are made, therefore, while they may be fewer, instead of being made to carry out the selfish aims of kings, will be made in obedience to the affiliations and tendencies of the people, and will be, in the most civilized States, more voluntary and less violent.

Thus, by a slow process of natural separation and reunion, based upon the recognition of national affiliations and the "government of the people by the people for the people," resulting in the adjustment of the boundaries of States by natural lines, a new balance of power will be gradually built up, destined to be as strong and lasting as that which the Congress of Vienna sought to establish was weak and transient. Each State having found its own proper limits and sphere of growth as determined by community of origin, language, and interests, will conform to them, will find its legitimate and most satisfactory field for the exercise of its energies within its own territory, its most prolific springs of power and renown in the building up of its own resources. No State will have reason to fear aggression from its neighbor, for all will be alike busy within themselves; and a rivalry among the nations in industry, in the culture of the arts and refinements of civilization, and in promoting the happiness and comfort of their own people will take the place of the ceaseless conflicts of dynasties which have too long interrupted the progress of mankind.

CHAPTER VIII.

COMPLICATIONS ARISING AT THE CLOSE OF THE WAR.

Leaning of the Turks toward the Russians—Austrian Note to Russia on the Treaty of Peace—British Objections to the Treaty—The British Fleet passes into the Sea of Marmora—Austria Issues an Invitation for an International Conference—Prince Bismarck's Declaration in the German Parliament—Russia's Opposition to the Conference—England Demands the Submission of the entire Treaty—Threatened Rupture between Russia and England—Ignatieff Visits Vienna—British Circular to the Powers—The British Reserves Called Out—Intimate Relations of the Russians and Turks

THE slow progress of the negotiations between the Russians and Turks was watched from the beginning with concern by all the powers, and with an anxiety which amounted to little less than alarm by Austria and England. It was evident that Russia had Turkey completely at its mercy. The Russian armies continued to advance, apparently irresistibly and without meeting even a show of resistance, notwithstanding it was understood that hostilities were suspended, and conferences had taken the place of battles. Every day they were coming nearer to Constantinople, and approaching positions whence they could command the navigation of the Straits. The danger seemed gradually to rise before the eyes of the watchers, and finally appeared imminent that Russia, in spite of the Treaty of Paris and its own promises often repeated, would seize Constantinople and the Straits, and dispose of the whole of European Turkey and its people, before any one could prevent it, and without consulting the views or interests of the two powers which imagined themselves immediately concerned. The delay which took place in the negotiations after they were begun was unaccountable, and became an object of suspicion, all the more because of the continued progress of the Russians. The British and Austrian Governments took the earliest opportunity to intimate to the Russian Government and the Porte that they would not recognize conditions of peace in contravention of the terms of the Treaty of Paris in which Europe did not participate. The Russians answered with assuring words, that all points in the treaty which were of European concern

(673)

would be submitted to a review of the powers, and continued to treat and to occupy points nearer to Constantinople. The Turks seemed to have no longer any will of their own, but to have thrown themselves entirely into the arms of the Russians. Crushed on every battle-field, having seen the British Government witness their utter defeat without moving a step in their favor, they seemed to have undergone one of those revulsions of feeling which often attend extreme disappointment, and turned the cold shoulder upon the old friends who they fancied had deserted them, to make friends of their former enemies—and the probability of a Russo-Turkish alliance against England began to be talked of. The excitement was intensified by the rumors which were circulated concerning the points of the treaty which were under discussion. Some of them were so represented as to seem to touch European interests very sharply. The mystery which shrouded the negotiations all through January added to the force of these rumors.

On the 30th of January, the Austrian Ambassador at St. Petersburg delivered a note to Prince Gortchakoff, embodying a declaration on behalf of the Austro-Hungarian Government, that it in no way disputed Turkey's right to conclude treaties in its own interest, but must consider the arrangements then under consideration, so far as they might modify the present treaty or touch Austrian interests, as not falling within the right of Turkey until new arrangements had been made with the signatory powers of the Treaty of Paris. At about the same time it was stated that Count Andrassy had taken steps with the object of bringing about a joint action of Europe to prevent a prejudicial policy on the part of Russia, and that Austria-Hungary would take the initiative in assembling a European Conference to discuss and determine all the points affecting the common interests of Europe. It was also said that the differences that had arisen between Austria and Russia were of so serious a character that the German Emperor had been obliged to interpose in person, and entreat his two brother Emperors not to break up the Tri-Imperial Alliance. The Austrian objections to the treaty were unofficially stated in a telegram from Vienna, February 4th, to be, in substance, that the Russian conditions were rather calculated to sow seeds of fresh troubles than promote a real and lasting peace. They destroyed Ottoman power in Europe without substituting anything in its place possessing guarantees of stability. The smaller States would receive just enough to make them wish for more, while Bulgaria, the largest of them in extent and population, would become little more than a Russian dependency. Restoration to the Czar of Bessarabia, without due equivalent to Rumania, would make Russia mistress of the mouths of the Danube. Thus, in the very preliminaries themselves there was much that must lead to discussion between Austria and Russia; and the same must be the case, though perhaps to a lesser degree, with the other powers. Rumania had announced its claim to take part as a belligerent in the conclusion of peace; the Servians were disappointed with the rectification of the frontier allowed them by the Russian preliminaries, and insisted upon the possession of Old Servia down to the Lom; and the Greeks had committed an act of war. "Thus the Eastern Question had been raised to its full extent."

Sir Stafford Northcote, the Chancellor of the Exchequer, had made a statement of the British objections in the House of Commons on the 28th of January. The terms, as they had been reported, were very sweeping. The character of the autonomy for Bulgaria was not that agreed upon by the Constantinople Conference. Administrative autonomy was then conceded; now, there was provided total separation from Turkey, under a Prince. Under the Russian plan, the southern boundary of Bulgaria would be brought almost to the seas, and if the Prince for the new State was to be chosen by the Czar, as was reported with some appearance of authority, a powerful State would be established in the very heart of Turkey, with a Prince devoted to Russian interests. Regarding tributaries becoming independent he would say nothing, but it must raise difficult questions, since it touched other interests. The indemnity condition was very elastic. How Russia might elect to take the indemnity and what territory she might ask were highly important to Europe. European concert was, therefore, necessary. The understanding regarding the Straits might mean something or nothing, but it was a European—an English—interest. The conditions were matters upon which no separate understanding between the belligerents could be acknowledged by the powers. "We can not disguise the vast importance of the question now raised; the keystone of South-eastern Europe is being removed."

On the 8th of February it was announced in the British Parliament, that a part of the English fleet had been ordered to proceed to the Turkish capital for the protection of British residents there. The Russian Government answered this by sending notifications to

37

all the powers that in consideration of what the British Government had done, and of a similar course which it was said the other powers were adopting in the premises, it would be obliged, on its side, "to take into consideration the proper means of protecting those Christians whose life and property might be threatened, and in order to attain this result, to contemplate the entry of a portion of our troops into Constantinople." The Porte, however, refused to permit the English fleet to approach Constantinople, and the Russians had no excuse for occupying the city at that time.

On the 3d of February, the Austrian Cabinet issued formal invitations to the Governments of the signatory powers of the Treaty of Paris, to send representatives to a conference to be held at Vienna. The invitation was accepted by all the powers. Russia objected to the Congress being held at a large capital, and presented a definition of the task of the Conference, reserving some very important questions for the decision of Russia and Turkey, to the exclusion of the signatory powers, among which were the reorganization of Bulgaria, the occupation of that country by Russian troops, and the re-annexation of Southern Bessarabia.

This effort to limit the functions of the Conference, together with the appearance that the Russians would find some pretext for entering Constantinople, threw a cloud for a time upon the prospects of the Conference, and the Austrian Cabinet began to consider the subject of mobilizing its army. A rupture between Austria and Russia and an alliance of the former power with England seemed probable, when Prince Bismarck performed the office of mediator, and intimated to Prince Gortchakoff, in the name of the German Government, that Russia must not strain the situation beyond reasonable bounds.

Prince Bismarck made a speech in the German Parliament on the 19th of February, in which he defined the policy of the Imperial Government. The interests of Germany were not affected by the preliminaries of peace in such a manner as to oblige it to deviate from its previous attitude. The apprehensions respecting the Dardanelles were not justified by the actual situation. He did not believe in a European war, as the powers which opposed Russia would have to assume the responsibility of the legacy left by Turkey. A Russian official communication made it certain that the chief interest of Germany, namely, the freedom of the water-ways, as the Straits of the Dardanelles, for commerce, would be maintained.

He believed it was Russia's interest to come to an understanding, and not have the fear of complications with Austria or England constantly impending. He denounced the idea of Germany engaging in a war with reference to the Eastern Question, declaring that nothing should induce him to hazard a rupture with any power respecting questions in which Germany had no direct interest, and rejected, emphatically, all suggestions that Germany should intervene, declaring that it was willing honorably to mediate, but did not wish to exercise the office of arbiter of Europe. Germany was on the most friendly terms with Russia and Austria, and had not a single interest, except friendly rivalry in trade, antagonistic to England.

Russia having objected to the meeting of the Conference in Vienna, Baden-Baden was selected as the place of meeting. It was afterward understood, however, that it would meet in Berlin.

The question arose during the negotiations whether the meeting should take the form of a conference of the representative members of the Cabinets of the several powers, or of a Congress of Plenipotentaries appointed especially to attend it. Questions arose respecting the admission of the smaller powers—Rumania, Servia, and Greece—to the Conference. Rumania sought to be represented in order to protest against the retrocession of its Bessarabian territory to Russia, Servia to press its claims for Old Servia which the treaty gave to Bulgaria, Greece because it felt neglected by having had no provision made for it, and wronged by the inclusion of Greek communities in the new principality of Bulgaria. It was suggested that the vassal States should have the privilege of sending delegates to represent their interests, without having a voice in the ultimate decision.

Formidable differences arose concerning the scope of the Conference. Russia desired to have submitted to it only those points of the treaty which were manifestly of European concern. Great Britain insisted that the whole of the treaty should be submitted, without reservation. Russia professed not to dispute the right of the Conference to decide what clauses of the treaty involved European interests, but declined to concede *a priori* its right to pass upon all the points.

France expressed a wish that the Conference, or Congress, be confined in its deliberations to the Eastern Question, fearing that otherwise it might claim the right to sanction all recent territorial changes. It also desired to have all questions concerning the holy places excluded, as introducing a needless complication and touching Syria, which France expected to have offered it some day in compensation for England's occupation of Egypt.

Italy avowed its intention to preserve its neutrality on the Eastern Question, but to exert to the utmost its influence in the Conference to oppose Russian preponderance in Europe, by seeking to extend the Hellenic Kingdom and constituting other Christian nationalities.

The demand of England for the submission of the whole agreement between Russia and Turkey was based partly on the apprehension that special and secret arrangements had been entered into independent of the principal treaty, and it would be useless to examine the latter except under a guarantee that it contained all that had been done. Russia, while denying that any secret engagement existed, avoided giving a direct answer to the British demand, but replied that an obligation to submit all the clauses of the treaty was quite unnecessary, as the whole treaty would be known before the Conference met, and the plenipotentiaries could discuss which clauses should be submitted for consideration. The English objected to this, that, by its adoption, the previous question would be raised on every clause of the treaty, except those which Russia brought forward of its own accord. The difference between the two Governments was apparently one of words and diplomatic prestige, rather than of essentials, but their experiences of Russian diplomacy had taught the English that, with those experts in the use of terms of double significance, the most trifling terms of expression may involve great distinctions of hidden meaning.

While the attempt was making to settle these questions, the time of the meeting of the Conference was put off from the early part of March till the last of that month, then till the middle of April.

As the differences between England and Russia became more and more evident, the Russians directed their efforts to making terms with Austria. Notwithstanding the opposition of the Hungarians to having anything to do with the Slavs of Turkey, the Austrian Government had been led to look favorably upon the occupation of Bosnia and Herzegovina as an offset to the extension of Russian influence in Bulgaria, and had been encouraged by Russia in the idea of such occupation. The Austrian Government had also applied to the Chambers for a credit of six millions florins, similar to the credit which the English Government had obtained from Parliament. General Ignatieff was dispatched by the Russian Government to Vienna toward the end of March, in an effort to remove the Austrian opposition to the schemes of the Czar. This done, England would be isolated, and Russia could venture to defy it. The negotiations failed to secure the desired result. Count Andrassy informed General Ignatieff that the whole tendency of the treaty was in opposition to the interests of Europe, and that no lasting peace could be concluded without the sanction of all the powers. General Ignatieff rejoined that Russia had altogether abandoned the idea of a congress in consequence of the difficulties raised by England. He urged Count Andrassy to state Austria's demand. The Count declined, as he still hoped for a congress, but declared that if he had to consider the treaty solely from an Austrian point of view, he would demand far greater concessions than if he had to consider it in relation to the general interests of Europe. Having received this decided rebuff, General Ignatieff returned to St. Petersburg, and the Russian organs stated that his object had been to ascertain just how Austria felt, and that having accomplished this, the purpose of his mission had been gained.

It was afterward stated that the Austrian views were regarded as so exorbitant by the Russians that the Chancellory, in order to prevent an offensive alliance between Austria and England, was about to make another attempt to come to terms with England.

The Servian Government, on the last day of March, ordered the immediate remobilization of the whole of its forces.

The English Government, having decided to call out the reserves, Earl Derby offered his resignation as Secretary of State for Foreign Affairs on the 28th of March, and was succeeded by the Marquis of Salisbury.

The correspondence between the British and Russian Governments concerning the Conference was published on the 30th of March. From it, it appeared that Austria was the only Government which had expressed an opinion about England's demand for the submission of all the articles of the treaty to the Conference. It thought the reservation of full liberty of action by the powers a sufficient guarantee, and that it was not to the interest of England or Austria to raise difficulties on this point. Prince Gortchakoff had said to Lord Loftus, in a conversation at St. Petersburg, that if the Congress made any modifications in the treaty they would be subject to further arrangements between Russia and Turkey.

The British Government issued a circular to the powers, which was published on the 1st day of April, complaining of the terms imposed by Russia on Turkey. Its objections to the details of the treaty, which were clearly given, were intensified by the reservations of Russia relative to their discussion by the Conference. Every material stipulation of the treaty, it said, involved a departure from the treaty of 1856, and by the declarations of 1871, her Majesty's Government could not acquiesce in a withdrawal from the cognizance of the powers of articles which were modifications of existing treaties. The combined effect of the stipulations upon the interests of the powers also furnished a reason against the separate discussion of any part of them. By the articles relative to Bulgaria, a strong Slav State would be erected under the auspices and control of Russia, who would thus secure a preponderating influence in the Black and Ægean Seas, and a considerable Greek population would be merged into a Slav community alien to it. The stipulations for the better government of Thessaly and Epirus, in themselves highly commendable, were accompanied by provisions the general effect of which would be to increase the power of Russia to the prejudice of Greece, and every country having interests in the Eastern Mediterranean. The territorial severance of Constantinople from its European provinces still left would deprive the Porte of any strength it might receive from them, and expose their inhabitants to serious risk of anarchy. The acquisition of Bessarabia and Batum made Russia dominant over the vicinity of the Black Sea, while the acquisition of the Armenian strongholds enabled it to arrest trade between Europe and Persia. Another combined effect of the treaty was "to depress, almost to the point of entire subjection, the political independence of the Government of Constantinople." The formal jurisdiction of that Government, including the control of the Black Sea Straits, the head of the Persian Gulf, the shores of the Levant, and the immediate neighborhood of the Suez Canal, extended over geographical positions which must, under all circumstances, be of the deepest interest to Great Britain. It could not be otherwise than a matter of solicitude that the Government to which this jurisdiction belonged should be so closely pressed by the political outposts of a greatly superior power, that its independent action, and even political existence, was almost impossible. These results arose, not so much from the language of any single article of the treaty as from the operation of the instrument as a whole.

While England would willingly have entered a congress in which the stipulations could be examined as a whole, neither British interests nor the well-being of the Turkish provinces would be consulted by the assembling of a congress restricted by Prince Gortchakoff's latest reservations.

On the same day that the circular appeared, the Queen notified Parliament that she was about to call out, for permanent service, the reserve force, and the militia reserve, or so much of them as should be deemed necessary. The order was issued on the next day, commanding the reserves to assemble on or before April 19th.

While the breach between England and Russia was thus widening, the Czar was drawing the Sultan of Turkey into close relations with him, and apparently forming an alliance of the two powers. On the occasion of the anniversary of the Czar's accession to the throne, March 3d, the Sultan sent him a message of congratulation, " with the desire of renewing our friendly relations." The Czar replied, thanking the Sultan for his congratulations, which he received simultaneously with the news of the signature of the treaty of peace, and perceived in the coincidence a presage of good and lasting relations between the two. The Grand Duke Nicholas, accompanied by twelve Russian generals, paid a visit of ceremonial to the Sultan, in the Dolmabaghtche Palace, March 26th, where he was received with the utmost courtesy and cordiality by the Sultan, surrounded by his ministers, and Osman Pasha and other Generals. He then went to the Beylerbey Palace, and was there called upon by the Sultan. On the next day he dined with the Sultan, the company including several Russian princes and generals, and Vefik, Savfet, Namyk, Rauf, and Osman Pashas. The Sultan was said to be having presents and an imperial order prepared for the Grand Duke.

APPENDIX I.

THE WILL OF PETER THE GREAT.

THE so-called will of Peter the Great, although it is now generally regarded as a spurious paper, has in the past made a prominent figure in the discussions of European politics, particularly with reference to Russia and Turkey. It assumes to mark out a policy for the weakening and gradual absorption of the East, and of all the neighboring States of the West, and the ultimate conquest of the whole West by Russia. The paper which assumed to represent such a will, was so ingeniously contrived by interweaving into its text notices of events which had already taken place at the time it was manufactured, as to seem to unfold a genuine policy, and make the scheme for conquests in the future appear real and plausible. Its appearance was calculated to create alarm, and it, no doubt, had its influence over the movements and combinations that were made and entered into while its genuineness was believed in. The "will" was first brought into notice in the year 1812, in a French work, entitled *Du Progress de la Puissance Russe, depuis son Origine Jusqu'au Commencement du XIX. siecle, by M. L.* (Of the Progress of the Russian Power, from its Origin to the beginning of the Nineteenth Century, by M. Lesur), which, according to Sir Robert Wilson, of the English army, was published under the direct oversight of the French Government. The abstract of the paper which follows, was given in this work, prefaced by the words : "I am assured that there exist in the private archives of the Emperors of Russia, secret memoirs, written in the hand of Peter I, in which are exposed without evasion the projects which that Prince had conceived, which he recommended to the attention of his successors, and which many of them have in effect followed with a persistence which may be called religious."

In 1836, M. Frederick Gaillardet published a work called *Memoires of the Chevalier d'Eon,* in which he gave what he professed was an exact copy of the will of Peter the Great, foreshadowing substantially the same policy that was indicated in the abstract of Lesur. It was asserted that d'Eon, while in Russia, had enjoyed the unlimited confidence of the Court, and the privilege of making unrestricted researches, and had used them to make the copy of the will of Peter, which he took to France, and gave to the Abbé de Bernis, Minister of Foreign Affairs to Louis XIV. The *Memoires du Chevalier d'Eon* is a romance, with but little foundation, in fact, for its incidents, and it is certain that the will was not known to the public till Lesur published his abstract in 1812. The present received theory of the origin of the document, is that Gaillardet elaborated his version from the abstract given by Lesur, that Lesur wrote his abstract by dictation from Napoleon I, and that Napoleon invented the whole concern. The evidences of the ungenuineness of the paper appear in certain phrases which a Russian would never have used, and the supposition that Lesur did not write or even edit the abstract he gave, is sustained by the fact that he avowed no responsibility or original knowledge of the will,

(682)

but merely said that he was assured that it existed; and by the style in which he gave it—which is crude and ill-connected—such a style as one might use in dictation, but which a cultivated author, as Lesur was, would never have written The following is the abstract given by Lesur, translated from the original as literally as the clearness of the sense will permit:

1. To neglect nothing that will give to the Russian nation European forms and usages , and with this view, to engage the different courts, and especially the scholars of Europe, whether by speculations of interest, or by the philanthropic principles of philosophy, or by other motives, to assist in this object.

2 To keep the State continually in order for war, so as to harden the soldier, and hold the nation always in breath and ready to march at the first signal

3. To stretch by every possible means toward the north, along the Baltic, as well as toward the south, along the Black Sea; and with this object·

4. To nurse the jealousy of England, Denmark, and Brandenburg against Sweden , by reason of which those powers will shut their eyes to the aggressions we will commit against that country, and which we will complete by subjugating it /

5 To interest the house of Austria in driving the Turk from Europe, and under that pretext, to maintain a permanent army and establish docks on the Black Sea, and constantly advancing, to stretch out toward Constantinople

6. To keep up anarchy in Poland; to influence its diets, and especially the elections of its kings , to take from it on every occasion that shall present itself, and finish by subjugating it.

7 To contract a close alliance with England, and cultivate intimate relations with it, by means of a good treaty of commerce, to permit it even to exercise a kind of monopoly in the interior; this will insensibly produce a familiarity between the English merchants and sailors and those of our nation, who, on their side, will favor all means of perfecting and aggrandizing the Russian marine, by the aid of which we must aim as soon as possible at the domination in the Baltic and the Black Seas, a capital point, on which depends the success and the acceleration of our plans.

8. The testator recommends to all of his successors to be penetrated with this truth, that the commerce of the Indies is the commerce of the world, and that whoever has the exclusive control of it, is the real sovereign of Europe , consequently no opportunity should be lost to excite wars against Persia, to accelerate its decay, to penetrate to the Persian Gulf, and then attempt to re-establish the ancient commerce of the Levant through Syria.

9. To engage at every cost, whether by force or by stratagem, in the quarrels of Europe, and especially in those of Germany , and for this object:

10 To seek and keep up a constant alliance with Austria; to flatter that power in its favorite idea of predominance; to profit by the least ascendency we may gain over it; to engage it in ruinous wars, so as to enfeeble it by degrees; even to assist it sometimes, and never to desist from secretly making enemies to it throughout Europe, and particularly in Germany, by exciting against it the jealousy and mistrust of the princes.

NOTE —We shall succeed in this the more easily, said Peter, because this proud house has already manifested more than once a disposition to domineer over the ancient States of Europe, and because on every occasion when it shall undertake it, we shall acquire some of the good provinces which border on Hungary; and we will finish by incorporating Hungary into an empire, as a compensation

11 Always to choose among the princesses of Germany wives for the Russian princes, and thus multiply our alliances by relations of family and interest, so as to increase our influence in that Empire.

12 To make use of religious ascendency over the disunited or schismatic Greeks who are found in Hungary, Turkey, and the southern parts of Poland, to attach them to us by all artful ways, so as to be called their protectors, and acquire a title to the sacerdotal supremacy. Under this pretext, and by means of it, Turkey will be subjugated; and

Poland, not being able to sustain itself any longer, either by its own forces or by political alliances, will submit itself to the yoke

13 Then, every instant will become precious. It will be necessary to prepare in secret all the batteries to strike the grand blow, and make them play with an order, a skill, and a celerity that shall give Europe no time to come to itself We must begin by proposing separately, and with great circumspection, first to the Court of Versailles, then to that of Vienna, to divide with one of them the empire of the world, accompanying the proposition with the remark, that Russia being already, in fact, sovereign of all the East, and having nothing more to gain except the title, this proposition on its part can not be suspected by them Doubtless the proposition will not fail to flatter them and to kindle a deadly war between them which would soon become general , for in view of the extended alliances and relations of these two rival courts and natural enemies, all the other powers in Europe would be compelled, by interest, to take part in the quarrel between them.

14 In the midst of this general fury, Russia would be asked for aid, sometimes by one, sometimes by the other of the belligerent powers, and, after having hesitated for a long while, so as to give them time to exhaust themselves, it would appear at last to decide for the House of Austria ; and while advancing its troops of the line to the Rhine, it would cause them to be followed immediately by a swarm of Asiatic hordes ; and as the former should advance into Germany, two large fleets should set sail—the one from the Sea of Azov and the other from the port of Archangel—charged with bodies of these same hordes, under the convoy of the armed fleets of the Black Sea and the Baltic. The fleets would appear suddenly in the Mediterranean and on the ocean to pour out all these nomadic peoples, ferocious and greedy for booty, and to inundate with them Italy, Spain, and France, of which they would pillage one part of the inhabitants, reduce another to slavery to people with them the deserts of Siberia, and subject the rest to such a condition that they would not be able to shake off the yoke. These diversions would then give complete latitude to the army of the line to act with the greatest possible vigor and certainty in conquering and subjugating the rest of Europe.

The version of Gaillardet, since it professes to be a copy of the original document, is more formal and finished in style, and a little, but only a little, more minute in detail than that of Lesur It is accompanied with an introduction, giving a general summary of the views of the supposititious testator, which does not appear in Lesur's abstract This is followed by the fourteen articles, the first twelve of which are the same in substance, differing only slightly in details and arrangement as those of Lesur, and only the last two articles show material variation. The document, as given in the *Mémoires du Chevalier d'Eon*, is entitled, "Copy of the plan of European domination, left by Peter the Great to his successors on the throne of Russia, and deposited in the archives of the palace of Peterhoff, near St. Petersburg " The introduction is as follows "In the name of the Most Holy and Indivisible Trinity, We, Peter, Emperor and Autocrat of all Russia, etc , to all of our descendants and successors on the throne of the Russian nation, the Great God, from whom we hold our existence, having constantly enlightened us with His wisdom and sustained us with His divine support, etc.

"Here Peter I. avers that, according to his views, which he believes to be those of Providence, he regards the Russian people as called in the future to the general domination of Europe He founds this belief on the fact that, according to him, the European nations have, for the most part, arrived at an age approaching decadence, to which they are rapidly marching; whence it follows that they could be easily and indubitably conquered by a young and new people, whenever the latter should have attained all its force and growth The Russian monarch regards this future invasion of the Western and Eastern countries by the North as a periodic movement decreed in the designs of Providence, which thus regenerated the Roman people through the invasion of the barbarians He compares those emigrations of Northern men to the overflow of the Nile, which at certain times fertilizes with its slime the impoverished fields of Egypt. He adds that Russia, which he found a stream and will leave a river, will become under his successors a great sea destined to fertilize impoverished Europe, which its waves will overflow in spite of all the dykes which feeble hands can oppose to it, if his descendants shall know how to direct its course. It is for this reason that he leaves to them the following instructions, and recommends them to their constant attention and observation, as Moses recommended the tables of the law to the Jewish people." Here follow the articles, of which the thirteenth and fourteenth are :

"13 Sweden dismembered, Persia vanquished, Poland subjugated, Turkey conquered, our armies united, the Black Sea and the Baltic guarded by our fleets, we must propose separately and very secretly, first to the Court of Versailles, then to that of Vienna, to share with them the empire of the world If one of them accepts, which can not fail to be the case, while flattering their ambition and their self-love, to make use of one to crush the other, then to crush in its turn the one which shall remain, by engaging with it in a contest which can not be doubtful, since Russia will already possess all the East and a large part of Europe "

"14. If, which is not probable, both should refuse the offer of Russia, it will be necessary to stimulate quarrels between them and make them exhaust each other. Then, taking advantage of a decisive moment, Russia shall pour her troops, assembled in advance, upon Germany, at the same time that two fleets shall issue—the one from the Sea of Azov, the other from the port of Archangel—charged with Asiatic hordes, under convoy of the armed fleets of the Black and Baltic Seas. Advancing by the Mediterranean and the ocean, they shall inundate France on the one side, while Germany is overwhelmed on the other, and these two countries being conquered, the rest of Europe will pass easily and without our striking another blow under the yoke Thus Europe may, and should, be subjected."

APPENDIX II.

THE TREATY OF SAN STEFANO.

1. In order to put an end to the perpetual conflicts between Turkey and Montenegro, the frontier dividing both countries will be rectified in the following way:—From the Jobrostcha Mountain the frontier will follow the line indicated at the Constantinople Conference to Korito, through Bilck, thence will go to Gatchko, Metochia, Gatchko belonging to Montenegro, toward the confluence of the Piva and Tara, rejoining the Drina northward to its confluence with the Lim. The Oriental frontier will follow the last-named river to Drijepolie and through Roskai and Sukhaplanina, leaving to Montenegro, Bihor, Roshai, taking in Rugowo, Slava, and Gusigne along the mountain ridge, through Shlieb, Saklen, along the north frontier by the mountain tops of Koprivnik, Babavitch, Borvih, to the highest summit of Prokled; then by the summit of the Biskoshik Scait to Lake Tchicenitlod, dividing it from Tchicenikastrati, it will cross the Lake of Scutari and join the Boyana, whose course it will follow to the sea. Niesic, Gatchko, Spuz, Podgoritza, Zabliak, and Antivari remain to Montenegro. A European commission, in which the Porte and Montenegro will be represented, will have to fix the definitive limits of the principality modifying the general outline when found necessary and equitable for the respective interests and tranquillity of both countries, the necessary equivalents being agreed to. The navigation of the Boyana, which always provoked contests between the Porte and Montenegro, will be the object of special regulation by the same European commission.

2. The Sublime Porte definitely recognizes the independence of Montenegro. An agreement between the Governments of Russia and Turkey and Montenegro will ultimately determine the character and form of the relations between the Porte and Montenegro respecting the agents of Montenegro in Constantinople and other localities of the Ottoman Empire where necessary. The Montenegrins will submit to the Ottoman laws and authorities whenever traveling in Turkey, according to international law and uses. A convention shall be concluded between the Porte and Montenegro regulating the relation of the inhabitants on the confines of both countries, and the military works on the confines at points where an understanding would be impossible, will be decided by Russian and Austrian arbitration. Should disputes or conflicts arise except respecting territorial claims, the Porte and Montenegro will leave the settlement to the common arbitration of Russia and Austria. The Montenegrin troops will evacuate the territory not included in the above-mentioned delimitation within ten days after the peace preliminaries have been signed.

3. Servia is recognized as independent. The frontier marked on the annexed map will follow the course of the Drina, leaving Little Zvornik and Zakar to Servia, along the ancient boundary to Decevas, near Storiac, thence along to the river Raska, and along it to Novi Bazar; thence across the villages Mekigne, Trooviste, to the source of the river, the line will go by Bazar Planita, in the Ibar valley, and follow the rivulet which flows into the river at Ribanic, whence it will follow the rivers Ibar, Pilnitza, and Lab, and the rivulet Balutza, to its source on the Grapatchtitza Planix, thence by the

(686)

summits separating the rivers Kriva and Veternitza it will rejoin by the shortest route the last-named river at Mivratzkas, will ascend it, cross the Miovtza Planix and descend toward the Morava, near the village of Calimanci, thence descend the Morava to the river Vlossina, near the village of Stalkovotzi, remounting the river Linberazda and the rivulet Koukavitza, crossing the Sukhaplanina, following the rivulet Vryls to Nihava, and so on to the village of Kruplatz, whence the line will join by the shortest route the ancient Servian frontier south-east of Karasulbare and follow it to the Danube Ada Kaleh will be evacuated and razed. A Turkish and Servian commission, assisted by a Russian commissary, will establish on the spot the definitive line of the frontier in the course of three months, and definitively regulate the questions of the Drina Islands. When the commission discusses the question of the Servian and Bulgarian frontiers, a Bulgarian delegate will be admitted.

4. Mussulmans possessing property in the territories annexed to Servia and wishing to settle out of the principality will be allowed to hold such property according to the existing tenure A Turco-Servian commission, assisted by a Russian commissary, will have to decide the question of sovereignty. In all matters respecting immovable property involving Mussulman interests the same commission will have to regulate, within three years, the mode of alienation of goods belonging to estates or vakufs, and questions of private interests, until the conclusion of a direct treaty between Turkey and Servia determining the character and form of their common relations. Servian subjects traveling or living in Turkey will be bound by international law. The Servian troops will have to evacuate within fifteen days from the signature of the peace preliminaries the territory above mentioned

5 The Sublime Porte recognizes the independence of Rumania, which will present its claim to an indemnity to be discussed between both parties Until the conclusion of a treaty between Rumania and Turkey, Rumanian subjects will enjoy in Turkey all the rights guaranteed to the subjects of the other European Powers

6. Bulgaria is constituted as a tributary Ottoman principality, with a Christian Government and a national militia The definitive boundaries of the principality will be determined by a special Russo-Turkish commission. Before the evacuation of Rumelia by the Russian Imperial army it will take notice of all modifications introduced on the spot in the general draft; the nationality of the majority of the inhabitants; the topographical necessities and practical interests of the local populations The territorial extension of Bulgaria is fixed in general sketches on a map, which will serve as the basis for the definitive delimitation From the new Servian frontier the line will follow the occidental boundary of Vranya to the Kara Dagh ridge. Turning westward it will follow the occidental boundaries of the Cazas Koumanovo, Mochani, and Kaldanelk to Mount Karab, thence from the river Velestchitza to its junction with the Blanck Alix, southward by the Drina and occidental limits of the Caza Ochrida toward Mount Linas, and along the occidental limits of the Cazas Gortcha and Starovo to Grammos, and thence by the Kastoria Lake it will rejoin the river Moglenitza, follow it, pass southward to Yannitza, continue by Wardars Mouth and Galoko toward Porga and Sarakoi, thence across the middle lake to Tchikguel Shoumas and Karasson, and by the sea-coast to Buruguel. North-westward toward Tchaltepe it will ascend by the Rhodope ridge to Oushovo, ascend the Kara-Balkans, Eshekkouladji, Tchepelion, Karakolas, and Tchiklar to the river Adla. Thence the frontier will go in the direction of the town of Tchirmen, and, leaving Adrianople southward, will go through the villages of Suguthod, Karahamze, Arnaoutkoi, Akardji, Eadnijie, to the river Tekederessi, following the Tekederessi and Tchoilonderessi rivers to Louleh Burgas, and by the river to the village of Serguen will follow through the mountains forward Hakim Tabiassi to the Black Sea. It will leave the sea-coast near Mangolia, pass along by Tultcha, down to the Danube above Rassova.

7 The Prince of Bulgaria will be freely elected by the population and confirmed by the Porte with the assent of the European Powers. No member of the reigning dynasties of the Great Powers can be elected Prince of Bulgaria In case of a vacancy the elec-

tion of a new prince will take place under the same conditions and with the same forms. An assembly of Bulgarian notables will meet in Philippopolis or Tirnova and draw up before the election of the Prince, under the supervision of a Russian commissary in presence of a Turkish commissary, the organization of the future administration. In localities where there are Bulgarians, Turks, Wallachians, Greeks, and others, account will be taken of the rights and interests of each population The introduction of new regulations and the supervision of their execution will be intrusted for two years to an Imperial Russian commissary. At the end of the first year after the introduction of the new regulations, and if an understanding between the cabinets be obtained, delegates, if found necessary, will be associated with the Imperial Russian commissary.

8. The Ottoman army shall no longer remain in Bulgaria. All the old fortresses shall be razed at the expense of the local Government The Sublime Porte shall have the right to dispose as it pleases of the war material and other articles belonging to the Ottoman Government which may remain in the Danubian fortresses already evacuated by virtue of the armistice of the 31st of January, as well as of any which may be in the fortified towns of Shumla and Varna, until the complete formation of an indigenous militia, sufficient to preserve order, security, and tranquillity, the number of which shall be fixed subsequently by agreement between the Ottoman Government and the Russian Imperial Cabinet The Russian troops will occupy the country, and lend armed intervention to the commissary in case of need. This occupation will also be limited to an approximate period of two years. The Russian effective army of occupation, consisting of six divisions of infantry and two of cavalry, which will remain in Bulgaria after the evacuation of Turkey by the Imperial army, will not exceed fifty thousand men, and shall be maintained at the expense of the country occupied. The Russian troops in Bulgaria will preserve communications with Russia, not only via Rumania, but also through ports on the Black Sea, Varna, and Burgas, where the necessary depots may be organized for the duration of the occupation.

9. The amount of the annual tribute which Bulgaria shall pay to the Suzerain Court, through the agency of a bank which shall subsequently be designated by the Sublime Porte, will be determined by an agreement between the Russian Government and the Ottoman and other cabinets. At the end of the first year a new organization of the tribute will be established, based upon the mean revenue of the whole of the territory forming part of the principality. Bulgaria will be substituted for the Ottoman Government in its charges and obligations toward the Rustchuk and Varna Railway Company, after an understanding between the Sublime Porte, the Government of the principality, and the administration of this company. A regulation relative to the other railways passing through the principality is also reserved for an agreement between the Sublime Porte, the Government of Bulgaria, and the administration of the companies interested.

10. The Sublime Porte shall have the right to make use of the Bulgarian route for the transport by roads to be determined, of its troops, ammunition, and commissariat in the provinces situated beyond the principality and *vice versa*. In order to avoid difficulties and misunderstanding in the exercise of this right, while guaranteeing the military necessities of the Sublime Porte a special regulation will establish the conditions within the space of three months after the ratification of the present document. By an understanding between the Sublime Porte and the Bulgarian Administration, it is well understood that this right will extend only to the Ottoman regular troops, and that the irregulars—Bashi-Bazouks and Circassians—will be absolutely excluded from it. The Porte reserves also the right to send through the principalities its mails, and there to keep up a fixed line of communication. The two points will be likewise regulated in the manner and at the time above indicated.

11. The Mussulman land-owners or others who may fix their personal residence outside the principality will be able to preserve their landed property by causing it to be administered by others Turco-Bulgarian commissaries will sit in the principal centers of population, under the superintendence of Russian commissioners, to administer as the

supreme power, for the period of two years, in all questions relative to the verifying of claims to landed property in which the interests of Mussulmans or others shall be involved   Analogous commissions will be intrusted to regulate during two years all affairs relative to the mode of alienation and management, or for the use on account of the Sublime Porte of the lands of the State and of the Vakufs.   At the expiration of two years all lands which shall not have been claimed will be sold by auction, and the product will be devoted to the support of the widows and orphans—both of Mussulmans and Christians—the sufferers by the late events   Inhabitants of the Bulgarian principality who may travel or remain in other parts of the Ottoman Empire will be subject to the Ottoman laws and authorities.

12. All the fortresses of the Danube shall be razed.   There shall henceforth be no more fortified towns upon the banks of this river, nor ships of war in the waters of the principalities of Rumania, Servia, and Bulgaria, save guard-boats and light vessels intended for the river police and coast-guard services.   The rights, obligations, and prerogatives of the International Commission of the Lower Danube are maintained intact.

13. The Sublime Porte undertakes the re-establishment of the navigation of the passage of Sulina, and the compensation of the private individuals whose property may have suffered on account of the war, and from the interruption of navigation of the Danube, assigning for the purposes of this double expense the sum of 500,000 francs out of the moneys due to them by the Danubian Commission

14. The European proposals communicated to the Ottoman Plenipotentiaries in the first sitting of the Conference at Constantinople, with the modifications which shall be determined upon by common agreement between the Porte and the Governments of Russia, Austria, and Hungary, shall be immediately introduced into Bosnia and Herzegovina   The arrears of payment will not be exacted, and the current revenues of these provinces up to the 1st of March, 1880, shall be exclusively employed to indemnify the families of refugees and sufferers by recent events, without distinction of race or religion, according to the local needs.   The sum which will annually revert afterward to the central government will be subsequently fixed by a special understanding between Turkey, Russia, Austria, and Hungary

15. The Sublime Porte undertakes scrupulously to apply in the island of Crete the regulation put in force in 1868, while paying regard to the wishes expressed by the indigenous population.   An analogous ordinance adapted to the needs of the localities will be also introduced into Epirus, Thessaly, and other portions of Turkey in Europe, for which there will be a special organization not within the purview of the present document   Special commissions, in which the indigenous element shall largely participate, shall be commissioned in each province to elaborate the details of the new ordinance   The result of these labors shall be submitted to the examination of the Sublime Porte, which will consult the Russian Government before putting them in execution.

16. As the evacuation by the Russian troops of the territories in Armenia, which are to be restored to Turkey, might give rise to conflicts and prejudicial complications in the relations of the two countries, the Porte undertakes to effect without further delay the ameliorations and reforms called for by local requirements in the provinces inhabited by Armenians, and to guarantee their security against Kurds and Circassians.

17. A full amnesty shall be extended to Ottoman subjects compromised in recent events, and all persons now incarcerated by reason of these or sent into exile shall be immediately restored to liberty.

18 and 19. The Sublime Porte shall take into serious consideration the opinion pronounced by the Commissioners of the mediating Powers with regard to the possession of the town of Khotoor, and undertakes to cause the execution of the work of definitive demarkation of the Turco-Persian frontier.   The indemnities for the war and the losses entailed upon Russia, which the Emperor of Russia claims and which the Sublime Porte has undertaken to reimburse, consist of : *A.* Nine hundred millions of roubles for the expenses of the war. *B* Four hundred millions of roubles for damage caused to the

southern sea-coast of the country, to its commerce, exports, industry, and railways
C. A hundred millions of roubles for damage caused to the Caucasus by invasion.
D. Ten millions of roubles for damage (with interest) caused to Russian subjects and
institutions in Turkey ; total, 1,410,000,000 of roubles   Taking into consideration the
financial embarrassments of Turkey, and in accordance with the desire of the Sultan, the
Emperor of Russia consents to exchange the payment of the greater portion of the
sums enumerated in the preceding paragraph for the following territorial concessions ·
A The sanjak of Tultcha—that is, the districts of Kilia, Sulina Mahumdie, Isaktcha,
Tultcha, Matchin, Baba Dagh, Hirsova, Kustendje, and Medjidie, as well as the islands
of the Danube Delta and the Isle of Serpents. Russia, not desiring to annex this territory or the islands of the Danube Delta, reserves the power to exchange it for the portion of Bessarabia alienated by the treaty of 1856, and bounded on the south by the arm
of the Kilia and the mouth of the Stary Stamboul. The question of the partition of the
waters and fisheries shall be regulated by a Russo-Rumanian commission within the space
of a year after the ratification of the treaty of peace. B. Ardahan, Kars, Batum, Bayazid, and the territory as far as the Soghanli Dagh. Roughly speaking, the frontier,
starting from the Black Sea, will follow the ridges of mountains which separate the
affluents of the river Hopa from those of the Tchonisk and the chain of mountains by the
town of Artvin to the river Tchoruk, near the villages of Ailat and Bechagesthst , then
the frontier will run along the summits of Mounts Derenik, Ghexi, Hortsheyar, and
Bedigindagh, by the ridge separating the affluents of the rivers Tortum Tchai, and
Tchoruk, and over the heights near Yali Vihim, coming out at the village of Vilim Kilissa
on the river Tortum Tchai ; thence it will follow the Sirri Dagh chain to the pass of the
same name, passing south of the village of Norman. It will then turn south-east and go
to Zewin, whence, passing west of the road leading from Zewin to the village of Ardost
and Khorassan, it will proceed south over the Soghanli chain as far as the village of
Gilitchman ; then by the ridge of Sharian Dagh it will reach a point ten versts south of
Hamaur, in the defile of Murad Tchai ; it will then follow the ridge of the Ala Dagh
and the summits of the Hori and Tan Dur, and passing south of the valley of Bayazid,
will rejoin the old Turco-Persian frontier south of Lake Gazil Gol   The definitive limits
of the territory annexed to Russia, indicated upon the map annexed, shall be fixed by a
commission composed of Russian and Ottoman delegates. This commission will take
into account, in its labors connected with the topography of the locality, considerations
for good administration, and proper conditions for assuring the tranquillity of the country. C. The territories mentioned in paragraphs A and B are ceded to Russia as an
equivalent for the sum of 1,100,000,000 of roubles. As for the rest of the indemnity, with
the exception of 10,000,000 of roubles due to Russian interests and institutions in Turkey,
or 300,000,000 roubles, the mode of payment of this sum and the guarantee to be given
for it are regulated by agreement between the Imperial Government of Russia and that of
his Majesty the Sultan   D. Ten millions of roubles, claimed as an indemnity for Russian subjects and institutions in Turkey, shall be paid by degrees, as the claims of the
persons interested shall have been examined by the Russian Embassy at Constantinople
and transmitted to the Sublime Porte

   20 The Sublime Porte shall take efficacious measures for the amicable settlement
of all the lawsuits of Russian subjects pending for several years, compensate the latter
if there be occasion, and cause the judgments delivered to be executed without delay.

   21. Those of the inhabitants of the localities ceded to Russia who may desire to
establish their residence outside those territories will be at liberty to depart, selling
their landed property. Three years' delay, dating from the ratification of the present
document, are granted to them for this purpose. Beyond that period those inhabitants
who shall not have left the country or sold their lands will be Russian subjects. Landed
property belonging to the State, or pious establishments situated outside the aforesaid localities, are to be sold within the same period of three years, by means which shall be determined by a Russo-Turkish special commission. The same commission shall be intrusted

to determine the mode of the withdrawal by the Ottoman Government of the war material, ammunition, provisions, and other articles belonging to the State, which may be in the towns, cities, and localities ceded to Russia and not occupied at present by the Russian troops.

22. Russian clergymen, pilgrims, and monks traveling or staying in European and Asiatic Turkey shall enjoy the same rights, advantages, and privileges as foreign clergymen belonging to other nationalities The right of official protection of the Imperial Embassy and Russian Consuls in Turkey is recognized both with regard to the persons aforementioned and to their possessions. Religious and philanthropic establishments and others, at holy places and elsewhere, of the monks of Mount Athos, of Russian origin, shall be maintained in their former possessions and privileges, and shall continue to enjoy, in the three convents which belong to them, and in their dependencies, the same rights and prerogatives as those assured to the other religious establishments and the Mount Athos convents.

23 All treaties, conventions, and undertakings previously concluded between the two high contracting parties relative to the commerce, jurisdiction, and position of Russian subjects in Turkey, which have been suppressed by the war, shall be put in force again, excepting those clauses which will be affected by the present document The two Governments will be reinstated as regards their mutual relations, for all their undertakings—commercial and otherwise—in the same situation in which they were placed before the declaration of war.

24 The Bosporus and Dardanelles will remain open in time of war as in time of peace, to the merchant vessels of neutral States arriving from Russian ports or proceeding to those ports The Sublime Porte undertakes in consequence not to establish henceforth in the ports of the Black Sea and the Sea of Azov a fictitious blockade, which shall depart from the spirit of the Declaration of Paris of 1856.

25. The complete evacuation by the Russian army of European Turkey, with the exception of Bulgaria, shall take place within a period of three months from the definitive conclusion of peace between his Majesty the Emperor of Russia and his Majesty the Sultan. In order to save time, and to avoid the prolonged maintenance of Russian troops in Turkey and Rumania, a portion of the Imperial army may proceed to the ports of the Black Sea and the Sea of Marmora for embarkation in vessels belonging to the Russian Government, or freighted for the occasion. The evacuation of Asiatic Turkey shall be effected within the space of six months, dating from the definitive conclusion of peace, and the Russian troops shall be at liberty to embark at Trebizond, to return by the Caucasus or by the Crimea. The operations for the evacuation shall commence immediately after the exchange of the ratifications

26. As long as the Russian troops remain in the localities which—according to the present document—will be restored to the Sublime Porte, the administration and order of things shall remain in the same state as since the occupation. The Sublime Porte shall take no part in it during this time, and until the entire departure no Ottoman troops shall enter the localities restored to the Sublime Porte. The latter shall not commence to exercise its authority there until, as each town and province shall have been evacuated by the Russian troops, the commander of those troops shall have given information to the officer appointed for this purpose by the Sublime Porte.

27. The Sublime Porte undertakes not to treat rigorously in any way, or allow to be so treated, Ottoman subjects who have been compromised by their relations with the Russian army during the war In case any persons may wish to depart with their families by following the Russian troops, the Ottoman authorities shall not oppose their departure.

28 Immediately after the ratification of the preliminaries of peace the prisoners of war shall be reciprocally restored through the agency of special commissioners named on each side, who shall proceed for that purpose to Odessa and Sebastopol. The Ottoman Government shall pay all the expenses of the support of the restored prisoners in

eighteen equal installments, within the period of six years, according to the accounts which shall be substantiated by the above-mentioned commissioners. The exchange of prisoners between the Ottoman Government and the Governments of Rumania, Servia, and Montenegro shall take place upon the same bases ; deducting, however, from the account to be drawn up, the number of prisoners restored by the Ottoman Government from the number of prisoners which they will receive in return.

29. The present document will be ratified by their Majesties, the Emperor of Russia and the Emperor of the Ottomans, and ratifications will be exchanged in fifteen days, or sooner, if possible, at St. Petersburg, or both place and time may be agreed upon, at which the stipulations of the present document may be invested with the solemn forms used in treaties of peace. It remains well understood, however, that the high contracting parties consider themselves formally bound by the present document from the moment of its ratification, in faith of which the respective plenipotentiaries have put their hand and seal to the present document.

Given at San Stefano, February 19 (March 3), 1878.

                                COUNT IGNATIEFF.
                                SAVFET.
                                NELIDOFF.
                                SADOOLAH.

CPSIA information can be obtained at www.ICGtesting.com
Printed in the USA
BVOW02s1104010714

357887BV00010B/683/P